THE WORKING CLASS UNDER THE IMF

THE JAMAICAN EXPERIENCE

LEON HOSANG

minna
PRESS

ISBN 978-1-7324034-7-5

Ordering Information – Quantity (Bulk) Sales: Special discounts are
available on quantity purchases by corporations, associations, and others.
For details, contact the publisher: sales@minnapress.com

Executive Editor: Lena Joy Rose

Cover and Design: Mark Steven Weinberger

Published by Minna Press

For my children
Anton, Cecile and Rosanne

Foreword

Jamaica's relationship with the International Monetary Fund (the IMF) – the subject of Dr Leon HoSang's excellent book, *The Working Class Under the IMF – The Jamaican Experience* – has generated considerable political and economic controversy. Some components of the controversy stem from the role of the IMF within the international capitalist economic system and Jamaica's ambivalent perspective on aspects of this system. The IMF exists, in large part, to facilitate international payments and to assist countries which have short-term balance of payments problems. As such, it helps to keep countries on track, and provides creditors with the assurance that countries will meet their foreign exchange obligations. But, the IMF does more than that, for, in practice, IMF support provides a seal of approval – if a State is backed by the IMF, this support provides a guarantee that the State is applying sound neoclassical economic principles in the macroeconomic sphere.

In order to provide this guarantee, the IMF has traditionally sought to place conditionalities on its loans. Accordingly, Jamaica – often in need of support – has had to accept constraints on its economic praxis. Some of these constraints proceed from the assumption that the country's consumption levels are in excess of our production – in short, that we spend more than we earn. And, starting with this assumption, the IMF has sought to dampen Jamaican expenditure in various ways. While this approach has significant support in economic theory, it has, in the course of Jamaica's relationship with the IMF, stirred controversy because limits on expenditure often result in a reduction of social spending. Thus, for example, governmental commitment in the 1970s to "free education" may have been perceived by the IMF as largely unaffordable; and similarly, other desirable social goods have had to be restricted because expenditure has had to be curtailed. With a large army of unemployed or underemployed persons, Jamaica has had the challenge of meeting IMF constraints while providing basic goods and services for the populace.

Against this background, IMF constraints are sometimes said to contribute to social pressure in Jamaican society. On the other hand, supporters of the IMF raise points in defence. To begin with, they suggest that the IMF is merely a bank, and as a bank, it must necessarily place conditions on its loans simply to ensure repayment. This argument was firmly advanced by no less a friend of Jamaica than Ambassador Andrew Young in January 1977. Young, the then American Ambassador to the United Nations, recommended acceptance of the IMF's terms, for such terms would bring about stability in the Jamaican economy, and safeguard our potential to honour our indebtedness. This is true, but, arguably, it misses a part of the point. IMF conditionalities may enhance our capacity to repay the loan, but some of these same conditionalities work heavily against the interests of the poor and traditionally dispossessed in society.

A second line of defence presented by supporters of IMF prescriptions is that the IMF works on the basis of tried and tested principles that bolster developing economies. This argument is not without its critics. From as early as 1975, Cheryl Payer, writing in *The Debt Trap: The International Monetary Fund and the Third World*, demonstrated that in several test cases, IMF prescriptions led to increased State dependence on the Western banking system and stifled indigenous potential to bring about economic improvement. So, for a long time, the argument has been that the IMF model does not work. As a part of this argument, it is sometimes suggested that the IMF is too dependent on a "one size fits all" approach. So, for example, the IMF has been inclined to rely on the devaluation of the local currency as a strategy to reduce domestic demand and to promote export-led growth. The problem with this IMF approach is that, even with significant devaluation of the Jamaican dollar, import levels will remain high because we are dependent on imports for essential goods such as medicinal effects and petroleum. And, simultaneously, some of our export items, such as tourism earnings, are denominated primarily in foreign currencies, so that consumers overseas will not benefit from lower prices attendant upon a devalued Jamaican dollar. Contrary, therefore, to the textbook theory, devaluation does not necessarily lead to an improvement in Jamaica's balance of payments situation.

Thirdly, supporters of the IMF approach to Jamaican economic problems are inclined to argue that local authorities do not stay the course. They point out that, since the decade of the 1960s, Jamaica's growth rate has been anaemic essentially because policy-makers succumb to demand-driven pressures, especially when elections are approaching. This has tended to drive up the inflation rate, and has led to significant governmental indebtedness. Accordingly, the IMF supporters say, it is not surprising that in 2013 Jamaica's government debt to GDP ratio was 135.5%, and that the average debt to GDP ratio was 126.57% between 1980 and 2017. With such ratios, economic growth has been stifled by the need to repay indebtedness, high interest rates and by "crowding out" of the private sector by government debt. Since 2013, the debt to GDP ratio has been declining, so that it reached 103.3% in 2017, and at the end of 2018/2019 it was reportedly at approximately 96%. This success — achieved through bipartisan collaboration and fixity of purpose – has placed Jamaica near the top of the IMF list of role models for small, open, developing economies. But the IMF story is not quite over. To be sure, domestic income levels remain skewed, wealth is unevenly distributed, and productivity levels are relatively low. Also, some traditionally important contributors to national income, including agriculture, have underperformed for various reasons. The current Jamaican growth rate – clocking in at 1.7% year on year in the first quarter of 2019 – continues, too, to be a point of concern.

Even so, however, IMF supporters are now on the rise. After years of uncertainty, Jamaica's balance of payments situation is not grim. Prices are relatively stable, to the point where there are now authoritative voices raised in support of a higher inflation rate, a suggestion that has justifiably prompted quizzical eyebrows. There is little doubt, though, that Jamaica will meet its debt obligations. We are poised on a positive footing, seemingly ready for take-off. If we can ensure that this take-off does not leave the poor and dispossessed waiting in vain, our relationship with the IMF — so ably assessed by the polymath Dr HoSang — will have been worthwhile.

—Prof. Stephen Vasciannie, CD
President of the University of Technology, Jamaica (UTech)
Former Jamaican Ambassador to the United States

Table of Contents

Abbreviations

ACTU	Australian Confederation of Trade Unions Bustamante
BTTU	Industrial Trade Union
BOJ	Bank of Jamaica
BJIR	British Journal of Industrial Relations
CBT	Caribbean Basin Initiative
CQ	Caribbean Quarterly
ESOP	Employee Share Ownership Programme
ESSJ	Economic and Social Survey, Jamaica (Annual Reports)
ETRPA	Employment (Termination and Redundancy Payments) Act
GATT	General Agreement on Tariffs and Trade
ILR	International Labour Review
IMF	International Monetary Fund
ISA	Industrial Stabilization Act (of Trinidad & Tobago)
JCTU	Jamaica Confederation of Trade Unions
JLP	Jamaica Labour Party
JTURDC	Joint Trade Union Research and Development Centre
LRIDA	Labour Relations and Industrial Disputes Act
NWU	National Workers Union
OECD	Organization for Economic Cooperation and Development
PBR	Payment by Result
PIOJ	Planning Institute of Jamaica
PNP	Peoples National Party
PREALC	Programa Regional del Empleo para América Latina y el Caribe (The Regional Employment Programme for Latin America and the Caribbean)
PSOJ	Private Sector Organization of Jamaica
SES	Social and Economic Studies
TUC	Trade Union Congress (British)
UAWU	University and Allied Workers Union
UNICEF	United Nations International Children's Emergency Fund
UWI	University of the West Indies
USAID	United States Agency for International Development
[ ]	Author's Insertion

List of Tables

List of Figures

Preface

In the 1970's and 1980's, Jamaica's borrowing relationship with the International Monetary Fund and the World Bank presented grave social and economic challenges for the island's political directorate, at a time of pronounced partisan polarization.

An explicit ideological orientation vigorously expounded, locally, was in collision with the muted orthodoxy of the International Financial Institutions; these agencies are still being depicted as propagating the, "...rabid, unbridled religiosity of the free market absolutists".[1]

Not significant in the determination of policy choices and their chances of success, was the location of the 'point of impact', in accordance with the relative strength of the contending forces, local social/political versus the international institutions and their tone setters. That policy responses, in a situation of deep economic distress, were destitute in terms of implementation capability, whatever the objective merit of project-proposals, was inauspicious for the 'alternative' ideological pathway.

The attitudes toward/opinions about the IMF intervention in Jamaica's economic affairs, and, as a direct consequence, its social system, constituted a central concern of the presented effort here. Having gone through purgatory, since the mid 1970's, Jamaica is now a star student, certainly when it comes to 'passing' IMF 'tests'. A press report in June 2018, declared, 'IMF pleased with Jamaica's economic performance',[2] no doubt partly because of the 'underperformance in capital spending' mentioned in the report.

Is Jamaica unique? The island would seem to be quite capable of consistently passing the IMF tests; somehow, it seems incapable of graduating.

This "hill and gully ride", under the IMF – its expectations/predictions, versus the people's experience – may be reason enough for the ideological orientation, as against the more conventional mode of review and analysis, adopted here.

If success in this 'affair' can be measured by indices/targets, perhaps the all-revealing one is that of the exchange rate: this moved from J$ 0.91 to US$1.00 in 1974 to J$35.45 to US$1.00 in 1997, a devaluation of the local currency of 97.4 % over the twenty-three year period. The rate is as of September 2018, J$138 to US $ 1.00.

The "human face", allegedly mediating the worst social consequences of the structural adjustment project, continues to fail to put the human *person* at the center of policy prescription.

It seems to be believed, in some quarters, that the more aggressive slaves on that abominable Trans-Atlantic journey, were sent to Jamaica, the more docile to Barbados. That may, even remotely and partly, be explanatory of the apparent pre-disposition to violence on display, as evidenced by the serious crime data, since the late 1960s.

Violence now targets individuals, no longer that particular manifestation of the capitalist ethic, the trade in human cargo involving the yoke, shackles and whip. Neither is aggression directed at the authors of the more current ravages and decimation brought about by the apparently more morally respectable international financially complicit system. This is despite the attendant further distress imposed on the usually, already debilitated, poorer sections of their client nations.

Legal or other mechanisms of control, of recent times, after political independence, have not animated revolt to any extent approximate to social upheaval. One of the central tasks of this work is to seek comprehensive answers to the obvious historical question posed, why not?

Leon HoSang

---

1. See 'The Free Market?', O. James, The Daily Observer, Thursday, May 17, 2018, p.12
2. The Daily Observer, Wednesday June 20, 2018, pp. 20, 22.

A race that is solely dependent upon
another for economic existence sooner
or later dies. As we have in the past been
living upon the mercies shown by others,
and by the chances obtainable, and have
suffered therefrom, so we will in the
future suffer if an effort is not made
now to adjust our own affairs

MARCUS GARVEY (1923)

Introduction

It has been claimed that recently published material on the International Monetary Fund (IMF/Fund) and the International Bank for Reconstruction and Development (World Bank/Bank) stabilization and structural adjustment programmes in Jamaica has consisted of largely descriptive chronological studies of political leaders and their failed policies. A later, more accurate assessment, however, would be that these agreements have, "...generated volumes of economic reports and analyses, focusing on the objectives, mechanisms and monitoring of these programmes ... followed by a growing literature on the welfare effects...."[1]

The recent perspective of Anderson and Witter is that of an analysis involving a, "...systematic examination of the range of alternative responses which may emerge as life-chances become radically altered".[2] Theodore is, nevertheless, of the view that, "...we are now almost at saturation point as far as discussions on structural adjustment are concerned".[3]

If the process is necessarily continuous and is pursued out of national self-interest, as Davies regards it,[4] then as the country seeks to confront an increasingly dynamic environment, its multi-faceted, complex, and contentious nature will increasingly be revealed.

The view taken here is that the consideration, under considerable economic duress and political pressure, of mechanisms and strategies of mediation between the state, powerful external interests, and internal sectoral and class-differentiated constituencies, has meant, less than warranted attention to the need to situate policy options within the screening device of the principles of a vision of society – or even the milieu of other countries' policy experimentation experience. Neither have the strategies in the industrial relations arena on which we shall focus, that is to say, issues pertaining to wage policy, been sufficiently scrutinized from a political science perspective.

These omissions gain in significance, in a context where there is yet to be developed any notable tradition in industrial relations theory. Further, preoccupation with economic problem-solving on a day-to-day basis,[5] in an atmosphere of unrelieved crisis, has led to the denial of the opportunity for broadly focused deductions as to the reasons for conspicuous failures of policy implementation.

The emphasis of previous work, macro-economic factors and their welfare effects, will be considered, apart from a consideration of the wages, inflation, employment relationship – given its importance for strategic pay policy determination – only to the extent necessary for a rounded treatment of the areas selected for attention.

The notion of the 'National Interest' is considered sufficiently important to be the subject of Chapter I. In 1981, Justice Parnell found that although, "The categories of what is deemed to be in the national interest are not closed ... (and although) public opinion may play a great part in shaping or refurbishing ... the national interest (nevertheless) it is the Government of the day which is competent to declare it".[6]

Whatever the merits of this view, based as it was on a certain interpretation of collective Cabinet responsibility for public policy under section 69(2) of the Jamaican Constitution, it shall be challenged by an analysis of Jamaican society, which rejects totally the idea of the "class-neutral state,"[7] and also the claim that IMF and World Bank programmes have no political bias.[8]

It is not without significance that the effect of the Senior Puisne Judge's ruling was that a wage award exceeding the limits set out in the Government's Ministry Paper No. 22 of 1978 was declared to be contrary to the national interest provision in Section 12(7)(b) of the Labour Relations and Industrial Dispute Act, 1975, (LRIDA), and was therefore void.

The struggle of differing interests, attitudes and values among and between the socially and economically contending forces for predominant influence in establishing 'the rules of the game', represent issues with which the survey instruments to be, referred to in Chapter 6, were concerned. As Weldon reminds,

> "Parties tend always to become more or less autonomous associations for advancing the interests of the sources from which they get their funds. ... Hence, they *may* [italics added] come to embody in their policy, compromises ... which are out of harmony with public opinion on more general issues".[9]

The use of the concept of hegemony, in the consideration of policy choice and institutional mechanisms of implementation, shall lead to a questioning of the reasons behind the somewhat self-contradictory conclusion that,

"Labour has, in effect, become a permanent opposition force of varying strength. Governments are locked (under the IMF) into putting the interests of profits, capital, international creditors, investors and job creation[10] above that of unionized workers, *in the national interest*" [italics added].[11]

Chapter 2, because of its central place in discussions about pay policy determination,[12] shall be devoted to a consideration of the Wage-Inflation-Employment relationship. Not only will the applicability of neo-liberal economic theory be questioned, but so shall the efficacy of a low-wage development strategy, against the background of the comparative economic performance of the East Asian "tigers" and the unemployment levels associated with wage compression policies in OECD countries in the 1980's.

Contention as to implementation methodology, policy design and the quality of results reflects, on one view,[13] not so much disagreement, as ignorance. 'Reality' will depend for its definition, in theory and practice, on cultural variables such as class, status and hierarchy, level of education, "... general political maturity and common-sense of the mass of the population".[14]

It has been argued, that even with the most up-to-date and accurate data available, all we can do in the field of economics is to make intelligent guesses as to the measures which are appropriate on issues involving satisfying a plural and highly differentiated public. This may explain the fact that although the cause identified for the inflation problem by the Government's monitoring unit are several, this has not restrained the political directorate from selecting the wage-push factor as the basis for inflation control policy prescription.[15]

If much of the commentary which shall be reviewed as to the virtues of wage restraint is based on questionable theoretical foundations, the question arises as to whether this is the result of alleged ignorance or rather deliberate strategy, motivated by interests of the hegemonic class and its agents.

Given the poor national productivity record, constantly expressed concern at governments' failure to contain inflation, and the rhetoric and exhortation about "producing our way out of our problems" and that "productivity is the only answer", *ad nauseam*, Chapter 3. shall deal with Productivity Incentive Schemes.

What does one make of the fact that although the IMF agreement of 1987 allowed for wage increases to exceed the wage guideline figure, if justified by increased labour productivity, this provision was hailed by the then Prime Minister, as late as 1990, as a "historic" new concession by the IMF.[16]

Well recognized by all levels of official leadership, is the importance of enhancing productivity for increasing output, thus reducing the unit cost of production and moderating inflation, thereby enabling the productive sector to meet competition in exports markets, improving the flow of foreign exchange earnings and, accordingly, the balance of payments position, and, not least, generating additional employment. It is proposed to include in the survey instruments, items which will allow an assessment of the extent to which the concept of a 'productivity culture' has been promoted and successfully communicated to the more relevant target groups.

Was the prolific and much quoted, the late Professor Carl Stone, correct in stating that,

> "For most unionized and non-unionized workers today (1990) the idea of wage increases beyond the guidelines [removed since 1991] that are based on increased productivity is entirely a matter of theory".[17]

And if he was correct, does the situation depicted of a dubious link in labour's thinking between wages and productivity still hold true at this time? (1994/95). A combination of the survey results and case studies together with Stone's summary of the experience of a sample of firms with incentive schemes will prove useful, one expects, for future policy design.

It is instructive that the Private Sector Organization of Jamaica (PSOJ) considers that, "The disclosure of remuneration levels whether for management or rank and file workers is a breach of confidence and an *anti-competitive* [italics added] practice".[18] The more likely situation is that pay structures are characterized by such gross anomalies that they cannot bear scrutiny, in many cases. But this attitude equally brings to the fore the problem of disclosure on a higher level, where accurate company accounts and business development plans are required for meaningful Productivity Bargaining, bearing in mind the relatively detailed and complex nature of that exercise. Productivity Bargaining has been stated, on occasion, to be something towards which management and organized labour ought to aspire, in a context of high inflation and low national labour productivity.

The attempt will therefore be made to identify the basic hurdles to successful policy implementation, whether in the form of administrative capability, technical skills, or conflict of goals and objectives, reflective of opposed vested interests and a manifestation of differences in underlying social and political philosophy. In this Chapter, the British experience of the 1960's and 1970's when, significantly, the Labour Party with its strong trade union link formed the Government shall play a prominent part in the treatment of the issue.

The approach to the subject matter of Chapter 4, Prices and Incomes Policy will, of course, differ according to ideological orientation. In Rowthorn's[1] view, a method has to be found for containing wages which, "…does not sacrifice employment to the point where it provokes social upheaval … (which) is the primary function of an incomes policy".[19] It should be added that neither can wages be so low as to preclude the purchase of capitalism products by too many of their producers. It is often overlooked, astonishingly perhaps, that workers happen to also be the consumers whose incomes determine demand for goods and services.

The treatment of the material covered in the Chapter will involve an implicit assessment of Corina's view that, "… the ultimate questions of incomes policy are not problems of labour economics but belong to the realm of social theory".[20] That of Demas that, "…the only explanation of the absence of incomes policies in the countries of the (Caribbean) region is to be found in the magnitude of the political problems involved in getting powerful vested interests and trade unions to accept such policies", also warrants consideration.[21]

From the perspective of free market principles, it does not seem to have been grasped, by its Jamaican proponents, that an incomes policy introduces into, and reinforces precisely those rigidities in the labour market which the application of the principles are designed to remove. And, in particular, that the allocatory function of wages is neutralized by a wage norm which is imposed, without discrimination, on expanding and contracting industries and firms alike.

If the effect of wage guidelines was to shift income to groups with a high propensity to import and consume expensive foreign goods, what are the chances, with the substantial gap in living standards, of popular acceptance of wage restraint, even if agreed by the leadership of the trade unions? And if one assumes acceptance, what would be required in exchange?

Answers to these and further questions, such as which classes are perceived to have borne the brunt of the cost of adjustment, will be presented from the responses to two survey instruments.

The Government has been forced to the conclusion that, "Any successful partnership must include a wages and prices component which would *call for a period* [italics added] of personal restraint and readiness to accept sacrifices of immediate personal benefits in the interest of future benefits".[22] Not only will the survey on 'Perceptions of the IMF' provide evidence against which such an assertion and expectation can be assessed, but it will be necessary to question, throughout, governments' inherent ability – in a society in which class/social status consciousness and divisions represent an essential aspect of cultural history[23] – to fairly allocate the costs of possible economic recovery and growth.[24]

What, if anything, has so changed since the removal of wage guidelines that will render incomes control, other than wages, less problematic as an exercise in the use of political power?

Within the varying contexts of some kind of social consensus, the experiences of Belgium,[25] Britain, Australia, and, most recently, Barbados will be briefly examined for policy development insights. In this, and other Chapters, a deliberate effort will be made to avoid the tendency to parochialism, associated with small island states which have suffered a significant degree of psychological damage from contact with foreign exploitative forces. The construction of a Wage Policy Summary which will feature data on the strike level, inflation, unemployment and the share of wages in the National Income will be presented at the end of the Chapter, for the IMF years, subject to data availability.

The attempts at the formulation of a Social Contract, after it was first mooted by the IMF in 1978, will be the focus of Chapter 5. After some eighteen years the document circulated for discussion and agreement, within a prescribed deadline of two months, consisted of twenty-three triple spaced pages: a classic case, it may be said, of much "too little, too late".[26]

One of the more remarkable omissions in all the documented proposals towards a tripartite national consensus, to date, is any serious attempt at quantification of the items that are to represent the subject matter of exchange, the costs or sacrifices as against the benefits and gains: the *quid pro quo*. The evolution of the Australian Accords stand in stark contrast as a model, against which the substance of the Jamaican proposals may be compared.

If as Freire contends, the concern with consensus and compacts is only in evidence when the hegemonic classes feel threatened, then only substantial tangible benefits, perceived as such by labour, will be likely to achieve agreement.[27]

The Social Partnership paper states that,

> "For the worker, probably the greatest advantages of having a social partnership are employment generation and improvements in living standards. With some social partnership on the level of wage increases (sic) labour becomes an increasingly more attractive factor of production".[28]

Noticeably, the greatest fear of the worker, job dislocation, is given scant attention, beyond the expectation that the private sector will seek to expand employment, in a policy environment, with respect to loan interest rates for example, that is decidedly adverse. Hobbes' warning that "covenants without the sword are but words",[29] has obviously been ignored.

While the Government blames the other 'social partners' for the excess money supply provided in response to price and wage increases above productivity gains, it is claimed by them that, indeed, it is Government's own macro-economic policies that are the primary cause of inflation. The attitude of the Jamaica Confederation of Trade Unions is that, "… similar promises have been made and the government has the mandate and the social responsibility as the elected representatives of the people to control inflation with or without the cooperation of the social partners".[30] The reasons for labour's ambivalence as to its role in tripartite national policy determination will be fully investigated.

The reasons for such disagreements on financial and economic fundamentals reflect from the perspectives adopted here, differences of social and political philosophy. These will be explored throughout on different levels.

A country-specific approach to the serious scrutiny of structural adjustment policies and their consequences demands empirical investigation. Just how, in fact, has the IMF been perceived, generally – but also, specifically, in relation to the strategy-options selected for consideration – by those most adversely affected by those policies.

The Stone Poll of 1986 found that responses to the question as to whether the country should break off the relationship with the IMF were given from partisan political positions: while a total of 56% favoured severance, this was broken down into 76% PNP and 37% of the governing JLP supporters.

Interviews by Kirton, on behalf of Oxfam, portrayed in 1991, a virtually totally negative image of the IMF's role in Jamaica; so have the vast majority of the articles in, and letters to the press over the years.[31]

The results of the surveys carried out as an integral part of this work, with a view to an assessment, for the first time, of public opinion, particularly of the working class, in a more detailed, structured manner on various aspects of stabilization and adjustment policy will be presented in Chapter 6, 'The IMF: Consequences and Perceptions'.

Impressionistic evaluation of the public's basic attitude to the IMF, while no doubt, correctly, very unfavourable, suggested changing opinions over different periods.[32] In the design of the initial survey instrument, the attempt was therefore made to elicit responses over periods which coincided with different political administrations.

The Chapter will be concluded with a report of six case studies of public sector redundancy arising from IMF sponsored privatization policy, the reduction of the budget deficit and the extent of the state's involvement in enterprise economic activity. This will substantially set the stage for the following Chapter on the determinants of policy resistance, in different forms and to differing degrees.

A study of strategies of wage and labour control, contemplated and adopted, under stabilization and structural adjustment cannot, it is argued, escape an analysis of the potential, and the reasons for the absence of, serious social upheaval during this very extended period of austerity.[33]

Policy response has not received the level of attention it merits in regional literature. This, an attempt will be made to remedy in Chapter 7. There has been little deep probing of the reasons for lack of strong policy resistance, organized or otherwise: what has been repeatedly reported is the resulting alienation, disillusionment, hopelessness, and loss of faith in leaders and the political system.

The examination of the factors responsible for the accommodation of severely harrowing policy consequences, when the attempt at fundamental systemic reform, or even destruction, might have been a more likely response, is useful for predictive and not just explanatory purposes. Treatment will be on the individual, historical-cultural, and institutional levels. Account will also be taken of such social features as the importance of external reference group approval.[34] For, given the inherently poverty-generating legacy of an overly dependent structure of production and consumption at Independence,[35] it can be argued that the results of self-government might have been otherwise, had the demobilization, which is the essential feature of the relationship between labour and the native ruling class, not prevented the formation of a, "…wider more resolute anti-colonial unity (and an elite radicalism), failing which the country entered the post-colonial period with an ambiguous sense of national identity".[36]

The role of the emergent multi-class political party alliances in the preservation of traditional class and production relations, in the absence of national inter-class unity mobilized around a common mission clearly deserves discussion.

Jamaica can be said to have suffered from the "Kuznets curve", grow now and redistribute later,[37] approach to development; but also, subsequently, the strategy of "benign neglect"[38] of the basic needs of the poorer classes by those designing stabilization and economic adjustment policies, from the latter half of the 1970s.[39]

As Lynette Brown has pointed out,

> "… structural adjustment is as much a social process as an economic one.
> Embedded in the prescribed measures … is a particular conception of
> the class structure and a set of expectations about the behaviour of the
> different social groups, and in particular the entrepreneurial classes".[40]

So what of the working class – "… the target of frequent public homilies and admonitions".[41] Having embraced the 'myth of Independence' will it, as governments have done – without the benefit of choice, it has been said – now also embrace, unconditionally, "this new American inspired myth", that the efficiency principle, central to the prevailing orthodoxy of economic technicism, will yield "self-generating social benefits, without recourse to human volition and social control?"[42] The task undertaken will include providing answers to such questions, explicitly and by necessary inference.

While recognizing the need for analytical and policy prescription differentiation, in keeping with situation-specific societal features, the comparative consideration of the selected strategy options will be constrained largely by material availability and accessibility,[43] and not by concern about allegations of contextual irrelevance. A comparative approach to a number of the major issues addressed has been dictated quite simply by the lack of local policy initiative, tradition and the accumulation of any significant body of literature on specific labour relations questions and problems.

1. Patricia Anderson, and Michael Witter, "Crisis, Adjustment and Social Change: A Case Study of Jamaica", in Elsie Le Franc (ed) Consequences of Structural Adjustment – A Review of the Jamaican Experience, Canoe Press, U.W.I., 1994, p.2.
2. Ibid.
3. Karl Theodore, "Structural Adjustment in the Caribbean" in ILO, The Role of Trade Unions in Periods of Structural Adjustment Programmes, Barbados Workers Union Labour College Dec. 1992, p.17.
4. Omar Davies, the Minister of Finance, was reported as saying, at the opening of a Seminar on "Employment and Training in the context of Structural Adjustment", in Kingston, "that Structural Adjustment should not be viewed as being imposed by external forces, as is often the case … as all economies if they are going to remain [italics added] vibrant and if growth is going to be maintained [italics added] will need to go through continuous structural adjustment – The Daily Gleaner, Nov. 9, 1994, p.38.
5. Michael Witter, "Some Reflections on the Economic Development of Jamaica", in Judith Wedderburn (ed) Rethinking Development, Consortium Graduate School of Social Sciences, U.W.I., 1991, p.113.
6. IDT ex parte Seprod, 1981.
7. Lionell Robbins, "The Economic Functions of the State in English Classical Economics", in Edmund S. Phelps (ed) Private Wants and Public Needs, W.W. Horton and CO, New York, 1962, p.100, where Adam Smith likened the functions of the state to that of the "night watchman"; Lenin saw the state, on the other hand, as "a machine for the establishment and maintenance of class rule – V.I. Lenin, The State, Foreign Languages Press, Peking: China 1975, p.ll; for the "guiding hand" approach of Keynes, see J.M. Keynes, The General Theory of Employment, Interest and Money, Harcourt Brace, New York, 1936, p.377; The role played by the state in the development of the E. Asian "tigers" is considered, by Dennis J. Gayle, in "Applying the East Asian Development Model to the English speaking Caribbean", in Jacqueline A. Braveboy – Wagner(ed) The Caribbean in the Pacific Century, Lynne Rienner Publishers, 1993, p.79. See also Michael Parenti, Democracy for the Few, St. Martins Press, New York, 1988, p.302.
8. Balogh in 1971 argued that neo-colonialist exploitation does not depend on open political domination, since agencies such as the IMF "fulfils the role of the colonial administration of enforcing the rules of the game which brings about the necessary consequences": cheap labour; cheap primary commodities, through devaluation; increased United States exports, in particular, through import liberalization; and increasing third world debt and dependency, through the effect of adverse terms of trade and increased international interest rates – T. Balogh, "The Mechanism of Neo-Imperialism", in K.W. Rothschild (ed) Power in Economics, Penguin, 1971, p.320; And as Nichols observed, the exploitation of labour, inevitable and necessary for capitalist production, "always takes place in a particular historical situation which, inter alia, has its own specific political and ideological components" – T. Nichols, The British Worker Question Routledge and Kegan Paul, 1986, p.31; See also Teresa Hayter, The Creation of World Poverty, Pluto Press, 1992, pp.84 et seq.
9. T.D. Weldon, States and Morals, John Murray Paperbacks, 1962, p.256
10. See "Toward Developing a Social Partnership", PIOJ, Feb. 16, 1996, Par. 40, p.20 for the emphasis on the employment generation obligation of the private sector. In contrast to intended policy consequences, past performance, as noted by the JTURDC and the JCTU, gives little cause to be optimistic in this regard.
11. Carl Stone, in The Daily Gleaner, Feb. 17, 1988.
12. Those founding the ILO in 1919 "stressed the need to attack conditions of labour involving such "injustice, hardship and privation to large numbers of people as to produce unrest so great that the peace and harmony of the world are imperiled" – ILO, Employment growth and basic needs: A one-world problem, Tripartite World Conference on Employment, Income Distribution and Social Progress and the International Division of Labour, ILO, 1976, pp.1,179 et seq.
13. Weldon, supra, p.253.
14. Ibid, p.255.
15. "Toward Developing a Social Partnership", Par. 16, p.10.
16. Report on a Symposium on: "The Impact of the IMF Agreement with Particular Emphasis on Labour", Kingston, in The Daily Gleaner Feb. 17, 1990 p.2.
17. Deregulating Labour, in The Daily Gleaner, Jan. 10, 1990, p.6.
18. PSOJ, "The Private Sector's Response to the Social Partnership Paper", Mimeo, undated, p.4.
19. Bob Rowthorn, "Unions and the Economy", in Robin Blackburn and Alexander Cockburn (eds) The Incompatibles: Trade Union Militancy and the Consensus, Penguin and New Left Review, 1967, p.220.
20. John Corina, "Can an Incomes Policy be Administered?", in British Journal of Industrial Relations, (BJIR), Vol.v No.3, Nov. 1967, p.310.
21. William G. Demas, Essays on Caribbean Integration and Development, ISER, U.W.I.,1976, p.47.
22. Towards Developing a Social Partnership", Par. 36, p.18; For a comparison with the measures adopted on a tripartite level in Barbados see the summary Barbados moves towards adoption of prices and incomes policy, in The Financial Gleaner, Aug. 27, 1993, p.24.
23. For an outline of the report of the 1968 Japanese Study Commission on Prices, Wages, Incomes and Productivity and the treatment of factors inhibiting consensus, see Taishiro Shirai, "Prices and Wages in Japan: Towards an Anti-Inflationary Policy", International Labour Review (ILR), Vol.103 No.3, Mar. 1971, pp.228-42.

24. In Par. 49, p.24 of the Social Partnership Paper it is boldly declared that "It is essential that policy on income addresses all incomes – wages and salaries, profits and dividends"; But see Danny Roberts in The Jamaica Herald, Dec. 20, 1994, p.7 where the charge is laid that "the supply side perspective of the Government accepts the existence of wide income differentials" and that, there has been no attempt to define "reasonable return in the form of profits and interest".

25. Roger Blanpain, Recent Trends in Collective Bargaining in Belgium, ILR, Vol.104, Nos.1-2, July - Aug. 1971, pp.120-21.

26. The Social Partnership concept contained in the long-awaited document "Toward Developing a Social Partnership", has been described as "more of the same verbiage with little or no substance", in Letter to the Editor titled, "Much ado about nothing" – The Jamaica Herald, Dollars and Sense Magazine, April 15, 1996, p.2.

27. See Carl Stone, in The Daily Gleaner, Jan. 1, 1988; Also, Paul Chen- Young, in The Jamaica Observer, Jan. 27, 1996, p. 3; The World Bank itself recognized in its study Poverty in Latin America, 1986, that "it would be unwise to wait on resumed economic growth before reforming government agencies dealing with education, health, nutrition and other social services targeting the most vulnerable groups", so as to ease the economic and social pressure on the bottom 40% of income earners in the region.

28. "Towards Developing a Social Partnership", Par. 40, p.20.

29. Hobbes Leviathan , p.105.

30. Jamaica confederation of Trade Unions (JCTU), Response to the PIOJ's Document "Toward Developing a Social Partnership", Mimeo, Feb.1996, p.4.

31. These views disclose not just the case of a people "too often led astray by false prophets and disappointed by broken promises", but political parties reduced to the role of "vehicles of resentment", that were nevertheless, at the same time, the instrument of the implementation of the objectionable policy – Gordon K. Lewis, Puerto Rico: Freedom and Power in the Caribbean, Monthly Review Press, 1963, pp.96,103. In the context of policy design in the earlier part of the period under review, Stone interprets "the bashing of the IMF" by radicals of the dependency school as an attempt to divert attention from themselves as the persons responsible for "the dismal failures of policies" adopted at their behest in the 1970s – Carl Stone, in The Daily Gleaner, Oct.8, 1990.

32. Forrest, for example, is of the view that during the 1980's the image of the IMF changed from that of an "ogre" in the 1970's to that of a "friendly face" – Raymond Forrest, in The Financial, Gleaner, Mar. 23, 1990, p.14.

33. Ralston Nembhard, Damned if you do damned if you don't, in The Jamaica Herald, May 9, 1996, p.6A.

34. Carl D. Parris, Capital or Labour ? The Decision to Introduce the Industrial Stabilization Act in Trinidad and Tobago, Working Paper No.11, ISER, U.W.I., 1981, pp.19,33; Jamaica, it seems, learned nothing from the Trinidadian experience; see also Katrin Norris, Jamaica – The Search for an Identity, Institute of Race Relations, London, Oxford University press, 1966, p.90.

35. Louis Lindsay, The Myth of Independence: Middle-class Politics and Nonmobilization in Jamaica, Working Paper No.6, ISER, U.W.I., Mona, 1991, PP.1-4,52.

36. Obika Gray, Radicalism and Social Change in Jamaica, 1960-72, University of Tennessee Press, 1991, p.46; 1966, pp.70-101.

37. S. Kuznets, Modern Economic Growth, New Haven, Yale University Press, 1966; Winston H. Griffith, "Appropriate Economic Theory for the Caribbean", in Hilbourne A. Watson (ed) The Caribbean in the Global Political Economy, Ian Randle Publishers, Kingston, 1994, p. 31;

38. Ralph M. Henry, "Inequality in Plural Societies: An Exploration", in Social and Economic Studies (S.E.S.) Vol.38 No.2, ISER, U.W.I. June 1989, p.70.

39. ILO, Development for Social Progress: A Challenge for the Americas, Report of the Director General I, Part 1, Tenth Conference, ILO, 1974. For the currently popular view held by the staff of international financial institutions, in spite of the work of Chenery et al., see Robin Broad, John Cavanagh and Walden Bello, "Development: The Market is not Enough" in Foreign Policy No.81, Winter 1990-91, Carnegie Endowment for International Peace, p. 144. Barber Conable, World Bank President in Feb. 1990 is quoted as saying that for the 1980's the most remarkable development was the "generation of a global consensus that market forces and economic efficiency were the best way to achieve the kind of growth which is the best antidote to poverty".

40. Lynette Brown, "Crisis, Adjustment and Social Change – The Middle Class under Adjustment", in Le Franc, (ed), 1994, pp.21-2.

41. Gordon K. Lewis ,1963, p. 224; David C. Korton and Felipe B. Alfonso, Bureaucracy and the poor: Closing the gap, Kumarian Press, (Asian Institute of Management), 1985, p.201. The authors remark that development programming and associated economic output policies continue to be dominated by methodologies in which the central focus is economic output and the allocation of financial resources, while "the people they are to serve remain a highly aggregated abstraction".

42. Bohuslav Herman, The Optimal International Division of Labour, ILO, 1975, p.132; Belinda Coote, The Trade Trap - Poverty and the Global Commodity Markets, Oxfam, 1993, p. 186, contends that "the need now is for governments in the South to prioritize poverty reduction when restructuring their economies".

43. Information and data requested from the BITU, UAWU and the Research Dept. of the Ministry of labour was not forthcoming. Neither was requested information on the trading in shares by employees under ESOP received from the National Investment Bank of Jamaica. The PNP declined to complete the "Party" Questionnaire submitted to them on three occasions, despite their several and specific promises to do so.

Chapter I
The National Interest

There are strong arguments that can be raised against the view that trade union leaders should regard themselves as exclusive custodians of the public interest for the simple reason, according to Shanks – and as unionized employed persons should have no difficulty accepting – that, "…this is not the job they are paid to do."[1] Union leaders who behaved in that fashion would very quickly lose control of their unions and sacrifice the confidence and dues of their members. This would be so even if there was no potential competition for members. Further, no one has yet seriously campaigned for union membership to be legally obligatory.

The irony is that while trade unionists are often castigated for not being 'patriotic', or for not putting the interest of the nation before the sectional interest of their members, few people, regardless of their social or political status, relate their own pay to the national interest. The apparently permanent need for sacrifice, in the form of remuneration forgone in the national interest, in the Jamaican context, is limited to wage earners, particularly those in the public sector and the unionized labour force. It has been found in India, for example, that despite overall GNP growth in the 1980's, the poorest members of the population had benefited little in terms of their standard of living. This, Bhandaric argues, is the result of, "… the policy bias of development planners in viewing the poor primarily as producers", and not as consumers.[2]

Shanks makes the still highly relevant point that in considering the issue of whether the average worker deserves an increase, the question which immediately occurs to the middle and upper-class person is whether the enterprise, industry or economy can afford it. The result is that, "… the worker's reward is judged by its effect, not on himself, but, on the national economy – a point of reference that is very unlikely to be chosen by the average middle and upper-class person in consideration of his own income. Yet, he is perpetually amazed at the obtuseness and selfishness of the worker"[3], in choosing not to do so.

Having conceded that, "… in ordinary circumstances voters cannot be expected to transcend their particular localized and self-regarding opinions", Lippman goes on to suggest that since government by referendum is not practicable, "… the public interest may be presumed to be what men would choose if they saw clearly, thought rationally, and acted disinterestedly and benevolently ...".[4] The problem, it goes without saying, is that not very many people can be expected to act disinterestedly.

As Stone observes:

> "The decolonization movement involved some very basic goals: the articulation of the notion of a "public interest", an expansionist view of the state, leading to increased revenues to government as well as public spending, a more active governmental administration that would in time challenge the private sector, the expansion of the bureaucracy and the promulgation of reform ideologies that would seek to maximize the public interest."[5]

Given the historical political linkages of the movement, the trade unions were expected to contribute to the development effort, based on arguments hinged to notions and sentiments of patriotism. But patriotic working class behaviour, in a state system characterized by entrenched middle class political hegemony, and the legitimized subordination of labour under an industrial relations ideology which sought to better ensure the realization of benefits by the preservation of traditional production relations,[6] was scarcely a good prospect.

Unlike the working class and its institutions in Jamaica and the Caribbean, the radical Palestinian labour movement is not duped into accepting a conceptualization of 'the public' or 'the nation' in which their interests are of no account. Since it is the working class and its dependents which constitutes the main component of "the people", it is, as Munck states, rather rhetorical to appeal to workers to restrain their demands on behalf of a collectivity that consists largely of themselves.[7]

Pressures for unions to be 'responsible' often leads to the undermining of internal union democracy. Union leaders can easily feel compelled by nationalist obligations to make decisions and adopt postures in conflict with their member's wishes and interests, even, which can only prevail by duress or the use of autocratic strategies.[8]

The basic conflict between democratic unionism, which most would consider to be in the national interest, and "responsible" unionism,[9] meaning responsible to interests other than those of its members, has not yet been recognized by that generation of business practitioners un-schooled in the ways of any other world but their very own. This failure has been betrayed in statements by two prominent and highly regarded members of the business community. Delroy Lindsay, the then

President of the PSOJ, who forcefully accused the unions of being anachronistic in their orientation to bargaining strategies and lacking the forward-looking attitude to the industrial relations problems thrown up by increased economic, financial and technological dynamism, which would be required for efficient problem-solving so as to achieve economic growth.[10] Robert Lightbourne, Minister of Industry and Trade during the period of rapid industrialization and economic growth in the 1960's, roundly blamed the unions for company closures, relocation abroad and the relative absence of new investments. He saw the unions as a threat to the "… social and economic fabric of the country", primarily because of their pursuit of power, both institutional and personal, claiming that,

> "… they fight like dogs over bones, each determined to win in a game in which the poor workers are the pawns and the country the hapless victim".[11]

As against this capitalist perspective, there is that of the late Arthur Lewis who suggested that the energy spent in preaching the virtues of social peace and brotherhood, and the dangers of envy and industrial and political strife, would be better devoted to removing glaring property inequality by legislative confiscation and redistribution.[12]

Access to, and capitalist control of the media places trade unions at a distinct disadvantage, vis-a-vis employers, in communicating with their own membership and the public, in situations where the sympathies and moral support of the wider population may be decisive.

More often than not, even if the media is not predominantly hostile, the listening and viewing public is bombarded, relatively speaking, with the employer's message, often professionally crafted by public relations specialists.

Lipset's well-chosen words, might, with advantage be given consideration by all vested interest representatives, many of whom probably suffer from authoritarian antecedents, at one level or the other,

> "Only the give-and-take of a free society's internal struggles offer some guarantee that the products of the society will not accumulate in the hands of a few power holders … democracy requires institutions which support conflict and disagreement as well as those which sustain legitimacy and consensus."[13]

There are those who will feel entitled to urge that with very skewed income distribution, the national interest requires more, rather than less, struggle against inequality.

Arthur Lewis, writing before the devastation of the 1970's and 80's, quite boldly declared, "All modern governments are egalitarian and seek to eliminate extremes of income."[14] His book, published under the auspices of the Fabian Society, was definitely not prophetic as to the policies – with the very opposite intention and effect – that were to be imposed less than a decade later, in the name of economic stabilization and adjustment.

Making an appeal for more equitable redistribution of property, Lewis remarked even then, that, "It is not merely that there are indefensible extremes of riches and poverty, with the ever-present threat of revolution promoted either from within or without. It is also that judgement on all other issues is distorted".[15]

As against the orientation which conceives of the national interest solely in terms favourable to capital, Clark Kerr, et al., take the position that human resource development is the most critical, "... of all the processes of development of industrial working forces".[16]

But the Jamaican experience has shown, conclusively, that the establishment of more committees, councils, secretariats and task forces, with the best of intentions and the most passionate rhetoric, has failed to provide the new industrial work force with the skill flexibility, in the numbers, and with the positive work ethic demanded by increasing global competition.

Yet. the massive resources necessary for the education, training, motivation and efficient national utilization of labour has yielded priority rating to 'cost recovery' and 'cost sharing' as a result of 'budgetary constraints', while permission is sought and obtained for the importation of Far-Eastern workers for the local garment industry, known to have been the fastest growing non-traditional export activity for several years.[17] And all because the middle class elite has typically assumed no direct managerial responsibility for unemployment, depending as it has increasing done – since the much abused and scandal-ridden Special Employment ("Crash") Programme of the 1970's – upon the invisible hand of the market economy to provide jobs in the Keynesian 'long run'.

Skidmore takes this perspective a step further in suggesting that, in fact, it is variations in the character of the labour movement (which may in turn be attributable to the level of economic development) which is, " ... the most important single variable in explaining the success or failure of stabilization programmes."[18] However, human resource development, on a national scale, has not figured prominently in the interpretations of the national interest under structural adjustment and IMF stabilization policies.

There can hardly be a better example of the possible conflict in the resolution of the question, as to what properly constitutes the national interest, as that which emerges between international financial institutions, intra-party ideological struggles, and intense inter-party rivalry than the situation described by Michael Foot,

> "What about the moment when the IMF was invited in, and that Labour Government [of the Harold Wilson-led British Labour Party of the 1960's to 1970's] agreed or was forced to inflict a whole range of cuts on the very services we wished to improve.... Thanks to his (Peter Shore's) advocacy and that of others, to the skepticism ... to the pressures from outside ... to Dennis Healey's own realism ... the original IMF propositions were at least mitigated, and the Labour Government retained the chance of seeking a new advance later. We were not prepared any of us, to risk the alternative: opening the gates to the Tory enemy, through resignations and the destruction of the Government."[19]

In contrast, that extraordinary nation-wide unity of purpose forged by the real threat of invasion and the prospect of military defeat and subjugation by Germany caused Cole and Postgate to conclude that,

> "The unity so frequently promised or appealed to in politicians' speeches was for some time a reality: it is for once not untrue to say that few in any class failed to do their utmost for the community."[20]

To put the situation in true perspective, however, it is to be noted that as the authors inform us:

> "Financiers on the Government's right clamoured for drastic retrenchment in public expenditure by cutting down the social services and especially by reducing benefits to the unemployed. ... They demanded that any domestic sacrifice necessary should be made by the poor. ... They badgered Ramsay McDonald with their prophecies of disaster until he came to believe with them that the Government should enjoy the fullest confidence of the capitalist class."[21]

This scenario can be said to have anticipated exactly the Jamaican experience under IMF and World Bank stabilization and structural adjustment programmes, in that the confidence referred to was that which would, in the crisis of capitalism, put the interest of capital before that of labour, the interest of capital being, to those international financial institutions, synonymous with that of the nation.[22]

It has been unfortunate that there has been no attempt to define the national interest in terms of the society's most serious social ills. In Toye's view, most people would consider the ending of large-scale poverty to be, "… what mattered ultimately."[23] It is the sickness, ignorance, and premature death, not to mention the violence, ugliness and despair of daily life which accompany poverty and unemployment, that, it is alleged, "revolt most people." Aggravated as these conditions have been by the Fund and, until relatively recently, by Bank designed policies, it comes as a relief - if somewhat late in the day for Jamaica – for it to be recognized that economic development should have as its fundamental objective the reduction of poverty.[24]

That the notion of, 'the national interest', however interpreted, flies in the face of the commitment to the pursuit of individual self-interest, on which the political economy of neo-liberalism is grounded, seems, strangely, to have escaped those former socialist intellectuals now reluctant converts to the prevailing free market ideology.[25]

Any status quo, as Lipset notes, embodies rigidities, contradictions and dogma, "… which it is the inalienable right of the intellectual to attack, whether from the standpoint of moving back to traditional values[26] or forward toward the achievement of the egalitarian dream."[27]

The role of the intellectual as catalyst is given additional significance by Mills' observation that it was apparently only at certain (earlier) stages in the industrialization process, and also under an autocratic political regime, that the working class can reach Marx's second stage of class consciousness by becoming "a class for itself".[28]

In the absence of action-oriented intellectual leadership, organized around a 'mission', the problem of converting popular distrust of the state[29] into the promotion of national well-being has been the subject of extensive comparative treatment which shall be considered below.

The Fund's strategy of unequal growth attempts, according to Harrison, "… to eliminate absolute poverty by increasing relative poverty, to reduce material want by increasing psychological want".[30]

One view which appears to be a rather perverse justification of growing asset ownership, and income and wealth inequality is not based on the usual IMF-type arguments in support of the need for highly favourable financial incentive-based entrepreneurial motivation for investment and capital accumulation. Rather – somewhat in the manner of Milton Friedman, – based, more fundamentally, on the need for the preservation of liberty, is Moore's proposition that,

"As we reduce economic inequalities and privileges we may also eliminate the sources of contrast and discontent that put drive into genuine political alternatives... There is, I think, more than a dialectical flourish in the assertion that liberty requires the existence of an oppressed group in order to grow vigorously".[31]

The obvious question that the oppressed would ask is: Liberty for whom? Toye, on the other hand, makes the observation that, whether Marx's account of the transcendence of capitalism is consistent with the political aspirations of the contemporary poor in the Third World, "...is a large question which those on the top do not seem to think requires an answer."[32]

For Gordon Lewis, the search for a new 'national interest', involving, as it does, the adjustment of values and patterns of behaviour necessary for service to the national community, is nothing more nor less than the search for a new cultural identity.[33] But that search, he maintains, by its tendency to become the 'private game' of the ruling elite, "... persistently obscures the important truth that neither national interest nor cultural identity of any genuine character can be achieved save as they rest on the foundation of social equality and economic justice."[34]

But to challenge the local politicians, according to Lindsay, can be taken to be, and often is interpreted as amounting to, indulgence in treasonable activities against the 'people' and the 'nation'.[35] This situation is, however, far from being an acknowledgement of the propriety of the position of the 'new political economy of development' - proponents of which equate Third World politics with the "... unbridled pursuit of self-interest, by rulers". Whatever the definition of the public interest, and however much allowance is made for the accommodation of private interests, as a constituent part of the wider community interest, it would, from Toye's angle of vision, "... have been more logical to question the competence of Third World politicians in explaining the persistent failure of the development effort, while, "... suspending disbelief in their good intentions". Otherwise, one ends up with the conclusion, which, "... belongs to the pathology of politics", that,

"... the political process is damned as incapable of serving any conception of the public interest".[36]

While it has always been an unreliable assumption that the individual will willingly sacrifice his interests in favour of those of the collectivity,[37] the role of interest groups in the political process was previously positively evaluated. This was on the basis of their moderating influence on the adoption and making of extreme positions and demands, reflecting the extent to which they represented countervailing forces towards compromise.[38]

It was formerly the accepted view that political competition of groups representing different interests served, "... not only to protect but actually to construct the public interest."[39] But under the influence of the new political economy, the contrary approach is now that political fragmentation, ideological incoherence, spatial dispersion and even temporal differences, all result in the general failure of disparate groups to coincide over an extended period.[40]

While those who see themselves as committed to the promotion of social justice inevitably emphasize redistribution towards the reduction of inequality, Galbraith, in the context of the period of the late 1950's, noted that both liberals and conservatives had indeed accepted that an alternative policy was that of increasing aggregate output.[41] What he failed to consider was the effect of the maintenance of traditional differentials in the allocation of the surplus, which, if established patterns were not disturbed, would simply result in unchanged relative inequality at a higher level.

In any event, Galbraith's option of increasing national output has not proved easy to grasp in Jamaica since the early 1970's, despite unceasing exhortations and admonitions. And, of course, when inequality increases faster than total growth the poor get poorer, in the meantime – and that may not be a short time.

Despite protestations of government representatives to the contrary, often convincing to the unlearned, the question of how the costs of adjustment are to be borne is one not entirely outside the discretionary decision-making power of the client state under an IMF agreement. In a society in which government, for most people, has represented, "... something from which to extract special privileges denied to others", and in which there is thus, "... little conception of government in the national sense",[42] the inter-class distribution of the cost of economic 'recovery' assumes critical importance for political survival.

Given the economics of retrogressive redistribution, and the persistence of liberal democracy, one is compelled to question the validity of Diamond's generalized statement that "Only the most autarchic of nations could build, "... even in principle, a democracy on a foundation of persistent poverty, and in a rapidly shrinking world such nations have all but disappeared."[43] It is not just that the economic and political upheavals and doctrinal revolutions of the decade of the 1980's were unanticipated, but that the observed crises of the 1970's seemed to offer no hint of the need for cautious predictions, in what was clearly a period defined by turbulence.

In the open, trade-dependent economies of the Caribbean, nationalism under the leadership of the middle-class elite, as a tool of popular mobilization, became blunted not long after the culmination of the process of constitutional decolonization in Independence. Thus, "... the identification of the national interest with the sectional interest of the creole ruling group" was assured.[44] And the rhetorical language of UNESCO, which in the mouth of a Jamaican politician would signal taking refuge from reality, was not likely to change this alignment. of interests. In its plan for 1977-82, UNESCO put forward the idea of 'endogenous development' to be designed and implemented within the context of national political sovereignty, and mirroring, "... its (the nation's) own choices and in accordance with the authentic values, aspirations and motives of its people."[45]

Whatever the worth of UNESCO's proposal, the more hegemonic IMF behaved otherwise. As Harrison documents, in relation to Peru,

"In 1961 the bottom 74% of land holdings occupied only 4% of the land while 88% of the land was held by 3% of landowners. Yet when the military government introduced serious land reform ... which by 1976 had seen the enormous feudal latifundia wiped out and one-third of all farm land taken over and distributed to landless peasants, the IMF [allegedly ideologically neutral and non-interfering in policy-making] found it. prudent to apply pressure to slow down the process of reform."[46]

Chenery et al., in seeking to shift attention from an exclusive focus on economic growth towards greater equity in the distribution of the accompanying benefits, argued for much more of the growth in national income to be invested in programmes to benefit the poor. They went further to recommend a redistribution of 2-3% of national income each year, which could be achieved if the rich sacrifice a 15-30% slower than normal rise in income.[47]

The obsessive concern to find alibis for inaction and, in typical colonial fashion, even deliberate evasion of responsibility, caused partly by the dismal heritage of slavery, colonialism, imperialism and now the austerity regime of the international financial institutions of world capitalism – have not allowed even this degree of 'politically feasible' sacrifice, proposed by Chenery, to be enforced by governments of the third world. There is no economic and social elite that is going to volunteer to take less so that the poor can get more; but some will engage m making donations to charity,[48] and thus earn national reputations as outstanding philanthropists and as model corporate citizens. This is a situation not dissimilar to the tokenism of debt relief and forgiveness which makes no noticeable dent in the debt service problem of the heavily indebted developing and not-so-developing countries.

The ILO calculation that, without redistribution, the developing countries would need to grow by 9-11% per year to be able to provide the basic, needs requirements of the poorest 20% of their populations by the beginning of the twenty-first century has proven to be a daunting proposition.[49] Any progressive internal redistribution has been frustrated by an elite that, if not 'totally ruthless in its egoism', has, to say the least, been substantially aided and abetted in its predatory tendencies by the policy consequences of stabilization and structural adjustment.

Stone observes that policy articulation in Jamaica is mostly symbolic manipulation, with factual representation a poor second.[50] The objectives of symbol manipulation have been to calm anxieties and fears stemming from a potentially explosive social stratification and to promise fulfilment of deep-felt aspirations and hopes. Here lies the explanation for the oft-repeated ritual of flight into non-specific mass-oriented rhetoric, holding out images of the prospective results of the state's, and, more lately, the private sector's, high performance capability. What therefore amounts to formalized wishful thinking may be easily verified by casual perusal of the last Five-Year Development Plan in relation to actual performance, as indicated below. The projection of loyalty symbols on which individual and group identities can be anchored provides emotional succour of last resort in the absence of a policy-based nationalist 'mission'. But, further, it constitutes an easily produced substitute for principled political mobilization.

The increasing public cynicism which greets, and now appears to be the standard response to, the announcement of public policy initiatives, no doubt has its genesis in that mass realization of the variance between appeals for sacrifice in the promotion of the spirit of self-reliance and national sovereignty, and demoralizing declarations such as: "... the economic programme is predicated upon continued inflows of external public *assistance* [italics added] ... and *foreign* [italics added] proceeds from the Government's divestment programme ..."[51]

Table: I	Jamaica Five Year Development Plan 1990-1995		
	Plan Forecast	Out Turn	Variance
Growth Rate (1990-93)			
GDP	+12.5%	+ 8.8%	-3.7%
Agriculture	+11.6%	+36.7%	+25.1%
Mining & Quarrying	+13.2%	+27.3%	+14.1%
Manufacturing	+12.4%	-6.4%	-18.8%
Construction	+25.2%	+ 2.1%	-23.1%
Trade (1990/91 - 1993/94)			
Exports (US$M)	5200	4414	-786
Imports (US$M)	7516	7583	-67
Trade Balance (USSM)	-2316	-3169	-853
Tourism Earnings (USSM)	2966	3160	+ 194
Job Creation			
High Forecast ('000)	228400	34500	-1193900
Low Forecast ('000)	100700	34500	-66200

Source: Bruce Golding, The Daily Gleaner, May 25, 1994, p.7; See also Martin Henry, "Innovation, S & T and Wealth creation in The Daily Gleaner, Jan. 12, 1995, p.6 re the nonfulfilment of the Science and Technology provisions under the Plan.

It is not surprising, given policmaker's penchant for vague generalizations, that the policy statement for meeting basic needs disclosed that over the current Five-Year Plan period provisions would be made to:

"... address the needs of the vast majority of persons and pay special attention to those that have fallen below or are in danger of falling below minimum standards; restore flow of funds to the social sectors which have been drastically reduced in recent years as a result of structural adjustment policies; direct resources in favour of those education and health services that are most likely to reach the poor."[52]

What, is remarkable about this statement is that the precise advantage to be derived from the basic needs planning strategy, that of quantification of targets within a specified time frame-work, has been totally ignored. We find in the Plan, under 'Social Security and Welfare', for example, the following statement of objective: "... to make benefits such as pensions more attractive in order to provide a higher level of income to beneficiaries".[53] But perhaps the most telling feature of the entire Plan is that concerning provisions for the railway, "... efforts will be made", it is said, "... to increase operating efficiency and expand its operation. The investment programme provides for track rehabilitation and renovation of existing equipment."[54] This, in connection with a utility which has been shut down since October 1992 and which has been on the divestment list for some years now and that, to date, after the end of the Plan period, is still inoperative.

It is interesting to note that the language of the Plan provisions, referred to above, reveals by implication what, has been described as the tendency, "... to hide behind the skirts of the wicked IMF in promulgating genuinely unavoidable, unpleasant adjustment measures". Janine Iqbal was among the few early commentators to contend that a structural adjustment programme is to be justified on the basis that it,

> "... constitutes a necessary assurance that hitherto profligate borrowers
> have put in place mechanisms to generate the requisite income to
> facilitate repayment".[55]

What is at issue, on this view, is not adjustment, but rather the pace and sequencing of various policy prescriptions, together with the more socially divisive question of the distribution of the costs of economic reorganization. Both JLP and PNP administrations have tangibly failed to recognize, except during the periods close to elections in their second terms of office, the need for social impact amelioration policies as a necessary countermeasure to structural adjustment dislocations and impoverishment. The "... provision of income supplement, subsidized health care and education, and temporary employment opportunities ..." have featured not even in rhetorical declarations of policy intentions, much less in the experience of the potential beneficiaries of a more human resource development orientation to economic restructuring.[56] In any event, in the absence of a cost/benefit analysis of tax revenue as against social welfare and other benefits provided by the State, from the taxpayer's point of view, it is clear that it must be meaningless to speak of 'subsidy' in this context.

Rather than the belated awareness of the need to promote adjustment 'with a human face' by the World Bank, and only quite recently by the IMF, and the deferred concern with poverty alleviation as a matter of party political survival, Thomas asserts the need for an alternative development model. This model calls for a changed system of resource ownership and control, primarily dedicated to the satisfaction of basic needs of the majority of the population. It, "... implies a systematic, conscious, deliberate and planned attack on poverty", as against traditional developmental strategies in which the concerns of the disadvantaged are, "... incidental items on an agenda for some other disembodied abstraction such as export-competitiveness, building an industrial sector, or developing a more appropriate technology ...".[57]

It is arguable, at the same time, that it is the abrogation of state responsibility for the development of national industrial and investment policies that has allowed the market allocation of resources, on the basis of decisions reflecting 'right price signals', to be presumed coincidental with the national interest. And foreign borrowing, if anything, allowed the non-execution of autonomous state-initiated adjustment measures[58] that might otherwise have occurred, if only by default. This in a situation where the borrowed funds were not invested in resolving the main resource constraint, the shortage of foreign exchange. The countries in the Organization of Eastern Caribbean States have managed, in large measure, to avoid the problems experienced by Jamaica because, in their case, transfers have been in the form of grants or foreign direct investment. Policy-makers and commentators, have failed to learn from the experience of others, even though, as shown in FIG. I, since 1984 there has been a net transfer of capital to private creditors and multilateral agencies, once interest payments are deducted from net inflows.[59]

In keeping with UNESCO's approach to development, Thomas, in reviewing the experiment of the PNP Government under a democratic socialist ideology in the 1970's, raises the possibility that, "Early and resolute decision" to pursue an economic path oriented to working class interests, as a priority, could have been successful.[60] Perhaps the most serious obstacle on this path was the existence of the multi-class party alliance which would inevitably have come under increasing pressure, internally and externally generated, in direct relationship to the degree of radicalism of the transformation attempted.

Ironically, the social havoc caused by structural adjustment policies that led to the UNESCO investigations which pointed to the need for the human implications, "... to be made an integral part of adjustment policy as a whole, and not to be treated as an additional welfare component",[61] started in Jamaica under the democratic *socialist* banner.

The price elasticities of demand for food being quite high, together with the fact that the poor spend a much larger percentage of their income on food, as compared to the rich, means that sharp wage declines result in significant reductions in food purchases by the poor. The coping strategies often identified are not usually available to the very poor for maintaining previous levels of consumption: reduction of savings, liquidation of assets, expanding family labour market participation and incurring debt.[62]

On the industrial policy front, 'learning by doing' has still not become a part of Jamaica's culture. Proximity to the island's largest trading partner, the United States of America, does anything but encourage the spirit of improvisation and creativity, without which local appropriate technology will never emerge, either indigenously or by adaptation. The call for a massive programme of scientific and technical, including agricultural and vocational, training for young people and the integration of school and the world of work has yet to receive a tangible response.

Figure: I

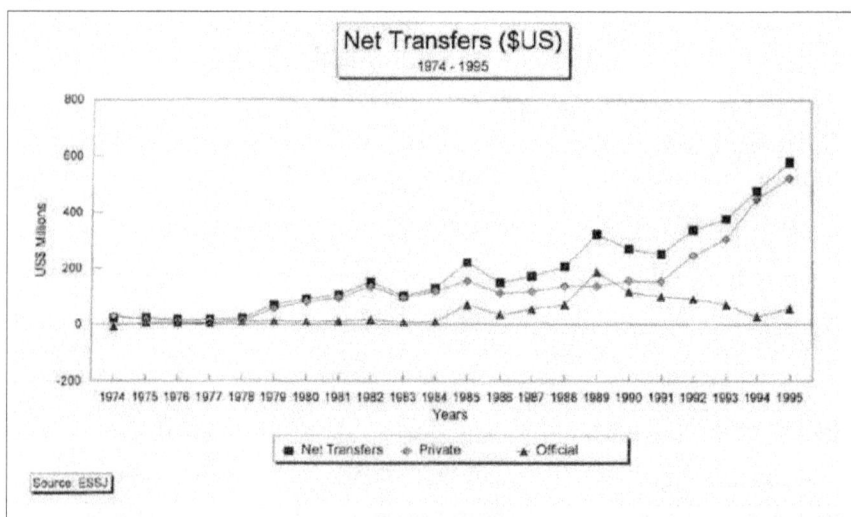

The economic vested interests with maximum media access, and which are organized into strong permanent professionally staffed pressure groups, not surprisingly, disproportionately influence the formulation, procedurally and substantively, of government policy, which is then portrayed, self-servingly, as being for the common good. This is all in keeping with the ideological sanctity of the *status quo*.

At the level of economic ideology, the development of a sense of 'community of interest' is not facilitated by free market individualism. This is unlikely, according to Gordon Lewis, to compensate for the increased social tensions and economic conflicts generated by capitalistic economic organization exacerbated by the disturbance of class composition and inter-class relations in increasingly dynamic domestic and international environments.[63]

The representative position of the government thus becomes more problematic: as it not only becomes more difficult to articulate an inherently distinct national interest, but the identification of 'the nation' as against changing coalitions of mutually potentially threatening interest groups[64] involves great indirect electoral risks.

As Salamon sees it, the national interest is an,

"… abstract concept which cannot be determined or assessed in any realistic way. It is whatever the government, mass media, or anyone else perceives it to be, and indeed may often be used by governments and others as an apparently self-evident and acceptable justification for what are in reality ideological based policies and decisions".[65]

The traditional view of the public interest is adopted by the Trinidadian, Zin Henry, in his consideration of the efficiency of compulsory arbitration as a method of resolving labour disputes. The premise on which public policy determination is seen to rest, is the internalized assumption that, "… public welfare transcends the sectional interests of labour and of employers"[66] – a contention that is regarded as being 'irrefutable'. It would appear that the bilateral resolution of industrial conflict through the process of 'free collective bargaining' amounts, on this approach, to 'collusion to the mutual advantage of employers and employees (and) to the detriment of society'. This would indeed appear to be the only sense in which the New Right and Thatcherite view that 'there is no such thing as society', is probably correct; for when the interests of labour and capital are removed there is really no significant 'public' remaining.

The idea, implicit in Henry's view, that there is somehow a 'fundamental identity of interest' between the contending groups in society is, for Tawney, an illusion that leads to the unrealistic expectation that industrial peace is achievable, "... merely by the exercise of tact and forbearance".[67]

And, specifically, the institutionalization of industrial conflict – through the machinery of compulsory arbitration takes for granted the equity, propriety, and stability of production relations of capitalist society. But if liberty is more precious than peace,[68] as Tawney would have it, then it becomes clear that it is precisely the question of equity that is at issue,[69] for,

> "... a body of workers who used their strategic position to extort extravagant terms for themselves at the expense of their fellow workers [italics added] might properly be described as exploiting the community.[70] But at present such a statement is meaningless ... before the community can be exploited, the community must exist[71] and its existence in the sphere of economic relations is today not fact but only an aspiration".[72]

Obika Gray sees the middle class, even within the context of multi-class political party alliances, as relating to the poorer, darker, (in colour) classes from a background based on class contempt and paternalistic relationships.[73] Given the fact that the ruling political elite has been drawn almost exclusively from the middle class, the emergence of any operational mobilizational notion of the national interest was most unlikely.

As a consequence, the popular condemnatory charge of 'holding the country to ransom',[74] when objectively considered, has been held to be "logically self-destructive," since little of the nation remains when workers, their dependents and sympathizers are deducted from it.[75] For therein lies the essence of inequality: the small number who control the economy.

But appeals to the "good of the nation", or some variant of the notion, persist because, if consistently applied, "... ideological pressures induce workers to conceive their interests, on the one hand in limited and parochial terms, on the other as merely part of some all-embracing national interest. Consciousness on the part of wage and salary earners that they [italics added] have substantial common interests is systematically inhibited".[76]

It is not, of course, only workers' interests that may be 'fused and confused' with the 'common good'.[77] Modernization theorists continue a line of traditional thought, given a more negative and cynical turn by the new political economy of development school.[78] Co-optation into a governing political administration is attractive enough "to blunt the edge of one's dissent", and "minimise the gulf which separates the would-be dissenter from his leaders",[79] thus allowing a free rein to the corrupt and mercenary politician to act as an intermediary in a spoils-seeking and distribution system. Politics in developing countries, on this view, "... is not defined by restraint and the protection of the public interest", but rather by "chronic instability and disorder".[80]

There are, of course, geopolitical aspects to the issue of the definition of the national interest. As N.W. Manley observed, with respect to 'Black Power', or any other such potential source of political instability, "... the United States would never tolerate a hostile revolution in its sphere of influence".[81] Perhaps another would be more accurate.

As with the policy implications of the British Labour Party's class character, according to Miliband, Jamaican multi-class parties have always sought to emphasize the nationalist nature of policies that have consistently failed to improve the lot, of the working classes. This is despite campaign slogans/promises of "Better Must Come" "Deliverance", and that "We Put People First". In Miliband's view, a different outcome is not to be expected in a society, "... whose essential social characteristic remains marked inequality",[82] and where, at the same time, the public, through a relentless and highly effective socialization mechanism, perceives 'good' industrial relations to exist when the working class foregoes, "... the one form of action employers tend to find persuasive". As a result, "... demands beyond certain limits at any point in time are protested against as being unnecessary, unpatriotic and socially unacceptable".[83]

That such indoctrination takes place within the nation's boundaries, is supportive of the claim that domination, whether by the IMF/World Bank, or otherwise, is possible only to the extent that there exists a thriving local comprador class.[84] Thus, despite conditions conducive to socially destabilization, widespread industrial action,[85] under stabilization and structural adjustment, relative peace has prevailed. But contrary to the Programa Regional del Empleo para América Latina y el Caribe (PREALC) prescription,[86] there has been virtually no economic growth and, most definitely, no equitable distribution of the surplus.

Rather than a vague general definition of the national interest, Chenery and others[87] have proposed specific policy objectives which, taken together, represent what, it is claimed, good government should seek to achieve in the pursuit of national development. The components of the basic needs strategy suggested by Chenery are:

- Productive employment for the poor
- Increased investment in traditional agriculture and the informal sector
- Access to basic services for the entire population
- Reduced disparities between households in their ability to consume basic goods and services
- Creation of institutions which would allow the poor majority to participate more actively in the development effort.[88]

It has, however, been charged that this approach to development is disarming of advocates of revolutionary change since the attempt to make capitalism more acceptable, by giving it a more 'human face', leaves unaltered the social, political and economic structures, "... within which poverty and inequality had their roots."[89]

Needless to say, for those who already have the capacity,

"to realize their personalities, policy preoccupation with basic needs satisfaction of the majority would have little appeal", [and since civil society is constructed by and for them and run by and for them], "... All they need do is insist that, "... the majority of themselves is supreme over any government, for a particular government might otherwise get out of hand."[90]

This looks remarkably like the minimization of the role of the state, under the prevailing free market paradigm promoted by the multi-lateral institutions, and taken as given, even by the ILO.[91]

But as Honderich suggests, "The principle of equality does not derive from a view of life as simply a race where all attention is given to an equal start, and no attention to some being lame".[92]

Rather than severe cuts of public expenditure, at the behest of the IMF, what this view calls loudly for is the provision of greater opportunities – in education, for example – for the disadvantaged, as an expression of a public interest, properly conceived. But this kind of prioritization, in a resource-scarce environment, with the dictates of a stabilization programme in force, is not likely, given the presence of,

"… the indigenous bourgeoisie and the professional strata (which) both look upon the state as their negotiating instrument with the rest of the capitalist world economy."[93]

In that narrow sense, the bourgeoisie are 'nationalists'; that is, "… they will always be ready to brandish the flag if they believe it has a blackmail effect, and to put the flag in cold storage for a price".[94]

Margaret Thatcher's claim to have changed British class relations, "… in some vague but fundamental way – ushering in a new and novel form of workers' capitalism",[95] has been matched, particularly on the official representative level of private sector leadership. Also, surprisingly, even in some sections of the trade union movement in Jamaica, one witnesses a degree of acceptance, if not enthusiasm, better reserved for an assault on economic-adjustment-induced-pauperization and the widespread sense of working class hopelessness. These are social consequences that remain untouched by the privatization prescription.

As V.V. Ramanadham submits, the trade union response might well be that the public, through the state, already owned the enterprises "divested", and that, "… all privatization has done is take away the people's stake in state enterprises and hand it over to the minority able to buy shares in *something they already owned*"[96] [italics added].

It had been intended to provide a report on the changes which have taken place in share-ownership by employees in divested state-owned enterprises, so as to be able to make a judgment of the effectiveness of privatization in broadening asset ownership on a more than short-term basis. However, it has proved impossible, to obtain data on the extent and changing levels of employee share ownership, through divestment, over time, from the Divestment Secretariat at the National Investment Bank of Jamaica.[97]

Be that as it may, when publicly owned entities are divested, the further objection can be made that,

"… it is the taxpayer's equity that is offered on soft terms (or gifted away) to the workers [or more meaningfully, those fortunate enough to be employed in potentially profitable entities] and largely discounted to capitalist interests, individual and institutional".[98]

In relation to the claim about the virtue of the creation of an asset owning working class, realism requires that attention be paid to the percentage of its share ownership compared to that of the traditional propertied classes in the total economy. Any temptation to prematurely celebrate a substantial change in the paradigm of privileged minority capitalism, must be held in check by the consciousness of the fact that its lower paid members, to say nothing of the vast number of 'outsiders' to the nation's economic life, can't buy adequate food, much less stocks and shares. Such a realization, prompted by a review of poverty-line data, ought to restrain any inclination in certain quarters to exaggerated expectations of greater working-class commitment to increasing the efficiency of 'their' enterprises, and greater involvement in productivity enhancement decisions, in privatized entities.

The record, [certainly in the United States of America] shows that man hour productivity is depressed by low levels of utilization, and that periods of movement towards full employment yields considerably above-average productivity gains.[99]

The implication is clear: improvements in Jamaica's historically low level of productivity need to be policy-related. Such policy requires integration with multi-portfolio government and private sector effort to reduce idle capacity by increasing demand, thereby also expanding output, hence lowering unemployment.

A perverse version of the 'national interest' has been virtually unrelentingly pursued since the 1970s. This is despite the policy-induced ravages invariably revealed due to the emphasis on personnel reduction in the public sector, rather than any concerted, positive employment-generating, tax-base-broadening national, multi-sectoral initiatives.

While state ownership might not have been, "... a necessary or sufficient condition for the prioritization of the national interest over sectional interests",[100] the state, Farrell claims, has to be made to identify and pursue the 'public good'. Farrell does not, however, venture to state the necessary or sufficient conditions to enforce the performance of this task. The most that is stipulated, is that achieving policy formulation consonant with the public interest is, "... arguably a function of a good sensible legal regime and an alert educated citizenry".

Stone,[101] Stephens and Stephens,[102] Norris[103], and others, have been obliged to refer to the educational and issue-comprehension limitations of the Jamaican populace, a finding also common to the United States of America[104] and Great Britain.[105] Against such a background – compounded by the alleged 'development by duress' approach of the IMF/World Bank, made possible by a low governmental resistance capability, arising from a diagnosed condition of 'debt fatigue' – it is difficult to contemplate the existence of effectively operating channels for influencing the design of national policy in the interest of the majority.

And if the citizenry cannot realistically be expected to have sufficient knowledge, to usefully engage in objective assessment of technical economic policy, then one must expect judgments on policy to be made on the basis of their perceived social consequences. The hope and expectation that leadership of the unionized sector will make up for the deficiency of its members, has to surmount the not inconsiderable hurdle that the national labour movement institutions, the JTURDC and JCTU, are only partially representative of the existing trade unions.

And, although the percentage representation by the JTURDC may seem high at 82.6%, as shown by FIG. 2, it must be remembered that this entails the unionized labour force only, which as a proportion of the employed labour force is said to be between 23-32%. Even more importantly, neither institution possesses effective sanctions to enforce compliance among member unions. For their part, the unions have little effective means of enforcing disciplined acceptance of policy, which may, on occasion, be acknowledged at the national tripartite level as being in 'the nation's best interests'.

As Peden enquires,

> "Even if trade union national leaders could be convinced by economic arguments that wage restraint [for example] was in the national interest, there seemed to be no-one capable of persuading workers on the shop floor that circumstances warranted sacrifice of their individual interest?"[106]

Figure: 2

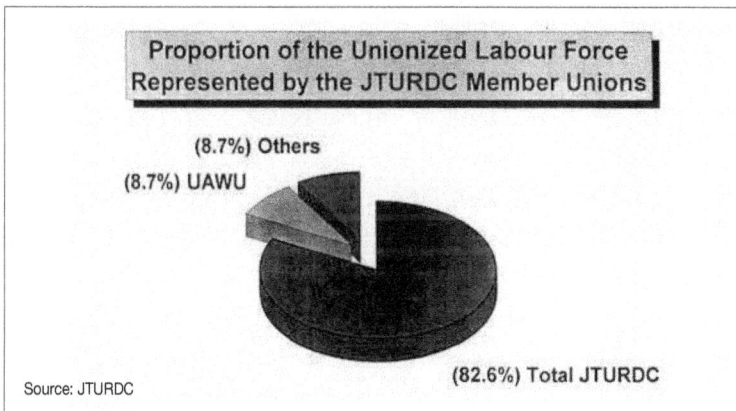

Proportion of the Unionized Labour Force Represented by the JTURDC Member Unions

(8.7%) Others
(8.7%) UAWU
(82.6%) Total JTURDC

Source: JTURDC

As a most effective sanction, the government can appeal to anti-union public sentiment, bolstered by well-funded, professionally organized mass media private sector public relations presentations. Increased potency is achieved when such campaigns take the form of saturation exercises in which the mass public consists of a combined number of self-employed, unemployed, and other non-union persons, which far exceeds the number of the unionized labour force. The consequence is that a majority of the population can, with effective government and private sector message presentation, distinguish between the interest of workers and that of "the nation as a whole", without a sense of betrayal.[107]

Lack of a sympathetic response by the working class for yet more sacrifices may be explained by the fact that it was not only social equity which was put in reverse during the, "lost decade of the eighties" and after. But, as Pantin observes, "... the evidence also shows that such growing inequality was not borne as a sacrifice for future aggregate growth",[108] despite the promises[109] and projections to the contrary.

The circumstances of regional governments, with an understandable obsession for political survival and a strong sense of their prerogatives, yet present what Nurse sees as, "... unlimited scope for trade unions to be caught in the national interest trap"[110] of being roundly condemned for failing to cooperate. This is despite the fact, as Nurse further observes, that they are provided usually with little opportunity to participate, beyond the level of symbolism, in broad policy decisions on social and economic management, although almost every decision made and action taken by the political directorate affects workers in one form or the other. Although it may be true that trade union leaders can cooperate, without being coopted, this is not an easy path to follow in countries with a tendency to an aversion to the adoption of independent positions and thought on electorally sensitive issues. And, most importantly, industrial relations and economic matters of controversy do fall within this category.

Short of participation in national policy formulation or, at the minimum, consultation prior to the making of major decisions, the scope for the exertion of working class influence is limited to collective bargaining. With the island's size and trade union history and structure, bargaining – which as a consequence occurs largely at the enterprise level – does not facilitate national agreements on strategies of interest mediation, such as a prices and incomes policy or a social contract. But with respect to working class articulation of the public interest, the process of collective bargaining is as distant from the daily experience of the masses as elections[111], and, indeed, any form of 'representative democracy', involving relatively large numbers of members of permanent institutions.

It is precisely this mode of working class organization, within a capitalist economic framework, which demobilizes the unionized element of the working class; and it is this element which sets the tone and pace for the defense of the general interests of a labour force in constant internal competition for a larger share of the surplus and greater job security.

The fragmentation of worker unity is further facilitated by segmentation of the labour force by industry, job category and even method of wage payment, to the extent that survival often involves intra working class competition on the individual, departmental, enterprise and sectoral levels.

The notion of common interests, to put it differently, does not come naturally to the working class. On the other hand, as Przeworski has observed,

> "Universalism is the natural ideology of the bourgeoisie, since as long as people living in the same society are thought to have some "general" or "public" economic interests, capitalists as a class represent those interests".[112]

The very conception of society based on a harmony of interests[113] was fiercely denied by the ideology of class conflict in the movement for socialism.[114] For it is objective production relations which, in this orientation, defines class interests and determine the substance of political action. In explaining the phenomenon of the working class playing by the rules of the capitalist game,[115] Gramsci notes that capitalism enjoys the active consent of the exploited, reflecting the central role of ideology in maintaining the hegemony of the dominant- classes.[116] The compromises represented by the diplomatic use of coercive power[117], in the form of collective agreements, are accommodated well within the existing system's tolerance limits.

All governments need to achieve a minimum level of policy tolerance for the purposes of implementation. This requires and, "... ensures that extreme demands will – to the extent that they cannot be conveniently ignored, politically be moderated" by those mutually accommodating bargaining outcomes, "... while the reasonable expectations of minorities would be respected in the process of coalition building".[118] But this accomplishment is never easy, with structural-adjustment-lending assuming the features of,

"... the offspring of Janus, smiling with one face as it delivered welcome foreign exchange (and) frowning with the other as it insisted on the performance of politically dangerous and administratively complex tasks".[119]

Thomas Paine's version of this scenario would be described in terms of making it more costly to live, on the one hand, and at the same time taking away the means of survival, on the other.[120]

And if there is 'a hostile industrial relations climate', normally attributed to heightened worker militancy and rarely to provocative factors such as substantial real wage erosion or actual/threatened retrenchment, the capitalist response is the counter-threat of a reduction in investment. But, "... whereas investment is in the order of things, perceived to be in the national interest, the same cannot normally be said about increases in nominal, much less real wages".[121]

In the Jamaican context, given the IMF policy assumption of a trade-off between wage restraint and increased employment-creating investment, it is well established that extra profits derived at the expense of wages can be unproductively 'invested': consumed, in the form of non-essential imports, or, 'exported'.

With the low level of confidence in the developmental capability of the private sector,[122] together with the weakness of patriotic sentiments noted by Manley,[123] Stone,[124] and Lindsay,[125] it is remarkable that the authors of the 'alternative' to the IMF, "The Emergency Production Plan/The People's Plan for Socialist Transformation", nevertheless placed faith in the possibility of economic reconstruction which required national unity based on, "... solidarity among the working class[126] and the (sic) cooperation with and by patriotic national capitalists".[127]

Despite the view of Beckford, et al.,[128] the sound radical position, it is submitted, is against the presumed viability of such class collaboration.[129] The ambivalence of this reformist, as against radical, posture is fully exposed by the statement that,

"It does not mean that labour should cease to struggle against capital. But it implies that workers and their organizations have a responsibility for avoiding unnecessary disruptions of the production process".[130]

It was no doubt precisely this compromised attitude to the reality of class relations which constituted the main weakness of President Allende's socialist Chilean experiment.[131]

The capitalist platform suffers from no such conflict on fundamental structural objectives:

> "Demands beyond certain limits at any point in time are protested against as being unnecessary, excessive, holding the nation to ransom, greedy/selfish, unpatriotic or socially unacceptable".[132]

There is no shortage of normative incentives in the form of recurring assurances of benefits to come[133], 'in the long run' in return for labour shouldering the cost of economic adjustment. A major trade union task is therefore to, "... demystify the doctrine of National Interest",[134] as formulated by capitalist interests and their class-related representatives at various levels of the state machinery – a principal example of which is the state's institutionalized control of trade union militancy under the 'national interest' provisions of the LRIDA.[135] In Harrod's view such control and subordination is seen as being legitimized by the labour movement itself, as it looks to the political directorate for defence and promotion of its social and economic interests.[136] Such a posture thus compromises any claim to independence and autonomy[137] in the determination of its modus operandi.

Trade union leadership is probably aware, beyond the level of instinctive distrust, that the periodic bargaining advantage they may enjoy in the context of a fragile free market economy is the explanation for the Social Contract project which seeks to, " ... integrate trade unionism into official administrative structures and thus [further] control it".[138] It has certainly been true that under the IMF/World Bank programmes, as Marx noted, "... the only part, of the so-called national wealth that actually enters into the collective possession of modern peoples is their national debt",[139] put in 1994 at some US$1700 plus per person.[140]

It is worthy of note that the self-employed in the formal and growing informal sectors, the unemployed, as officially defined and otherwise,[141] the peasantry, the youth and the aged have no voice in the formulation of a social contract between the Government the private sector and the trade unions represented by the JTURDC and the JCTU. Parenti's words, in such a context, need to be examined against the statistical reality of the distribution of the burden and wealth under structural adjustment:

> "The conflicts between plutocratic elites [caused by the disturbances and dislocation of economic change, due partly to what Havelock Brewster calls an "inclement external environment"] seldom work to

the advantage of the masses of the people. They are conflicts of haves versus haves – often resolved by collusion rather than competition at the expense of the public interest – higher prices; higher taxes; environmental devastation and inflation … The demands of the have-nots may be heard occasionally as a clamour outside the gate but the goals of business-growth, high profits, and secure markets become the goals of government … [while] … Proponents of the ideologically neutral mixed [and, more so, free market] economy assume that the government operates in a class vacuum".[142]

Taking into account the obstacles to national cooperation,[143] the probability of a dominant class being able, "…to articulate its hegemonic principle by absorbing *all* [italics added] the national popular ideological elements", is, at best, quite remote; for as noted by Edwin Jones, governments contend with, "… policy substance challenges from powerful classes, powerful opposition parties [certainly in Jamaica] and powerful bureaucrats",[144] not to mention the often seemingly overwhelming external constituency.

Until "a novel historical synthesis" occurs, in which the desired consensus becomes a reality, workers faced with, "… higher utility costs, transportation, medical and drug bills and education for their children … are not prepared to roll over and die … national interest cannot go to the supermarket."[145] This working-class scenario persists at a time when other observers see,

"… all those professionals and business people benefitting from the present state of affairs, or who see their snout getting closer to the trough as not to want anything to be changed; what else explains the tolerance among them, who should know better, for what prevails in Jamaica, for the abuse of the so-called small man?"[146]

Geoff Brown was, in the face of IMF austerity, since 1977, still capable of the comment: "Jamaicans just don't seem, on the whole, to understand the necessity for personal sacrifice and belt tightening when national survival is at stake".[147]

In similar vein, Ian Boxill argues that where election results depend on the spreading of the 'spoils', politicians are motivated, not so much to seek national policy consensus and display a concern for accountability, but, rather, to, "… defend their fiefdom at all costs from external threats", which negates any real chance of the adoption of, "… a model of development in which the relationship is established where capital and labour work in the national interest".[148]

If, as Katherin Norris and Hugh Sherlock allege, as reported elsewhere, there are two Jamaicas, needing to be "welded together", as evidenced by the gross materialistic disparities disclosed by FIG.3, what chances of success could possibly attend official strategies of labour control, however well-intentioned and designed?

Those who point approvingly to the traditional Swedish model of labour relations need to be made aware that the relatively low level of class conflict in Sweden made it easier for trade unions (representing between 80 - 90% of the labour force) to gain recognition from employers and to conclude collective agreements. Those agreements operate within a well-established framework. Legislation such as the *1976 Co-determination Act* on Employee Participation in Decision-making, "with its extensive repertoire of instruments for workers' control",[149] is indicative of the extent to which working class interests are accorded a central place in national policy-formation.

Further, in Sweden, most of the unions are members of national representative labour associations, "... to which they partially transfer their right to make decisions and to work on major issues." In such a context, some doubt that the foundations of the model will stand the strain imposed by internal structural and international production changes. It is nevertheless felt that, "... strong organised labour market parties freely cooperating on a basis of responsibility to the community at large"[150] will, in the absence of additional regulatory legislation, enable the preservation of the consensus that it is primarily the duty of the parties to the industrial relations system. The ultimate duty of the parties is to respect the interest of society and those within it who will be most directly affected by their actions. This is a very far cry from the extent of the radius of responsibility guiding behaviour in the Jamaican industrial relations system.

Of major significance to the interpretation given, in that country, to the 'national interest' is the fact that in a society usually committed to, and enjoying full employment, there is a *Promotion of Employment Act* (1974) on the statute books. And when, "... a severe deterioration in the economic situation ... subjected the legislation to unforeseen pressures, the result was that, "Government and the social partners have had to concentrate their efforts on safeguarding employment" [italics added].[151] The contrast in the Jamaican situation under so-called stablilisation policies cannot be more extreme.

It might, appear highly cynical, however accurate, to say that what Jamaica has borrowed from the model has been confined to the terminological: the phrase 'social partners' without even the beginning of the evolution of the essential features of a partnership relationship. Given the non-existence, in Jamaica, of the Swedish industrial strain and stress accommodating tradition and framework, it is appropriate to next consider the economic factors which have constituted the backdrop for strategic labour policy conceptualization and implementation.

Before doing so, however, it is highly instructive to compare the treatment of the national interest under Jamaican law with the Swedish situation.

Figure: 3

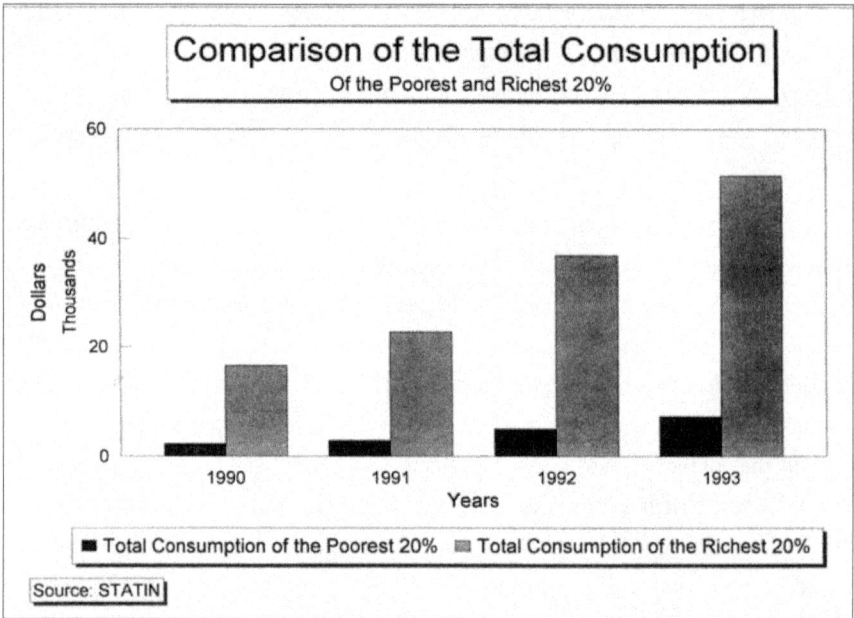

Comparison of the Total Consumption
Of the Poorest and Richest 20%

■ Total Consumption of the Poorest 20%   ▨ Total Consumption of the Richest 20%

Source: STATIN

Legislative provisions intended to protect the national interest on the labour relations front are mainly to be found in Sections 9 (2) and (5); 10 (1) and (2); 12(b); 29 (1) (b); and 32 (1) of the LRIDA. The intended effect of the sections is, firstly, to limit the right and freedom to take disruptive industrial action in those services Scheduled by the Minister of Labour as 'Essential'. FIG. 4 gives an indication of the level of disputes in these services as against the others, between 1982 and 1993.

Secondly, very extensive discretionary power to refer any disputes to the IDT is vested in the Minister, where it appears to him that, "... any industrial action in contemplation or furtherance of that dispute is likely to be gravely injurious to the national interest", being action which, "... has caused or (as the case may be) would cause, an interruption in the supply of goods or in provisions of services of such a nature, or on such a scale, as to be likely to be gravely injurious to the national interest".

Under Section 12, one finds, fourthly, the wage award restrictive feature, referred to earlier, in connection with the approach taken to the determination of 'the national interest' by Justice Parnell in the Ex-parte Seprod vs. IDT case. The Tribunal is here obliged not to "make any award which is inconsistent with the national interest", if the wages, hours of work or any other terms and conditions of employment which constitute the subject matter of the dispute being adjudicated, "… are regulated or controlled by or under any enactment".

This last restriction clearly allows the legal enforcement of statutory wage guidelines. As the Fire Services vs. IDT case at the Appellate level demonstrates, this requires a distinction between legislated wage control and Ministerial and Government declarations on pay bargaining positions, whether in Ministry Papers or otherwise, which latter are not legally binding on the IDT.

The fifth control measure, contained in S.29, is the extension of the provision of S.12 to cover disputes referred for settlement to, "… any person other than the Tribunal".

Finally, as is not unusual, there is the Ministerial power to apply to the Supreme Court for an order "restraining the parties from commencing or from continuing the industrial action; and the Court, may make such order, "… thereon as it considers fit having regard to the national interest". The section may be invoked where it appears to the Minister that industrial action which is threatened or taken is, "… likely to be gravely injurious to the national economy [italics added] to imperil national security or to create a serious risk of public disorder [italics added] or to endanger the lives of a substantial number of persons or expose a substantial number of persons to serious risk of disease or personal injury.

It will be seen that, with there already being the Public Order and the Emergency Powers Acts on the statute books, which adequately cover the situations contemplated in this latter section of the LRIDA, these provisions are meant to repress tendencies to mass resistance and revolt – not unfamiliar consequences of IMF/World Bank programmes. Those who are familiar with the dynamics of management/labour relations will be aware that it is labour that normally, in the nature of things, finds it necessary to react to management decisions, action or omission. Although the enactments appear to be class-neutral, in that they could equally be enforced against the interests of capital, they are clearly intended to hobble trade unions and control the distribution of the surplus in a manner inimical to labour.

Figure: 4

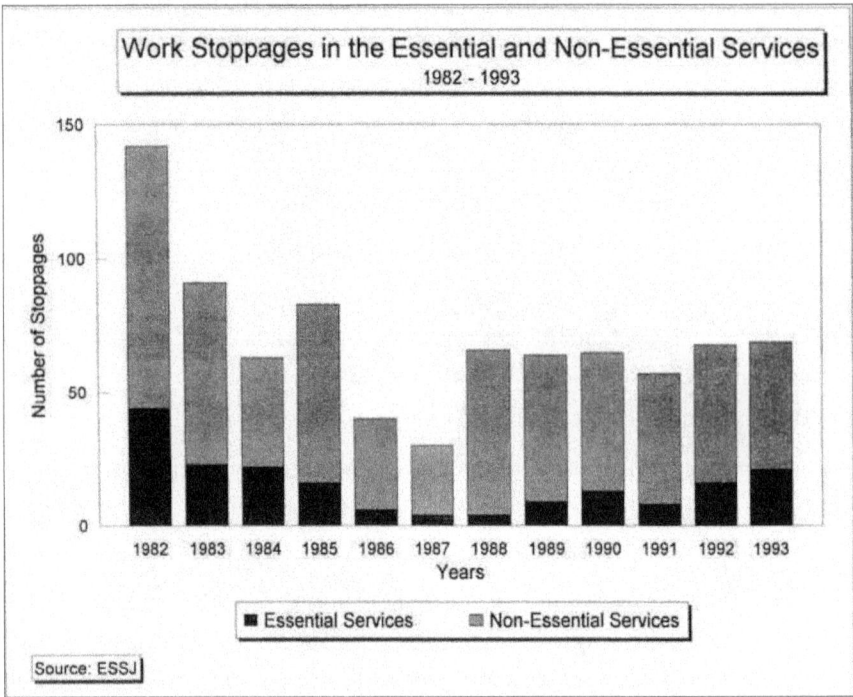

Work Stoppages in the Essential and Non-Essential Services
1982 - 1993

Source: ESSJ

For despite the adoption of the free market system, the wage-award provisions of the LRIDA have not been repealed – as against the position with price controls, which was one of the earliest features of the IMF/World Bank economic liberalization regime.

If there can be no tripartite agreement on an operational definition of 'the national interest', it is submitted that it is just as well if all references to the concept be omitted from the LRIDA, amendment of which, it is generally agreed – if for very different reasons – is long overdue.

---

1. Michael Shanks, *The Stagnant Society*, Pelican, 1964, p•116•
2. Labdhi Bhandari, "The Poor as Consumers", in David C. Korten and Felipe Alphanso, *Bureaucracy and the Poor: Closing the Gap*, Kumarian Press, 1985, chap. 10, especially p.171.
3. Shanks, supra, p,55.
4. Walter Lippman, *The Public Philosophy*, Mentor Books, 1962, p.40.
5. Carl Stone, *Class, State and Democracy in Jamaica*, N.Y: Praegar, 1986, p. 14.
6. Ronaldo Munck, *The New International Labour Studies*, Zed Books, 1988, P.131.

---

7. Ibid, p.170.
8. Seymour Lipset Martin, *Political Man*, Heinemann, London, 1983, p.391.
9. Ibid.
10. The Daily Gleaner, Jan. 22, 1995 p. 14A, "JCTU responds to attack by PSOJ President". For a more recent expression of private sector views in the same vein, see The Jamaica Herald June 19, 1996, p. 3A, "Unions threaten industrial climate in Jamaica – Emil George.
11. The Sunday Gleaner, Feb. 5, 1995, p. 22A; For response of JCTU to Lightbourne's attack, see The Jamaica Herald Feb. 13, 1995, p.6; Lightbourne's reply to the JCTU can be seen in The Sunday Gleaner Feb. 19, 1995, p. ID.
12. Arthur W. Lewis, "The Principles of Economic Planning", Unwin University Books, 1969, p.39.
13. Lipset, 1983, p.439.
14. Lewis, supra, p.31.
15. Ibid, p.38.
16. Clark Kerr, John T. Dunlop, Frederick Harbison and Charles A. Myers, *Industrialism and Industrial Man*, Oxford University Press, 1964, p.148.
17. The Daily Gleaner, Nov. 23, 1994; The Jamaica Herald, Nov. 18, 1994, p. 3A.
18. Thomas Skidmore, The Politics of Stabilization in Post war Latin America, in J. Malloy (ed) *Authoritarianism and Corporatism in Latin America*, University of Pittsburg Press, 1977, p.179.
19. Michael Foot, *Loyalists and Loners*, Collins, 1986, p.114.
20. G.D.H Cole, and Raymond Postgate, *The Common People*, University Paperbacks, Methuen, London, 1966, p.661.
21. Ibid, p.591.
22. Ibid, p.589.
23. John Toye, Dilemmas of Development, Blackwell Publishers, 1993, p. 36.
24. World Bank 1990, World Development Report, Washington D.C., p.24.
25. Included in the Government at the present time are: Dr. Omar Davies, Minister of Finance; Dr. Paul Robertson, Minister of Industry, Investment and Commerce; Dr. Peter Phillips, Minister of Health; and Dr. Richard Bernal, Ambassador to the United States, all being former members of the radical academic community of the University of the West Indies, who nevertheless found comfortable enough accommodation within an administration committed to "Continuity" with respect to basic macroeconomic strategy under the IMF, following the electoral defeat of the reputedly pro-capitalist, comparatively conservative, JLP in 1989.Lipset predicted that, the participation of intellectuals in politics also marks their increasing commitment to institutions of the *status quo* and their political transformation into apologists – Seymour Martin Lipset, *Political Man*, Heinemann, London, 1983, p.334.
26. Not only has the Communist Worker's Party of Jamaica (WPJ) been disbanded but leading ideologues of the radical left, and the WPJ's officers and founding members, like Don Robotham, to a somewhat lesser degree than Michael Manley perhaps, seem to have declared an indefinite armistice with capitalism; See Ian Boyne "The Growth Versus Equity Debate". The Sunday Gleaner, July 17, 1994, p. 30A.
27. Lipset, 1983, p.549.
28. C. Wright Mills, *Power, Politics and People*, New York; Ballantine Books, 1963, p.256.
29. Norman Girvan, Review of C.Y. Thomas, "The Poor and the Powerless", Monthly Review Press in *Social and Economic Studies*, Vol.37 No.4, ISER, U.W.I., Dec. 1988, pp.269-270.
30. Paul Harrison, The Third World Tomorrow, Penguin, 1991, p.288.
31. Barrington Moore Jr., Political Power and Social Theory, Harvard University Press, 1958, p.183.
32. Toye, 1993 , p . 13 2; See also Girvan, supra, pp.253-273 .
33. Gordon Lewis, "The Challenge of Independence in the British Caribbean", in Hilary Beckles and Verene Shepherd (eds) *Caribbean Freedom*, Ian Randle Publishers, Kingston, 1993, pp.512-514.
34. Ibid, p.51b.
35. Louis Lindsay, "The Myth of Independence": Middle class Politics and Non-Mobilization in Jamaica, Working Paper No.6, UWI, 1991, p.53.
36. Tove, 1993, p.136.
37. Lawrence Herson, *The Politics of Ideas: Political Theory and American Public Policy*, Homewood; Illinois, 1984, pp.235-37.
38. M. J. Ulmer "Economic Power and Vested Interests" in K.W. Rothschild, *Power in Economics*, Penguin Books, 1971, p.250.
39. See Parnell J., Ex-parte Seprod vs. IDT.
40. Nigel Haworth, "Proletarianization in the World Order: The Peruvian Experience", referred to in Ronaldo Munck, *The New International Labour Studies*, Zed Books, 1988, p.88.
41. J.K. Galbraith, *The affluent Society*, Boston: Haughton Mifflin, 1958, pp . 97,119.
42. Lewis, 1993, p.514.
43. Larry J. Diamond, The Social Foundations of Democracy, The Case of Nigeria, Ph.D. dissertation, Dept, of Sociology, Stanford University, 1980, p.106.
44. Lewis, 1993, p.517.
45. Harrison, 1991, p.40.

46. Ibid, pp.56-57.
47. Ibid, p.291; See also Colman and Nixson, 1994, pp.97-100.
48. Ibid, p.291.
49. Ibid pp.289-90.
50. Stone, 1980, pp.78-79.
51. Jamaica Five Year Development Plan 1990-95, PIOJ, July 30, 1995, p.19.
52. Ibid, p.37.
53. Ibid, p.115.
54. Ibid, p.141.
55. Janine Iqbal, "Adjustment Policies in Practice: Case Study of Jamaica 1977-91" in Stanley Lalta and Marie Freckleton (eds) *Caribbean Economic Development*, Ian Randle Publishers, 1993, pp.47-48.
56. It has been argued that while the J curve is usually descriptive of the adjustment experience, failure to anticipate and provide for the economic and social "fall out", as stressed by Iqbal, "effectively contains and conditions the positive and developmental impact of any programme".
57. C.Y. Thomas, 1993, p.317.
58. Marie Freckleton, "Jamaica's Balance-of-Payments Performance 1975-1988", in Lalta and Freckleton (eds) 1993, p. 123.
59. Helen McBain, *Foreign Capital Flows and Caribbean Economic Development*, in Lalta and Freckleton (eds), 1993 , p.134.
60. C.Y. Thomas, 1988, p.228.
61. Giovanni Andrea Cornia, Richard Jolly 8 Frances Stewart (eds) Adjustment with a Human Face UNICEF, Clarendon Press, Oxford, 1990, p.2.
62. Ibid, p.38.
63. Gordon K. Lewis, *Puerto Rico: Freedom and Power in the Caribbean*, Monthly Review Press, 1963, p. 185; Salamon argues that the divisions within society over major government decisions and policies reflect a lack of agreement as to what constitutes the national interest in respect of such contentious matters – Michael Salamon, *Industrial Relations: Theory and Practice*, Prentice Hall, 1992, p. 253. One example of the situation alluded to by Lewis is the purported extension of individual and collective rights to union representation under the LRIDA while in the same Act, as amended, the use of collective working-class power is restricted in favour of Ministerial discretion to refer disputes for arbitration to the IDT – Section 4 and Section 11A respectively, of the Labour Relations and Industrial Disputes Act 1975. The precedent had been set by the British Labour Party Government which established the Donovan Commission in 1965. Despite accepting most of its recommendations, including maintenance of the principle of voluntarism, the government still wanted to create new Ministerial powers of intervention in industrial "crises" which appeared to put the "national interest" in jeopardy. Compulsory Arbitration as Tawney (p. 9 5) argues, "takes for granted the stability of existing relationships, and intervenes to adjust incidental disputes upon the assumption that their equity is recognized and their permanence desired" – The attempt to install government as the natural arbiter of the public interest is taken a step further by the exercise of its law making function: class serving legislative measures of social control are given the aura of impartiality simply by their definition as "unlawful" – see for example, Section 10 (8) of the LRIDA, which it is here contended effectively introduces the injunction into labour relations, "through the back door". To those who are inclined to obey a law simply because it is the law, through the process of socialization, the merits of the actions taken in the context of economic and social power relations is hardly relevant: the "unlawful" label is to them sufficient for such actions to be condemned on "moral" grounds. Ted Honderich in Violence for Equality: Inquires in Political Philosophy, Rout ledge, 1989, argues that "It is only the amoral person who obeys the law because it is the law, regardless of its consequences, who accords to his government the right of obedience to the extent that the citizen is deprived of the right of resistance – to be morally responsible means acting for some "good" reason and certainly not against one's conscience".
64. Salamon, 1992, p.253; It may surprise some to learn that despite the great sensitivity on the issue of national sovereignty in the 1970's, the Cubans as "accepted ideologues" were asked to bring their influence to bear on recalcitrant members of the PNP's left wing, with a view to gaining their acceptance of the change in attitude towards seeking IMF funding – Maxine Henry, quoted in Evelyne Huber Stephens and John D. Stephens, *Democratic Socialism in Jamaica*, Princeton University Press, 1986, p. 182
65. Salamon, Ibid, p.253.
66. Zin Henry, Labour Relations and Industrial Conflict in Commonwealth Caribbean Countries, Columbus Publishers, 1972, p.222; Fox adopts the opposed view, that one should not expect certain and automatic working class compliance with arbitrated decisions and awards because, "… lacking moral adhesion to the system, their attitude is less likely to be able to take the strain of unfavourable outcomes – Allan Fox, "The Myths of Pluralism and a Radical Alternative", in Tom Clarke and Laurie Clements (eds) Trade Unions under Capitalism, Fontana, 1977 p.147.Recent IDT awards relating to pay claims for Firemen, Teachers, and Desnoes and Geddes Co. Ltd. provide compelling support for Fox's prediction.
67. R.H. Tawney, The Acquisitive Society, Fontana, 1964, p.40.
68. Ibid, p.95.
69. Ted Honderich, Violence for Equity: Inquiries in Political Philosophy, Routledge, NY, 1989, pp.6,17.
70. Milton Friedman's, views, denying the existence of "community" from the perspective of planned economic state-initiated action as set out in Freedom to Choose and Capitalism and Freedom, Chicago, University of Chicago Press, 1962 are referred to in

Herson, 1984, pp. 285, 290. Friedman's view was echoed some two decades later by Margaret Thatcher, as Toye reports, that 'there is no such thing as society' – Toye 1993, p.134.

71. Katrin Norris, speaks, with reference to Jamaica of: "… two nations sharing the same space but hardly touching each other. The first task a Government bent on creating a nation had to perform was weld these two nations together" – Katrin Norris, Jamaica – The Search for an Identity, Institute of Race Relations, London, Oxford University Press, 1966 p.42; – Obika Gray, Radicalism and Social Change in Jamaica – 1960-72, University of Tennessee Press, 1991, pp.75,115—16, 134. The problematization of public policy and posing of alternatives which might have been forthcoming from the New World Group of regional intellectuals, to the island's benefit, had to contend with the perceived elitist and enclave nature of this source of ideas and criticism. Further, ideological tensions and "impractical rhetoric" between, and of, its leading members in "an environment which was inhospitable to the expression of independent political ideas", and the desire, according to Best," to protect intellectual inquiry from the pressure of party political expediency", as against the wishes of some to test their ideas and prescriptions through actual political involvement reduced the Group's ability to function as a catalyst for change.

72. Tawney, 1964, p.134.

73. Obika Gray, Radicalism and Social Change m Jamaica, 1960 - 1972, The University of Tennessee Press, 1991, p.71.

74. In 1959 in Mexico the union involved in a railway workers strike was prosecuted criminally at the instance of the Government for an offense "against the economy" and "social subversion", in a situation where it was considered that strong political motives were present. The Supreme Court found in favour of the Government. – The Settlement of Labour Disputes in Mexico, ILR, Vol.103 No.5, May 1991, pp.477-98.

75. According to Toynbee, t.hr "nation" or 'country" never seems to be taken to mean the majority of the population, since "it is precisely the poor majority who are always told to stay poor in the interest of the country – Toynbee, Philip "The Language of Inequality" in Robin Blackburn and Cockburn, Alexander (eds) The Incompatibles: trade Union Militancy and the consensus, Penguin and New Left Review, 1967, p.99.

76. Allan Fox, in Blackburn and Cockburn (eds) Ibid, p.156; For Clements, the function of the dominant orthodoxy of pluralism is to legitimize the "existing distribution of economic power and rewards in capitalist society by ignoring the multiple dimensions of inequality provides an in-built justification for the integration of working class organizations within the prevailing power structure" – Laurie Clements, "Reference Groups and Trade Union Consciousness", in Tom Clarke and Laurie Clements Trade Unions Under Capitalism Fontana, 1977, p.310.

77. Engels is reported as having responded to a reference to the "people in general" with the question "who are they?" – Ralph Miliband, Parliamentary Socialism, Merlin Press, 1987, p.348; R. Hyman and R.H. Fryer, Trade Unions: Sociology and Political Economy" in Clarke and Clements, Ibid, p.156.

78. See Michael Todaro, Economic Development in the Third World, Longman, 1981, Ch.6 See W.A. Macmillan, The Road to Self-Rule, London, Faber and Faber, 1959; Miliband refers to the role played in development by leaders who are "bourgeois politicians with, at best, a bias towards social reform" (a bias increasingly determined, as the practice of politics becomes more of a career/ profession, by electoral considerations), which is weakening rather than becoming stronger. The originally reformist PNP has, it can now be argued, joined the JLP to become agents of the multi-lateral lending institutions for the "management and distribution of poverty" – In any event, as D.K. Duncan, the radical ex-General Secretary of the PNP, was to learn, and as Miliband concludes, "it is self-deception to believe that radical transformation can best be achieved "from the inside"; Andre Gunder Frank deals with the similar phenomenon in Latin America in "Dependence is dead, long live dependence and the class struggle: an answer to critics". World Development, No.5 & No.4, 1977.

79. See Ralph Miliband, Parliamentary Socialism, Merlin Press, London, 1987, pp.375-76.

80. Gray, 1991, p.l; Stone on the other hand suggests that what has been remarkable is that the degree of deprivation pauperization and suffering caused by IMF policies has failed to more substantially erode industrial peace and political stability – Stone, 1987, pp.119-20.

81. The Daily Gleaner, Nov. 11, 1968, report of Norman Manley's farewell speech at the PNP's Annual Conference. Lloyd Best referred to this diplomatic/military concern as a problem of the state of the consciousness of the islands political leaders, who suffered from a "self-imposed unwillingness to stop being intimidated by the Marines" – The Daily Gleaner Nov 10, 1968, quoted in Gray, supra, p. 167; See also Thomas, 1988, pp. 200, 224.

82. Miliband, supra, p. 348.

83. Zin Henry, 1972, pp. 113, 119, 143, 222; J. Harrod, "Social Relations of Production, Systems of Labour Control and Third World Trade Unions" in Southall, 1988, p.47; Stone, Power and Policy Making in Jamaica, undated Mimeo, p.23; also his "Labour's Pain", in The Daily Gleaner, June 1, Although the strike weapon may provoke more meaningful managerial response in dispute situations, it at the same time ensures that "Resentment is not permitted to accumulate explosively" to an antisystemic degree – Hyman and Fryer in Clarke and Clements, 1977, p.158.

84. David Colman, and Frederick Nixson, Economics of Change in LDC's, Harvester Wheatsheaf, 1994, p.55.

85. A capitalist class, referred to as "the tenants of present advantage" in Immanuel Wallerstein, The Capitalist World Economy, Cambridge University Press, 1993.

86. Owen Jefferson, The Post-War Economic Development of Jamaica, ISER, U.W.I. 1977. pp.26,145, suggests that the effect on the level of chronic unemployment be used as the criterion for judging the success of national development plans: whereas between 1956-68 investment incentive programmes yielded only 1300 new jobs, the labour force was then increasing by 25,000

per year; Michael Manley, The Politics of Change, Heinemann Caribbean Ltd. 1990. p.90; Dennis Partin, The Economics of Sustainable Development. Dept of Economics, U.W.I., Trinidad, 1994, p.5.

87. See for example B. Balessa and Associates. Development strategies in Semi- industrial Countries, Baltimore, John Hopkins University Press, 1982; P. T. Bauer, Reality and Rhetoric: Studies in the Economics of Development, London: Weinenfeld and Nicholson, 1984; Brandt Report 1980/North – South: A Programme for Survival, The Report of the Independent Commission on International Development Issues, London and Sydney, Pan Books; R. Findlay 1989, "Is the New Political Economy Relevant to Developing Countries?", PPR Working Papers, (WPS 292) World Bank Washington D.C.; A.C. Hirschman, A Basis for Hope: Essays on Development and Latin America, Yale University Press, 1971; C. Kay, Latin American Theories of Development and Underdevelopment, London, Routledge, 1989. D. Lai, The Poverty of Development Economics, London: Institute of Economic Affairs, Hobart Paperback 16, 1983; W.A. Lewis, Economic Development with Unlimited Supplies of Labour, The Manchester School, 22 (2), May, 1954; G.M. Meier, Politics and Policy in Developing Countries, San Francisco, ICS Press, 1991; M.K. Nabli and J.B. Nugent, "The New Institutional Economics and its Applicability to Development", World Development 17 (9) 1989; A.K. Sen, Employment, Technology and Development, Oxford: Clarendon Press, 1975; H.W. Singer, "The Strategy of International Development: Essays in the Economics of Backwardness" in Sir Alec Cairncross and Molmder Pun (eds) Basingstone: Macmillan, 1975; R.W. Solow, Growth Theory: an Exposition, Oxford: Clarendon Press,1970; F. Stewart, "The Fragile Foundations of the Neo-classical Approach to Development", in Journal of Development Studies 21 (2) Jan. 1985; UNDP, Human Development Report, 1991, Washington, DC - Works by the ILO, PREALC and Caribbean Scholars in this area are referred to throughout.

88. The Chenery et al variation on the basic needs strategy with its emphasis on growth with redistribution has been described as highly politically biased in the sense that it assumes the continuation of property, power and production relations, i.e. Redistribution with Growth "takes the position that not only is half a loaf better than none, but that so is the struggle over the crumbs" – See Colman and Nixson, 1994, p.98.

89. Colman and Nixson, Ibid, pp. 98-99, 153; Bauer, on the other hand, would see the approach of Colman and Nixson as "the work of politicians and intellectuals who have articulated and provided a veneer of respectability to envy and resentment" – See John Tove 1993, "Bauer's Dissent and the New Vision of Growth", Ch. 3, especially p.69; See also Ayn Rand, The New Left: the Anti-industrial Revolution, Signet Books, 1975, especially pp.152- 86; As with Friedman, for Locke the individual right of appropriation was seen as overriding any moral claims of the society- thus undermining the traditional liberal view that property arid labour power were social functions and that their ownership attracted social obligations – C.B. MacPherson, The Political Theory of Possessive Individualism: Hobbes to Locke, Oxford University Press, 1962, p.221.

90. Ibid, Macpherson, p.256.

91. Linden Lewis refers to (multi-lateral) "donor duress" to maximize state owned enterprise divestment, "gleefully supported by the native bourgeoisie who are interested in determining in more direct ways the functioning of the capitalist state through the vehicle of free market norms" – Linden Lewis, "Restructuring and prioritization in the Caribbean", in Hilbourne A. Watson (ed) The Caribbean in the Global Political Economy, Ian Randle Publishers, 1994, p.176.

92. Honderich, 1989, p. 61.

93. Wallerstein, 1993, p. 105.

94. Ibid.

95. V.V. Ramanadham, (ed) Privatization in the U.K., Routledge, 1988, p. 75.

96. Ibid.

97. It is suspected that the small employee shareholder (total employee share allotment rarely exceeds 5%) reeling from the adverse economic conditions of IMF stabilization and adjustment, would be under more frequent pressure to dispose of shareholdings, "would be less talented in investment portfolio management, and would face far higher transaction costs when selling" – Ramanadham, Ibid pp. 250-51. The clash of interests between the individual, in the dual roles of worker and consumer, is, of course, also a matter of concern, particularly as in Jamaica, where there is neither provision for competition, nor the timely establishment of adequate regulatory mechanisms – a consideration which unfortunately, for the consumer, tends to receive attention after the divestment event.

98. Ramanadham, supra, p. 252.

99. See Arthur M., Ed., The Battle Against Unemployment, W.W. Norton & Co., Inc., 1965, p.20

100. Trevor M.A. Farrell, "The Caribbean State and its Role in Economic Management", in Omar Davies (ed) The State in Caribbean Society, Dept, of Economics, U.W.I., Jamaica, 1986, p. 18.

101. Ibid, Farrell, p. 22; Stone on the other hand in tracing the revolution of the role of the state in Jamaica notes that "in effect, it became an instrument of the development of modern capitalism ... replacing the planter interests The political directorate treated the class interests of the new entrepreneurs as equal to the interests of the economy as a whole as the future seemed to hinge on their continued expansion" – Stone, 1987, p.80; But, as Przeworski argues, working class sacrifices for "future generations" or in "the national interest" are in no way guaranteed to benefit the present or future members of that class – Adam Przeworski, Capitalism and Social Democracy. Cambridge University Press, 1989, p. 139.

102. Ibid, Stone p. 93.

103. Stephens and Stephens, 1986, p. 171.

104. Katrin Norris, Jamaica: the search for an identity. London, Oxford University Press, 1962, p. 70.

105. Lawrence J.R. Herson, The Politics of Ideas, The Dorsey Press, 1984, p. 246; Lipset, 1983, pp. 196-207.

106. David Butler and Donald Stokes, Political Change in Britain, St. Martins Press, 1974, p. 22.

107. G.C. Peden, British Economic and Social Policy, Philip Allan, 1991, p. 170; Pantin is concerned that the "crafting of macro-economic policies supportive of growth" (in identified priority sectors and industries as an essential component of an appropriate national industrial policy) be accomplished in such a manner and with such content as to "trigger the desired behavioural response and actually steer micro-economic actors in the desired direction" – Dennis Pantin, The Economics of Sustainable Development, Dept of Economics, U.W.I., Trinidad, 1994, p.37. The effect of the presence of delegates at union negotiations in reducing leadership flexibility and sympathy with wider macro-economic issues is recognized in Stone, 1987, p.110. Intense union rivalry, it is argued, by Stone enables members to exercise "a powerful lever of control and accountability over union leadership".

108. Ibid, Stone pp. 111-12.

109. Dennis Pantin, "Resolving the Foreign Debt Crisis of the Caribbean in the 1990's: A Menu of Options", in ILO, The Role of Trade Unions in Periods of Structural Adjustment Programmes, Regional Seminar, Barbados Workers Union Labour College, ILO, Dec. 1992, p.11. Pantin remarks, that at US$21 billion plus, the Caribbean's total foreign debt was of "little global significance" and as such, "There really is no problem, therefore, in global creditors virtually writing of all of this debt or permitting large scale and generous rescheduling". Pantin is apparently unaware that, the United States, with the strongest influence in IMF/World Bank policy-making, refused even in the grievous war ravaged conditions of Great Britain after World War II, despite the "special relationship" between the two countries and the emotion of the times, to extend further credits until previous loans had been fully repaid; The present irony is that the United States – the most indebted country in recent times - can be said to now have "… no moral right to dictate economic policy to indebted countries of the third world", whose problems partly stem directly from policies pursued by, and conditions existing in, the developed world – See the Arusha Initiative, in Development Dialogue, 1980: 2, Dag Hammerskjold Foundation, Sweden, 1980, pp.14-19.

110. Such promises are usually contained in appeals for present sacrifice "for future prosperity",/ "national survival" etc. The sacrifice in the form of a lowered standard of living has not however been matched by any compensating growth in GDP and employment. But promises, in the Jamaican context, retain their potency not only because of the "distortion of workers consciousness by the power which comforts them", but by the tradition of a clientelistic/patronage based political culture which could conceivably elicit desired electoral behaviour in inverse relationship to the objective capacity of the system to deliver benefits.

111. Lawrence Nurse, "Managing Institutional Change During Structural Adjustment: Does Labour have a role ?" in ILO, Regional Seminar 1992, p. 21.

112. Przeworski, 1989, p.14.

113. Ibid, p. 139.

114. Malcolm Cross, and Gad Heumann, (eds) Labour in the Caribbean, Warwick University Caribbean Studies, MacMillan Press, 1988, p.228; Salamon, 1992, pp. 36-39, refers to harmony between the classes as nothing more than "an article of mere middle class folk memory"; Tawney, in his usual forthright manner, declares that the claim of capitalists to be the self-appointed guardians of the public interest is "a piece of sanctimonious hypocrisy" – Tawney, 1964, p.135; For John Locke and others of his era, it was not that the interests of the working class should be subordinated to those of the wider community: that class was not considered to be part of civil society, so that the only interest of consequence was that of the propertied class, which became ipso facto the national interest – Macpherson, 1962, p.245.

115. Przeworski 1989, p. 21.

116. Under these "rules", business confidence is not to be jeopardised, which results in a government usually "… confining itself to establishing the conditions in which private enterprise can flourish" – Peden, 1991, p. 113.

117. Antonio Gramsci, The Prison Notebooks, Qumtin Hoare and Geoffrey Howell Smith (eds) N.Y., International Publishers, 1971, p. 180.

118. Allan Flanders, quoted in Michael Salamon, 1992, p. 41.

119. Paul Mosley, Jane Harrigan, and John Toye, Aid and Power, Vol.1, Routledge, 1991, pp. 38-39.

120. Ibid, p. 15.

121. Thomas Paine, Rights of Man, Penguin, 1969, p. 279.

122. Przeworski, 1989, p. 188.

123. Stephens and Stephens, 1986, pp. 94, 123, 160; The Daily Gleaner, May 20, 1982, The Daily News, Feb. 12, 1982, The Daily Gleaner, Aug. 10, 1988. Several references to this effect are provided elsewhere reflecting the consensus of almost all of the academic community. See for example Jefferson, 1972, Girvan, 1971; Farrell, in Omar Davies (ed) p.21; Stone, 1987, pp.65-7; D.J. Harris, "Capital Accumulation and Resource Allocation in an Import-Constrained Economy: A Framework for Analysis of Recent Experience and Current Trends in the Jamaican Economy" - PIOJ, Kingston Symposium June 25-26, 1990; The Caribbean Development Bank, "The Adjustment Problems of the CARICOM States" in Lalta and Freckleton (eds) 1993, pp.42-4; Michael Witter, "Some Reflections on the Economic Development of Jamaica" in Judith Wedderburn (ed) Rethinking Development Consortium Graduate School of Social Sciences, U.W.I., 1991, pp.101 et seq; Hilbourne A. Watson "Global Restructuring and the Prospects for Caribbean Competitiveness: With a Case Study from Jamaica" in Watson (ed) The Caribbean in the Global Economy, Rienner/Randle Publishers, 1994, p.73 et seq.

124. Manley, 1990, p. 81.
125. "The Trade Policy Debate", in The Daily Gleaner, Mar. 23, 1988; Stone, pp. 116-120.
126. Lindsay, 1991, p.50.
127. Stephens and Stephens, 1986, p. 8.
128. George Beckford, Norman Girvan, Louis Lindsay, Michael Witter, Pathways to Progress: The Peoples Socialist Plan, Jamaica, 7977, Maroon Publishing House, Morant Bay Jamaica, 1985, pp. 8-9; PNP: "Principles and Objectives" Feb. 1979, p. 14; Stephens and Stephens 1986, p. 237 ; The Role of a strong state pursuing economically rational policies and "... standing above class interests is considered in Eddy Lee (ed), Export- led industrialization and development, ILO, 1981, p. 14; For the developments in Singapore during the 1960's and 1970's, see Everett M. Kassalow and Ukandi G. Damachi, The Role of Trade Unions in Developing Societies, International Institute for Labour Studies, Geneva, 1978; See also, ILO, Eleventh Conference of American States, Report of the Director General on Growth, Employment, and Basic Needs in Latin America and the Caribbean, ILO, Geneva, 1979, pp. 74-76; Karl Kautsky, The Class Struggle, Charles H. Kerr, and Co., Chicago, 1910, pp. 163-4 deals with the difficulty of ".. bourgeois idealists developing into genuine socialists, requiring, as it does, breaking with their own class as against being merely moved by the insights acquired sufficient to begin the search for a peaceful solution that will reconcile the interests of the capitalists (with) ... their consciences".
129. Beckford et al., 1985, p. 37.
130. Albert Memmi, The Colonizer and the Colonized, Earthscan Publications, London, 1990 pp.61-62, speaks of middle class leadership being forced to fight in the name of theoretical justice for interests which are not its own and may even be incompatible with them; Stephens and Stephens, 1986, p. 105, emphasize the need for not only a class analysis of society, but specification as to the class whose interests are to be accorded priority in a situation characterized, over an extended period, by severe resource constraints. See also PNP: "Principles and Objectives", 1979, p. 15, where it is stated that: "At all times every decision which is taken and every programme implemented, must ensure that the interests of the working people predominate".
131. Beckford et al. 1985, Chap.11, "Financing the Plan", p. 74, called for the burden of taxation to be borne by capital, "For it is The Capitalist Class who have created the crisis and they have the capacity to pay". But see Stephens and Stephens, 1986, p. 322 and especially p. 41 for a discussion of the negative effect of the close links between the parties and the private sector leadership, for state sponsored development in the interest of the majority of the population.
132. Kassalow and Damachi, 1978, pp. 76,85,88; But see pp. 143-160 for comparison with the situation in the Republic of Korea, in the same period.
133. Section B.9, "National Interest" in Noel E. Cowell, A Summary of Test Cases in Jamaican Labour Law, JTURDC, undated pp. 63-68. The Full Court decided in a landmark judgment – in the appeal of the unions, the NWU, JALGO and UAWU, on behalf of Fire Service workers, against an IDT wage award – that in fact the Tribunal must exercise its discretionary functions free from any obligation to necessarily conform to governments wages policy as announced by its spokesman. See, The Sunday Gleaner, Mar. 5, 1995, p. 13B for a report of the case, also The Jamaica Herald, Feb, 2, 1995, p. 1. The Tribunal, the Full Court said, should display the independence "... that can only add to the confidence of the persons who use it" – "The Daily Gleaner, July 3, 1995, p .3. The appeal centered around the IDT's decision to reduce to 15%, in keeping with the stated wage position of Government, the 25% wage increase recommended by the Government's own Permanent Salaries Review Board established to deal with the salaries of public servants. It. is instructive to note that the LRIDA enacted by the Democratic Socialist PNP in 1975, Stephens and Stephens 1986, p. 215) had in fact been originally proposed, under the JLP in 1968. The proposals were never, however, committed to the statute book during the JLP's term of office. For the details of these earlier proposals see etc. The Jamaican Weekly Gleaner, Aug. 14, 1968, p. 23.
134. J. Harrod, "Social Relations of Production. Systems of Labour Control and Third World Trade Unions", in Roger Southall, Trade Unions and the New Industrialization of the Third World, University of Pittsburg Press, 1988, p. 47.
135. James Petras and Dennis Engbath, "Third World Industrialization and Trade Union Struggles", in Roger Southall, Trade Unions and the new Industrialization of the Third World, University of Pittsburg Press, 1988, p. 104.
136. Sections 12 (7) b 29 (1) (b) of the LRIDA prohibits the making of awards that are inconsistent with the national interest or any regulations or enactment controlling, wages, hours of work or conditions of employment. The effect was to directly apply the force of the law to government's prices and incomes policy – see Sections 10 (1) and (2) which give the Minister of Labour the power to direct the parties to any dispute to adopt "such means as are available to them for the settlement of the dispute ...", if it appears to the Minister that, any industrial action has begun or is likely to begin [italics added] which is likely to be gravely injurious to the national interest [because such] industrial action has caused, or would cause an interruption in the supply of goods or in the provisions of services of such a nature, or on such a scale, as to be likely to be gravely injurious to the national interest". These provisions are further bolstered by s.32 which allows the Minister to apply to the Supreme Court for an Order "... restraining the parties [italics added] from commencing or from continuing (the) industrial action which is likely to be "gravely injurious to the national economy, to imperil national security or to create a serious risk of public disorder or to endanger the lives of a substantial number of persons or expose a substantial number of persons to serious risk of disease or personal injury". It needs little emphasis that the above provisions are not only class-biased, but that they are clearly intended to restrain any impulse towards social transformation through labour- capital confrontation. In a brief forwarded by the writer to the JTTRDC in 1995, for presentation to the Eaton Committee on Labour Market Reform, it was proposed that all references to the "national/public interest" in the LRIDA be struck out. In Tanzania in the 1980's the wage policy of the National Union

of Tanganyika workers was expected to be based on national economic needs as spelt out by the Government, but further, its officials' role was specified to be that of eliciting the sacrifices necessary for nation building rather than concern with fearsof exploitation of their members – Rhoda Howard, "Third World Trade Unions as Agencies of Human Right: The Case of Commonwealth Africa" in Southall, 1988, p. 239; Emmanuel argues that legislative references to the National Interest "implies a contrary interpretation (from the Marxist bourgeois dominated state thesis) of the necessary relation between the state and the ruling class" – Patrick A. M. Emmanuel, The Role of the state in the Commonwealth Caribbean, Working Paper No. 38, ISER, U.W.I., 1990, p.11.

137. See J. Harrod, "Social Relations of Production, Systems of Labour Control and Third World Trade Unions" in Southall (ed) 1988, especially pp. 49-50.

138. Petras and Engbath, in Southall (ed) Ibid, pp. 109-110.

139. Karl Marx, Capital Vol.I, Peking Foreign Language Publications, 1975, p.11.

140. With respect to the unorganized public "their wants" seldom become marketable political demands since those who have an interest in fundamental change lack the power and those who possess it lack the interest, "being disinclined to commit class suicide" Michael Parenti, Democracy for the Few, St. Martin's Press, N.Y., 1988, p. 305.

141. See M.G. Smith, Poverty in Jamaica, 1989, pp. 34-50.

142. Michael Parenti, supra, p. 302. See Emmanuel, supra, pp. 1-2 for the Caribbean leftists' views on collusion of imperialist elements and local class forces to "subvert formal democracy into class rule"; For a discussion of the conditions leading up to the passage of the strike control legislation and the establishment of compulsory arbitration vide an Industrial Court, and for the author's treatment of the national community/business interest, see Carl D. Parris, Capital or Labour? The Decision to Introduce the Industrial Stabilization Act in Trinidad and Tobago, Working Paper No. 11, ISER, U.W.I., 1981, p. 33.

143. Manley, 1990, pp. 26—36; Norris, 1966, pp. 98-99.

144. Edwin Jones, Class and Administrative Development in Jamaica, SES, No. 3:3, ISER, U.W.I., Sept. 1981, p. 10.

145. Carl Wint, "Inflation arid Wage claims", in The Daily Gleaner, Oct. 11, 1994, p. 6.

146. Franklin McKnight, "What have you done for me lately", in The Jamaica Herald, Jan. 1, 1995, p. 6A; The PNP, m The Sunday Gleaner, Oct. 16, 1994 p. 23A urged to the contrary that "... we need to come to understand that we cannot separate individual survival from national survival", something that deliberate IMF policy inducing growing inequality had very obviously succeeding in furthering.

147. Geoff Brown, "Hold the line – save the country", m The Daily Gleaner, Sept. 9, 1994, p. 6; See in contrast, the Editorial, "Social Justice", The Daily Gleaner, Nov. 1, 1994, p. 6, where governments' asking citizens to continually tighten their belts and "hold strain" is said to "smack of unfair privilege and hypocrisy"; See also Leon HoSang, 'Strikes and the public interest", in The Sunday Gleaner, Nov. 26, 1978, pp. 14,21; Further, see Stephens and Stephens, 1986, p. 129, on Manley's call for tough sacrifices in 1976. Twenty years later we have an unchanged scenario with the present Prime Minister warning the people to "Brace yourselves" for tough times, as reported in The Jamaica Herald, Nov. 8, 1995, p. 1.

148. Ian Boxill, "Capital, Labour and Feudalism", in The Daily Gleaner, Nov. 16, 1993, p. 6; With respect to the problems of implementation of the well-conceived populist programmes of the 1970's, see Stephens and Stephens, 1986, pp. 102-103. Conflicts between the "general interests", purportedly represented by the state in national social policy, and sectoral interests under collective bargaining are considered in ILO, 12t.h Conference of American States, Labour Relations and Development in the Americas, Montreal, ILO, 1986, pp. 38,44.

149. Sten Edlund and Birgitta Nystrom, Developments in Swedish Labour Law, The Swedish Institute, 1988. p.45.

150. Ibid, p.6.

151. Ibid, pp.79-80.

Chapter 2
Wages, Inflation and Employment

Within months of private sector representatives expressing satisfaction with Government's neo-liberal economic policies[1] in 1994, the Jamaica Chamber of Commerce (JCC) was voicing great concern at the slide in the value of the local currency vis-a-vis the currency of the island's major trading partner, the United States dollar.[2] There are many in the business community, and elsewhere, who seem to have believed that, with deregulation and liberalization, within the context of a free market framework, plus the build-up in the net international reserves position, the economy was on 'the right track'. The implications of the absence of real overall growth, failure of the export-sector to expand significantly, and lack of any substantial increase in investment were ignored in the newly-found mood of optimism.

Very quickly, however, Government's inflation policy came to be regarded as being "inconsistent with reality and cannot be sustained".[3]

Further, the JCC charged that "it is abundantly clear" that with the repetition of a cycle that started twenty years ago, "the financial policy framework adopted by Government has not worked to stabilize the economy ... nor is it likely to do so in the future".[4] In a renewed atmosphere of economic instability, after a brief period of apparent relative stability[5] during the 1993 period, it is now being declared that there can be no long-term planning or investment in such a climate.

A policy of wage restraint, and even an industrial policy, becomes more difficult if not impossible to implement, given the persistent fundamental structural weaknesses in the economic system. Such weaknesses perhaps justify what may otherwise appear as irrational and inexplicable trade union wage bargaining behaviour: 'confidence' in the system is important in determining behaviour not only on the part. of entrepreneurs, but workers and their representative organization as well. And it is imprudent to repose confidence in a system that is chronically unstable, and which produces outcomes that are opposed to expected policy consequences.

Ample illustration of the trade union difficulty of appearing to adopt a 'reasonable' wage bargaining posture, in the midst of uncertainty as to projected inflation levels, is given by Goodleigh of the JCTU in his response to questions as to the possibility of achieving the targeted inflation rate of 12% for 1994/95. The Government, he said, was making the same mistake as in the previous year when the rate achieved was some 27% as against the projected 6.5%.

One of the reasons for the divergence, as is being highlighted by similar developments at the present time (August 1995), was the assumption that the stability of the exchange rate, which had no basis in increased output, either for import replacement or expansion in exports, would be sustained.[6]

With this level of scepticism, and lack of confidence in targeted inflation rates, it becomes very doubtful that the minimum foundation for the emergence of an agreed tripartite plan for national growth and development will materialize in the foreseeable future.

But perhaps there are even more fundamental obstacles. Wilmot Perkins, for example points to differences in motivation between Singapore, often held up as an appropriate model, and Jamaica: whereas in the former there is a positive work ethic, Jamaica, he claims, has "a leisure ethic" derived from the plantation slavery experience which inculcated an aversion to work. This work attitude has been generalized to all levels of the population, as observed by many commentators, to the extent that it was ingrained in the national psyche that, since, "… plantation work was exploitation, freedom therefore came to have incorporated into its meaning the avoidance of work."[7]

As late as June 1995 it was being assumed that,

> "… from all accounts we have had our devaluation with the dollar sliding over 600% in six years … enough medicine for anyone to stomach in so short a time … it would be downright cruelty to contemplate any more medicine in the short run or even the medium term."[8]

Within a matter of weeks of that view being expressed, the dollar had moved from J$30.00 to US$1.00 to J$35.00 to US$1.00. Firemen, civil servants and teachers had only recently, with great bitterness and reluctance, accepted a wage 'settlement' on the basis of Government's projected inflation rates.[9] Already, there is a chorus of voices predicting, warning of, threatening, and actually imposing a wide range of price increases in an economy still very much import-dependent and still short of earned foreign currency. This was after nearly twenty years of stabilization and structural adjustment,[10] intended to stimulate an export-led economic recovery through output growth.

Inflation between 1990-94 totalled some 207.2%, as shown in TABLE 2, thus averaging 41.44% annually. It may well be that the maintenance of accepted and historical levels of profit and returns on equity, which benefited under stabilization redistribution policies in the interest of increasing investment and job creation, will be increasingly questioned and challenged; the more so, since, from the working-class point of view, there has been little to show for the. sacrifice made in the deliberate transfer of wealth from the relatively poor to the relatively rich.[11]

The price for the absence of serious revolt, given that there will be no significant productivity enhancement in the near future, may well have to be borne by the owners of substantial assets in the society. The prospect, then, is for a repetition of the capital flight, migration, and disinvestment of the second half of the 1970's and mid-1980's.

If increases in the cost of labour are not absorbed within firms, then exports will obviously suffer, as very much lower inflation rates prevailed among the island's major trading partners who will be placed, automatically, in an even more advantageous competitive position, given our status as price takers. As TABLE 3 indicates for 1992/93, the CPI for Jamaica was several times higher than that of most of the CARICOM countries. In relation to the industrialized countries – the country's main trade flows being with North America and Britain – it was some 26 and 7 times higher in 1992 and 1993, respectively.

Table: 2		Inflation				1974-1994	
Year	Inflation	Year	Inflation	Year	Inflation	Year	Inflation
1974	20.6	1979	19.4	1984	31.2	1989	17.2
1975	15.7	1980	28,7	1985	23.4	1990	29.8
1976	8.1	1981	4.6	1986	10.4	1991	80.2
1977	14.3	1982	6.5	1987	8.4	1992	40.2
1978	49.4	1983	16.7	1988	8.5	1993	30.1
Source: ESSJ						1994	26.7

Of equal importance is Shirley's observation that,

"as we have come to realize locally, competitive advantage based on the presence of natural resources and low-cost labour and a constantly devaluing currency is often associated with lower productivity and is notoriously unstable?"[12]

He further restates the popularly accepted wisdom that,

"… the highest order advantages associated with high levels of productivity are those which accrue from a steadily rising level of technology. Consequently, government policy must begin to shift to prod firms to move in this direction".

The emphasis on science and technology and national productivity, urged by increased global competitiveness and capital mobility, it is confidently predicted, "will require a new philosophy on labour relations".[13]

Inflation control by wage suppression, resulting in low wage levels has been used by apologists of various ideological hues as the explanation, and sometimes even as the justification, for the, "… gross inefficiency and staggeringly poor service in the public and private sectors in Jamaica…".[14]

Those who entertain the greatest positive expectations from the employee share ownership programme seem to foresee a worker response that will bring 'dividends' in the problem area of poor quality service identified by Boxill. But it is the substantial players in the booming stock market, up to 1993, who have really benefited from the redistribution of income away from the poor, traditional and new, since stock market activity has created little new real wealth through new productive investment.

Table: 3	Comparative Inflation (C.P.I.)				Rates	
	1992	1993			1992	1993
Antigua	6.3	3.5	St. Kitts and Nevis		1.5	1.4
Barbados	6.0	3.7	St. Lucia		3.2	0.7
Dominica	4.4	1.5	St. Vincent		3.1	4.5
Grenada	4.6	2.8	Monsterrat		1.4	2.8
Guyana	14.2	7.7	Trinidad & Tobago		6.5	10.8
Jamaica	77.7	22.1	Industrial Countries		3.3	3.2

Source: Headley Brown, in The Financial Gleaner, Nov. 11,1994, p.9.

The observed fact of the high incidence of contemptuous treatment of customers by staff in the public and private sector calls into question the presence of any link between pay and performance,[15] quantitative and/or qualitative. But also demanding attention, is the nearly monopolistic/oligopolistic market conditions which tend to characterize small economies susceptible to cartelization, particularly where there is a marked concentration of asset ownership in the hands of a small socio-economic class.

It is usually the occupational categories which interact with the public most frequently on a day to day basis, the lower and middle-income earners, on whom the tax burden of adjustment and stabilization has disproportionately rested. In the absence of effectively compensating benefits, this has meant not just low morale and productivity, but poor service in the formal sector, particularly, "… where it is difficult for workers at certain income levels to earn undeclared income." Where the scope for such additional income is present, or is created, it is often at the expense of the primary occupation in terms of time, effort, and commitment. In such a situation of a vicious circle of low productivity, the Japanese enterprise feature of lifelong employment and loyalty is of little relevance to Jamaica, contrary to the suggestion put forward by Alleyne.[16]

But policy makers seem oblivious of the nature, extent, and the form of the manifestation of poor morale, in a work environment afflicted by the frustrations and disenchantment, at the micro level and alienation generated by the consequences of policies pursued at the national level.

There can be little doubt that the unrestricted inflow of motor vehicles into the island since 1993 contributed substantially to the disequilibrium in the external accounts, thus ultimately causing the exchange rate to come under increasing pressure, given the slow response of the export sector to the various incentives offered. It is therefore somewhat ironic that the Minister of Finance, in the very political directorate which implemented such a motor vehicle policy, found it appropriate to interpret the build-up of vehicles on the wharves – as a result of the private importers financial inability to clear them – as evidence that the strategy of mopping up liquidity was succeeding. The government's policies were alleged to be working, which suggested, he said, that, "… we must be doing something right".[17]

This interpretation of failure as success, particularly on this sensitive matter of private motor vehicles, given the acknowledged dismal state of public transportation, led Mark Ricketts to prophesy, no doubt tongue in check, that, "Before long if people are having problems buying medication or purchasing basic food items the government might jump for joy saying that its policy is working"[18]

On a rather personal note, Ricketts noted that, "In being happy that people can't buy cars Minister Davies has one advantage as he watches the natives standing waiting late at night for public transportation, he can easily make his observation from his chauffeur driven limousine with its plush interior and automatic windows".[19]

It is to be noted that if there is in fact one commonly agreed obstacle to efficient production, that is external to the parties directly engaged in the production relationship, it is the state of public transportation .[20]

One commentator on the troubling subject of inflation, Jacques Bussieres, Governor of the Bank of Jamaica, called attention to an IMF study of 88 indebted developing countries. It was found that those with inflation levels in excess of 15% in the period 1983-89 had an average investment ratio that was one-third lower than that of low inflation countries. Further, real income per capita tended to stagnate in the former economies while it increased by more than 49% on average in economies with low inflation. The conclusion drawn was that a certain minimum degree of monetary stability is essential in controlling inflation and promoting investment.[21] The Central Bank Governor might be criticized for the failure, in his, "... almost textbook-like defence of current monetary policies", to advise as to how, even with monetary stability, a low level of inflation was achievable under the high interest rate regime,[22] over which he has continuously presided.

While Government Ministers, Davies and Robertson, in late 1994 and early 1995, were announcing how ripe the country was for foreign direct investment,[23] not long before that their ex-colleagues of the academic community, Levitt and Best, were making yet another negative assessment of the development strategy of 'industrialization by invitation'. Low wage levels under such a strategy had induced neither the adoption of labour-intensive technology nor any change in the rate of domestic savings, the increase in domestic product notwithstanding.[24] For the future, it is likely that the new sites for labour intensive production activities will be countries like China, India, Sri Lanka and Vietnam, as the international division of labour continues in a permanent state of flux, responding to changes in wage and skill levels and technology".[25]

On the other hand, high wage rates in sectors which are capital intensive, or which cater to export markets and therefore benefit from steep devaluations, exert a strong pull on wages in other sectors, both public and private. Because the higher the income earned the easier it is to maintain an accustomed life style, despite inflation, the consequence has been the failure of growth in new jobs. Instead there has been the persistence of the propensity for high consumption of 'non-essential imports, resulting from the 'demonstration-effect'.[26] It is evident that the domestic price level will reflect the degree of imported inflation arising from this lopsided sectorial high-wage and consumption paradigm.

Constant foreign currency scarcity would seem to dictate the need for prioritization in its allocation by state intervention. Secondly, the regulated inflow of imports both in terms of composition and volume is, it can be argued, an alternative to wage restraint or increased taxation in a situation where devaluation and heightened inflation would otherwise be virtually inevitable.[27] The not insubstantial hurdle in the way of such a policy choice is, of course, the standard import liberalization dogma of Fund and Bank programmes, which has proven to be not a subject for meaningful negotiation, despite its potential "advantage of being more selective and discriminatory in its impact".

Downes, Holder and Leon, utilizing co-integration theory to estimate the wage-price-productivity relationship for Barbados, concluded that changes in productivity have a positive impact on the growth of real wages, but changes in prices (domestic and tradeables) have negative effects on real wage movements.[28] Given the low level of development of consumer consciousness, and therefore the weakness of the consumer lobby together with market imperfections, one would also expect to find Jamaica, as in Barbados, that where there were increases in the productivity of labour, the benefits would be shared between profits and wages to the exclusion of the consumer.

As long ago as 1969, Brewster, in his study of similar relationships in Guyana, had arrived at the conclusion, which is of great contemporary relevance, that, "... trade unions were demanding higher wages that the economy could afford with unfavourable consequences on the price level, the growth of exports and the rate of investment".[29] Even earlier, W. Arthur Lewis, (1958), had pointed to the need to control the upward movement in nominal wage rates in order to ensure international competitiveness, which would be further promoted if productivity was increased at a higher rate than money wages, as, in relative terms, this would amount to a fall in the domestic cost of production.[30]

Regional research indicates that real wages fall more than proportionately with prices. The effect of short term money illusion and the fact that wage-induced unemployment, or the threat of it, in the short term, is not significant in determining wage levels, is that workers and their unions feel compelled to seek pay rises that exceed the current rate of inflation. This strategy is regarded as necessary just to maintain purchasing power, given the very steep upward movement in the CPI over the past several years, and not necessarily to 'catch up' with what living standards would have been if the movement in wage rates had fully compensated for increased inflation. To get back to the living standards of 1972, the kind of wage increase that would now be required would be in the three-figure order.[31]

This kind of situation was faced and handled very differently by the Germans some thirty years ago. Their approach to achieving price stability was to put industry under heavy government pressure – and not just the unions – to meet increases in production costs out of efficiency improvements and increased production. What this meant was that the squeeze was put on both wages and profits, but the focus was a positive one, namely general efficiency enhancement.[32]

In the case of Britain, Shanks observed that, "… a tough competitive spirit need not be bought by mass unemployment…" In the Jamaican situation, one might modify that to say that international competitiveness need not be bought by increased poverty, 'starvation wages', nor a sense of hopelessness.

Whereas the Germans concentrated on price stability through increased productive efficiency, Shanks, in typical British (mother country) and Jamaican style, places the main emphasis on wage restraint, since, "…without it", (wage planning), "… no long-range plan for economic growth has much hope of success". Although he did add, "supplemented by some use of controls on prices and profits".[33]

However, a wages policy cannot be designed in a vacuum, but must be set within the context of the inflation, interest, and exchange rate regimes. In this connection, it is to be noted that liberalization of the exchange control system in September 1991 was witnessed by a fall of the value of the local currency *vis-a-vis* the United States dollar from JS8.00 to US$1.00 to JS32.00 to US$1.00, at the end of 1994. This was a depreciation of some 400% in three years.

Clearly, any wage benefits contained in two-year collective agreements negotiated towards the beginning of this period, however generous, were overtaken, by a wide margin, by increases in the CPI, resulting from this level of currency devaluation.

Prior to liberalization, the strategy of protecting selected producers and the consumers of certain basic items from the additional cost effects of devaluation, by the use of multiple exchange rates, was not only costly in administrative terms, but provided loopholes for the unscrupulous. As Jefferson states, it also meant that, "… certain foreign exchange earners have to bear the burden", which is guaranteed not to gain any government popularity. This is especially so, bearing in mind the severe scarcity of, and therefore inordinately high value placed on, foreign currency,[34] in an import dependent society with a highly developed taste for foreign consumer goods.

On the other hand, liberalization without a large enough cushion of reserves, to allow market intervention to prevent plummeting of the exchange rate, and without any rate differential, caused a massive increase in the prices of such necessities as medicines, educational, and construction materials, most of which are imported. It is the poorer classes who would be most affected by the high prices of these categories of goods.

The deteriorating spending power of the working class and the unemployed, the poor and pensioners was very seriously aggravated by the removal of subsidies and the 'progressive' introduction of user fees and cost-sharing in the health and educational systems. This was with a view to meeting budgetary performance targets of the IMF stabilization agreements.

While the Government's 1990-95 Five Year Development Plan ambitiously declared that, "… education and training would be given the highest priority, particularly after the second year of the Plan",[35] the notice board at a leading high school in the second city in the island could be viewed displaying the message: "NOTICE: Students whose fees are not paid will not be admitted after half-term, Signed: Principal".[36] Naturally, only students from poor families would be the targets of such a warning. In considering the effects of inflation on the purchasing power of wages, attention must also be paid to interest rate levels. In a situation in which, traditionally, most businesses are under-capitalized and rely very heavily on bank loans and overdrafts for survival, a high interest rate regime – as part of an IMF demand management policy – is clearly a threat: firstly, with respect to general price stability in the economy, and, secondly, in terms of the acceleration of bankruptcies and closures. This is particularly the case, bearing in mind the declining productivity levels which have persisted since 1972. In pursuing a high interest rate policy with the intention of 'mopping up excess liquidity' and thereby, theoretically, reducing the demand for foreign currency, the cost of credit has been pushed to levels where it is conceivable that it represents a more costly production input than labour.

It is at the same time that a high exchange and interest rate policy is being pursued, with its negative consequences for the consumption capacity of labour, that the working class is expected to entertain appeals for wage restraint, in the interest of the foreign exchange earner/holder who converts his funds into Jamaican currency. The "... average Jamaican bombarded over time by strategies of manipulative mystification"[37]; often takes refuge from their deprivation and' frustration, as the rich get. richer and the poor get poorer under IMF retrogressive redistribution of income, by resignation to the apparent fulfilment of Biblical prophesy: "... for unto everyone that hath shall be given, and he shall have abundance; but. from him that hath not shall be taken away, even that which he hath".[38] Benefits from increased competition in the form of lower prices, to compensate for wage maldistribution and erosion have failed to materialize, with constant massive devaluations.

Lewis noted that in the free market economy, market responsiveness, the search for increased efficiency, and keeping profits at a low level all flow from the heightened state of competition. After the further observation that high inflation, as is well known, creates a seller's market which prevents the proper functioning of the market economy, he goes on to propose that, "... the smooth way to increase wages relative to profits is to have low taxes on wage earners and high taxes on large and unearned incomes".[39] As with many others sympathetic to the cause of the working class, Lewis takes the level of profits in relation to wage movements as given. To put it differently, he adopts the position that if there is price control, and wages are increased relative to prices, then this triggers unemployment and distortion in the structure of production. He does not seem to conceive of the possibility of wages being raised at the expense of profits, since, like the capitalist, he believes in profits control through maximum business competition.[40] This in an environment where increased costs, of whatever kind and level, have been passed on without hesitation, to a public which suffers from limited consumer lobby organization and a weak will to effectively resist.

Even without technological advances, Domar argues that wages might be improved, without undue inflationary consequences if there is sufficient capital accumulation to raise labour productivity to a certain level. But, as FIG. 5 shows, not only is the level of capital formation still below 30% of GDP but for almost the entire period 1976-86 was below 20%. More capital per workman may not only be utilized with benefit at the level of an industry or firm, but this should also bring into play the allocatory function of wages. There will usually be a shift of labour to such firms and industries that use more capital and can afford to pay higher wages.[41] Jackson considers one of the principal objections to the concept of an incomes policy from the following perspective:

> " . . some see the role of wages in the economy to be an allocator of labour between the many different jobs that need to be done. They believe that industries which are expanding and so needing more labour should be free to offer higher wages. They fear that if such industries are tied to the norm of an income policy [such as prevailed in Jamaica during the IMF wage guideline regime for some 14 years] they will not be able to recruit the additional labour they need".[42]

On a somewhat different level, Hamilton, in analyzing the real wages, prices, and productivity relationship, specifically takes account of the 'scars' of slavery as revealed by Stone's Worker Attitudes Survey.[43] It was found that the area of human relations was consistently considered by workers to be the least satisfactory in the work environment. The finding that human relations concerns were ranked as being of greater importance than material rewards, was greeted with some surprise, even by those familiar with Maslow's needs hierarchy, since in the occupational categories surveyed it might have been expected that lower level needs would have predominated. Hamilton's assumption seems to be that dissatisfaction with the state of human relations necessarily translated into negative productivity consequences,[44] which, as is well established, is not inevitably so.

> It is also claimed that, "... as the number of state employment opportunities grow, private sector workers tend to increase their resistance to management pressures to speed-up, due to the availability of alternative employment provided by the state".[45] Given the significant disparity between public and private sector wages for comparable jobs, plus the lack of any evidence of any increases in productivity with declining public sector employment, under IMF government expenditure cuts, the validity of the propositions derived from such premises is clearly questionable.

Figure: 5

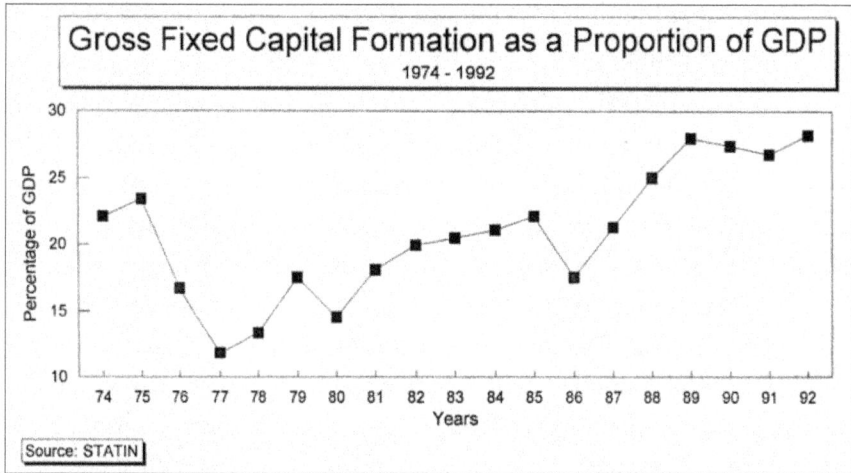

Gross Fixed Capital Formation as a Proportion of GDP
1974 - 1992

Source: STATIN

It is not denied that greater sensitivity to, and awareness within the country of the need to export and 'earn one's keep' represents an intangible benefit of the adjustment experience. This is a benefit, however, that appears, with the lack of effective communication and worker education, to have been confined to a minority of the upper social, economic and political strata. And, in any event, 'knowing' what. is 'necessary' has never translated, outside of utopia, automatically into appropriate action, as is adequately borne out by consistently disappointing export performance.

A market-determined interest rate regime has led to the level of rates virtually prohibitive of any form of productive long-term investment to be financed by loan capital.

In a parallel development, the policy of a market-determined exchange rate, since exchange control liberalization, has led to movement of the exchange rate to a level in excess of J$30.00 to US$1.00 a devaluation of nearly five hundred and fifty percent in the five-year period, 1989-94. And the trend has been slowly upwards. There is thus every reason to expect resulting lay-offs and a continuing pressure to maintain and improve the purchasing power of wages.

One of the consequences of import liberalization, devaluation, and wage restraint, noted by Stone, is the decline in sales and profit margins experienced by businesses producing for local consumption. The reduced rate of return naturally led to reduced investment and job creation and an increased sense of job insecurity.

One is left to speculate as to what role this sector of the business community, producing for the local market, and the small business and informal sector, generally, would have played had violent, deep-seated, determined policy protest occurred. To which class would their loyalties and support have been inclined?

What has caused the retrogressive income redistribution to be so unceasingly questioned, by those whose social conscience is still uncorrupted by greed and who refuse to accept notions such as the 'non-existence of society', is not just the failure of any significant-increase in investment to take place. Equally importantly, in small and even medium-sized businesses, in particular, which are typically under-capitalized, workers, as wage earners and as consumers, have suffered substantial reductions in real income. Those on fixed incomes such as pensioners, have, of course, been the hardest hit. Spirited attempts to have pensions indexed to movements in the CPI have met with little else besides official sympathy.[46] Many pensioners have now to try to seek work in order to have an income on which mere survival is possible.[47] And it is often overlooked that the level of pensions is normally tied to the level of wages earned at retirement.

Hedging against expectations of continuing high, and at times hyper – inflation, by the business community, in the setting of prices – particularly where imported goods received and sold will be paid for in the future – at what could be significantly adverse rates of exchange, has exacerbated the inflation problem.

It should not be surprising if labour seeks to similarly protect itself against the probability of real income erosion.

Whereas pricing policy in these circumstances goes uncondemned as 'prudence', trade union and working class militant bargaining that seeks to cope with the identical threat is often seen as behaviour that amounts to 'holding the country to ransom', 'irresponsible', 'self-defeating', 'destroying the climate for investment''', 'sending the wrong signals to foreign investors', 'damaging the country's international competitiveness', if not a downright 'lack of patriotism'. The 'game' would seem to have 'different rules' for different 'players'.

In anticipating what the exchange and/or inflation rate might be in the future, one has to consider not just the phenomenon of the 'self-fulfilling prophecy', but also the 'natural' tendency to use the maximum figure that, the rate could possibly be, in one's own favour, to the detriment of an already burdened consuming public. This is, of course, one of the prices a country pays for economic uncertainty.

As long as uncertainty persists with respect to the extent and likely movements in the essential prices which determine the behavioural responses from the vested interests in the economy, the attempts to 'catch up', 'keep up', or 'stay ahead' of inflationary consequences must be expected to continue.

Reflecting on this situation, Stone's conclusion is thus that both sides, capital and labour, tend to see themselves as victims rather than villains in causing high inflation in economies like Jamaica's".[48]

Crisis in the country's foreign exchange reserves position, (until 1995/96) declining investment, and increasing inflation, combined to produce a level of economic decline which signalled the start of the almost unbroken period of negative GDP growth from 1976 onwards. What growth there was in the latter half of the 1980's was modest, on average, as can be observed from FIG. 6.

It has been reported[49] that, as reflected in FIG. 7, profits and inflation increased faster than wages during the second term of the Manley regime in 1976-80. The situation of the workers certainly deteriorated further after the introduction of IMF-sponsored wage guidelines in 1977.

It is also to be noted that although the worsening position of labour continued into the 1980's under Edward Seaga's allegedly more procapitalist JLP, there was a substantial decrease in the disparity between movements in wages and the CPI. With this development, one would expect that it would be reflected in the incidence of disruptive industrial action. What would seem to be supported here is not paralysis of the trade unions, by fear of Seaga's tough, no-nonsense leadership that was determined to pursue anti-trade union and working-class IMF policies, by way of a managerialist leadership style. Rather, the interpretation is feasible that the fundamental changes in the state of the economy resulted in altered relative economic power positions of capital and labour, which partly determined the law degree of trade union militancy and the level of industrial action.

Figure: 6

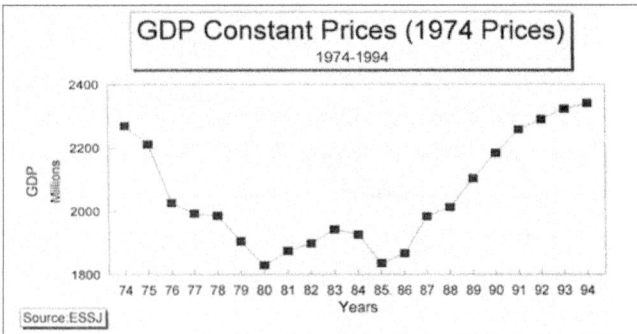

GDP Constant Prices (1974 Prices)
1974-1994

Source:ESSJ

Figure: 7

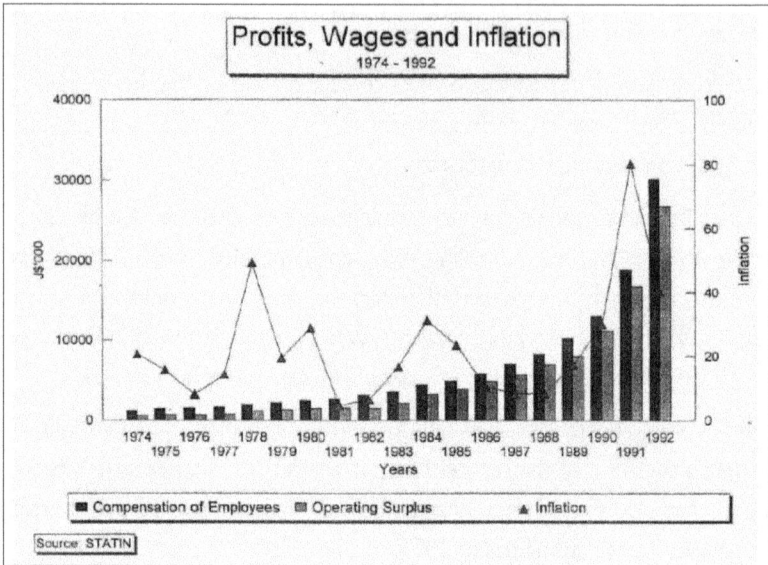

Profits, Wages and Inflation
1974 - 1992

Source: STATIN

Labour-intensive foreign investment has been largely confined to the export garment assembly sector, concentrated almost entirely in the Kingston and Montego Bay Free Zones, notorious for anti-union management and a low-wage, predominantly female, work force.

Such is the image of the export garment industry in terms of wages, in relation to effort and working conditions, that with a largely unskilled national labour force, in which the highest levels of unemployment are among the youth and females, and with the general level of unemployment being in the high teens, officially, and high twenties, unofficially, there is a sufficient labour shortage for the importation of workers to have been allowed to fill the outstanding vacancies .[50] The phenomenon of an informal economy of some size, and the additional cultural features of the extended family and 'hustling', explained such a situation.

It is worth keeping track of the essential point that is being made, namely, that in capital-intensive industrial development under industrialization by invitation, it is a contradiction in terms to suggest that labour costs are a major cause of inflation.[51] In the labour-intensive enclave export sector, international competition is so intense that any significant change the economics of production, including currency re-valuation, can quickly lead to closure and relocation of operations. The profit motive has no national loyalty.

Whatever else has been achieved by the low-wage IMF economic strategy, it has certainly not led to significant new investments with accompanying job creation. Yet the theory of low wages as a factor generating the creation of more jobs is a consideration which employers and their organizations often claim that militant, wage- maximizing, 'irresponsible' and 'selfish' trade unions and their members fail to accommodate in their bargaining strategies.

Instability of the exchange rate and astronomically high interest rates could more be expected to account for the disincentive to invest than would 'excessive' wage rates, which, when converted to United States dollars, are just above those of Haiti.

This is not meant to dismiss altogether, the argument that wage levels have inhibited investment. There can be little doubt that low wages, creating new, and deepening traditional poverty, is partly responsible for the substantial increase in the crime rate – both against the person and property. That cannot be a factor encouraging to prospective investors, or those who might otherwise expand existing operations, whether local or foreign-owned.

Whereas the fall in labour's share is greatest, comparatively, in the case of Jamaica, the Jamaican labour force, generally, was not 'compensated' by any substantial additional investment, in terms of new decent paying jobs, as was the case in other countries, such as Mexico, Chile, Argentina and Brazil. This is compounded by the fact that, compared to Mexico and Brazil, Jamaica's hourly wage rates for semi-skilled production workers was in fact significantly lower, as indicated in Table 4 below.

Table: 4   Wages in Manufacturing restricted by wages guidelines under stabilization/structural adjustment have declined as a percentage of value added.

% VALUE ADDED

	1972	1988		1972	1988
Jamaica	43	18	Mexico	44	20
Chile	19	17	Peru	30	18
Argentina	30	18	Bolivia	43	26
Brazil	22	15			

Source: Carl Stone/in Headley Brown (ed) *The Jamaican Economy in a Changing World: The Way Forward 1993/94 and Beyond,* Headley Brown & Co. Ltd., 1994, p.130

While the Government has been operating a wage-norm policy, with some effectiveness, with respect to the public sector, so far – since the removal of the guidelines in 1991 – its policy in relation to the private sector has been one of propaganda and exhortation amounting to a warning of the possible inflationary repercussions of unusually large wage increases.[52]

But *action* needs to confront the very real perceived risk of redundancy. For it is this real fear in a labour surplus, demand compressed economy which explains what might otherwise appear as irrational behaviour on the worker's part when he persists in expending less energy, initiative and skill than he is capable of, thus appearing to put his job, at an individual level, on the line, and denying himself the opportunity of earning higher wages and upward job mobility in the process.

Manhertz, in writing on price determination in Jamaica, reports that the contribution of wages to cost of production between the research period 1956 to 1974 was small: 96% of the increase in prices being due to the high cost of imported inputs.[53] There are hardly any acceptable reasons to doubt the soundness of the belief in the current relative importance of these factor prices in the inflation equation – given the massive levels of devaluation since the late 1970's. The effect of devaluation has been exacerbated by the trend downwards of world market prices for developing country primary products, over which there is little supplier control (what with the failure of the mission for a New Industrial Economic Order, and UN sponsored proposals to bring a greater measure of 'justice' in favour of third world commodity exporters in international trade relations with industrialized nations).

Persistent, low labour productivity puts Jamaica, according to Ross, in danger of becoming a low-wage but high labour cost country which is unlikely to attract investment. Having identified the explanatory factors as low levels of education and skills, he nevertheless goes on to suggest that the primary reason for low productivity is due to, "… severe rigidities in the labour market caused by restrictive labour legislation". The claim is made that the combination of very aggressive trade unions and such a management-fettering situation, as, "… the total absence of an exit clause in the island's labour laws, makes it "extremely difficult to dismiss a worker even if one is prepared to fully compensate them [sic] for that dismissal".[54]

The authors of *Structural Adjustment with a Human Face*, report that they found strong evidence in five out of six country studies that, in fact, the index of food prices, or the CPI calculated on a basket of goods consumed by the poorer classes, revealed faster rates of growth than-the CPI or the GDP deflators, which are normally used to calculate real income. They then point out that, "… what this means, of course, is that the degree of income loss is greater than that based on the real wage calculated on the basis of the average CPI".[55] It is difficult to believe that Ross, the Executive Director of the PSOJ, is unaware that adequate nutritional standards have important productivity implications.

A family of five with two wage earners, it was estimated in 1984, would have to spend as much as 75% of their income to purchase only 50% of the foodstuff contained in the minimum basket which would be nutritionally acceptable.[56] In the space of eighteen months, October 1984 to March 1986, the price of the minimum basket increased by some 45%, with the increase for 'basic' imported foods such as flour and rice being substantially higher. In the Jamaican context, what this meant was a parallel increase in locally grown root crops, which might be of benefit to the local farmer but certainly not the poorer consumer, whatever his status: unemployed, worker or pensioner.

Not only have investments in labour-intensive activities not positively responded to the attraction of low wages, but neither has marked inequality m income distribution fostered a significant increase in domestic savings.[57]

Those presumed to have a high propensity to save, have clearly not been saving to anything like the extent for which they have theoretically been given credit. And yet, the presumption as to the strategic developmental benefits of retrogressive income redistribution has continued unshaken under IMF inspired policies.

Low-wage production is no guarantee of increased export sales. There will always be lower-wage countries, unless a particular country permanently occupies the bottom position, a distinction hardly to be sought. And it goes without saying that it is the lowest wage countries that also fall into the poorest country category. The alternative approach is the search for product innovation and market diversification, with the promotion of unique items, even at higher costs, which will always find niches in increasingly discriminating, differentiated, and sophisticated global markets .[58]

A.N.R. Robinson's Budget speech in Trinidad and Tobago (1964), quoted by Lloyd Best, is of particular interest and relevance in the Jamaican context at this time, given certain parallel developments:

"… firstly, strike consciousness on the part of businesses which is inhibiting the impetus to grow; secondly, unsatisfactory industrial relations... have struck at the root of confidence in investors [sic]; and thirdly, rapid wage increases are reducing the competitiveness of local labour".[59]

The conclusion that these factors together neutralized the effect of investment incentives was among the reasons, if not the primary one, for the passage of the labour restrictive *Industrial Stabilization Act* through both houses of Parliament in one day in Trinidad.

Echoes of such speeches have recently been heard from such persons as Delroy Lindsay[60] the President of the Private Sector Organization of Jamaica and the late Robert Lightbourne,[61] former Minister of Trade and Industry, whom many regard as having spearheaded Jamaica's process of industrialization in the 1960's.

It is not without a measure of anxiety, therefore, that trade unionists' are watching the outcome of the recently established Eaton Committee on Labour Market Reform. Official references to the need for changes in the Industrial Relations System, in keeping with the movement to a free market economy have come from none other than the Minister popularly regarded as being most concerned about and committed to the cause of the masses the present Minister of Labour herself, Portia Simpson. Naturally, this has provided cause for concern, allaying fears, as to a possible intention/attempt to 'discipline' the unions under new statutory 'reform' provisions.

The claim – has been made – that trade union militancy compensates for loss of national economic control which has passed to the multinational corporations; increases net income at the expense of profits; and asserts the popular will in the face of otherwise unrestrained government or foreign influence and control. On this assessment, trade unionists should perhaps suffer feelings of guilt for the extent of capital intensive technology in the productive sector, by having, allegedly, driven up wages to the point where capital is substituted for labour, thus making them partly, if not largely, responsible for growing unemployment.

The crescendo of protest at rising money wage rates, highlighted by the occasional large wage increase gained in union negotiations, is usually not articulated in the form of an argument that the 'trickle down' effect is taking place too rapidly. This would be too unsubtle a provocation to working class anger, guaranteeing graphic verbal responses, if nothing more. Instead, the standard, seemingly objective, impliedly disinterested basis for protest is usually stated in terms of the negative consequences for local, but particularly foreign, investment and by implication employment. But these investments, at the best of times, have failed in their primary policy objective – apart from the plant construction phase in the bauxite industry – of catalyzing further industrial development and absorbing surplus labour, thereby generating revenues for infrastructural development and social service provision.

In any event, as DeLisle Worrell argues,[62] investment rates of return in the typically capital-intensive enterprise will be influenced only within narrow limits by comparative wage rates. Assuming that certain basic prerequisites are in place, Worrell insists that investors will choose products, processes and technologies that compensate for any major wage disparity between alternate production locations. Obviously, this will depend on the extent to which the existence and prices of the other basic prerequisites, such as energy and taxes, compensate for a higher labour unit cost of production.[63]

If managers are to justify *their* level of salaries, and the sixteen to one disparity in Jamaica between the highest and lowest incomes, which is a feature of the wages and salary structure in private industry, then they must be prepared to accept responsibility for results, including the level of labour productivity both at the enterprise level, directly, and average national productivity, indirectly.

Simply pointing to the negative consequences for inflation when wages outstrip productivity contributes little to the problem's solution. A workforce demotivated and demoralized by substantially declining real wages cannot be a desirable alternative scenario. What is indeed striking is the total failure on the part of almost all non-union commentators to recognize the legitimacy of the notion of the 'betterment factor' as an ultimate goal of social and economic policy. It is only those lacking in ambition who are satisfied to be 'marking time' in relation to their future life-prospects. And without needing to employ actuarial expertise, it is apparent that with the trend of inflation in the 1990's, prudent consideration of tolerable retirement needs compels a highly materialistic orientation on the part of the mass of the labour force, who are unlikely to be the beneficiaries of any form of worthwhile 'golden handshake'.

As enterprise managers expect to be lauded for improved profit performance, so it ought to be that workers and their representative organisations should take, and be given, credit for achieving a continually improving standard of living and quality of life for the labour force.

Yet in an economy where the exchange rate has been devalued from J$5.50 to US$1.00 in 1989 to J$33.00 to US$1.00 in 1994, and where, as reported by STATIN, (ESSJ, 1995, Ch.4.1) the CPI has moved from 108.5 in 1989 to 332.7 in 1994, it is as if workers, who are fortunate enough to be unionized in enterprises and/or industries where their bargaining position is strong, should forego the use of that leverage for the nebulous 'common good'. On this view, labour should not try to keep up with the cost of living, much less begin to recover lost ground, due to the massive erosion of living standards during the late 1970's and for most of the 1980's. Instead, they should, on the basis of this view, feel responsible for and guilty about the rate of inflation and unemployment.

But the greater the extent of privatization and the more deregulated and free from state intervention the economy becomes, the less possible it is to predict, much less guarantee, the purposes to which accumulated capital is deployed. There can be no assurance, under unregulated capitalism, that current wages foregone, 'in the national interest', will accrue in the future to those presently making the sacrifice. Nor does the private sector's labour absorption track record instil hope, much less confidence, that there will be substantial working-class benefit in term of increased employment, improved social wages or lower prices.

"Deceleration in prices", seen as being,

".. heavily dependent on ongoing fiscal restraint." is elaborated in this blinkered view, into a repetition of the call for wage restraint, without limitation of applicability to the public sector. "Wage restraint" thus becomes synonymous with "fiscal restraint".[64]

An examination of the data discloses that, in fact, as wages as a proportion of the national income has been declining, (FIG. 8) the movement of wages as a percentage of the cost of production, as indicated in TABLE 5, has also declined.

Table: 5	Cost of Input as % of Total Production Coat				
	(sample of large manufacturing firms)				
	1964	1991		1964	1991
Wages & salaries	15%	8%	Service & misc. costs	9%	12%
Material, fuel, power	47%	58%	Services of contractors etc	1%	1%
Transportation	2%	4%			

Source: Carl Stone, in The Daily Gleaner, June 8, 1992.

Forthright statements to the effect that wage restraint is critical for price suppression are usually made without any supporting empirical statistical foundation.

The 'big stick' of the threat of redundancy is displayed not unexpectedly, in the next step of the development of the wage-inflation-employment argument of neo-liberal economics protagonists. So, the country is treated to the prediction of a 1993/94 Budget which is expected to almost certainly involve layoffs.[65] This is despite the fact that the last public sector pay settlement did not involve significant violence to the salary allocation provisions of the previous recurrent budget, nor were the increases awarded in breach of the IMF agreement then in force.

Basic comparative regional economic performance indicators cast serious doubt on the premises and elements of IMF stabilization policy. It is noted, by Blackman, that the three countries adopting devaluation as an adjustment/stabilization tool, Trinidad and Tobago, Guyana, and Jamaica all managed, during periods of regular substantial exchange rate adjustments, to achieve negative GDP growth. On the other hand, countries which avoided the strategy, such as Belize, the Bahamas, Barbados and the Organization of Eastern Caribbean States all recorded positive, if low, growth. This growth performance was matched in a reverse relationship with rates of inflation, over the decade of the 1980's.[66]

Figure: 8

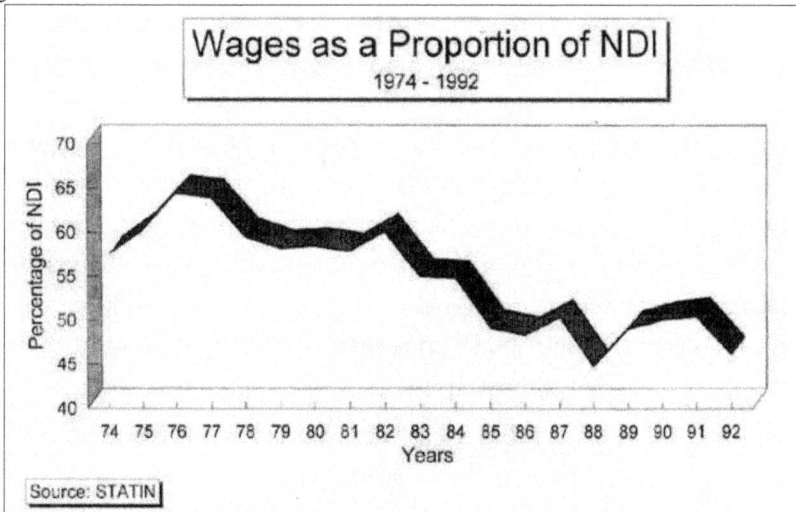

Wages as a Proportion of NDI
1974 - 1992

Source: STATIN

It is not high or rising wage levels but the 'overhang of foreign debt' which hangs like an albatross around the neck of the Jamaican economy. And the only thing that the working class has to show for all this foreign borrowing is the per capita debt in excess of U$1700 in 1995, after peaking at over US$2,200 in 1989, (FIG. 8). This may seem to provide confirmation of Marx's exaggerated dictum that the only part of the national wealth shared by the masses is in fact the national debt.[67]

The findings of a study by Witter and Reid, investigating the share of wages in the total costs of production, are interesting, if not entirely novel. Given the state of wage data, the authors were unable to disaggregate the wages and salary totals into compensation for different occupational levels, or even into management categories.[68]

Contrary to the traditional wisdom, and as strenuously argued,[69] it was confirmed by the authors that the percentage of wages in the cost of production is some would expect this average to represent a balance between a low range for capital intensive operations, such as in the bauxite/alumina industry, and a high range for labour-intensive activities such as export garment assembly.

The main causes of inflation are identified by those authors as resulting from the policies associated with borrowing with 'aiding' from multi-lateral agencies, namely: the end of price control, removal of subsidies, and the determination of the rate of exchange by market forces. It will be seen from TABLE 6 that it is only for four years 1979, 1980, 1987 and 1991, that it has been concluded that wages was a principal cause of inflation during the sixteen year period 1977/1993. In those four years, 1987 had an inflation rate of 8.6%; it is also note-worthy that wages in the aggregate represents remuneration to all employee categories.[70] In other words, for the few years in which wages may be said to have contributed to inflation, an element in the equation was managerial remuneration. And yet, instead of there being a campaign for managerial wage and fringe benefit restraint, tradition has it that any such move will remove the incentive for performance – in convenient defiance of Maslow's need hierarchy, which postulates the greater importance of non-material motivators at managerial occupational levels especially, one would expect, in a situation of such gross income disparity as exists in Jamaica.

Conversely, devaluation is revealed, by the study, to be a principal contributor to inflation. In 1980, with an inflation rate of 28.6%, other causal factors were: severe shortages of consumer goods and raw materials, taxation, growth in money supply and oil price increases. In the other high inflation year in which wages figured, 1991. influence of devaluation imported inflation, taxation (GCT), money supply, and the removal of subsidies was significant in accounting for the very high 80.2% rate.

Figure: 9

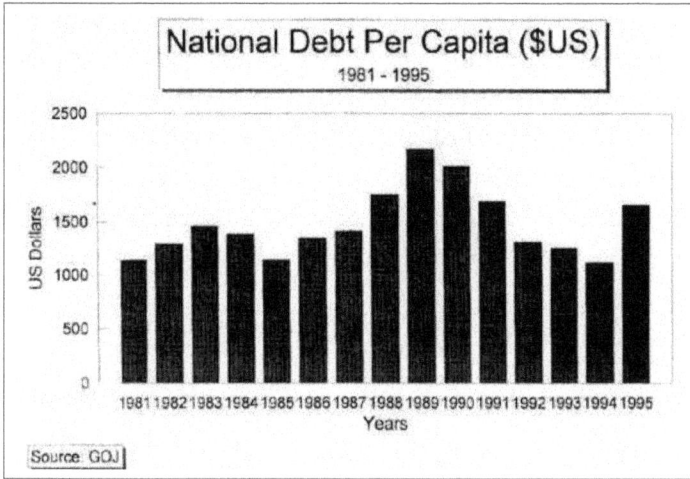

National Debt Per Capita ($US)
1981 - 1995

Source: GOJ

Table: 6	The Causes of Inflation		Key to Table

YEAR	RATE OF INFLATION %	CAUSES
1977	14.1	1,2,3
1978	49.4	1,4,10
1979	19.8	1,2,3,5,6,8,9
1980	29.6	2,4,5,7,8
1981	4.7	3,8
1982	5.2	2
1983	16.7	I
1984	31.3	1,7
1985	23.1	1,4,6,10
1986	10.4	2,4,7
1987	8.6	2,3,5,7
1988	8.8	2
1989	17.2	1,3,4,5,7,9
1990	29.8	1,3,9,9,10
1991	80.2	1,3,4,5,7,9
1992	40.2	7
1993	30.1	1,4,7

Source: PIOJ, Economic and Social Survey, Various Years

Key to Table

#	CAUSES
1.	Exchange Rate Shortages
2.	Imported Inflation
3.	Taxation
4.	Wage Increases
5.	Interest Rates
6.	Mindey Suppy
7.	Oil Prices
8.	Sybsidy Remoival
9.	Price Liberalization
10.	Exchange Rate Shortages

The performance of wages in 1992/93 is due largely to the substantial increases achieved after the lifting of the guidelines in 1991 together with large increases to the public-sector work force in 1993/94. But even with these good years for labour, as the last column in **TABLE 7** shows, the rise in wage levels was only some 74% of the increase in the CPI for the period 1988-93. The fact that the wage data includes professional, technical, management and other higher level salaried groups, which all managed to improve the purchasing power of their wages, means that the fall of the disaggregated real wages for the working class was greater than the figures indicate.[71]

Table: 7   Growth in Average Weekly Earnings (%) / Inflation Rate

	1989	1990	1991	1992	1993	1989-93 Average	1988-93 % change
Wages	12	20	32	51	47	32.4	295
CPI	17	30	80	40	30	39.4	400

Source: Witter and Reid, p.11 from ESSJ, various years.
* excludes Public Sector, Agriculture and Freezone employment.

This fall in the consumption capability of labour was not peculiar to Jamaica, nor indeed the third world, despite charges of mismanagement by economists of the New Right and multi-lateral lenders. In The Organisation for Economic Co-operation and Development (OECD) area, as a whole, the economic performance was far from flattering: for the period from the mid 1970's to the early 1980's, the average annual inflation rate doubled; and the number of those without jobs was twice that for the 1966-72 period.[72]

In a situation where the island's level of per capita income was less than US$1,500 at the end of 1992, the second lowest in the Commonwealth Caribbean,[73] it is not surprising that a journalist — not known for the radicalism of his views — went as far as to declare that, "... the constant strikes and threats of strikes demonstrate that they ('big business people') do their utmost to keep the salaries of their staffs a couple of jumps behind the rate of inflation ... while the big employers get richer".[74]

As the Guardian Weekly notes, with reference to the glaring anomaly, at British Gas, "It is curious how, when 'market forces' are invoked to settle levels of remuneration, those at the top are always aligned upwards — while those at the bottom go down".[75] It is reported that whereas the chief executive of British Gas was given a pay rise of 75%, taking his salary to 475,000 pounds per year, at the same time 2650 showroom staff, earning "an unprincely average" of 13,000 pounds per year, were to suffer a pay cut of up to 16%, in addition to reductions in holidays and overtime. The new ratio of top salary to show room staff thereby became 36.5 to 1, despite declining efficiency of operations – which in a situation of egalitarian treatment, would have suggested that the director's salaries be reduced and that they be put on bonuses related to efficiency, as with the show room staff.[76]

While in the case of the United Kingdom, the Bank of England could express concern that companies failed to adjust target rates of return in keeping with, "… the collapse in inflation and interest rates over the last few years",[77] the interest rate and inflationary situation is somewhat different in Jamaica. That was although a lack of confidence that inflation was effectively under control was common to both countries. Ironically, for the OECD countries, the cost of the reduction in inflation and real wage increases, although limited to 1.5% in 1986 and 1% in 1987, was a substantial increase in unemployment,[78] and, indeed, long-term unemployment as reflected in TABLE 8 below.

Using the combination of two approaches: firstly, the direct impact of increased wages on total costs and, secondly, the resulting increased consumption, Witter and Reid[79] give the results for the Jamaican economy of a 10% increase in the cost of labour as amounting, to a percentage in total costs of 1.7% - 1.8%. This was when the cost approach was used which caused a 2.8% in increase in total GDP, assuming a propensity to consume of 66%.[80]

Another perspective on the question of the appropriateness of regional wage levels is adopted by Gonzales, who grounds his view on the existence of a substantial divergence between private and social costs, resulting from labour market and other distortions.

With the high level of unemployment (TABLE 9), he concludes that the actual price of labour, "… may be way above its opportunity cost"[81]from the point of view of wage policy design. This needs however, to be balanced by the existence of a reserve price for labor.[82] This price may be so low that it prohibits the acceptance of 'low wage' employment by the unemployed. Such a seeming anomaly, in work environments suffers from such a sweatshop notoriety as to give rise to the importation of workers in the context of the labour-surplus Jamaican economy.

Whatever the opportunity cost of labour, low wage rates as a factor in attracting foreign direct investment may, as Theodore suggests, be outweighed as a determinant of production location decisions by higher, but still 'relatively competitive wages', associated with attributes of the labour force, in a high-tech world. These could include labour productivity, trainability, and the type, level, and flexibility of the skills possessed, as well as the lack of over-rigidity in the labour market.[83]

In an environment of persistent high and hyper-inflation, causing crippling real wage erosion, it would probably take an ex-Governor of the Central Bank to so doggedly focus on the 'danger' of 'excessive' wage adjustments. Referring to the Mexican economic crisis of 1994, Headley Brown makes the point that where real wage increases are not matched by increased labour productivity or increased national output - amounting to the 'real wage gap – this not only leads to retrenchment, resulting from lowered investment,[84] but, "... firms react by raising the prices of their outputs thus passing the higher wage costs on to consumers in the form of higher prices".[85] Such pricing behaviour appears to be taken as given – no doubt, as one of 'the rules of the game'.

Table: 8   Long-term Unemployment Rates (12 months or more) in Selected Countries, 1980 and 1986.
As Percentage of Total Unemployment

	1980	1986		1980	1986
			Italy	37	56*
Australia	20	28			
			Japan	16	17
Austria	9	13			
			Netherlands	26	56
Belgium	58	68*			
			Norway	2	7
Canada	3	11			
			Spam	35	57
Finland	15	21*			
			Sweden	6	8
France	33	48			
			UK	19	41
Germany	17	32			
			USA	4	9
Ireland	35	41*			

* 1985.

Source: OECD: Employment Outlook, Paris, 1987.

Table: 9			Unemployment Rate		
Year	(Oct.) by Year	Job Seeking Rate	Year	(Oct.) by Year	Job Seeking Rate
1974	22.8	n.a.	1984	25.6	15.9
1975	22.4	n.a.	1985	22.3	12.7
1976	20.7	n.a.	1986	20.8	13.4
1977	21.0	10.5	1987	18.9	12.7
1978	24.2	11.8	1988	16.8	13.3
1979	23.8	11.0	1989	15.7	10.8
1980	26.0	12.9	1990	15.7	9.6
1981	31.1	14.9	1991	15.9	8.3
1982	26.8	12.6	1992	16.0	8.1
1983	25.6	11.3	1993	22.8	6.9

Source: STATIN, reported in letter to the Editor, The Daily Gleaner, October 27, 1994, p.8

Note: It is interesting to note that during the years of the Socialist PNP government between 1972-1980, the average rate of unemployment was 24.3 and, despite the ideological polarization between the parties and within the society, the average during the JLP years of 1980-1989 was £3.3%. This is as good an indication as one could probably find as to the existence of any real difference of economic philosophy policy between the contending political elites.

This traditional approach to the wage-inflation relationship continues to ignore the fact, that productivity is, by the nature of production relations and organizational structure, a management-responsibility[86] and, further, seems to regard profit levels as inviolable.

The excessive growth in money supply, the massive increase in net domestic credit of 54.9%, between August 1993 and August 1994 – interest rates to the productive sector at a level as high as 70% in 1993-94, substantially higher utility and transportation costs and, not least, the constant adjustment of the exchange rate resulting in the increased cost of capital goods, are all factors alluded to by Brown.[87] There is, remarkably, however, no attempt to provide statistical evidence as to the causal weight no be attached to them in the inflation equation. Nor is there any prescription tendered for controlling these 'other' costs.

Brown's contribution to the raging wages debate is difficult to reconcile with his earlier stated view that, since inflation feeds on expectation, as is widely recognized, given the nation's inflation experience, "... steep increases in wage rates and pay scales are inevitable".[88]

Table: 10 Targeted Inflation Rates vs. Actual

	Targeted	Actual
1990/93	18	29.8
1991/92	25	80.2
1992/93	15	40.2
1993/94	11.4	30.1
1994/95	6.5	25.1

Source: ESSJ

There is a contradiction in the treatment of the wage-inflation question, which is evident in the editorials of the island's leading newspaper, *The Daily Gleaner*, depending on whether the primary focus is on 'inflation' or 'workers real wages'. For example, in one editorial, it is stated that with an average annual increase in inflation of about 56.6% for the previous three years, "... the case for wages to 'catch up' may be perfectly justified".[89] This is in contrast to another editorial, headed, "Wage Rise Folly", where the following observations are made:

> "The Government, however, cannot abandon its demand management measures which are central to its adjustment programme with the IMF.
> "... wage increases of the magnitude being demanded would serve only to generate additional demand "... for it means absolutely nothing to workers to be given wage increases only for it [sic] to be swallowed up by more inflation ...

In a backhanded kind of way, the trade unions seem to be vested with the responsibility for promoting the strong economic growth based on macro-economic stability, which is seen as the way out of the ambivalence which typifies much of the wages/inflation debate. This is further reflected in another editorial which, after relating the Government's 9% public sector wage offer to the estimated 40% rate of inflation, went on to remark that,

"... while there is much to the 'catching – up' argument, wage increases that are not the result of productivity are inflationary and cannot be in the best interest of workers and of the vulnerable groups."[91]

In what is perhaps the most peculiar tack on this issue, however, one finds in a Financial Gleaner editorial (Sept 9, 1994, p.6) the recognition, firstly, that of the nine groups listed on page 83 below, only the Judicial and security forces kept ahead of inflation, running at 390 per cent. Secondly, it was noted that those groups that had fallen behind would naturally try to make up, " ... for what they did not get the last time"; and thirdly, that wage settlements in the private sector were averaging some 50%.[92] This last fact is against the background of Government's undertaking to bring public sector pay more in line with the private sector on a job evaluation/ reclassification and comparability basis.[93] Yet the editorial, headed "Fairness to all", ends: "... therefore some semblance of fairness must set in and soon, so that normality can be restored in the interest of the nation, *if not that of public sector workers.*"[94] [italics added].

It cannot be accepted as true, as Brown obviously does, "... that whether the profits of the industries, where wages are raised first, have been exorbitant or moderate does not make much difference to the outcome", since, "... there will be other groups who will insist on similar raises".[95] Not only does this approach forbid, by necessary implication, the upward movement of wages in relation to productivity at the enterprise level, not to mention the union – favoured ability to pay factor, but even more fundamentally, it seems to take for granted that pay demands will be met as a matter of course by management.[96] If the latter were the case there would naturally be no point in any discussion of the issue of wage restraint.

A strikingly opposed view on the wages question was taken by the late Carl Stone. He dismisses the allegation of there being excessive real wage increases, in the face of which it is claimed that the Minister of Finance's targets are not achievable. Stone notes that the working class in Jamaica and in the region had been patient in 'holding strain' in the 1980's, and therefore, rightly expects the agenda for the 1990's to be one changed from austerity and stabilization to increased investment, production and growth. This is necessary, "... so that labour can begin to increase its real income and purchasing power", in the context of increased national income, and, thereby "catch up with inflation".[97]

Data on the changes in real wages for selected Latin America and Caribbean countries, proved by stone, shows Jamaica being the fourth worst in the list of eleven countries during the 1980's.

Against the background of this negative performance in the previous decade, it should perhaps not come as a surprise to find that not only inflation, but also wage bill targets, even for Government's own employees, that have been agreed with the IMF, have been missed by substantial margins.

Table: 11   (Negative) Percentage Change in Wage Worker's Buying Power (1980-90)

Colombia	15%	Argentina	9%
Barbados	13%	Venezuela	18%
Chile	13%	Jamaica	26%
Uruguay	6%	Honduras	30%
Costa Rica	6%	Dominican Rep.	46%
		Brazil	48%

Source: Carl Stone, The Daily Gleaner, Sept 30, 1992.

The Letter of Intent to the IMF of October 1992 contained the following wage/inflation provisions:

	1993/94	1994/95
Wages	Government's Wage Bill to exceed 1992/93 more than 20%	Government's Wage Bill to rise in keeping with Inflation
Inflation target	11.5%	6.5% revised to 12%

As against these provisions in the 1992/93 period, in fact for 1993/94 Government's wage bill increased some ten times more than the level specified, being $5.0 billion, as against $522 million the previous year, and inflation was actually 57.5%. In 1994/95 the inflation level was more than double the revised figure of 12%.

It is in view of this 1994/95 pay stipulation in the Government's Letter of Intent to the IMF that the Leader of the Opposition, and Opposition spokesman on Finance, has challenged the size of the increase offered to public sector workers," on the ground of inability to pay,[98] given inflation running at the annualized rate of some 40%.

On the question of 'the ability to pay' constraint, the Government's cause and credibility suffered by the increase of the "maximum offer possible" and payable from 9% to 12.5%, and finally to 16%. In the case of teachers, in particular, the Permanent Salaries Review Board had recommended that they be given priority treatment, represented by an offer of 16% in the first year and 14% in the second. This was priority treatment with which, according to Carl Wint, the Jamaica Teachers Association, "remained unimpressed".[100]

It is worthwhile to take note, in this context, of Robinson's view on the issue of a strict resource availability criteria in pay determination in the British public sector:

> "The effects on pay determination would be far-reaching. If the cash limit system prevails it means in effect that the main component of pay bargaining is determined in the House of Commons and not at the bargaining table. The cash limit figure is the crucial decision. All that is left for the bargainers are questions affecting the distribution of the cash limit increase and any marginal effects of slippage or jobs trade-off".[101]

It is significant that neither the Minister of Finance's statement, nor the governing party's newspaper articles, indicating the seemingly enormous public-sector wage increases between 1990 and 1994, provide cost of living data allowing meaningful assessment, on a real wage-level. From a comparative perspective, the similarity between the British and Jamaican public sector pay issue is remarkable: in almost identical journalistic language the British Chancellor, Kenneth Clarke, is reported to have,

> "... stepped up his campaign of psychological warfare against wage-led inflation last week when he reminded 5 million public sector employees that they cannot expect an automatic pay rise in 1995/96 – for the second year running".[102]

Claiming inability to pay, also – whereas the British Employment Secretary conceded the return to a "public sector pay policy" – the Jamaican Minster of Finance strongly denied a re-institution, 'by stealth' of public sector wage guidelines.

The information on pay increases provided by the Minister is prefaced by the singularly sleight of hand observation that, "Whilst there has been inflation, the fact is that increases over the period have been significant". The following are examples of the level of public sector salary increases granted at the time.

The categories shown below are only a part of the total public-sector bargaining units, which together submit anywhere between 40 and 70 (there being 42 in the

1993/94 period) wage and fringe benefit claims, on a biannual basis 'Leap frogging' is, needless to say, rife in this situation. Again, the inherently contradictory position is adopted – not unlike the Gleaner editorials referred to above – that,

> "Public Sector Workers do have a right to make the claims they have but at this time the economy is delicately poised, "… [and thus] any rocking of the boat could lead to disaster. This is not to minimize the economic survival [sic] of the individual … but it is necessary for us at this time to understand the reality and cooperate in the interest of a better future for us all",[105]

Public sector group		Percentage Increase
1. Judicial and legal group	-	401
2. Security forces	-	390
3. Teachers	-	268
4. Health service group	-	815
5. Professional, admin, and clerical	-	207
6. Weekly and daily paid group	-	202
7. Fire services	-	215
8. Local Government	-	184
9. Prison services	-	210

Brown claims that it is precisely the level of real wage increase of some 112% granted in 1993/94, by Government, as indicated above, ranging from 401% to 184%, which laid, "… the foundations for workers success in securing unaffordable adjustments in pay throughout the economy which have been running at over 50% per annum".[106]

To put these increases mentioned by the Minister in context, however, reference is appropriate to the data indicating that over the period inflation in fact increased by 390%.[107] *The Gleaner* editorial stated,

> "We suspect that he (the Prime Minister) would not hesitate to increase taxation, but his intelligence on the ground would have informed him that such a move at this time would certainly be met by a revolt" there

had been massive tax increases, consumption and property tax in particular, the previous year. The editorial then continued,

> "But we must ask, on what moral or economic authority can the Prime Minister be asking workers to act within the constraints of increases in single digit percentage movements, when inflation for the 12-month period from July to July (1993-1994) now stands at 39.6% per cent?".

It is in this context of the morality of the wage/inflation dilemma, that it was no doubt politically convenient for the Opposition spokesman for the Ministry of the Public Service (which has portfolio responsibility for salary negotiations for public sector employees) to describe as "perverse" the Government's "threat" that meeting the level of wage claims submitted would mean a reduction of staff by 50%, when it is considered how generous the increases have been for members of the public service over the last two years".[108]

The trade union position has perhaps been most fully argued by Danny Roberts, Vice President of the NWU and the Jamaica Confederation of Trade Unions. Roberts refutes the implied claim by Government that labour costs, as against other factors, are a major contributor to inflation observing that between 1977 and 1991 wage increases averaged under 12%, causing a transfer of income from labour to capital resulting in the top 20% of income earners getting 50% while the bottom 20% received only 9% of the total national income". The workers experience had been such that he predicts that they,

> "… would no longer favour an argument predicated on the notion that modest wage increases will promote the maximisation of investment[109] … For the market competitiveness and investment expansion never materialized[110] during the halcyon days of excessive profits under wage guide lines"[111]

Citing a World Bank Country Report of April 1994, Roberts insists that the ability to pay existed, since there was not only a budgetary surplus, even after taking into account Central Bank "losses", but collections from the recently imposed General Consumption Tax (GCT) significantly exceeded projections – by nearly 50%, or $3.9 billion.[112] In any event, higher wages, it is proposed, ought not to be viewed as a cost item, but rather as an investment in the increasingly important area of human resource development.[113] The probable production and productivity consequences of low morale induced by a sense of grievance over low wages must be added to the "alarming decline in basic educational levels of the Jamaican population (which has had a devastating impact on the country's growth prospects".[114] But this is exactly what IMF-inspired government policies, including spending cuts in the social services, which contributed to this deterioration of the educational system, was intended to remedy – by crowding in[115] the private sector, the so-called engine of growth.

It is to be noted that it is precisely the policies of deregulation and full liberalization of the foreign exchange regime which led to the precipitous devaluation of the local currency and the consequential increase, of the foreign debt servicing burden on the national budget. This was to the point where nearly 50 cents of each tax dollar is being spent on debt service, for which the country has virtually nothing to show. Repeating a trade union sympathizer's opposition to what appears to be the re-introduction of wage guidelines "by the backdoor", Munroe regarded such wage policy developments as a retrograde step. As he pointed out, Jamaican labour had already been 'Haitianised' to the extent that certain categories of the so-called 'aristocrats of the working class', the bauxite workers, still earned less than the minimum hourly wage prevailing in the. United States.[116]

Other trade unionists have opposed what they interpret, as the official n on-statutory re-introduction of wage guidelines. They are viewed as being "inappropriate in relation to the public sector, since "they (wage guidelines) are not acceptable" in a free market economy, where prices are de-controlled and the foreign exchange market is liberalized,[117] but also because,

> "Workers need to catch up after taking a battering since deregulation and liberalization, therefore we will never agree to wage guidelines, (as) we firmly believe in the process of free collective bargaining".[118]

Munroe was to further argue that,

> "... it could not be right that Government spends billions of dollars pumping up the Net International Reserves way above the programmed IMF targets,[119] thereby itself fuelling inflation (by buying up large quantities of foreign currency on the open market) pre-empting resources that could otherwise have gone to propose more reasonable settlements to the police, to the teachers, the nurses and to other public-sector employees".[120]

It would seem almost facetious therefore, on Munroe's view, for the claim to be made that if the IMF's September 1995 performance test was failed, this would be as a direct consequence of granting the wage increases sought. The Government's determination that the present IMF Agreement shall be the last, is being equated in a subtle and novel manner as evidence of the *inability* to pay.[121] The lack of long-term *earned* foreign exchange reserves to cushion the dislocation of the ending of the borrowing relationship with the Fund – and therefore the risk of continuing financial instability after the break – might be advanced as a good enough reason to, allow more time for, consolidation of the reserves position. That might also provide the environment for a more comfortable accommodation of the government workers' wage claims.

In any event, the 'ability to pay', as a ground for failure to meet a claim, must meet the objection of the Civil Service Association's President that, "… there is a large percentage of the populace which does not bear its proper share of the tax burden".[122] There has also been the allegation that in respect of 'artificial' price increases, some retailers in Jamaica … would hoard the milk of mothers if they could".[123]

For Hugh Shearer, acknowledged to be the senior trade unionist in the island, the wage policy of the Government in setting maximum limits *below* the likely inflation out-turn – and bearing in mind that labour contracts are for two years and do not normally contain inflation adjustment clauses – represented nothing less than the "compromising (of) the integrity and impartiality of the Permanent Salaries Review Board". In support of this allegation of a serious breach of principle, the case of the Civil Service Association offer/award was cited, in which a 15% increase was 'granted' even before the Association had an opportunity to present its case.[124] This level of increase was exactly what Government claimed was the maximum it could afford.

Although the Minister of Finance sought to dispel working class fears that it was the intention to re-impose wage guidelines,[125] it is difficult to interpret the wage offer parameters, characterizing the negotiating stance on the management side, otherwise. The ranges of offers happen strangely to replicate, rather suspiciously, the declared official limits said to be payable. Indeed, the public-sector wage increase levels proposed, as economically feasible by Government have been applied to such statutory corporations and non-civil service enterprises as the Jamaica Public Service Company, National Water Commission, The National Housing Trust, The

Ex-Im Bank, non-academic workers of the University of the West Indies, and the Governments investment promotions agency, JAMPRO.

The issue of public sector wage levels has been related to private sector wage settlements by the Minister of Finance, who reacted very strongly against private companies granting increases which were, "... not only out of tune with those granted by the government, but out of line with inflation".[126]

The Minister took the trouble to make it known that, since his party had been built on the trade union movement, the Government "would not 'pick a fight with trade unions unless it was necessary".[127] Perhaps the classic reaction, in the context of Finance Minister Davies' statement, was that of the Vice President of the UAWU, Clifton Grant, who, against the background af his union's 150% wage claim on behalf of the University's non-academic staff, made it known that, "... nine percent (Government's initial and allegedly maximum affordable offer) is nothing on top of nothing".[128]

The workers and unions in Jamaica have been protesting against attempts to keep wage increases in line with some unilaterally determined norm that has no justifiable basis from labour's point of view. By comparison, the situation in Barbados was one where a freeze – and, even worse, a cut – in public sector wages was imposed under their version of an incomes and price policy, despite protest – demonstrations lasting for two days. One of the early populist moves of the new Owen Arthur-led government, was to amend the constitution so as to make such a wage policy procedure illegal in the future.[129]

Despite the opposition of workers and their unions to the alleged 'back door strategy' of the re-introduction of wage guidelines, Stone cited changes in prices as against wage data in 1992, to show that in fact the working class was, "... better off in the 1980's when the wage guidelines were in force,[130] as against after their removal in 1991.

Guidelines, in Stone's view, will not effectively limit wages in the face of cost of living increases, simply because,

> "... unionized workers push up wage increase levels to survive, guidelines or no guidelines".[131]

Nor, Stone continued, will Government's "jaw-boning" about the need for wage restraint and a social contract elicit the desired response, while failing to control inflation.

It is now the case that in a high inflation scenario, and with some amount of trade union unity, (evidenced by the creation of the JTURDC and more recently the JCTU, unions are no longer apologists for Governments as a result of the traditional party/major unions linkage.

Unions now seem to realize that whereas there is the tendency for the constant relationship between factor incomes to persist in the long run, under 'normal' conditions, it is favourable conditions in the economy and the labour market, together with the mood of the labour force, from a bargaining point of view, which gives unions the chance to raise slightly the share of wages in the national income. There is thus no longer a sense of guilt in pursuing higher wages aggressively; unions must tangibly assist in providing increases in material and social-psychological benefits and rewards substantial enough for their members, to make the cost of membership a worthwhile investment,[132]

Table: 12 Wage/Price Increases Before and After Removal of Wage Guidelines (1991), 1987 - 1992

Year	Wages	Prices (Statin)	Prices (Stone Surveys)
1987	15%	8%	12%
1988	15%	9%	11%
1989	15%	17%	15%
1990	17%	30%	35%
1991	30%	80%	120%
1992133	40%	51%	80%

Source: Carl Stone, in The Daily Gleaner, Oct, 14, 1992.[133]

As against the mood of the masses, the mood of the hegemonic local capitalist class is not dissimilar to that reflected by the main conclusions of the meeting of the leaders of the European Union in December 1994. The key areas identified as appropriate for policy action included,

> " . . a wage policy which encourages investment and wage agreements *below* [italics added] increases in productivity; reducing non-wage labour costs; reforming labour market policy by avoiding practices which are detrimental to readiness to work . . .[134]

That was, seemingly, an echo of the words of the Director General of the Confederation of British Industry, Howard Davis, who had, some two months previously, voiced the opinion that "While the increase in pay awards is marginal, the slight upward shift over the last six months gives cause for concern".[135] This, it can be argued, is perhaps a good enough indication of the essential unattractiveness of free market ideology under which policy and statistics, *per se*, without any apparent concern for social consequences, is made to appear to take priority, over the condition of the majority of the population.

In the Jamaican context, the relevance of the inflation factor, in assessing the 'appropriate' level of wages, has been negatively described as,

> "... not a mistake nor an accident, nor even a measure of governmental mismanagement in the strictest sense of action being improperly related to objectives or having unintended consequences".[136]

Positively, it is seen as,

> "... an instrument of a deliberate policy, the object of which is to shear from productive labour a substantial portion of the value of its product, which then becomes available to the Government for distribution elsewhere. In short, inflation is employed as a form of taxation ... to expect that the practitioners of such a politics can come up with policies to quell inflation is not unlike expecting a Bengal tiger to preside over the increase of a flock of sheep".[137]

Nor, as Will Hutton argues – citing the work of David Blanchflower and Andrew Oswald (1994) on the cross-country survey of 'The Wage Curve (the relationship between wages and employment in a sample of 3.5 million spread over 12 countries) – is there any empirical evidence that employment is highest where real wages are lowest or lowest where real wages are highest.[138]

For the Jamaican case amply demonstrates that,

> "... unemployment does not lower real wages to price the unemployed into work".[139]

It could hardly be expected to do so, despite abstract traditional supply and demand price determination theory, given persistent high and hyper-inflation. According to Hutton, the dynamic component of the labour market is the demand for labour as against the payment terms the unemployed will accept. What he refers to as the "efficiency wage" is comprised of an effective mix of incentives, recruitment costs, the value of knowing the capacity of the firm's existing work force and its marginal productivity – all of which is traded-off against output.[140] This scenario portrays quite accurately the Jamaican experience, which never ceases to baffle the visitor: as to why it is difficult to get workers to fill what are perceived to be low-pay jobs.in the midst of so much unemployment.

The OECD based their forecasts of the effect of the level of unemployment on wage disinflation, in the industrialized countries, on the view that,

> "… the dis-inflationary impact of constant, high unemployment diminishes over time as the actual level of unemployment is increasingly perceived to be 'normal, and accordingly exerts less influence on wage negotiations".[141]

Contrary to the thinking by which official employer and trade union wage policy was formerly expected to be influenced, Hutton concludes, that, "unemployment… instead acts to discipline the wages [sic] and behaviour of those who are employed". Such discipline in a country like Jamaica, may well be constrained by the contextual social and cultural peculiarities, which allow people to choose unemployment, at tolerable standards of existence even in the absence of any meaningful system of public welfare benefits.

This line of argument provides confirmation for Stone's[142] conclusion that the existence of minimum wage standards does not in fact, have negative consequences for employment.[143] Minimum wage adjustments are only likely to lead to the loss of jobs where the rate is set above the efficiency wage-ignoring, for now, any attempt to calculate its value in containing social unrest.

From the point of view of trade union wage-strategy, it should be acknowledged that they, like others, do not have a sophisticated knowledge of the elasticity of demand for labour. Neither is there any assurance that increase in wages forgone will result in the employment of additional workers, thus enlarging the pool of prospective union members. And while it is true that marginal increments of employment will increase the total wage bill, this is a difficult kind of rationality to pursue.[144]

Additionally, the shape of a union's/wage preference path shows that its first responsibility is to its *existing membership*, especially in a situation where union competition is high. As a consequence, it is only when a substantial number of *union members* are unemployed that it can, realistically, be expected that priority will be given to additional employment rather than increased wages. This is particularly so, since the employment consequences of a wage change show up only through an indirect chain of actions and reactions. Adjustments in bargaining behaviour, based on changes in the psychological position of the parties, are thus made on the basis of actual experience in the labour and product markets, together with technological considerations, and not on the basis of predictions from theoretical principles.

Whatever the negative consequences of this state affairs for revolutionary potential, the society's notorious lack of a predisposition to theoretical formulation, suggests caution in designing Social Contract and Prices and Incomes Policy, in accordance with established neo-liberal 'rules of the game'.

1. The Jamaica Herald, Aug. 25, 1994, p.2.
2. The Jamaica Herald Aug. 14, 1995, p.4.

3. Ibid

4. Ibid
5. The Sunday Gleaner, Dec. 24, 1995, p.84; The changing position of the private sector will be apparent from a comparison with the earlier "Realistic economics – JCC's position", in The Sunday Gleaner, Feb. 6, p.5E; See also Keith Thompson, "Economic Policy in a Liberalized World" in The Financial Gleaner, May 28, 1993, p.13; Lloyd I. Wright "Case for a new Private Sector" Parts I and 2 in The Sunday Gleaner, Nov. 21, 28, 1993.
6. Lloyd Goodleigh, Chairman of the JTURDC, in the Money Index, No.416 May 3, 1994, p. 11.
7. Wilmot Perkins, "A Matter of Motivation", Money Index, No.297 Nov. 26, 1991, p . 43.
8. Mark Ricketts, "Devaluation, Wages and Profits", in The Money Index No.454 June 6, 1995, p.5.
9. Whereas inflation was projected, after revision, at 12.5% – in keeping with Hyman's observation as to "government's chronic instability to control inflation (which is) why the country's macro-economic environment is so unstable" – the actual rate was some 100% higher, i.e. 25.1% for 1995. Public sector work groups almost all eventually settled wage claims at the level of 15-16%. See The Daily Gleaner, Dec. 23, 1994, p. 8R and The Jamaica Herald, Dec. 9. 1994, p. I. In the case of the teachers, the governments offer of 30% over two years was the exact level of award handed down by the IDT, raising serious doubts as to its independence from government influence, and therefore its integrity.
10. Given the country's severe import dependence the depreciation of the local currency against those of its main trading partners, particularly the United States, automatically triggers rounds of price increases with widespread ripple effects throughout the economy. Not being anywhere near self-sufficient in food, for example, many of the "basic" food items of popular consumption are subject to substantial devaluation – induced price increases. Apart from basic foods, fertilizers, animal feeds, farm implements, energy sources, raw materials and almost all capital goods and spares are imported.
11. Ricketts, supra, p.5.
12. Gordon Shirley, Professor of Management Studies, University of the West Indies, Mona, "Productivity in Services", in The Money Index, No.313, March 31, 1992, p.23.
13. Danny Roberts, Letter to the. Editor, The Daily Gleaner, Oct. 20, 1994, p.lE, see also "Labour market reforms", in The Jamaica Herald, April 9, p.7A.
14. Ian Boxill, "Inefficiency, impoliteness and economic backwardness", in The Money Index No.353, January 26, 1993, p.10.
15. Ibid, pp.10-11.
16. Dillon Alleyne, "Personal Income Taxes and Work Effort in Jamaica", in The Money Index No.338, Sept. 22, 1992, p.39.
17. Reported by Mark Ricketts, in "Failure as success", The Money Index No.392, Oct. 26, 1993, p.3.
18. Ibid.
19. Ibid, p.5.
20. Cedric Wilson, "Policies and Productivity", in The Money Index No. 325 , June 23, 1992, p.7.
21. Jacques A. Bussieres, "The Role of Monetary Policy in The Structural Adjustment Process", in The Money Index No.383 Aug. 24, 1993, p.20.
22. Ibid, Bussieres, p.19.
23. The Jamaica Herald, Oct. I, 1994, p.5 and The Daily Gleaner, May 8, 1995, p.lC.
24. Kari Levitt, and Lloyd Best, "Character of the Caribbean Economy", in Hilary Beckles and Verene Shepherd (eds) Caribbean Freedom, Ian Randle Publishers, Kingston, 1993, p.412.
25. Paul Harrison, The Third World Tomorrow, Penguin, 1991, p.30. The location of manufacturing industry will to some extent depend also on comparative inflation levels and the degree of changes in its rate in the short to medium term.

26. Ibid, p.415.

27. Levitt and Best supra, p.418.

28. Andrew S. Downes, Carlos Holder and Hyginus Leon, "The Wage-Price - Productivity Relationship in a Small Developing Country: The Case of Barbados", in SES Vol.39 No.2, ISER, U.W.I., 1990, pp.69-70.

29. Havelock Brewster, "The Pattern of Change in Wages, Prices and Productivity in British Guyana, 1948-62", SES, Vol.18 No.2, ISER, U.W.I., p.107.

30. W.A. Lewis "Economic Development with Unlimited Supplies of Labour" Manchester School of Economic Social Studies, Vol. xxii, May, 1954.

31. Inflation between 1974-1995 totalled 515,2% (Source: Statin Publications).

32. Michael Shanks, *The Stagnant Society*, Pelican, 1964, p.21S.

33. Ibid, p.121.

34. Owen Jefferson, "Liberalization of the Foreign Exchange System in Jamaica", Seventh Aldith Brown Memorial Lecture, ISER, U.W.I., Nov. 26, 1991, p.10.

35. Jamaica Five Year Development Plan, (Education) 1990-1995, PIOJ, July 30, 1995, pp.2-4.

36. Cornwall College, Montego Bay, May, 1995.

37. Louis Lindsay, *The Myth of Independence: Middle Class Politics and Non-mobilization in Jamaica*, Working Paper No.6, ISER, U.W.I. 1991, pp.51-52.

38. The gospel according to St. Matthew xxv:29.

39. W. Arthur Lewis, *The Principles of Economic Planning*, IJrwin University Books, 1969, p.87.

40. Ibid, p.88.

41. E. Domar, "Capital Expansion and Growth", in Amartya Sen (ed) *Growth Economics.* Penguin, 1970, p.67.

42. J.M. Jackson, "Wages: Just Reward or Efficient Allocator", BJIRs, Vol.v No.3, Nov. 1967, p.375.

43. Carl Stone, "Work Attitudes Survey: A Report to the Jamaican Government", Earle Publishers, Jamaica, 1982.

44. Rosalea Hamilton, "Analysing Real Wages Prices and Productivity and the Effects of State Intervention in Caribbean Type Economics", SES, Vol.43 No.1, ISER, U.W.I., March 1, 1994, p.7.

45. Ibid, p.9.

46. For the appeal by Hugh Shearer of the BITU and JCTU for indexation of pensions to the rate of inflation, see The Sunday Gleaner, Dec. 4, 1994, p.2A; "Shearer calls for Drug Stamp implementation", in The Daily Gleaner, Oct. 23, 1994, p.4A; "Trade unions dissatisfied with 'lop-sided development.' in The Daily Gleaner, Dec. 2, 1992; "Poverty leading cause of death – WHO report" in The Sunday Herald, April 30, 1995, p.4A; "More students going hungry", in The Daily Gleaner, June 1, 1992, p.l; "Plea for Poor" in The Jamaica Herald, Mar. 22, 1995, p.l; "Golden Age Home in dire need", in The Daily Gleaner, April 11, 1995, p.2; "Budget not for the poor" in The Jamaica Herald, April 26, 1995, p.l; "$250ra more for poverty alleviation in The Jamaica Herald, April 24, 1995, p.4; "Jamaica 65th on UNDP Human Development Index (HDD" in The Sunday Gleaner, July 3, 1994, p.5E; "More Householders for food stamp programme" in The Daily Gleaner, May 11, 1995, p.4C.

47. Richard Browne, "Pensioners on the job: Cost of living hits hard, in The Sunday Gleaner, Aug. 28, 1994, p.lA.

48. Carl Stone, "Wages Policy and the Social Contract" in Headley Brown (ed) *The Jamaica Economy in a Changing World: The Way Forward 1993/94 and Beyond*, Headley Brown and Co. Ltd, 1993, p.123.

49. The data reported here is taken from "bridling the wrong horse", by Desmond Richards, in The Jamaica Herald, Oct. 15, 1994, p.10, who referring to the 1995 UNDP Human Development Reports informs that "Jamaican workers ranked only above Haiti in terms of low wages, and the country is ranked number three in the world in terms of income inequality. Gini Coefficient figures are not ready available. However the figures quoted indicate that "between 1975 and 1980 average wages increased by only 55% compared to the very high 185% increase in the cost of living … the picture remained dismal as between 1980 and 1985 wage levels increased by 33% compared to a 110% increase in the cost of living In contrast to the period 1970-75 when wages increased faster than gross profits, this position was reversed during the 1980's when gross profits double – contributing to the widening of the gap between labour and capital which begun during the 1970's under Manley regime.

50. Catherine A. Sunshine, The Caribbean Survival, Struggle and Sovereignty, EPICA, Publications, 1994, p.148.

51. Stone, 1982, p.126.

52. See "Davies (Omar Davies, Minister of Finance) lashes big wage hikes" in The Daily Gleaner, Jan, 18, 1995, p. 9R; "Reserves good but no big pay increased – Davies" in The Jamaica Herald, Sept. 19, 1995, p.3A; "Davies addresses wages" in The Jamaica Herald, Nov. 3, 1995, p.2A, "We have no more – Omar" etc, etc; For contrasting perspectives see Edward Seaga (Opposition leader and spokesman on Finance!" "Accuracy of the published record" in The Daily Gleaner, Nov. 26, 1994, pp.6,8 and also Will Hutton "A Nobel vision of fair shares for all" in The Guardian Weekly, Jan. 7, 1996, p.19;

53. Huntley Manhertz, "The Price Determination Process in A Small Open Economy – The Jamaican Experience" in Compton Bourne (ed) *Inflation in the Caribbean*, ISER, U.W.I., 1977, p.ll.

54. Charles Ross, Executive Director, The Private Sector Organization of Jamaica, Labour Productivity and Competition" in The Sunday Herald Oct. 16, 1994, p.3B.

55. Giovanni Andrea Cornia, Richard Jolly and Frances Stewart, *Adjustment with a Human Face*, Clarendon Press, Oxford, 1990, p.27.

56. Cornia and Stewart "Country Experience with Adjustment", in Cornia et al Ibid, p.114.

57. Levitt and Best, 1993, p.36.

58. Ibid p.54.

59. Lloyd Best, "A Biography of Labour" in George L. Beckford (ed) *Caribbean Economy*, ISER, 1984, p.147.

60. Unfortunately for Lindsay the new President of the PSOJ, his bank, "Workers Bank", was involved in the dispute which was referred to the IDT, which made an award in favour of the workers represented by the BITU, headed by Hugh Shearer, the President of the JCTU. Lindsay in the Jamaica Observer, of which he is Co-Chairman was accused of having launched an unwarranted attack not only on the IDT and the union involved, but also on the entire labour movement (and) "... pulled the organization of which he was recently named as president, into his personal vindictive attacks against Trade Unions. He has boldly declared that he will devote his presidency of the PSOJ to reforming labour practices" See "JCTII responds to attacks by PSOJ President", in The Daily Gleaner, Jan. 22, 1995, p.14A; Lindsay's concern was to have the customary "normal" work week of Monday to Friday changed to meet the flexibility required by the so-called "demands of current business trends", where more firms are opening on Saturdays and Sundays.

61. Robert Lightbourne, "The Unions are Killing us!" in The Sunday Gleaner, Feb. 5, 1995, p.22A.

62. DeLisle Worrell, "Exchange Rate Policy for Less Developed Countries" in SES, Vo 1.2 9, Nos. 263, ISER, U.W.I., June/Sept: 1930, pp.138, 140. But see Andrew S. Downes, Carlos Holder and Hyginus Leon, "The Wage-Price- Productivity Relationship in a Small Developing Country: The Case of Barbados" in SES Vol.39 No.2, ISER, U.W.I. June 1, 1990; where it is stated that "As in the Jamaican Case ... Wage policy was considered to be important because it was believed that "trade unions were demanding higher wages than the economy could afford with unfavourable consequences on the price level, the growth of exports and the rate of investment" (p.52) but further on, "Thus to maintain real wages, workers need to bargain for a nominal wage increase that is higher than the current rate of inflation" since "..The negative coefficient on the. lagged inflation variable suggests that real wages fall more than proportionately with prices and that some money illusion exists in the short run" (p.70). See also Rosalea Hamilton "Analysing Real Wages, Prices and Productivity and the Effects of State Intervention in Caribbean Type Economics" in SES Vol.43 No.1 ISER, U.W.I. Mar. 1994, pp.16,30 . Worrell, Ibid.

63. Headley Brown, "The Jamaica Economy: Performance and Prospects 1992/93 – 1993/94" in Headley Brown (ed) 1993, pp.75-76.

64. Ibid, p.82.

65. Courtney Blackman, "Exchange Rate Policy in the Context of Liberalization", in Headley Brown (ed), 1993, p.89.

66. Per capita debt is now about US$1,700. Jamaica's external debt has been reduced to some $3.3 Billion from over $4 Billion in the late 1980's; See "Third World debt drains Third World Health" in The Sunday Gleaner, Dec. 4, 1994, which refers to the "Millstone of Debt"; Raymond Forrest, "Managing that debt burden" in The Financial Gleaner, Aug. 5, 1994, p.9 at which time the debt service ratio was down [italics added] to 25% (of export earnings including services) as against some 40% in the late 1980's; The reduction came about as explained in "Jamaica taking serious steps to reduce international debt" in The Daily Gleaner, Mar, 16, 1992, P.10.

67. Michael Witter and Rodney Reid, "The Inflationary Impact of Wage Increases in the Jamaican Economy", undated Mimeo, p.1.

68. Ibid p.22 – a study commissioned by the JTURDC.

69. Perhaps because the Witter and Reid study was specifically commissioned and unpublished, the method of calculating this figure is not disclosed. Although the term "total compensation" is used it is nevertheless unclear if non-monetary benefits are included.

70. Witter and Reid employ a Labour Force Survey-derived, proportion of 5% for Management, Professional, Technical and other top job categories to 35% labour in 1973, moving to 12% and 88%, respectively, in 1992.

71. For details of the percentage changes in the earnings of these comparatively privileged occupational strata relative to inflation rates see annual JEF salary surveys covering this period.

72. Robert Kyloh, "The Wage Inflation – Unemployment nexus". Occasional Paper 1, Labour Law and Labour Relations Programme, ILQ, 1988, pp.4,7.

73. Douglas Orane, then President of the PSOJ, "Jamaica's per capita income low", in The Daily Gleaner, Western Bureau, reporting on a speech at the Jamaica Professional Secretaries Association at the Holiday Inn Hotel, 1993.

74. Morris Cargill, in The Daily Gleaner Sept. 18, 1994, p.9A.

75. The Guardian Weekly, Dec. 25, 1994, p.S.

76. In relation to pay in privatised entities in the UK, generally, it has been remarked that "a sharp distinction must be drawn between management, especially top management and the rest of the labour force" – V.V. Ramanadham led) *Privatisation in the UK*, Routledge, 1938, p.79. For those who have placed great hope in ESOP as a means of stimulating improved worker morale, and the motivation to increase productivity, this book adopts the view that with the small percentage of shares held by workers, "their essential interest continues to be in wage benefits which far exceed the dividends on their slender share quantum", P.252.

77. The Guardian Weekly Aug. 7, 1994, p.13.

78. Kyloh, 1938, p.6.

79. Witter and Reid, supra, p.25.

80. If 100% of the wage increase was spent, it is calculated that the change in consumption would be some 4.2% What appears to be faulty computation, i.e. the simple addition of the estimates for both the cost arid the demand approaches leads to a total ranging from a low of 4.5% to a high 6.0%, purportedly representing the overall inflationary impact of a 10% rise in labour costs. This is assuming productivity to be constant, and presumably profit levels. Since wages do not have a ripple effect on other costs of production it would hardly be expected that the over-all inflationary impact of a 10% wage increase could be anywhere as high as some 50%, and should in fact be more like 2%.

81. Anthony Gonzales, "The Caribbean and South – South Trade", in Ramesh Ramsaran (ed) *Caribbean Economic Policy and South – South Cooperation*, Warwick University Caribbean Studies, Macmillan (Caribbean) Ltd, 1993, P.53,

82. Owen Jefferson, The Post-war Economic Development of Jamaica, ISER,1977, p.33. fsee also pp. 17, 36).

83. Andrew Green, Free zone factory seeks 300 foreign workers, The Jamaica Herald, Aug. 18, 1994, p. 1; 'Expatriates small percentage of free zone workers', The Daily Gleaner, November 23, 1994, p.24.

84. Karl Theodore, "State Policy and the Role of Private Foreign Investment in a World of Increased Capital Mobility – The Salient Issues", in Ramsaran (ed^ op cit, 1993, p. 251. The contrasting private sector and trade union positions are stated by Charles Ross and Danny Roberts, respectively, in the Sunday Herald, Oct. 16, 1994, p.3b, and The Daily Gleaner, Oct. 20, 1994, p.lE.

85. It is worth recalling that the erosion of the "real wage gap" – the excess of real wages over labour productivity growth – has even now not resulted in a return to full employment in Western Europe, since the early 1980's, although the increasing use of labour-saving techniques is relevant. In the radical view, "Real wage flexibility" has become a euphemism for downward movements in real wages. And wage settling institutions, such as the Jamaican IDT, tend to be seen as an "enemy of working class", in the eyes of the trade union movement. It is acceptable, as a general conclusion that the whole issue of labour's wages, existing levels, appropriate increases, its share in the national income, and its relation to productivity, "is surrounded by much ambiguity, controversy and ideological fervour" – See European Trade Union Institute: *Flexibility and Jobs – Myths and Realties*, ETUI, Brussels, 1985, p.43.

86. Headley Brown, in The Financial Gleaner, Jan. 27, 1995, p.9. Or they may of course, simply reduce their labour force and produce less, especially under IMF demand compassion macro-economic policies – See M. Bruno and J. Sachs, Economics of Worldwide Stagflation, Harvard University Press, Cambridge, Mass 1985.

87. Ashwell Thomas, "Creating a Productive Working Environment" in Caribbean Labour Journal Vol.l, No.2, Dec. 1991, pp.48,50; Jacques Bussieres, then Governor of the BOJ, "The Role of Monetary Policy in the Structural Adjustment Process", in The Money Index No. 383, Aug. 24, 1993, p.20; But see Leon HoSang, "Importance of Productivity" in The Daily Gleaner Nov. 6, 1991, p.6; and Danny Roberts "Labour Market Reforms" in The Jamaica Herald, April 9, 1995, p.7A.

88. Headley Brown, supra, (Note 84).

89. Headley Brown, in The Financial Gleaner, July 3, 1994, p.7,

90. The Daily Gleaner, Jan. 20, 1994, p.6.

91. The Daily Gleaner, Oct. 12, 1994, p.6.

92. The Daily Gleaner, Sept. 12, 1994.

93. The Daily Gleaner, Oct. 26, 1994, p.3.

94. The President of the Civil Service Association, Eddie Bailey, stated that "the Association was holding. Government to its word that salaries of public sector workers would be brought within 80% of what now obtained in the private sector. This should be done by March 1995".

95. The Financial Gleaner, Editorial, Sept. 9, 1994, p.6.

96. Headley Brown, supra, (Note 34).

97. The increased level of strike action over wages since 1991 is, of course, a clear indication of managements' resistance to wage demands. And certainly not everyone tries to keep up with pace-setters.

98. Carl Stone, in The Daily Gleaner, Sept. 30, 1992.

99. The Daily Gleaner, Editorial, Oct. 23, 1994, p.6A.

100. The Minister of Finance declaring that, "the future economic survival of the whole country was at stake", continued by expressing "confidence that the public sector workers and their trade union representatives will, in the national interest, moderate their demands consistent with what the country is able to afford", in The Jamaica Herald, Sept. 6, 1994, p.6A; The Prime Minister took this affordability line of argument a step further by emphasizing that the Budget could not be devoted entirely to the payment of debt and public sector wages, adding that if the Government's wages targets were exceeded the result would be redundancies, cutting capital expenditure, or increasing taxes – The Jamaica Herald, Oct. 15, 1994, p.2; To the Prime Minister's list of possible negative consequences should be added cuts in social services, previously mentioned by the Minister of Finance, in The Jamaica Herald, Sept, 5, 1994, p.6; A possible solution of the wage/ inflation problem by way of indexation (wages moving automatically in line with the CPI) was specifically dismissed by the Prime Minister – see The Daily Gleaner, Oct. 15, 1994, p.2: "There is no cash hidden or locked away in safes at the Ministry of Finance or vaults of the Bank of Jamaica. We cannot allow the printing press to roll"

101. The Daily Gleaner, Nov. 11, 1994, p.6.

102. D. Robinson, *Monetarism and the Labour Market*. Clarendon Press, Oxford, 1936, p.426.

103. The Guardian Weekly, Sept. 25, 1994, p. 6.

104. Statement by the Minister of Finance, Dr Omar Davies, in The Jamaica Herald, Sept. 5, 1994, p.6.

105. See PNP: Taking care of the worker" in the. Daily Gleaner August 21,1994 p.l0B.

106. Ibid, As one commentator said, statements such as that of the PNP that, "Public sector workers do have a right to make the claims they have but at this time the economy is delicately poised [as it has been since the early 19 70f s] and any 'rocking of the boat', could lead to disaster", can't pay the cashier at the supermarket.

107. See Headley Brown, "The twelve month up-trend in inflation", in The Financial Gleaner, Sept. 30, 1994, p.7, where the remedies advanced, for persistent acceleration of the general level of prices, "by observers and analysts and published by the media", were described as ranging from fantasy to pipe dreams". For Brown, the effective remedy is, not surprisingly, the containment of wage increases, and productivity improvement.

108. The Jamaica Herald, Editorial, Sept. 5, 1994, p.7.

109. The Daily Gleaner, Sept. 10, 1994, p.3; See also Clifton Segree "The tip of the iceberg" in The Jamaica Herald, Dec.1, 1994, p.7A, where there is concurrence with this view in that "it (the government) has no moral authority to ask its workers to hold strain. The Members of Parliament have looked after themselves very nicely, they have fixed themselves a nice cushion against double-digit, inflation". Like many other commentators, the current situation, to this columnist, put. the. Government on a head-on collision course with labour. For a contrary position see James Walsh "Public Sector wage talks" in The Daily Gleaner, Oct. 21, 1994 p.6, where the matter is seen net in terms of morality or leadership by example, but from a resources quantum perspective, i.e. Members of Parliament are too few for their salaries to make a difference on the national financial level, so too for the number of ministries.

110. Basil Buck, has repeatedly emphasized that the incentive to invest is considerably reduced by the cost of money and the heightened prices of capital goods and raw materials due to devaluation-induced inflation – See Basil Buck, "Cool it Mr. Minister", in The Financial Gleaner, Sept. 16, 1994, p.3. The fact that over any particular time-period from the short to even medium term the exchange rate has been stable cannot, be expected necessarily to result in the absence of price increases: the full effect of exchange, rate depreciation will be lagged over different periods for different goods and services, depending on credit arrangements for purchases, and most certainly on expectations as to how long such stability is expected to last.

111. The point has been made that once there is declining national output, inflation is inevitable, i.e. even if wages were to be frozen, Delroy Chuck, "Wage settlements and inflation", in The Daily Gleaner, Oct. 5, 1994, p.6.

112. Danny Roberts, "Inflation and public sector wages" in The Jamaica Herald, Nov. 14, 1994, p.7; See also Ian Boxill, "Management by Crisis", in The Daily Gleaner, Feb. 7, 1995, p.4.

113. See The Daily Gleaner, Oct. 31 , 1994, p.l, under the heading "Charles: Government capable of bigger pay rise". Charles' argument, as reflected in the article's caption, is based, on the fact of the Government's collecting more revenue than budgeted for, because of inflation.

114. Ibid

115. A conclusion from a 1994 study of Jamaican labour force problems, reported in summary in The Sunday Gleaner, Feb. 12, 1995, p.2C.

116. Byron Buckley, "Wage restriction by stealth", in The Daily Gleaner, July 3, 1994, p.9A.

117. The Financial Gleaner, Jan. 14, 1994, p.2.

118. Ibid.

119. Ibid; See also The Jamaica Herald, Jan, 1, 1994, in which Senator Navel Clarke advanced the view that, "in a free market economy, competitive salaries was the only way to ensure production and efficiency in the sector".

120. See The Daily Gleaner, Oct. 28, 1994, in which the Opposition leader established that for every US$100M bought up by the Bank of Jamaica, the money supply is thereby increased by an additional J$3,300M, which of course defeating the Governments attempt to control inflation.

121. The Daily Gleaner, Oct. 31, 1994, p.3A,

122. Duke Douglas, "Trade Union pressure mounts against 9% guideline", in The Jamaica Herald, Oct. 7, 1994, p.3.

123. Gary Spaulding, "Wage battle lines drawn", in The Daily Gleaner, Sept. 3, 1994, p.l.

124. The Daily Gleaner, Oct. 27, 1994, p.l.

125. Allan Rickards, "No considerations for consumers", in The Jamaica Herald, Dec. 9, 1994, p. 7A; This is after the startling statement that "the people demanded less government and they have got it … no more price controls … no more price inspectors. The country's *consumers* have therefore got what they have called for, total private sector freedom". This can only be described as taking the functions of a public relations consultant to the governing party too far. One could with not a little justification have "the private sector and/or the IMF/World Bank" substituted for "consumers".

126. The Daily Gleaner, Jan. 20, 1994, p.6.

127. The Jamaica Herald, Jan. 12, 1995, p.2; The Daily Gleaner, Jan. 13,1994 p.9B.

128. The Jamaica Herald, Sept. 19, 1994, p.3A.

129. The Daily Gleaner, Sept. 29, 1994, p.2.

130. The Daily Gleaner, Mar. 4, 1995, p.3.

131. Carl Stone, in The Daily Gleaner, Oct. 14, 1992. Stone's prices surveys take into account the fact that the basket of goods used in computing the official CPI is now too narrow and does not reflect the actual consumption range of goods, and the CPI (statin) is thus understated. Headley Brown on the other hand supports the use of the Implicit GDP Deflator as a measure of inflation containment policies in Jamaica since he holds that in small open trade dependent economies more meaningful measures of inflation from the perspective of recovery and growth "are best informed by export competitiveness", The Financial Gleaner Nov 4, 1994, p.8.

132. IIbid.

133. Leon HoSang, "Wages and the working class" undated mimeo.

134. Extrapolated from Jan - Aug data: although there was a 10% guideline, wages increases exceed this official limit.
135. Reported in "EU summit conclusions", in The Jamaica Herald magazine "Dollars & Sense" Dec 12, 1994 p.12.
136. See "British pay awards raise concern", a Rueter report in The Jamaica Herald magazine, "Dollars & Sense" Oct 31, 1994 p.4.
137. Wilmot. Perkins, "Of inflation and Bengal tigers", in The Jamaica Herald, Oct 16, 1994, p.bA.
138. Ibid.
139. Will Hutton, "Minimum wage offers maximum returns", in The Guardian Weekly, July 23, 1995 p.21 Nowhere in the Blanchflower and Oswald study has "lowering real wages led to higher employment", contra Headley Brown in the Financial Gleaner, Sept 30, 1994, p.7.
140. Hutton, Ibid.
141. OECD: Economic Outlook: June 1987, p.42.
142. The Financial Gleaner, Editorial, "Minimum Wage" July 8, 1994, p.4: "$500 (the new minimum wage) can hardly meet 50% of the cost of feeding a family of five a basic weekly diet, let alone pay for children's education ... if the minimum wage is higher than the market clearing wage rate, excess labour will result, thereby effecting a reduction in employment of low-wage, non-unionized workers ... although all indications are that the minimum wage of $500 is much below the market rate...therefore the fear that the minimum wage would derail employment will be unfounded."; See also The Daily Gleaner, April 27, 1994, p.27, June 13, 1994, p.2A; 'Minimum wage not affecting jobs', in The Financial Gleaner, July 8, 1994. p.3.
143. See David Card and Alan Krenger, *Myth and Measurement*, Princeton University, 1995, where it is established that it is only when the minimum wage is set above the "efficiency wage" that a loss of jobs is likely to ensue.
144. Leon HoSang, "They (the unions) must deliver, but how?", undated mimeo, also "Productivity Bargaining" in The Daily Gleaner, Nov. 22, 1991, p. 4D; Carl Stone, 1987, p.102; James Hinton, "The First Shop Stewards Movement", George Allen and Urwin, 1973, pp.275-97 reprinted in Clarke and Clements, "The Theory of Independent Rank-and-File Organization" 1977, p.116; R. Hyman and R.H. Fryer, "Trade Unions: Sociology and Political Economy" in J.B. McKinley *Processing People: Studies in Organizational Behaviour,* Holt Rinehart and Winston, 1975, pp.160-3, 182-91. Shanks argues that "There are two overwhelmingly strong arguments against this view that trade union leaders should regard themselves as exclusively custodians of the public interest ... a trade union leader who tried to behave in this way would in fact lose control of his union. ... Quite simply, a trade union official is paid by his members to do one thing only – to look after their interests" Michael Shanks, The Stagnant Society, Pelican, 1964. This observation is no less true today as the fall off in union membership during the labour retreat of the 1980's proves.

Chapter 3
Productivity Incentives Schemes

If low productivity is given as the explanation for wage-push inflation, the question of providing a work climate conducive to the kind of motivation necessary for the evolution of a culture of productivity should be foremost in the minds of those concerned with rapid economic growth and development.

Instead, the attempt to promote the straightforward use of increases in productivity as a justification for exceeding the limits imposed by IMF wage guidelines was announced by the then Prime Minister, Michael Manley, in February 1990. "For the first time", Mr Manley was reported as saying, "... there is a historic new understanding that we are to try and explore ways of building in a productivity factor outside of the wage guidelines".[1]

The then Deputy Prime Minister and Minister of Industry and Production, expressed the view that, "... the purpose of the wage policy was to reward increases in production and productivity" and that the IMF had been persuaded by the Government that, " profit-sharing and productivity bonuses should be permitted".[2]

The Prime Minister's further observation that, "... there was very little to guide the country in terms of known procedures from other countries," did little credit to a party that had thirteen years to acquaint itself with at least the British experience during the decades of the 1960's and 1970's.

As this writer has noted elsewhere,[3] this is a failure that has blighted the island's two-party system: Little policy study, much less identification of all policy options, has taken place while parties have been in opposition. When in government, they have apparently been 'too busy' with the job of governing. 'Think-tanks' in either period of the governance cycle seem to be regarded as luxuries.

More accurately, Winston Lewis, at a forum sponsored by the Mona Institute of Business at the University of the West Indies, noted that even though bonuses are usually paid on the basis of production, Jamaica had no significant tradition of labour productivity bargaining.[4]

It is perhaps typical of the way policies are implemented in countries such as this, that the new opportunity of using productivity improvements to justify pay rises, above the guideline, could be hailed as 'historic', at the same time that the admission of procedural ignorance is made. And this was, despite the fact, that the 'concession' had actually been allowed by the IMF three years before, in the 1987 agreement. The change of Government which took place in 1989 can scarcely be given as an excuse for ignorance of these pre-existing arrangements with the IMF.

But it is a gross over-simplification of the issue to propose that what is required, as a component of a workable incomes policy, is the development of comprehensive productivity incentive policies, on a sector by sector basis, with a view to increasing capacity and energy utilization efficiency.[5]

There has been little local attempt at a comprehensive in-depth treatment of the productivity question, either with a practical or academic orientation. What there has been is the occasional contribution of articles exposing varying levels of comprehension of the issues.

Having frankly admitted the country's ignorance as to the procedures for the introduction of productivity incentives schemes, and by implication, also, the appropriate substantive components of such schemes and the nature of the associated bargaining processes associated therewith, Manley did not see it necessary to establish a task force to study the problem as a matter of priority on a comparative basis. This would have been a useful exercise, even if restricted, in terms of the number of country/company experiences reviewed, so as to gain the operational knowledge lacking in the Jamaican labour relations environment.

In manifestation of the syndrome of setting up a new institution, body/ committee each time a problem emerges, the Prime Minister established the much-heralded Productivity Council under the Chairmanship of Robert Lightbourne, a former Minister of Trade and Industry. The preparatory work necessary for the successful implementation of such a project which represented a major policy innovation had not been attempted, and the Council's terms of reference did not remedy this omission. Lightbourne, although reported to have been a highly effective Cabinet Minister, in speeding the process of industrial development during the 1960's and earlier, and a successful manufacturer himself, was not in a position to personally shed light on the areas of ignorance. His experiences, gained as an entrepreneur industrialist in post-World War II Britain, were hardly relevant to the problem of low productivity in Jamaica in the 1990's. Indeed, they would not have been relevant for Britain from the late 1960's to the mid 1970's. While the appointment could be understood in terms of image, it was difficult to justify, functionally. Being impressionable as a people, the general reaction from the business community, in particular, was however one of strong approval.[6]

Having been conceived in 1990, with great expectations and considerable support from the trade unions, understandably, the Productivity Council so ineffectively performed, if at all, after its very auspicious beginning, that its presumed early demise may be excused. It is true to say that very little has ever been heard of its work. The choice of Chairman, it is felt, has usually been reflective of poor judgment: the person selected seem to have been a case of *status* based on lineage and general business reputation than issue-specific accomplishment (productivity-related accomplishments).

The fact that wage guidelines were removed, officially, in 1991 is not without significance for the Council having faded out of existence in the public mind. The notion of productivity and productivity incentive schemes was very clearly seen, initially, as not having much greater merit that as an IMF approved means of exceeding the wage guideline limit.

Thus, one finds that what little eulogizing there has been over the Councils apparent demise has tended mostly to be from trade unions. In fact, there has been a peculiar dichotomy of emphasis as between managements and the trade unions: the former concentrating on increased productivity, *per se*, the latter on the incentive pay aspect.[7] The survey results reported below should perhaps therefore be not surprising.

Whatever the past or present concerns about pay and productivity, or different vested interest emphases, there was little illumination of this aspect of industrial relations up to the time of the Productivity Seminars sponsored by the Joint Trade Union Research and Development Centre in 1993.[8]

To date, for example, the distinction is yet to be widely recognized, among those whom one would expect to be most knowledgeable, between a productivity agreement and payment by results systems,[9] or even between increased production and productivity.[10]

Increasing the pay of workers beyond the then (1990) existing guideline figure of 12.5%, in accordance with increased performance under a piece-rate payment system, would clearly not have amounted to a breach of the guideline, since this so-called 'effort-bargain' involves an increase in effort, not the rate of pay. That is on the assumption that technology, organizational and other factors remain the same. The consequences of pay increases under this heading should therefore be of little worry to policy makers and administrators, their effect being inflation-neutral, as long as wage *rates* remained unchanged.

When the Prime Minister therefore said that,

> "… At least this (exceeding the guideline on the basis of increases in productivity) is a sign that we are trying to act in a more just and equitable manner as far as the worker's experience is concerned under the IMF programme".[11]

The focus from the national point of view needed to have been on productivity with much greater/broader implications for changes in work practices, methods, organization structures and technology.

Changes of these types, resulting in increased efficiency, would be an integral part of the bargain, and would be expected to substantially pay for the cost of whatever benefits are conceded to workers, whether in terms of money wages, fringe benefits, or additional leisure.[12]

In the Jamaican context, where talk tends to take precedence over action – as is often manifested by government by exhortation – it is useful to note the point made by Flanders that,

> "… when unions are asked to cooperate in introducing measures that will raise productivity, they cannot decide their attitude on general grounds of national interest or economic theory".[13]

The restriction on the level of wage increases under the IMF guidelines could also have been circumvented, with no inflationary consequences by a deliberate policy of converting time rates of pay, which one suspects would have applied to most of the working population, into production-based payment systems. That would have required the setting of output targets on the basis of which remuneration would be calculated. This would certainly have raised the level of productivity consciousness on a wide scale in quite a dramatic fashion.

One would still have had to contend, of course, with a major problem arising from the way in which incentive payments systems work, especially over a long period of time. This is the fact that they become susceptible to 'decay' because of 'loose' rates, the constant pressure on rates, and the effects of the 'learning curve'.

Put differently, earnings can well increase with *decreased* effort that is unaccompanied by a corresponding downward rate adjustment.

In another respect, incentive payment systems put pressure on incomes policies that lack mechanisms to deal with the sense of injustice and grievance felt by those categories of workers whose work is not amenable to easy measurement, and who are aware of substantial wage increases gained from productivity increases by other categories. What may be 'just and equitable' for one set of workers might well constitute 'injustice' from the perspective of a different category, including supervisors who see established wage differentials, with occupational and social status significance, being substantially reduced. The trend towards expansion of the services sector relative to other sectors of the economy will tend to aggravate this potential problem.

To be properly operated, an incentive payment system may not only be costly to administer but places a heavy burden on supervisors to resist strenuous efforts to 'rig the rates'. The point has been made, on the basis of British research, that,

> "… This difficulty obtains no matter whether the effort to control inflation is through inducing a higher level of employment or through an incomes policy or through a combination of both courses".[14]

Manley's choice of words sums up the general attitude to productivity incentive schemes, under the IMF wage guidelines, "restraint avoidance". In this regard, it would have been useful to have conducted studies of the impact of incentive schemes on productivity.[15] Empirical research on this issue would need to focus on enterprise level situations and would probably not be amenable to aggregation for the purposes of providing insights of significance at the national level. Relevant here, is Stone's informed impression, that,

> "… the fact is that only a few companies have developed the productivity and payment by reward systems necessary to implement that idea (allowed wage increases in excess of the wage guidelines figure) and the trade unions have not been aggressive enough in pushing for productivity payments in areas of the economy where they represent workers."[16]

Trade union action has been limited by their traditional reactive posture and role under strong historical and cultural influences emphasizing management prerogatives. Further, they have been faced with a situation of a declining level of unionization and union political influence under IMF economic stabilization and adjustment programmes. The problem of data availability and accuracy, in any such project would present a major obstacle, together with the reluctance to provide information and to welcome investigation of 'private' company affairs in a society which, on both the personal and corporate level, is instinctively suspicious of the motives of anyone, official or private, seeking to scrutinize their activities.

The Jamaican economy is a small, labour-surplus, low-wage one, where consumer price competition in the market place is not strong, due to the existence of monopolistic or oligopolistic conditions. With market-information inadequacies, and the absence of an effective consumer lobby, the motivation to focus on increasing labour productivity is, perhaps understandably, not high. It is no doubt easier to maintain profit levels while passing on increased production costs – including the costs of inefficiency – to the consumer, rather than offsetting them by initiatives to raise productivity levels.

Productivity incentive schemes must be recognized as having limited applicability if the goal is substantial, as against marginal, efficiency enhancement in order to make incomes policy an effective instrument of inflation restriction.[17] With the imposition of IMF demand management policies on more than a short-term basis, rigidities of several kinds in the export sector, and the small size of the internal market, any substantial increase in worker productivity would, ironically, have disastrous consequences, all other factors remaining unchanged, for employment. The influence of a well-established trade union movement, increasingly liberated from the influence of party political affiliation, together with the disinclination to technological innovation, are phenomena of relevance for achieving marked productivity growth in a free market economy which, despite the propositions of theory, has failed to generate investment creating meaningful new employment.

Not usually noted is the positive relationship between output and productivity which suggests that much of the input by labour is essentially a fixed cost for fairly substantial periods. Okun provides the reminder that high output levels thus permit the spreading of labour overheads and *low production levels* [italics added] raise unit fixed costs of labour.[18]

It is here suggested that the following conditions are conducive to the successful introduction of productivity bargaining and incentive payment schemes:

(a) where the power of union delegates on the shop floor is significant and there is a high level of unionization.

(b) where the technology in use is outdated thus providing the opportunity for large increases in efficiency due to possibly substantially increased capital input.

(c) where there is a general shortage of labour, or of the particular skills required to meet the demands of proposed changes.

(d) where the demand for the enterprise's products is highly price elastic.

(e) where the firm's stock level and delivery schedules are such as would make disruption of production unacceptable.

(f) where the organizational culture emphasizes consultation and joint job regulation, rather than the unilateral exercise of "management prerogatives".

(g) where work practices, methods and organization are markedly inefficient, and

(h) where labour costs form a relatively small part of total costs.[19]

The delusion that productivity can be raised by propaganda still needs, at the present time, to give way to work study, job evaluation and the systematic evaluation of different systems of wage payment to fit the particular needs of the enterprise or industry.[20]

In this regard, the Productivity Council could have served an important function as a central source of information and expert advice; arrange for necessary research into known productivity issues, problems and concerns as they arise; maintain a reference service for the use of the private and public sectors, consisting of local and international comparative material of a procedural, organisational design, technological and analytical nature; and providing a vital link between government, employers, trade unions, teaching, research and technical institutions, professional bodies and consulting firms.[21]

Status distinctions based on formal authority and class related factors would, consciously or subconsciously, be expected to negatively affect the attitude of the parties in the industrial relations system, at both the micro and macro level. It is possible that unsatisfactory productivity performance might be minimised, if not eliminated, along the lines of limited British company policy- experimentation in the decades of the 1960's and 1970's. This took the form, for example, of making the basis of manual workers' pay the same as that of white collar workers, that is to say, an annual salary and possibly, also, equality of treatment on such employment benefits as holiday and sick pay and rights to notice of termination.[22] With the 'slave driver' and 'exploitation' mentality which persists in the Jamaican work culture, this kind of development could well have very significant positive psychological consequences for productivity improvement.[23]

The 'pressure' to develop productivity bargaining and to introduce incentive schemes deriving, not from statutory or official but from persuasive, voluntary incomes policy considerations, has led, and could be expected to lead, in a society characterized by a marked tendency to attach more importance to form, as against substance, to, "... concessions dressed up as productivity bargains for the sake of appearances".[24]

In contrast to the British approach to productivity bargaining, in an incomes policy context, the traditional American and Canadian approach has been for negotiation of fixed-term collective agreements to be conducted on the basis that increased efficiency during the life of an existing agreement increases the scope for the application of the 'ability to pay' criteria in the future. This can obviously provide a very effective incentive for the acceptance of changes which are expected to yield wage increases under a new contract. The advantage of this direct linking of pay with enterprise efficiency, especially in a first world society, is that it reinforces the principle, over time, "that higher wages have to be earned".[25]

As with other policy initiatives, productivity incentive schemes are introduced in circumstances which may be more or less favourable for success. In Jamaica's case, the general macro-economic conditions have been less than propitious: high unemployment; depressed demand; cheap labour; high interest rates which discourages capital expenditure for retooling; and the absence of effective market competition and a robust consumer lobby.

Apart from the incomes policy implications of productivity bargaining and incentives schemes, policy makers, enterprise management, and trade unions will equally be concerned at the employment consequences. Contrary to popular belief, there might very well be favourable outcomes with respect to job creation. If the enterprise was previously of marginal viability, a significant productivity increase could just be 'the shot in the arm' needed to put the business on a sound financial footing, through increased production and sales or, perhaps, by improving customer satisfaction through improved supply reliability, in terms of volume and delivery dates, or by realizing the cost benefits of scale economies. Rather than increased productivity leading inevitably to redundancies, therefore, what could possibly result is business and employment expansion instead.

It is thus essential that those responsible for policy design, IMF/World Bank and Governments, ensure that growth and investment-oriented macro-policies are in place so as to maximize the acceptability of productivity enhancing measures.[26]

Without such policies, productivity efforts are likely to be viewed as threatening by workers, however 'enlightened' and 'progressive' the positions that their union leaders may adopt.[27]

The process and results of effort-wage bargaining will be further determined by factors such as:

- the state of the local labour market
- certain internal factors, such as the strength, number and tactical bargaining skill of trade unions
- the competitive position of the enterprise, depending on whether the market is local and/or overseas
- cultural and sub-cultural values as to the factors to be taken into account in the determination of what a fair day's work ought to be
- the efficiency of the disputes procedures available
- the family circumstances of the worker; the level of skills required for the tasks to be performed
- the technology being utilized
- and even such factors in the external environment as the quality of public transportation and the crime level.[28]

Gloria Kirton has emphasized the need to act rather, than continuing to talk, about the one thing—productivity—on which she believes there is consensus among politicians, economists, academicians, the IMF, the private sector, the church and the man in the street. According to her, this consensus centres on the realization that, "... our economic survival hangs on our ability to improve our productivity and increase production."[29]

As part of the price for union acceptance and cooperation, the Fawley Productivity Agreements, which represented the British model of its kind, included a clause under which management promised the unions, representing the *total* workforce, that there would be no redundancy as a result of the agreements.[30] This did not, however, exclude the possibility of a reduction of the work force; but this was to be achieved over time, as necessary, by the process of attrition.[31]

In a high unemployment economy, such as Jamaica's, it is worth noting that in respect of this 'no redundancy' promise, Flanders concluded, after interviews with representatives of both sides, that, "... no employer in his senses would expect to win consent to such (fundamental and far reaching) changes without giving such a pledge".[32] Indeed, in giving reasons for the negotiations culminating in agreement, one union delegate simply made the comment in relation to the "no redundancy" clause, that, "that could be taken for granted". Peace, in other words usually has a price and a sense of security is highly relevant to the acceptance of far-reaching changes.[33]

Trade unions in Jamaica, individually and collectively, have been, with little result, leading the call for the introduction of productivity schemes. In this respect, it has been claimed that proposals had been submitted to various companies for a period as long as one year without approval and agreement.[34]

The various members of the political directorate, private sector leadership, and the academic community have, with varying degrees of emphasis, pointed to the importance of improving the level of national productivity. There has, nevertheless, failed to emerge any sense of problem-specific crisis and mobilization around any 'great leap forward' with respect to productivity levels at the individual, enterprise, or national level. The consistently declining national trend portrayed by TABLE 14 and FIG. 10. provides another example of the failure of exhortation and rhetoric to be acceptable substitutes for focused policy and its effective implementation.

This disappointing trend over a 20-year period was perhaps to be expected when it has been stated by Robert Gregory, Executive Director of the HEART Trust/National Training Agency that,

> "Amidst the muddled industrial relations climate in Jamaica in recent times, over 76 per cent of the labour force has no training for the job which they occupy"[35]

Indeed, given the tendency to imitate North American fashions and fads, it is instructive that the Jamaican industrial relations scene has yet to be invaded by the notion, if not the practice, of concession bargaining – a relatively recent development in the United States of America, as a strategy to cope with the dislocations of the free market economy and the effects of increasing global competition at all levels, nationally and sectorally.

In a Daily Gleaner report, Hugh Shearer, President General of the BITU and President of the JCTU, complained that rather than being told the reasons for the delayed response to union submission of productivity incentive proposals,

> "Instead, we hear about imposing a social contract... . It must be recognized that merely fixing productivity targets in the board rooms of companies or by mere arithmetical calculations will not enhance economic development".[36]

The continued conflict in the conclusions about the state of the Jamaican economy is well demonstrated, albeit unintentionally, by Frank Kerber, an officer in the Political and Economic Unit of the United States Embassy in Kingston. Kerber is reported as saying that Jamaica continues to get high marks from the IMF; had made "incredible improvements" in macro-economic performance, such as reduction in the rate of inflation; had achieved a substantial increase in international reserves and stability in the value of the currency as against the currency of our major trading partner, the U.S. dollar; experienced increased availability of foreign currency; and, because of all these positive developments, earned an improved international credit-rating.

But Kerber was compelled to further observe that these improvements had, nevertheless, failed to improve:

- the trade balance or to stimulate investment
- job creation which remained at a very low level
- productivity growth
- performance of the export sector
- efficiency level, generally, at the micro level
- production of home grown substitutes for expensive imports.

- the waste of scarce resources; and

- severe labour relations problems"[37]

Against the background of these remarks, it is difficult to believe that Kerber was unaware of the negative and well-documented consequences of the stabilization and structural adjustment policies such as import liberalization, a high interest rate regime, and demotivating wage guidelines in a hyper-inflation situation.

The structural factors which account, to some degree, for the less than desired responses noted by Kerber, have been written about *ad nauseam* in academic, popular media, and every conceivable form of publication. It would be incredible if the government of the United States of America appoints Embassy personnel to such positions without ensuring that they satisfy an appropriate test of adequate familiarity with the basic characteristics of the economies of the countries to which they are posted. Unlike the IMF, the United States government does have a permanent 'mission' in the island. It is well known that it is not without influence with the IMF.

Figure: 10

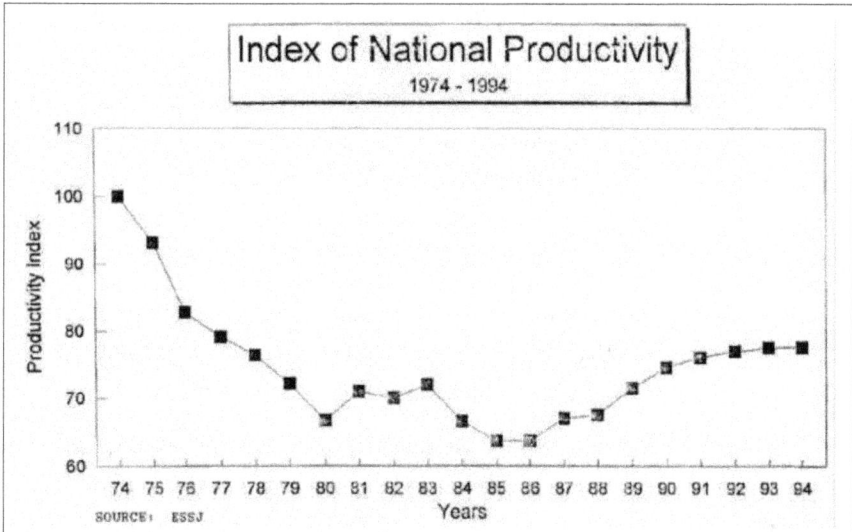

Index of National Productivity
1974 - 1994

The 1994 Business Behaviour Survey sponsored by the Private Sector Organization of Jamaica (PSOJ) found that 80% of the firms participating pointed to poor employee work habits as the major constraint on efficiency and productivity: the level of hardship and demoralization suffered during the IMF years, should make this result hardly surprising to the realistic. Neither are the findings of the USAID commissioned study of labour force problems comforting, with respect to the prospects for national productivity. The study group agreed, unanimously, that,

> "... the two most fundamental causes of Jamaica's work force problems [were]: the lack of strategic vision among Jamaica's managers [italics added] and the decline in literacy, numeracy and work ethic of the workforce".[38]

Apart from faulting the poor "growth mentality" of managers, it was reported that their basic orientation was suited to a static, rather than a dynamic view of their industry,

> "... with very little thought or planning for the future growth or diversification of their enterprises, the implications for the workforce ... are readily apparent: workers do not see clear career paths for themselves and have difficulty in focusing on developing technical skills to improve their own growth prospects. ... Top Management's preoccupation is compensating for the deficiences of a weak middle management structure that is unable to lift the productivity of the production process and maintain quality."[39]

As is usual with those who adopt the technicist approach to social and economic problems in a developing country, where the working class is without the buffer of unemployment insurance or any form of a social safety net, Kerber's contribution to the analysis and solution of the problems identified is simply to note that.

> "... the country's workforce still lacks most of the basic competencies and technical skills needed to build a modern prosperous economy that can compete efficiently in regional and international markets".[40]

This being the case, assuming Kerber is correct, how then could significant export expansion and productivity increases be expected to materialize?[41]

The IMF and World Bank programmes in Jamaica have failed to generate growth, much less development. In the context of the negative economic growth experienced, almost without interruption since the 1970's, it must be borne in mind that "business productivity may make the downturn worse if the trade-off is rising unemployment". Marmor, a contributor to the *"Investor's Daily"*, continued,

"... 800,000 workers [in the United States of America] are not applauding the rising trend in manufacturing productivity. They are displaced workers – those whose jobs no longer exist, largely because strong manufacturing productivity gains have made their skills obsolete".[42]

In the same article, Steve Dean, economist for the San Francisco Federal Reserve Board, makes the point that the increase in unemployment due to productivity improvements, "... compounds weak economic conditions adding to the nation's economic contraction and output decline".[43] If this kind of development can be a source of anxiety in the United States, because what may be good from a broad societal view can be quite painful from an individual perspective, then the extent to which unregulated markets can be expected to work in achieving desired results must be much more problematic in Jamaica, with the various market imperfections and high unemployment level which exist.

If talk about productivity incentives schemes is to be of any value, it is imperative that certain basic principles be agreed and operationalized.

Since profits are generated by the combination of resources, including labour and capital, it seems remarkable that as late as 1991 it should be thought improper for there to be disputes, "... where workers demand a share of labour cost savings, even when the savings arise solely from capital investment or other action taken by management". Winston Lewis, in concluding that, in fact, schemes may fail for this reason[44] would, one suspects, take for granted the right of capital to share in any incremental surplus value created exclusively by improved *labour* performance.[45]

Perhaps, even more surprisingly, Gordon Shirley, has expressed the same unbalanced sentiments in his statement that, "... the productivity of human resources determines their [sic] wages".[46] Again, the combination of inputs is recognized in the earning of the surplus, but is apparently forgotten in its distribution.

The limit to this 'cycloptic' perspective though was perhaps reached when Gloria Kirton, in her presentation entitled "Government's Proposed Policy on Productivity Incentives", reminded her audience that it was Prime Minister Manley who had in the previous year announced that, "... as an incentive towards increasing productivity and investments consideration would be given to offering income tax relief".[47] Of all the reasons for offering companies tax relief, this seems the most peculiar. One would have expected that the benefits of improved efficiency would in themselves have been adequate to justify the effort. Further depriving the Treasury of Revenue to effect much needed infrastructural *employment creating* development is simply to continue the discredited investment-attracting incentive regime associated with the industrialization by invitation developmental approach relentlessly pursued in the 1950's and 1960's. That approach was not distinguished by the achievement of the desired and expected employment and inter-sectoral linkage effects.

The figures for annual real output per worker set out in TABLE 13, records virtually a continuous decrease since 1972. Improvements since 1988 have been quite marginal. Thompson notes that in 1972, only 611,300 workers were employed to produce a level of output valued at J$2,218.2M (in 1974 prices). After 19 years, it required 907,700 workers to produce the almost identical output of J$2,188.6M at constant (1974) prices.[48]

An explanation of this 'phenomenal' reduction in productivity of some 34%, between 1972 and 1991, is attempted by seeking to link its movements with the level of industrial disputes. "It can be observed", Thompson concludes,

> "... that, when industrial disputes is high [sic] and rising in a particular year labour productivity tends to fall faster, while when industrial disputes is low [sic] or declining then labour productivity is either falling slowly or is indeed rising".[49]

It is in his identification of the causal variable that issue may be taken with Thompson's arguments. Labour productivity, he says, is therefore significantly dependent upon the level of industrial disputes because disputes have the effect, firstly, of causing a loss of production man-hours and, secondly, they have a demotivating effect on the workforce. Obvious as it may seem, it has not occurred to Thompson that the argument could well be reversed: low productivity is caused by low and falling real wages, low morale, inadequate retooling – due either to inefficient production methods and planning or the prohibitively high cost of capital – or the fear of producing oneself out of a job. With declining sales under the IMF demand compression strategy, the scope for 'voluntarily granted' pay rises could very well have been limited to an extent where increased agitation and disruptive militant action was the natural result.[50]

Noting that, "... for the first time in decades no trade union leader is prominent in government and politics", Buckley reports Danny Roberts, a deputy Island Supervisor of the National Workers Union, (NWU) the second largest union, as indicating that his union will be attempting to link productivity,

Table: 13 National Labour Productivity/Dispute Level

Year	Productivity Real output per per Employed Worker ($)	Industrial Disputes
1991	2411.10	-
1990	2436.90	103
1989	2413.30	308
1988	2302.20	372
1987	2341.90	370
1986	2312.70	391
1985	2348.90	83
1984	9471.90	62
1983	2616.10	86
1982	2596.00	129
1981	2568.10	625
1980	9618.20	557
1979	9847.50	608
1978	2853.80	678
1977	2909.30	679
1976	3009.30	514
1975	3224.90	551
1974	3347.60	443
1973	3568.10	371
1972	3628.70	395

Source: Keith R., calculations from STATIN data, measured by productions levels, The Financial Gleaner, Feb. 26, 1993, p.22.

profitability and pay through the means of payment-by-results systems, in a new relationship between management and workers, characterized by shared information and "democratic dialogue".[51] While Roberts noted the consequential requirement for more training and a, "... reorientation of worker delegates into business aspects of the work place", he left, unacknowledged, the existence of a similar need on the part of union officials, if any kind of performance-based bargaining is to stand a reasonable chance of being conducted in an efficient manner.

Another respect in which the union movement is at odds with the spokesmen for Government and its agencies is in the assessment of the degree of success attending the efforts to stimulate productivity improvements. In early 1993, Valerie Veira claimed that the Productivity Centre and Council, revived in July 1990, as an element of the National Five-Year Plan, 1990-95, was achieving some of its goals – raising the level of productivity consciousness and developing measurement s techniques .[52]

However, Hugh Shearer, just a matter of some six months earlier, since when nothing had changed significantly – had expressed disappointment that the strategy of increasing production by the use of payment systems based on performance was not working.[53]

As if to directly refute the claim that the Productivity Centre was achieving some of its goals, some eighteen months later the Minister of Labour, in seeking ILO assistance in addressing problems encountered at the Export Free zones, expressed the desire, "… to examine successful programmes (of productivity incentives) implemented by the ILO in other countries…".[54]

If, as Charles Ross maintains, productivity suffers because of strict adherence to job descriptions by trade unions,[55] then the blame ought to be placed on those drafting the job descriptions, for omitting a work/skill flexibility clause; and, secondly, on management for the failure to seek out innovative bargaining strategies to elicit acceptance of, and cooperation in, operating at efficient manning levels with the optimum use of human resources, generally. This may best be regarded as a matter of high principle.

In any event, the degree of unionization of the total labour force is limited to some 21.1% and of the employed labour force 24.9%, (FIG. 11).[56] Further, any growth in employment has been more than offset by the increase in the total labour force, together with retrenchment resulting from structural adjustment policies, under which increased labour-force-participation has taken the form of small scale self-employment or non-unionized informal sector activity.

But the blinkered, traditional private sector approach to labour problems is exposed when in the context of drastically reduced working class, and even the 'traditional' middle-class living standards – making many workers unable to bear the costs of educating their children – it is proposed that workers should remedy their own education and training inadequacy, "… even if this has to be done at their own

Figure: II

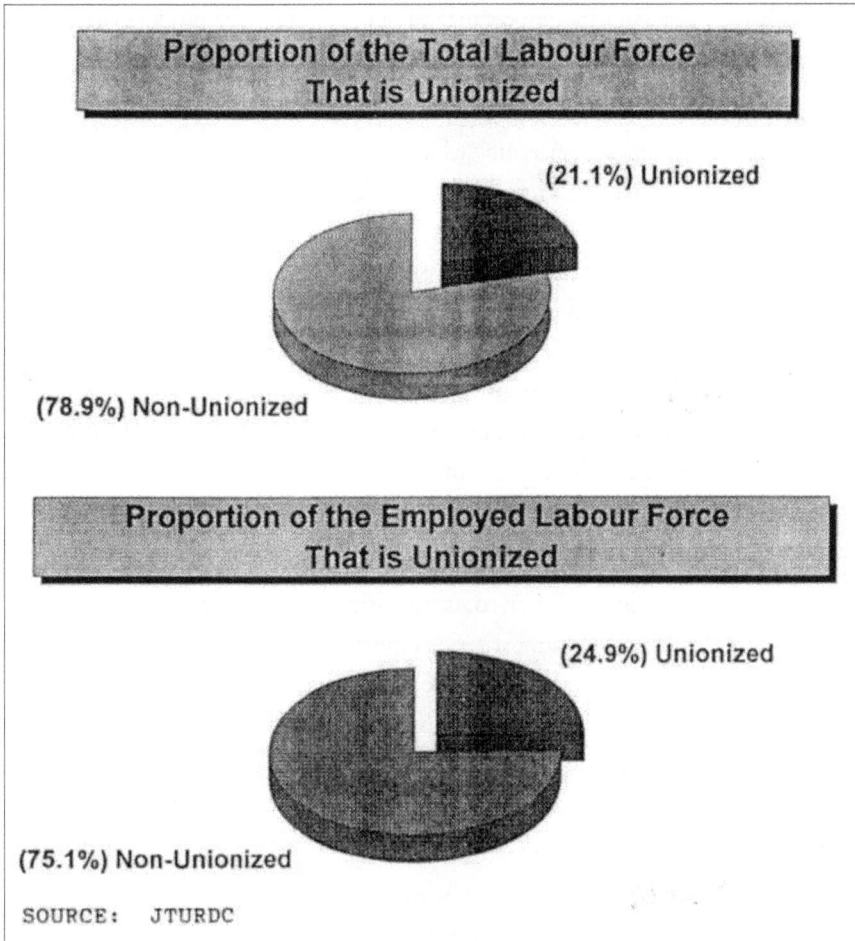

Proportion of the Total Labour Force That is Unionized

(21.1%) Unionized

(78.9%) Non-Unionized

Proportion of the Employed Labour Force That is Unionized

(24.9%) Unionized

(75.1%) Non-Unionized

SOURCE: JTURDC

cost". Having earlier complained of the difficulty of adjusting the work force to meet the requirements of efficient operations, Ross, then Executive Director of the PSOJ, later disclaims managements' responsibility for employee training, citing the reason that training is for life and therefore the worker will be able to take his skills, and enjoy the benefits derived therefrom, "elsewhere …".[57]

In challenging Ross' position, Danny Roberts cited positive real wage movements for South Korea, from a base of 100 in 1970 to 284 in 1984, noting further, that the rate of increase was higher for production workers than for professional, technical, or managerial employees. He observes that with respect to real wage increases and its occupational group distribution, "Quite the opposite has been the Jamaican experience".[58] Roberts concluded that a union or union officer who fails to understand the importance of improving labour productivity, "... is writing his own epitath".

The benefit of the historical perspective is demonstrated by Walsh's focus on the Industrial Revolution, concerning which he notes that, "... the wellspring of the modern world was, at its core, a revolution in productivity". Without being particularly technically oriented, this approach leads Walsh to a consideration of the factors responsible for the unprecedented increase in production and productivity which characterized that revolution. Briefly noted, are the tools, equipment/machinery, processes and social organization.[59] The awareness of the causal importance of improved technology, in its various aspects, that is so readily identified as critical to one's understanding of the revolutionary industrial changes by a student of 18th century British economic history, is lost on many businessmen and politicians. For the official focus, and that of most of the private sector, continues, misguidedly, to be exclusively on more intensive worker effort, if only by necessary implication.

Little attention is being given to such a critically relevant factor as investment in research and development – a most serios omission in the present global industrial, technological and trading environment.[60] But then, in the now established orthodoxy of Government recovery strategy, is it reasonable to expect more than symbolism in the form of the drafting of another policy position? After all, a central plank of multi-laterally approved economic stabilization has been substantial cuts in the funding for basic education under successive government budgets.

Not surprisingly, perhaps, what with the scope for connivance inherent in Government's proposal to grant tax concessions on earnings from productivity incentive schemes, the promise has been withdrawn, earning the displeasure of the President of the Jamaica Employers Federation, George Phillip. Because implemented too recently for proper development, in his view, Phillip felt compelled to, "... call on my colleagues in the private sector to raise their voices and call on the Government to give the programme a meaningful chance".[61]

Minister of Finance, Omar Davies, had in fact disclosed in his 1994/95 Budget presentation that Government intended to substitute a general tax concession, in the form of an increase in the income tax threshold figure, [which brought wage earners into the income tax net] instead of the earlier proposed benefits under the *Income Tax Act* to approved productivity schemes.[62]

In Phillip's opinion, the incentive effect of a rise in the basic rate of pay, "... is consumed within three months", an argument which, presumably, he regards as being of equal application to the moving of the income tax liability threshold. However, it is claimed that an incentive scheme "of the nature that existed" enables the worker to make a closer connection between reward and output,[63] and is therefore more effective in motivating improved performance.

What is of some significance in regard to this development is, firstly, that the decision to abandon the original proposal was taken and announced without any prior consultation with employer organisations, and presumably the labour movement, also; and, secondly, that this failure of prior communication occurred while Government was strongly urging consensus in the form of a social contact. This must be taken as further confirmation of the lack of consciousness at the highest policy- making level of the degree of bargaining and negotiating skill requirements involved in the process of winning tolerance of, if not passionate enthusiasm for, the elements of any meaningful model of a social contract.[64]

While Phillip was lamenting the discontinuation of the productivity incentive project, the Executive Director of his Federation was reported as saying, "To tell the truth, I don't know much about it", (productivity incentive schemes). He then, in elaboration, alleged that the qualifying conditions were never stipulated by Government. The result was that some companies which applied for approval of their schemes were told, for reasons that are not convincing to them, that they did not qualify. There was also, he claimed, disagreement over the restriction of the project's application by Government to the export sector only.[65]

As against the attitude of employers' organizations, some trade unions reportedly refused to sit on the Productivity Council because of dissatisfaction with certain aspects of the project; the civil service, on the other hand, was still trying, after two years of the project's existence, to prove that its contribution to economic development was measurable for productivity incentives purposes.[66]

Perhaps a good indication of a Government's ideas as to its economic priorities can be obtained from the nature of its first budget at the beginning of a new term in office. In the instant case, the Government's first Budget, after gaining power in the 1989 election, drew the following comment:

> "One would have thought that the new Government would have used
> their first Budget to try and motivate the populace to achieve record

high production targets during the present fiscal year. ... In contrast (sic) there is very little in there to stimulate the individual worker to higher levels of productivity, especially if he/she is employed in the public service".[67]

Reflecting the usual preoccupation with its IMF rating, the Government's major concerns seemed in 1989 — when the tone of its term of office, as it correctly turned out, was being set – to have been the maintenance of "fiscal prudence" and improvement in the balance of payments position. This was even at the risk of sacrificing any real prospects for economic growth. The higher taxes and interest rates imposed could scarcely have been expected to act as stimulants for increased productive investment, output, and productivity in an already overtaxed, capital-scarce economy.

The case for productivity incentives was put very simply by Stone, in 1989, when he argued that,

"Structural adjustment policies seek to make capital more productive by providing more incentives for investment. The emphasis on incentives for capital need to be balanced by emphasis on incentives to reward productive labour".[68]

Apparently, he has ruled out a revolutionary response by the working class to, "... the situation in which labour has become a sort of hostage to economic reforms rather than a participant in both its initiatives and its benefits". Instead, he arrives at the conclusion that cuts in their living standards, set against expanding profits and the lavish lifestyles of top level salary earners and the business and professional classes, will not elicit the kind of effort necessary to yield the productivity increases needed to bring about economic recovery or transformation.[69]

The oft-repeated emphasis on the need for increased productivity, probably wrongly couched in the typical exhortatory language of the need for the nation to 'produce or die', seems always to have the opposite effect to that desired. The period since the 1970's has been noteworthy for the consistent decline in labour productivity. The people have not produced, and yet have not died, at any extraordinary rate.

This feature partly explains the failure of various policies intended to stimulate economic recovery and places the island in a special, if unenviable position, of having experienced a decline in per capita output of some 34% between 1972 and 1991. Thompson's attempt to establish a causal link between per capita output and the number of industrial disputes annually is clearly discredited by the very statistics he reports in TABLE 13. Substantial fluctuation in the level of industrial disputes from year to year produce only marginal annual changes in per capita output and not always in the expected direction – a point long established from a comparison of strike propensity and growth and prosperity among selected countries including Australia, France, United States of America and Britain from the period of the 1960's to 70's.

The Stone survey of 1985,[70] carried out for the Seaga Government, showed that of a sample of 97 enterprises only 14 were regarded as having satisfactory work attitudes, a feeling of trust between workers and management, positive work norms, and adequate levels of work effort. It is reported their performance overall was only some 60% of worker capability.

Under the first Five-Year Development Plan, the promise was that, "Government will participate as much as necessary in the productive sector in order to ensure that necessary production is not neglected or abandoned by unresponsive private efforts".[71] However, the flurry of state enterprise activity under Democratic Socialism between 1974-1980 saw no fundamentally new major public investment projects. As is well known, during the decade of the 1980's, under 'policy continuity' after the 1989 election, there was, and has since been a reversal of the policy of state investment initiative to the point where former radical intellectuals now see the essential function of government as that of the 'honest broker' or, more popularly, 'the facilitator'.

In an economic and entrepreneurial culture where the private sector's appetite for incentives and concession appears insatiable, the "engine of growth" in neo-classical, if not New Right, economics has devoured the incentives, and produced stagflation rather than growth. That has been in combination with the effect of the free market policies of the international financial institutions, as shown in FIG. 12.

It is not as Basil Buck, of Buck Securities, has claimed that the Government is trying to do the impossible of, "... fine-tuning an engine with a broken piston,"[72] but more a case of trying to fine-tune an engine without connecting rods and a drive shaft.

The fundamental weakness with virtually all the suggestions for incomes policies has been the very notable absence of the *quid pro quo* element. The promise of reduced inflation is hardly worth considering in return for the actual loss of purchasing power and increased unemployment consequent upon reduced sales and output, particularly when, even if there is a reduction in the rate of inflation, that rate will still – from experience over the IMF years – be in excess of any movement in wages. The point being made is that a persistent situation of declining purchasing power of wages is not conducive to motivating increased labour productivity.

And those who are at, or near, the poverty line cannot reasonably be expected to show patience in 'catching up', especially given the vast income maldistribution. In the absence of conditions actually generating productivity-related pay increases, one can expect pressure to be intensified to move basic rates, whether calculated on a time or piece rate basis, substantially upwards.

It seems obvious that the implied simplicity of an incomes policy, as put forward by its several proponents, is indicative of the lack of any attempt to arrive at a well thought out framework with quantification of its various elements attached. It is this fact, it is here asserted, which has precluded the negotiated reconciliation of conflicts of policy objectives, necessary for vested-interest group acceptance.

Without this reconciliation and the offer of benefits/rewards to labour to substantially offsets the costs of the sacrifices - virtually demanded as proof of *patriotism* – the negative, sceptical, and cynical trade union response which has greeted the social contract proposal is not likely to change, whatever its productivity incentive payment elements may be,

Figure: 12

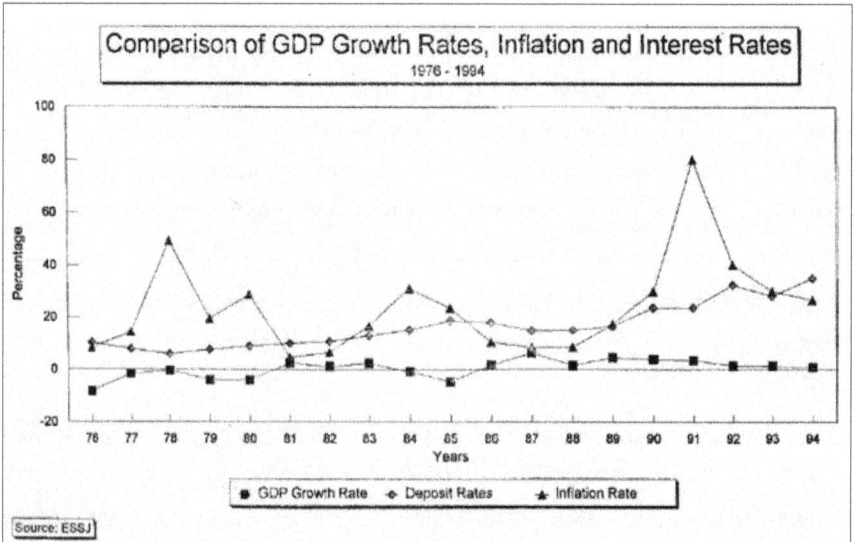

Comparison of GDP Growth Rates, Inflation and Interest Rates
1976 - 1994

A sense of unease always seemed to exist on the part of policy makers, about the enthusiasm of the private sector and trade unions to move positively towards the formulation and implementation of agreed incentive schemes, despite Government's encouragement of the use of such schemes as an 'escape route' from the rigidity of the wage guidelines. This led to the commissioning of a survey of private sector opinion towards incentives schemes and to assess any tangible progress made in the development of schemes which satisfied the provisions of the IMF agreement.[73]

Although forms of Payment by Results (PBR) had for a long time been practised in Jamaica on a limited scale, the heavy-handed imposition of the controversial wage guidelines provided the impetus to seek varieties of incentive systems which were applicable to the various sectors and labour force categories which felt the impact of the guidelines. The aim was to avoid the pay rise limits imposed, without fuelling inflation and destroying the island's capacity to be competitive in international markets and in a manner consistent with the preservation of enterprise profit levels.

It was found, quite surprisingly, that about 24% of the 136 medium to large companies surveyed had attempted to introduce some form of incentive scheme, as a reaction to the guidelines.

The three types of problems highlighted, as reasons for lack of greater initiative in implementing schemes were identified as:

(1) **The adverse economic environment:**
many companies were going through rough times and were therefore reluctant to innovate (high interest rates, reduced sales, increased overhead costs, uncertain overseas markets increased competition from imports etc). 42%

(2) **Technical problems:**
measuring productivity was difficult in many enterprises. 54%
no access to expertise or information on how to implement schemes 28%

(3) **Attitudinal problems:**
employer opposed to sharing profits. 11%
distrust between workers and management. 25%
scepticism as to whether incentive payments will work or show results in Jamaica 14%

Source: Carl Stone, in The Sunday Gleaner, July 8, 1990.

Stone offers the quite questionable assessment that only problems in the technical category are amenable to the effects of policy innovation. On the contrary, it is possible that focus on the benefits derived by management, tangible and intangible, in a strong sustained publicity campaign highlighting 'success stories' could well evoke significant changes of attitudes, after which the 'demonstration effect' could conceivably come into play.

It is ironic that the adverse economic environment should be regarded as being intractable to the extent that no significant change is thought possible in the short run: the very policy initiative being surveyed was meant to achieve precisely that general objective at the level of the national economy.

The views and opinions of the 24% of firms that had attempted implementation of schemes, as to the problems faced and the quality of results achieved are set out below:

I. PROBLEMS
   Main Problems encountered in establishing incentive payment schemes / % mentioning problems

   - Workers suspicious of changes   31%

   - Workers feel that rewards not big enough to justify
     extra work effort   30%

   - Problems of measuring worker/employee productivity   24%

   - Workers unhappy whenever income fluctuates downwards
     in periods when productivity falls   18%

   - Shortages of raw materials and declining sales often limit
     the opportunity that exists to increase worker output   22%

2. RESULTS
   Opinions on results achieved from setting up payment by incentive schemes % expressing these opinions among managers of companies which have implemented payment by incentive policies

   No results as yet, too early to tell   56%

   Seen evidence of increased worker output, cooperation,
   and more positive attitudes to work   44%

Additionally, the survey disclosed the following information:

No. of problems experienced	Percentage of enterprises
I	64%
0	36%
3	"many"

Source: Stone, Ibid. (The Sunday Gleaner, July 8, 1990).

Information was also sought on the attitudinal response of, and the role played by, trade unions. It was found that 70% of managers involved with the productivity schemes, from the 80% of the enterprises which were unionised, replied to the effect that they received full union support, cooperation, and beneficial ideas and suggestions. Cooperation was not forthcoming from unions in only 10% of the over 100 unionized firms participating. The lesson is clear: unions can and will cooperate, if they are convinced that change, however fundamental, is in the direct interest of their members. Given skepticism over the promises of benefits in some unspecified 'future' – based on experiences of eighteen years of belt-tightening under IMF austerity – few, excepting those politically responsible for policy adoption, would regard such a stance as unreasonable. As Roberts puts it,

> "The trade unions have a vested interest in improving the efficiency of the workforce and increasing productivity and profitability.[74]

It was thought useful to investigate, where possible, and report the findings on the experiences of those enterprises which attempted the implementation of Productivity schemes, from a more operational approach than that of the Stone study. The Interview Schedule is contained in APPENDIX i.

Unfortunately, of the 33 firms which submitted schemes to Jampro's Productivity Unit, with a view to gaining Certification so as to be approved by the Ministry of Finance as being eligible for the tax concession, only 10 were forwarded to the Ministry, after analysis. Of that 10, five were large foreign-owned capital-intensive type operations, with four being bauxite/alumina companies. These are, needless to say, not typical organisations in the Jamaican context, especially given the scarcity and very high cost of capital.

Comparison between the experiences of entities in different sectors would have been interesting and instructive. A special attempt was therefore made to access information from the agricultural sector, as there were four such entities among the 10 schemes approved. The Sugar Producers' Federations case was found, on investigation, to have in fact been a production as against a productivity incentive scheme. However, the necessary co-operation and availability of detailed information was not such as to allow meaningful investigation of the other agricultural entities (all banana growing operations).

The rather limited information which was accessible and obtained by telephone contact and interviews with companies industrial relations and trade union personnel is presented below.

EXAMPLES OF PRODUCTIVITY INCENTIVE SCHEMES

Case I: Goodyear Jamaica Limited

Goodyear established a productivity incentive scheme in 1993. This scheme was primarily introduced in response to the company's need to increase production levels. Initially, a goal of producing 1,800 tyres a day was used to mobilize the work force. This was packaged and presented to the workers in the form of a "Project 1,800".

The idea of setting up this productivity scheme came initially from the top managers of the company and the leaders of the union representing the workers coming together to address the issue of the survival of the company in the newly liberalized Jamaican economy. The liberalization of tyre imports meant that Goodyear, which once monopolized the Jamaican tyre market, was facing stiff competition from imported tyres. In response to this challenge, the top managers and the union leaders, through a process of consultation, developed and introduced the incentive scheme. All the workers in the production bargaining unit, which the UAWU represented, were included in the productivity scheme, as well as their supervisors. In all, over 95% of the work force at Goodyear was covered in the scheme. Apart from the overall target of 1,800 tyres per day, a number of performance standards in pursuit of this target were established, and workers were rewarded for achieving these standards.

Reduced wastage was also a factor in the determination of productivity levels. Increased productivity under the scheme was rewarded by way of a quarterly pay-out, which was included in the workers' salary. Because the company is basically numbers-driven, the production statistics needed to measure productivity were already being generated on a regular basis.

A joint management and worker production committee had the responsibility of monitoring the scheme. In the event that obstacles occurred during production that hindered the achievement of the targets, off-time shift meetings were held among the workers and supervisors to address and correct the problems.

As a result of the scheme, productivity and efficiency increased and the scheme had a positive impact on the morale of the workers. After the initial target of 1,800 tyres per pay was met the target was revised upward.

After successfully operating this productivity scheme to the benefit of the company and the workers for two years the scheme came to an abrupt halt in 1995. This happened as a result of the transfer of the manager who had established the scheme to another Goodyear plant in the region, outside of Jamaica. The new manager who replaced him in an attempt to "prove himself", began tinkering with the scheme (as well as other benefits and terms of employment of the production workers). This led to a break-down in the fairly good relationship that had existed up to then between the managers and the union. Numerous conflicts developed between the two parties that, after a particularly serious dispute over wages and working conditions, led to a prolonged strike at the company. The company decided to cut. back on production of tyres and import them instead from other Goodyear plants in the region. As a result, car tyres are no longer produced in Jamaica and the local plant manufactures only truck tyres.

One of the lessons learnt from Goodyear's experience with its productivity scheme is that for the scheme to work progressive management is essential. The other major lesson is that it is important to involve the worker/his representative organisation in the decision-making process when establishing and modifying productivity schemes.

Case 2: Alcan Jamaica Company Limited

Alcan introduced its productivity scheme in 1991, largely in response to the government's decision to grant tax concessions to wage increases that were the result of increased productivity. Prior to its introduction, Alcan had an incentive programme which had been in place since the mid 1970's. This early scheme was one where workers were invited to make suggestions to improve efficency or reduce costs and were given awards for accepted suggestions. The company also had a biannual awards programme under which workers were rewarded on the basis of performance appraisals.

The idea to establish a productivity incentive scheme from the management at Alcan. Through a process of consultation between the top and middle managers and the union leaders, officers and delegates (production workers at Alcan are represented by NWI)) the scheme was developed. Although the scheme was said to be non-negotiable, managers were nevertheless willing to discuss the union's concerns.

All categories of the workers at Alcan were included in the scheme; over 90% of the workforce, which included production workers, supervisors and administrative (clerical) workers, participated in it. Only the top managers were excluded, as they already had a special management incentive scheme.

The performance standard was primarily based on a production target set by the company. This also included a measure for efficiency, which factored in things such as oil and caustic soda usage, the impact of production operations on the environment, and health and safety accident aspects. Targets in these areas were set on a quarterly and annual basis. As a result, poor performance in one quarter could be compensated for by improved performance in the following quarter.

No special mechanisms were put in place to monitor the scheme, since the company already produced statistics on the performance criteria.

Increased productivity was rewarded by way of a direct cash benefit given to each worker in the scheme. The size of the benefit was weighted according to the level of the salary of the individual worker. The last payment as a result of the scheme was made in 1993, since when the productivity levels have not warranted any benefits being given.

In 1993, as a result of government's policy change, productivity incentive schemes lost their tax-free status which contributed to a lower level of interest in the scheme. It is estimated that in 1993 of a wage bill of approximately US $30 million, the benefit from the productivity scheme was only US $1 million. As a result, the typical worker would get only 3% more on his/her salary as a consequence of improved productivity. Because the payments were perceived to be relatively small, compared to regular salary, the productivity scheme had little or no future impact on the morale of the workers.

Over the period of its existence, some minor changes were made to the way the scheme operated. Instead of developing special production targets, the standard company production targets were used, and time lost due to industrial action was included as one of the performance criteria.

The major lessons to be learned from the productivity incentive scheme at Alcan are that the schemes should be specific and more direct. Too many criteria were used, and many of them were beyond the control of individual workers. Also, for schemes to be effective, the incentive payment must be large enough to make a real difference to the workers' take-home pay. A 3% increase in pay is negligible, especially given the inflation trend, as reflected by the CPI; at least a 15% increase would have had to be obtained for it to have had an impact in the union's view.

Case 3: Kaiser Jamaica Bauxite Company Limited

The productivity incentive scheme at. Kaiser was introduced in 1995. The idea of introducing a productivity scheme had been discussed by the management and the union (UAWU) before its implementation. In 1995, however, during wage negotiations the company stated that it could not meet the wage claim made by the union and, as a result, negotiations became deadlocked. At this stage, the idea of a productivity scheme again surfaced, and it was presented as an alternative to a straight wage increase.

As a result of consultation between top management and the union leaders the scheme was developed; at the later stages of the consultations, lower level union officers, delegates and workers were involved. During the consultations there was a general atmosphere of distrust between the workers and the managers (this distrust was by no means restricted to the discussions surrounding these specific issues) and as a result a number of conflicts arose. These conflicts stemmed from the workers' reservations about getting into the scheme, since they thought that any benefits to be enjoyed by them would be sabotaged by the managers. Workers also had doubts about the ability of the trucks, used to transport the bauxite ore, to cope with the increased pressure and usage they would come under. These conflicts and doubts were resolved, however, and the scheme started in October 1995.

This scheme applied solely to the production bargaining unit, which made up 70% of the total work force. Supervisors were not included. The performance standard centered around a target number of tons of bauxite that should be mined per day. In practice, on an informal basis, workers were able to measure this by the number of trips made by the trucks each day.

Based on the changes in productivity, the hourly wage of the workers would be adjusted on a half-yearly basis.

A special Productivity Council was set up to monitor the scheme, which had the final say on the scheme's operation, and consisted of six union and three management representatives. The vice-president of the union and the general manager of Kaiser were ex-officio members.

After the scheme started near the end of 1995, it operated for three months and paid a benefit, before beginning its standard six-month measurement cycle. During the first three months productivity increased significantly and the minimum hourly rate moved from $161 to $206. This placed the Kaiser workers among the highest paid in the bauxite industry. In the next measurement period (of six months on this occasion) productivity fell and the hourly wage rate decreased from $206 to $200. The initial increase followed by a decrease had a negative impact on the morale of the workers. This was heightened by the fact that the workers felt that factors outside of their control, such as rain, were the main causes of the lower productivity. The workers also felt that the supervisors were sabotaging the scheme by not fulfilling some of their responsibilities (the feeling was that this was the case primarily because the supervisors got no benefit from the scheme).

As a result, the Productivity Council assumed many of the responsibilities that the supervisors were not fulfilling – but this led to conflicts between the Council and the workers.

Since the scheme was introduced, minor changes have been made to it, the main one being an adjustment for the distance that the trucks had to travel.

Based on the experience with the scheme, the workers are not favourably disposed to the idea of productivity incentive schemes in general and would rather not have another one. This dissatisfaction is also adversely affecting the workers' relations with their union and, as a consequence, they are currently approaching another union with a view to changing their representation.

Apart from the importance of consideration being given to the effect of factors affecting productivity which are beyond the control of workers, another insight provided by this experience is clearly the need for lower level supervisor commitment. Further, more emphasis needs to be placed on the 'work smarter' as against 'work harder' approach, if a more lasting positive worker response is to be expected (perhaps particularly for workers who are deemed to constitute the Jamaican 'labour aristocracy').

There does exist the cynical view, perhaps, that the problem of low productivity is "embedded in our culture, history and social structure... ."[75] to the extent that anti-productivity sentiments are too deeply entrenched in the national psyche to be susceptible to meaningful change in the forseeable future.

Unlike their Jamaican counterparts, South Korean policy-makers showed that, as Kaown Ishikawa, the noted quality management specialist, declared, "... the only culture that matters is the one management creates within the enterprise".[76]

Whereas the tendency on the part of the political directorate has traditionally been the use of exhortation as the means of inducing improved productiveagain efficiency, to workers suffering from IMF stabilization fatigue, the appeal is increasingly likely to be interpreted as further attempts at greater exploitation. The historical levels of suspicion, distrust, and antagonism is such that it should be obvious that positive trade union endorsement and cooperation is a vital element in the successful implementation of any productivity-based payment system.

If workers are not to equate the productivity drive with the historical slave-driver's attempt to get the worker to work harder and more intensively for no appreciably greater reward, then it becomes even more important for emphasis to be placed, at the very outset of a scheme's design, firstly, on technological and organisational aspects of efficiency enhancement, and secondly, the equitable sharing of the benefits between shareholders,[77] workers and consumers.

In contrast to most commentators, Ashwell Thomas, saw the wage guidelines as presenting, "... a wonderful opportunity to develop a comprehensive and meaningful productivity incentive programme".[78] What he found however, was that some companies were using the schemes simply as a means of circumventing the guidelines by granting higher wage increases than permitted, without any corresponding productivity improvements, so that the relationship between wages and productivity continued to be blurred in the eyes of the worker.

An additional barrier to scheme implementation, is the fact that payment by results systems have historically emerged in an economic climate characterized by buoyant demand, and low-level unemployment, hence the need for increased output and a more effective deployment of a scarce, resource, labour. The conditionalities in effect in the country for very nearly the entire IMF period have had the very opposite objectives and consequences[79] to those facilitative of the introduction of performance-based methods of wage payment. It would be interesting to see how many of the incentive schemes, inspired by IMF wage guidelines, exhibited the national penchant for 'beating the system'; put differently, to what extent was increased labour costs absorbed by increased efficiency?[80] The Ministry of Labour's productive council should, functioning properly, be constantly providing such answers.

Apart from anomalies, due to imperfection of techniques of work measurement; learning curve effects; and the perverse erosion of skill differentials, whereby unskilled or semi-skilled workers on a PBR scheme earn more than skilled workers, not to mention supervisors, there is the problem of 'justice' and 'fairness' in resolving the pay problems of 'indirect' productive are workers who are not usually paid by measured results, but on a time basis, who are engaged in the provision of auxiliary services feeding those directly engaged in production. 'Lieu bonuses' of various types, implicitly or explicitly keyed to production-line earnings, can go some way towards meeting the problem of income relativities, thus enabling the enterprise to end up with a more rational wage structure.[81]

The psychological aspects of pay and productivity on the part of the average worker are reflected in Clive Dobson's observation that, during years of acquaintance with the shop floor it was his experience that a lot of the lethargy and low productivity which is blamed on bad work ethic among the rank and file, is nothing more than the manifestation of, "... low levels of industry, low levels of competence, and low levels of innovation at the managerial level".[82] What is at issue here is simply the matter of leadership by example.

C.Y. Thomas makes the almost self-evident point that if productivity is seen by employees as a means of satisfying their needs, high productivity is likely to result.[83] Despite the passage of time, however, Maslow's hierarchy of needs seems relevant in determining the potentially motivating factor in the work environment most likely to yield the desired worker attitude to productivity and efficiency, generally. Somewhat surprisingly – in the face of the low level of industrialization achieved, the fall in real incomes among the lower socioeconomic strata, and the vast income disparity between the lower and upper classes – the 1982 Stone survey found that in ranking working-class dissatisfaction with their work environment, low wages was placed behind opportunities for promotion, which was ranked first, and of educational and skill-upgrading opportunities. These factors seen by workers as most important in their enterprises as good or bad places for which to work and for getting ahead in life.[84] Wages, contrary to traditional managerial philosophy and conventional wisdom about low level working class motivation, in the context of persistent real wage erosion in a third world country, was placed only third in importance by the sample.

Also, it is necessary to consider environmental influences on productivity. However conducive the internal organizational culture to maximizing its members focus on increasing efficiency, if there are strong negative forces operating in the wider external social, political, and economic environment, then positive internal factors may well be neutralized. Concern with the relationship between pay and performance has therefore to take into account, for example, the state of public transportation, the level and nature of crime and violence,[85] and the quality of social services.

It may be easier to adopt the position from the productivity enhancement perspective that the only culture that matters is the one created internally by the enterprise's management, when one is dealing with a homogeneous population, devoid of deep-seated antagonistic class divisions, and where relevant infrastructural requirements for operational efficiency are securely in place, quantitatively and qualitatively.

One can clearly place greater acceptable, or at least more tolerable, restraint on nominal wages in an inflation-prone economy, the more adequate the social wage provisions.[86] But this has not been the case in Jamaica. The working class has been battered from two sides: substantial reduction in its income capacity to consume and the considerable decline in government's social services expenditure as reflected in the imposition of so-called 'cost-sharing', user fees, and the removal and withdrawal of most subsidies and certain services previously provided by the state.

Barbados' strategy in designing a programme around IMF support is interesting in the extent to which certain of its elements vary from the Jamaican experience. The measures introduced as the price for obtaining IMF foreign exchange assistance included: an 8% statutory reduction of public sector salaries and wages; an increase in social security contributions; a reduction in unemployment and redundancy benefits; lay-offs in parts of the civil service; and price increases on a number of consumer items.[87]

Similarities in the approaches are also noticeable: such as the disproportionate share of the stabilization/adjustment burden that public service workers are expected to shoulder. Again, this is without any serious attempt to provide an avenue of amelioration through the adoption of innovative approaches to achieve pay-linked productivity increases.[88]

To be noted also, is the ideologically contradictory use of the law, within the context of a free market economy, to regulate wages. Two recent sets of wage negotiations, those of the firemen and later the teachers, have been examined in the chapter, "The National Interest." At this point, it will suffice to note the use of institutional arrangements, in these instances the Industrial Disputes Tribunal, and the legislation under which it was established, as an instrument of suppression of working class interests.[89] As against the position with wage claims which may involve militant industrial action, there is no similar provision for any Ministerial reference of price increases for adjudication before any tribunal.

Despite the intentions behind The Administrative Reform Programme, and its desired effects on the quality of the civil service, the treatment of the issue of pay in the public sector reflects very clearly the nature of the island's production culture. In Hussey's words, it, "... has never placed emphasis on efficiency and productivity".[90]

It is perhaps as a direct result of this type of 'production culture' that it was found by Hussey that, "... neither they (the trade unions) nor management were ever clear as to the mechanisms and import of such (productivity incentive) schemes." If this was the experience in the private sector, where generally speaking the scope for, and relative ease of implementation of more precisely quantifiable performance-related reward systems is much greater, it becomes understandable that little effort has been expended on increasing the directness of the link between productivity and pay in the public service.

The unfounded, naive, and misleading assumption has been given national publicity, to the effect that in some mysterious way a leaner civil service as a result of substantial repeated shedding of staff will result in a more efficient service. It is not as if massive pay increases were being given to the reduced number of the workforce with a view to motivating heightened performance levels of a degree to more than compensate for the loss of the effort of those made redundant. On the contrary, public service wage negotiations have, particularly in recent times, been characterized by acrimony, crises, worker disillusionment, and indeed, deep despair.

Being numbered among those who support the idea of performance-related payment systems, the major justification given by Hussey for their continuation is that, "... they remind us that we need to earn our wages", as, he continues, "Too many people are paid for work not done".[91]

As against the need for such a reminder, in the view of Clive Dobson, President of the NWU, "no serious sustained effort …" had been made to increase the level of labour productivity. Implying that work done on overtime could contribute to productivity, as against production, he charged that making overtime earnings subject to tax had led to the abandonment of the productivity incentive programme, having, "… wiped away any possible incentive".[92] One of the primary objectives of comprehensive productivity bargains, has in fact, been the reduction, if not the complete cessation of overtime work.

When in January 1994, the Minister of Finance announced a projected monthly inflation rate of 1% for the fiscal year 1993/94, there were few, who were knowledgeable, who thought this was achievable. In the very week that the announcement was made, the price of gasoline jumped significantly, which could be expected to have the usual ripple or "flow through" effect throughout the economy. Following soon after, was the flour (and naturally bread) price increase, behind which one could expect, as did Ricketts, a substantial rise in the price of sugar, in keeping with the post-divestment price paradigm.[93]

Not even in this unwelcomed scenario for consumers, was it found possible to allay the fears of a substantial section of the working class as to imminent further pressures on their ability to keep pace with the cost of living. Instead, the workers in the public sector were issued the warning that any "excessive" upward wage movements, could only be met, against the background of IMF agreed budgetary provisions, from increased taxes,[94] in an economy agreed to be already at its taxable limit, a further cut in staff, or an even greater decline in social service budgetary allocation.

As it turned out, the inflation rate for 1994 was 26.9%, and the implicit target 12%, as against the Minister's forecast of 10.5%, revised from the original target rate of 6.5%. Money supply and interest rates, both still held to be within the ambit of Government influence, seemed from all assessments, to have been primarily responsible for the significant divergence,[95] as appears from FIG. 13.

So far, the prodding done by governments has been largely by way of rhetorical exhortation. Although the country, according to the received wisdom, has no real choice at this stage but to "produce its way out of its difficulties", according to Perkins, the declaration that "Production is the key" by the Prime Minister has been repeated too often, without effect, to be worthy of serious notice. What the appeal really means, in his view, is that "the industrious minority must, as a patriotic duty, redouble its efforts at production so as to provide the resources with which the Government can then fulfil its plantocratic obligations."[96]

Figure: 13

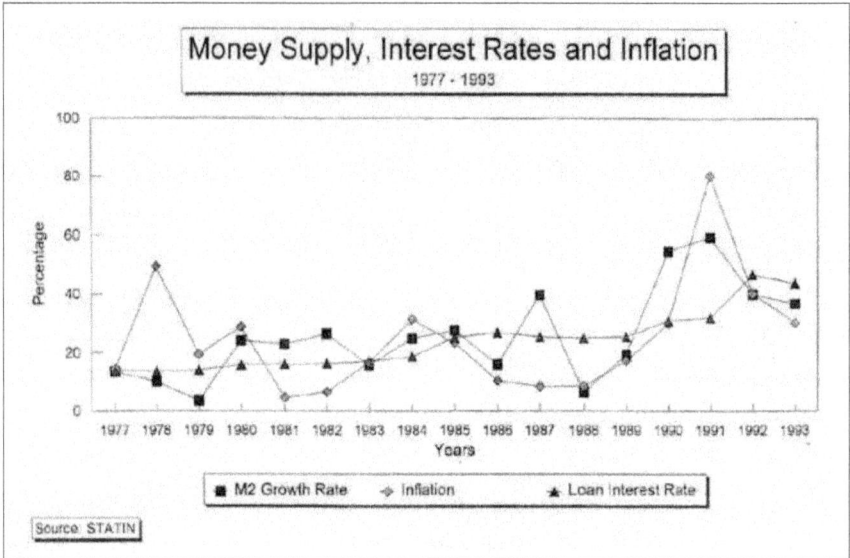

Money Supply, Interest Rates and Inflation
1977 - 1993

Source: STATIN

Observing that consumption rights involve, automatically, commensurate obligations to produce, the problem of motivating increased productivity is seen, in post-plantation terms, as the lack of effective means of "compelling" work, with the abandonment of physical coercion in 1838 – the year of the abolition of slavery in Jamaica, And, by having adopted the Westminster parliamentary political system, indolence cannot, he elaborating argues, be abandoned to its own consequences of increasing poverty, malnutrition, illiteracy, ignorance and disease.[97]

Dobson, in on his initial response to the enquiry by Government into the causes of inflation, deemed the motive behind government's low projected inflation rate to be the attempt "to justify the low wage increase that the government has used to calculate the 1994/95 Budget".[98]

"Past experience", Dobson continued, implying that projected inflation levels have been deliberately manipulated, "has taught us to take the government's inflation projections with a grain of salt". He warned that the unions would not be fooled by this tactic and, further, that perhaps the government itself was not too serious about, nor interested in, making accurate inflation projections, since they were apparently directed at fulfilling the expectations of the international lending institutions, and the IMF in particular.[99] It is remarkable that with all the talk about developing a 'productivity culture', what we find is the preoccupation with the time-honoured link between the cost of living and wages.

Whatever else "the magic of the market" under the sponsorship of the Fund and Bank has achieved, it has certainly not improved productivity levels. This, "… naive and in some cases superstitious belief in the free market economic ideology as a panacea" might, in Wilson's view, prove to be the greatest obstacle to productivity. All the NICs of South East Asia, and, for comparative purposes, Singapore, in particular, and Japan earlier, experienced strong, systematic, strategic direct state intervention in their economies, not only in the form of the design of industrial policies and the sponsorship of large public productive investments, but also in the development of specific programmes for increasing productivity and greater workforce discipline – sometimes by the use of methods, it must be conceded, that were less than democratic, to the Western eye.[100] They might also have been less than appealing to the descendants of ex-slaves under colonial regimes.

The blinkered approach to the issue of productivity, that is to say the focus on greater *effort*, which is the norm in Jamaica, is to be contrasted with the stance taken by Jain who, perhaps due to his accounting bias, proposes that apart from the labour component, other areas of cost worthy of use as efficiency indices are energy utilization, floor space, volume of raw materials, and so on. The possible advantages of this approach should be readily apparent: firstly, other costs of production might well be more critical in terms of cost, availability, and the degree to which they are amenable to management control, than the labour input; secondly, focus on other such factors might provide more useful data for purposes of inter-firm comparison; and thirdly, and consequentially, cost-consciousness is more likely to extend over a wider spectrum of costs, thus keeping in constant view the need for seeking out ways of achieving savings on a multifactor basis.[101]

Needless to say, savings so derived might form an element of an incentive scheme and be distributed between the parties accordingly.

Achieving savings by the more efficient utilization of all inputs in the production process becomes important given the disappointing record of generating additional investments from the greater profits accruing from IMF retrogressive income distribution. The Governor of the Central Bank ought, therefore to have been armed with suggestions of issue-specific initiatives to mobilize investment in research and development, having raised the question of firms needing to be more efficient and productive. Neither was much assistance offered as to how the. need to find ways of raising the level of internal savings might best be satisfied or even approached.[102]

What is beyond dispute is that given the unrelenting inflationary pressure on wages and salaries, household savings will be nowhere near large enough to satisfy productive investment requirements, simply because the majority of the population is living at the subsistence level with some 40% at the very least being below the poverty line,[103] between 1989 and 1993, the rural towns being in the worst position, as revealed by FIG. 14.

Instead of the suppression of demand, as is typical of IMF policy prescription, in the interest of productivity, employment creation and global competitiveness, it needs to be recognized that demand, as Harrison emphasizes, has always been the strongest stimulus to technological innovation. The urge should, bearing this in mind, be to implement strategies creating buoyant demand for local manufactures by increasing, in the least possible inflationary manner, the incomes of the working classes and small and peasant farmers. Nondiscriminating IMF/World Bank import liberalization leaves little scope, however, for this policy choice in the short run, at least.[104] The effect is clearly to improve the potential for increased production and productivity in industrialised countries from which most of these imports originate.

The 1990-95 National Development Plan quite boldly stated that, "The Government, with the help of the trade union movement and the private sector will develop appropriate ways of linking wage movements with changes in productivity".[105] Whereas the Council was established, "... to support and improve production in industry",[106] after five years the search is presumably still on to find acceptable methods of wage payment based on performance. It is, at the very least, fair to say that the results of the Council's investigations into the variety of schemes and systems available for selection have been with-held, it would seem, quite unwisely, from the general public, from which not only the labour force but management are drawn.

Figure: 14

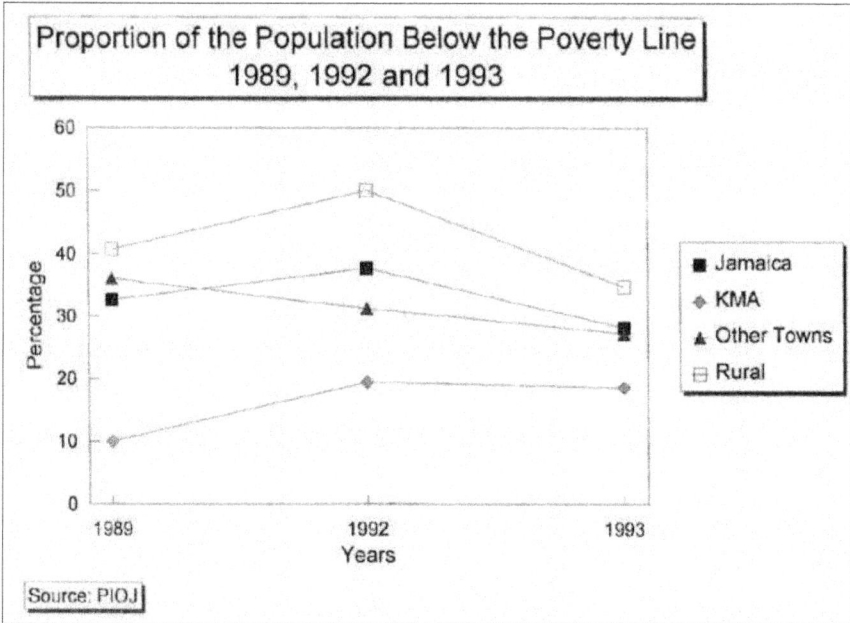

Proportion of the Population Below the Poverty Line
1989, 1992 and 1993

Source: PIOJ

Considerations which caused a negative response from trade unions and workers, particularly in the labour-intensive sugar industry to attempts at mechanization are not less relevant in the present context. The drive for greater efficiency, especially through increased labour productivity resulting from technological upgrading, in an increasingly competitive globalized market place, and in a national economic environment lacking new substantial investments, will clearly come into collision with employment-creation policy expectations.[107]

Apart from the effect on the wage earner's pay packet of user fees and charges, "cost sharing" in the health and education sectors and the removal of subsidies on food items of mass consumption, one must consider, also, the consequences of these budgetary initiatives for productivity, viewed broadly. It needs little emphasis that the standard of the health of the labour force directly effects its productive capacity. Of equal, if less obvious, importance is the attempt to get- answers to questions such as: how is the volume of expenditure on education correlated with national output? and what part of the country's economic growth can reasonably be attributed to its educational and/or research efforts?[108]

Despite the current preoccupation with the formulation of an industrial policy and the "illusions of (planned) progress" in education set out in documents like

Five Year Development Plans, serious economic and social planners ought, perhaps, to heed Gill's words to the effect that an illiterate society is unlikely – however much the rhetoric about meeting global competition – to be in the forefront of technological creativity. Such a society may not even know how to use new cutting-edge techniques, even if they exist for the taking.[109]

Without the emergence of an intellectually and scientifically curious sector of the population which leads the search for and builds confidence in the expectation of finding improved methods of production, to the extent that these attitudes become embedded in the fundamental psyche of the society, the scope for the design and implementation of incentives scheme is destined to remain limited. Cuts in the share of the national budget allocated to education and training, before factoring in the effect of inflation, seem decidedly ill-advised from a medium and long-term productivity perspective.

In a period of high inflation, profits, as the Nobel Laureate, the late West Indian, Arthur Lewis, puts it, "... are so easy [to be made] that employers become careless of costs" – the consequences, equally importantly, being that the stimulus to find avenues to increased productivity is reduced, if not removed.[110]

With all the recent emphasis on technology, research and development and 'working smart', it is interesting to note that Lewis, as long as a quarter of a century ago, noted that, "Efficiency depends in the first place upon research and upon its application," and, further, that, "... the real issue is not to get people to work more or harder, but to get their agreement to working more effectively."[111]

Lewis goes further than Roberts of the NWU in pointing out that trade unions have a particularly vital role to play in this area of their members' work experience as, instead of being passive spectators, or reluctantly reactive, they can become, "... authorities on managerial techniques", production systems, aspects of industrial engineering and organizational structure and management, in general. Thus, they can bring, "... pressure to bear on inefficient firms that are wasting men's labour".[112]

To those who bemoan the prevalence of a poor work ethic, the suggestion may be made that they should consider the merit of the statement that high labour turnover and absenteeism, major obstacles to productivity enhancement, "... is endemic wherever modern economic enterprise ... has at least not offered sufficient inducement to capture the working man's loyalty".[113]

When productivity is very low, as Furtado notes, the basic consumption requirements accounts for a large proportion of the goods and services produced, whereas increasing productivity provides for real income increases and demand diversification, which are likely to result in the generation of new investment opportunities.[114]

Given the verbalized concern in Jamaica with increasing national productivity, it would with little doubt be regarded as nothing short of heresy for one to note, as Bottomore has done, and as many did before him, that, the more socially sensitive, "… have become increasingly aware that technological progress [the surest way of generating increasing productivity] is not an unmixed blessing. "Compulsive innovation" and "growth addiction" consequences guarantee that doubts do, and should always exist, about the essential nature of 'progress', or economic development. It will almost certainly be decades before questions such as, "… what kinds of new technology and economic growth are likely to add most to the sum of human happiness and to the quality of life" register themselves on the consciousness of our policy makers, public and private.[115]

One of the previously noted problems of Productivity Bargaining and incentive schemes which becomes a central factor within the context of wage guidelines – as discovered in the United Kingdom[116] – is precisely that the sometimes quite substantial wage increases resulting from such bargaining or schemes provoke heightened dissatisfaction from the disturbance of established differentials among other workers who do not enjoy the benefits of those kinds of wage arrangements. A high level of innovation in the design of different types of payment systems for different categories of workers is clearly an essential management requirement for broad acceptance of changes particularly in larger, more complex, task-diversified production sites.

This is particularly so, where, "… work groups utilize orbits of coercive comparison", in the sense that they operate under the influence of their own unofficial version of wage guidelines, based on some notion of equity and justice.[117] This might, in many situations, be, "… the most potent force in wage negotiation".[118]

Downes has argued, by implication, that the Productivity Council ought not to have concerned itself exclusively with the private sector. This was because reduced staff and low productivity in the public sector can interfere with the performance of certain essential bureaucratic tasks necessary for efficient private enterprise operations.[119]

The functions of the Productivity Council, properly conceived, ought, it is here suggested, to have explicitly included the monitoring of technological developments and their applications among the pace setters in relevant production activities, "... with close attention being paid to the pursuit of competitive advantage, by lobbing for information, knowledge and markets".[120]

While Ventura stresses the need for Jamaica to develop an, "... astute, dynamic work-force committed to innovation and efficiency" in order, rather ambitiously, to, "... become an influential player in the new paradigm of world competition",[121] Girvan, more soberly, issues a reminder as to the "... culture of technological passivity," which has largely characterized the business environment.[122]

The holder of either view is unlikely to receive much comfort from the declining budgetary provision to education reflected in such perverse strategies as "cost sharing" in education. This is against Bernal's call for, "... the financial requirements of what is needed for a well-educated work force to be the first charge on the governments' budget",[123] if the production requirements of increasing skill flexibility are to be met.

Some seem to harbour optimistic expectations of employee share ownership programmes (ESOP), to the extent that they see them as a variant of productivity incentive schemes. The justification for offering equity, at a discount, is said to be the greater effort that will be forthcoming from labour when reward, in the form of dividends, is linked directly to profitability.[124]

On a different tack, at least one eminent person, Professor Rex Nettleford, of the Trade Union Education Institute at the University of the West Indies in Jamaica, has held up the Accord in Australia as evidence of the kind of cooperation that is achievable by the parties in the industrial relations system.[125]

Some twenty years ago, it is interesting to note, it was found that Productivity Bargaining in Australia was inhibited by such factors as management's conservative approach to negotiations; the then current notions as to the wide boundaries of management prerogatives; low level negotiating skill on the part of management and unions; weakness of union structure and leadership, and unsatisfactory union-member relations; easy access to arbitration; and, of no little importance, the emphasis on wage uniformity and the maintenance of occupational and inter-industry relativities. As Yerbury and Isaac observe, at that time, "The egalitarian notion referred to as 'comparative wage justice' traditionally underlined by arbitration authorities runs counter to the 'bargaining power' concept of Collective Bargaining".[126]

The negative impact on productivity of the undiscriminating nature of IMF wage guidelines, as implemented in the island, reinforced by the orientation of trade unions to seek across the board increases,[127] regardless of the differences in inter-industry productivity levels, might well have been mitigated by properly conceived and designed incentive payment systems.

Apart from the British experiment with Productivity Bargaining and Incentive Schemes, there was also the alternative – contrary to Manley's claim as to the absence of any available precedent – of the Polish model of advanced worker participation. Workers there were given the scope to take initiatives for improving methods of work and solving day to day problems, thus directly determining their enterprises' efficiency and improving working conditions. The degree of success in the implementation of enterprise plans, which dovetailed into the national development plan, would be reflected in the size of the enterprise fund available for distribution at the end of each year. Apart from the material incentive of performance bonuses, there would also be the allocation of funds for the provision of additional housing and social and cultural amenities for enterprise workers. Clearly, this represented one way of reconciling the interest of the working class, enterprises, and the national economy.[128] As Coates has prescribed, the best remedy for the 'roll-on-Friday' attitude could well be to involve the workers, actively and vitally, in the processes of decision-making.[129]

Among the factors identified by Stettner as being responsible for the stimulus to Productivity Bargaining are the pressures of a changing industrial structure, the pace of technological innovations, increased (skilled) manpower shortages, and an emphasis on both domestic and international competitiveness.[130] In the Jamaican context, the primary concern is, of course, with inflation control, as well as the increasing mobility of capital and the location of production, internationally.

Trade unions, therefore, according to Petras and Engbath, need to be sensitive to the requirements for adaptation in an increasingly competitive environment, not only with respect to developing the capacity to exploit emerging opportunities, "... opened through considered linkages with the world economy... ", but also, "... to promote utilization of more advanced and efficient production processes".[131]

In the United Kingdom, after the 1966 six months wage freeze, followed by six months of severe restraint, one month's notice of wage increases had to be given. Increases could then be referred to the National Board for Prices and Incomes for decision as to the merits of the claim on the basis of the assessment of its productivity element. As Paden points out, in keeping with observed practice, a lax attitude to Productivity Agreements was not only one way of avoiding conflict with strong unions,[132] but also of showing sympathy with the plight of workers pressured by the erosion of wages as a result of galloping inflation.

For Luxemburg, any cooperation between capital and labour, and especially the participation of labour unions, "… in fixing the scale and cost of production", amounted to their solidarity against consumers, and certainly against business competitors[133] – particularly in cases, as tends to be the rule in Jamaica, when the efficiency gains, resulting from such a 'cartel', are not passed on in the form of downward price adjustments.

For as Okun has reminded us, productivity enhancing schemes might tend to create "perverse incentives" to collude, so as to hold down the performance norm, or to sacrifice quality, safety considerations, and even "civility in the workers' conduct." The function of labour market conditions in determining wages, he argues, is diluted by reward systems which are based on worker performance. Given that the employer's responsibility is to create the conditions – the rewards and sanctions – for satisfactory productivity standards, this is often neutralized, as in Jamaica, by a plentiful cheap supply of prospective workers.[134]

It has been observed that if the least productive workers are laid off in any job category, as a result of increased, productivity – and if the selection processes is demonstrably objective – then "the longer-run impact of layoffs on quit rates [labour turnover] of the best workers may be reduced (and the short-run benefits enhanced)".[135] But, as is well known, there is strong attachment, certainly on the part of labour, to the 'last in first out' selection principle for redundancy purposes.

The concern in Jamaica with labour productivity improvements has, perhaps unfortunately, been strongly linked, at least on the trade union side, with the preoccupation of finding ways around actual or proposed restraints on wages.[136] One doubts that there is an appreciation of the productivity implications from an on-going, long-term, national economic perspective – certainly not on the part of the labour force. As a result of this limited focus, important aspects of the productivity-wage relationship have been de-emphasized, if not ignored. These include the balance between direct and indirect compensation; current and deferred wages (e.g. annual bonuses); financial and non-financial rewards; the need for security in wage incomes;[137] and the provision of incentives for workers to work "smarter" and not only "harder".[138]

Uncertainty in the economic environment about the level and stability of demand at both the macro and micro levels would, one would have thought, provoked firms into showing greater concern for varying the wage bill, according to output levels. Despite the scarcity and very high cost of capital, however, one suspects that the low and declining percentage of labour costs in total costs of production explains the lack of emphasis on getting maximum output from capital equipment.[139] The state of competition in product markets, clearly also constitutes a further reason for the failure of management to prioritize productivity issues.[140]

It is instructive that the observation, that,

> "... since one cannot speak of wage determination with any meaning without regard to the faltering economy, collective bargaining, it seems, will have to shift, its goal from one of mere comparisons with consumer price indices and external relativities to that of productivity bargaining"[141], was made in 1978.

However, seminars for trade unionists, explaining the basic concepts of Productivity Bargaining, were only being held in the island in the first half of the 1990's. That, after a period of some fifteen years, leading trade unionists were admitting their ignorance and confusion on the subject,[142] is a sufficient indictment of the island's policy implementation capability and the adequacy of its training and skill-upgrading facilities. Even more fundamentally, the relevance of its educational system at the tertiary level to a problem-solving approach in priority areas of national concern was clearly open to question.

The implication is that the Jamaican employers' 'ability to pay' can be considered a function of the ability to pass on labour costs to consumers, or to achieve higher levels of productivity.[143]

What might have seemed a rather bold statement in 1975, that,

> "It is moreover, high time that trade unions stopped supporting marginal entrepreneurs in their pleas for protection and subsidies, hopeless remedies which in the long term cannot prevent the closure of factories".[144]

This has proven prophetic, given the effects of the import-liberalization and subsidy removal planks of the IMF/World Bank economic restructuring programmes, in the context of the developments in global finance, production and trade.

The following table, which needs little, if any, comment is evidence, if more were required, that the decade of the 1980's was 'lost' in more than one sense.

Table: 14	Labour Productivity 1980 – 1990		
Year	Average labour Force (Million)	Real GDP (Jamil)	
1980	0.991	1829	1845.6
1981	1.015	1875	1935.6
1982	0.97 8	1893	1935.6
1983	0.974	1942	1993.8
1984	0.978	1925	1716.0
1985	1.042	1835	1761.0
1986	1.059	1870	1765.8
1987	1.070	1983	1853.3
1988	1.077	2013	1869.1
1989	1.063	2104	1979.3
1990	1.059	2184	2062.3

Source: Cedric Wilson in the Money Index, No 325, June 23, 1992, p.7.

The treatment of issues relating to Productivity Incentive Schemes, before the Chapter on Prices and Incomes Policy. is considered appropriate given the fundamental importance of the national productivity level for facilitation of the trade-offs required in the negotiation of meaningful and orderly income and price adjustment strategy. The lack of policy coordination and the weakness of implementation capability has meant that, while there have been various degrees of control exercised at different times over incomes and prices at the national level, such attempts were never dovetailed into a national programme of enhancing productivity at the micro level. As could be expected, this has tended to frustrate Prices and Incomes Policy formulation, acceptance and implementation – a matter which will next be considered in detail.

---

1. The Daily Gleaner, Feb. 17, 1990.
2. Ibid.
3. See *Money and Politics*.
4. Winston Lewis, Corporate Industrial Relations Manager, Alcan Jamaica Limited, at Mona Institute of Business Forum, University of the West Indies, Mona, Jamaica, Oct. 2, 1991.
5. Carl Stone, "Wages and the Social Contract", in Headley Brown (ed) p.128.

---

6.   As Minister of Trade and Industry, Mr. Lightbourne was closely involved with the initial establishment of the Productivity Council, in 1966.

7.   See Brown's "Labour productivity and export growth: Sources of concern" in The Daily Gleaner, June 24, 1994, pp .7,11; The total misconception of the strategy and purpose of the "initiative was disclosed in reported remarks of the very person in charge of administration of the resuscitated Productivity Council to the effect that, since giving the incentive tax benefits for approved incentive schemes to only a few and *not to everyone* [italics added] – as Cezlev Sampson, the new chairman, pointed out: "there are other types of incentives that *companies can explore* [italics added] apart from money. Those included environmental improvement and human resource development" – Claire Clarke in The Daily Gleaner, Jan. 31, 1993; "Jamaica's labour force problems", in The Sunday Gleaner, Feb. 12, 1995 where the survey concluded: "Little attention is devoted to product quality, packaging, or export market positioning – Production uses very low technology, is labour intensive and uses outdated capital equipment" – "Private Sector Focus" in The Sunday Gleaner, Feb. 12, 1995, p.2C; The worker perspective is given, for example, by The General Secretary of the PNP, "Creating a productivity culture in '95", in The Jamaica Herald, Jan. 3, 1995, p.6, where the emphasis is on deepening the process of worker participation, improving earnings through improved motivation, so as to protest workers against "further erosion of their Standards of Living". He continued, "Equally, it must have implications for the workers as consumers as well, where (sic) they must remain vigilant against unscrupulous businessmen who change excessively high prices for goods and services"; See also Hugh Shearer "Unions Want productivity schemes finalized". The Daily Gleaner, Aug. 19, 1993, p.2, where it was claimed that "Instead, we hear about imposing a social contract". Danny Roberts of the NWU made the observation that "in most of the South East Asian countries real wages increased ... over the years ... In South Korea] for example the index of real wages increased from a Base of 100 in 1970 to 284 in 1984. Ours, I am sure over that period fell. The rates of increase in South Korea were higher for the production workers than it was for professional technical or managerial employers. Quite the opposite has been the Jamaican experience", as disclosed by the JEF Salary surveys. See also "Private Sector Focus" on "Improving Worker productivity" in The Sunday Gleaner, Oct. 16, 1994, p.2E, pointing to the difficulty of dismissing a worker and job demarcation inefficiencies in the deployment of labour.

8.   Held at the Jamaica Conference Centre, Kingston and attended by trade union officers, company executives, and in which the writer participated as a presenter on Aug. 20, 1993.

9.   Leon HoSang, "The Importance of Productivity", Daily Gleaner, Nov* 6, 1991, p.6.

10.   R. Marriott, Incentive Payment Systems, A Review of Research and Opinion, Industrial Psychology Research Unit, British Medical Research Council, Staples Press, London, refers to the terminological confusion in respect of which some assistance is provided by the ILO Report (1951) pp.7-25 urging the need for a comprehensive classification of the various systems/schemes. Raymond Forrest, "Raising Labour Productivity", in The Financial Gleaner, Mar* 8, 1991, p*10; "Fooling Ourselves" by Marjorie Stair, in The Daily Gleaner, Nov* 19, 1994, p.6; Carl Wint, "On production and productivity", in The Daily Gleaner, May 10, 1994, p.6*

11.   The Daily Gleaner Feb. 17, 1990.

12.   Allan Flanders, *The Fawley Productivity Agreements*, Faber, 1964, p.239.

13.   Ibid, p.240.

14.   National Board for Prices and Incomes, Report No.65, *Payment by Results Systems*. HMSO, London, 1969, (CMND.3627)

15.   The Daily Gleaner Oct. 7, 1991, p.2.

16.   The Daily Gleaner, Jan. 10, 1990, p.6.

17.   Leon HoSang, "Importance of Productivity" in The Daily Gleaner, Nov. 6,1991, p.6.

18.   Okun, supra.

19.   Ibid.

20.   Flanders, supra, p.239.

21.   National Board for Prices and Incomes Report No.65 supra, p.62; Generally, see the study of productivity agreements by the National Board for Prices. Incomes, Report No.36, (Cmnd 3311) which shows that the undertakings which engaged in this type of bargaining secured considerably more efficient use of manpower. Paragraph 134 of the Report states: "Outside the industries covered by this reference, we have encountered wide scope for increasing the pace of economic growth by the more effective utilization of manpower and existing capital equipment. There are examples in the printing industry, in road haulage, in railways, in buses, in the industrial Civil Service and in local authority services and hospitals". Other industries studied included the docks, Committee of Inquiry under Lord Devlin, (Cmnd 2734), Aug. 1965 and the Court of Inquiry into the printing industry under the Chairmanship of Lord Cameron, published in Jan. 1967, (Cmnd 3184).

22.   The Royal Commission on Trade Unions and Employers' Associations, 1965,1968, London H.M.S.O., 1969, Par.322.

23.   Ibid, Pars. 85-86,131,293-295,313-329.

24.   Ibid, Par. 325.

25.   Ibid, Par. 327.

26.   Leon HoSang, The Daily Gleaner, Nov. 22, 1991, p.4D.

27.   Derrick Rochester, of the National Workers Union, in The Daily Gleaner, Jan. 2, 1992, p.lb,

28.   Leon HoSang, "Pay and Productivity", in The Financial Gleaner, Jan. 24, 1991, p, 13.

29.   Gloria Kirton, Senior Manager at Price Waterhouse Associates, Kingston, Jamaica in Caribbean Labour Journal Vol. 2, No. 1 Spring 1992, p.28.

30. Flanders, 1964, pp.14, 96,138.
31. Ibid, p.80.
32. Ibid, pp.136,138.
33. Ibid
34. Hugh Shearer, President General of the Bustamante Industrial Trade Union, and former Prime Minister, in The Daily Gleaner, Aug. 19, 1993, p.2.
35. The Jamaica Herald, Jan. 25, 1996, p.5.
36. Hugh Shearer, at the Productivity Seminar sponsored by the JTURDC, Jamaica Conference Centre, Kingston, Aug. 18-21, 1993,
37. Frank Kerber, in a speech at the Nova Southeastern University MBA graduation ceremony in Kingston, Jamaica, reported in The Daily Gleaner, Mar. 23, 1995, p. 12A.
38. The Sunday Gleaner, Feb. 12, 1995, p.2C.
39. Ibid.
40. Ibid, supra.
41. Ibid.
42. Investor's Daily, Vo 1.7 No.182, Los Angeles, Dec. 26, 1990.
43. Ibid.
44. Ibid.
45. Laurie Marmor, Ibid p.l.
46. Ibid.
47. Winston Lewis, in a paper entitled "The Pros and Cons of Productivity Incentive Schemes", at a Mona Institute of Business Forum U.W.I., held at the U.W.I., Mona, Oct. 2, 1991.
48. Keith R. Thompson, "The Role of productivity in Production Growth", in The Financial Gleaner, Feb. 26, 1993, p.22.
49. Ibid.
50. The Daily Gleaner, Oct. 7, 1991.
51. The Financial Gleaner, April 23, 1993, pp.10,17, "NWU linking productivity and pay".
52. Thompson, supra, pp.5,22.
53. Claire Clarke, op cit.
54. Clinton Pickering, in The Daily Gleaner July 25, 1992, reporting on a closed-door meeting between the Prime Minister, senior public-sector officials, and two specially invited guests, Hugh Shearer, Chairman of the Joint Trade Union Research and Development Centre, and Dennis Lalor, President of the Private Sector Organization of Jamaica, at the Jamaica Conference Centre, Kingston, on July 22, 1993.
55. Charles Ross, "Improving worker productivity". The Sunday Gleaner, Oct. 16, 1994, p.2E.
56. The Jamaica Herald's Magazine, Dollars and Sense Sept. 26, 1994 p.2, (Strangely enough there existed a serious shortage of labour in the garment industry due to the "sweat shop" image of the Freezone firms and the existence of a reserve price for labour despite the high level of unemployment).
57. Charles Ross – supra. But see also Private Sector Focus – "Jamaica's labour force problems" in The Sunday Gleaner, Feb. 12, 1995, p.2C, where a USAID sponsored study concluded that "Companies invest only minimally in creating proper technical skills, in part because of the aptitude of the work force, but also in part because management remains stagnant in the low technology, low value-added part of the industry".
58. Charles Ross, Private Sector Focus: "Labour Productivity and competition", The Sunday Herald, Oct. 16, 1994, p.3B.
59. Danny Roberts, "Mere economic development is not enough", in The Daily Gleaner, Oct. 20, 1994, p.lE.
60. James Walsh, "Workers and Production", in The Daily Gleaner, Dec. 23, 1994, p.6A.
61. David T. Coe, & Elhanan Helpman, "International Spillovers", National Bureau of Economic Research, U.S.A., 1994. This study which focused on the period 1970-90 introduces the concept of a "Research and Development capital stock" of knowledge on a country-wide basis, determined by R & D capital stock based on the R & D expenditure of a country's trading partners. The authors also compute a measure of total factor productivity based on estimates of output minus a weighted average of labour and capital inputs. The effects on total national factor productivity of domestic and foreign R & D capital stocks is then estimated. The study reports that smaller countries with more open economies benefit more from foreign R & D than larger countries. Not surprisingly, it was found that the spillover of R & D benefits in the form of productivity increases is largest from the United States and Japan, with a 10% increase in the capital stock in these two countries increasing total factor productivity in their trading partners by an average of 0.04 and 0.01% respectively. It is concluded that a country's own R & D efforts enhances its benefits from foreign technical advances and "the better a country takes advantage of technological advances in the rest of the world the more productive it. becomes".
62. Dr. George Phillip, at a Productivity Seminar at the Medallion Hall Hotel. Kingston, on May 24, 1994.
63. Ibid.
64. Dr. Omar Davies, Minister of Finance, when opening the 1994/95 Budget Debate, Gordon House, Kingston, April 28, 1994.
65. The Daily Gleaner, May 25. 1994. p.2.
66. The nature of the reported employer and trade union responses indicate a lack of appreciation that their associations can play a most important role in facilitating successful bargaining and, more generally, in gaining support and acceptance of the project.

This aspect of the matter is treated in Leon HoSang "The Role of Employer Organisations and Union Associations", in The Financial Gleaner, Dec. 27, 1991, pp.4,6,

67. Grace Virtue, "Growing dissatisfaction with Productivity Incentive Schemes", in The Sunday Gleaner, May 23, 1993, p.lA.

68. Raymond Forrest, in The Financial Gleaner, June 16, 1988, p.10.

69. The Daily Gleaner, Aug. 2, 1989, p.6.

70. Ibid.

71. Jamaica Five Year Development Plan, 1970-75, PIOJ.

72. Basil Buck, "PM fine-tuning a broken engine" in The Financial Gleaner, Feb. 4, 1994, p.3.

73. Survey by Carl Stone, Pollster and Professor of Political Sociology, University of the West Indies, Mona, Kingston, Jamaica, in April 1990, the results of which were reported in Carl Stone, "Rewarding productivity: The private sector's view". The Sunday Gleaner, Public Affairs column, July 8, 1990.

74. Danny Roberts, in The Daily Gleaner Oct. 20. 1994, p.l E, and Oct. 16, 1994, p.7A.

75. Dr. Henley Morgan, in an address at the Jamaica Employer's Federation's annual convention, Ocho Rios, Jamaica, May 5-7, 1995, reported in. The Investor's Choice, July 22, 1995, p.12; Frances Coke, "Barriers to Excellence" in Caribbean Labour Journal, Vol.1 No. l, Sept. 1991, pp. JO-24.

76. Morgan, Ibid, p.13.

77. See Ian Boyne, "The Growth Versus equity debate" in The Sunday Gleaner, July 17, 1994, p. 30A; Leon HoSang, "Productivity Bargaining", in The Sunday Gleaner, June 13, 1976, p.5C; Lloyd Goodleigh, "Creating a productivity culture in '95" in The Jamaica Herald, Jan. 3, 1995, p.6; "Draft Outline of Social Contract/Understanding" for Discussion purposes only, The National Planning Council, undated mimeo, pp.2,3. See in contrast Tom Clarke, "The Raison d'etre of Trade Unionism", in Clarke and Clements 1977, pp.19-20 and J.H. Goldthorpe, "Industrial Relations in Great Britain. A Critique of Reformism" in Clarke and Clements, p.224. Basil Buck refers to the prospect offered under the 1994 Budget presentation, to "stagnate with equity" The Financial Gleaner, May 6, 1994, p. 3.

78. Ashwell Thomas, "Creating a Productive Working Environment" in the Caribbean Labour Journal, Vol.1 No.2, Dec. 1991 p.13; Bentham H. Hussey "Performance Pay vs Status Related Pay" in Caribbean Labour Journal, Vol.1 No.2 Dec. 1991, p.36.

79. Leon HoSang, "Productivity and PBR systems: The Jamaican Solution?" in Caribbean Labour Journal, Vo 1.3 No.4, Dec. 1993, p.30.

80. Ibid, p.3 I.

81. Ibid, p.32.

82. Clive Dobson, Vice President of the National Workers Union, "The Case for Consultative Management", in Caribbean Labour Journal, Vol.1 No.l, Sept. 1991, p.40; Ibid: Ashwell Thomas, "Productivity: Whose Responsibility?" Caribbean Labour Journal, Vol.1 No. I Sept. 1991, p.12; USAID Survey on Jamaica's labour force, summarized in The Sunday Gleaner, Feb. 12, 1995, pp.2C,6C.

83. Thomas, supra, p.47.

84. Carl Stone, "Work Attitudes Survey: A Report to the Jamaica Government", Earle Publishers, Jamaica, 1982.

85. Thomas, supra, p.48.

86. Dillon Alleyne, "Personal Income Taxes and Work Effort in Jamaica", in The Money Index, No.338, Sept. 22, 1992, p.39. Additional scope for the broadening of trade union objectives would thereby be created.

87. The Financial Gleaner, Aug. 27, 1993, p.24.

88. Lawrence Nurse, "Organized Labour at the Crossroads", in Caribbean Labour Journal, Vol.1 No.2, Dec. 1991, p.58.

89. The Labour Relations and Industrial Disputes Act (1975) S.9 provides for industrial action in the so-called "essential services" to be declared unlawful unless certain conditions are met; s.10 bestows wide discretionary powers on the Minister of Labour to refer any dispute to the IDT which is adjudged by him as being likely to be "gravely injurious to the national interest; S.lla allows the Minister the discretion of referring any dispute to the Tribunal for settlement, where he is satisfied that such a dispute should be settled expeditiously; and S. 12(4)(c.) provides, not surprisingly, that "An award in respect of any industrial dispute, referred to the Tribunal for settlement shall be final and conclusive and no proceedings shall be brought in any court to impeach the validity thereof, except on a point of law"; S.32(I) (b)(i) provides that the Minister may apply to the Supreme Court for an injunction to restrain actual or threatened industrial action where it appears to the Minister that such action "is or is likely to be – gravely injurious to the national economy "

90. Hussey, supra.

91. Ibid, p.40.

92. Clive Dobson, making his submission to the Eaton Committee on Market Reform, reported in The Friday Herald, Aug. 18, 1995, p.3.

93. Mark Ricketts, "Inflation" – "The Way I see it" in The Money Index No. 401, Jan. 18, 1994, p.3.

94. Ibid.

95. Ibid, p. 5.

96. Wilmot Perkins, "Cataclysmic Politics", in The Money Index, No.299, Dec. 10, 1991, p.55.

97. Ibid.

98. "Budget 1994/95", in The Money Index, No.416, May 3, 1994, p.ll.

99. Ibid.
100. Cedric Wilson, "Policies and Productivity", in The Money Index, No.325, June 23, 1992, p.7; Reuter Report "Japan Stresses Bigger Role for Government" in the Money Index No.302, Jan. 14, 1992, p.18; Dr. Sang Sung Park, Former Governor, Bank of Korea, "Korea's Economic Development and its Relevance to Jamaica, Part II", in The Money Index No.352, Jan.19, 1993, pp.26-33.
101. Sushil K. Jain, "Does Profitability prove the Productivity of an Organization?", The Money Index, No.350, Dec. 15, 1992, p.18.
102. Jacques A. Bussieres, Governor, Bank of Jamaica "The Role of Monetary Policy in the Structural Adjustment Process", in The Money Index No.383, Aug. 24, 1993, p.20.
103. Sung Sang Park, supra, 1993, p.29.
104. Paul Harrison, The Third World Tomorrow, Penguin, 1991, p.178; PREALC, Adjustment and the Social Debt, ILO, 1987, pp.65 et seq.
105. Jamaica Development Plan, 1990-95, PIOJ, July 1995, p.8.
106. Ibid, p.14.
107. Ibid, p. 31; Tom Bottmore, The Socialist Economy: Theory and Practice, Harvester Wheatsheaf, 1990, p.108.
108. I Richard T. Gill, Economic Development: Past and Present. Prentice Hall, 1967, p.18.
109. Ibid, p.18.
110. Arthur W. Lewis, The Principles of Economic Planning, Urwin University Books, 1969, p.41.
111. Ibid, p.90.
112. Ibid.
113. Wilbert E. Moore, "Industrialization and Labour', in Industrialism and Industrial Man, Kerr et al., 1964, p.173.
114. Bottmore, 1990, p.67.
115. Celso Furtado, Development and Underdevelopment, University of California Press, 1967, pp.63-65.
116. Tony Topham, "New Types of Bargaining", in Robin Blackburn and Alexander Cockburn (eds) The Incompatibles: Trade Union Militancy and the Consensus, Penguin and New Left Review, 1967, p.134.
117. Przeworski advances the view that "concern with justice is not immediately [italics added] compatible with increased productivity", since one has to produce before there is anything to distribute and "a just distribution of poverty was (certainly) not the socialist promise" – Adam Przeworski, Capitalism and Social Democracy, Cambridge University Press, 1989, pp. 41-43; For Hobbes justice itself was reduced to a market concept, rather than the principle of reward according to need or the social value of the different effort and contributions to social life – see C.B. MacPherson, The Political Theory of Possessive Individualism: Hobbes to Locke, Oxford University Press, 1962, p.64.
118. A.M. Ross, Trade Union Wage Policy, University of California Press 1948, referred to in Tom Clarke and Laurie Clements (eds) Trade Unions under Capitalism. Fontana, 1977, p.312.
119. Andrew Downes, in ILO, The Role of Trade Unions in Periods of Structural Adjustment Programmes, Regional Seminar, Barbados Workers Union Labour College, Dec. 1992 ILO, p.15.
120. Hilbourne A. Watson, "Global Restructuring and the Prospects for Caribbean Competitiveness: with a case Study from Jamaica" in Hilbourne A. Watson (ed) The Caribbean in the Global Political Economy, Ian Randle Publishers, Kingston, 1994, p.89.
121. Arnold Ventura, "Technology: Creating Competitive Advantages in Production", in Patsy Lewis (ed) Jamaica: Preparing for the 21st Century, Ian Randle Publishers, for PIOJ, Kingston, 1994, p.191.
122. Norman Girvan, "A Strategic Approach to Technology", in Patsy Lewis (ed), 1994, p . 200.
123. Richard Bernal, "Recent developments in the Western Hemisphere", in Patsy Lewis (ed) 1994, p.233; On the issue of budget allocation priorities, see The Jamaica Herald, Sept, 5, 1994, p.6, where the Minister of Finance claimed that "excess" public sector wage increases would mean further cuts in social service expenditure, including education already afflicted with "cost sharing". The Prime Minister was to state in connection with the public service pay dispute that the Budget could not only be devoted to wages and debt service.
124. Christopher Adam, William Carendish and Percy S, Mistry, Adjusting Privatization, Ian Randle Publishers, Kingston, 1992, pp. 53-55. In the author's view "… the qualitative importance of these links is dubious" as the main function of ESOP is to buy out opposition, especially where significant redundancy is anticipated in the entities to be privatized. That there seems to be no evidence of any such productivity change is the conclusion reached (p.140), with respect to a particular case where the inducement was supposed to have been embodied in a contract, i.e. the Caribbean Cement Co; For a valuable contribution to the literature on Privatization, see Paul Cook and Colin Kirkpatrick (eds)Privatization Policy and Performance International Perspectives, Prentice Hall, Harvester Wheatsheaf, 1995, p.71, which deals with employee share schemes; see also World Bank, Privatization: The Lessons of Experience, Country Economics Department, Washington D.C., World Bank, 1992, p. 9. See also Carl Stone "Worker Participation in Industry – A Survey of Workers' Opinion", in Carl Stone and xAggrey Brown (eds) Essays on Power and Change in Jamaica, Dept, of Government, UWI and Extra Mural Centre, UWI, 1976, pp. 456-60. Stone reports a low level of interest in profit sharing and share ownership schemes due to "the high cost of living which placed a premium on certain, short-term income, the risk and uncertainty of profits, and the desire of workers to exercise discretionary choice over their limited financial resources".
125. As against Jamaica's tradition of collective bargaining, a legacy of the British influence, the situation in Australia was defined as one in which "the entire socio-legal framework has been not only inappropriate for 'free' and independent Collective Bargaining

and fraught with formal barriers for those who prefer its operations, but also in a very real sense hostile to the values which underlie it: "Yerbury and Isaac, Recent trends in Collective Bargaining in Australia, ILR, Vol. 103 No.5, May 1971, p.422.

126. Ibid.

127. Huntley G. Manhertz, "The Price Determination Process in a Small Open Economy: The Jamaican Experience", in Compton Bourne (ed) *Inflation in the Caribbean*, ISER, UWI, 1979, p.22.

128. Edward Marek, Worker's Participation in Planning and Management in Poland, ILR, Vol.101 NO.3 March 1970, p.271.

129. Ken Coates, (ed), *Can the workers Run Industry?* London: Sphere Books, 1968.

130. Nora Stettner, *Productivity Bargaining and Industrial Change*, Pergamon Press, 1969.

131. James Petras, and Dennis Engbath, "Third World Industrialization and Third World Struggles", in Roger Southall (ed) *Trade Unions and the New Industrialization of the Third World*, University of Pittsburg Press, 1988, pp.104-109.

132. G.C Peden, *British Economic and Social Policy*, Philip Allan, 1991, p.172. "Productivity agreements", Peden notes, "became increasingly spurious".

133. Rosa Luxemburg, Reform or Revolution, Pathfinder, 1988 edition, p.22.

134. Arthur M. Okun, Prices and Quantities: A Macroeconomic Analysis, The Bookings Institution, 1981, p.74; J.R. Hicks, The Theory of Wages, London: MacMillan, 1932, pp.39-40.

135. Ibid, p.103.

136. T.H. Patten Jnr, Pay, Employee Compensation and Incentive Plans, New York, The Free Press, 1977, p.197.

137. See Flanders, supra. Standing supports attention to job security as a proper element of productivity oriented workplace relations, in that the economic benefits could include increased worker motivation and sense of commitment to the employing organization which might well result in the raising of productivity; lowered rates of labour turnover; greater receptiveness to efficiency increasing rationalization and modernization and to with the concomitant changes in work organization, methods and techniques; induce a greater awareness of the need for rational disciplinary provisions; encourage managers to find other means of raising efficiency than laying off workers; and reducing the probability of frictional unemployment: Guy Standing Structural Adjustment and Labour Market Policies: Towards Social Adjustment?, Workshop on Labour Market Issues and Structural Adjustment, ILO, Geneva, 1989, p.42; With respect to modernization of techniques, See UNESCAP, Technology Atlas: An Interim report, Asian Pacific Centre for Transfer of Technology, Bangkok, March 1987, part 16 for the design of an elaborate index of national technological capability; Jamaica is yet to develop a skill profile of the labour force or carry out any study of the impact of skill availability on choice of technology despite a great deal of talk on the need for a highly skilled, flexible, easily retrainable work force given increasing globalization of production and competition at all levels; David J.C. Forsyth Appropriate National Technology Policies a manual for their assessment, ILO, 1989, p.67.

138. ILO, *Wage Determination in English-speaking Caribbean Countries*, ILO/ DANIDA Regional Seminar, Kingston, Jamaica, March 1978, p.27.

139. Capital-intensive industrialization favoured by Galenson and Leibenstein even if inefficient, on the grounds of the higher rate of savings, is questionable not only on the ground that a country should economize on the raise of those resources that are in short-supply, but that incentive wage system arrangements can, together with innovative taxation policy as Bhagwati has argued, allow achieve the same results by direct concentration on production efficiency.

140. ILO. supra, 1978, pp.28-29. For the several disadvantages of Payment by Results Systems, see p.29; The Report of the Royal Commission on Trade Unions etc. GR – PIS The suitability of introducing a production incentive payment systems depends on factors such as: the nature of the work, the size of the undertaking and the motivational assumptions inherent in management's philosophy; ILO, supra, 1978, p.66.

141. Ibid, ILO

142. This became apparent at a JTURDC Seminar in Kingston on Aug. 20, 1993 on Productivity Bargaining.

143. Ajeet. N. Martbur. *Industrial Restructuring and Union Power – Micro Economic Dimensions of Economic Restructuring and Industrial relations in India*, ILO – ARTEP, ILO, 1991, p.10.

144. Bohuslav Herman, *The Optimal International Division Labour*, ILO. 1995, pp.132-33.

Chapter 4
Prices and Incomes Policy

It should be apparent that any call for the introduction of an incomes policy would, of necessity, have to take account of the effect of devaluation on the level of inflation and movements in real wages. The positive relationship between devaluation and the rate of inflation as against the negative effect on real wages is demonstrated in FIG. 15.

Given the very high levels of inflation during years of wage restraint under the guidelines, the conclusion is inescapable that any intended effect of an incomes policy to restrain inflation will not just be neutralised, but overwhelmed, by other stronger inflation-generating forces in the economy. That would be regardless of whether such forces are internally or externally generated.

Wage guidelines have thus not just failed to have the desired effect but that failure, it has been said, has consequently, made them become, "… mechanism of oppression".[1]

If, as one would expect, increased labour productivity were to be one of the basic elements of a prices and incomes policy, under a social contract, it should not be surprising if this failed to materialize in the existing circumstances.

What did materialize under the effect of wage restraint was disaffection, alienation and the low levels of morale in the world of work, aroused by a sense of exploitation and inequity.

Better certainly came for Banks up to 1993. They, and other financial institutions, benefited from high interest rates and made huge profits from foreign currency trading; large hotels and almost all enterprises engaged in foreign exchange earning activities enjoyed substantial windfall gains. Speculators in real estate and investors in government paper, yielding interest rates which make investments in problem-prone productive ventures economically and financially foolhardy, in the absence of and genuine commitment to national development and any effective direction from the Minister of Finance or the Bank of Jamaica. They made fortunes which they could hardly have accomplished through investment in productive, especially manufacturing employment-creating activity.

That the tremendous windfall gains have not been too readily shared with workers is evidenced by the intense militancy which has characterized the collective bargaining process and the relatively high level of industrial action in recent times, as borne out by FIG. 16. There was a high level of disputes in almost all the above-named industrial/commercial sectors, in which significant improvements in terms and conditions were conceded.

Deliverance of the nation, "into the arms of the IMF" by the purportedly Socialist PNP in 1977 has meant that the rich have become richer at the expense of the poor who have become poorer. This situation was to worsen under the JLP Government led by Edward Seaga. His initial impact on the national political scene dated back to his Parliamentary speech focusing on the wide disparity between the "haves" and the "have nots", and whose 1980 campaign slogan, ironically, was *Deliverance*.

Under Michael Manley, who had promised *Better Must Come* in 1972 and that he would *Put People First*, in 1989, the transfer of income from the poor to the better-off was begun and continued under subsequent administrations. There is little chance of a change from that experience under IMF prescriptions.

Figure: 15

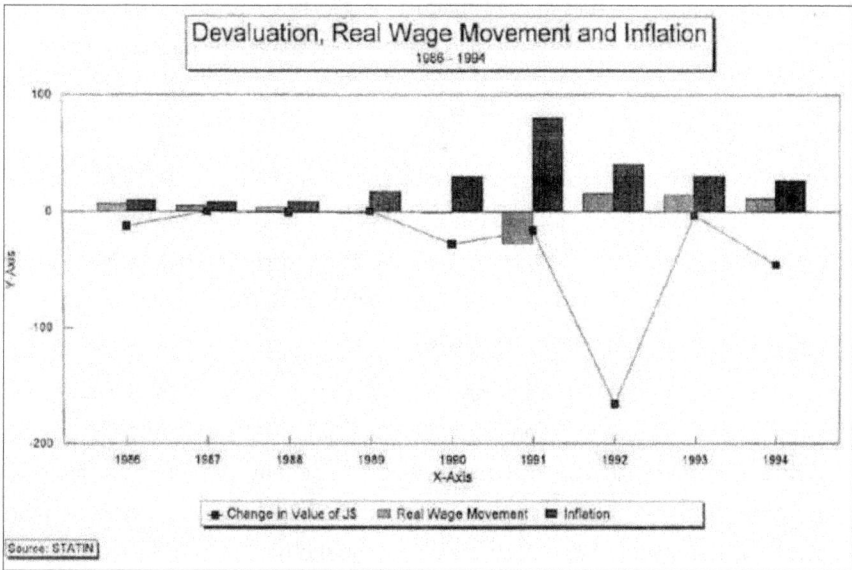

Inflation, largely caused by continuous devaluations, has, in, practical terms meant that the poor cannot afford school books for their children, after the exchange rate of the Jamaican dollar to the British Pound climbed from the initial J$2.00, to £1.00 in 1969 to J$52.00 to £1.00 in 1991/95.

Members of the poorer classes who suffer the double misfortune of also being sick have been unable, as a direct result of the staggering increases in the prices of medicinal drugs, due to devaluation, to fill prescriptions often containing three, four and even more items. So, they have in many cases been forced to resort to the purchasing of a part only of some of the items prescribed the consequences for the health of the poorer classes of the 'nation' is obvious.

This trend was confirmed by the Stone survey of 1991 which showed that consumption of basic food items by the majority of the poorer classes fell by between 30 and 40 percent, while purchases of non-essential; items decreased by some 50 to 60 percent.[2] What has become a disturbing feature of stabilization policy with respect to the three critical prices under IMF programmes, i.e. foreign currency, credit and wages, is that the only one 'successfully' controlled has been wages.

Positive interest rates in an environment of galloping inflation has pushed the price of credit to a level where banks not only advertise heavily for borrowers but have adopted promotional strategies more traditionally associated with the retail trade, namely, prizes, raffles and all manner of giveaways to attract business. The irony is that as the banks advertise the availability of loans, the increased incidence of foreclosures on and auctions of defaulting borrowers property is a daily feature in the newspapers.

Redistribution of income downwards in the first half of the 1970's, despite the adoption of Democratic Socialism in 1974, was 'put into reverse' by IMF dictated wage guidelines of 1977/8. Wage increases were limited to $10.00 per week in the first instance and then to 15%. As TABLE 15 shows, inflation for those two years was 14.3 and 49.4%, respectively.

Under the present Government, in power since 1989 under the campaign slogan *We Put People First*, inflation moved from 17.2% in 1989 to 29.8, 80.2, 40.2, 3.1 and 26 to 1994 – an annual average rate of 37.3%. This was largely the result of a lack of control over money supply, as revealed by FIG. 17. Also, the loss of value of the local dollar against the United States dollar and the British Pound caused the increase in the CPI to jump well above the movement in wage rates.

The country was thus, again, confronted with a situation from 1989 which – on the basis of past experience, properly interpreted – was likely to generate increased industrial conflict.

Until there is greater convergence between the rate of inflation and wage increases, those urging restraint by workers and unions are likely to be ignored – not so much because of malice on anyone's part, but simply as a consequence of the 'logic of the situation' and/or the 'rules of the game', from the other teams' perspective.

Figure: 16

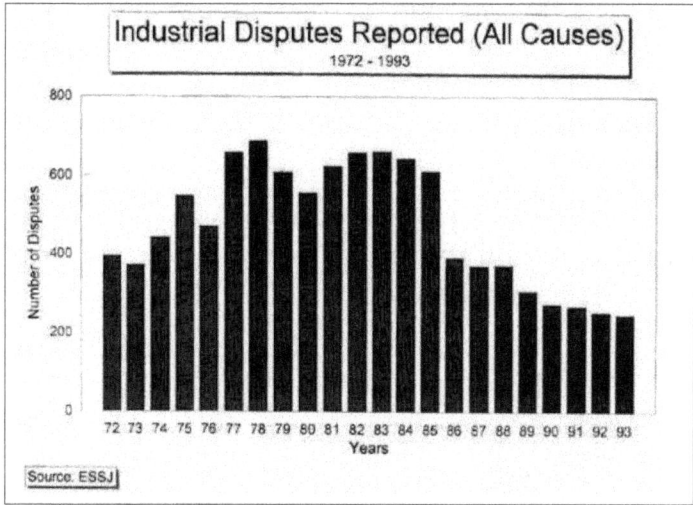

Industrial Disputes Reported (All Causes)
1972 - 1993

Source: ESSJ

Table: 15   Wage Guideline and Inflation 1976 – 1990

Year	Wage Guideline	Inflation
1976	$10 per week	8.1
1977	$10 per week	14.3
1978	15%	49.4
1979	10%	19.4
1980	10%	28.7
1981	10 - 15%	4.6
1982	10 - 15%	6.5
1983	10 - 15%	16.7
1984	10 - 15%	31.2
1985	10 - 15%	23.4
1986	10%	10.4
1987	10%	8.4
1988	10%	8.5
1989	10%	17.2
1990	12.5%	29.8

Source: ESSJ

From a trade union bargaining strategy perspective, despite the 1982 official statement as to management's responsibility to provide 'ability to pay' information,[3] the failure of employers to provide financial statements for the purposes of negotiations, (contrary to specific Swedish provisions) means that aggregated data on average gross profits, relative to the rate of inflation, is useless in applying the ability to pay criterion. This was the same as when wage guidelines were enforced as a maximum/minimum, rather than an average. So that although gross profits increased by some 56% in 1991, this was exceeded by more than 25% by the figure for inflation.

As with wages, the nominal increase in profits was more than offset by the loss of value of the local currency which moved from J$5.51 to US$1.00 in 1989 to J$21.57 TO US$1.00 in 1992.

Increases in the income tax threshold and the zero-rating of certain "basic" items, making them exempt from The General Consumption Tax, (GCT), will not gain peaceful acceptance of wage restraint in the public or private sector in the 1990s. That is unlikely, despite the formal removal of wage guidelines in 1991 and Government's determination to enter into no further agreement with the IMF after the present Agreement expires in September 1995.[4]

GCT increases, a continuing inability to keep within inflation targets – in relation to which levels of wage increases for public sector workers, in particular, are set and budgetary provision made – makes for recurring crises in new contract negotiations with each of the numerous categories of public service employees. And the large number of bargaining units inevitably makes for delay and consequential frustration.

Elevation of an unofficial guideline by Government, now approximately sixteen percent for the public sector, into a unilaterally determined figure, representing what is said to be "affordable in the national interest", has led to interesting developments.

In fact, it. would be instructive to see the results of a study showing the correlation between wages as a proportion of the total cost of production for different industries and sector and labour disputes. Would one find, for example, that business activities in which wages are a significant item of total cost are also those experiencing a higher incidence of labour management conflict? Without information of this kind it is difficult to contemplate the formulation of a "coherent, comprehensive, precise incomes policy" grounded in realism, rather than conclusions based on misinformation and faulty analysis. It is not difficult for persons with an anti-working-class bias, which might well exist on the level of the subconscious, to put forward policy proposals more reflective of vested interests than being based on an objective appraisal of all the relevant explanatory variables.

Figure: 17

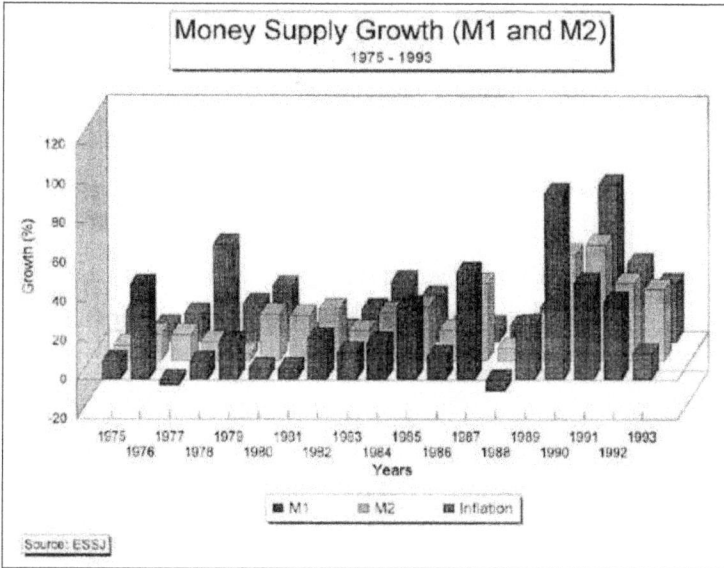

Data on the numbers below the poverty line, as indicated in FIG. 18, while the subject of dispute for partisan political or methodological reasons, from almost any source, suggest the need for a significant general increase in wages for those in the lowest forty percent of the income strata. Those who are full-time employed who cannot meet the cost of the basic necessities, generally considered appropriate for their traditional job and social status, are most unlikely to be motivated to be good producers.

It is of significance that despite the fact that the wage rates of Hong Kong, Taiwan and South Korea are approximately three times that of Jamaica's, those countries achieved a substantial increase in employment opportunities, while there has been little to show for the sacrifice of the Jamaican working class.

There are, of course, those who allege that there is no place for incomes policies, and certainly not the limited and crude class discriminatory wage guideline/restraint variant, in a free market economy. The market is, it seems, selectively/discriminatingly 'free'.

The acknowledgement of the context of wage negotiations as being "tough economic times when everyone is concerned about inflation and the rising cost of living" is noteworthy. Carl Welsh, a senior company manager, went on to express pleasure at reaching an agreement "generally considered fair and equitable" under which the National Workers Union won a historic level of increase even for the "aristocrats of (Jamaican) labour", the bauxite and alumina workers; in this case, an increase of 112% on all wage rates over the period October 1st 1991 to May 31st 1994 was agreed at the Alumina Partners of Jamaica plant.[5]

What is perhaps 'historic' about the agreement is management's recognition of the need to, "... remain mindful of the economic problems that face our people from time to time".[6]

It is obvious that while the attitude of concern for the consequence of inflation on employees' well-being could be generalized, the level of the resulting wage increases in individual enterprises will be constrained by the 'ability to pay' factor, as well as the cost of labour as a percentage of the total cost of production. In the case of bauxite/alumina, the percentage cost of labour is relatively small in an industry known to be highly capital intensive.

Figure: 18

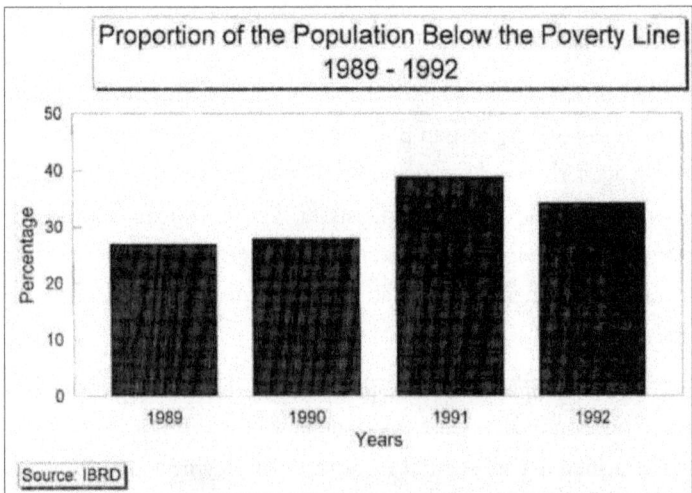

Proportion of the Population Below the Poverty Line 1989 - 1992

Source: IBRD

After wage guidelines, were abolished in 1991, the Prime Minister, P.J. Patterson, proceeded in May 1992 to issue a call for wage restraint and the, "... passing on of the benefits of the dollars (recovery to the consumer". The removal of price controls was followed by the fixing of prices by 'market forces', under the IMF. As there has never been a profits guideline policy, after the short-lived Social

Contract experiment in 1978/79 under the PNP's Mixed Commission, there is in fact no institutional arrangements for ensuring – with the state having much less of a role to play in the regulation of the economy – that any such benefits will in fact, be passed on to consumers. Recent experience confirms that prices do not go down very readily.[7]

In wage negotiations on behalf of the electricity generating and distribution company (The Jamaica Public Service Company) workers, the union involved, (the Union of Technical Administrative and Supervisory Personnel) put in a claim, in 1992, for a 230% wage increase. Wesley Hughes, who was to become the Director General of the PIOJ, in a letter to the Editor of the Daily Gleaner, wanted to know if this claim was backed by a similar increase in productivity. He then quoted figures for the latter half of the 1970's showing that whereas the CPI had moved by an average of 15% per annum, private and public-sector wages had increased by 17.2% and 29.8%, respectively between 1974 and 1977. It was this excess increase in wage movements over the rate of inflation, in a period of union militancy which led, it is claimed, to the imposition of wage guidelines at the behest of the IMF in the first place.[8]

Hughes, who writes "as a consumer", would appear not to be a worker; most definitely not an ambitious one who seeks to achieve an ever-improving standard of living and quality of life for himself and his family. For there can be no progress for the working class unless the rate of wage increase exceeds that of inflation on a sustained long-term basis.

Proof that the high level of inflation, and even the failure to raise productivity, is primarily the fault of labour has yet to be provided. "Nevertheless", the consumer/letter-writer continues, "In a chaotic situation of inflation driven by wage cost it would be very hard for the government to resist calls for the re-imposition of wage guidelines".[9]

The unions, it is claimed, by Ministry Paper 47/91, have a "responsibility in national economic management", so they are expected to shun short-term advantage which might damage the interests of "the wider community".[10] The extent to which wage guidelines, whatever the reason for their introduction, caused severe worsening of the social and economic well-being of workers in the long run is quite conveniently overlooked. The observation omitted would obviously run very much against the grain: the need to control profits under the IMF free market philosophy.

Having recognized that restraint needed to be exercised on prices, profits and dividends the Paper continued that it, nevertheless, "... focuses primarily on wages and salaries",[11] It might well have substituted "exclusively" for "primarily". There has been no real attempt to control any other form of income but working-class wages and salaries, since then. Indeed, even where there are existing legislative controls as under the Rent Restriction Acts, there is little effective enforcement.[12]

The new proposed unofficial guideline of 12.5% was grounded in no other justification, economic or social, than containment of wages, within the limit of 15%, as specified by Government in its latest Letter of Intent to the IMF. This clearly amounted to the removal of the guidelines, officially and an attempt to re-introduce them, virtually in identical form, "by stealth".[13]

There having been the prior introduction of a private sector 'Adopt a School Scheme', a 'Friends of the Hospital' movement, and a private sector funded 'Crime Stop' programme, this Ministry of the Public Service Paper goes on to propose that wages *foregone* by the comparatively highly paid in the *private* sector be applied towards "a social project to benefit the disadvantaged". This from a governing party that is yet to publicly disclaim its professed socialist founding principles. Significantly, no mechanisms for implementation of this very novel, if fanciful social welfare proposal were specified. Perhaps that was to be the task of the capitalistic 'invisible hand'.

Those employees who received pay increases above an "agreed" percentage level in the previous year were expected to forego further rises, while discretionary or nominal increases were recommended for those not receiving an increase over the 1991/92 period.

The traditional language of ineffective non-mobilizational exhortation, almost totally lacking in quantification, is applied even more to prices, profits, and dividends: the advice in this area is simply to practice, completely out of character, "complementary restraint".[14]

Since wage awards are to be related to present and expected, rather than past inflation rates, the message is clear: appeals for sacrifices at any "present" time are unattached to the prospect of the receipt of compensating benefits in the future, whatever the current rhetoric may promise. For target rates of inflation are usually substantially exceeded. Quite apart from this consideration, how can Government expect to be taken seriously when it withdraws, without a fight, a paper which declares that, "Government will have to be resolute with the unions with regard to any industrial action that may result from, "... strict adherence to the policy outlined for the Public Sector ...".[15]

Because of the economy-wide objectives of wage guidelines, such as maintaining/improving export competitiveness, the private sector up to the time of the removal of the guidelines, used their imposition in the public sector to moderate offers in response to wage increase demands. This was regardless of 'ability to pay' and the maintenance of 'wage relativity' considerations. One resulting "anomaly", cited by Forrest, was the phenomenon, in certain years, of average public-sector wage increases actually outstripping increases in the private sector.[16] This was despite the fact that one of the principal objectives of the guidelines, under the IMF stabilization programme, was to reduce pressure on the fiscal budget. But, with the latter aim in view when the government re-introduced the notion of a social contract in the 1992 Budget debate, it was claimed by the trade unions that this was being done prior to any discussions with them.[17] The idea had thus been greeted with little enthusiasm. Rather, there has apparently been a 'wait and see', 'lip services' reaction, instead.

That such an allegation of lack of consultation could have been made was conclusive enough proof that the Government was unaware of the kind of preparatory *quid pro quo* negotiations and bargaining that are required so as to establish the basis for even morally binding consensus. This is more important on the trade union side, since getting members to conform to wage-restraining provisions is difficult at the best of times. The difficulty arises, not because union officials are wanting in integrity or a sense of responsibility, necessarily, but primarily because of the nature of trade unions as voluntary associations and the consequential absence of effective sanctions for enforcing discipline. This is of particular significance in a context where the 'closed shop' does not prevail in practice – and where existing legislation would seem to preclude its enforcement[18] – where the level of unionization is low (FIG. 19), and where union rivalry has traditionally been keen.[19]

Marjorie Stair and others have, with obvious sincerity, sought to evade reality by questioning the reasonableness of unions making wage claims in the order of, "... 80 and in excess of 100 percent when the rate of inflation, ... is running somewhere around 45 to 50 percent ... unless productivity, output, and therefore profit"[20] are on a similar level. It does not seem to have been taken into account that collective agreements are usually for a period of two years and usually do not contain an inflation indexation clause. The consequential movement in the period rate of inflation over two years following a 50 per cent increase per year one is not 50 per cent but rather a compounded increase of 125 percent at the end of year two. The trade union leader who was ignorant of this factor in conducting wage negotiations would not retain his members for very long and would not deserve to do so. His members may not be accountants, but they do go to the supermarket.

As it happened, concern about increasing productivity was highlighted by Lloyd Goodleigh, General Secretary of the N.W.U., in his 1995 New Year's message, when he noted that,

> "... the battle against inflation will continue to pose a challenge to the unions, for the workers must *at all costs*, [italics added] be protected against further erosion of their standards of living. The simplistic and transient solution so readily offered to restrain wages, is a recipe for industrial conflict ... until and unless we create a productivity culture, where there is a national effort and will to greatly improve the level of production and productivity.... . The implications of a National productivity drive must-be understood by the social partners ... must mean profound changes to the present labour-management relationship ... transparency and trust. Equally, it must have implications for the workers, as Consumers as well, where they must remain vigilant against unscrupulous businessmen who charge excessively high prices for goods and services".[21]

One of the few contributors to the debate on incomes policy who recognized the basic flaw in the typical Jamaican approach to this 'wage restraint' strategy of inflation control, was the late Professor Carl Stone. In noting that, "... past and present concentration of policy makers, analysts, economic and financial journalists has been almost exclusively on wages, not profits nor low productivity", he outlines a case for a new approach.[22] The concentration on wages has not been sufficiently sympathetic to include concerns with ensuring the earning of a living wage, (which will ensure the adequate satisfaction of 'basic needs').

In this view, a viable incomes policy needs to be, "... coherent, comprehensive, acceptable, and consistent with a liberalized, more market-driven economic environment".[23]

Figure: 19

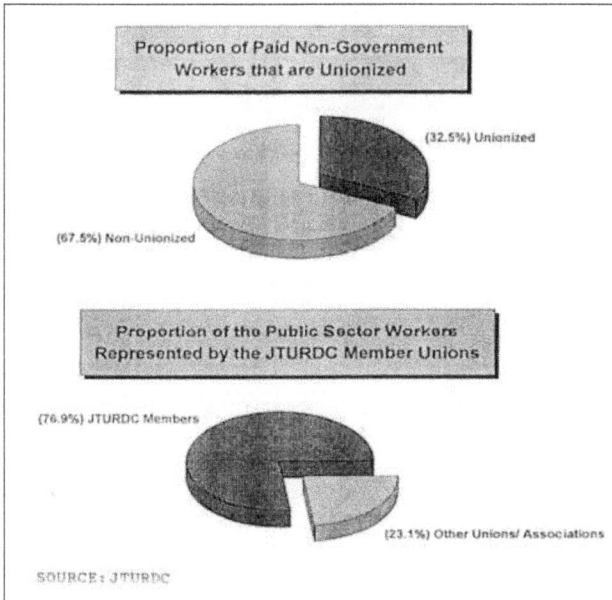

Again, very noticeably, there has been no direct mention, officially, of the need for prices control. It appears to be assumed that if there are national guidelines established for setting profit levels – and in fact there have been none – and if desired productivity levels are attained, then price levels will automatically come out 'right' for goods and services. But it is difficult to see how an incomes policy without some form of official price regulation, which goes beyond appeals for reasonable or complementary restraint, can be acceptable, as coherent and comprehensive, by an astutely-led labour force. Further, it would appear that any incomes policy that won the approval of labour on those grounds would be most likely to contradict fundamental, free market economic principles.

For the very notion of a "more market-driven economic environment" would seem, for example, to rule out controls restricting profit margins. Indeed, this would run completely counter to the traditional domestic savings/capital accumulation and investment attraction strategy of IMF stabilization and structural adjustment programmes: a redistribution of income from wage to profit earners.

Effective implementation of any kind of profit control mechanism would probably present insurmountable problems, in any event, given the well-established predisposition of the population, on a whole, to excel at finding ways of 'beating the system'. The level of ingenuity and innovativeness displayed in attempts to circumvent United States visa requirements, local customs regulations and anti-drugs provisions, for example, makes it virtually impossible to predict success in the implementation of profit restriction provisions in a business environment notorious, in general, for its moral and ethical indifference.

As long as the cost of capital remains very high and the local currency continues its downward trend, policy makers must accordingly act to prioritize attention measures for inflation control.

One of those persisting in stating the need for wage restraint/incomes policy was Headley Brown, Governor of the Central Bank from 1985 to 1989, who was a casualty, given the nature of party politics and despite the theme of continuity, of the change of political party administration after the general election of 1989.

For Brown, as for many who see the economy and the results of its functioning from an almost chillingly technical perspective, even when employment is the subject under discussion, "... labour costs generally, unconstrained by wage guidelines, accelerated in 1991-92 as unions sought to catch up with inflation,"[24]

Despite the absence of any conclusive evidence that in the 1990's the wage factor has been the principal or even one of the major causes of cost-push inflation, nevertheless, by implication, the blame for any inflationary spiral is clearly being placed on aggressive trade union activity. There is no indication that incomes policy, to those of this orientation, must necessarily contain any element of 'social justice' or of 'sharing the cost of adjustment', or of allocating the benefits according to any 'principle of distributive justice'. Incomes policy for them, is little more than naked wage restraint. Restraint from this perspective is effectively limited to public sector and unionized private sector workers at the lower occupational levels: precisely those among the employed who have been most severely impoverished by social service expenditure cuts, the introduction of user fees and cost sharing, the removal of subsidies, increases in consumption tax, and inflation in general.[25]

Although the effects of interest rates (above fifty percent at times), the massive increases in utility charges, and, above all, the 'pass through' effect of substantial, continuous devaluations on prices, are mentioned by Brown, the primary solution for inflation control is nevertheless still seen as wage restraint. Indeed, the upward movement in wages is blamed for negating the, "... inducement to export expansion",[26] which, it is assumed, would apparently have otherwise inevitably followed exchange rate adjustments.

Production rigidities, as a constraint in the response to price incentives to increase exports, have been completely ignored; so has the factor of the abnormally high import content of Jamaican exports: raw materials, energy, spares, machinery; and so too has the problem of identification of, gaining access to, and efficiently servicing export markets in an. increasing competitive international trading environment.

While Brown has no hesitation in proposing wage restraint/incomes policy to curb inflation, he has no such ready and easy prescription for dealing with the phenomenon of negative job creation in a situation of a declining labour force participation rate. His contribution, in this regard, is restricted to the descriptive: the changes in the employment/unemployment situation being viewed as, "... depressingly unimpressive."[27]

As against the preoccupation with wage restraint as the essence of incomes policy, Stone's departure is reflective of that balanced concern without which the notion of a social contract is destined to remain just one more item on a "wish list". In his treatment of the problem, the "need" for incomes policy is generalized: "... all economies need income policies which try to ensure an adequate rate of return to labour and capital so as to provide incentives and motivation for production and increased productivity".[28]

The narrow view traditionally taken of incomes policies has already been exposed. Some of the broader aims that are possible, and which are at the same time possibly contradictory, and even objectionable, deserve mention:

(a) by encouraging the use of profits for new investment or the expansion of existing operations by the provision of appropriately designed incentives; such incentives may be partially tied to the solution of basic economic and social problems, such as the degree of employment creation, earning or saving of foreign exchange, the use of local raw materials, and the geographical location of industry;

(b) inflation control by way of voluntary (institutionalized) restraint on wages, price increases and profit levels; or

(c) officially enforced profits/price stabilization by controls and regulated wage levels by thorough guidelines or norms of one form or another;

(d) the deliberate creation of a low-wage labour market, with a view to attracting increased investment, improving the competitiveness of exports and thereby increasing employment;

(e) the creation of a sense of equity, social justice, public morality – however called – so as to make the road to consensus-achievement smoother, thus enhancing the effectiveness of policy formulation and implementation.

But a not unfamiliar problem in the design of an incomes policy, in developing countries such as Jamaica, is that of the existence, timely availability, and reliability of data.

Detailed statistics on profits and price movements, and wages for different job categories by sector, for the wholesale/retail trade are not officially collected. This, as much as ignorance of other countries' experiences with incomes policy experiments, explains the crude nature of the wage guidelines which have been attempted. Lack of political will, coupled with the failure to accurately anticipate and provide for the consequences of policy, including the need for adequate resources for effective enforcement, has also discredited what was meant to be important aspects of an incomes policy which would contribute to greater working-class acceptance, such as rent control legislation, personal income tax relief and increased public housing provision.

As an example, it is scandalous that for some time now it is only members of the middle class who have been able to afford houses purportedly built for low-income earners in the National Housing Trust schemes, which was originally conceived as a *quid pro quo* element of a prospective social contract.[29]

Under the 1990-95 National Development Plan,[30] the targeted inflation rate for 1990/91 was 16.5%, with the goal being an eventual reduction to single digit levels. The Government intended to apply, "… from time-to-time … appropriate fiscal and monetary policies supported by the application of wage guidelines". Although the guidelines have been lifted, the public has not been informed, through Parliament or otherwise, of the consequential modification to the Five-Year Plan that this will entail. There was, too, the Plan's promise that monetary or fiscal policies will be, "… adjusted in response to *actual* [italics added] price movements and the need to maintain international competitiveness". The implication here is clearly that, as a matter of policy choice, prices, except for labour, are beyond control.

Repeated failure to contain inflation to the targeted levels has not only put pressure on wages but raises the important question as to whether any policy of incomes restraint, based on a nationally applicable guideline, is at all defensible.

The macro-economic polices geared to increasing investment, exports, and the creation of an efficient import substitution development model have all failed to materialize. This failure has largely been due to grossly excessive interest rates, the effect of devaluation on the cost of inputs into the production of exports, production rigidities, problems of market access, and competition from cheap, sometimes subsidized, imports facilitated under the IMF and World Bank import liberalization measures. Cuts in the budget deficit has also meant that neither the social nor economic infrastructure have been progressively enhanced.[31] And, of course, as the experience of the NIC's amply demonstrates, spectacular industrial development is facilitated by priority state attention to infrastructural investment.

While, therefore, the Productivity Council was expected to spearhead an innovation and productivity drive, we find such institutional arrangements being neutralized by the effects of monetary policy in stifling investment, and therefore causing the deferment of the technological upgrading and modernization of industry contemplated by the Plan.[32]

The relevance of the state of technology for incomes policy may not be immediately apparent to those whose focus is on enterprise bargaining. It is easy to lose sight of the fact that in a situation where production statistics and wage data is late, incomplete, unreliable, or even just not available, it becomes even more important that absolute priority be placed on technological advancement. The figures on labour productivity mentioned in the Five-Year Plans show, a decline, on average, of 2% per year between 1980-88, which would be moderated by the Plan's implementation to a level of 1.5% per annum. Alternatively, a moderate increase of 1% per year between 1989-94 – assuming success of the technological upgrading, modernization and investment policies – could mean that what might be reported and taken for a successful outcome could easily, in fact, be really failure, given the minimal room for any margin of error in the data.[33]

In addition to the problem of data constraints, the formulation of a more than rudimentary Prices and Incomes Policy is made less than easy by the uncertainty generated by wide fluctuations in interest rates and the exchange rate. With respect to the latter, Jefferson lists eight different mechanisms utilized up to 1991, noting that, "... almost every permutation and combination of available systems have been employed at some time."[34]

If worker protest, with potential as a revolutionary force, is time and situationally determined,[35] then Michael Foot's comments as to the opportunities for significant social reform (by the British Labour Party) are more readily understood. He informs that,

> "One such initiative and one such moment was in the winter of 1974, just after the election victory, when we had the chance … to launch the only kind of Incomes policy which could have worked; a much fairer, more egalitarian policy than anything subsequently attempted, *starting at the top*", [italics added].[36]

Working class response to incomes policy proposals will be determined not by government's convenient "flight from reality into statistics", which, "… detracts attention from the broader aims of economic policy and tends [particularly with preoccupation with passing quantitative IMF performance tests] to become a substitute for them".[37] Its response will more likely be moulded according to the general mood and impressions as to the state of the economy derived from intra-class communication and from the media, as well as upon "direct changes of individual well-being that result from changes of employment or income or prices".[38]

The modern British experience with wage control coincides with the special conditions of World War II, which saw an "enormous extension of the area of wage regulation", with provision for settlement of claims by the National Arbitration Tribunal, in the event bilateral negotiations between employers and their associations and trade unions failed to result in an agreement. The extreme risks to survival as a distinct sovereign nation, posed by the threat of invasion, was enough to justify even direct reference of wage issues to the Government or the Department concerned,[39] for determination.

Fortunate to be deprived of the 'benefit' of that kind of stimulus, Jamaica's recent experience has been for any past tendency for the relative income gap to narrow to have been put very contentiously into reverse.[40] Since the early 1980's, under IMF/JLP free market dogma, that retrogression has, dubiously, been made conventionally respectable, with labels such as 'pragmatic', 'non-ideological', and 'the rules of the game'.

The conclusion is unavoidable. The attempt to enforce wage and price guidelines – whether by conservatives such as Heath and Nixon or the radical Michael Manley, following extensive debate over incomes policy – succeeded in exacerbating the income inequalities. The deepened and increased spread of poverty was to such an extent as to compel the World Bank's attention in the second half of the 1980's. For economists on the right, the lesson that was there to be learned, as to the "undesirable" consequences of "the overriding of market forces" and the alleged failure to analyse inflation correctly, was that Keynesianism needed to be overthrown.[41]

On the diagnosis of this anti-Keynesian development counter-revolution, in which Lal was a principal spokesman,[42] one of the major reasons for poor economic performance in developing countries was the extension of state regulation into almost every facet of economic life. Yet it is notable in Jamaica that the more progress was made with the removal of price controls, the more insistent the calls from certain quarters for some form of wage regulation – whatever the form of the 'ideological disguise' in which they have been clothed.

Downes, et al., recommend that for a small open economy, the policy implications of their study of the wage/price and productivity relationship, in Barbados, seem to be: firstly, the need to take action to 'accommodate' the effects of imported inflation by the application of selected price controls in the short run; and secondly, designing a wages policy which takes account of the influence of wages rate movements on prices and the effect of increases in productivity on wages.[43]

The two glaring omissions in this approach to the wages and prices relationship are, on the one hand, the complete failure to explicitly consider other forms of income, apart from wages, and on the other dimension of the vicious circle: the effect of price increases, past, current, and anticipated, on wages. It might have been expected that despite the traditional view of development economists which holds that, "... wages are too high and are rising too fast, relative to prices and productivity to enable the growth of output to facilitate the development process",[44] that view would by now have been sufficiently discredited, by the rebellion mounted by the facts[45] of hardship, hunger, and poverty. Downes, et al., might therefore have been expected to feel compelled to argue for progressive redistribution as an essential prerequisite to working class acceptance of any sacrificial wages policy proposal.

Further, an expansionary, rather than a demand compression policy to stimulate growth, would establish the economic foundation for that feeling of optimism and buoyancy in which the productivity related non-economic human relations variables are more likely to flourish.[46] This should create a climate more conducive to that spirit of cooperation which would facilitate incomes policy acceptance, particularly where there is a mechanism which strongly relates wages to productivity, and which forces attention to productivity-enhancing factors, other than labour's effort.

The functions of an incomes policy, as seen by Demas, are not only that of keeping prices low, "as far as is economically feasible", but also to cut down on wide and increasing income differentials within countries. Further, to his credit, he gives the additional reason that the richer foreign and local companies can thus be made to pay their fair share of taxes.[47] He might well have added, with respect to almost every category of enterprise operations, in the Jamaican context, "as far as is administratively possible". This would have taken into account the phenomenon of 'transfer pricing' by multi-national firms and the penchant for 'beating the system' by members of the local entrepreneurial class. With the limited attempts at the formulation of prices and incomes policy – the latter half of the 1970's not excluded – it is not difficult to position the Jamaican experience within the range from "intermittent recourse to weak devices which scarcely amount to a coherent system, to strong and comprehensive ... systems". Those features of weak systems listed by Gorina,[48] which may be said to have constituted elements of the local experiments over the years, appear to be the following:

(a) government exhortation on wage and price developments, in the attempt to influence collective bargaining processes

(b) policies to determine national legal minimum wages, and more recently,

(c) national economic goals for mainly working-class incomes, and prices – without the establishment of criteria for enterprise wage and price decisions.

Absent, significantly, have been: sustained attempts to curb abuses of economic power by direct sectoral intervention, in keeping with national overall economic/industrial policy priorities in income and price market determination mechanisms – (there have not even been functioning employment, i.e. recruitment, services at the Ministry of Labour offices). Neither have there been reliable frameworks for the analysis and forecasting of income and price changes in the economy, except for politicized projections as to the expected rate of inflation; and surprisingly – within the last two decades under the free market philosophy – no consistent policies to affect, *indirectly*, general price and wage movements through *market* adjustments.

Stone enumerates several requirements, which deserve quotation at length, that are considered essential for a new approach to incomes policy formulation, among them being:[49]

1. The collection of relevant income data, sector by sector, especially in those activities in which the cost of labour as a percentage of the total cost of production is high. [One would add that for wage planning, or informed negotiating purposes, data needs to be timely, but also, should best include all forms of income, earned and unearned, and price and productivity statistics.]

2. In line with the thinking of trade unions represented by the JTURDC[50] the anti-inflationary emphasis should be countered by equal concern for fostering increased production and growth and thereby generating additional employment- opportunities.

3. Inflation control through effective fiscal, monetary and exchange rate management so as to check the erosion of real wages and living standards, thus improving the chances of a more positive employer, trade union, and working-class response to policy proposals.

4. Instead of incentives being provided for the establishment of new businesses (primarily in the export sector) they should be broadened to cater to existing businesses involved in major plant, equipment and systems upgrading, [bearing in mind the existence of idle capacity and the United States experience that substantial productivity growth comes usually from technological advances.][51]

5. Comprehensive and accurate data collection to measure the effect of incomes policy, in the short, medium, and long term, on incomes, profits, productivity, prices and employment, [important for monitoring performance and facilitating necessary corrective action.]

6. The attempt at a tripartite approach to incomes policy design and development, rather than one imposed by government. [Policy design on a sectoral basis has yet to be contemplated.]

7. Finally, the depoliticization of money supply, [as treated by Blackman, with the objective of reducing Government/Central Bank created inflation].[52]

The JTURDC has indeed challenged the assertion by the Government in the *Draft Outlines of Social Contract/Understanding, 1993*, to the effect that,

> "... the discussion among the social partners involved the setting of the economic targets, choosing the policy instruments, and quantifying

their magnitudes to reach the targets.[53] The desirable balances between real income, consumption and investment, the desirable level of prices, international reserves, exchange rate (sic) are policy objectives that were agreed among the partners".[54]

It seems evident that consultation and communication is less than efficient.

One role of an effectively functioning state, in Okun's view, is to use some variant of anti-trust regulations and/or incomes policy to restrain wage acceleration and price mark-up widening, brought about by the exercise of monopoly/cartel power. In the case of trade unions, the "danger of adverse economic consequences" would, in itself, be more of a deterrent if the entire labour force were unionized; there would obviously be greater overlapping of the status of union member and consumer/citizen, and a greater sharing of the social costs of the action of the major power wielding groups.[55] This is clearly not the case here, given the low level of unionization and consumer consciousness in Jamaica. there are those who expect that incomes policies can be operated without friction, although the disturbance of established practices of wage emulation and wage relativities, " ... fondly cherished by personnel managers and other practitioners in the area of industrial relations",[56] is more often than not, their direct consequence. Avoidance of this kind of problem would require a degree of design sophistication and detail elaboration undoubtedly beyond the state bureaucracy's administrative capability. This is likely to be the case, especially given the budgetary constraints involving substantial public-sector staff retrenchment under IMF stabilization programmes.

This observation holds true, one suspects, for that aspect: of the early wage policy of the latter half of the 1970's which came into effect on March 1, 1976. Under those provisions only those pay increases which conformed to the guidelines were allowed as expenses, for the purposes of the determination of employer income tax liability. Beating the tax system is an activity for which all levels of the society in Jamaica are notorious. It is highly unlikely that there was the effective monitoring that would have required detailed and expert examination of wage data and accounting statements, for even this limited purpose.

Contrary to the voluntarist British tradition,[57] under which has evolved the preference for self-imposed, or at least consensual, restraint, Okun would rather place reliance on legislative provisions as a means of eliciting greater compliance with a policy of wage and price control.[58]

With respect to this question of the role of the state, the adoption of an incomes policy was once thought to rest essentially on the decision as to whether the state's significant involvement in the labour market – in fixing national minimum wages, through its disputes settlement machinery, and also its price regulation role – should continue on an ad hoc, or be coordinated on a systematic basis.[59] With the virtually complete absence of price intervention under the IMF/World Bank policy of minimum state control and economic regulation, what is in effect left for state action in this segment of the policy arena is 'inflation control'. This to many of the less than adequately informed, particularly those in the relatively privileged classes, is simply a matter of restraining wages.

The only global objective sought to be explicitly achieved under the IMF guidelines was control of the rate of increase of wages. There was neither a target set for the general level of wages nor any planned change in their structure.[60] The result of this blinkered approach has been the data-supported allegations of the Haitianization of the cost of Jamaican labour, concurrent with concerns for the trade and employment consequences of a 'high' wage economy, where continuing 'excessive' wage demands, in both the public and private sector, is the: norm.

What has also been lacking is any emphasis on a projected increase in Gross National Product, per capita, adjusted for price movements, as a guide to wage adjustment decisions.[61] Neither did the crudity of IMF guidelines allow for discrimination in favour of the lowest levels of wages, as an expression of concern for meeting the majority's basic needs,[62] excepting under Ministry Paper No.23 of 1979.

And it most certainly has not been the case that priority has, instead, been directed to the generation of mass productive employment for the under, and unemployed, as against increasing the real incomes of those fortunate enough to already have jobs.

Traditionally, the exception to the. implementation of wage policy, which ensures that money wages keep abreast of price movements, has been in periods of economic crisis, characterized by hyper-inflation and/or rapidly accelerating and serious balance of payments disequilibrium. It was a notable feature of the IMF guidelines that in such exceptional circumstances the objective pursued was in direct opposition to that of "an equitable sharing of the sacrifices." As TABLE 16 indicates, income was distributed away from the working class for virtually' the entire period.[63]

The failure to integrate wages policy into any well thought out national development plan, grounded in an appropriate consensus-based[64] industrial policy, has meant that there has been no attempt to incorporate features into the policy on incomes which would serve a labour allocative function.[65] Some five years after the removal of wage guidelines, the Minister of Industry, Commerce and Investment was expressing concern about the continuing incidence of rural-urban migration and the need for policy to reverse the trend.[66]

It should, against such a background, be expected, perhaps, that recent awards of the IDT have lent support to the proposition that attempts by government to influence collective bargaining wage results represent the, "... most, controversial aspects of prices and incomes policies".[67]

In one case (UAWU vs Desnoes & Geddes Ltd) the union's Vice President declared the Tribunal to be "the enemy of the working class", while another union leader vowed "never (to) appear before the IDT again while I am alive". This reaction was aroused by the IDT's award which was below the company's offer, which the union had previously rejected.[68]

In the case of the Jamaica Teachers Association's claim for an increase of 150%, the increases awarded over two years by the IDT were exactly in keeping with the maximum that Government spokesmen had long claimed that the Government was able to pay, which was 16% in year one and 14% in year two.[69] This "Award" coinciding with the Governments' "final offer", as it turned out, was not confined to the teachers' claim but was applied, without significant adjustment, to the public sector generally.

The very prolonged, and at times, emotional and acrimonious teachers' pay negotiations and dispute, involving the burning of the normally relatively popular Minister of Education's effigy at one point, had extensive coverage in both daily newspapers, The Daily Gleaner and The Jamaica Herald over the 1994/95 period. From all indications, the public was predominantly sympathetic to the teachers' cause, despite media saturation with, and Parliamentary exposure of the Government's considered and fully-argued position. This episode seems to have answered the question as to who is, if not who should be, the final arbiter on industrial relations issues with sufficient fiscal consequences to have major national budgetary importance.

Table: 16   National Income and Wages 1974 - 1992

Year	National Disposable Income ('000)	Compensation Employees ('000)	Compensation % of National Disposable
1974	2035.2	1170.2	57.5
1975	2408.7	1450.2	60.2
1976	2380.6	1531.0	64.3
1977	2589.6	1653.1	63.8
1978	3266.3	1942.5	59.5
1979	3750.4	2181.2	58.1
1930	4154.7	2426.5	58.4
1981	4726.7	2733.4	57.8
1982	5256.8	3156.0	60.0
1983	6508.3	3573.1	54.9
1984	8041.0	4399.1	54.7
1985	10000.7	4906.9	49.1
1986	11949.3	5768.3	48.3
1987	13875.7	6971.6	54.2
1988	18444.1	8221.3	44.6
1989	20908.2	10231.1	48.9
1990	26100.3	13043.3	49.9
1991	37457.5	18869.0	50.3
1992	65750.0	30231.7	45.9

In opposition to the trade union view, it can however be argued that with the efficacious selection of fiscal and monetary measures supported by prices and incomes policies formulated to confront the nation's priority problems in a manner consistent with addressing the problems faced by labour, the cost of bringing about changes in economic performance can be reduced. It has also been suggested that of an appropriate wage policy, and the establishment of the attendant institutional arrangements, are a means of reconciling the practice of collective bargaining with the requirements of development policy,[70] But an ever-important question, often ignored by the ruling elite and its agents, should be, of course, "development policy" for whose benefit?

Source: STATIN

Brown, in 1978, observed that, "… it is important that there be a mechanism which ensures that some of the results of pay restraint are passed on in moderate price increases".[71] But given the difficulty of policing the pricing process and the weakness of administrative capability, it is hardly surprising that prior to price de-control there was no evidence of the operation of any such mechanism. Eighteen years later, the proposal for a Social Partnership is presented on the same level of generality: "The Private Sector", one is told, "is expected to play a role in increasing efficiency and lowering domestic costs";[72] and further, that "Production gains should be shared in terms of reduced prices and wage increases".[73]

In somewhat similar vein, in the 1991 Observations on ILO Convention No.98, the ILO Committee of Experts on the question of the Application of Conventions and Recommendations, is reported as having reminded the Government of Peru that:

> "… if wage rates cannot be fixed freely by collective bargaining because of economic stabilization or structural adjustment policies, such restrictions should be imposed only as an exceptional measure, *and* only to the extent necessary without exceeding a *reasonable* [italics added] period. They should be accompanied by adequate safeguards to protect workers living standards[74] … (to be implemented through consensus) rather than by unilateral imposition".[75]

The final sentiment expressed by the Committee of Experts clearly has implications for Minimum Wage administration. If the safety net is such that too many fall through or, put another way, a minimum wage level that is too far below the average earnings of the lowest paid groups is likely to further harm those intended as its beneficiaries. On the other hand, if the minimum is too high, given the state of the labour market, further unemployment could obviously be a direct conse¬quence. TABLE 17 would seem to indicate that, although the JLP's slogan at the last general election was that " It takes cash to care", the beneficiaries of minimum wage legislation have done better under the party with the image of caring more about the poor since the 1979's, the PNP. This impression is, however, put into perspective by the data in FIG. 20, which relates the minimum wage to movements in inflation for the period of JLP rule, 1980 – 1989 as against the current term of the PNP administration which began in 1989; the relatively large increase since 1991/92 has clearly been to the advantage of those whose pay is set relative to the statutory minimum. The full picture is however only revealed by FIG. 21.

Table: 17	Minimum Wage		
	Effective Date	Weekly($)	Hourly($)
	November 2, 1975	20	0.50
PNP	February 5, 1978	24	0.60
	August 6, 1979	26.40	0.66
	June 16, 1980	30	0.75
	July 16, 1984	46/40	1.15/1.00
JLP	January 7, 1985	60/52	1.50/1.30
	June 6, 1988	80/72	2.00/1.80
	January 2, 1989	100/8 4	2.50/2.10
	June 4, 1990	130/110	3.25/2.75
PNP	July 1, 1991	160/140	4.00/3.50
	July 6, 1992	300	7.50
	July 4, 1994	500	12.50

Note: General/Household (minimum rate)
Source: Dawn Johnson, The Financial Gleaner, May 24, 1996, p.2.

Figure: 20

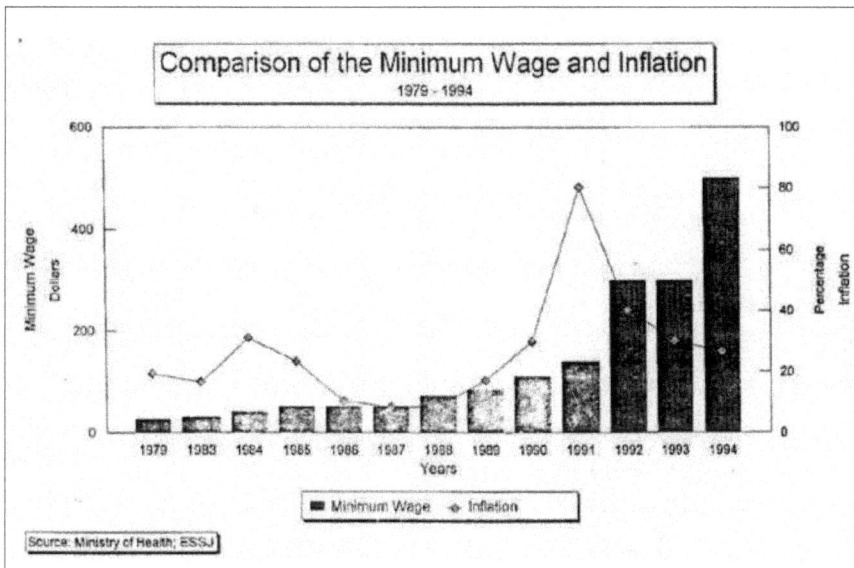

Comparison of the Minimum Wage and Inflation
1979 - 1994

Source: Ministry of Health; ESSJ

Figure: 21

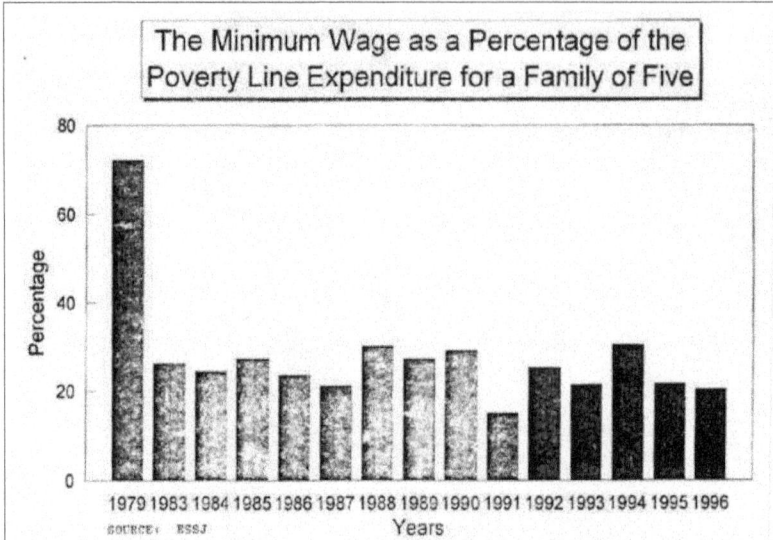

The Minimum Wage as a Percentage of the Poverty Line Expenditure for a Family of Five

With respect to the more general issue of consensus-based incomes policies,[76] it has been held that "social concertation in the 1980's[77] has been easier, not surprisingly, where the governing party has had traditionally close links with a trade union movement that is not split along partisan or ideological lines"[78] Also well known, are the examples of the United Kingdom, where there has existed the traditionally close relationship between the Labour Party[79] and the union movement and in Australia between the Australian Labour Party and the Australian Confederation of Trade Unions (ACTU).

It is perhaps the combination of co-optation of trade union officers plus Governments' attempt at control by gentle coercion/moral suasion which has had negative consequences for the relationship between unions and their members in terms of trust and confidence. This is especially so under IMF World Bank austerity policies, calling, as- they invariably do, for sacrifices by the working class and those already poor. It is this which partly provides an explanation for the growing relative independence of unions from direct political affiliation and influence.[80] At the same time, such a development facilitates incomes policy negotiation and formulation, with increased labour movement unity and the increased prospect of labour leadership participation in economic policy discussions at the national level.

Given the tradition of extreme political polarization, party-specific individual union affiliation and intense inter-union rivalry,[81] the IMF nevertheless, under the agreement of 1978, pressed for action in achieving a social contract, embracing the government and the political opposition, unions, farmers, professionals and the private sector, in the interest of maximizing production.[82] An essential aspect of this contract was to be a further reduction in the size of the budget in real terms, 'crowding in' of the private sector, and the restriction of both wage and price movements to 10%, replacing the unilateral restraint on wages in a context of high inflation.[83]

The trade unions aggressively resisted the guidelines, what with the intense competition for members, and for other member welfare-related reasons. This naturally resulted in a high level of strike activity.

The result was the expansion of the powers of the Minister of Labour to refer disputes to the IDT for arbitration, under a 1978 amendment of the LRIDA, which powers were to be in frequent use[84] from then on.

This development provides a good example of the function of law – not just generally, in terms of the entrenchment of the interests of property in the legal system, but in relation to specific legislation – as a means of class control and for protecting the position of the hegemonic economic and social elite, by preserving the fundamental class relations in the society through institutional arrangements. The supreme irony is that this particular statute, the LRIDA, was heralded as bestowing fundamental rights on the working class.

Islanders have been regarded as tending to suffer from a self-imposed limitation on the range of options or models from which they make a selection for internal policy application.[85] This is an inhibition which does not apply to Jamaica when it is a matter of keeping up with the latest trends in fashion, gadgets and novelties. Bearing this predisposition in mind, it was interesting to learn of reference to the possible relevance of the Australian experience, under their "Accords", to recent and current Jamaican industrial relations problems and concerns, central among which are the twin issues of wages and prices.

The main elements of the seven Accords to date, as outlined by Senator Cooke of Australia,[86] indicate the comprehensive nature of the agreements[87] and, equally importantly, the adaptability displayed in responding to macroeconomic changes – changes themselves dictated by a reaction to, and in anticipation of, developments in the international capitalist economy. From a highly centralized wage fixing system[88] directly linked to the level of prices, there has been a major departure to what is regarded as 'managed' decentralization, with an enterprise-level productivity orientation.

A conspicuous feature of all the Accords, and the factor which has, without doubt, accounted for their unusually lengthy survival – apart from the quite important fact of the close affinity between the Australian Labour Party and the trade union movement – is the all-important recognition of the essential requirement, often overlooked or down-played by Jamaican commentators, of what, in the Law of Contract, is called "valuable consideration",[89] or *quid pro quo*. This notion entails the exchange of promises to do or refrain from doing acts, or of the conferment of benefit or reward by either party, perceived as sufficiently attractive to justify the compromise or sacrifice involved in the "bargain".

The first Accord agreement, Mark I, between the Australian Labour Party government and the ACTU in 1983, sought to deal with the problems of inflation and unemployment, while restoring profit levels and promoting the social wage.[90] This agreement provided for the maintenance of real wages through full wage indexation,[91] established the Prices Surveillance Authority, introduced Medicare, and included income tax reform with the objective of easing the burden on low and middle-income earners.

With the fall in the value of the Australian dollar, Accord Mark II of 1985 aimed at insulating wages from the effects of devaluation,[92] by providing personal tax cuts and employer-funded super-annuation in exchange for a one-off 2% discounting of the CPI-wage indexation increase, due the following year. It is important to note that after-tax real disposable incomes were protected.

The principle of productivity-based wage movements, signifying a move towards the establishment of a productivity culture, was accepted in Accord Mark III of March 1987. This agreement marked the end of formal indexation, as greater labour market flexibility was pursued in the interest of increasing the country's international competitiveness in response to adverse trade consequences flowing from global market changes.

Under Accord Mark IV, the "structural efficiency" principle was established, as a central element in wage formation, with the objective of rewarding unions[93] and workers for cooperating in the reform of, "… the highly specialized award regulation of the work process to encourage multi-skilling and to try to minimize demarcation disputes".[94s]

Pay increases were made available under the system proposed by the Australian Industrial Relations Commission to workers represented by unions which gave a commitment to, "… a fundamental review of the industrial awards with a view to implementing measures to improve efficiency and provide workers with access to more varied, fulfilling, and better-paid jobs." This later became known as "award restructuring".

The current agreement, Accord VII which covers the period March 1993 to March 1996, therefore represents the culmination of a process of adaptation and modification, reflecting learning by experience and the changes in the national economic and social context, as affected by external financial, economic and trade developments.

Looking at the agreements of more recent times, the Accord Mark V, in 1989, was intended to secure wage restraint, while providing improvements in real disposable income. It was based on a combination of moderate wage increases, substantial cuts in personal income tax,[95] and improvements in the social wage.

The Accord of February 1999, Mark VI, amended in November of the same year, emphasized the restructuring of the award system in the direction of enterprise level pay settlements. Incorporated in this agreement was a wage-tax-superannuation trade-off, together with a $12 pay rise, applicable from May 1991, an 'equal pay' understanding,[96] as well as lower inflation and productivity enhancement aspects.

The breadth of coverage of social issues of concern, not just to the working class, *per se*, but the poorer sections of the population, generally; the inherent principle of review, flexibility, and adaptation; together with clear specification of policy objectives are features deserving of careful consideration. These features may be compared with the Jamaican Government's proposal, *Towards Developing a Social Partnership*.

In contrast to the official spirit of the Australian arrangements, Panton appears to have identified a dubious benefit from the Jamaican guideline strategy: that of widening the large income gap between the formal and informal sectors.[97]

It could be persuasively argued that instead of the spreading of poverty represented by this development, what would have been more equitable was policy innovation to increase the level of earnings of workers in the informal sector and the small scale self-employed – the largest growing segments of the labour force under the structural adjustment regime.

But governments in capitalist economies rarely pursue pro-working-class policies, except under the influence of electoral or other duress. Venner's sentiments, now typical of the New Right, that, "... the dependence of the citizen on the state has become virtually parasitic ..."[98] while not novel, begs the question: what resources does the state possess that are not merely the accumulated contribution of its citizens? The identification of the wages and prices questions as, 'the most critical public-sector issue at this time', could predictably, with such a perspective, be expected to result in state action biased in favour of prices and, by extension, those who benefit most from their deregulation.

In fact, Harrigan concludes that both the PNP and JLP regimes' strongest area of policy disagreement and resistance to the IMF was that of the use of currency devaluation as a mechanism for achieving a low-wage economy that was expected to lead to heightened international competitiveness and the attraction of foreign direct investments. But with the devastating fall in real incomes, anyway,[99] one is left to ponder what the fall would have been had there been enthusiastic compliance[100] by the political directorates.

By comparison, the Barbadian Protocol[101] sought to defend the exchange rate so as to protect the living standards of the majority. A general income freeze at all organizational levels was called for in both the. public and private sectors, including fringe benefits, except in areas where pay was deemed to be sub-standard by the three parties to the industrial relations system. It further sought to establish an environment which "would bring Barbados' goods and services into a more competitive position at home and abroad," by imposing restraints on wages and "other compensation payments", as well as prices.

The restructuring of the Barbadian economy on a more sustainable basis was expected to proceed on the principle of greater capital and labour involvement in the planning process. Attraction of foreign investment was made to depend, not only on the wage policy, but, also, "the promotion of a national commitment to improved productivity and increased efficiency".

The policy, effective from April 1, 1993 to March 31, 1995, should see increases in wages and salaries – outside the agreed sub-standard areas – solely on the basis of profit-sharing arrangements or productivity bonuses, "based on the assessment of profitability". Monopoly pricing on the other hand was to be kept under review by a monitoring committee made up of the social partners, "so that increases may be limited to legitimate cost increases".

Major inherently contradictory provisions were that consideration would immediately be given to "indexing wage adjustments and tax allowances to increases in the cost of living and, despite the wage freeze (and indeed salary cut), the declaration that "collective bargaining will still be maintained within the period to address conditions of work, as well as the sharing of productivity gains".

Review provisions are contained in section 7.1, subject to the important proviso that "any decision taken to further the objectives of this protocol shall be unanimous."

Highly significantly, from the comparative Jamaican perspective, it was recognized at the outset that the climate for a Prices and Incomes Policy must be based on mutual respect [which is hardly amenable to legislation] and on a clearly definable national commitment to,

(a) Protect workers' security of tenure [without any specification of the intended mechanism)

(b) Reduced labour disputes [the provision triggered a two-day national strike and protest and led to the ultimate demise of the Prime Minister and later his party's defeat at the polls]

(c) changing labour terms and conditions only if this "assists in effecting the long-term improvements in the conditions of those employed and [italics added] create jobs for the unemployed,"

(d) the pursuit of full and adequate information sharing on matters relevant to proposed labour market changes.

With the change of Government, subsequent to these reforms, wage cuts and freezes were prohibited by Constitutional amendment. This the first Vice President of the Jamaica Civil Service Association thought unnecessary for Jamaica, since "we have always had players in the labour movement high up in the Government". Massive real wage decline under wage guidelines and devaluations seemed to have been placed by this worker representative in a quite different policy arena,[102] apparently beyond the sphere of influence of co-opted labour leaders.

An assistant Island Supervisor of the NWU, Vincent Morrison, reacted to the Barbadian development to the effect that "Jamaica's politicians are more sensitive of labour's contribution to the economy…" and, in any event, it is claimed that Jamaica's industrial relations climate "is much more mature".

For Morrison, a 30% wage award to civil servants, over two years, with inflation at a high 20% level, obviously does not qualify as an effective wage cut.

What appears little short of heresy is put forward as feasible for Jamaica, as against sub-Sahara Africa: that,

> "… the potential exists for a coalition in the form of the agricultural sector, exporters, the unemployed and those in weakly unionized sectors to fight for real wage reductions [italics added] in selected sectors of the economy and for the continued removal of rents and subsidies which have given rise to highly skewed income distribution".[103]

In this regard, the JTURDC's focus has been on the relationship between wage guidelines and poverty. As the organization sees it, the following are the important negative consequences[104] of a statutory wage norm:

1. Redistribution of income away from the poor to the asset-owning classes.

2. Deterioration of health and nutritional standards as real disposable income declines.

3. Decreased employment generation, due to compression of demand, resulting in a less than optimum level of national savings (see FIG. 22)

4. Worsening rural/urban migration.

5. Increased outward migration some have, on the contrary, seen this as a principal economic strategy i.e. exporting people.[105]

Figure: 22

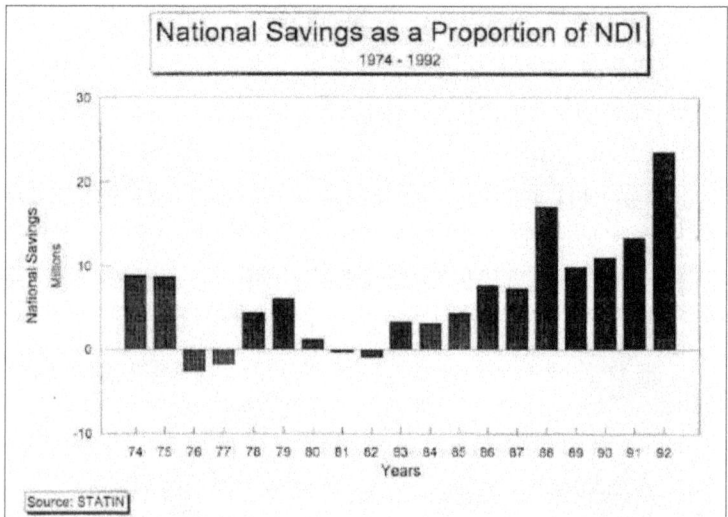

National Savings as a Proportion of NDI
1974 - 1992

Source: STATIN

For the period 1974-90, the JTURDC observed that both National Income and National Disposable Income reflected, "… the general excoriation of incomes available to the wider population", with an average change in percentage terms of some 0.86% with respect to the former and with the latter moving in a similar direction.[106]

The decline in labour's share in the surplus is shown in TABLE 13 and FIG. 23

Table: 18	Wages as % of GDP		
1974-77	1970-82	1983-87	1988-9
56	49	44	47

Source: STATIN

The redistributive effect of guidelines enabled the top 10% of income earners to enjoy an average consumption that was 17 times that of the bottom 10% whose consumption was only 1.9% of the total.[107]

Nor has the provision of a safety net for the employed, in the form of an effectively enforce minimum wage machinery, effectively safeguarded the living standard of the poorer sections of the working class from erosion.[108]

As disclosed by TABLE 19, the minimum wage as a percentage of the minimum cost of feeding a family of five has declined from 105% in June 1979 to 36.6% in June 1991. By 1994, the basic food basket cost 410% more than the minimum wages of $300 per week. The worsened situation since 1990 can be seen from TABLE 20.

In workers purchasing power terms, it has been observed by the political opposition that the difference between 1989 and 1992 is reflected by the purchases listed in the endnote being possible with $100 over the two periods.[109]

Reduced budgetary allocation to the social services to satisfy IMF conditionalities has added to the pressure on working-class incomes, constrained by government/IMF wage policy. This is as governments have sought to 'recover the cost' of services by the introduction of 'user fees' and 'cost sharing' in areas as basic to any planned development effort as health, education, and training. The quality of the services for which citizens now have to pay (in addition to their contribution to the budget as tax payers) is likely to suffer seriously from poor maintenance, and the failure to replace and upgrade equipment. But perhaps the worst consequence of all is the demoralization of personnel whose remuneration, limited by unofficial – meaning non-statutory – public sector wage policy, has failed to satisfy the 'betterment factor' expectation and has instead been over-run by inflation, "... the judge and jury of financial policies",[110] according to Nigel Lawson, ex-British Chancellor of the Exchequer. In the Jamaican context, the *exchange rate* is a serious/related rival.

Figure: 23

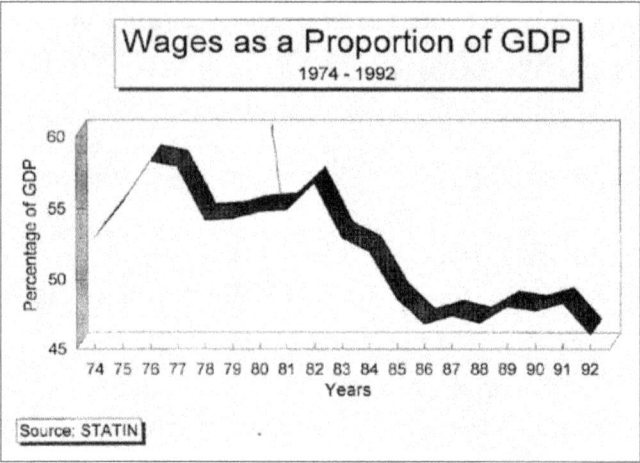

Wages as a Proportion of GDP
1974 - 1992

Source: STATIN

Table:19 Food Costs and Minimum Wage June 1979 - June 1991

Year	Cost of feeding a family of five for a week($)	Minimum Wage($)
Jun. 1979	24.27	26.00
Dec. 1983	77.00	30.00
Aug. 1984	110.00	40.00
Jul. 1985	128.43	52.00
Sep. 1986	148.72	52.00
Dec. 1987	196.60	52.00
Dec. 1988	160.03	72.00
Dec. 1989	207.04	84.00
Mar. 1990	221.67	110.00
Jun. 1990	220.60	110.00
Sep. 1990	239.86	110.00
Dec. 1990	253.34	110.00
Mar. 1991	285.94	110.00
Jun. 1991	382.13	140.00

Source: **Ministry of** Health (reported in The Daily Gleaner, July 22, 1991, p. I.)

Table: 20   Items Which Could be Purchased With J$100

	1989		1992
I pound flour	I chicken		I chicken
I pound cornmeal	I pound salted cod fish		I loaf bread
I pound sugar	I pack crackers		
I pound rice	I soap		
I loaf bread	I toilet tissue		
I bottle cooking oil	I box matches		
I tin milo	Kerosene oil, with change		

Source: Mark A. Wignall, in quoting opposition leader Edward Seaga, in The Jamaica Herald, Nov. 19, 1995, p.7A.

And, of course, guidelines, official or unofficial, adversely affect not just weekly pay, but all benefits calculated on the basis of the current weekly pay rate, such as holiday, sick, and redundancy pay.

As the JTURDC has pointed out, trends in the labour force composition have established that guidelines are not easily applicable to what has been the fastest growing segment, the self-employed and informal sector workforce, which comprised some 38% of the total in 1989.[111]

This further confirms the unscientific, arbitrary nature of this kind of wage policy, in which standards are set without reference to any appropriate economic variable.[112] Indexation to the CPI, as proposed by the JTURDC, while guaranteed popular worker support is not an entirely satisfactory answer.[113] The CPI affects different income groups differently, as the weights given to the items in the basket of basic goods, which itself no doubt needs review, is different for different socio-economic classes.[114]

With the abandonment of CPI-based wage indexation in Australia, in favour of the encouragement of decentralized productivity-related bargaining, the concern for the continued protection of the most vulnerable in the society was sustained by the provision of an award safety net pay increase, currently varying between $8 to $12 for those unable to obtain a raise in pay through localized bargaining.[115]

As has been shown, quite dramatically, with public sector wage negotiations, under any form of wage guidelines – centralized negotiations, under government-controlled wage policy administration through arbitration in the Industrial Disputes Tribunal (IDT) – threatens the independence of trade unions, if not their very existence. But as Henry observes, arbitration properly conducted is in the nature of judicial proceedings.[116] And if the integrity of the system is to be maintained, then impartiality and freedom from external influence must be evident to the participants, if their respect and compliance are to be forthcoming, as confirmed by the judgment in the *Fire Services vs. IDT* case.

At the same time, impartiality is not easily practiced in the context of the economic crisis of capitalism, which usually triggers the search for incomes policies. For the situational logic demands, according to Topham, that local working-class power be curbed on the maximum number of fronts possible, if national policies are to be successfully implemented.[117]

One eagerly awaits the report of the *Eaton Committee on Labour Market Reform*, in view of what appears to be contrasting vested interest expectations, with the trade unions being wary of the attempt to 'discipline' them.[118] This they have vowed to resist. On the other hand, the employers are seeking increased management flexibility in the use of labour,[119] and quicker labour market responsiveness to changed and changing macro-economic circumstances.

It must be admitted as strange, that within a deregulated, free market economic environment, the attempt, through the mechanism of incomes policy, is being made to curb the exercise of bargaining power and the operation of forces conducive to wage movements, whether or not in excess of productivity. Where such pay increases are nevertheless well below the trend in inflation, the paradox of an incomes policy becomes even more conspicuous, in that if it is to gain acceptance by labour, "… it has to make concessions to social justice which may destroy or even reverse its effectiveness".[120]

Whereas Crosland, and others in Britain, argued that an incomes policy, by introducing an element of planning into an otherwise unplanned economy, represented progress towards socialism, that particular illusion was never possible in Jamaica. Guidelines were here introduced as a part of an IMF stabilization package,[121] revolving around the free market ideology.

And the later variants of the policy had, "… nothing to commend it to the unions".[122] Capital benefited, rather than the community or the working class, as income restraint — because of prevailing price setting practices and the state of the consumer goods market — removes "a serious cost pressure from employers and allows them to get by without seriously examining their methods of production".[123]

The factors influencing productivity are yet to be thoroughly investigated from a wage policy perspective, despite rhetoric about productivity and incentive schemes.

It is not impossible that the state of the nation's economy would be healthier if the effort at wage restraint had been diverted to productivity enhancement. Despite the relative abundance of unutilized labour in Jamaica and, in the absence of any substantial demonstrable benefits from the emphasis on the importance of national savings, investment and employment creation, there is scarcely any justification for a policy which encourages and perpetuates inefficiency, by keeping wages low. But then, like the British government of the time, the IMF in Jamaica has encouraged the "pursuit of inequality as a conscious act of social [and economic] policy", the somewhat perverse thinking being that, "... increasing the incomes of the better off, will improve the life chances of the worse off".[124]

As against the Australian Government Senator's favourable portrayal of the major effects of the earlier Australian Accord policies, they have been assessed, in marked contrast, by Watts as being a big increase in unemployment and a consequential rise in the incidence of poverty. He makes the observation that, in 1990,

> "... the commitment to mutual consultation around wage-fixing although battered and bleeding, is still in place if only because the ACTU remains convinced that it can continue to lobby a Labour government to make it behave like one".[125]

Watts has described as, "... the essential contradiction and mystery of the Accord", the self-proclaimed commitment to equity, giving the pursuit of real wage restraint in the interest of encouraging economic growth, as a result of increased capital accumulation and heightened levels of investment, which failed to occur. The results of the Accords, from this angle of vision, are rather strikingly similar to those of structural adjustment and stabilization under the IMF/World Bank in Jamaica, despite the Accords' declared concern with "equity".[126] For despite this concern, to qualify for family allowance benefits there was a means text; for old age benefits, an income test; and for pensions, an assets test. In this scenario, Watts concludes that, "... no category of welfare benefit recipient improved its position (1983-87) in relation to the poverty line".[127]

As against this assessment of the Australian Accords, Miliband regards past incomes policy in Great Britain as, "... a matter of people earning 1000 pounds per month (or more) telling people earning 1000 pounds a year (or less) that they must stop being greedy".[128]

In line with such a sentiment, Colman and Nixson refer to the work of Adelman and Morris (1973), showing that the top 5% received a smaller percentage of total income in countries with a dominant public sector and a large state enterprise sector than in countries where the private sector played the major role. These authors' conclusion was that their, "... analysis supports the Marxian view that economic structure, not level of income or rate of economic growth[129] is the basic determinant of patterns of income distribution".[130]

In direct contrast to IMF retrogressive redistribution, Colman and Nixson argue that redistribution in favour of the working classes and poor would lead to the greater use of labour intensive methods which are more appropriate to the production of essential goods consumed by this sector of the population. The demand for such goods and services would be expected to increase with increased purchasing power, with obvious favourable employment consequences. Of equal importance, assuming significant income elasticity of demand, redistribution in this direction would mean less income for the non-essential imports which have a negative impact on the balance of payments.[131]

The approach adopted by Colman and Nixson, and others, invites consideration for the reason that, as Watson notes, wage restraint driven by an incomes policy will not necessarily encourage the capitalist beneficiaries of such a policy to invest the extra profits, so occasioned, in capital goods, thereby generating greater output and also upgrading the nation's technological capabilities.[132]

Nor, on the other hand, will the relatively low wage levels resulting from restraint guarantee, without more, a reduction in the rate of capital-for-labour substitution in industry and commerce. Low wages, most definitely, does not encourage or promote, much less guarantee efficiency, and cannot be expected to, from any vantage point.

On a somewhat broader level, Wallerstein advances the view that,

> "... the framework of the capitalist world system limits critically the possibilities of transformation of the reward system within it, since disparity of reward is the fundamental motivating force of the operation of the system as it is constructed".[133]

Rather than the growing inequality which has been a prominent feature of structural adjustment and stabilization, it has been forcefully suggested that, "From an equi-distributive viewpoint, all social sectors should have experienced a decline in living conditions at rates similar to the rates of reduction in real incomes of the countries".[134]

When the usual retrogressive distribution of the surplus is allowed to flow from standard IMF policies,[135] the reduction in per capita income of the poorer sectors naturally adds to the buildup of pressure,[136] in relation to different adverse policy consequences, at some point in the future. "For this reason, the target of at least preserving the workers' share in the National Income in a period of crisis should be foreseen".[137] Failing this, the preservation of social stability may require a greater than average fall in the incomes of the non-poor. For the lower paid only apply the principle of comparability to their own wages as against managerial and other relatively privileged groups' salaries, in dispute circumstances of high emotion,[138] or what is perceived to be scandalously excessive salary increases to high-status persons.

Contrary to Manley's view,[139] Salamon suggests that however ambitiously or sincerely an incomes policy is designed, of itself it cannot achieve an equitable distribution of the burdens and rewards flowing from economic changes.[140] For this reason, Davies has concluded that a voluntary policy of restraint with the. active support of those affected, and largely administered by them – as was the case in Britain under the social contract of 1975-79, which came closest to this pattern – "… is likely to have the greatest chance of success".[141]

Experience has shown, in fact, that whether a policy of wage restraint is consensus-based or not, aggressive industrial action, often in the form of militant strike activity in defense of substantial, if not 'excessive' wage and salary claims, tends to heighten significantly, "… at the point of return to 'normal' collective bargaining". Unions and workers invariably attempt to, "… make up for losses sustained during the period of restraint".[142]

Further, labour's wage strategy will undoubtedly be influenced by inflationary expectations over the short, to medium term.

The consensus and active support, which Davies regards as being essential for policy effectiveness in this area, is precisely the missing factor on which Jude reported in *The Daily Gleaner* as being identified by Roberts of the NWU as justifying unionized worker resistance. Between 1977 and 1991, the unionized working class, he argues, were the ones called upon to, and who did in fact, make sacrifices by complying with wage guidelines. Other groups were, "… allowed a free hand to take (the) wage increases they desired". If the 9% wage offer to public sector workers in 1994 was not accepted, then all hope held by the government, "… of ridding itself of the IMF are over", according to a government source, the report concluded.[143]

As it turned out, the 9% was raised to 12.5% and was finally "accepted", or "settled" at 16%, by the public-sector unions at the IDT. Resolution of the conflict between the level of the Government's wage bill's effect on the budget, and the severing of the borrowing link with the IMF, took the form of a special surtax of 23% on the island's banks. The Minister of Finance spoke, in justification of the levy, in terms of "asking" a sector that had made "huge profits" [legitimately under his Government's own free market and financial sector/exchange rate liberalization policies] to contribute to, "… easing the IMF budgetary constraints" on government. The purpose of the surcharge was to simply recover the difference between the targeted wage bill involving the 9% increase and the settlement at 16% — nearly twice the original offer.[144]

The highly contentious public expenditure funding innovation not only allowed this Government to exceed "the *maximum* that it could afford", but also enabled the avoidance of the choice between what had been regarded as the *only* possible alternatives: taxing an already overtaxed populace, additional public-sector work force retrenchment, or a still further cut in social services expenditure. The lesson warrants emphasis: despite protestations to the contrary, there are always policy alternatives.

To the leadership of the private sector, however, this selective taxation which was viewed as, "a punishment for success" was described as being like,

> "… a secular replay of Christ driving the money changers from the temple, to thunderous applause [of the public] "… the Minister of Finance has announced his dashing determination to overturn the money tables of the bankers".[145]

However popular a measure, with poorer members of the population, what is not certain is its long-term effect on confidence in Government's *modus operandi* on the part of the financial sector, and its possible interpretation as a precedent, as an aspect of strategy, in wage bargaining by government employees. Public servants might well feel that if they are resolute enough again, in the future, government could be coerced into resorting to this or some other novel, "arbitrary", and "discriminatory" solution, perhaps with a different sector as the "target" or "source". This could clearly adversely affect investment, as the question could well be asked, "whose turn next?"

The PSOJ in 1985, with little amendment in this area of its Progress Report in 1992, regarded it as, "… an essential element of successful adaptation to economic growth and development that relative *prices* [italics added] be free to change. Administrative control of prices is therefore impossible to reconcile with a dynamic economy…". Such a statement conveniently ignores the fact that there had been consistent annual negative/negligible GDP growth since the mid 1970's; that despite its simplistic appeal, bordering on the self-evident, all prices, except for labour, tend to change in one direction only, in Jamaica, which is upward. As a result, overall price stability has been unknown for more than two decades, with single digit inflation achieved in only 5 of the 20 years covered by TABLE 2.

Finally, price regulation in the public utility services sector cannot be considered an example of the, "… special cases … in which market mechanisms cannot be expected to function efficiently".[146] On the contrary, market imperfections throughout the economy are so pronounced, and pricing policy deviates so significantly from the practices in mature free market economies, to the detriment of the consumer, that there is little merit to the attempted distinction between utility and general pricing practice considerations.

If inflation continued unchecked, and the "even moderately intelligent" average citizen tries to keep his wage up with the CPI trend, the consequences, according to PSOJ reasoning, would be,

> "… equivalent, in economic terms, to anarchy in the political sphere, where no police force exists to prevent armed robbery, and the average citizen is at the mercy of brutal marauders".[147]

This analogy from the crime and national security arena is not applied, unsurprisingly, to the effects of,

> "… the reality of *rising prices* [italics added] that are the result of inflationary pressures, previously created by unwise policies and suppressed by price controls and exchange controls and quota restrictions".[148]

The PSOJ declared its opposition to price control and incomes policies, "whether voluntary or statutory", and by necessary implication to a social contract, one would think. Yet there is no known case of its failing to support the call for worker and union restraint in wage negotiations, whether in the public or private sector, much less to ever dispute any claim by any of its members of their inability to pay. This is despite much higher eventual settlements that have never caused bankruptcy. The policy on distribution of incomes, taking its cue from "Reaganomics" and "Thatcherism",[149] must, it is claimed, be determined by market mechanisms, modified compassionately in a seeming attitude of philanthropic eccentricity by a system of public welfare, "… that does not destroy incentives to economic efficiency".[150]

In this conception, Hutton sees the market portrayed as an,

> "… impersonal arbiter of economic fortunes. The great forces of power and equity that lie at the bottom of market relations, and the social and political institutions through which they are mediated, are abstracted away".[151]

The austerity programmes of stabilization and structural adjustment left little room for compensating increases in social wage provisions in such important areas as education and health, much less for social support based on 'compassion'. As Friedman, and others, would argue, free market economics and this kind of Titmussian public welfare sentiment are a contradiction in terms.[152]

While not adopting a formal incomes policy, Austria, Norway and Sweden, engage in extensive and intensive mediation and consensus-seeking "… consultation to ensure that wage decisions serve the objective of full employment, low inflation, economic growth, equitable distribution of income, a stable exchange rate and the maintenance and improvement of international competitiveness".[153] What results from this kind of comprehensive multi-party approach to policy design is, it is said, a *de facto* incomes policy.

With respect to the importance of consensus, Metcalf has concluded that countries adopting such an approach, "… suffer smaller increases in unemployment in response to things like an upsurge in militancy or a rise in real interest rates."[154] And they need, he concludes, a smaller increase in unemployment to obtain a given reduction in real wages.

Consensus, without the requisite comprehensiveness, will not, of course, guarantee policy success. Neither will the proverbial weakness of implementation capability, and an absence of the necessary structures, facilitate the adoption of the 'second-best' solution, in a context where wages levels are sensitive to the price level – thus, making the struggle for low unemployment and low inflation a vital subject of dialogue".[155]

Despite the observation that "capitalism does not require that even one person be unemployed", concern under the prices and incomes policy attempts has not tangibly taken the form of focus on their employment-consequences. Preoccupation has tended, rather, to be with inflation, per se, hence the alleged death of Keynesianism. The most unflattering comment that could, in good conscience, be made in respect of Government's unemployment and inflation performance in the current decade, is that speculation as to what the situation would have been, without Government's ill-fated purported prioritization of those two indices of economic well-being, is likely, as in virtually all such cases, to be inconclusive.

In the absence of some major external threat, sufficient to call forth national unity, in response to the community survival instinct, or ideological affinity and/or a symbiotic relationship between a strong government party and the labour movement in a situation where a high degree of unionization prevails, consensus is only likely to be promoted by strong emphasis on equity in the structure of wages.[156]

In responding to forcefully argued, and international data-supported anxieties about the extent of local income and wealth inequality, the Minister of Finance, an academic economist of some standing, found refuge of sorts by again stressing the island's alleged uniqueness. In his view, the solutions will not come from abroad,

> "… and even while we benefit from international comparisons the solutions will have to be developed here".[157]

If, as the Minister suggested, taking from the rich to give to the poor,[158] as a solution to the problem of poverty[159] was a "fallacy", one cannot help but wonder as to how he would describe the government/IMF connivance over nearly two decades in taking from the poor to give to the rich. How does he view the real effect of the more recent World Bank's "poverty amelioration" policies of taking from the poor to give to the poor, (as, for example, by the indiscriminate removal of subsidies on even basic life-preserving items, to be replaced by woefully inadequate school feeding and food stamps programmes). Further, with respect, one suspects that this shield against considered policy experimentation represented by the 'country uniqueness' argument, is, in the mouths of many, nothing more than a more sophisticated variant of the *manana* mentality.

At the other extreme of the range of attitudes to policy emulation, we find the late Headley Brown, on the basis of classical economic theory, and entirely without any supporting evidence from the island's experience since 1975, putting forward the notion that,

> "*Everyone* [italics added] must now agree that in Jamaica, pay guidelines have an essential role to play in the context of the current efforts towards growth in a stable economic environment".[160]

Those efforts were outlined in Ministry Paper No. 6 of 1987. In relation to "Everyone", here, one might be justified in again enquiring – as Engels did to the use of the term "the public in general" – "who are they?" Clearly, the poor and the working class are not included.

The limit of absurdity was probably reached with the provision of "the employment creation" section of the Ministry Paper (6/87) to the effect that, "… an increase in the total wage bill arising from an increase in the numbers employed during the current twelve-month period will not be included as part of the ten percent [wage guideline] limit".[161] Shallow thinking, sometimes reflected in policy, is clearly not a charge to which policy designers and legislators can always successfully plead innocent.

Having emphasized the importance of inflation control for incomes restraint acceptance by the working class in 1990, Brown, by 1994, was championing the cause for the introduction of an incomes policy on the ground that it was necessary to the achievement of price stability, generally, and to maintain export competitiveness. He urged that, "… efforts should be made to address the moderation of domestic cost increases, a major component of which is the wage bill[162] – with no attempt to substantiate the alleged phenomenon of cost (wage) push inflation. Contrary to Brown's claim, a weakening of the link between wages, production costs, and prices would only be facilitated by increased scale economies from utilization of idle capacity,[163] if the resulting additional production is achieved without a proportionate increase in the workforce.

Given the Government's conspicuous failure to control inflation, one consumer group has felt obliged to call for a four month "Price-Increase Freeze", while others have demanded the re-introduction of price controls – against the background of the variables of price determination all moving in a favourable consumer direction, while prices continue inexorably upwards.[164]

But the 'hands off' prices policy can be traced back to the days when the allegedly radical middle, class Minister of Industry, Commerce and Production, Hugh Small, in 1991, seemed to limit the government's function with respect to the price level to that of taking steps to, "... ensure that the consumers are getting more information than they are currently getting as to how the price of the various products are currently made up". This dubious role would, it appeared, devolve on the government by default, since it was explained that, "... the government cannot go out and form consumer bodies and it cannot go out and become the stimulant for consumer consciousness ...".[165]

Three years later, the Minister of State in the Ministry of Labour and Welfare was reported in the press as having made 'the offending statement', that, "... there is a definite need to review and monitor the profit margins of companies, but without returning to *de facto* price control..." The press editorial continued,

> "... maybe this honourable Member of Parliament is either not committed to a system of free market price determination or that he still holds on to the virtues of socialism ... the people of this country do not want to witness the consequences of price controls again".[166]

No doubt, to the editor, the consequences of *wage* controls can be more comfortably contemplated.

This issue of individual and interest group ideological commitment raises the question of the extent to which incomes policy can, "... create consent where social valuations of incomes within a given incomes distribution[167] are confused and often obscure...".[168]

This suggests that policy design has to reflect an appreciation of relevant conditions such as:

> "... the political climate, social conflict patterns, the misadventure of [IMF/World Bank/Governments] general economic policies, the lack of effective fiscal means and commitment to reduce extreme income inequality, the lack of union cohesion and centralization, and the absence of voluntary cooperation between employers, unions and the government. ... The expectational environment [might well]—under the problem of wage restraint prove almost intractable".[169]

As Gayle has noted,

"... the prototypical pluralist political system is composed of constantly changing coalitions and cross cutting interest groups".[170] In the Jamaican case/this was particularly true after the 1972 election, followed in 1974 by the intense short-lived ideological polarization of party politics and then the dislocation and reordering of social classes and class relations under stabilization and structural adjustment. In such an environment, it might be realistic to expect that "a syndrome of policy failure", exemplified by inadequate wage guideline design and implementation, and the absence of any comprehensive mechanism of *prices* and *all-embracing* incomes control, should represent the nation's frustrating experience.

The British experiments and accumulated experience with wage restraint, and various forms of incomes and prices policy, has been summarized by Peden as depending for success on the following factors,[171] on the basis of which it would be highly interesting to assess the recent Barbados experiment with its incomes policy/social contract:

1. Employers' [and Government's] willingness to resist wage demands.
2. The relative degree of cohesion and of organization on both the union and employer side.
3. The side favoured by legislation in the conduct and settlement of disputes
4. The degree of difficulty associated with the raising of prices.
5. The extent and attitudinal consequences of workers' fear of unemployment (which in the 1980's probably "cowed" the unions more effectively than repressive legislation could have done".)
6. Inflationary expectations.
7. Acceptance/rejection by workers of existing wage structures/differentials.
8. The ability of trade union leaders to control their members.
9. Access to information on employers' ability to pay.

The probability of having these several factors, or even enough of them tending in the positive direction, that is to say, in favour of incomes policy success, must be low in an unstable economic environment characterized by uncertainty and frequent conflicting policy changes and reversals. Friedman's advice that prices and incomes policies should be avoided, as the market is a more efficient allocator of resources,[172] has generally been heeded under the hegemony of free market ideology; hut in practice one finds, and certainly in Jamaica, that the new-found freedom of the market has, for the most part, been effectively restricted to the movements in prices, only.

SUMMARY OF THE ASPECTS OF PAY POLICY 1976-1994

CHART LEGEND FOR DATA ON THE FOLLOWING PAGE

CPT	Consumer Price Index
D&S	Dismissals an Suspensions
FPP	Emergency Production Plan
LRIDA	Labour Relations and Industrial Disputes Act
MW	Minimum Wage
MP	Ministry Paper
MPS	Ministry of the Public Service
PC	Prices Commission
TDT	Industrial Disputes Tribunal
U	% Unemployment
WG	Wage Guidelines
* WSC	Wages and Conditions
**W/NDT	Wages as % of National Disposable Income

* The Publication in which this data was contained has not been produced since 1992
** There was no breakdown of strikes by Cause for the years before 1979

YEAR	DISPUTES	PUBLIC-SECTOR PAY POLICY	STRIKE - CAUSE		
			W&C	D&S	MISC
1994	227	The Industrial Relations Division of the former Ministry of the Public Service put under Ministry of Finance. Industrial action by public sector workers increased by 53.89% with 11 ending in strikes	62	13	20
1993	248	The MPS handled 80 wage claims 45 of which were settled. The Police got 85% in yr. l and 45% in yr. 2; teachers 60% in yr. I and 30% in yr. 2. civil servants 35% in yr. I and 50% in yr. 2. This caused a massive increase in the Government's wage bill in 1993/94 over 1991/92	46	8	15
1992	254	Permanent Salaries Review Board established (MR 18/92). There were 103 wage contract negotiations for the first-time unions (10) presented joint claims (JTURDC)	41	13	14
1991	269	Wage guideline abolished (MP 47/91) Public sector workers who are fully funded from the Budget will have their wage determined by availability of budgetary resources. The MPS handled 75 wage negotiations	30	12	15
1990	275	As below	13	15	19
1989	308	The 10% Wage guideline was continued (MP 33/89) which had been instituted from 1/1/87- 31/3/88 and extended to 31/11/89. The WG were said to have helped to contain inflation, expand exports and improve the BOP	38	8	18
1988	372	As below	23	15	26
1987	370	MP6/87 stipulated 10% limit over previous 12-month wage fund	16	8	6
1986	564	The pay package for 1985 was applicable, this being the second year of the 2-yr. contract	21	9	10

U%	WG%	MW$	CPI	PRIVATE SECTOR PAY POLICY
1994 15.4	-	500	26.7	Although operating officially on the basis of free collective bargaining ,concern with the failure to control inflation led the Minister of Finance to strongly criticize private sector companies which granted "excessive" increases beyond the inflation level thus setting a pace that would create problems for public sector negotiations *W/NDI.
1993 16.0	-	300	30.1	See (1) Fig 7 on p. 65 (2) W/NDT
1992 15.9	-	300	40.2	See (1) above (2) W/NDT : 45.9%
1991 12.5	12.5	160	80.2	See(1) above (2) W/NDT : 50.3%
1990 15.7	12.5%	130	29.8	See (1) above (2) W/NDT : 45.9%
1989 18.9	10	100	17.2	See (1) above (2) W/NDT : 48.9%
1988 18.9	10	80	8.5	See (1) above (2) W/NDT : 44.6%
1987 21.7	10	60	8.4	See policy under "Public Sector". The 10% limit over the previous 12 months wage fund applied to each enterprise. Incentive and retroactive payments were excluded from the 10% limit.
1986 22.3	-	60	10.4	Up to 31/12/86 the principle applicable was that of free collective bargaining, comparability, ability to pay and "the national interest" W/NDT : 48.3%

YEAR	DISPUTES	PUBLIC-SECTOR PAY POLICY	STRIKE - CAUSE		
			W&C	D&S	MISC
1985	790	In an attempt to reduce its house keeping expenses, Government offered increases of between 10-18% for 1985-1986- 87 under a staggered system of regrading introduced in 1983/84 (ESSJ,1985,17.6)	44	20	18
1984	643	The size of the public sector was scheduled to be reduced by 6,200. The wage fund was not expected to exceed that for 1983/84 by more than 10%	35	10	18
1983	662	A two year pay plan was implemented on 1/7/83 involving a staggered system of regrading. Professional and technical personnel were offered 29-63.3% increases; others were offered 12.5% or $780, whichever was the greater for yr. 1 and across the board increases for 1983/84 was some 14% above that of the previous year	49	20	18
1982	659	The Pay Plan for workers in institutions supported through current account transfers from the Budget provided $15 p.w. increases from 1/7/81-31/3/82 and $14 p.w. from 1/4/82-31/3/83. In the remainder of the public-sector wage increases were to be determined as in the private sector: ability to pay, rate for the job, national interest	58	20	61
1981	706	The quantitative WG of MP 23/79 was abandoned. However, the policy of restraint on pay rises was maintained in keeping with budgetary constraints. The acceptance of the Pay Plan by the Civil Service Association resulted in lowered labour unrest	65	29	47

U%	WG%	MW$	CPI & PRICES POLICY	PRIVATE SECTOR PAY POLICY
1985 25.6	-	60	23.4	As for 1983. W/NDT : 49.1%
1984 25.6	-	46	31.2	As for 1983. Increases based on the projected rate of inflation were expected to average 15%. There was nevertheless a high level of lay-offs and redundancies in various sectors of the economy. New jobs created in agriculture and industry, pushing up the total employment by some 150,400,partly explained the relative calm prevailing in the industrial relations climate. W/NDT : 54.7%
1983 26.9	-	30	16.7	Wage negotiations were to be governed by "the usual forces of demand and supply", never the less with the expectation that increases would be within the expected inflation rate of 15%. Tax relief on O/T pay was granted as of 23/5/83 W/NDT : 54.9%
1982 27.9	-	30	6.5	The principle of free collective bargaining was to be applied "having due regard to the national interest." There was no attempt to spell out what constituted "unfair labour practices". W/NDT : 60.0%
1981 25.6	-	30	4.6 Free Market approach adopted, but price controls kept on essential goods and monopolies	Wage negotiations to proceed on the basis of ability to pay. Wages in private sector moderated by the acceptance of the public sector Pay Plan. The effect of pay and fringe benefits increases on product costs was to be taken into account, bearing in mind investment and employment creation implications W/NDT : 57.8%

YEAR	DISPUTES	PUBLIC-SECTOR PAY POLICY	STRIKE - CAUSE W&C	D&S	MISC
1980	557	Uncertainty as to the continued applicability of the pay guidelines resulted from the socialist PNP's break from the IMF in March. Labour unrest continued due to Government's inability to formulate and implement major policy in the turbulent political and economic climate in the year of the "IMF election"	56	26	57
1979	608	MP 23/79 (Min. of Labour) established pay guidelines of 10% as from 1/6/79 for two years. All wage Agreements expiring after 31/5/79 were subject to the WG. But the Government itself as an employer exceeded the 10% limit under trade union pressure, especially since the sanctions were "either weak or impracticable"	68	18	87
1978	687	The minimum of 15% increase for a 2-yr. period applied to both the public and private sectors.			

U%	WG%	MW$	CPI & PRICES POLICY	PRIVATE SECTOR PAY POLICY
1980 26.8	10	30	<u>28.7%</u> Prices. Policy Price control was in effect on three levels: list A prices could only be increased with Ministerial approval; B list if no objection was made by the P.C. and C list items having stipulated markups under various Price Orders: 20% before or 15%, after interest, as the rate of return on capital	See "Public Sector Pay Policy". Non-enforcement of sanctions for breach of pay monitoring provisions plus the "wait and see" attitude after the "IMF election led to increased ineffectiveness of the WG. Only 1 of 48 reported collective Agreements fell within the 10% limit. The Social Contract therefore had little effect, as production costs and inflation were not held to 10% target. W/NDT : 58.4%
1979	10%	26.40	<u>19.4%</u> Attempts were made to limit price increases influenced by local and external factors (ESSJ, 1979 5.2). Social Contract price policies were outlined in M.P. 17/79. Apart from direct price control, the policy rested, it was said, on co-operation, consultation and consumer education	The guideline figure applied to a firm's total wage fund but did not have the force of law. Lower paid categories of workers were recommended for favourable treatment and provision was made for productivity incentive schemes to be taken into account in exceeding the 10% limit. Higher pay increases were obtainable from IDT awards as the IDT was not bound by the guidelines and has never been given directions as to how to interpret the national interest and so is free to use its own interpretation "(ESSJ, 1979, 5.5). The WG presented within the framework of a social contract were not supported by the unions W/NDT : 58.1%
1978	15%	24	<u>49.4%</u> There were steep price increases due to domestic factors. A price stabilization fund was in effect, also the provision of subsidies on items in the "basic needs basket" and imposition of a rent freeze for most of the year. Special shops (AMC) offered basic goods (food) at ?5- 30% less; but volume handled was a small proportion of the total	Wage restraint was an element of the IMF Agreement (M.P 22/78) Devaluation and the removal of subsidies on items of mass consumption caused real wages to fall by some 30% accompanied by a fall in Governments social services expenditure- The Ministry of Labour could now send wage disputes to the IDT for settlement WITHIN the guideline limit as a result of an amendment to the LRIDA. Collective Agreements were limited to 2 yrs. instead of being open- minded and a wage monitoring unit was established within the Min. of Labour. The upper limit bof 15% was imposed on total pay and became the norm, although it was exceeded in cases. W/NDT : 59.5%

1977 659   The Wage guideline was $10 p.w.

1976 514   As for 1977: $10 p.w.

U%	WG%	MW$	CPI & PRICES POLICY	PRIVATE SECTOR PAY POLICY
1977	$10	20	<u>14.3%</u> The number of items directly under price control was increased with scope for additions. There were also controls on profits, dividends, rent, interest, and professional fees	The data shows increasingly higher percentage wage increases after 1973 under the socialist PNP Government, with a leading trade unionist as party leader and P.M. But 1973 was also the year when the first oil price crisis generated serious international inflation. (ESSJ, 1977, p.462) Income guidelines were in- introduced in Sept. 1975 and March 1976, Under the EPP of April 1977 there was a $10 p.w. limit on pay increases. The inter-industry comparability clause was also abolished (M.P. 27/77) Strenuous trade union opposition led, however, to the withdrawal of these policies. Under MP 12/77 wage increases were to be now based on:CPI, ability to pay, comparability and a proficiency allowance, which might justify increases above $10 p.w. A pay moratorium extended collective Agreements for a further six months and specified that retroactive pay for the extension period should be in the form of cash for 25% and savings bonds for the balance.(The bonds idea was to be re-introduced under the same party W/NDT : 63.8%
1976	$10	20	Price guidelines comprised two lists: A list items were directly controlled, whereas applications for increases had to be made in respect of items on the B list. Profits, dividends/ rents and professional fees were also controlled.	The guidelines were those which applied for 1977 under MP 12/76. Also stipulated, was a graduated' reduction of increases available to higher income groups. Allowances and fringe benefits were frozen at the levels of October 1975. Whereas in the' 1972-73 period 15.5% of the 107 Agreements contained increases of more than 30%/ by 1975/76 the percentage had risen to 90 of a total of 86 wage agreements, especially in this sector. The apparent substantial reduction in average percentage increases granted during 1976 (an election year) was not necessarily due to the effectiveness of the guidelines (ESSJ, 1976, p.391) The main stated objective of the wage policy was to allow wages to recover to the level of real incomes in 1973.

Source: Economic and Social Survey, Jamaica, PIOJ, Several Issues (Compiled by the author)

1. Carl Stone, "Wages and Social Contract", in Headley Brown (ed) *The Jamaican Economy in a Changing World: The Way Forward: 1993/94 and Beyond*, Headley Brown c Co, Ltd, 1993.
2. Stone, Ibid, p.122.
3. ESSJ, 1982, p.182.
4. The Daily Gleaner, May 12, 1995, Letters to the Editor, The Sunday Observer, April 30, 1995, pp.8-9.
5. The Daily Gleaner, May 16, 1992.
6. Ibid.
7. See The Financial Gleaner, June 12, 1992, p.5; "Lalor lashes those who favour control", in The Daily Gleaner, June 1, 1992; Byron Buckley, "Why aren't prices falling", in The Daily Gleaner, Aug. 28, 1994, p.9; Godfrey E. McAllister on chicken meat price, in The Daily Gleaner, Sept. 17, 1994, p.12; Byron Buckley, "Retailers resisting market forces" in The Daily Gleaner, July 24, 1994, p.9A. See in contrast the drastic price control policy of Venezuela in "Venezuela get tough on price violators", in The Financial Gleaner, Aug. 26, 1994, p.24.
8. Wesley G. Hughes, in The Daily Gleaner, June 19, 1992, p.7.
9. Ibid.
10. Ministry of the Public Service Paper No. 47 of 1991 which superseded Ministry Paper No.33 of 1988 the operation of which was extended to 1989/192 saw the establishment of the Permanent Salaries Review Board for the public sector.
11. Ibid.
12. The Rent Restriction Act, 1983, seeking to control substantially escalating rents nationally, lacked human and financial resources so the rent assessment boards were unable to enforce the tenets of the Act. This left landlords with their freedom in determining the rent on their promises, which often meant increases of well over 100%.
13. Despite the removal of wage guidelines Government has, with IMF prodding, sought to have public sector wages increases kept in the 15% region. Similar wage, policies for the private sector are being sought in the negotiation of a Social Contract, See working papers: "A Brief on the Social Contract. National Planning Council Meeting, July 14, 1993 and "Draft Outline of Social Contract/Understanding" mimeo. See "IMF wants wage limits", lead story in The Daily Gleaner, Mar. 9, 1994, p.l, but see also, "Seaga: breach of IMF pact" in The Daily Gleaner Oct. 26, 1994, p.l; "Letter to the IMF on EFF" The Daily Gleaner, Sept. 4, 1994, par. 8. For government's latest position see "The Social Partnership" P.M's. broadcast to the Nation Feb. 26, 1996, JIS, p.8.
14. Ministry Paper 47, supra.
15. Ibid.
16. Raymond Forrest, "Reformulated Incomes Policy likely", in The Financial Cleaner, June 11, 1993, p.9.
17. Ibid.
18. Section 4 (I) of the Labour Relations and Industrial Disputes Act (1975) provides: "Every worker shall, as between himself and his employer, have the right (a) to be a member of such trade union as he may choose, …"; Section 4 (2) further stipulates: "Any person who – (a) prevents or deters a worker from exercising any of the rights conferred on him by subsection (I); or (b) dismisses, penalizes or otherwise discriminates against a worker by reason of his exercising any such right shall be guilty of any offense"
19. With the emergence of the union umbrella organizations, the JTURDC and JCTU, there is now an understanding among member unions against poaching of members* Significantly, the relatively new, aggressive, ambitious, and expansive UAWU is not affiliated to either body.
20. Marjorie Stair, "Fooling Ourselves", in The Daily Gleaner, Nov. 19,1994, p.6.
21. 1995 New Year's message from the General Secretary of the National Worker's Union, Lloyd Goodleigh, published in The Jamaican Herald, Jan. 3, 1995, p.6.
22. Carl Stone, supra, p.128.
23. Ibid.
24. Headley Brown, "The Jamaican Economy: Performance and Prospects 1992/93 - 1993/94 in Headley Brown (ed), 1993, p.56; Headley Brown, "Major Changes in Wage Policy" in The Financial Gleaner, Oct. 21, 1994, p.S; Leon HoSang "Wage Restraint/Incomes Policy" in The Daily Gleaner, Dec, 13, 1991, p . 14 .
25. Headley Brown, The Jamaican Economy: Performance and Prospects 1992/93 - 1993/94, Ibid.
26. Ibid.
27. Ibid, p.61.
28. Carl Stone, in Headley Brown (ed) 1993 , p . 117.
29. Ibid, p.119. For the effect of skewed income distribution on the housing market in Jamaica, see Michael G. Salmon and Celvin McDonald, *Caribbean Labour Journal*, vol.1 no.2, pp.22-28.
30. Jamaica Five Year Development Plan 1990-1995, PIOJ, July 30, 1995, p.14.
31. Ibid, p.12.
32. Ibid, p.31.
33. Ibid, pp.31-33.
34. Owen Jefferson, "Liberalization of the Foreign Exchange system in Jamaica", Seventh Aldith Brown Memorial Lecture, ISER, U.W.I., 1991, p. 5.

35. J. Hinton and R. Hyman, Trade Unions and Revolution, Pluto Press, 1975, p.59; Tom Clarke and Laurie Clements Trade Unions under Capitalism, Fontana, 1977, p.29.

36. Michael Foot, *Loyalists and Loners*, Collins, 1986, p.49.

37. E.J. Mishan, *The Costs of Economic Growth*, Pelican, 1969.

38. David Butler and Donald Stokes, *Political Change in Britain*, St. Martin's Press, New York, 1974, p.373.

39. G.D.H. Cole, and Raymond Postgate, *The Common People*, University Paperbacks, Methuen, London, 1966, p.632.

40. John Toye, *Dilemmas of Development*, Blackwell, 1993, p.34.

41. Ibid, p.45.

42. D. Lai, The Poverty of Development Economics, Institute of Economic Affairs, 1983.

43. Andrew S. Downes, Carlos Holder, and Hyginus Leon, "The Wage-Price Productivity Relationship in a Small Developing Country: The case of Barbados", SES, Vol.39 No.2, ISER, U.W.I., June, 1990, pp.71-72.

44. W. Arthur Lewis, "Jamaica's Economic Problems", The Daily Gleaner, Sept. 1964. John C.H. Fei and Gustav Ranis, "Innovation, Capital Accumulation, and Economic Development" in American Economic. Rev., Vol.53 No.3, June 1963, pp.283-313.

45. Toye, 1993, p.74. See also the poverty line statistics in Figs. ???

46. Rosalea Hamilton, "Analyzing Real Wages, Prices and Productivity and the Effects of State Intervention in Caribbean - Type Economies", SES Vol.43 No.1, ISER, U.W.I., March 1994, p.7.

47. William G. Demas, "Situation and Change in Caribbean Economy", in George L. Beckford (ed), *Caribbean Economy*, ISER, U.W.I., 1984, p.72.

48. John Gorina, "Can an Incomes Policy be Administered?", in *British Journal Industrial Relations*, Vol.v No.3, Nov. 1967, p.287.

49. Stone, in Headley Brown (ed) 1993, pp.128-136.

50. JTURDC, "Response to Discussion Document on Social Contract/Understanding", Mimec, JTURDC, 1993, Kingston, Jamaica.

51. R.W. Solow, "Measuring Contributions to Growth", in Amartya, Sen (ed), *Growth Economics*, Penguin 1970, p.418. For the 1909-1949 period in the U.S.A. a crude application of a simple method of segregating shifts of the production function from movements along it, which rests on the assumption that factors are paid their marginal products showed that gross output per man-hour doubled over the period: 37.5% being due to technological change and the remainder to increased use of capital.

52. In fact, in relation to the targeted inflation rate of 6,5% for 1994/95 the JTURDC had this to say: "By setting unrealistic targets in the Contract and then making projections (wage increase levels, etc.) based on those unrealistic targets the contract is destined for failure". See JTURDC "Response to Discussion Document on the Social Contract/Under- standing" JTURDC Mimeo, 1993 p.l.

53. Draft Outline of Social Contract/Understanding: For Discussion Purposes Only, National Planning Council, 1993, p.5.

54. Professor Walter Eltics is quoted to the effect: "the ultimate effect of the deficit financed expansion in highly open economies is to destroy the balance of payments" – "The Failure of Keynesian Conventional Wisdom", in Lloyds Bank Review, No.122, Oct. 1976.

55. Arthur M. Okun, Prices and Quantities: A Macroeconomic Analysis, The Brookings Institution, 1981, pp.340-41.

56. Okun, Ibid; See also John T. Dunlop, Wages and Price Controls as seen by Controller, Labour Law Jnl. Vol. 26, August 1975, pp. 457-63, and Royal Commission on Trade Unions and Employers Associations, Cmnd 3623, HMSO, 1969, par. 90-91; The inadequacy of the administrative capacity to implement a tax-based incomes policy effectively rules it out of serious consideration. For details of such a policy, see Henry C. Wallich and Sidney Weintraub, "A Tax-Based Incomes Policy", Jnl. of Economic Issues Vol.5 June 1971, pp,1-19.Okun, 1931, p.351, proposes the possibility of a reward-based tax credit system instead, to meet criticisms as to the anti-labour bias of the penalty method.

57. For evidence of the British experience of voluntarism, see G.C. Peden, *British Economic and Social Policy*, Philip Allan, 1991, pp.121,14344,203. The TUC agreed to wage restraint in 1949/50 on condition that wage differentials were maintained; pay was raised where it was below a reasonable standard of subsistence; and the cost of living was kept to within 5% of its 1949, predevaluation level. The essential point is that consensus must be grounded in a sufficiently valuable exchange in the perception of the industrial relations parties

58. Okun, 1931, p.347. The cost of blocking loopholes "for subtle violations" when the policy is based on voluntarism will, for Okun, tend to "exacerbate the misallocation of resources likely to be caused by the programme".

59. ILO, Wage determination in English-speaking Caribbean Countries

60. The guidelines of 1975 did stipulate lower rates of wage increases for ranges of pay on an ascending scale between $7000 and $16000 per year, with salaries above $16000 being frozen. In 1976 certain changes were introduced which, while favouring labour's interests, appeared to dilute the purpose of the guidelines as an anti-inflationary measure: additional wage adjustment was allowed where the movement in the cost of living was more than $10; and increases were allowed on the basis of job comparability on an inter-firm level. Further, having allowed "extra" cost of living increases, Ministry Paper No.38 reflects conflicting objectives inherent in the policy by providing that. ".. all other pay increases must be accommodated either by way of improvements in productivity or a reduction in the rate of return on capital employed" – both sources of accommodation being highly unlikely to materialize.

61. ILO, 1978, p.23.

62. Compton Bourne, "Wage determination in the Caribbean Countries, trends and issues", in ILO, Ibid, p.39.

63. Originally the guidelines did apply to profits, dividends, professional fees and rents – see Headley Brown, "Prices and Incomes Policy in Jamaica" in. ILO, Ibid, 1978, p.84. For the distribution of the employee labour force by income groups for the period 1968-73 see Carl Stone and Aggrey Brown (ed) *Essays in Power and Change in Jamaica*, Dept, of Government/Extra Mural Centre, U.W.I., Feb. 1976, p. 263 which reported statistics from the ESSJ showing the top earning groups being paid as much as 20 times the bottom groups.

64. On the. question of the need for tripartite policy consensus. See ILO/ DAN I DA Regional Seminar on Labour Relations in the Caribbean Region, Port of Spain, Trinidad, ILO, March 1973, Geneva, 1974, p.23.

65. Guidelines agreed in Fiji in 1977 included special provisions dealing with the low wage sectors, skills scarcity, wage anomalies and productivity incentives, providing another example of Jamaica's failure to benefit, from an outward-looking approach to policy design.

66. British Journal of Industrial Relations, Vol.v No.3, Nov. 1967, pp.375- 335 .

67. Jamaica, according to Manley, and every other country which "claims concern about social justice, must face the issue, of an incomes policy". Incomes policy he describes as "the most difficult of all strategic requirements of social justice" and as being "bedeviled by controversies …" and suffering from the existence of "mutual distrust of all the elements of the society which might, be affected by restraint in the national interest" – Michael Manley, *The Politics of Change*, Heinemann Caribbean Ltd, 1990, pp.116-17; Peden concludes, with reference to Britain in the 1970's, "that. the. struggle over Stage III (of the. Conservative's incomes policy) had been a 'searing experience'. "It is not. surprising that the experiment of a statutory prices and incomes … returned to peer in 1979, the Conservatives preferred to revert to their original policy in 1970 of relying on the discipline of the market", G.C. Peden, British Economic and Social Policy, Philip Allan, 1991, pp.202-3.

68. "IDT under fire", lead story in The Daily Cleaner, Dec. 5, 1995, p.l; "Sam Tyson questions IDT's future" in The Jamaica Herald, Dec. 6, 1995, p.3; Philmore Ogle, President of the Jamaica Chamber of Commerce, "IDT: butt of government's contempt.", in The Daily Gleaner, Aug. 7, 1994, p. 10E, "At the bottom of the barrel" by Nova Gordon-Be.il, in The Daily Gleaner, June 16, 1995, p.5A.

69. The Daily Gleaner, June 6, 1995, p.l.

70. ILO, Background Paper Prepared by the Labour Law and Labour Relations Branch of the ILO, Wage policy issues facing developing countries", in Wage determination in English-Speaking Caribbean Countries, ILO/DANIDA Regional Seminar, Kingston, Jamaica Mar. 1-7, 1978, p.26; Sec also the recommended "Structure, power and wage-price policy in the West Indies" by Compton Bourne, in ILO/DANIDA, Caribbean Project on Workers' Education and the Trade Union Education Institute: Labour Economics for Caribbean Trade Unionists, which highlights the difficulties of incomes policy implementation based largely on the Jamaican experience: See also Bourne, Caribbean Development to the year 2000: Challenges Prospects and Policies; CARICOM/Commonwealth Secretariat, 19SS, p.49.

71. "Prices and Incomes Policy in Jamaica", in ILQ, 1973, p.85.

72. Towards Developing a Social Partnership , PIOJ, Feb. 16, 1996, par. 36, p. 13.

73. Ibid, par. 46, p.22.

74. Roger Plant, *Labour Standards and Structural Adjustment*, ILO, 1994, pp. 40,43,

75. Ibid.

76. See Manley, 1990, p.117, where "broad national consensus on incomes policy is regarded as a "pre-condition both of orderly development and of the hope for a society resting upon the just distribution of wealth". Why then, one wonders, have the trade unions been so intransigent?

77. "Concerted" income policy instruments in Latin America are typified by the extension of control beyond wages to prices, profit margins interest rates and rents etc. Curbing excessive mark-ups on goods and services and on the cost of money, whether for capital investment or operating expenses, makes it possible "to create room for raising real wages" PREALC, Adjustment and the Social Debt, A structural approach, ILO, 1987, pp.35-86; Such real wage increases or parts thereof, can, of course, be placed in investment funds for the benefit of workers, and "excess" profits be reinvested in the same or some other enterprise, thus improving the investment rate and the production of tradeable; In the UK under the Labour Party in the 1970's the TUC in 1973 accepted incomes restraint within the context of an agreement covering prices, food subsidies, rents, taxes, pensions, steps to mitigate the erosion of living standards of the working class plus repeal of the Industrial Relations Act. Such apparent willingness to make concessions to labour was not enough to avoid the "Winter of Discontent" triggered by a demonstration against a public sector pay ceiling of only 5% by over one million civil servants desperate to 'catch-up'. The social contract was undermined by external fears about the stability of sterling, as the result of increased public expenditure in the effort to improve the social wage, provide income support for the poor, and cement the social contract with the unions. As was the case with Michael Manley's PNP, later in the decade, the Labour Party's reputation as the party of the working class was severely damaged – see Peden, 1991, p.205,

78. Nora Lustig, Mexico, *The Remaking of an Economy*, The Brookings Institution, Washington D.C. 1992, p.7.

79. But see "Battered British unions rethink Labour Party link" The Daily Gleaner, Sept. 10, 1994, p. 9 and the Guardian Weekly, Sept. 13, 1994, P. 9.

80. Carl Stone, "Trade Unions and Politics" in The Daily Gleaner, Feb. 3, 1938, and Jan. 6, 1938; Stone 1937, p.103. See also Lewis

and Nurse, "Caribbean Trade Unionism and Global Restructuring" in Watson (ed) 1994, p.206; Danny Roberts, "Defending the link between politics, and trade unions" in The Jamaica Herald, July 11, 1994, p. 6; For the somewhat similar development in Britain see "Battered British unions rethink Labour Party link", in The Daily Gleaner, Sept, 10, 1994, p.9,

81.   Rawle Farley, "Trade Unions and Politics in the Caribbean", Guyana: Daily Chronicle, 1957; William H. Knowles, Trade Union Development and Industrial Relations in the British West Indies, Berkeley and Los Angeles: University of California Press, 1954; H. Orkando Patterson, "Outside History: Jamaica Today", New left Review, London, No31, 1965; Carlene J. Edie, Democracy by Default - Dependency and Clientelism in Jamaica, Ian Randle, Kingston, and Lynne Rienner Publishers, Boulder and London, 1991, pp.105-107; For the tumultuous period of the 1970's See Girvan, Bernal and Hughes Development Dialogue 1930:2, Dag Hammerskjold Foundation, Sweden, pp.147-48,152; Evelyne Huber Stephens and John D. Stephens, *Democratic Socialism in Jamaica*, Princeton University Press, 1986, p. 51.

82.   This was a repeat of the monetarist prescription in the British situation of the mid 1970's causing the Labour Government to adopt and "announce policies acceptable to those (IMF) from which it wished to borrow" – see Peden, 1991, pp.205,210, The IMF doctrines based on public expenditure cuts, etc., which have now been played out in several countries, effectively ended the reign of Keynesian economies See also Paul Mosley, Jane Harrigan and John Toye, *Aid and Power*, Vol.l, Routledge, 1991 p.10: Not only was there the desire to abdicate responsibility for unemployment but IMF monetarism "reflected the spirit of the times: a weariness with the complexities and multiple and conflicting responsibilities of government".

83.   Stephens and Stephens, 1986, p 203

84.   By the insertion of a new Section, 11A, the Minister could now refer to the IDT on his own initiative, as against at the request of the parties, any dispute in any undertaking, once satisfied that an industrial dispute existed that should, in his view, be settled expeditiously.

85.   There is evidence in Jamaica of an obsession with a sense of social and cultural uniqueness to a degree verging on the unwillingness to objectively evaluate policy precedents established elsewhere. The attitude is almost as if nothing that has worked elsewhere, can work if adopted, in the island.

86.   The very brief treatment of the successive Accords to date is meant to bring out the degree to which they contrast with the efforts of the Jamaican authorities in the formulation of proposals for a Prices and Incomes Policy within the framework of a Social Contract. The details are taken from and the source is limited substantially to the "Background information to accompany the address by Senator Peter Cook, Australian Minister for Industrial Relations, at the London School of Economics and Political Science, June 13, 1991. This information was kindly provided on request by the Department of Industrial Relations, Central Office, Canberra, Australia.

87.   See also Stone, in Headley Brown (ed) 1993, pp.118,128.

88.   See also Corina, in British Journal of Industrial Relations, Vol.V, No.3, Nov. 1967, p.300.

89.   A necessary ingredient for a Contract to be binding in the English legal system which looks somewhat askance at altruistic commitments.

90.   The Accord Between the Australian Labour Party and the ACTU, Background Information to accompany the address by Senator Peter Cook, Australian Minister for Industrial Relations at the London School of Economics and Political Science, June 13, 1991, p.2.

91.   Ibid.

92.   Ibid.

93.   Ibid p.3; For a provision of a similar nature offering incentives for unions to keep the. peace (Wildcat Strikes, in particular) see Roger Blanpain, "Recent Trends in Collective Bargaining in Belgium", ILR Vol.104 Nos.1-2, July-Aug. 1971, p.125: "This peace obligation is generally accompanied by a clause providing benefits for union members only and gearing the payment of benefits to the faithful observance of the collective agreement and the maintenance of social peace during the life of the agreement". A brief summary of the position in Sweden is reported in Mats Hallvarsson (id) translated by Victor Kayfetz, *Swedish Industry Faces the 80's*, The Federation of Swedish Industries/The Swedish Institute, 1981, p.75.

94.   Under the Australian Accord,(Note 90 above) p.3 – "the aim was to reform the highly specialized award regulation of the work process" and promote more efficient deployment of the work force, somewhat along the lines of the British Productivity Bargaining/Agreements episode of the 1960's and 70's; See *Royal Commission on Trade Unions and Employer's Associations*, 1965-1968, (The Donovan Report) Cmnd.3623 Hmso,1969, Ch. 6, and in particular Research Paper, 4 on Productivity Bargaining and Restrictive Labour Practices, HMSO, 1967; Allan Flanders, The Fawley Productivity Agreements, Faber and Faber, 1964 reports fully on what became known as a model/classic case of this kind of bargaining and agreement.

95.   Concern with an equity, social wage, and family benefits package significantly distinguished it from Thatcherism.

96.   The Equal Pay law passed in 1975 with much fanfare and shoulder patting was largely ignored in terms of enforcement. The Australian Accord, supra, p. 4. One of the pieces of progressive pro-working-class legislation, for which the government of the day rightly takes much credit, was the Employment (Equal Pay for Men and Women) Act 1975. As with much well-intended statutory provisions the Act has not received the benefit of effective enforcement in a resource scare country with a substantially reduced role for the state and substantial reductions in the complement of public service staff under IMF required budget deficit cuts. See the Australian Accord (Note 39 above) p.4.

97.   David Panton, "Dual Labour Markets and Unemployment in Jamaica: A Modern Synthesis, SES, 42:1, ISER, U.W.I., 1993, p.97; Patricia Anderson, "Informal Sector or Secondary Labour Market? Towards a Synthesis", SES, Vol.36:3 ISER, U.W.I.,

pp.149-76; Michael Witter and Claremont Kirton, "The Informal Economy in Jamaica: Some Empirical Exercises, ISER, U.W.I. Working Paper No.36.

98. Dwight Venner, "The State in the Caribbean with Special Reference to a Mini-Economy", in Omar Davies (ed). The State in Caribbean Society, Dept, of Economics, UWI, Jamaica, 1986, pp. 52-53 .

99. For example, within three months of the IMF Extended Fund Facility Agreement of 1977, arrived at after dialogue between the Fund, Cover; …meat and unions , resulting in the wage guide policy, real wages fell by some 30%, described as "a brutal adjustment by the standards of the 70's" – Jane Harrigan, "Case Study of Jamaica" in Paul Mosley, Jane Harrigan and John Toye, *Aid and Power*, Vol.II, Routledge, 1991.

100. Harrigan, Ibid, p.355.

101. Reported in the Financial Gleaner, Aug. 27, 1993, p.24.

102. "Barbados-type wage measure not needed here, unionists say", The Daily Gleaner, Mar. 4, 1995, p.3.

103. Harrigan, Ibid.

104. JTURDC, The IMF and the Jamaican Labour Sector 1977-90. *A Study of the Impact of Wage Guidelines*, Occasional Paper, 1993, Section 3, pp.22 et seq.

105. Ibid, p.3.

106. Ibid, p.3.

107. Kari Polanyi Levitt, "The Origins and Consequences of Jamaica's Debt Crisis, 1970-1990, Consortium Graduate School of Social Sciences, 1991, p.11. According to Levitt," If the highest quintile consumes 49 of total national consumption, it is indeed likely that they earn at least 60a/ of the income. … This places Jamaica in a category with such notoriously inequitable societies as Ecuador, Peru, Mexico and Brazil".

108. Claremont Kirton, *Jamaica: Debt and Poverty*, Oxfarn, 1992. Subsidies on food items of mass consumption were abolished in May 1991 to meet the demands of Fund/Bank conditionalities, having been categorized by the IMF as "market distortions".

109. Mark. A. Wignall, "Row much is your dollar worth?" in The Jamaica Herald, Nov. 19, 1995, p.1A.

110. The impact of inflation is of course greater on those who are more likely to be affected by guidelines ~ the low paid with a higher marginal propensity to consume, and without the benefit of any form of income support.

111. JTURDC, 1993, p.42. See the labour market segmentation framework developed by Anderson and Witter as used to reveal the share of employment by sector – Patricia Anderson and Michael Witter, "Crisis, Adjustment arid Social Change: A Case Study of Jamaica in Elsie Le Franc (ed) *Consequences of Structural Adjustment: A Review of the Jamaican Experience*, Canoe Press, U.W.I., 1994, pp.28-30.

112. JTURDC, 1993, p.42.

113. The policy of appeasement of workers and their union organization, the ACTU, in the earlier Australian Accords, which represented a powerful incentive for cooperation, was in fact abandoned under Accord Mark III in March 1937. It is notable that under Accord Mark V the attempt was made to effect improvements in the social wage. The change, not surprisingly, from the policy of wage indexation reflecting the competitive situation in the global marketplace.

114. Huntley G. Manhertz, "The Price Determination Process in a small open economy: the Jamaican Experience" in Compton Bourne (ed) Inflation in the Caribbean, ISER, UWI, 1937, p.5; Headley Brown, "How meaningful is the published inflation rate?", (meaning CPI) in The Financial Gleaner, Nov. 4, 1994, p.8.

115. See News Releases, Minister for Industrial Relations, Government of Australia, 21 Sept. 1994 and 16 Aug. 1994. Pricing practice in Jamaica shows a "strong tendency for an exaggerated immediate upward adjustment in prices" in response to input cost increases, and, on the other hand, the fact that a price change in the opposite direction is either "lagged over an appreciable time period" or altogether lacking when input costs move downwards – Manhertz Ibid, pp.5-10. With the removal of price controls under the IMF regime, it is in such a situation even more urgent for consideration to be given to some form of safety net provision for members at the lower levels of the working population who are excluded from government's Food Stamp programme.

116. Zin Henry, *Labour Relations and Industrial Conflict in Commonwealth Caribbean Countries*, Columbus Publishers, Trinidad, 1972, p.244.

117. Tony Tophan, "New Types of Bargaining", in Robin Blackburn and Alexander Cockburn (eds), 1967, pp.149-155.

118. Danny Roberts, "Labour Market Reforms" in The Jamaica Herald, April 9, 1995, p. 7A; "Unions will resist 'discipline'" – JCTU, in The Daily Cleaner, April 3, 1995, p. 2. Lloyd Goodleigh, General Secretary of the JCTU is reported as calling on government and capital to say exactly what they mean by "labour market reform … many of the industrial relations practices that are now standard have been identified by various elements of the society as standing in the way of investment. Some people argue that regulations that protect workers are standing in the way of economic growth … (if labour market reform was a code word (sic) for an exercise to discipline unions, "it will not work".

119. Delroy Lindsay, President of the PSOJ, "Jamaica's industrial climate: a disincentive to investment and growth" in The Sunday Gleaner, Dec. 24, 1995, p.8C.

120. Rowthorn, op cit, pp.220-21.

121. Ibid, p.222.

122. Victor Allen, "The Paradox of Militancy", in Blackburn and Cockburn (eds) 1967, p.246; See also Tom Clarke and Laurie Clements (eds) Trade Unions under Capitalism, Fontana, 1977, p. 19; The wage restraint of the late 1970's sought to protect real wages from the effect of devaluation through the mechanism of a dual exchange rate policy. Subsequently, however, the extent of devaluation required by the IMF was directly linked to the level of wage increases. For a chronological treatment of the social and

economic policies and their consequences in the second half of the decade of the 70's, see Norman Girvan, Richard Bernal and Wesley Hughes "The IMF and the Third World: The Case of Jamaica", in Development Dialogue 1980: 2 Dag Hammerskjold Foundation, Sweden, p.124.

123.   Ibid, p.256.

124.   Alan Walker, "Strategy of Inequality" in Ian Taylor (ed) *The Social Effects of Free Market Policies*, Harvester Wheatsheaf, 1990, p.30.

125.   Rob Watts, "Living Standards and the Hawke Government, 1983-89", in Ian Taylor (ed) 1990, p.153.

126.   Ibid, pp. 154-167.

127.   Ibid.

128.   Ralph Miliband, *Parliamentary Socialism*, Merlin Press, London, 1987, p. 364.

129.   It is not economic growth, *per se*, which determines income distribution, Fields argues, but the type of growth "as determined by the environment in which growth occurs and the political decisions taken" – G.S. Fields Employment, Income Distribution and Economic Growth in 7 Small Open Economies", in The Economic Journal, Vo 1.94 No.373, 1980, p.94. In this regard, "the consumption preferences of those groups benefitting from income redistribution will need to be 'directed' towards those goods considered essential for subsistence" – a David Caiman and Frederick Nixson, *Economics of Change in LDC's*, Harvester Wheatsheaf, 1994, view which Girvan regards as perhaps not feasible in Jamaica – See Norman Girvan, Review of C.Y. Thomas, *The Poor and Powerless*, in SES, Vol.37 No.4, Dec. 1988, pp.264-65,269-71.

130.   Colman and Nixson, 1994, p.77.

131.   Ibid, pp.85-86.

132.   Hilbourne A. Watson, "Global Restructuring and the Prospects for Caribbean Competitiveness: With a Case Study from Jamaica", in Hilbourne A. Watson (ed), *The Caribbean in the Global Political Economy*, Ian Randle Publishers, Kingston, 1994, p.85.

133.   Immanuel Wallerstein, *The Capitalist World Economy*, Cambridge University Press, 1993, p. 73; Watson puts the matter in rather more terse language "It is naive", he declares, "to expect any capitalist state to guarantee equitable distribution of income and wealth" – Hilbourne A. Watson, "Beyond Nationalism: Caribbean Options under Global Capitalism", in Hilbourne A. Watson (ed) 1994, p.230.

134.   PREALC, Meeting the Social Debt, ILO, 1988, p.7.

135.   Girvan describes such IMF policies in the 1970's as being those that would "appease the very social and economic groups that were diametrically opposed to its (government's) political programme" – see Norman Girvan, "Swallowing the IMF medicine in the 1970's", in Development Dialogue 1930: 2 Dag Hammerskjold Foundation, Sweden, p.66.

136.   Norman Girvan, Richard Bernal and Wesley Hughes, op cit, pp.113,132-152; The authors who remark that "the IMF program clearly contributed to dissolving the class alliance ... discrediting the government's record of performance and undermining Its authority", at p. 147 report Michael Manley as referring to the "... internal price of social betrayal ... the outcome in an open society is political catastrophe", in his address to the management of the Inter-American Development Bank in May 1979. The catastrophe was to be manifested on only the personal and party-political electoral level in elections in 1930, and again in 1989 when the traditional pattern of two-term administrations was preserved, but with landslide victories for the rival parties on both occasions.

137.   PREALC, 1938, pp.48-49; Employee compensation in Japan was 41.3% of National Income in 1950 but 69% in 1990 – Japan: Profile of a Nation Kodansha International, 1994, p.104.

138.   138.   Elliott Currie, "Free Market Policy, Inequality and Social Provisions in the United States", in Ian Taylor (ed) op cit, p. 314; Laurie Clements, "Reference Groups and Trade Union Consciousness" in Clarke and Clements (eds) 1977, p.312; See also "Huge pay gaps fuel NWC labour dispute", in The Jamaica Herald, Aug. 24, 1994, p.3; The Guardian Weekly, Jan. 22, 1995, p.9, reports that "The Government did try with the idea of legislating executive pay, but considered this incompatible with its free market ideology". Workers union leaders are said to have warned of anger amongst all at the obscenely high pay rises given to top management. The right of the business community to call for wage restraint was clearly in question; The 1994 Jamaica Employers Federation's Wage Salary and Benefits Survey disclosed that some heads of private sector businesses were being paid up to J$4 million per year – The Daily Gleaner, July 26, 1994 p.3.

139.   Michael Manley, *The Politics of Change*, Heinemann (Caribbean) Ltd. 1990, pp.116-18.

140.   Michael Salamon, *Industrial Relations – Theory and Practice*, Prentice Hall, 1992, p.274; R. Hyman, *Industrial Relations: A Marxist Introduction*, MacMillan, 1975, p.125; See, generally, B. Towers (ed) A Handbook of Industrial Relations Practice, Kegan Paul, 1989.

141.   R.J. Davies, "Incomes and Anti-inflation Policy", in G.S. Bain, *Industrial Relations in Britain*, Blackwell, 1983, p.439.

142.   See Salamon, supra, pp.271-75; John Corina, "Can an Incomes Policy be Administered?", BJIR, Vol.V No.3, Nov. 1967, p. 305; Leon HoSang, "Wage Restraint/Incomes Policy", in The. Financial Gleaner, dec. 13, 1991, p. 21; For a variant of wages policy for the purpose of allocating labour, see J.P. Hutton and K. Hartley, The Selective Employment Tax and the Labour Market, BJIR, Vol. IV No.3, Nov. 1966, pp.289-303.

143.   George Jude, in The Daily Gleaner, Sept. 8, 1994, p.l; Danny Roberts of the NWU represents an example of the younger, more well-read, articulate and better educated of the current trade union leadership.

144.   The Daily Gleaner, Editorial, Nov. 11, 1994, p.6.

145.   The Hon. Dennis Lalor, in The Daily Gleaner, Dec. 18, 1994, p.4E.

146.   PSOJ, A Policy Framework for Economic Development in Jamaica, PSOJ, Kingston, Jamaica, Aug. 1985, p.22.

147. Ibid, p.22.
148. Ibid.
149. Will Hutton, "Minimum wage offers maximum returns", in The Guardian Weekly, July 23, 1995, p.21.
150. In the Jamaican Case, it. is the IMF and World Bank that effectively fulfil the roles of "the social and political institutions" in the Hutton quotation.
151. Hutton, supra, p.21.
152. Norman Girvan, "Rethinking Development", Consortium Graduate School of Social Sciences, U.W.I., April, 1991, p.9.
153. Robert Kyloh, The Wage - Inflation - Unemployment nexus, ILO, Geneva, 1988, p.45.
154. See D. Metcalf, Labour Market flexibility and jobs: a survey of evidence from OECD countries with special reference' to Great Britain and Europe, London School of Economics, Discussion Paper No. 254, 1986. Despite the focus on OECD countries, one would expect the same to apply in developing countries with IMF inspired or self-imposed guidelines that had been the subject of negotiated *quid pro quo* agreement; See also in this connection, K. Schott, *Policy, Power and Order – the Persistence of Economic Problems in Capitalist States,* Yale University Press, New Haven and London, 1984.
155. Kyloh, 1988, p.60.
156. Headley Brown, also stresses quite rightly, the importance to acceptance of pay policy of the inflation rate being contained at a level below the increase in the wage rate - see Headley Brown "Requirements for Social acceptance of pay guidelines", in The Daily Gleaner, Jan. 7, 1990; Some attempt at distributive justice might also have been made by interpreting guideline figures as an average and permitting increases above and below the guideline on the basis of "merit", the criteria for which could be established by agreement – see Leon HoSang "Wage restraint/ incomes policy" in The Financial Gleaner, Dec. 13, 1991, pp.14,16. This would require the provision and computation of accurate and comprehensive wage data, at both micro and macro levels, which requirement could easily frustrate such an approach. The alternative would, of course be, centralized planning of wages on the national level, which is unlikely for structural, institutional, and ideological reasons.
157. Jeffrey Sachs, in a 1985 study has argued that social conflict caused by large income inequalities constituted a serious barrier to economic success in Latin America. It was found that countries in which the ratio of the income of the richest 20% exceeded the income of the poorest 20% by more than 10 to 1 – in which group Jamaica would fall, almost invariably had to seek debt rescheduling in the 1980's – See J.D. Sachs, Social Conflict and Populist Policies in Latin America, NBER paper No. 2897, Harvard University, 1985.
158. Ted Honderich, *Violence for Equality – Inquiries in Political Philosophy,* Routledge, 1989, p» 14: this class of agents of inequality [the hegemonic ruling elite] ... actively obstruct change individuals who by their own actions do make for the distress of identifiable victims of inequality. ... These agents, he notes, do not set fuses to bombs, rather they are a member of a large anonymous class who read books, so their feeling about inequality has little to do with its agents ourselves) but not so with respect to our feelings about the *violence* of agents for *equality.*
159. The solution, according to the Minister in 1993, is not simply giving those in low paying jobs more money for the same performance either, but rather by relating rewards to productivity – a sound enough principle, but one rarely applied to management. Additionally, however, there are many obstacles to production and productivity enhancement that are beyond remedial action by the labour force. With so large a number of the population below the poverty line, it is evident that many in the lowest paid categories must be unable to afford the dietary requirements necessary for efficient productive physical activity – Dr. Omar Davies, then Minister without Portfolio in the Prime Minister's Office, later, Minister of Finance, the "The Economy: There are Things to Cheer About" in *The Money Index,* No.380, Aug. 3 , 1993 , p. 17; The "betterment factor", whereby workers expect a continuous improvement in their standard of living and quality of life, appears to have been of no great concern to Minister Davies, then Minister without Portfolio in the Prime Minister's office, later Minister of Finance. "The Economy: There are things to cheer about", in The Money Index, No.380, Aug. 3, 1993, p. 17; The "betterment factor", whereby workers expect a continuous improvement in their standard of living and quality of life, appears to have been of no great concern to Minister Davies.
160. Headley Brown, "Requirement for social acceptance of pay guidelines", in The Daily Gleaner, Jan. 7, 1990.
161. Ministry Paper No.6, 1987, Section B.2. on Public Sector Wage Policy.
162. Headley Brown, "Income policy needed in Jamaica", in The Financial Gleaner, Jan 3, 1994, p.13.
163. Ibid, This assumes, against the weight of the data on the rate of domestic investment, that the capitalist class will respond positively to investment opportunities. Carl Stone, on the other hand, has asked "How can the government and private sector leaders be talking about wage restraint unless they are going to offer in exchange a massive roll back in prices ..." – See Carl Stone, "The politics of prices", in The Daily Gleaner, June 15, 1992, and Carl Stone "Deregulating Labour", in The Daily Gleaner, Jan. 10, 1990, where it is asserted that, "The current incomes policy reflected in the wage guidelines is misconceived because it makes the false assumption that the cost of labour in Jamaica is a major factor influencing inflation levels and that price stability can be achieved by controlling wages".
164. See Dawn Ritch, "Bring back price controls", in The Daily Gleaner, May 31, 1992, p.9A; Godfrey Me Allister, President of The United Consumers in Action, "Swap lower prices for higher wages", in The Jamaica Herald Sept. 17, 1994, p. 7; The Jamaica Herald, Jan 4, 1995, p.3.

165. The Sunday Gleaner, Aug. 18, 1991, p. 38, reporting the speech of Government Minister, Hugh Small, at the Long Service Awards Presentation of the Best Dressed Chicken Division of the Jamaica Broilers Croup Limited, Kingston, Jamaica, on Aug. 16, 1991.

166. The Financial Gleaner, Editorial, Sept. 23, 1994, p.6.

167. For a treatment of the conflict between optimality concepts of income distribution and normative perceptions of the labour market mechanism, see Jan Tinbergen, "On the Theory of Income Distribution", in Selected Papers, North-Holland, 1959, pp.243-63.

168. John Gorina, "Can an Incomes policy be Administered?", in British Journal of Industrial Relations, Vol.v No.3, Nov. 1967, p.310.

169. Ibid, p.296.

170. Dennis J. Gayle, "Applying the East-Asian Development Model to the English-speaking Caribbean", in Jacqueline A. Braveboy-Wagner, *The Caribbean in the Pacific Century*, Lynne Rienner Publishers, 1993, p.94.

171. Peden, 1991, pp.169-71.

172. Milton Friedman, 'The role of monetary policy' American Economic Review, Vol.58, pp.1-17; Friedman's fear of overload of the welfare system, thereby undermining the citizen's independent spirit leading to increased dependence on the state and increased 'crowding in' of the state into the economy is contained in Milton and Rose Friedman, *Freedom to Choose*, New York, Avon Books, 1981, pp. 23,83. His earlier work *Capitalisim and Freedom*, University of Chicago Press, 1962 laid the foundation for his advice in 1963 against statutory incomes policy, which advice has aptly been described, in the then British context, as "attractive to Ministers who wished to be relieved of responsibility for unemployment".

Chapter 5
Social Contract

With the question obviously inviting agreement that there is just no conceivable alternative, Errol Ennis, the Minister of State in the Ministry of Finance and Planning, some two years ago asked, "If not a social contract then what?" A social contract is now, however, no nearer agreement, much less implementation: the concept has remained as general and nebulous as ever.[1]

The Junior Minister found it possible to inform his audience that "We in Jamaica are having an exciting economic and social revolution."[2] This was despite his observation that the private sector and the trade unions had harboured, in recent times, unrealistic expectations of the future. After some two decades of unrelieved inflation it was claimed that the trade unions and the private sector, in their reluctance to embrace the idea of a social contract, were reflecting a "lack of understanding of inflation and its effect on the economy."

But talking about the "ratchet" effect in the movement of wages and prices is of little usefulness, unless one demonstrates convincingly the direction in which the causal relationship operates. In fact, it is common knowledge that a constant rate of profit, with input price increases, whatever the reasons for them, which are built into the selling price of the product, can mean a larger surplus, even with a lower volume of sales. What can upset this scenario is the level of interest rate for businesses operating on a high ratio of bank loans/overdraft as against equity: and that, (interest rates levels), has been the responsibility of governments and the government-influenced Central Bank.

The commitment to deregulation and the determination of the essential prices, except wages, by market forces has not prevented the trend in loan interest rates being effectively set in relation to the rates on Government treasury bills, as FIG. 24 abundantly demonstrates.

On the other hand, as against the situation that is possible with profits, when the rate of wages remains stationary and costs to the worker increase, his real wage falls.

It is therefore a matter of ignorance, lack of thought, or an intention to mislead that accounts for this approach to the explanation of inflation. With respect to its control, as against its explanation, the only alternative to the social contract, of which Ennis is aware, is the Japanese Bonus system, where "one-third of salaries was paid as bonuses which were wiped out when there were "shocks" in the system"; this is a system said to be "not available to us", due to cultural differences. No mention whatsoever is made of the impracticality of the scheme, given the degree to which working-class living standards have already been ravaged by some twenty years of shock in the case of Jamaica.

The social contract solution requires, it is said, that labour and capital "come together and offer to share some of the reduction in real wages."[3] Put somewhat differently, although the working class has been "sharing" the considerable fall in real wages amongst its members, under government-imposed IMF income maldistribution, it must look forward to more of the same deprivation and hardship under the version of a social contract contemplated by a Government elected on its pledge to "Put People First", and that has given a recent commitment to the alleviation of poverty. One response to this conception of the long-awaited social contract was that of Hugh Shearer who, in speaking at the graduation ceremony of trade union delegates at the Joint Trade Union Research and Development Centre, made, special reference to "the social contract being spoken about." Cooperation of the unions, he suggested, could only be realistically expected, in arriving at "national understandings", if their range encompassed such matters as "control of price increases, profits, dividends, professional and other fees, mortgages, rents and interest rates."[4]

Figure: 24

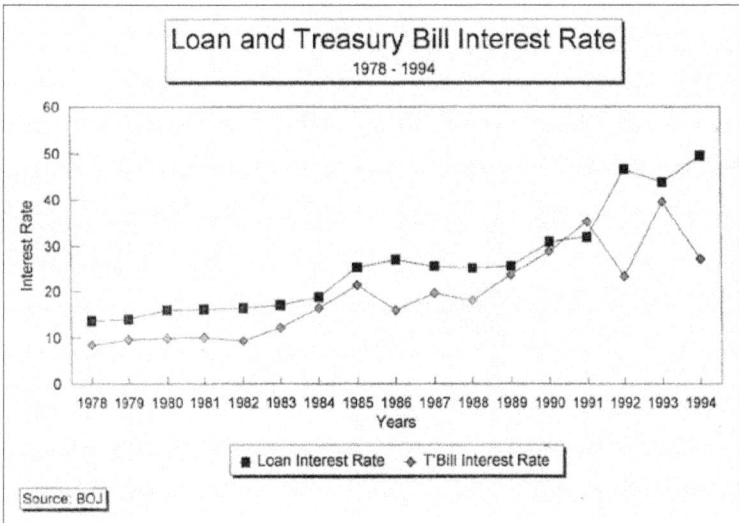

Loan and Treasury Bill Interest Rate
1978 - 1994

Source: BOJ

It has been suggested by Wilson that among these "prudent" triangular national understandings, basically involving wage restraint and price rise moderation, should be included "the missing dimension" of productivity. He strongly makes the further point that stability is but a means to an end, i.e. growth.[5] However, it is always also to be remembered that no matter how genuine and wide-ranging the consensus, and no matter what its specific elements, instability m the economic environment, and in particular with respect to consumer prices and the cost of capital and foreign currency, will cause the collapse of any social contract – regardless of the good faith of the representative parties directly involved in its formulation. If the economic foundations on which such a consensus rests shifts substantially, the degree of consultation with, and participation of, the various interest groups is not likely to preserve the consensus from disintegration.[6]

Political tribalism has, if anything, exacerbated the pronounced inequality in the system of asset ownership and wealth distribution as well as the lack of opportunities for social mobility under IMF austerity measures. While the numbers of the poor have been increasing, the resources available for the Social Well-being Programme of the 1980's and the Social and Economic Support and Poverty Alleviation Programmes of the 1990's have not been enough to make any real difference to the target groups. A clear indication of this has been the poverty line numbers, as disclosed by FIG. 18, while the allocation of the percentage share of public spending has shifted against working-class interests as indicated in TABLE 21 in percentage terms.

Spread as thinly as they have been, the benefits provided are more likely to harm than reward the political parties, in electoral terms. There has hardly been any period of significant length when the sample of opinion polls has reported predominantly optimistic feelings about future prospects, or the feeling of being currently better off than before. The Don Anderson poll of October 1994, for example, is not unusual in its finding that the volatility of the voting population is demonstrated by the marked changes of response on the question of their satisfaction with, the Prime Minister's running of the country:

Views on Own Personal Situation Now Compared to a Year Ago

Worse off now	36.6%
Just the same	43.0%
Better off now	14.2%
No response	6.2%

Source: The Don Anderson Poll of Oct. 1994r reported in the Daily Gleaner, Oct. 18, 1994, p. 2.

Table: 21		% Share of Public Spending	
Date	Debt Service	Social Services	Economic Services
1973-74	11%	33%	28%
1980-81	25%	22%	28%
1985-86	46%	23%	14%
1992-93	50%	20%	5%

Source: Carl Stone "Spending on the poor", The Dairy Gleaner, Jan. 4, 1993, p.6.

The more deprived the lower social classes perceive themselves to be, the more aggressive they are likely to become in the various forms of anti-social behaviour in which they can possibly engage. This will make it even more difficult for the spirit

Date	Satisfaction %	No	Not Sure
Feb. 1993	67	29	4
Sep. 1993	50	44	6
Feb. 1993	27	59	14

Source: Stone Poll, Mar. 1994, reported in The Daily Gleaner, Mar. 23, 1994, p.2.

of tolerance and mutual respect for rights, essential for an agreed social contract, to prevail.[7] The Stone Poll of December 1994 reported the public's perception of the prioritization of social issues in order of importance as being: education, crime, unemployment, health, and the management of the economy;[8] these are all areas requiring state attention.

In the 1990-95 Development Plan a major goal of Government was said to be to begin the process of creating the social climate that will allow the evolution of national consensus. Ensuring that "the welfare of people is given primacy in the development process", stated as the Governments' mission, was thought to require, surprisingly in a free market environment, the achievement of this allegedly discredited. "Keynesian consensus".

At the end of the planning period the observation that no progress whatsoever has been made in this aspect of the Plan would probably meet with little opposition, except from the Government and those with administrative responsibility in this specific area of policy determination. The same may be said in relation to the commitment "to the development of a social contract, through the operations of the National Planning Council and by means of public consultations to be launched from time to time."[9]

In seeking to gain maximum image differentiation from its predecessor – the JLP under Seaga – the present administration has taken the public participation and consultation approach to a point where policy formulation is being seriously delayed. The lesson has still not been learnt that contribution to policy making can better take place during a party's opposition years: disclosing one more instance of adopting the form of the Westminster parliamentary model, but not the substance.

The terms of reference of the National Planning Council of most relevance to the evolution of the social contract was, the, "… coordination (sic) where, labour, the private sector and Government can meet to work towards overall improvement in the standard of living of the nation *as a whole.*"[10]

It is obvious that the people to be served by Plans of this kind are again being treated as a highly aggregated abstraction[11] – giving rise to the indictment that "seldom is there more than superficial effort to determine the characteristics of the poor who constitute the majority of the population: their location; their strategies for survival in their particular ecological setting; the barriers to improvement; how the development project will ensure that the benefits reach those most in need as against the most greedy or powerful or those with better contacts".[12] Given the scandalous and well-documented income and wealth inequality, the inclusion of the words of appeasement "nation as a whole" perhaps suffices to justify doubt as to the seriousness of the Government's commitment. If indeed the Government is to be taken seriously about its pursuit of a social compact, it must state in precise terms where the benefits and the costs will fall, if it is to avoid accusations of deception. As Harrison has put it, "… if change is really to benefit the poor and powerless, it has to hurt the rich and powerful".[13]

The projected annual growth rate under the Plan was 3% – on the basis of which one of the objectives of macro-economic policy was increasing consumption, "so as to achieve social and political consensus needed to support the economic programme."[14]

After several years of giving consideration to the notion of a social contract the economic and social targets disclosed in this the latest Five-Year Plan still lack quantification and are still couched in general terms such as: "long term growth"; "broadening the base of the economy"; "employment growth"; "improvements in basic social services".

The fact is yet to be squarely faced that, as Schumpeter remarked, there is the need for some kind of incentive (beyond the reliance on a purely altruistic sense of duty) to elicit the response desired by policymakers. Generalities, such as 'greater equity', 'and substantial and lasting human resource development improvements', have been heard too often, with little tangible results, to form the basis of national consensus involving 'belt tightening' and 'sacrifice'.[15]

This elusive 'national consensus' within the context of a free market economy does not seem to be recognized for the contradiction in terms that it is. Indeed, it would seem to fit more easily into the Marxist version of utopia, involving the withering away of the state[16] or William Morris' vision of a society, "… where affairs are conducted entirely by voluntary and spontaneous cooperation".[17]

For while competition and markets may have the potential for bringing benefits to the consumer by stimulating increased efficiency in production, Bottomore has cautioned that not only is technological progress not an un-mixed blessing, but also, that the free market mechanisms are likely, at the same time, to also bring greater instability, economic inequality, perhaps a deterioration of collective provision and the sense of community.[18]

Hayek, in opposition to the vision of a deliberately inclusive national society pursuing the goal of social justice, conceives of an ideal represented by a "spontaneous order", in which the freedom exists for the individual to use his knowledge for his own purposes. The very notion of a social contract, according to Hayek, is doomed to failure since,

> "… society in the strict sense in which it must be distinguished from the apparatus of government, is incapable of acting for a specific purpose … since it has no general will".[19]

As against Hayek's view, it may be recalled that the equivalent of a social contract in its basic form was, for however short a time, achieved in Britain in February of 1948 by the Atlee Government, whereby the TUC and a conference of trade union executives endorsed a programme calling for the voluntary stabilization of prices, profits, and wages. As Shanks asked some thirty years ago, "… why should usages be the one planned element in an unplanned society?"[20]

Under the outstandingly effective leadership of Sir Stafford Cripps, during peacetime in 1949, wage restraint was successfully implemented, in Britain, as one element in the austerity campaign. It is significant that his strong fiscal measures which applied to all classes, were ameliorated, mediated and balanced by relatively high budgetary allocation for the social services.[21]

Contrary to this post-war British approach and its results, the 1988 ILO study of South and Central America and Jamaica found, that workers share of the national income declined by 1.6% between 1980 and 1985; their consumption fell by 4.8%; the shift in income from labour to capital, instead of stimulating an increase in investment, was associated with a 6% decrease; and capitalist consumption rose by 8%.[22]

Attempts to remove food subsidies – unlike in Jamaica where they were met with the characteristic short-lived verbal opposition-led in Egypt, Algeria, Tunisia, Morocco, Sri Lanka, Haiti, Venezuela, and the Dominican Republic to the sort of riots which caused Pantin to remark that, "In its severity the prescribed medicine can be seen as major surgery without anaesthetics or antibiotics",[23] Removal of subsidies on not only basic food items but essential items like medicinal drugs, has not been an isolated choice of policy tending to militate against the achievement of national economic policy consensus. Massive layoffs in the public and private sectors has naturally led to union opposition and the creation of a mood in the labour movement that is not at all conducive to cooperation, much less voluntary restraint and sacrifice 'in the national interest – a national interest in which they see themselves as being regarded as having no stake.[24]

Proponents of a social contract/national consensus have not displayed a consciousness of the essential distinction between the need for substantive content in the form of subject matter appropriate for meaningful inter-class bargaining on the basis of modern concepts, as against what might have been adequate for philosophical formulations in the day of Hobbes, Rousseau, Locke and Hume. By founding the authority of government on the presumed consent of the people it was taken as an indispensable part of this "original" compact that the subjects had,

> "... tacitly reserved the power of resisting their sovereign, whenever
> they find themselves aggrieved by that authority with which they have,
> for certain purposes, voluntarily entrusted him."[25]

The consent necessary for the legitimization of governmental authority was not expected to be granted in the absence of the advantages resulting from the maintenance of peace and order by the government. As tangible benefits alone would justify a man foregoing,

> "... the advantages of his native liberty and subject(ing) himself to the
> will of another, this promise is always understood to be conditional

and imposes on him no obligation, unless he meet with justice and protection from his sovereign."[26]

Whereas,

> "... the conditions upon which (the subjects) were willing to submit were either expressed, or were so clear and obvious, that it might well be extremely superfluous to express them"[27] the same can hardly be said with respect to interest representation in the formulation of the national consensus/social compact framework attempted, to date, in Jamaica.

It goes without saying that, in a responsibility-avoidance and accountability-averse society, no thought has publicly been given to the matter of determining the locus of responsibility in the event the consensus is forthcoming, but its projected results are not achieved. Finger pointing has long been a favourite exercise among the tripartite so-called social partners.[28]

Arthur Lewis, one suspects, with the British wartime experience in mind, claimed that liberal democracy would prevent the imposition, of wage control in the absence of, "... the full consent and cooperation not only of the union leaders, but of the rank and file."[29] Clearly, such a statement does not apply to the Jamaican case in the context of IMF/World Bank stabilization and structural adjustment programmes. Lack of trade union unity and militancy due to industrial rivalry and political party affiliation; low level unionization; intimidation of the unions by a combination of the threat of the constant possibility of the withholding of loan tranches or the cancellation of project funding by the IMF and World Bank; and political leadership under which there is the gradual reduction of economics to politics (a tendency noted by Karl Mannleim);[30] the loss of radical ideological commitment, with union establishment and maturation; the changed political and economic world environment; and an internal economic situation distinctly unfavourable to labour, all conspired to allow, if not welcome, in Jamaica in the 1970's and 80's precisely what Lewis had thought impossible in England at the end of the 1960's.

Being conscious of the need for a worthwhile *quid pro quo*, Lewis does observe that wage restraint would not be accepted until workers felt that other egalitarian measures were being pursued, that there would be substantial employment creation, and that the government "has the activities of capitalists well under control." For

Lewis' time and place, it might have been valid to conclude that, "these things take time to demonstrate", and so, "... there is little prospect of achieving a planned wage structure in the near future".[31] In the Jamaican situation, "these things" have not happened for eighteen years and are no more imminent now than at any time since Independence, in 1962, not to mention universal adult suffrage in 1944.

The greater the class distinctions in the old culture, according to Kerr, Dunlop, Harbison and Myers, the more intense, as might be expected, the industrial conflict.[32] In the absence of crisis, prompted by the threat of, or actual aggression against the country, or the affiliation of the majority of the unions in the labour movement to the political party forming the government, it seems doubtful that the conditions will be perceived to exist to the extent necessary for agreement on a social contract to emerge – taking these authors' conclusion and the guidance of historical evidence from different country settings into account.

Additionally, Kerr, et al., argue that, "... the greater the reliance on the constriction of domestic consumption the greater the control over the relations of workers and managers",[33] which fits very neatly the IMF scenario. But it is precisely the attempt at greater institutional regulation of industrial relations which in an ex-colonial cultural setting, suffering from the further disabilities of the experience of slavery, which will aggravate the contradictions of capitalism and erect the most forbidding hurdle to a genuinely voluntary national 'understanding'.

Demand management, as a key IMF macro-economic strategy, has meant intended sustained reduced consumption by the working class and the poorer sections of the population. The way has been smoothed for the implementation of the strategy by the statutory imposition of institutional constraints on labour's freedom to resort to industrial action. Those provisions have come under the pressure posed by a combination of the effects of inflation, mass disillusionment with traditional party politics, and increasing trade union unity resulting in the greater representation and articulation of labour concerns and interests at the national level.

One suspects that this has led to the recent establishment of the presently sitting Labour Market Reform Committee. It should not be surprising if, despite the predominance of the free market ideology, new strategies and mechanisms of labour control are proposed. As Kerr, et al., have argued:

"The quicker the adjustments required of the work force, the greater
the potential protest, and the greater the technical need for control over

the workforce, labour organisations, and the labour market, if latent protest is not to be explosive"[34]

It seems not to be realized that the greater the level of existing control, the less the room that is thereby allowed for the kind of maneuvering space required for fruitful social consensus negotiations.

There has been some broadening of the focus of concern of Jamaican trade unions, over historical periods, from an almost exclusive emphasis on wages and basic working conditions in the 1930's and 40's, to the consideration of national economic issues in the 1970's to the present. This development has occurred as the direct relationship between macro level economic policies and the prospects for the welfare of the working class became better appreciated. The present conjuncture between militancy at the enterprise level, a reaction against prolonged frustration of the objective of a better quality of life under structural adjustment, and the desire of the political directorate to achieve a new level of cooperation within a social contract framework, seems also to confirm the observation that sharper divisions tend to arise in industrial conflict between the issues of the work place and those of the larger community at certain stages of economic development.[35]

The dilemmas faced by labour organisations: increased wages versus capital formation; strikes versus production; grievance handling versus discipline; and organisational prestige versus political subservience[36] are all issues, save perhaps the last, which need to be high on the agenda of discussions seeking national economic and social policy agreement.

To say, as Boxill does, that "Politicians are able to maintain control and avoid accountability because their largest constituency is divided", is not of great assistance: in every multi-party-political system division is the very reflection of the benefit of choice. The existence of choice can scarcely, in itself, explain permitted weaknesses in the system. "Because, there is a divided nation, vertically and horizontally, civil society is stifled, and, attempts", Boxill contends, "... to reach a national consensus on issues such as an industrial policy are stymied."[37]

If consensus on industrial policy, in particular, is elusive, it is false analysis to suggest that the reasons are the divisions in society, together with the presence of political patronage, deriving from the political system's clientelistic features. As slavery and later colonialism were, and still are, used by some to explain virtually all the ills, and weaknesses in the society, so, on this dispensation, the source of all shortcomings in the political system – particularly as represented by a less than desired response from the mass of the electorate – is to be traced to 'pork barrel/ personal benefit' politics. It is here suggested that the conflict of views as to the proper substance of an Industrial Policy is to be expected: indeed, it would have been remarkable if it were otherwise. It is also to be observed that the chosen method and expected level of participation by the general public could not have been more ill-conceived by those responsible for policy formulation.

Holding public forums on technical issues in a disillusioned semiliterate society is to try to camouflage lack of clear policy leadership with 'people participation' public relations activity. The embarrassingly small attendance at parish capital venues testified adequately to the widespread indifference to many such participatory strategies and "remotely relevant" subjects by, "… a people preferring strong leadership and involvement at a level where their *personal* [italics added] interest is immediately apparent."[38] As it has been put by Butler and Stokes, with reference to Britain,

> "… understanding of policy issues fall away very sharply indeed as we move outwards from those at the heart of policy decision-making to the public at large".[39]

It is instructive that, as in Australia in the 1980's, the nearest that Britain got to a social contract covering more than the barest minimum of issues was during the union-affiliated Labour Party government after the 1974 election. This was when the nature of the party/labour movement relationship was such that Michael Foot could, on reflection, declare that,

> "Even during the so-called 'winter of discontent' in 1978-9 the lines of communication with the trade unions were never broken, and the concordat agreed after it, was a fresh intelligent way of seeking a solution to common problems, especially for the lower paid workers whose discontent had been so real."[40]

The expectation that with a history of authoritarianism, a public nurtured on a psychology of dependency, paternalism, and more recently on home-grown patronage, would eagerly make worthy contributions to policy content ignores the reality that the general population is often incompetent to fill the 'informed spectator' role which call for the ability to make the connection between ends and means.[41] In addition to this inability, Butler and Stokes argue that,

"... having but a weak sense of how a particular policy line will have an influence on anything it values, the electorate may form only weak ephemeral preferences even among the policy alternatives it does perceive."[42]

What is suggested here is the need for selective public participation in policy formation – for the process of participation and consultation is likely to be generally devalued and made the target of public cynicism, if misapplied.

Within the framework of the population's experience and perception of the IMF and World Bank and their policies, historically, not unassisted by delinquent governments, any new public policy proposed within the life of the IMF regime is likely to be tainted by, and negatively prejudged as a result of that experience. This will, of course, cause a shift in focus from policy content and potentialities to conditioned expectations as to consequences. "[Unfavourable] changes of personal economic condition are overwhelmingly salient to the mass of electors and evoke in them strong and definite attitudes".[43] Calls for a social consensus, to surmount or circumvent the hurdle of cynicism, and negative predisposition on the part of a disaffected public, need to offer very attractive positive incentives to have any chance of being heeded.

Under the British war-time coalition government, the state assumed wide powers of control over private property, including land and banks; powers of inspection of the books of private companies; and employees could be forced to any location and to do any task.

Bilaterally, a Joint Council had the function of preventing disruptive industrial action, while the Ministry of Labour and other Government-Departments worked together to fix rates of wages and other terms and conditions of employment.[44] Not unexpectedly, in such a situation where austerity was not "unerringly reserved for the working class", the public was more disposed to favourably respond to appeals for cooperation and sacrifice in the national interest.

The failure by Caribbean governments to implement their own proposals can be traced, as Gordon Lewis has done, to, "... one of the crippling handicaps of West Indian Life" which,

"... has been the deceptive sense of security engendered by colonial rule – like Mr. Micawber [they] have been incurable optimists waiting for something to turn up. Their capacity for positive action rooted in a frank appraisal of the reality of things was thus seriously undermined. They were lacking the one single incentive, the knowledge that they were on their own in an uncertain and frequently hostile world, calculated to nurture that capacity."[45]

No one could, with justification, accuse the Jamaican poor, of being impatient to find a sanctuary, having endured purgatory at the hands of their governments and the international financial institutions for nearly two decades. Indeed, they could be excused for thinking and acting as if their turn had come to inherit the earth. But the perspective which linked economic growth and equity in the distribution of income, promoted under the auspices of the World Bank, by the Institute of Development studies at the University of Sussex, has had little tangible results in improving the lot of the poorest, including the working poor members of the population.[46]

Contrary to the concerns of those sensitive to the need to achieve some measure of social justice, the sister institution to the World Bank, the IMF has guided and supervised the design and implementation of economic 'development' policy, the direct result of which has been the very opposite of maximizing the growth of incomes of the poorest groups in the medium term.[47]

In any model of a social contract some form of the ILO promoted concept of the 'basic needs' approach to public policy formulation can, with advantage, be incorporated. Instead of platitudinous declarations, in vague general terms, of the intention to improve the living conditions of the poor,[48] the political directorate will, adopting this approach, be forced to set targets with time schedules for improving the life circumstances of specific groups. Perhaps this would help to minimize indulgence in rhetoric about "progress in the abstract", which is so difficult of measurement, and, therefore, of being disproved.

Focusing on strictly economic rather than social considerations, Morrison expresses the view that a viable accumulation model is lacking, based on majority political and consensual social support, by which the process can reproduce itself with continuously increasing levels of investment, production, and living standards.[49] He sees the construction of the tripartite social contract taking place within the context of a "culture of partnership" prevailing in an economy operating along the lines of the general market model.

The nature of the commitments required from the parties relate to matters such as: the role of the state in economic development;[50] the aims of adjustment policies – whether emphasis should be exclusively on stability/demand compression or increasing production through investment and thereby generating growth; measures to encourage re-investment of profits, perhaps through the mechanism of "investment wages", as proposed by PREALC and as implemented in Sweden; the identification of investment priorities under an agreed industrial policy; the reform of production relations along more participative lines; strategies for manpower development; and, not least, the appropriate returns to capital and labour .[51]

From this perspective, the effectiveness of the social contract will be largely a function of the degree of determination exhibited in the pursuit of investment priorities, bearing in mind the dynamism and degree of competition in international markets, among other factors.

Morrison regards the abandonment of what he calls "predatory" party politics as essential, if there is to be a move towards cooperation for investment maximization and away from the political oppositional attitude which seeks electoral victory by default.

If the Asian "Tigers" provide a model worth emulating, then on the World Bank's evaluation, there may be a strong case for a strong state, since a strong private sector may well need a strong state to drive the development process. Monetary policies, discriminating in favour of investment, such as differential interest rates; the setting of overall investment and savings targets, conspicuously absent from the National Planning Council's Social Contract Discussion Paper;[52] and insisting that venture capital be diverted towards productive investment projects are all factors, it is argued, which would enhance the social contract's effectiveness.[53]

It is in order to suggest that a fundamental error being made by the ruling political elite is the apparent belief that, given the society's social history and culture, the classes will somehow optimally apportion the burdens of accumulation for investment, voluntarily, among themselves. It may be that it is necessary to make use of,

> "... the coercive power of the *state* [which] provides a means of enforcing the cooperation that we all desire, of ensuring that each of us bears his share of the investment burden instead of attempting to shift it onto the shoulders of others."[54]

This is a failure exhibited at the very outset, if in a slightly varied form, in the *Draft Outline of Social Contract/Understanding*, a document prepared for discussion between the so-called "social partners." The goal of domestic investment and national cooperation is stated to be improving the living standards of *all* [italics added] who contribute." Policy makers continue to attempt to appease all classes – and, in so doing, ignore the reality that, given the pattern of extreme income and wealth inequality, the relatively wealthy can be called upon to make sacrifices for the benefit of the relatively poor; in other words, there are some whose standard of living deserves, perhaps, to fall.[55]

The matter is put into perspective by noting the different treatment given the issue of poverty. *The Draft Outline of Social Contract/Understanding* reserves the consideration of Poverty Abatement for the very last section of the Paper, begun with the admission that, "The government recognizes the negative impact on certain disadvantaged groups, that the necessary structural reform programme has caused." While we are informed that total spending on programmes to help these groups was close to 1% of GDP during the previous financial year (1991/92) and that there was a commitment to maintain this level of expenditure "during the period of this understanding and beyond", there is no indication as to the inadequacy, or otherwise, of "this level of expenditure".[56]

It is significant that although it is recognized that the real solution to poverty depends on the level of growth and employment in the economy, whereas the targets were 2-1.5% real GDP growth for 1992/93 and 1993/94, actual performance was 1.4% and 0.8%, respectively.[57] Of even greater interest, perhaps, in a document purporting to convey the fact of tripartite agreement, we are advised that "The social partners have reached consensus on the following broad policy objectives, "... 5. Increasing new employment by '000 (sic) jobs in each year."[58] In marked contrast, the JTURDC in the second paragraph of its response to the Draft Outline, targets, "... the dramatic increase in the levels of poverty in the country" as being primary among the concerns of its member unions and the labour movement, generally.[59]

It is arguable that the psychological basis for a social contract will not exist until there is acceptance of the realities, as put by Farrell, that,

> "... as a country we have failed; it is decisions at government level
> (mismanagement) that largely explain this failure; our failure is, in the
> final analysis, our responsibility. To blame everything imaginable for our
> failure after two decades and more of independence is silly ... [since]
> enemies, rivals, obstacles and capricious fate are facts of life that one has
> to live with, overcome, or get around."[60]

The promoters of the free market ideology have yet to convince the masses that the assumption, from Independence, that the state had the principal role in social and economic transformation in the interest of the majority,[61] is no longer valid. Therein largely lies the explanation for the present disenchantment with the two political parties which have shared power in Jamaica since 1944, but, more particularly, since 1972. The appearance of consensus and the perception of the state as the appropriate representative and leader for the benefit of the majority of the population seems in fact to have been shattered by the adjustment experience. It may not be an unreasonable interpretation, therefore, that the attempt to arrive at a social contract really represents the continuing, "... search for an appropriate strategy of transformation of the inequitable, unjust and unproductive relationships ..."[62] which have long existed, and which have been substantially worsened by the borrowing relationship with the IMF. Such an interpretation needs to be highlighted because there are those who seem to seek consensus and continuity without regard for the social merit of the policies being agreed or maintained. The argument based on the need for preservation of 'the basic rules of the game' and "consistent policy fundamentals" over time, so as to create the environmental stability which will allow "those policies needing a longer gestation period" the time to take hold, despite its superficial appeal, certainly needs to meet the social merit test.[63]

Workers were being told that while it was understandable that they were demanding more wages as the local currency lost value and as their standard of living fell, in consequence, this response did not amount to a real solution to the problem. By demanding less in wages, and, better still, no increase at all, the message of neoliberal economics seemed to be that workers would somehow be better off.

And if self-discipline on their part was not sufficient t o p rovide t he 'real' solution, then that solution was to be found in a social contract between workers, employers and Government. The real solution as far as public-sector workers were concerned, was an announced staff reduction by a further 8000 – a reduction that according to the Minister of the Public Service had the objective of "achieving efficiency in the spending of taxpayers money." But the repeated use of this tactic has been described as,

> "... the band-aid of redundancy that is always pulled out of its first
> aid kit every time the Government has to reduce its budget deficit".[64]

Without attempting to specify the elements of a social contract in such circumstances, in respect of which "the time has come for the parties to reach consensus", Mr. Patterson, the Prime Minister, is reported to have continued, "If each group can keep its part of *such* [italics added] an agreement, we are well on our way".[65]

Instead, then, of the details of the "something" to be sacrificed by each party – the *quid pro quo* of the compromise or, at the very least, the proposed mechanism to ensure price restraint – what we are provided with is another instance of government by exhortation: "companies should refrain from charging higher prices *simply* [italics added] to maintain and increase their profits". To the unconverted this would seem to signify a version of the free market economy, without the freedom.

In similar vein, the Governor of the Central Bank urged workers to accept a fall in their living standards as they should avoid seeking pay rises in keeping with the expected upward movements in prices.[66]

These expressions on a social contract directly followed substantial wage gains by bauxite/aluminum and banking sector employees. In the case of bauxite/alumina, the reason, already adverted to, was ability to pay – the direct result of substantial devaluations; in banking, massive windfall gains had been made and well publicized in the Financial sections of the press in recent years, arising from removal of exchange controls, deregulation of the exchange rate and liberalization of the financial sector, particularly with respect to the setting of interest rates.

Whereas McIntyre referred to the planned "next-leap", in Singapore, a Government of Singapore publication has stated that one of its major objectives was the creation of a "German quality workforce at two-thirds of the wage rate". What policy-makers and vested business interests in Jamaica seem to be seeking is the German quality at the Haitian/Jamaican wage rate; that is to say, at the 1987 comparative wage rates shown in TABLE 22, below one-twenty fifth, or 4% of the German wage rate.[67]

Table: 22   Hourly Compensation for Semi-Skilled Production Workers
in Export Manufacturing (1987)

	US$ Per Hr.		US$ Per Hr.		US$ Per Hr.		US$ Per Hr.
U.K.	8.67	Mexico	0.84	Taiwan	1.84	Jamaica	0.63
Canada	11.94	Costa Rica	0.95	S. Korea	1.54	Barbados	1.72
U.S.A.	13.66	Dom. Rep.	0.79	China	0.15	Trinidad	
Germany	15.93	Hong Kong	1.98	Brazil	1.14	& Tobago	1.66
Haiti	0.58	St. Lucia	0.92	Antigua	1.40		

Source: Stone in Headley Brown (ed), 1993, p.129.

In relation to Prime Minister Patterson's dual call for "lumping together" wage restraint and passing on of the benefit of the dollar's revaluation to consumers, in the late Terry Smith's judgement the former was, in the then prevailing circumstances, only a "minority irritant". But the latter he saw as constituting, "... a majority issue of deeply entrenched market deception, if not out-right trade fraud". Smith argues that what we need is not the "ILO ism" of a social contract between workers, employers and Government but one between the *community* (including the workers and their unions) the private sector and government.[68]

As far as Smith was concerned, "production or other incentive bonuses remains paper talk", because the unions take no responsibility for finding answers, which they view as "always the business of somebody else". He therefore did not find it surprising that the two major unions rejected the call for wage restraint in the interest of cost-push inflation control and international competitiveness – neither of which moved in the desired directions despite fourteen years of wage guidelines – but insisted instead on conducting wage negotiations on the 'ability to pay' criteria.[69]

Smith then made the rather startling suggestion that the trade union attitude could, with impunity, be ignored "once he (the Prime Minister) brings the overriding interests of the wider community into the social contract equation, to keep certain other minority self-centered demands in check". Who or what institution would effectively, whether *de jure* or *de facto*, represent the views of this wider community is never stated, and there is no hint of reference to a referendum. As the property-less labourer was not considered a part of Locke's civil society, so it seems that for this "doyen of labour journalists" the unionized working class and their leadership is not an important element in the 'community'.

The Government, pointing to the potentially inflationary consequences of the extraordinarily large pace-setting wage increase of over 100% at Alumina Partners of Jamaica in 1994 could not be less than pleased by this journalistic performance. The pay rise was justified by company management on the basis of concern for equity and justice. The more cynical, but perhaps realistic, view could however be taken that it represented "a strong element of desperation" and even strategic accommodation of union demands for the sake of maintaining industrial stability, m a context of extremely aggressive, acrimonious inter-union representational rivalry between the incumbent union and one determined to challenge for bargaining rights, the more left-leaning, UAWU.

As it turned out, the level of wage increase granted by the bauxite company did nothing to remove the representational challenge, nor alter the bitter nature of the violence-threatening inter-union conflict. Action based on expediency rather than principle, whether in relation to pay rises or the resolution of community conflicts of interest, is usually unlikely to prove a satisfactory long-term solution to basic industrial or social issues.

Disappointingly, but true to the Jamaican tendency to clientelism, patronage and to personalization of issues, the trade unions are by implication condemned for ingratitude. The argument seems to be that since the Prime Minister, a Queen's Counsel, had given distinguished legal service to the workers and their trade unions, those workers and trade unions "possessing very short memories", were not about to tear up their IOU's "with any emotional trauma". The strong probability of accusations by members of a "sell-out"[70] by their trade union leaders in a scandal-riddled, rumour-mongering society, did not appear to have been a matter of concern to those, like Smith, who are untroubled by the question as to where the occupational commitment and loyalty of union leaders ought properly to be.

"By this strategy", of tearing up IOU's, allegedly outstanding in favour of the then and current head of the then governing party, "the trade, unions could attempt to have it all their way in any social contact – "... if they had the strength".[71] The most that can be done with contributions of this kind to the Social Contract debate is to leave them to confront the challenge of the data on real wages, profits, investment, unemployment, the deterioration of the social services and price movements from 1977 to the present.

Essentially, the point being made is that trade union and worker behaviour on wage-related issues needs to be constrained, within the framework of any form of compact, by "the supportive attitudes of the whole community". Yet again, trade union members, non-unionized workers and their dependents – to say nothing of the vast army of the unemployed – appear not to be counted among this mysterious "whole community". It is in facing this perspective on these issues that one can gain an appreciation of the import of Engel's reply, "Who are they?", when reference was made to the entity, "the people in general".

In September of 1992 Terry Smith returned to the subject of wages and the elusive search for a social contract". Mention is made of a document[72] circulated to the unions by the Ministry of the Public Service. This document called for a national wage increase of not more than 12.5%, a public sector and selective private sector wage freeze, and price, profits, and dividend restraint.

Recalling the crisis brought on by similar developments in 1985, which led to protest and defeat, the unions, through a more united front in the form of the Joint Trade Union Research and Development Centre, "donning their battle fatigues, examining weapons and strategies and even uttering bunker epithets", were successful in negotiating the document's withdrawal within a matter of four weeks.

It had been thought necessary by the Ministry of the Public Service to "dampen wage expectations and achieve national consensus on what level of wage increase will afford *reasonable* [italics added] standards of living, without fuelling inflation".[73] Under the Social Contract – National Wage/Income Policy for Fiscal year 1992/93, (Ministry of the Public Service Paper 78/92), the crucial question is, of course, deciding what is 'reasonable'. The workers of the Bank of Jamaica, the Central Bank, who should be 'in the know', are persons one would expect to be guided by rationality. They nevertheless claimed increases of 260% in year one and 500% in year two. They no doubt entertained the belief that it was legitimate and desirable to attain/regain a standard of living formerly considered appropriate, given their status, in pre-IMF days. Viewed in this manner, 760% increase in two years would not be at all excessive. 'Greedy and selfish' militant workers and their unions who are condemned for 'holding the country to ransom' had nevertheless failed up to the first half of the 1990's to regain real wage levels of the late 1970's, as is clearly indicated by TABLES 16 & 18 and FIG. 29.

If, as the Ministry paper stated, "Achieving a social contract is crucial to the success of the Governments' efforts in reducing the rate of inflation"[74] this would signify failure in that major policy objective. The social contract has yet to move beyond the 'talking' stage up to the end of 1994,[75] and beyond.

The Government, in the Ministry paper, called for a freeze and voluntary reduction, in salaries above a "certain level" in the private sector. This appeal was unmatched by any similar restraint or any such undertaking on the part of members of the Government. Instead, the self-decreed salary increase of 250% to Members of Parliament did not fail to generate popular denunciation and accusations of hypocrisy.[76] The Minister of Finance ill-advisedly perhaps, disclosed that on his salary of $708,000 (plus the allowances which he failed to mention) per annum, he is only able to survive because his wife works. When teachers are awarded a 16%[77]

increase which would bring a trained teacher's salary up to $169,431.00 per annum, without the enjoyment of the various benefits, allowances, and concessions enjoyed by MP's and Government Ministers, the working class and masses generally are unlikely to sympathize with the Minister's call to "hold strain".

Figure: 25

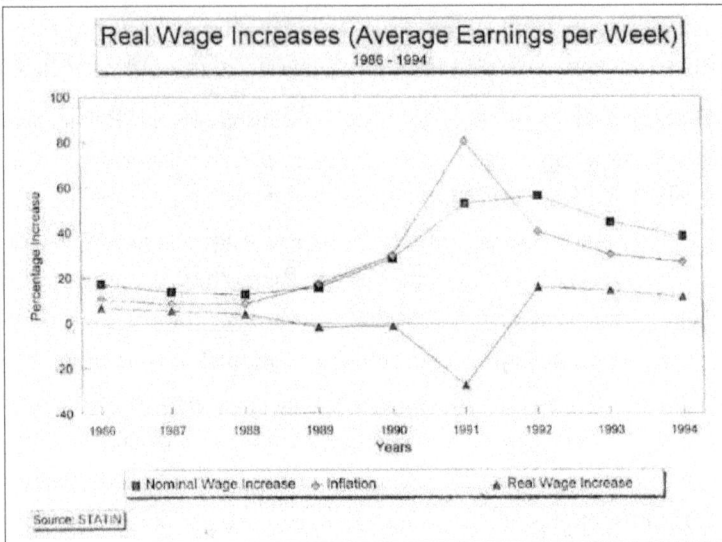

Real Wage Increases (Average Earnings per Week)
1986 - 1994

Source: STATIN

The trade unions, in any event, took the view in their response to Government's declaration of intention that the very idea of a social contract was anachronistic, given the prevailing free market ideology.[78] As it was, the promise of the lowering of the income threshold for the purposes of determining personal income tax liability was no doubt offered with the March 1993 general election in mind. This concession, without agreement on the concept, much less the specific cost/benefit details of a social compact/consensus, in any form, naturally meant that the Government would have less to offer by way of inducement to labour in the future. For discussions, and most definitely any form of contract negotiations, to be of value, they must be conducted within a context determined by the real benefits to be exchanged, that are of sufficient importance to the negotiating parties.

One has therefore to monitor the likely effect on bargaining postures of such variables as the agricultural terms of trade, wage rates, food prices, changes in aggregate demand, and the type, targeting and size of public expenditure, in order to draw meaningful conclusions about changes in income distribution resulting from an adjustment exercise. For, it is such factors which, together, will constitute the context in which bargaining occurs.

Policy configuration will reflect the relative effective political power of different socio-economic groups: workers, self-employed, small farmers, rentiers and capitalists, the unemployed and destitute.

While attention to income distribution, balance of payments, inflation, and growth can be appreciated, the effects of stabilization and adjustment policies on overall poverty rates may be said to be 'the crucial issue'. For when demand restraint policies predominate, as in Jamaica, programmes tend to strongly affect poverty levels, and the number below the poverty line, quite significantly. And it is largely in these terms that the majority's response to policy is effectively determined.

Consensus and agreement by efficient communication allowing the exploration of alternatives, in a spirit of enquiry, in the context of a pluralist political democracy, in the search for a rationally defined objective, may be possible in academic circles or societies less class stratified and tribally polarized.[79] In the case of Jamaica, the public's inclination to favour strong fearless leadership was confirmed by their admiration for Castro, Thatcher and Reagan as disclosed by the Stone Poll of 1987.[80]

If governments experience tension between the pursuit of trade union objectives and national development and employment goals, in particular, it would seem, without more, that there may be a case for consultation with interest group leaders on economic and social policy determination at the national level.

The notion of a social contract as a mechanism of class rule mediation, when proposed by the joint IMF/state regime, may be viewed as the attempt to disguise co-optation of potential antagonists. This is achieved by giving the appearance of sharing responsibility and authority through participation in joint decision-making on policy at the highest level. The, "... displacement of the state from narrow ruling class interests",[81] by the process of interest-group leadership incorporation into an inter-class "hegemonic consensus", represents the classic reformist device of self-deception. It is precisely this which ultimately destroys working-class confidence in leadership, whether of trade unions, or otherwise.

Apparent attempts at the reconciliation of ruling class and national/public interests will arouse working -class suspicion the more vociferous the calls for consensus; and the greater will be the felt need for vigilance the less related the source of such calls to persons and institutions with unquestionable working-class credentials.

Concern with social stability under IMF/Bank sponsored structural adjustment took the form of the Social Well-being Programme in the 1980's and the Social and Economic Support Programme – and currently the emphasis on Poverty Alleviation – in the 1990's. Such concern seems to seek the answer to the question: what level and kind of social welfare provisions is necessary to maintain, not social stability, as Green suggests,[82] but rather to regain and/or increase political favour with the disenchanted poor and disadvantaged in the electorate and in the population at large.[83]

One lesson of the Democratic Socialism experiment of the 1970's was indeed the extent to which those normally considered to be on the periphery of, and even outside, the electoral process could nevertheless profoundly affect the outcomes of electoral contests.

So far, (1990's), the trade unions have shown little enthusiasm "to be educated" into any formal inter-class consensus. This is despite the repeated statements by government and some private sector spokesmen that the time and circumstances are appropriate for a social contract.[84] The trade union attitude may no doubt be related to the fact that the terms, or even an outline of the contemplated compact have been very conspicuously left unspecified, beyond the persistent implication of the necessity for wage restraint. Chen-Young sees the essence of the social contract tripartite collaboration as resulting in,

> "… a more caring, better society, where the quality of life can be improved through economic cooperation, creating more employment, economic growth, more opportunity for advancement where people feel there is hope and equity (sic) for improvement."[85]

Declaring that "self-interest must be sacrificed for the greater good", this then highly successful financial mogul was not reported as venturing to share any specifics on questions as to: how much, when, by whom and for whom? as appropriate to the several issues raised.

Prime Minister Patterson, no doubt with one eye on the private sector's need for "an industrial relations climate conducive to investment", and the other on elections, due by 1998, regards the Social Contract policy being developed (since 1978) as having the essential purpose of restoring industrial stability and improving conditions in the social services.[86] This is to be facilitated by establishing the criteria necessary for achieving productivity growth and a stable economy; all of which has been said by many persons and groups, on many different occasions over the years, ever since the radical intellectuals' proposed Emergency Production Plan of 1977.

While the functionary's role is not necessarily ideologically explicit, there is little doubt that the role of the intellectual has had negative consequences for the working class. Their field leadership potential has been severely compromised by conflicting class, family and interpersonal relations[87] in a small society where relations are highly personalized and there are interlocking and overlapping social roles, occupational positions, or organizational membership and patterns and circles of friendship and acquaintances.

The pre-IMF-engagement legislation of the mid 1970's, the praises of which are still sung (with the exception of the *Labour Relations and Industrial Disputes Act,* and the *Employment Termination and Redundancy Payment Act* in more recent years) has proven to be little different, in terms of its welfare ineffectiveness, as against other legal regulation. This may not be surprising in a society more concerned with form than substance, and in which more energy is expended in rhetoric, or just plain 'talk', than action. Machinery for enforcement has been woefully inadequate. This is despite the importance of the statute's provisions relating to such matters as wage awards in conformity with the national interest; the settlement of disputes in essential services; the establishment of the IDT; and the wide discretion given to the Minister of Labour, as extended by amendments, to institutionalize labour/management conflict by referring disputes, on his initiative, to the Tribunal for settlement.

Even one, who cannot usually be accused of inaccuracy or lack of objectivity, such as the late Carl Stone was led – by the extensive public relations exercise which even now accompanies references to statutes now twenty years old – to declare that the Employment (Termination and Redundancy Payments) Act, (1975) "protected workers from unfair and arbitrary dismissals and provided for redress and compensation in circumstances of unfair dismissals".[88] This claim was totally without foundation, as a perusal of the Act, in fact, discloses no such provisions.[89]

The Employment (Equal Pay for Men and Women) *Act 1975,* has not had the benefit of enforcement, partly a casualty, as with governmental regulations, generally, of the massive lay-off of public sector staff and cuts in public expenditure under stabilization and structural adjustment. Enforcement requires 'Enforcers'.

What this lack of effectiveness of legislation, *per se,* and of its administration has meant, is that the value of intended pro-working-class provisions, as items around which bargaining towards an early Act 1975, has not had the of the massive lay social contract could have proceeded, has been effectively negative.

The greater efficiency which it was promised would flow, in an unexplained fashion, from a 'leaner public service' has, not surprisingly, failed to come to pass.

It was undoubtedly true that "both political parties became captives of organised labour" in the 1918 to 1950 period. However, it is apparent from an examination of the trend in real wages between 1970-90 and the movement in per capita income, as shown in FIG. 26 for the period 1974-92, that the gains of those years have been utterly negated by the ravages of the policy effects of IMF/World Bank loan conditionalities.

All the sacrifice and the struggle which gave birth to the trade union movement, the spirit of nationalism, and ultimately independence, have, it has been occasionally claimed, put to waste by the policies promoted under the election campaign banners, "Better Must Come"; "Power to the People"; "Deliverance"; and "We Put People First".

Dubin's, *Power Theory of Conflict*, appears to provide an explanation for changing levels of industrial conflict, trade union militancy and economic gains by labour at the expense of capital in the Jamaican context. Indeed, it has been observed that differing levels of conflict must be seen and assessed against the changes which occur in the political climate, depending on, among other things, the ideological taint of the governing party over different political periods.[90] Whereas work stoppages decreased significantly during the JLP's term in office in the 1980's (FIG. 27) it is interesting to note the increase in the number of disputes over dismissals during most of those years, as shown by FIG. 28.

Labour's declining influence during the IMF years of the 1980's, in particular, would suggest, firstly, that the feeling of the economic and political elite, then, would have been that a social contract was hardly necessary with capital being dominant. And, secondly, that whatever prestige might have appeared to be attached to national joint economic decision-making for trade union leaders, who might have been co-opted into some formal tripartite body, was far out-weighted by the fear of charges of a 'sell-out', and "betrayal". This would have been compounded by unions having to accept moral, if not legal, joint responsibility for the anti-working-class consequences of any policies formulated with their active participation.

The formulation and implementation of national economic policy became more complex with increasing consultation with, and guidance and monitoring by the IMF, World Bank, and USAID. Together with increasing interest group

Figure: 26

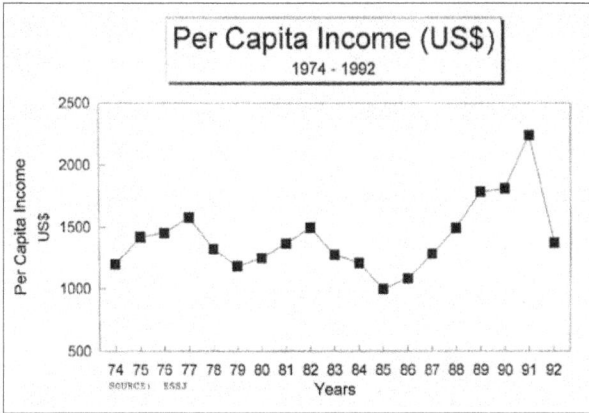

Per Capita Income (US$)
1974 - 1992

Figure: 27

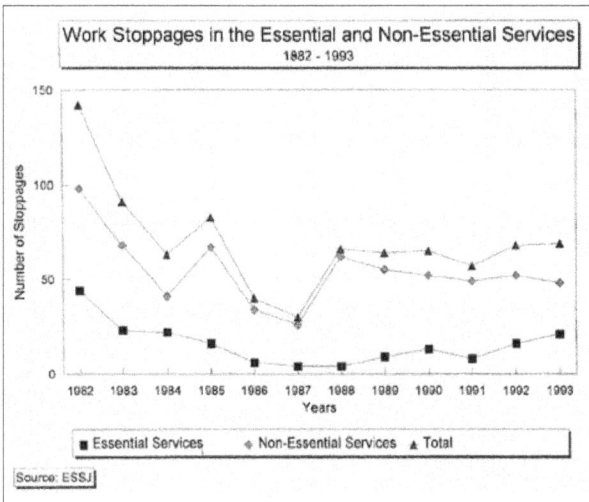

Work Stoppages in the Essential and Non-Essential Services
1882 - 1993

Figure: 28

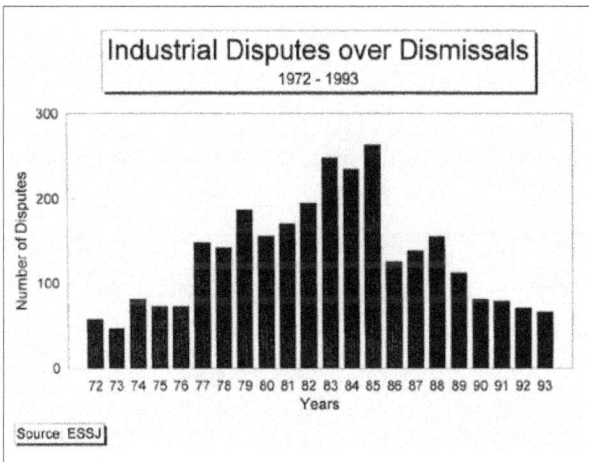

Industrial Disputes over Dismissals
1972 - 1993

differentiation and representation, this caused a, "... parallel loss of intensity of populist politics catering predominantly in its rhetoric to a mass constituency".[91]

There is, however, nothing in this development to support the conclusion that the ruling class was now being, "... forced to think in terms of what was best for the national interest as a whole".[92]

It would be interesting to relate the changing degree of unionization, to levels of GDP, per capita income movements, and the level of industrial action. Data on union membership, however, is notoriously unreliable and are in fact unavailable from sources such as the Ministry of Labour. The information assessed was so outdated and of such doubtful accuracy that the decision was taken to forego the attempt at this particular exercise.

It is worthy of note that, contrary to popular perception, the formation of the Joint Trade Union Research and Development Center, the first trade union umbrella organization of its kind that, is likely to be active and permanent – given the short active life of the Independent Trade Union Advisory Council, (ITAC) – reflected weakness rather than strength on the part of individual trade unions.

Of greater significance though, is the point that up to the time of the formation of the JTURDC[93] it might have been misleading to speak of a trade union movement, despite the existence of several well established, recognized and active individual unions. It is only these national labour organization developments which makes it worthwhile to raise the issue of a social contract at all, in spite of Terry Smith's views; and that opens the ruling elite's definition of 'the national interest' to organized institutional systematic challenge.

The "social consensus on the broadest possible properties of policy and implementation strategy", regarded by Jones as being necessary for successful development administration, has proved elusive. In fact, one wonders whether such consensus would be meaningful: agreement can be on such a broad, general level as to mean very different things to different persons when the stage of conversion into specific regulatory detail is approached.[94]

It is likely to be national, non-partisan mobilization – around comprehensively worked out, all-embracing and reasonably detailed policy – that will remove the "challenge of having to cope with almost permanent opposition". There is usually no violent disagreement with 'policy' at the level of generality at which fundamental objectives are traditionally stated, in a society where vigorous thinking tends to be limited to an academic community which is somewhat remote from the arena where ideas are tested by their application and consequences. It is evident that if the built-in tendency to oppose persists among almost half the population (with the two major parties being of roughly equal strength, normally), any government – to achieve effective transformation – will require great counter-mobilization capacity. The chances of ever arriving at a substantive social consensus are obviously not outstanding in this environment.

Whenever the usual exhortations are made to invest, "because the conditions are right/ideal"; to increase production, "since we must produce ourselves out of our problems", or "produce or die", or "acquire the culture of production"; and "to practise the norms of good corporate citizenship", such exhortations have invariably been interpreted, by those to whom they are directed, as targeting a public interest that is not defined on behalf of the masses.

The answer to the private sector's reputed negativism is unlikely to be contained in a recipe for the preservation of the *status quo*: "a doctrine that is ... socially non-threatening and that also promises or guarantees basic rewards for social support", without discrimination between social and economic classes.[95]

But a sufficiently technical orientation and the development of generalized bargaining skills necessary to support the task of national mobilization is yet to be achieved – hence the apparent ideological collision between the policies of redistribution and wealth creation. The "dilemmas of policy choice" inherent in the process of industrialization, regardless of the type of ruling elite, has yet to be consensually resolved, either in terms of a commitment to a favoured class or the striking of a strategic time-bound balance between contending class interests.[96]

Given the generation of increasing income and wealth inequality by adjustment policies, it might have been anticipated that the calls for a social contract or some form of 'consensus' would have made the need for greater public perception of increased opportunities for economic advancement and social mobility obvious, even in the medium term. Bell concluded, from the American experience, that if there is the belief that there is equality of opportunity through the openness of the educational system, then a society will tend to exhibit greater tolerance for existing inequality, than otherwise.[97]

The first deliberate attempt at arranging the coalition of forces with a view to consensus building, if not agreement on a social contract as such, with the implication of enforceability, was the establishment of the National Advisory Council in 1978. Instrumental in shaping economic policy, as is almost always the case in conditions unfavourable to labour, the National Council, chaired by the Prime Minister, had representation from the Cabinet, the private sector, and the trade unions.

This kind of institutional arrangement, however, could not survive the contradiction between the attempt at inter-class cooperation and the emission of ideologically aggressive anti-capitalist "messages and symbols" which were perceived to be also threatening by the substantial, ambitious, status-conscious, and desperately socially mobile middle and upper middle classes. Socialist rhetoric, interpreted as hinting, at least, at a belief in the scientific version of socialism, by the Ministry of National Mobilization, established in 1977, and defunct within one year, exposed the lack of methodological preparation for any serious socialist project.

Resulting disaffection and alienation was sufficient to destroy the foundation on which a social contract could be built.

The objectives of the tripartite Mixed Commission as set out in Ministry Paper 18/1978 were to,

> "… consider the more important matters of business, industrial and economic concerns by research, presentation and publication of papers in order to stimulate and reach a consensus and commitment to agreed economic strategies and to assist the Government to promote the economic wellbeing of the nation".[98]

Much was promised in the Commission's first year of operation: concentration would be on strategies for development, not complaints; sectoral committees would review policies and programmes and make recommendations towards the goal of economic recovery; there would be an assessment of the assumptions on the basis of which projections under the Five Year Plan, 1978-82, had been made, sectorally; the search for economic growth through involvement in overall planning of the economy would be pursued; there would be the engagement in various aspects of productivity enhancement, including "the design of a programme to sell productivity to the nation", and to provide a forum for ideas on economic development "and matters of concern to workers".

Perhaps the membership of the Commission was too large: 9 Government, 9 private sector and 3 trade union representatives. The range of issues considered might also have been too wide, certainly with so little experience of participation at this level and of working together "in an organization where the main focus is on the national interest rather than on the representative groups only".

Among the issues covered were:

(a) A national production drive involving traditional agricultural crops, tourism, construction and manufacturing

(b) Foreign trade and investment in their various aspects

(c) Labour, employment and conditions of work including wage guidelines and a proposed Disclosure of Information law.

(d) Taxation and Government Contracts

(e) Energy

(f) Prices

(g) Relationship between Government and the media

Additionally, the Commission performed a consultative function; monitored Social Contract developments; lobbied for procedural and administrative reforms; evaluated socio-economic policy; and made remedial economic policy proposals.

Apart from poor attendance at meetings, preoccupation with mounting day-to-day economic problems, "inadequate and inconsistent support" from some of its members, especially government, small business and the trade unions, the Commission acquired the image of being a "rap session" for big business, or a forum to be used on the basis of expediency. That it attempted all that it did without a full-time secretariat was not the least remarkable feature of its brief existence.

This might well have been a strategy to have the state internalize the potential to "operate beyond the narrow confines of class service". The attempt to embody "a practice, discourse and institutions" of and for the development and renewal of a national consensus has not. yet met with success. Green's explanation would be that,

> "... whatever the fractional interests and conflicts of the bourgeoisie, its class-affiliated political practitioners and visionaries have self-consciously sought to reconcile the interests of the class with those of the nation and to establish overall bourgeois hegemony in preference to naked and fractional (and therefore precarious) class rule"[99]

If the society was to be transformed, other than through this kind of compact, then mobilization of the majority, the working poor, unemployed, and marginalized would clearly be required. However, the effort at political education was limited by its ideologically polarizing partisan nature. Further, rhetorical references to "class struggle", "rapacious capitalists", "sufferers", "progressive and patriotic forces" and, most importantly, "social justice" raised expectations of immediate personal benefits and patronage. Not only did such expectations prove incapable of satisfaction, given the resource constraints, but of more fundamental long-term consequence, their existence perverted the very notion of radicalism, which the attempt was being made to ingraft onto the public consciousness.

Thus, while the doctrine of 'self-reliance' was being expounded from every government platform as a mobilizational strategy, it was also used as an article of faith and as the basis of a philosophy of development: a tool with which to defy the 'reactionary' and 'fascist' forces of 'oppression' and 'exploitation'.

Against the background of this kind of ideological environment, if popular political pressures are to be ignored, in the interest of free market structural adjustment doctrinal purity, one wonders how the consensus embodied in a social contract could ever have been arrived at.

It appears that what is contemplated is a "compact" which represents agreement or *consensus ad idem* not between principals but, rather, agents who in the case of trade union leaders may not even have *de jure* much less *de facto* authority to represent their members.[100] And to continue with the legalistic perspective, briefly, the public at large, excluding the private sector, can scarcely be vested, even morally, with vicarious liability for the acts of its presumed representatives.

How can the masses, especially the unionized workforce, be expected to support and abide by terms of a "social contract" of which they may well strongly disapprove? For the policies pursued under stabilization and structural adjustment are essentially the very opposite of the kinds that one would expect to form the basic structure of any compact or social contract. It is well established that, certainly with respect to any particular client-country, the Funds and Banks orthodoxy which has prevailed is that there is only one "right" policy mix.

Nor did the mix of policies between the Barbadian social partners in 1993 constituting the Protocol for prices and incomes policy within the context of a compact framework, described as "unique" in the Barbados Advocate of August 30, 1992, prove of any electoral advantage to its initiating political administration.

There is unlikely to be much controversy regarding the observation that,

"... inattention to basic human needs in a poverty-ridden context seems destined to subvert the social support at the base which a developmental administrative regime definitely requires".[101]

Explanations of differing levels of returns to labour that are based on the trade union or non-union background of political leaders, their accessibility to trade union influence, and their populist as against managerialist leadership styles are questionable. Countries – such as Trinidad and Tobago have had long periods of government by the same party and have nevertheless experienced marked differences in the welfare of the working class over time. The relative unimportance of the leadership variable is especially to be, expected the greater the subjection of the economy to IMF influence, with Tanzania being the supreme example. The state of the economy would appear to us to be the determining factor: if anything, Michael Manley became more rhetorically committed to the working class, the poor, and the down-trodden after the declaration of his party and Government as Democratic Socialist in 1974. It was after this that their social and economic condition progressively and very rapidly worsened, parallel with the deepening economic deterioration.

Both Downes[102] and Nurse[103] have been critical of trade unions for failing to adopt a more pro-active role in the formulation of economic and social plans and policies at the national level. Nurse, in particular, argues that the unions, by not actively participating m decisions determining the design of stabilization and structural adjustment programmes, have cemented themselves in the traditional reactionary posture which leaves them open to attack. On the one hand, the question has been asked: "Where is labour's clout?";[104] and on the other, it has been assumed that trade unions and their members would automatically support adjustment policies, once they are declared to be in the national interest.

It might well be that the absence of more active trade union participation in policy formation is due partly to the reason alluded to by Munroe which is that there are few significant values and behaviour patterns common between the subcultures in the society. It is claimed that, as a result, "... the cement of consensus which binds together more homogenous societies is lacking".[105]

Contrary to the regional, and, in particular, the Jamaican Government's approach to the introduction of adjustment policies, in the case of the United Kingdom in the 1960's the Trade Union Congress and the Confederation of British

Industries signed a Declaration of Intent undertaking to vet individual applications for wage or price increases, so as to decide and advise whether such applications were in the national interest.

Significantly, this was after the Government had consulted with management and unions and arrived at agreement as to the definition of the 'national interest'. It was perhaps the novelty of this kind of "treaty" being agreed and signed by traditional rivals, if not enemies, that caused the then Minister of Economic Affairs, George Brown, to declare that that historic event, "... heralded the end of the class war".[106]

Rather than focusing on changes in class relations it might be more realistic to use a political-economy analytical approach to explain changes in the distribution of income and arriving at a common yardstick of what is 'right', 'justifiable' or even just 'acceptable'.[107] One is required to face the fact, that the problematic absence of agreement on these ethical matters has its basis in different class interests as determined by different levels of education, income, wealth and social status.

As Colman and Nixson urge, "Equity is an ideological construct about distribution and is therefore political in the sense of an intervention in the struggle of political ideas".[108]

Girvan, Bernal, and Hughes[109] record that the context in which the IMF first requested government's commitment to the formation of a social contract was not propitious: wage movements were to be directly linked to the extent of exchange rate devaluation and vice versa; the severe foreign exchange shortage resulted in the widespread scarcity of most categories of goods, including basic items of mass consumption; lay-offs; steep price increases of some 40% over a 12 month period; real wage decline of approximately 25%; sluggish exports and great pressure for imports, including raw materials for production, spare parts, and capital equipment – all resulting in heightened social tension, short-lived protest demonstrations, looting and vandalism.

The following elements of this first attempt at a social contract are of particular interest:

1. There would be no further devaluation as long as the level of wage increase was in line with that, of the island's mam trading partners.

2. Business confidence was to be promoted by greater harmony and trust

between government and the private sector. (No formulae was however provided to bring this about)

3. Trade unions were expected to reduce the number of industrial dispute, especially those arising from inter-union rivalry. (There was no breakdown of strike statistics to determine the mam causes of industrial action; the approach adopted conveniently ignoring the structurally reactionary nature of unions' responses in conflict situations.)

4. The private sector was to undertake to reinvest profits with a view to increasing the provision of new jobs. (Incentives have never seemed adequate to elicit the desired response.)

5. Both wage and price increases were limited to 10%, arbitrarily.

6. Government was to reduce the real size of the budget. (In a clientelistic political culture this had a direct negative impact on the dependent poorer classes.)

In comparison, the Barbados Protocol presented to the House of Assembly on August 24, 1993, declared, as the bases for its implementation, the following major objectives:

a) the safeguarding of the existing parity of the rate of exchange, recognising that any deterioration in this rate would lead to a significant reduction in the living standards of the vast majority of Barbadians;

b) the expansion of the economy to satisfy the need for improved competitiveness; to provide the. right of access to employment, to reduce the threat of social dislocation caused by an unacceptably high level of unemployment; and thereby to ensure the security and well-being of the community as a whole;

c) the establishment of an environment which would bring Barbados goods and services into a more competitive position at home and abroad;

d) the promotion of mechanisms which, within this search for a competitive position for Barbados, would achieve restraints in wages and other compensation payments as well as prices;

e) the restructuring of the economy on a sustainable basis with opportunities being given for workers and employers alike to make a greater contribution to planning and development and also to share in the fruits of that improved economy;

f) the promotion of a national commitment to improved productivity and increased efficiency, so that by reducing wastage and by enhancing national performance, the country would be able to heighten its attractiveness to investors, thereby further expanding the opportunities for employment, with the establishment of a National Productivity Board.[110]

The absence of penalty provisions was not expected to jeopardize the policy's success as,

> "… the continuing spirit of co-operation and mutual respect between the Social Partners in the best, interest of all the people" was taken to be a "demonstration of Barbadian common sense and pragmatism, personal and sectoral difference being put. aside for the common good".[111]

In contrast to the goals of this earliest Jamaican and recent Barbadian attempts at a national 'understanding', it is highly instructive to peruse the basic social policy objectives pursued under the Australian Accord initially signed in February, 1981 between the Labour Party and the[112] ACTU, as indicated below:

1. To maintain real wage levels and improve them to the extent feasible.

2. To close the gaps and remove the anomalies in welfare coverage.

3. To foster social equity by efforts to improve the relative position of the most disadvantaged.

4. To adopt measures as a matter of urgency to restore the standards of unemployment benefits.

5. To develop automatic wage indexation provision (later to be discontinued) and restore the relative value of pensions to the basic rate of 25% of average male earnings and develop the basic rate of wage indexation provisions (later to be discontinued).

6. A commitment to the re-introduction of a national health insurance scheme, the improvement of child care, income support provisions, and the introduction of a rental subsidy scheme.

It is immediately apparent that there was no adequate quid pro quo provisions in the Jamaican formula to elicit acceptance, much less enthusiastic compliance.

To the cynic, the Barbadian statement of policy objectives seems little more than platitudinous exhortation, being noticeably averse to quantification, except in relation to "the existing parity of the rate of exchange". In contrast, an emphasis on positive benefits for workers and their dependents stands out as the striking feature of the Accord arrangements. One suspects that it might have been a deliberate strategy of the Australian approach that in the first instance, at least, the pill should be so heavily sugar-coated as to virtually avoid all taste of the medicine. The initial agreement was subject to continual modification in keeping with internal macroeconomic conditions, as influenced by general global developments. Of particular importance were factors influencing financial and economic interest rates, terms of trade, exchange rate implications for international competitiveness and, more specifically, by the circumstances prevailing in Australia's major trading partners.

Needless to say, it was understood that consent to social contract terms was unlikely to last indefinitely, in the best of conditions, given the increased dynamism and longer-term instability in national and international economic affairs.

What is implied here is that the Accord's survival is to be explained on the basis of political affinity and hope, rather than as the consequence of a favourable cost-benefit assessment.

The results of the Accord policies, as assessed by Watts, disclose a quite remarkable similarity with the Jamaican experience under structural adjustment and stabilization programmes. As it turned out, the more perceptive accurately predicted defeat for the Keating-led Labour Party,[113] which was routed in the 1995 general elections. This provided some confirmation that "Legitimacy is just suspension of withdrawal of consent", which is always likely to disappear after results fail to correspond, for any significant period, to the perceived real interests of those consenting.

Tony Blair, the British Labour Party leader, was advised to avoid guidance from the Australian Labour Party by Peter Reith M.P., Shadow Minister of Industrial Relations, in Australia, who saw the Accord not as the Grail its proponents made it out to be, but rather as,

"... a pact between the political and industrial wings of the labour movement ... which institutionalized union influence at the heart of government and as a result a low wage/low productivity relations (sic) system. Concluded over the heads of Australian Workers it has cost them dear".[114]

One suspects that this advice could equally be tendered to the Jamaican Government, especially since the *Social Partnership Paper* makes favourable mention of the Australian system, as an example of the experience of countries where some form of a social contract has generated stability which would "provide a catalyst for growth and development".

Unfortunately, the GDP growth figures under the Accord, which are cited in support of the improvements achieved, relate to the 1986-88 period. Since eight years can be like an eternity in politics, it would have been more convincing as a case for emulation, if evidence of the more recent performance of tine Australian economy had been provided – bearing in mind the decimation of the Labour Party Government in the 1995 election.

The effects of these Accord policies as indicated in TABLE 23 exposed, as fantasy, the belief that a win-win situation could be forged. In the words of Watts,[115]

> "... the real point of the Accord was to ... increase capital accumulation through retrogressive redistribution [which made the stated objective of social justice an exercise in the] legitimacy (sic) of fiction".[116]

Gramsci would explain this situation by asserting that the reproduction of a particular form of social relations is determined by, and represents the results of, inter-group conflicts. Such conflicts being ones in which outcomes are perceived to be sufficiently beneficial to warrant system maintenance – an essential aspect of which is socialization into a predisposition to consent to existing hegemonic relationships.[117]

The early Jamaican social contract provisions, in the not inappropriate language of horse racing, in a country where gambling is now one of the most prosperous types of business activity,[118] might well be described as an "early non-starter". To relate the island's level of wage increase to the situation of its main trading partners such as North America and, to a lesser extent, the United Kingdom, without any regard for the divergencies in the rates of inflation seemed to question, fundamentally, the sincerity of the programme's sponsors.

It is worth bearing in mind, also, that at that particular time (1978) the island suffered significantly from imported inflation.[119] Additionally, unlike the Accord provisions, there was not even implicit recognition of the need for new "social wage" arrangements to cushion resulting real wage losses. Indeed, the opposite was the case, as budgetary cuts were – as is almost always the case with IMF prescriptions – a central plank of the programme.[120] The lesson had clearly not been learned that 'sacrifice' comes easier in an environment characterized by a concern for equity in the form of economic distributive justice. equity and economic distributive justice. As with most social and economic problems, where the missing variable appeared to be psychological in nature, the authorities placed reliance for successful change on the promotion of "business confidence"[121] in a mixture of Australiaope and exhortation.

TABLE: 23   Social Security Payments as a Percentage of Total
Budget Outlay (TBO) and of Gross Domestic Product (GDP) 1976 – 89

Year	Social Security as percentage of TBO	Personal percentage
1967-77	26.5	8.9
1977-78	27.8	9.1
1978-79	28.0	8.8
1979-80	27.9	8.6
1980-81	27.5	8.5
1981-82	27.9	8.7
1982-83	28.9	9.8
1983-84	29.1	10.1
1984-85	28.0	10.2
1985-86	27.2	10.0
1986-87	27.3	8.1
1987-88	28.6	7.9
1988-89	28.9	7.3

Source: Budget Statements No.1, 1989-90. – Australia.

It can be argued, further, that, implicit condemnation of inter-union rivalry completely ignored the reality of the symbiotic relationship between political parties and trade unions,[122] at a time when union rivalry conformed not just to patterns of electoral contestation, but-had the objective positive function of enabling the actual and potential members of the organized sector of the working class to exercise a measure of influence over their leaders.[123] This was largely otherwise lacking, by virtue of the internal structures and administrative practice of those 'representative' labour institutions.

But perhaps the element of policy which most exposes the naivete of the policy designers was that relating to private sector investment. It has been forcefully suggested that austerity should only be agreed in exchange for control over investment. In this regard, the 1971 Conference of the Irish Trade Union Confederation laid down the principle that,

> "All workers must be guaranteed that wage restraint will lead to productive investment beneficial to workers and not towards even further increase in the personal incomes of the privileged classes in society"[124]

The Jamaican 'plural' social order has been described as being "characterized by descensus, "... resulting from race, class and caste distinctions", which are, "... pregnant with conflict".[125] Fortunately, or otherwise, there has been no perceived external threat to national security as in India in 1962, for example,[126] sufficient to mobilize commitment to the development effort, in compensation for the divisive effects of social and cultural heterogeneity and gross economic inequality.

The search for tripartite policy consensus in this inhospitable environment is often urged by Third World creditors who argue the case for the incorporatization of trade unions. This is despite its incompatibility with the promotion of the free market framework,[127] within which the unions are expected to nevertheless function as independent institutions.

Also negatively influencing the achievement of consensus is the fact that some policy contradictions of IMF/World Bank style capitalism become pronounced to the extent that, "... conservative goals are too successful, such as upward income distribution ..."[128] and, at the same time, the removal of price controls.

There are, as usual, no guarantees that "the underlying logic of cooperation", that future benefits to labour "will increase as a function of current profits disproportionately appropriated by capitalists", will hold. It thus becomes obvious that to claim that workers are necessarily better off cooperating and making less militant demands, so as to increase the size of the pie, rather than struggling, disruptively, to increase their relative share now, is reflective of ignorance as to the often experienced unfavourable results for labour of 'playing by the rules of the game'. The fact is that normally each group seeks to maximize its own current consumption and pass the costs of accumulation unto the other.[129]

At some point in the deepening working class consciousness of the removal of the bases for consent, confidence in their leadership and the integrity of the system begins to be eroded. The stage may well be reached where it is not just the economic system which is the arena of conflict, controlled as it is by institutional bargaining mechanisms, but, indeed, the political system might well be challenged[130] to accommodate structural changes in production relations, as against merely the distribution of the surplus. Collaboration can thus be at the risk of labour organization's well-being, if not survival. This is so, particularly in the seemingly insensitive and hostile environment of IMF conditionalities.

The participation of working class institutional leadership in the formulation and implementation of a social contract/partnership may thus represent yet another aspect of the system-maintenance function of a de-radicalized labour movement.[131]

There are those among the 'have-gots' who speak in biblical language about the trade union movement's need to eschew higher wages in exchange for the creation of more jobs, in pursuit of the high principle, applied to labour – but remarkably, and significantly, not to labour/capital relations – that "I am my brother's keeper ...".[132] This is a message, it is claimed, which could be carried with great effect, and, no doubt, one for which a place is reserved in the newest model of the eighteen-year-old proposal for national consensus.

However, this kind of appeal to working class selflessness is turned around by Sir Philip Sherlock. Perhaps reflecting the wisdom of the ages, octogenarian that he is, he asserts that,

> "It's indeed for the "have-gots", the upper class and upper middle class,
> to make Jamaican nationhood meaningful by bringing the two Jamaicas
> together ... (since) ... to the 40% of the Jamaican people who are
> below the poverty line, talk about 'galvanizing the national spirit'[133] has
> no meaning".[134]

In looking at the problem from this moral perspective, Macpherson asks, "Can an obligation based only on enlightened self-interest [if enlightened it is in this particular context] be expected to bind when it conflicts with short-term interests?" Self-interest, he argues, being based on reason, means that for some such as Hobbes, "Morality enters the argument *not* [italics added] at the late stage of the making of the social contract but at the early stage of deduction of equality of right from the stated equality of ability and need".[135]

What is implied is that there must be some commonly shared value by virtue of which citizens "come to see themselves as equal in some respect more vital to them than all their inequalities", if a sense of obligation to comply with the demands/sacrifices required by any social compact is to prevail. But the strength of this sense of obligation is likely to be inversely related to the degree of social and economic inequality existing in society.

Such inequality Bonderich sees as a product of the procedural and substantive content of the legal system, other settled institutions and customs, and involves – as others have asserted – the assent of the disadvantaged. It is nevertheless questionable if these observations justify such statements as that, "... the vast majority of those who are worse off do not resist. Because they cannot".[136] This is a question which will be treated in some depth in the Chapter on Resistance.

The issue of inequality reduction immediately raises the question of the need for some sort of prioritization in the deployment of resources. Those who have studied the problem over the past two decades in Latin America conclude that payment of the "social debt" to the worse off,[137] internal and external debt service, plus the need to increase investment, when put together, are beyond the countries' capacity to generate the required volume of national savings. One of the relevant items for tripartite and indeed international negotiations thus becomes the pace at which different targets are met, guided by the principle of the cost of adjustment being borne by all.[138]

The Social Contract agenda for negotiations, by implication, if it is to be realistically pursued, would thus be expected to include questions as to the resources to be allocated and the mechanisms to be established to deal with the more pressing social welfare problems within a specified time frame: the creation of an adequate number of jobs at reasonable rates of pay with decent working conditions; wage policies geared to the recovery and growth of real wages; the use of taxation and other methods to cut back consumption of non-essentials, in particular by the higher income groups; and perhaps through the formation of a debtor cartel, the effective re-negotiation of foreign debt repayment terms, (not excluding the now non-negotiable repayment of multilateral debt.)

In the absence of such structural modifications, together with the easing of the debt burden, programmes such as the Social Well-being project of the late 1980's and the Social and Economic Support Programme and Poverty Alleviation of the 1990's are likely to be of marginal effect only. If the social debt is acknowledged, there is simply not enough resources to fully meet obligations to the multi-lateral institutions and the poor, at the same time.

In a situation of widening and deepening poverty, sooner or later, for some, the point is reached when survival is at stake. And with increasing competition for jobs, the growing numbers of the marginalized find that even the informal economy excludes them[139] as it cannot meet, the reserve price for their labour.

And when survival is at stake in combination with a lack of marketable skills, financial resources, and the fabric of social support, then the choice if often perceived as one between poverty and criminal activity – activity which, "… begins to resemble an opportunity rather than a cost, work rather than deviance".[140] The type of 'contract' that is relevant to some in that kind of setting is sometimes highly antisocial.

What may appear to be a negative, if nevertheless realistic perspective, which may be of surprising applicability to the current Jamaican "Social Partnership" proposal, is that adopted by Goldthorpe commenting on the British labour relations scene in the mid-1960's:

> "Unless the norms implicit, in the new regulative arrangements are ones to which the mass of those *regulated* [italics added] felt some degree of moral commitment, which would scarcely seem likely on the evidence of the degree of labour unrest [similar to the situation in Jamaica from 1992-95] then the acceptance that any reformed institution would command would be of no more than a pragmatic, provisional kind; that is to say, these arrangements would in turn be exposed to distortions and 'decay' as they were found to conflict with the values and interests of those subject to them, and order would once again be problematic".[141]

It is therefore appropriate at this point to take note of some public responses to the notion of a social pact/contract/compact/partnership[142]/understanding/ consensus that have been articulated:

> "The social contract is a sneaky way of passing off the mismanagement of the country on the unions and private sector. All this government now has to say is that it is the lack of cooperation between union and management why the country is in the mess it finds itself".[143] (sic).

> "What we have today is an unravelling of what might have existed of such a contract. Inflation is running at over 15%, way ahead of

governments projections. Prices have remained extraordinarily high despite an apparent stabilization of the exchange rate. Daily, consumers are being battered by the ravaging effects of inflation . . ."[144]

"The most striking thing about this proposed partnership has been that all three [government, some unions and some members of the private sector] have only expressed what each expects of the others. I am yet, and still very anxious, to hear what each of them will bring to the table that will make it work."[145]

The contribution expected from each social partner was concisely reported for public information as follows:[146]

The Government *will* [italics added][147]

- Keep the exchange rate stable for an extended *period* [italics added]

- *Look at* [italics added] increasing the "social wage" to stop the decline in living standards

- Reduce Government spending on debt (How this is to be done with a very high interest rate regime which has the effect of increasing debt service was not indicated)

- Ensure that the Bank of Jamaica (BOJ) is not used to fund Government spending

Employers/producers/private sector *must:* [italics added][148]

- Hold down prices while the exchange rate and wages rates are stable

- Include workers in making decisions about productivity

- Reduce the length of the distribution chain, and price margins at each stage. (No mechanisms were put in place or suggested)

- Start new enterprises to create more jobs. (Why the capitalist class should do so merely in response to governments suggestion was not explained, given the high interest rates on Government paper and commercial bank loans and some types of deposits)

- Share production gains by reducing prices and increasing wages. (No monitoring procedure was established or proposed)

Trade Unions *must:* [italics added][149]

- Negotiate for wages based on increased productivity and not high inflation of the past. (The issue of a high *current* rate of inflation was not addressed)
- Obey industrial procedures and laws, and collective labour agreements signed. (Specific reforms strenuously lobbied for were not offered as incentives)
- Adapt to the multi-task approach and avoid restrictive practices. (The consequences for possible redundancy was ignored)

Not surprisingly, noticeably absent was any mechanism ensuring or even promoting compliance, despite the mandatory tone of the language used.

Walsh sees the social partnership idea as one contributing,

"... to de-tribalizing the society on a more general level than just its most extreme visible manifestation ... [and as] one measure which can make a major contribution to the removal of this acidic edge (to interpersonal and inter-sectoral economic relations) ... and defusing some of the potential for confrontation and explosion".[150]

The economist and regular columnist, Ralston Hyman, takes a decidedly different view:

"There is currently a lack (of) trust in so far as the private sector and the unions are concerned ... the government cannot be trusted to keep their end of the bargain by taming inflation as history indicates. The current climate (industrial relations) ... makes (it) almost impossible for any national understanding [which] has been proposed ad nauseam ... to be developed (it) is extremely useful to remember that it is precisely because of government's chronic inability to control inflation why the country's macro-economic environment is so unstable".[151]

To support his point Hyman provided the following inflation data:

Inflation Rates

Year	%	Year	%	Year	%
1989	17.2	1992	40.2	1995	25.1
1990	29.8	1993	10.1		
1991	80.2	1994	26.9		

Source: Ralston Hyman in The Jamaica Herald, Feb. 20, 1996, p.7A.

Carl Wint, the editor of the leading daily newspaper took the view that,

> "Mr. Patterson (The Prime Minister) expects that the Government, labour, and business can seriously forge such a partnership in so short a time (two months).[152] ... Clearly there is need for a Social Partnership. What is troubling is whether the players have the vision, the strength, the street smarts and the sincerity to forge an agreement that will be adhered to in good faith. One cannot help but feel that there are too many wild cards in the pack. And the intellectual bankruptcy of so many of our leaders, the selfishness of the vested interests, the indiscipline which pervades the society does not augur well for success of this Social Partner ship".[153]

In the long-abandoned mysticism of the Hobbesian tradition, Chuck submits – Attorney-at-law that he is – that to call for a social contract, "... is tautologous, since effective government is underpinned by the hidden and undeclared parameters of a social contract". The plea for a social contract, he contends, is only necessary because government has not succeeded in its business of governing and, in any event it, "... should be *preceded* (italic added) by the setting and achievement of clear and easily verifiable macro-economic targets".[154] This seems to be calling for some sort of a trial run, no doubt, in the hope of earning credibility.

In his special broadcast to the nation, the Prime Minister issued the charge:

> "Finally, my fellow Jamaicans and friends, as we enter this *new and exciting* [italics added] phase of nation building and together seek to work at a Social Partnership that will meet our special needs and bring a feeling of renewed hope to our people, let us use the unique gifts with which God has blessed us. Let us devise our own solutions as we face today's special challenges".[155]

An ILO study of fairly recent experience in industrialised market economies reports that there is,

> "... considerable evidence that countries pursuing a corporatist or consensus approach to macroeconomic policy formulation have performed much better in key areas than many other countries."[156]

Metcalf is cited to the effect that the consensus approach results in less unemployment, as a consequence of high worker militancy and, further, that real wages is more sensitive to unemployment levels.

With unions in Jamaica being organized and conducting negotiations very largely at the level of the enterprise, this, when put together with the low level of unionization, places Jamaica in the non-corporatist country category.[157] These countries tend to lack machinery for routinized cooperation among the major interest groups through institutions of interest mediation[158] for policy design, implementation and, most importantly, on-going modification reflecting the vigilance and flexibility required by an increasingly dynamic environment.

In Sweden, mechanisms and procedures for constant dialogue and cooperation are an inherent part of the industrial relations tradition and the administrative processes of the national economic system accommodates policy consultation, flexibility and review. As a result, the benefits of devaluation, contrary to the Jamaican experience, were fully gained, as against being, "dissipated in a wage-price spiral". The Swedish alternative has been largely successful because of extensive experience in the institutionalisation of interest mediation in the context of a national concern for social justice. Their economic and industrial relations practices have been characterized by a, "… genuine egalitarian commitment informing a set of interlinking social investments, social security, [integrated] labour markets and national economic policies". This sense and practice of social justice is the cement which no doubt holds the Swedish system together and is clearly, in this case, more than a spray-on placebo".[159]

For a country such as Jamaica, which has a far way to go to achieve the routinization of cooperation between capital and labour, Miliband's seemingly negative perspective may yield a more accurate portrait of class attitudes: "… businessmen", he thinks,

> "… are not very likely to find much merit in policies which appear to run counter to what they conceive to be the interests of business, much less to make themselves the advocates of such policies, since they are almost by definition most likely to believe such policies to be inimical to the national interest".[160]

And if Marx's 'typical capitalist' suffers only from the "Faustian conflict between the passion for accumulation and the desire for enjoyment",[161] then the ideological explanation for this blinkered view of reality is offered by Friedman, for whom,

"The political principle that underlies the market mechanism is unanimity. In an *ideal* [italics added] free market resting on private property, no individual can coerce any other, and cooperation is voluntary, all parties to such cooperation benefit or they need not cooperate. There are no values, no "social" responsibilities in any sense other than the shared values and responsibilities of individuals. ... But the doctrine of "social responsibility" taken seriously would extend the scope of the political mechanism to every human activity ... I have called it a "fundamentally subversive doctrine" in a free society and have said that in such a society, there is one and only one social responsibility of business – to use its resources and engage in activities designed to increase its profits so long as it stays within the rules of the game".[162]

The congruence between Friedman's 'crusading rhetoric' and the IMF's implicit free market principles was highlighted by the terms and conditions for the second year of the 1978 Agreement between Jamaica and the Fund. In exchange for an increase in the level of funding over a three-year[163] period, the Government had to undertake to reduce public expenditure as provided for in the budget, thus "crowding in" the private sector. While it can be conceded that goal-specification requires a high level of political consensus, the sincerity of the IMF's proposal that an agreement on a social contract be sought, then, was open to question. The trend rate of inflation was some 20 percent, while the wage-price policy called for the quite crude, arbitrary and "unscientific"[164] limit of 10% to be applied to both wage and price increases. The country's economic circumstances, from the point of view of the living standards and life chances of the masses, has not improved significantly since then.

To put the matter forthrightly, the case can certainly be made that the IMF's principal concern as a creditor was to ensure repayment, rather than catering to the demands of national development for the benefit of the majority.[165]

Although the Fund had envisaged a coordinated effort of "all social and political forces" in exercising restraint and to maximize production, when the private sector and the unions predictably rejected the social contract,[166] the Minister of Labour, through the IDT, nevertheless enforced the wage guideline,[167] with a tax sanction against employers who granted increases in excess of the guideline figure.[168] It is hardly justified, in retrospect, to interpret this policy as an attempted, "... trade-off of excessive wage claims against the promise of long-term stability in employment and real income".[169]

The situation with respect to experienced inflation levels, should make it obvious that at least one of the important conditions necessary to elicit working-class cooperation would not be present, namely: "... the confidence [as against the hope] that current sacrifices will ultimately yield a fair *share* of future benefits".[170] This, then, was a very inauspicious start to policy consensus experimentation under the guidance and the watchful eye of the IMF. What was necessary to aid the parties' search for "stable, mutually non-destructive, recognizable patterns" of behaviour was clearly absent: participation in the creation of *traditions*[171]. It was an experience of policy failure that was to characterize the entire period of Jamaica's borrowing relationship with that institution.

Adopting, with little modification, Goldthorpe's view, it may be said, with considerable relevance to Jamaica – despite locational and time differences – that,

> "Since the society falls far short of the consensual model[172] suited to the emergence of [widely accepted] normative institutional forms, and in fact is one in which economic life is a matter of individuals and groups exploiting as best they can their positions within a generally unprincipled structure of power and advantage, the divergence of interest and values among the 'partners' to industrial relations [and the parties to the proposed Social Partnership] will tend always to militate against the possibility of their concerted action towards [anything other than cosmetic] reform".[173]

As an ILO Report has suggested, it is unreasonable to expect individual groups of workers to moderate their wage demands voluntarily (or for individual companies to hold down their prices) in order to contribute to the collective goal of reduced inflation, unless they have credible reasons for believing that others will do the same. This is unlikely in a situation where the level of unionization of the employed labour force is only about 23%. If other workers and companies behave differently, as Friedman would allow, then the group which exercises moderation will suffer a real wage [and profit] loss without affecting inflation.[174]

For the elites' call for harmony between the classes, is, "as if classes were fortuitous agglomerations of individuals curiously looking at a shop window on a Sunday afternoon". In certain historical conditions, when people begin to threaten the dominant elites, usually. manipulation, Freire has argued,

"... is accomplished by means of pacts ... which if considered superficially might give the impression of dialogue between the classes ... these pacts are not dialogue between the classes ... but rather represent the expression of the unequivocal interest of the dominant elites".[175]

The latest word on the social partnership, from the trade union side, coming from the President of the JCTU, is simply and forcefully put: in any agreement reached, the workers' interests cannot be subsumed in the national interest.

1. Errol Ennis, in a speech opening the seminar sponsored by the Caribbean Association of Indigenous Banks in Kingston, Jamaica, on Oct. 6, 1992.
2. The Financial Gleaner, Oct. 9, 1992.
3. Ibid, 1992.
4. The Daily Gleaner, Dec, 2, 1992.
5. Cedric Wilson, *Policies and Productivity*, The Money Index No.125 June 21, 1992, p.7.
6. Ibid, 1992, p.7.
7. Carl Stone, Class, *State and Democracy in Jamaica*, N.Y., Praegar, 1986, P. I 90.
8. Reported in The Jamaica Herald, Dec. 4, 1994, p.1A.
9. Jamaica Five Year Development Plan 1990-1995, Planning Institute of Jamaica, July 10, 1995, p.8.
10. Ibid, p.8.
11. See David C. Korten in David C. Korten and Felipe B. Alphanso, (eds) *Bureaucracy and the Poor*, Closing the Gap, Kumarian Press, 1985, pp.201202.
12. Ibid p.202.
13. Paul Harrison, *The Third World Tomorrow*, Penguin, 1991, p.304.
14. Jamaica Five Year Plan, 1995, p.13.
15. Tom Bottomore, *The Socialist Economy: Theory & Practice*, Harvester Wheatsheaf, 1990, p.67.
16. Karl Marx, *Capital, Vol.1*, New York: International Publishers, 1975, pp. 237, 582; Lipset, 1983, p.5.
17. See William Morris, News from Nowhere, London: Longman Green, 1914, and *A Factory As It Might Be*, London: Twentieth Century Press, 1907, for the ideas of Syndicalist Utopianism, which then enjoyed a measure of popularity.
18. Bottomore, 1990, p.79.
19. Hayek, Law, Legislation and Liberty, London: Routledge & Kegan Paul, 1982, Vol.II, pp.56-64; As a matter of historical philosophical interest see Jean-Jacques Rousseau. The Social Contract and Discourses, Everyman, J.M. Dent, 1993, pp.132-308, also xxv, xxvii, xxxi, xxxii.
20. Michael Shanks, *The Stagnant Society*, Pelican, 1964, p.121.
21. Henry Pelling, *A History of British Trade Unionism*, Pelican, 1965, P.227.
22. PREALC, Meeting the Social Debt, ILO, 1988, pp.6,23; Dennis Pantin Into the Valley of Debt: An Alternative Road to the IMF/World Bank Path. Gloria V. Ferguson Ltd, Trinidad & Tobago, 1989, p.55.
23. Ibid p.27.
24. The 1988 Stone survey of working-class opinion disclosed widespread worker dissatisfaction over: wages, union representation; lack of worker's power and influence at the workplace; employers' treatment of workers; the JLP Government's treatment of the labour movement; and the role being played by the IDT. The results of the survey showed that 56% of the sample felt that workers did not get a fair deal from the IDT; 50% were not satisfied with the quality of trade union representation; 94% felt they did not get a fair deal from employers; 62% harboured feelings of wage – related exploitation; 90% saw it necessary for greater worker involvement and influence in the running of the country – See Carl Stone, Politics vs Economics: The 1989 Elections in Jamaica, Heinemann Publishers (Caribbean) Ltd, 1989.
25. David Hume, Theory of Politics, Frederick Walkins (ed) Nelson, 1951, p.193.
26. Ibid, p.196.
27. Ibid, p.195.
28. See Introduction, section headed "Social Contract", p.6.
29. W. Arthur Lewis, The Principles of Economic Planning, Unwin University Books, 1969, p.83.
30. Karl Mannheim, *Ideology and Utopia*, New York: Harcourt Brace Jovanich, 1955.
31. Lewis, 1969, pp.83-84.

32. Clarke Kerr, John T. Dunlop, Frederick Harbison, and Charles A. Myers, *Industrialism and Industrial Man*, Oxford University Press, 1964, p.79.
33. Ibid, p.92.
34. Ibid, p.184.
35. Ibid, p.177.
36. Ibid, p.201.
37. Ian Boxill, "Global Trends" in The Money Index No.395, No.16, 1993, pp.13-14.
38. Carl Stone, "The Reagan/Thatcher Factor", in The Daily Gleaner, Feb. 17, 1988.
39. David Butler, and Donald Stokes, *Political Change in Britain*, St, Martin's Press, New York, 1974, p.277.
40. Michael Foot, *Loyalists and Loners*, Collins, 1986, p.116.
41. Butler and Stokes, 1974, p.278.
42. Ibid.
43. Ibid, p.370.
44. G.D.H. Cole and Raymond Postgate, *The Common People*, University Paperbacks, Methuen, London, 1966, p.661.
45. Gordon Lewis, "The Challenge of Independence in the British Caribbean", in Hilary Beckles and Verene Shepherd, (eds) Caribbean Freedom, Ian Randle Publishers, Kingston, 1991, p.512.
46. The Jamaica Herald, Sept. IS, 1995 p.1.
47. Harrison, 1991, p.29.
48. See, Jamaica Five Year Development Plan 1990-95, Planning Institute of Jamaica, July 30, 1995, p.33.
49. Dennis E. Morrison, "Economic Imperatives: An Effective Investment and Manpower Strategy 1991/94 and Beyond", in Headley Brown (ed) *The Jamaican Economy in a Changing World: The Way Forward 1991/94 and Beyond*, Headley Brown & CO. Ltd, 1991, pp.152,166.
50. The conditions for Pareto Optimality of Fiscal Neutrality are given by E. S. Phelps as: the existence of competitive equilibrium; perfect information about present and future prices, wages and supplies of public goods; producers have perfect information about current technology over the lifetime of the population; there are no externalities in production; consumers have perfect information about present and future – and unchanging-tastes; and, finally, there are no externalities in consumption other than the public goods whose production is taken as given – E.S. Phelps, "Growth and Government Intervention: a Critique of Neutralization" in *Fiscal Neutrality Toward Economic Growth*, McGraw Hill, 1965, ch.4, reprinted in Amartya Sen (ed) *Growth Economics*, Penguin, 1970. It goes without saying that such conditions do not exist in any one economic context at the same time, or at all, and certainly not in Jamaica.
51. Morrison in Headley Brown (ed), 1993, p.167.
52. The rate of savings (and investment) is, according to Phelps, unavoidably political. "The ballot box", he says, "or something else, must be substituted for the price mechanism" – E.S. Phelps, op cit, p.504. As happened with the NICs, and Japan before that, Phelps proposes government participation in the financing of risky but developmentally strategic investments or, otherwise, the provision of state subsidy for investments promoting substantial exports production or employment creation, (p.510).
53. Morrison in Headley Brown, 1993, pp.168-70.
54. S.A. Marglin, "The Social Rate of Discount and the Optimal Rate of Investment", The Quarterly Journal of Economics, Vol.77, 1961, p.104.
55. Draft Outline of Social Contract/Understanding p.1.
56. Ibid, pp.8-9.
57. The missing of growth and inflation targets naturally influences the level of policy credibility and commitment.
58. Ibid, The Draft Outline of Social Contract/Understanding p.4.
59. JTURDC, Towards a National Understanding, JTURDC, 1993, p.1.
60. Trevor M. Farrell, "The Caribbean State and its Role in Economic Management", in Stanley Lalta and Marie Freckleton, (eds) *Caribbean Economic Development*, Ian Randle Publishers, Jamaica, 1993, p.201; See also Farrell, "Some Notes Towards a Strategy for Economic Transformation" in Lalta and Freckleton, (eds), p.330.
61. Peta-Anne Bilker, "Search for Transformation Strategies – a Perspective from the NGO Sector", in Stanley Lalta and Marie Freckleton (eds), 1993, p.348.
62. Ibid.
63. Apart from C.Y. Thomas this approach to developmental policy design is reflected in the work of others such as Trevor Barker in his Development Planning - Reflections and Reconsiderations, in Lalta and Fredileton (eds) Caribbean Economic Development, Ian Randle Publishers, 1993, p.356.
64. Byron Buckley, in The Daily Gleaner, May 31, 1992.
65. The Daily Gleaner, May 27, 1992, p.1.
66. G. Arthur Brown, in The Daily Gleaner, May 27, 1992, p.2.
67. Sir Alister McIntyre, in an address at the dinner in honour of two former Prime Ministers and trade union leaders, the Rt. Hon. Michael Manley and Rt. Hon. Hugh Shearer, in Kingston on Jan. 22, 1992.
68. Terry Smith, a specialist industrial relations journalist, in The Daily Gleaner, May 31, 1992.
69. Terry Smith, "PJ's Pre-Budget Kite", in The Daily Gleaner May 31, 1992.

70. See Leon HoSang, "Wage Restraint/Incomes Policy" in The Daily Gleaner, Dec. 13, 1991, p.16; Carl Stone, "Deregulating Labour" in the Daily Gleaner, Jan. 10, 1990, p.6.
71. Terry Smith, in The Daily Gleaner, May 31, 1992.
72. "The Social Contract – National Wage/Income Policy for Fiscal Year 1992/91", Ministry of the Public Service May 16, 1992, revised June 12, 1992.
73. Ibid.
74. Ibid; Jamaica Five Year Development, p.8.
75. A pay rise of 5% to British MP's generated as much resentment in circumstances where public sector workers were limited to a wage increase linked to the cost of living which had then increased by only 2.3%.
76. Davies in The Daily Gleaner, May 1, 1995, p.1. See for the similar British scenario, The Guardian Weekly, Sept. 4, 1994, p.8.
77. Salary per annum for a Trained Teacher with 2-3 years' experience is $14,119.25 and allowance is $3723.75.
78. The Financial Gleaner, June 11, 1993, p.9.
79. Ramesh Deosaran, "The Caribbean Man: A Study in the Psychology of Perception and the Media", CQ Vol.27 No. 283 p.78; Charles Steinberg, The Communication Arts, New York, Hastings House, 1970, pp.26-27.
80. Reported in The Daily Gleaner, Feb. 17, 1988.
81. Cecelia Green, "Advanced Capitalist Hegemony and the Significance of Gramsci's Insights: A Restatement", SES, Vol.42 No. 283, June and Sept. 1993, ISER, U.W.I., p.186.
82. Ibid, p.175.
83. Ibid, pp.57-8,263 .
84. Paul Chen-Young, The Jamaica Observer Jan. 27, 1996, p.1; P.J. Patterson, Prime Minister, The Jamaica Herald, Jan. 29, 1996, p.3.
85. Which is what politics is held to be essentially about by Harold Laswell and others.
86. The Jamaica Herald, Jan. 29, 1996, p.3.
87. Paulo Freire, Pedagogy of the Oppressed, Penguin Books, 1972, pp.36,119.
88. Carl Stone, Power and Policy Making in Jamaica, undated mimeo, p.12.
89. All that the Act in fact does is to stipulate required periods of notice for the termination of employment under 5,3,4,
90. Carl Stone, Class, State and Democracy in Jamaica, Praegar, 1987, pp.109,119.
91. Ironically, increasing social and economic polarization coincided with the proposed search for a social contract.
92. Carl Stone, Power and Policy Making in Jamaica, undated mimeo, pp.24-25.
93. The Jamaica Confederation of Trade Unions (JCTU) was formed in Jan. 1994 and the JTURDC in Sept. 1980.
94. Jones, 1992, p.124.
95. Ibid, p.40.
96. Kerr et al Industrialism and Industrial Man, Oxford University Press, 1964, pp.178-91,233.
97. C.L.G. Bell, "The Political Framework" in Hollis Chenery et al., Redistribution with Growth, Oxford University Press 1974 p.61.
98. ESSJ, 1979, pp.26.1-26.5.
99. Cecelia Green, "Advanced Capitalist Hegemony and the Significance of Gramsci's Insights: A Restatement" SES 42: 2-5r3, June and Sept. 1993, p. 187.
100. The status of a trade union as agent of the worker is a matter of some uncertainty in relation to the terms and conditions of an individual's contract of employment as affected by the provisions of a collective agreement negotiated by a union of which the individual is a member since one is obliged to raise the issue of incorporation to withdraw, although briefly, from membership of the PSOJ; and given the recent low rating of the Government in public opinion polls, who can it really effectively claim to represent in any tripartite policy formulation.
101. Jones, 1992, p.159.
102. Trade Unions may be afraid of being held jointly responsible for failed policies.
103. Lawrence Nurse, "Managing Institutional Change during Structural Adjustments Does Labour Have a Role", in ILO, The Role of Trade Unions in Periods of Structural Adjustment Programmes, ILO Seminar, Barbados, Dec. 1992, pp.28-31.
104. Such a question by Daily Gleaner columnist, Byron Buckley, was being asked at the same time that the unions were being accused by private sector leaders of over indulgence in militancy.
105. Trevor Munroe, The Politics of Constitutional Decolonization, Jamaica, 1944-62, ISER, U.W.I., 1984, p.7.
106. Ralph Miliband, Parliamentary Socialism, Merlin Press, 1987, pp.365,369.
107. David Colman &Frederick Nixson, Economics of Change in Less Developed Countries, 1994, pp.8-9,70,79 et seq. There are unfortunately no available Gini Coefficient figures for recent years.
108. Ibid, p.103.
109. Girvan, Bernal and Hughes "The IMF and the Third World: The Case of Jamaica, 1974-80" in Development Dialogue 1980: 2 Dag Hammerskjold Foundation, Sweden p.128.
110. Reported in The Financial Gleaner, Aug. 27, 1993, p.24.
111. The Barbados Advocate, Aug. 30, 1993.
112. Rob Watts, "Living standards and the Hawke Government 1981-89", in Ian Taylor (ed) The Social Effects of Free Market Policies, Harvester Wheat-sheaf, 1990, p.161.
113. "Toward Developing a Social Partnership", p.19.

114. Guardian Weekly, "Poor lesson from Australia, Jan. 7, 1996 p.2; See also Guardian Weekly, Oct. 16, 1994 p.2, "Swedish model explained" which gave as the reasons for the electoral return of the Social Democratic Party in the 1994 elections, the massive jump in unemployment to 14% in three years; "hefty" tax cuts for the better-off; increased user charges for social services; "higher and higher salaries and obscenely generous redundancy compensation for senior managers and directors; and government, (taxpayer) bail out on overly generous terms of the banking sector during the financial crisis of 1992. The letter writer, one Nick Quantock, referred, significantly, to the sense of solidarity between Swedish citizens who as "a condition for making these sacrifices (demand) that they be fairly shared by all sections of society, rich and not so rich alike".

115. Watts, 1990, p.163.

116. bid, p.167; Przeworski argues that because conflicts of interests under capitalism become politically prioritized during economic crises – unbroken in Jamaica since the 1970's – the political directorate is under pressure to mitigate their disruptive consequences by the negotiation of social contracts, understandings, and other forms of decision-making by consensus, in a context which is "certainly the most propitious in terms of a favourable working-class response" – Adam Przeworski, *Capitalism and Social Democracy*, Cambridge University Press, 1989, p.134.

117. Antonio Gramsci, The Prison Notebooks, Quint in Hoare and Geoffrey Nowell Smith (eds), N.Y. International Publishers, 1971, p.243.

118. Kerr et. al, 1964.

119. Girvan, Bernal, Hughes 1980, pp.147-154. 1994.

120. Walsh has made the point that "willingness to sacrifice is likely to be a scarce quantity in circumstances where perceptions of reality differ as sharply as they do here and the sense of common interest is so weak"-James Walsh, "Something's gotta give", The Daily Gleaner, Sept 16, 1994, p.6; Beckford sees the population as one having "a limited and constrained confidence in the future". George Beckford, *Persistent Poverty*, 1983, p.124.

121. For the function to be served by "business confidence" in neo-liberal ideology, see G.C. Peden, *British Economic and Social Policy*, Philip Allan, 1991, p. 113 where the. views of such leading proponents as Milton Freedman are considered.

122. Zin Henry, Labour Relations and Industrial Conflict in Commonwealth and Caribbean Countries, Columbus Publishers Ltd, 1972, pp.55-57. Arthur Lewis "The 1930's Social Revolution" in Hilary Beckles and Verene Shepherd (eds) Caribbean Freedom, Ian Randle Publishers, Jamaica/James Currey Publishers, London, 1993, p.387; G. E. Eaton, Alexander Bustamante and Modern Jamaica, Kingston Publishers Ltd. 1975, pp.79 et seq; William H. Friedland Unions and Industrial Relations in Underdeveloped Countries, New York State School of Industrial Relations, Cornell University, Bulletin 47, Reissued May 1966, p.19; Munroe, 1984, P . 5 6 .

123. Carl Stone, in The Daily Gleaner, Feb. 3, 1988, Jan. 6, 1988 and Mar. 21, 1988.

124. Przeworski, 1989. Since ultimately, capitalists do not just want to reinvest profits but to consume them, it would appear risky to leave the matter of investment to a private sector said to suffer from the "absence of a capitalist class capable of technological innovation" – Dennis Pantin "Techno-industrial Policy in the Restructuring of the Caribbean: the Missing Link", in Hilbourne A. Watson (ed) *The Caribbean in the Global Political Economy*, Ian Randle Publishers, Kingston, 1994 p.7Q; Farrell concludes that the state has to play the role of entrepreneur by default as "the local private sector has neither the resources, the skills, the organization, nor the will to undertake the job of economic resources transformation – Trevor M.A. Farrell "The Caribbean State and its Role in Economic Management" in Omar Davies (ed) *The State in Caribbean Society*, Dept, of Economics, U.W.I. Jamaica, 1986, p.15; As a member of the private sector saw fit to put the matter of timely state action: "… politicians have a way of coming to reality late" – The Jamaica Herald, Feb. 6, 1994, p.1B.

125. George L. Beckford, Persistent Poverty, Maroon Publishing House, Jamaica, 1988, p. 204; The State itself in Jamaica may indeed be regarded as the expression of a compromise instrumental in defining the tolerable boundaries within which the interests of the multiple classes in the coalition will be allowed legitimate pursuit. It could well be, however, that the societal contradictions are so severe as to deny the probability of an agreement of substance on the major socio-economic essentials of class conflict. Even at the early stages of the experience of IMF imposed austerity it was recognized that "such basic questions as how to reconcile social consensus with accumulation strategy and how to harmonize revolutionary expectations with actual possibilities, or production efficiency with popular participation, need to be adequately resolved in both technical and political terms – The Arusha Initiative – Development Dialogue 1980: 2, Dag Hammerskjold Foundation, Sweden, pp.10 et seq.

126. After the outbreak of border hostilities with China, the Industrial Truce Resolution of Nov. 1962 produced dramatic results in increased production and management-labour cooperation reflected in a significant reduction in work stoppages. In Belgium during the last month of World War II a pact of social solidarity was signed between union leaders and employers' organizations representative which amounted to a blue print covering the principal areas of social reform which were due for attention in the post-war years: wages, working hours, social security, pensions health and invalidity provisions, family allowances, unemployment benefits annual holiday pay, the establishment of union delegations, joint, committees, a joint national council and machinery for the settlement of industrial disputes. This developed in the 1960 into "social programming" between employers and unions consisting of national and industry level agreements setting out the social improvement targets based on a realistic assessment of economic conditions – Roger Blanpain, Recent Trends in Collective Bargaining in Belgium, IFR Vol.104, No.1-2 July-Aug. 1971, p.112. Apart, from increased union security an important *quid pro quo* offered to the workers was the establishment of objective criteria for determining labour's share in the growth of the national wealth.

127. Roger Southall, (ed) *Trade Unions and the New Industrialisation of the Third World*, University of Pittsburg Press, 1988, p.43; Clarke and Clements quote Trotsky to the effect that "trade unions can either transform themselves into revolutionary organizations or

become lieutenants of capitalism in the intensified exploitation of workers" in the name of sacrifice for the common good – Tom Clarke and Laurie Clements (eds) *Trade Unions Under Capitalism*, Fontana, 1977, p.29.

128. Michael Parenti, Democracy for the Few, St. Martins Press, N.Y., 1988, p.312.
129. Przeworski, 1989, pp. 144-145.
130. If trade union leaders are perceived by their members to be acting as merely agents of the state this will obviously offer additional/new opportunities to any already existing militant left, or for its emergence-depending on the ideological environment – see Ralph Miliband, *Parliamentary Socialism*, Merlin Press, London, 1987, pp.51,152. For Przeworski, a model of irreconcilable class conflict (as portrayed for Jamaica by George Beckford in *Small Garden: Bitter Weed, Struggle and Change in Jamaica*, ISER, 1991, p.124 and Beckford, *Persistent Poverty*, Maroon Publishing House, Jamaica, 1933, p. 153;) "... leads to the conclusion that capitalism could not have survived as a choice of the working class ... [unless the working class was] a passive victim of oppression, a perpetual dupe of ideological domination, or at best, ... repeatedly betrayed by its leadership" – Adam Przeworski, 1989, p.202.
131. V.I. Lenin, *The State*, Foreign Language Press, PQ, China, 1975, p.31.
132. Headley Brown, "Requirements for social acceptance of pay guidelines", in The Daily Gleaner, Jan. 7, 1990; Honderich makes the point that "it is easier to argue against violence [as a means of achieving social, economic, and political equality] from a premise about things being better for future generations as a result of non-violent progress, if one's place in the present generation is satisfactory" – Ted Honderich, 1989, p.12.
133. Katrin Norris, Jamaica: The search for an Identity, Institute for Race Relations, London, 1966, p.101, speaks of "two nations sharing the same space", (needing to be welded together).
134. Sir Philip Sherlock, in The Daily Gleaner, Aug. 22 1994 p.6.
135. C.B. MacPherson, The Political Theory of Possessive Individualism: Hobbes to Locke, Oxford University Press, 1962, pp.76,87.
136. Honderich, 1989, p.18.
137. The "social debt" refers to the excess resources captured by those who benefited from structural adjustment/stabilization, as socio-economic agents – the "debtors", and to the deficit of the remaining agents – the working class and poor who bore the brunt of the burden of change – the "creditors".
138. PREALC, Meeting the Social Debt, ILO, 1988, p.8.
139. Stuart Henry and Jeffrey Brown, "The Informal Economy Outcomes of Free Market Policies", in Ian Taylor (ed) 1990, p.319.
140. M. Harris, *America Now: The Anthropology of a Changing Culture*, Simon and Schuster, N.Y. 1981 p.126.
141. J.H Goldthorpe, "Industrial Relations in Great Britain: A Critique of Reformism", in Tom Clarke arid Laurie Clements (eds) *Trade Unions under Capitalism*, Fontana, 1977, pp.213-4.
142. Toward Social Partnership presented as a paper identifying the broad issues for discussion – after the idea has been mooted on and off for some eighteen years – seeks to identify the causes and consequences of inflation, promises social and economic stability as the essential benefit of compliance, citing the growth in employment achieved under the Accord in Australia, in an obvious pitch to the trade unions no doubt correctly targeted as the main source of potential reservations/opposition. See the Social Partnership Feb. 1996; Broadcast to the nation by Prime Minister P.J. Patterson Feb. 26, 1996 (Jamaica Information Service); The Daily Gleaner, Feb. 19, 1996 reports the Prime Minister's presentation to Parliamentary.
143. Phyllis Marsh, The Daily Gleaner, Mar. 16, 1996, p.8A. Lewis and Nurse have observed that it is the state that will face increasing pressure from local and international capital to provide the environment most conducive to the extraction of the surplus value from labour ... mediating these contending forces can become so problematical that both capital and labour, perceiving un-met. needs, may unleash their hostilities on the state" [as well as on the each other] – Linden Lewis and Lawrence Nurse, "Caribbean Trade Unionism and Global Restructuring" in Hilbourne A. Watson (ed) *The Caribbean in the Global Political Economy*, Ian Randle Publishers, 1994, p.196.
144. Ralston B. Nembhard, The Jamaica Herald, Sept. 13, 1994, p.7A; The Government is said by Raymond Forrest to have had its most "... distinguished failure" in the very area declared to be its priority concern: containing inflation – The Financial Cleaner July 22, 1994, p.7; On an optimistic note, Girvan holds out the possibility of the nation becoming internationally competitive under a social contract which guarantees all social partners a *reasonable and just* [italics added] share of the national pie – Norman Girvan, "Eight Lessons of Liberalization in Jamaica", in Lloyd Best, Norman Girvan, C.Y. Thomas, Liberalization and Caribbean Development, ISER, IJ.W.I., 1993 p. 31.
145. Christopher Garwood, The Jamaica Herald, April 4, 1996, p.7A.
146. The Daily Gleaner, Feb. 27, 1996 p.1; There is clearly no attempt to indicate where the frontier should be drawn between one group's interests and another – J. Joblin, S.J. "Mastering the Future" ILR, Vol.104 No.3, Sept. 1971, p.227; In the language of Hobbes, the parties to the social contract need the "sovereign" to serve the purpose of keeping their 'invasions' on each other within non-destructive bounds – C.B. MacPherson, 1962, p.100; See also Wallerstein, 1993. pp.53-4; Those who fault the Social Partnership for its vagueness need to be mindful of Stone's observation that political parties have to be decidedly vague in their policy commitments in order to disguise class emphases ... so as to appear to be all things to all classes" Carl Stone Class Race and Political Behaviour in Urban Jamaica, ISER, U.W.I., 1993, p.26.
147. See The Jamaica Herald Jan. 3, 1995, pp.1,3, "$15 not enough", say welfare beneficiaries, in relation to the gross inadequacy of welfare provisions, exacerbated by increasing introduction of user charges for social services used by "the growing army of the new poor"; while Food Stamps have become a way of life for 320,000, there are still tens of thousands who cannot get into the

programme, it is reported and the proposal for Drugs Stamps for the elderly is yet to be accepted by the government – Daily Gleaner, Oct. 23, 1994, p.4A.

148. It would appear that the labour movement would rather the issue of an investment policy be not left to "the. invisible hand", as the government would seem prepared, and the private sector would be happy, to have it – see JTURDC "Towards a national understanding", undated Mimeo, p.4. Heller's statement that "A capitalist economy does not require that even one of its workers ever be unemployed" can only be described as fantastic, even for 1964, given the experience of the Great Depression – Walter W. Heller, "Employment and Manpower" in Stanley Lebergore (ed) Men Without Work – The Economics of Unemployment, Prentice Hall, 1964, p.44. For Tawney on the other hand "unemployment is not an act of God, but a disease accompanying a particular type of industrial organization" R.H. Tawney, *The Acquisitive Society*, Fontana, 1964, p.140.

149. Gordon K. Lewis, speaks of one conception of the role of trade unions as being that of "marshalling a docile and malleable labour force for service under capitalism" Southall, 1988, p.12, sees the global expansion of capitalism and trans nationalization of production requiring and generating repressive political institutions and social formations in the third world whose role is to educate, discipline and mobilize the potential and actual labour force for servitude; In the United Kingdom during World War I, moderate union leaders who called a truce ending considerable industrial conflict when war broke out, found that it was one thing to reach agreement with government, it was another to persuade the rank and file to abide by the agreement. Peden, 1991, pp.42-4; see Perry Anderson, "The Limits and Possibilities of Trade Union Action" in Robin Blackburn and Alexander Cockburn (eds) *The Incompatibles: Trade Union Militancy and the Consensus*, Penguin and New Left Review, 1967 pp.273-4. For a discussion of the neo-capitalistic attack on trade union autonomy, in which Anderson arrives at the conclusion that the threat to subordinate unions to the state through the method of corporatism/concertation, under some variant of a social contract, ultimately might just have the opposite effect of catalyzing working-class consciousness in revolt against the perceived betrayed of its leadership.

150. James Walsh, The Daily Gleaner, Feb, 23, 1996, pp.4A,8A; Michael Manley Regards the Jamaica people as being disputatious almost to the point of destructiveness, distrustful of authority, and resentful of discipline to the extent that "the question of a sense of unity in national purposes becomes confused with the totalitarian method. He nevertheless finds it possible to remark that " it is the politics of participation which will the mobilization of people and institutions behind national programmes", print – Michael Manley, *The Politics of Change*, Heinemann (Caribbean) Ltd. 1990, pp.27,30,35,36,64,67 .

151. Ralston Hyman, The Jamaica Herald, Feb. 20, 1996, p.7A; See the Daily Gleaner Dec. 13, 1995, p.2C where Opposition Senator and a leading trade unionist expressed the view that there is little chance of agreement being reached as "… every inflation target set by the present government has been exceeded by several hundred percent … preventing the unions from being able to make any binding guarantees about wage restraint".

152. The Jamaica Herald, Feb. 15, 1995, p.3.

153. Carl Wint, The Daily Gleaner, Feb. 20, 1996 pp.4A,15A; Beckford regards the population as one dwelling in a conflict-prone society, with a limited and constrained confidence in the future characterized by strong individualism entirely divorced from cooperative action – Beckford, 1988, p.204; For Nurse, the notion of Social Partnership becomes farcical when employers refuse to share vital information, do not engage in joint problem-solving or otherwise behave as if trade union practice amounts to an unnecessary but unavoidable irritant – Lawrence Nurse, "Managing institutional Change during Structural Adjustment. Does Labour have a Role?" in ILO, *The Role of Trade Unions in Periods of Structural Adjustment Programmes*, ILO, Seminar, Barbados Workers Union Labour College, Barbados, Dec. 1992, p.17. Whether consent to any pact will hold depends on, among other factors: the degree of unionization, the level and traditions of collective bargaining; union unity/rivalry, the voluntary/coercive nature of the compromise attained in relation to the extent of the domestic political experience, stability of the internal/external economic environment, especially exchange rate; price behaviour and interest rates.

154. Delroy Chuck, The Daily Gleaner Feb. 21, 1996 p.4A; see also for reference to the relevance of Rousseau's ideas, Clifton Segree "The ultimate Social Contract, The Daily Gleaner, June 3, 1992 p.6.

155. P.J. Patterson, Prime Minister, Broadcast to the nation, Jamaica Information Service, Feb 26, 1996 p.10; The editorial of the Daily Gleaner Feb. 5, 1996 p.4A, suggested that the Prime Minister "needs to come with something much more concrete much more specific than an idea whose time has already come and which has yet. to show that it is capable to successful translation into realty … moral leadership is one thing; pragmatic political leadership is quite another. Appeals to people's "better nature are not generally guaranteed to achieve success". Larry A. Bailey is of the view that when politicians lead the call for a "social partnership" or a social contract we know (from experience) that either the country or the politicians, or roost, likely both are in trouble. When things are going relatively well we never hear the call for a social partnership. More is the pity – The Financial Gleaner, Feb. 16, 1996 p.7; In "The Parties Speak" in The Daily Gleaner, Oct 16, 1994 p.23A the JLF asserts that when trade unions during its tenure of office in the 1980's were asked to accept wage guidelines of 12.5%, this was on the basis of an achieved target of inflation of under 10% … It is upon this type "of social contract", if you will, that the JLP Government of the eighties proceeded to institute and maintain wage guidelines; The late highly respected Carl Stone wrote that "The generation therefore of genuine national consensus on any sensitive position issue with partisan implications is rendered quite impossible … Public opinion exchanges on such sensitive, controversial issues, therefore get narrowed, simplified, distorted and confused by party polarization – Carl Stone, *Class, State and Democracy in Jamaica*, Praeger, 1987, p.137. In 1992 the then Minister of Finance, Hugh Small, indicated, in opening the Budget Debate for 1992/93, the Government's intention of cutting the flat, rate of income tax from 3 3.3% to a flat, rate of 25% on all incomes and also the rate of inflation from the unofficial figure of over

100% in the previous year to 15% (a figure that was nearly tripled, at 40.2%, as it. turned out.) – The Daily Gleaner May 29, 1992, p.1. The idea that employers would develop financial instruments enabling greater worker equity ownership, or a housing fund, in lieu of wage increases, never progressed beyond the conception stage.

156. Robert. Kyloh, The Wage-Inflation-Unemployment nexus, ILO, Geneva, 1988, p.47; One must of course beware of the effect, of "policy stacking" in trying to disentangle the effect, of different policy interventions the more so with highly complex economies.

157. Particularly in such situations, it's confidently predicted by Przeworski that, social pacts cannot last "unless they are coercively enforced because capitalist democracy puts any group in the situation of a prisoner's dilemma" – Przeworski, 1989, p.144; It may be, Immanuel contends, that the interests of classes are substantially irreconcilable, in which case notions of coalitions of classes are mythical – Patrick A.M. Emmanuel, *The Role of the State in the Commonwealth Caribbean*, Working Paper No.38, ISER, U.W.I. 1990, p.4; In the case of Kenya, tripartite "agreements were entered into which involved the amalgamation of small unions into a central labour organization, prohibition of strikes, measures to increase employment by some 10% and a wage freeze in exchange for union financial security in the form of an official check-off system – Rhoda Howard, "Third World Trade Unions as Agents of Human Rights" in Southall (ed), 1988, p.233.

158. A central plank of the "Swedish alternative" is the solidaristic wage policy, "perceived as a way of not only accelerating structural adjustment and economic growth, but also achieving equity objectives" Under this policy the principle of comparability – the rate for the job-is consistently applied, regardless of inter-industry or firm productivity or ability to pay, differences, Centralized collective bargaining has, further, facilitated the raising of wages in the low-wage labour intensive sector at the expense of the high productivity and profit industries and firms, while the actual size of wage adjustments was determined by export competitiveness considerations. To deal with consequential retrenchment, transfers was encouraged by the measures taken to provide training, skill upgrading, information and financial support so as to minimize personal, enterprise, industrial, and national dislocation – Kyloh, 1988, p.48.

159. Rob Watts, "Living standards and the Hawke Government, 1933-89," in Taylor, 1990, p.167.

160. Ralph Miliband, The State in Capitalist Society, Basic Books, 1969, pp.58-9.

161. K. Marx, *Capital Void*, N,Y, International Publishers, 1975, p.594.

162. Milton Friedman, "The Social Responsibility of Business is to Increase its Profits", The New York Times Magazine, Sept., 13, 1970; See, for an opposed view to that of Friedman, Trevor M.A. Farrell "The Caribbean State and its Role in Economic Management", in Omar Davies (ed), *The State in Caribbean Society*, Dept, of Economics, U.W.I., Jamaica, 1986, p.20, where Farrell speaks of "… the anarchy of individual (American) firms … pursuing their individual short-run interest over the long-run social interest and even over their own long-term interest while their intellectual apologists in the universities babble about the "Invisible Hand" and "the magic of the market".

163. G. Benveniste, The Politics of Expertise, Berkeley, California, Glendessary Press, 1972, p.70.

164. The JTURDC was to argue that the wage guidelines were set "without any regard for notions of equity and that there was "no synchronization between the aims and objectives of labour and those of the adjustment policies. – JTURDC, *The IMF and the Jamaican Labour Sector 1977-90, A Study of the Impact of Wage Guidelines*, JTURDC Research Dept. 1993, pp.40-41.

165. For the totally different Argentinean orientation of the 1990's pledging each party to a joint effort to achieve a greater measure of social justice, particularly for the least well off, see ILO, Report of the Director General, Tenth Conference of America States Members, Mexico City, ILO, Nov-Dec 1974, p.19.

166. Rondinelli notes that where decisions are "made and implemented through the interaction of groups with different interests, objectives, sources of power, and capacities to undermine or block the action of others" it is highly unlikely that comprehensive planning and control-oriented management will be successful – Dennis A. Rondinelli, Development-Administration and US Foreign Aid Policy, Boulder, Colorado: Lynne Reinner Publishers, 1987, pp.159-60.

167. The United Nations Research Institute, for Social Development's field investigations in the late 1960's indicate that per capita income correlate strongly with indices of social well-being such as calorie intake and the quality of health, educational and housing standards, which "suggests that, if handled carefully, growth of income may be a good approximation to satisfaction of the aspirations of developmentalists … there cannot be solidarity between partners of unequal economic power. Solidarity therefore implies a more rapid growth in the income of the poor – Bohuslar Herman, *The Optimal International Division of Labour*, LO, Geneva, 1975 p. 32, Miliband suggests that given capitalist control of financial, economic, social and communication resources, to argue and even worse, formulate plans on the basis of the class-serving fiction that capitalists are only one of many more or less equal contending groups, amounts to nothing less than "a resolute escape from reality" Ralph Miliband, 1969, p.155.

168. Stephens and Stephens 1936, p.216; Okun proposes a reward version of a tax-based incomes policy which he claims "also shades into proposals for tax reductions as a way to lubricate a social contract and increase the acceptability of voluntary or mandatory standards for restraint on wages and markuptey" – Arthur M. Okun, Prices and Quantities – A Macroeconomic Analysis, The Brookings Institution, 1981, p. 152.

169. Alan Adelman and Reid Reading (eds), Confrontation in the Caribbean Basin University of Pittsburg, 1984, p.101. There could scarcely have been any doubt that the consequences of the initiative would have been demand suppression, reduced, investment, and business contraction, particularly, since the rate of price increase to which wages were tied was well below the actual rate of inflation. See PREALC, Adjustment and Social Debt, ILO, 1987, pp.66-68,71,78,88.

170. Roger Plant, *Labour Standards and Structural Adjustment*, ILO, 1994, p.68; For details of the Mexican Economic Solidarity Pact see Plant, pp.104-5. Commentators in the Jamaican press held up the model of the Mexican economy as a "miracle" to be emulated

not long before its latest major economic and financial crisis, which incidentally demonstrated the very considerable advantage gained in negotiating with the IMF as a member of a trade block which includes the U.S.A. in this case NAFTA.

171. Thomas C. Schelling, *The Strategy of Conflict*, Harvard University, 1994, p.106.

172. Norris, 1966. p.42; Munroe, 1934, pp.56-7, where it is noted that the powers of the Governor 'Under Proclamation) were used not to protect the colonial regime from anti-colonial assaults, but to keep Jamaicans from attacking themselves.

173. J.II. Gold Thorpe, "Industrial Relations in Great Britain: A Critique of Reformism", in Clarke arid Clements, 1977, p. 214; One is left to wonder if the 'big leap' to 'social partner' is really possible in the near term. Paulo Freire, *Pedagogy of the Oppressed*, Penguin, 1990, pp.113, 119. The Capitalist Class, Kautsky contends, rules but does not govern (since) ... it contends itself with ruling the government" ... Karl Kautsky, *The Social Revolution*, Chicago: Charles H. Kerr, 1903, p.13. This ensures that there is no attempt to, apply radical solutions to fundamental problems which are likely to be damaging to interests of the privileged classes; in this predisposition, as Miliband notes, "the economy" acquires a life of its own, becomes an end in itself and "is part of the idiom of ideology". Miliband, 1969, p.79.

174. ILO. Report to a Symposium on Employment, Trade, Adjustment and North – South Co-operation, ILO, Geneva, 1985, pp.26-27.

175. Freire, 1990, p. 117.

Chapter 6

International Monetary Fund,
Consequences and Perceptions

Jamaica having become a member of the International Monetary Fund (TMF/ Fund) and the International Bank for Reconstruction and Development (World Bank/Bank) on gaining Independence in 1962, the Agreements establishing both institutions are incorporated into the Laws of Jamaica as The Bretton Woods Agreements Act[1] which sets out the purposes, functions, organization, and management of the Fund and Bank under Part I and II, respectively.

Since membership is voluntary it must be assumed that the prospective benefits of belonging to this so-called "rich man's club"[2] outweigh the possible disadvantages. The protagonists of third world interests who bemoan the fact that they are subject to rules which they did not formulate – having become members some years after the founding of the organizations – suffer the common fate of the new citizens of their own countries[3] and indeed new members of any organization, society or association, whatever its nature, purpose, or importance.

It is generally agreed that the weaknesses of the Bretton Woods system (Art I (I)) for ensuring effective consultation and collaboration on global monetary matters was exposed by "the unrelenting, costly chaos in world currency markets" in September of 1992;[4] nor can there be said to have been "... the expansion and balanced growth of international trade" required for "the promotion and maintenance of high levels of employment and real income", (Art.I(11)).

With respect to employment the industrialized world has experienced sustained levels of unemployment traditionally associated with developing countries; the trend in OECD real unit labour costs was on the decline from the 1980's as indicated by TABLES 8 & 24, respectively. The data for Jamaica as set out in FIG. 29 & TABLE 9, provides abundant evidence of the IMF's dismal failure to carry out its mandate under Article I (II)[5] – the more significant for its virtually unbroken monitoring and influence over policy design for the island's economy for almost two decades. The authority to provide balance of payments support to members is contained in Article I(V) which stipulates,

"... thus providing them with the opportunity to correct maladjustments in their balance of payments without resorting to measures destructive of national or international *prosperity*,[6] [italics added]

But balance of payments support has been usually conditional on repeated substantial devaluations of the value of the local currency, having the effects on the exchange rate indicated by FIG. 30.

The island, far from being a "success story"[7] as in 1992[8] Mexico was also held out to be by IMF Managing Director Michael Camdessus, has suffered from trade protectionism by the industrialized countries. This the IMF has seemed powerless to remedy. As Teresa Hayter has said, "free trade has never existed in the real world"; but apart from the vagaries of international trade, other salient factors which explain the island's less than impressive economic performance are the adverse *terms* of trade, (FIG.31), and recession in the industrialized countries.

Table:: 24	Real Unit Labour Costs[9] in the EEC. 1975-1987 (100 - 1961-73 average)							
Country	1961-73	1975	1981	1982	1984	1985[1]	1986[1]	1987[2]
Belgium	100	110.0	115.0	112.9	111.9	110.2	106.1	104.6
Denmark	100	104.6	100.5	99.2	96.1	94.4	92.9	93.5
France	100	105.9	108.1	107.3	105.3	104.4	102.1	100.2
Germany, Fed. Rep.	100	105.9	103.5	102.2	98.9	97.8	96.1	95.7
Greece	100	90.2	106.4	106.1	107.2	109.2	101.2	98.9
Ireland	100	104.6	101.3	99.5	95.2	92.9	91.4	91.3
Italy	100	110.9	108.6	108.6	109.4	108.5	103.2	101.7
Luxemburg	100	123.4	124.9	120.4	111.2	109.3	106.4	107.5
Netherlands	100	108.8	102.5	101.1	95.8	94.3	95.4	97.8
Portugal	100	136.2	116.1	100.6	100.5	96.9	92.0	90.6
Spain	100	104.0	102.9	100.7	94.4	91.8	89.1	87.7
United Kingdom	100	110.1	100.3	98.5	98.8	97.9	99.9	100.3
Total EEC	100	107.2	104.3	103.0	101.1	99.9	98.1	97.1

[1] Ratio of real wage costs per employee (wages and social security contributions) to GDP per employed person. Estimates and forecasts.

Source: Commission of the European Communities: Annual Economic Report, 1986-87.

Note: The EEC blamed the level of unemployment on "the failure of real wages to adjust to the levels warranted by the crisis in productivity and the terms of trade that occurred during the 1970's"

However, we are advised that the European Trade Union Institute strongly contested this view," arguing that "there is no direct correlation between movements in the real labour cost gap and the level of employment, "since the two countries with the worst employment performance have seen the gap move in opposite directions."

The Table shows that in the case of the U.K. the gap decreased significantly, between 1975 and 1981, from 110.1 to 100.3. For Belgium, on the other hand, there was an increase from 110.0 to 115.0 over the same period (The average unemployment for the U.K. (1975-86) was 8.48 and for (1983-86) 11.53. For Belgium it was 9.60 and 12.10, respectively.

Even more to the point, as Kyloh points out, while "the wage gap has disappeared in most countries yet labour markets have not rebounded". The implications for trade union strategy is obvious.

Figure: 29

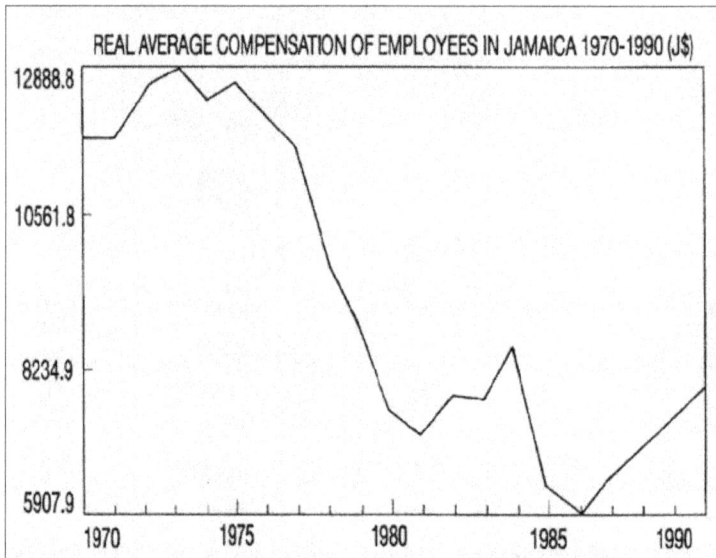

Source: STATIN

Both have proved to be inhibiting factors in the implementation of policy having electoral implications, which is perhaps inevitable in a competitive parliamentary political system. Other consequences have been the underdevelopment of the entrepreneurial class; disparity in the returns to labour as against capital; insufficient promotional attention and assistance to the small business and informal sectors;[10]

and in the earlier years of the global economic crisis, recession, inflation, and the steep upward adjustment of international interest rates.[11]

Rather than the success story that Jamaica has occasionally been claimed to be,[12] the combination of the above factors has led McDonald to complain that,

> "... successive governments continue to apply the economic stick of austerity to the overburdened backs of the black working man and woman through rising prices, reduced living standards and increased poverty... Reduction on spending on education, health, housing and other social services increasingly establishes the conditions for class warfare, (since) it is only the social and economic policy actions by government, (through budgetary welfare/patronage provisions, which) ... allow the poorer classes of people some economic redress".[13]

There is a striking example, given the ideological affinity of the two countries, then, of Jamaica's political and administrative elite's failure to benefit from the British experience. From 1964 the British Prime Minister, Harold Wilson, had recognized the fact, that,

> "If you borrow from some of the world's bankers you will quickly find you lose another kind of independence because of the deflationary policies and the cuts in social services that will be imposed on a government that has got itself into that position".[14]

For budgetary allocations to the social services, as against the amount devoted to debt service, see FIG. 32. Thomas, by implication, seems to accept this statement of reality in view of his observation that, "... politicians increasingly try to use these multilateral institutions as the whipping boy",[15] since they do not take responsibility for allowing their countries to get into the "debt trap". This, he says, is what Levitt protests[16] against, much more than the Fund/Bank medicine, *per se*, to which they (the politicians) are said to respond as "hopeless victims".

When IMF designed policies are implemented and fail, the government is blamed and the poor, in particular, are punished. And while there are no negative consequences for either the fund or its officers and experts,[17] the social disintegration which ensues, Thomas asserts, "... invariably has a negative effect on the social psychology of the masses".[18]

Gordon reports on the phenomenon of downward mobility arising from IMF policy-induced large scale redundancies in both the public and private sectors.[19] He

Figure: 30

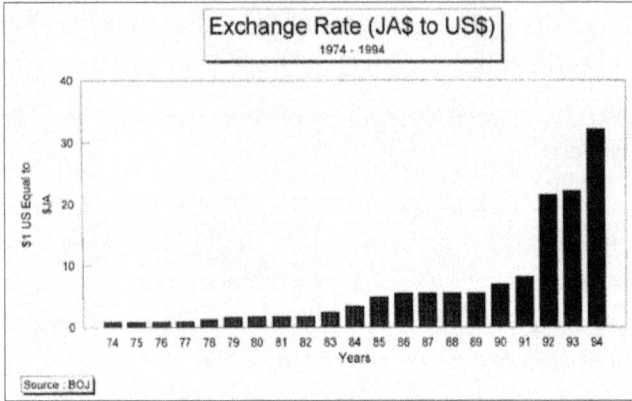

Exchange Rate (JA$ to US$)
1974 - 1994

Source : BOJ

Figure: 31

Terms of Trade
1973 - 1992

Source: World Bank
Index: 1987 = 100

Figure: 32

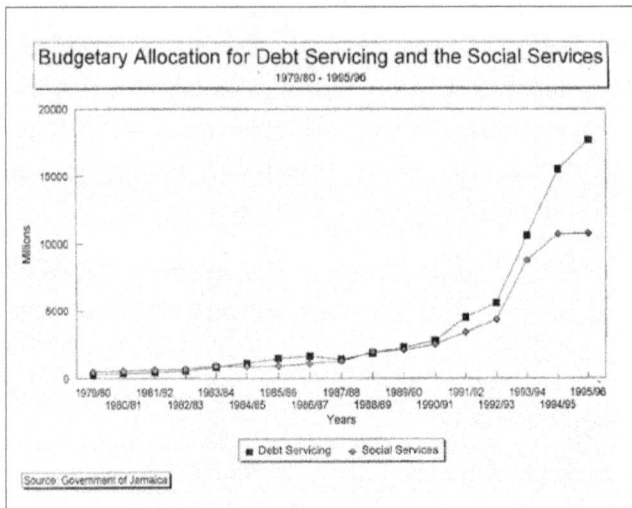

Budgetary Allocation for Debt Servicing and the Social Services
1979/80 - 1995/96

■ Debt Servicing ◆ Social Services

Source: Government of Jamaica

found that as many as one-third of the male and one-fifth of the female middle strata, according to traditional labour market segmentation, experienced dislocation into the working class, "... although only about 5 out of every 100 actually descended into its mainly unskilled and casual lower section".[20] The type of job creation which occurred during the period under Gordon's study, especially in the second half of the 1980's, led to the proletarianization of sections of the formerly petit bourgeois clerical 'white collar' categories, whereby more and more 'members of staff' became 'workers', without being aware of this occupational status change. As both Gordon Lewis and Carl Stone have noted, and as Gordon emphasizes, the stagnation in the economy, virtually unbroken since the early 1970's,

> "... could mean a sharp decline in upward mobility by the hitherto conventional routes[21] for the children of the ambitious hardworking peasant sector, thus disturbing an important part of the social foundations of the island's reputed political stability."[22]

It is this kind of IMF-type 'development' that has caused many, like Cavanagh and Beio, to conclude that the Fund and Bank, "... have adjusted economies to the short-term benefit of narrow elite interests",[23] by the use of strategies developed by and for advanced capitalist economies.

Nor has the World Bank been noticeably more successful, in the Jamaican case, in fulfilling its mandate of, "... encouraging international investment for the development of the productive resources of members, thereby assisting in raising productivity, the standard of living and conditions of labour ...".[24] This is despite several structural adjustment loans since 1983,[25] each with its intended reform conditionalities attached.

The failure to achieve improved living standards and conditions of labour was explained, as recently as the beginning of 1990, by Downer of the PSOJ as being the consequence of the,

> "... prescription of an antacid for a heart condition which requires by-pass surgery (as) The IMF... allows us to get away with a gradualist, and piecemeal approach (which) ... has not worked".[26]

So, one had the Prime Minister reporting to the nation that the Fund's advice to the government was to "give the society a shock".[27] The "bottom line", it was stated, was that "we must go on a foreign exchange diet and work harder to cure this 'bang-belly' economy"; this was, and is, in the midst of the policy implementation of the removal of exchange controls and abolition of import restrictions. The IMF – faceless as it is, and its officials removed by distance and life experience from poverty and deprivation – has refused to recognize that the more severe the "shock", the more likely the occurrence of serious social unrest; but perhaps the violent death of the poor is not too high a price to pay for the administration of social and economic "shocks." What is portended in this seemingly cavalier fashion is malnutrition, poor health and education, disease, crime and violence.

The indulgence in colloquialism to describe the malaise in the economy would suggest that Manley may well have accepted the IMF's diagnosis, if not, the treatment. It. is in this context, however, that the oft- repeated – but. as often conveniently ignored – exhortatory maxim, restated by Iqbal, demands attention: "... even in the absence of multilateral institutions there are limits to the extent to which a country can live beyond its earning ability".[28]

More intensive adjustment has resulted, in Latin America, in the increase in cyclical and structural unemployment; restriction of job creation to low wage and productivity sectors (in Jamaica to intensive production and non-unionized, largely female-dominated type work); and the relatively novel experience of an increasing number of the labour force earning wages which places them below the poverty line. This is so, even in the formal sector.[29] The logic – in a situation where poverty and increasing inequality appear to be inevitable and consistent policy consequences, whatever the declared intention, only for this to be followed by concentration on "social well-being" and "poverty alleviation" programmes – is certainly not obvious. And the situation is likely to remain so with the persistence of interest rates prohibitive of increased legitimate productive investment activity, and the continually widening external trade gap, evident in FIG. 37, due largely, to the IMF/ Bank policy of non-discriminating import liberalization.[30]

The principal beneficiaries have been the local comprador merchant capitalist class and the country's trading "partners" from which most of the island's imports come, especially the United States.

The lesson of economic adjustment in Latin America and the Caribbean would seem to be that the challenge of, "... how to harmonize – in the short and medium term – an *increase* [italics added] in worker's share of income with a rise in the investment rate"[31], is one that needs to be confronted without regard for "exceptional circumstances". The same was true of the Puerto Rican experience of industrialization under United States political and economic hegemony, which caused Gordon Lewis to refer to,

"... the full blast of a socio-economic revolution that was allowed to run its course ... with little effort ... to channel it into more desirable social directions or to shield the more defenceless local groups from its consequences".[32]

He further observed that,

"... both American reform liberalism and British Labour socialism had very little need to preoccupy themselves with the difficult problems of initial capital formation and technological development because they came into power, in their respective societies, in economies where the problems had in large part been solved earlier"[33] [although they were to be rediscovered to some degree with the triumph of free market economics, international capital mobility and the transnationalization of production].

The principal objective of the 1977 Emergency Production Plan[34] – representing the elaboration of an alternative to IMF style stabilization[35] – was to find solutions of a more self-reliant nature to the current Jamaican economic problems. The countries from which the programme designs were taken and which were then applied to Third World countries like Jamaica were vastly different on almost every important social and economic index. Those problems include reducing dependence on imports of capital goods (where possible, given the virtual absence of capital goods industries in the smaller and more industrially/technologically backward territories), consumer goods and raw materials; diversifying economic relations; changing the structure of the economy to minimize foreign currency requirements; maximizing job creation (if anything, labour shortage was the problem faced by the industrialized economies once the process of industrialization had begun in earnest); and increasing the production of goods and services catering to the satisfaction of the basic needs of the mass of the population, first and foremost, with the export thrust being an extension of such a production strategy.

Bertram suggests by implication, that the country would have fared better by following the lead taken by the ruling PNP's National Executive Council in January 1977 of opposing the IMF's "entry into the Jamaican economy at the invitation of the PNP government... on the basis of its irrelevance to Jamaica's economic progress... a crime worse than a communist conspiracy",[36] (in the eyes of the dominant economic class, it is suggested). What is certain is that while the political ideological struggle has subsided with the omnipotence of the free market paradigm all but conceded, and thus with its virtual omnipresence assured, economic debate still rages, although not again, against a background of intense ideological polarization.

Whether the country would have been better off without having been "IMF'ed" will always, of course, be a matter of debate.[37]

What is reasonably certain is that the course of electoral political events is likely to have been ruptured by the major changes that would, without doubt, have resulted from the adoption of a non-IMF path.[38] The opinion of Stephens and Stephens,[39] and Stone,[40] is that electoral results follow the mass public's perception of their personal economic circumstances under current political regimes, regardless of the merits, or otherwise, of the opposition party's campaign platform or manifesto. This increasingly became the case, as the ideological gap between the parties continued to narrow under the influence of standardized substantive and procedural arrangements of Fund/Bank policies. But this attitude was reinforced also to a significant extent by the political developments in Eastern Europe, which effectively removed for the new PNP government of 1989 any possibility, however remote, of delinking from the world capitalist system.

In a small, open, highly vulnerable economy where autarky is totally inconceivable, there was little chance of identifying more ideologically compatible sources of aid and trade. The changes in the Soviet Union had also, of course, automatically devalued the strategic importance of the Caribbean, diplomatically and militarily, to the extent that United States aid scheduled for Jamaica was diverted to Romania instead.[41]

Perhaps partly because of these developments, together with a reassessment as to the preparedness of the Jamaican electorate for radical ideologically-crusading politics, the new government after 1989 was more predisposed to try to work along with the international financial institutions, to the extent that Hugh Small, one of the reputedly more left-leaning in the party and then Minister of Finance, found it appropriate to state that,

> "We are convinced that the reforms that we are making, we have to make,
> not because the IMF is advocating them or the World Bank has been

advocating them, but we are convinced from our own experiences that we have to do them for our own sakes ... We need to take responsibility for harsh decisions: one of the aspects of our political culture that we have to face up t:o".[42]

Given Jamaica's performance under Fund/Bank programmes, on the evidence of the data provided throughout, however, a high level of skepticism would not be out of order. For although, "... thinking of a history without the IMF may be wishful thinking/fantasy"[43], as recently as 1992, it was still fitting for the UNDP in its Human Development Report to ask, "... in a period of rapid economic globalization, who will protect the interest of the poor?"[44] For the columnist, Guy Arnold,[45] "... the short answer to that is no one".[46]

If Small's view is accepted, then it should not be difficult to agree that a general non-partisan verdict on the political parties which had introduced and presided over the implementation of free market policies, and on the assessment of the political system itself would, by implication, be a reflection of the public's perception as to the nature and consequences of those policies.

The result of the relevant public opinion poll were as follows:

QUESTION: If an Election was called now which party would you vote for?

JLP	20.9%
PNP	21.0%
NEITHER	58.1%

Source: Stone Poll, reported in The Jamaica Herald, Dec. 5, 1994, p.1E

That, too-brief, respite of the 1986-87 period, when significant growth was achieved, was not enough, however, to even begin to reverse the persistent trend in inequality in income shares and asset ownership characteristic of stabilization and economic restructuring in a supposedly self-regulating market economy. This provided, according to Thomas,

"... a clear reminder of how easy it has been for social forces of underdevelopment and dependency to reproduce themselves and how, under conditions of negative growth and declining per capita real income, a minority can still prosper",[47] [under the political direction of those who are distracted and diverted by class compromises and who seek refuge in the addiction to sloganeering.[48]]

This is one perspective from which to assess the perception of the camouflaged version of the 'new political economy of development,' as applied with varying degrees of 'diplomacy' by the IMF to the Jamaican situation. It is now therefore appropriate to report our survey findings on public perceptions of the IMF and case studies of public sector redundancies resulting from budget deficit reduction Fund policies, as well as views as to the proper role of the state.

Prior to this, there have been, as far as we are aware, two attempts to gain an insight into the public's perception of aspects of Jamaica's relationship with the IMF. The more recent, the Kirton interviews,[49] conducted on behalf of Oxfam, did not seek responses to structured questions; the earlier effort was restricted to a question in the 1986 Stone Poll on the public's view as to whether the IMF relationship should be terminated. Both attempts shall be referred to, as appropriate. A summary of Jamaica's performance under IMF programmes is presented in APPENDIX II .

The late decision to undertake the opinion surveys to be reported here was prompted by the concern to test, however tentatively, the validity of the many "accepted truths" about the IMF, its structural adjustment programmes and their perceived consequences. The almost total absence of research in this area, in spite of the voluminous literature which has accumulated around the technical macro-economic aspects of the various Fund and World Bank programmes and their welfare effects, invested the project with particular interest.

Given the nature of the subject matter under investigation, it seemed a challenge to make an assessment of Stone's view that because of,

> "... the low level of awareness of macro economic forces the logic, purpose and rationale ... of the economic policies formulated by the government are neither understood nor grasped ...".[50]

Further, it was hoped that questions which sought to provide some indication as to the people's interest in, and understanding of, certain specific proposals, encouraged and supported by the IMF, would thereby serve not only to explain past failures of policy and policy formulation but would prove valuable for predictive purposes m relation to the proposed "Social Partnership", for example. This aspect of the research gains in importance, being one of the often-neglected issues in the study of IMF/World Bank economic stabilization and structural adjustment-prescriptions against the background of Cooper's observation that,

> "... the relevant public must be persuaded that the program can work

and that the government is determined to see that it will do so. How the rationale and content are presented will affect the way the public receives the program, as will the reputation of the public leaders responsible for seeing the program through. The quality of political leadership,[51] as well as the past experience of the public is crucial in establishing favourable dynamics.[52]

Statements by the Bank of Jamaica (BOJ) to the effect that the only alternative to the IMF,

> "… in the context of a country with chronic resource imbalances, is increased international generosity or default and mendicancy … (since) Without an IMF programme … an economy … which does not adjust voluntarily will face painful impoverishment through an inflation, devaluation spiral."[53]

Admittedly, that would not be likely to enhance national self-esteem and confidence. It is precisely the IMF programmes that are perceived by the vast majority of our sample as being responsible for exacerbating the conditions they are supposed to prevent, or at least ameliorate, as borne out by FIG. 33.

Figure: 33

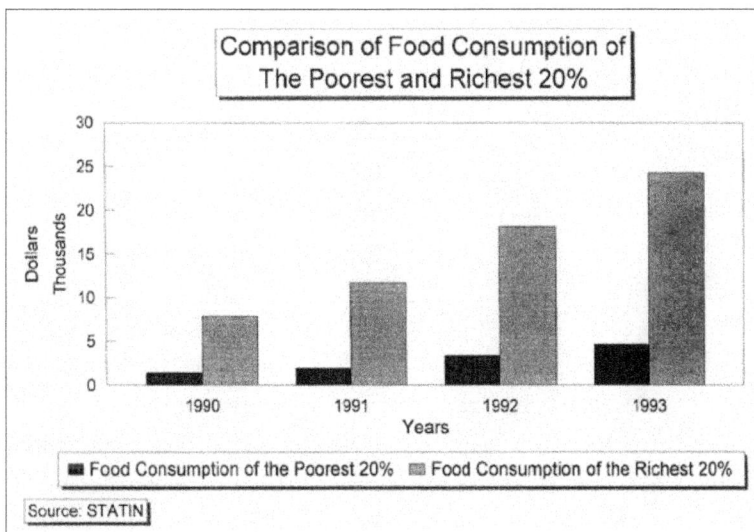

By his comments, the then Senior Deputy Governor of the Bank of Jamaica, seemed to associate economic success with continuity of current "technically correct" IMF policy implementation, *per se*, without regard for policy outcomes in terms of the quality of life of the majority of the population.[54] At the same time, a director at the Government's Economic Planning Agency, the PIOJ, was declaring that the prospect of breaking off the IMF borrowing relationship meant that, "Now is the time for real independence".[55] And, although the then Senior Deputy Central Bank Governor saw economic programme success as depending on "our implementation capabilities", there is nothing to suggest that the importance of the public's experience, attitude, and role, as emphasized by Cooper, has yet been grasped by such vitally positioned officials. What was regarded as essential was the recognition of the importance of the time-worn platitudes concerning resource constraints and the need to contain inflation and increase output.

Bearing Cooper's strictures in mind, the question becomes how well have governments sold policy proposals, such as Productivity Incentive Schemes, Prices and Incomes Policy and a Social Contract to the public, without whose support, up to a certain level, these policy prescriptions must fail. And, fundamentally, are governments perceived as being legitimately vested with the authority to be the arbiter of the 'national interest' as social and economic classes struggle to shift the balance of power in their own favour.

As Butler and Stokes have reported, with respect to Great Britain, the average citizen's level of comprehension of technical policy issues is low.[56] This is, not surprisingly, more so the case in an underdeveloped society with a high rate of functional illiteracy, made worse in the past two decades by severe cuts in government expenditure in education.

This situation was aggravated in the design of the survey instrument by the relatively sophisticated and technical nature of the issues being investigated, bearing in mind, particularly, the intention of focusing predominantly on workers.

METHODOLOGY

In an attempt to develop a questionnaire that was likely to elicit adequate meaningful responses which would be amenable to relatively easy processing for tabulation and summary forms of presentation, a preliminary instrument was designed and interviews carried out in August and September 1995 in the parishes of Tre lawny, St. James, St. Ann, Manchester, Clarendon, St. Elizabeth and Hanover. But for the omission of the Kingston Metropolitan Region (KMR) (which includes the parish of St. Andrew), these 8 parishes out of a total of 14, could be safely said, on the basis of an informed observer's knowledge of their socio-economic status, to be nationally representative. It was nevertheless subsequently decided to include the parishes of St. Mary and St. Thomas on the island's North East and East coasts together, of course, with the KMR in further surveys. A copy of this test-instrument is displayed in APPENDIX iii.

Feedback from the administration of this preliminary instrument-suggested the need for substantial changes as a result of the following factors:

1. The questionnaire was found to be frustratingly lengthy for the typical respondent

2. Most interviewees were unable to make genuine choices as against stating "gut feelings" from the alternate responses suggested (Questions 4, 5, 6, 15, 24.)

3. Specific Questions (e.g. 8 and 13) which were considered to be of particular interest drew little definite comment.

4. With the widespread feeling that the formation of a third political party, by the former Chairman of the JLP, was imminent there was a noticeable reluctance. to cooperate on the part of interviewees especially in those constituencies where the third-party agitation was strongest. Despite denials at the introductory stage of the interviews, it was still felt by many that the study was politically sponsored – this led to a revision or omission of questions perceived as having partisan political implications (Questions 3, 9, 13)

5. Where one managed to get a response to a question requiring a Yes or No answer, it proved extremely difficult to have reasons provided. The "whys" and "hows" attached to several questions, therefore required reconsideration. (See Interviewer Guide – APPENDIX iv.)

6. The level of comprehension and literacy of worker and small business respondents clearly suggested that most questionnaires for these segments would probably be more effectively administered by experienced opinion survey personnel. (Hence the time and expense constraints referred to below in connection with the sample.)

7. It was discovered that interest in, awareness of, and therefore competence to respond to IMF related issues was a function not only of individual characteristics but reflected the state of relative development or backwardness of the geographical areas.

8. Tabulation of the data would prove unduly difficult.

In a view of the above, the first instrument was substantially modified, as evidenced by Questionnaire No. 2 at APPENDIX v. Changes also reflected the fact that at least two items, Questions 5 and 12, had previously been investigated with similar results in the existing I iterature.[57]

While this second version of the survey instrument proved a great deal easier to administer, there was a strong element of dissatisfaction that questions centering on certain areas of the wider study, had been omitted. It was for this reason, ultimately, that a small experienced interviewer team was contracted to do the data collection on the basis of Questionnaire No. 3, as exhibited at APPENDIX vi.

The process of survey instrument redesign, and the reasons therefore, in itself proved to be a valuable learning experience.

THE SAMPLE

Time and budgeting constraints dictated that the sample size for the survey, using the Questionnaire No. 3, be kept to about 600 (see TABLE 25), In fact, the actual number of instruments administered and completed was 562, spread over 12 parishes, with only the parishes of Westmoreland and Portland being omitted. On the basis of preliminary findings in relation to parish socio-economic profiles from Questionnaires Nos. I and 2, this was not expected to affect the results significantly.

An early decision was made that, although the survey was to be of worker opinion, primarily, it would nevertheless be useful to include a small number of small and big business persons. This would give some indication as to whether perceptions on the issues covered appear to be economic class-related, and if so, on what issues and to what degree. The data forthcoming from the big business and small business respondents can clearly point the way to further research, using representative samples, it being recognized that such data is highly tentative and is useful only on the indicative level.

The persons to be interviewed were determined through the *purposive* selection process. This is a non-probabiIity sampling process which is often referred to as an *availability* sample and represents the approach in which persons are interviewed on the basis of their availability and accessibility to the interviewer. The nature of the issues being investigated, and the focus being primarily on workers, makes the technique appropriate for our purposes.

The decision to conduct interviews in particular geographical areas of the country flowed from a consideration of the factors which emerged from the initial instrument, which strongly suggested an inclusionary rather than exclusionary approach, given the many problematic elements identified, which might otherwise make it difficult to satisfactorily complete the project. Further, the purposive method entailed speaking to people at their workplaces and other locations where they could be accessed, without following the sort of procedure that would be appropriate for and typical of random sampling.

It was intended that every effort would be made to gain access to individuals and businesses in a range of settings, occupational categories and sectors. It was felt that because of the nature of the Questionnaire it was best to have it administered during visits to different locations, to the greatest extent possible, there being little confidence that many prospective respondents would take the trouble to complete and return them on their own initiative. This can be gleaned from occasional concluding negative comments, obviously resulting from frustration, about the difficulty and length of the instrument, where concluding remarks about the survey issues were invited. Some interviews, especially among the small and big business segments, were conducted by telephone where this was more convenient to the interviewees, and some were completed without individual guidance in group situations.

Table: 25   Sample: Public and Private Sectors, by Category

Category of Respondents	Number	% Sample
Big Business	42	7.5
Small Business	91	16.2
Workers - Private Sector	399	71.0
Workers - Public Sector	30	5.3
TOTAL	562	100.0

As employment opportunities in the private formal and public sectors have contracted as a result of "tight monetary policies", together with the abandonment of deficit financing of government expenditures, more and more of the displaced labour force have adopted self-help survival initiatives since 1978/79. Unfortunately, these activities have tendered to be imitated and duplicated often to the point of over saturation, resulting in non-viability.

The significant growth in self-employment, as shown in Fig 34 below, was such as to justify the seemingly large number in the small business (formal and informal) segment of the sample, relative to the number of workers.

Figure: 34   GROWTH IN % OF SELF EMPLOYMENT

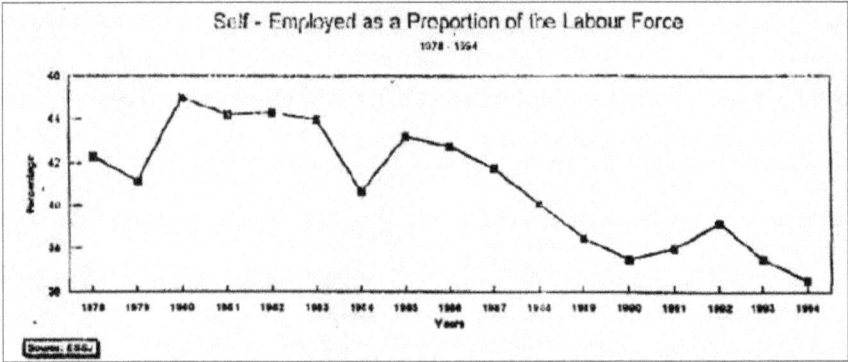

Self - Employed as a Proportion of the Labour Force
1978 - 1994

The selection of some big businesses was from general directory listings and background knowledge of them. The process involved contacting several companies in various commercial and production spheres of operation and attempting to arrange interviews, which did not prove easy. Proprietors and executives were not only busy but, reflecting the general negativism and apathy on IMF related issues, did not. see this kind of exercise as being worth their time. One also suspects, given their responses to questions on specific policy areas, that there may be some anxiety to avoid exposing lack of familiarity with certain of the national issues covered.

Large businesses were drawn from the commercial and manufacturing sectors and included, for example, enterprises involved in life insurance, travel, tourism, animal feeds, motor vehicle tyres, commercial farming, and banking.

In the case of small businesses interviews were conducted on an ad hoc, "door to door" basis. The unpredictable nature of small business operations ruled out interviews by appointment as even where these were pre-arranged they were either not kept or were so frequently disturbed as to prove of no great advantage, reflecting certain cultural traits as well as small-business practices.

The small business segment functioned largely in the retail sector. Among the activities represented are hardware, fashion (clothing, cosmetics, hairdressing) florists, jewellers, electrical/electronics, groceries, pharmacy, automotive (rental, garage) printing, building construction, and subsistence farming.

With respect to the worker segment of the sample, most were interviewed at work, in breaks between tasks. For the purpose of selecting worker interviewees, managerial and policy-making personnel were excluded. We are aware of the changing composition of the "working class", in keeping with the developments noted by Gordon[58] and feel that the categories of workers surveyed, as indicated in TABLE 26, sufficiently reflects these economic adjustment-induced class dislocations and realignments.

FINDINGS

The ending of the borrowing relationship with the IMF was thought in some quarters to constitute such an occasion for celebration that it was rumoured that the Government secretly planned to turn the moment of the break into a bacchanal (festival) that would signal a preelection 'spending spree' and the calling of an election soon thereafter.[59] This is despite overwhelming commentary indicative of a public mood characterized by deep-seated disillusionment, alienation, apathy, negativism, and skepticism. We were surprised at the high level of correct responses to the effect that the borrowing relationship had ended as shown in FIG. 35. It will be apparent that, not surprisingly perhaps, the level of awareness declines as one moves from the big business sector, 90%, through small business, 80%, to workers, 65%, with the percentage moving in the reverse direction for those stating, incorrectly, that the relationship had not ended. It is of interest to note that the results obtained from the administration of Questionnaire No. 2, (Question 7), had showed as many as 82% strongly agreeing that the IMF relationship should be terminated while 2.6% disagreed, with some 15% having no opinion.

Of those stating that the borrowing relationship had ended, most in answer to Questions 2 and 3, were pessimistic about prospects for the future, with only 38% expecting consequential benefits on a personal/national level, with workers displaying a higher level of optimism, 46%, as against big business 12.5%, and small business 19%, (TABLE 28). Perhaps, despite frequently verbalized sentiments to the contrary, it is more so at the level of the worker that it is felt that "things can't get any worse".[60] The response to the similar Question (8) on Questionnaire No.2 was markedly different, with no less than 75.4% of respondents anticipating improvements. The explanation for this divergence could well be the adverse experiences with respect to price movements, unemployment and crime, among other things, since the break with the IMF in September, 1995 and between the periods of the surveys – January, as against June 1996 – given the speed with which the public expects significant improvements to occur. It would seem that disillusionment has now partly shifted from the IMF and is totally focused on Government.

Table: 26   SAMPLE: WORKERS, BY CATEGORY AND NUMBER

Category of Workers	No. in Category
Bartender	12
Bus Operator	4
Cabinet-maker	3
Carpenter Chef	5
Chef	4
Civil Servant	8
Clerical (office)	92
Construction Worker	6
Cook/Higgler	2
Electrician/Electronic Technician	16
Fireman	8
General Worker (Hotel)	9
Hairdresser	4
Housekeeper	8
Library Assistant	12
Mason	13
Meat Vendor/Worker (Market)	3
Media Worker	7
Messenger	9
Nurse	10
Policeman	7
Sales Representative	17
Security Guard	19
Service Station Attendant	14
Shop Assistant	65
Sewing Machine Operator	15
Taxi Operator	6
Teacher	22
Truck Driver	4
Welder	5
TOTAL	429

Note: "Clerical (office)", includes, e.g., bank tellers and clerks, secretaries, postal clerks, general clerks, etc. "Shop assistant" includes, e.g., counter assistants in hardware establishments, pharmacies, clothing and gift shops, etc. Take, e.g., also the category, "taxi operator". It is not clear whether the persons owns and operates a taxi-cab, or drives a cab for the owner (which is quite commonly done).

Figure: 35

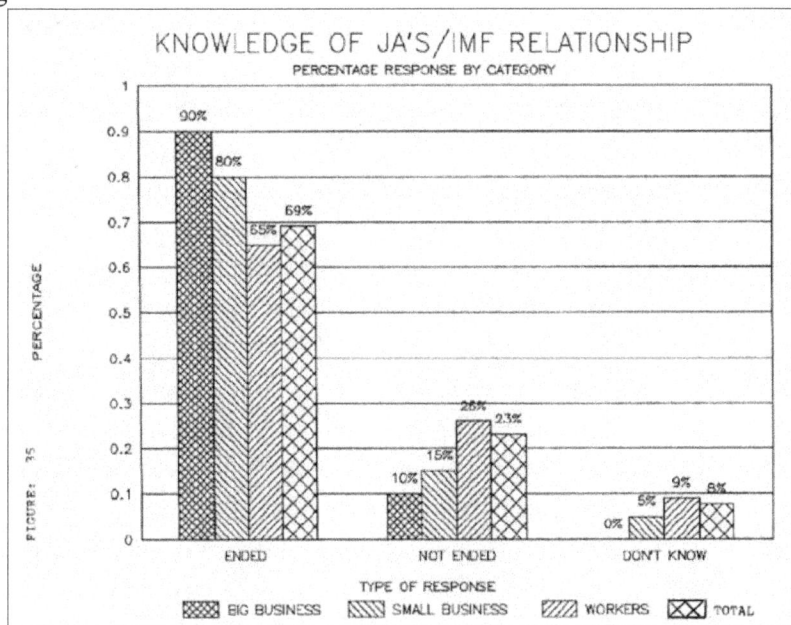

KNOWLEDGE OF JA'S/IMF RELATIONSHIP
PERCENTAGE RESPONSE BY CATEGORY

While the majority of the business segment, combined, associated increased wages with increased prices and unemployment, 73% and 40% respectively, the result for workers was 76% and 62%. It would seem that the much greater number of workers who link wage increases with unemployment explains labour's docility under IMF wage guidelines, lay-offs, and redundancy as a direct consequence of adjustment policies. This further provides reinforcement for some of the reasons given for the lack of serious class confrontation and protest. The fear of unemployment, both as an economic consequence and as an established capitalist management strategy is, of course, a phenomenon which afflicts not just the workers but their more "objective", "responsible" and "mature" union leaders.

Question 9, "What would you want in exchange for wage guidelines?" was directed only at workers. There was some hesitation on the part of a large number of respondents in offering a reply, as though the matter of wage guidelines (normally applied officially more directly to the public-sector workforce, and officially removed in 1991) was unclear. Answers were however forthcoming fairly readily, it was found, once a basic explanation was provided. Responses ranged from "Control of inflation", "price freeze", "better education and health system", "Workers' control", "reasonable profits" to "death". There seemed little hope that such "demands" (the *quid pro quo* of the Social Partnership) were likely to be met.

As mentioned earlier, replies to open-ended questions on technical issues, such as Question 10, on the likely effect of Prices and Incomes Policy on the economy, are usually quite vague, and so general, as in many cases to be of little meaning, even after the essential element of such a policy was fully explained. It was evident however that many in the business categories were against price control. On the related item, as to whether price controls should be introduced in a liberalized economy, Question 19, as shown, in FIG. 36, the view of the big business sector varied significantly from that of the other categories, being evenly divided, 50% for and 50% against, compared to 7 5% and 15% for small business and 86% and 10% for workers. In the interviewing process many respondents expressed a ready and deep disenchantment with price movements in the Jamaican economy. The few who raised the issue of the apparent contradiction between a liberalized free market economy and any move to impose price controls all belonged to the large business sector. One of the primary reasons for the level of price increases under the IMF has undoubtedly been devaluation of the local currency, together with non-discriminatory import liberalization, which proceeded, in fact, ahead of schedule. The consequences for the country's trade balance is revealed by FIG 37. As one of the Kirton interviewees remarked, "If you go into the supermarket you'll see American red peas there. People leave the local produce and buy that. So, we're helping to devalue our dollars . . . . In the Kingston area there are people who buy imported water from America".[61] When these results are combined with the strong generally affirmative responses to Items 11 and 20 as shown in TABLES 28 & 29, on the efficacy, firstly, of controls being imposed on rent, interest rates, dividends and profits, and, secondly, on the introduction of a fixed exchange rate, this seems to provide firm evidence of the public's rejection of major planks of Government/IMF policy and confirms the impressionistic view as to the large gap existing between policy makers and administrators and the people at large[62] relative to IMF policy commitment.

Q2 & Q3:

Table: 27   OPINIONS ON IMF AND DERIVATION OF BENEFITS
Responses by category among persons stating that borrowing ended

Category of respondents	Yes, will benefit	No benefit	Other response
Big business (38)	4	34	-
Small business (74)	14	42	18
Workers (279)	129	146	4
TOTAL	147	222	22
%	37.5	56.8	5.7

Note: The figures in brackets beside the categories of respondents are the total numbers stating that Jamaica had ended its borrowing relationship with the IMF.

In the context of Cooper's propositions, previously alluded to, one would not expect very knowledgeable, or, even merely specific responses to Question 25, asking "What does the idea of a Social Contract mean to you?" This proved in fact to be the case. Responses to this item included, "Agreement between workers, employers, and others, including the government". It is noticeable that one of the major hurdles to the formation and implementation of such a Contract/Partnership has not been recognized even in what was one of the more meaningful replies: precisely the fact that any agreement will not be between workers and employers but some of their representative organizations. Not long ago the Jamaica Manufacturer's Association withdrew from the Private Sector Organization of Jamaica, and neither are rural nor medium nor are many small businesses represented in that body. Further, the most aggressive, doctrinally oriented, trade union, the UAWU, is neither a member of the JTURDC nor the JCTU. Among the workers in the sample, only one in six said they belonged to a trade union.

The inclination to a negative stance with respect to the likelihood of agreement on, and implementation of, a Social Contract is clearly reflected in responses such as:

"I don't believe in it" (this from the interviewee whose reply is quoted above), "Don't listen to what government have to say", "Will not happen in Jamaica", "Farce", "Smokescreen", "Gives them time to stall", "Hog wash", "Political Junk", "It doesn't mean a thing", "I am the one putting money in my pocket".

Figure: 36

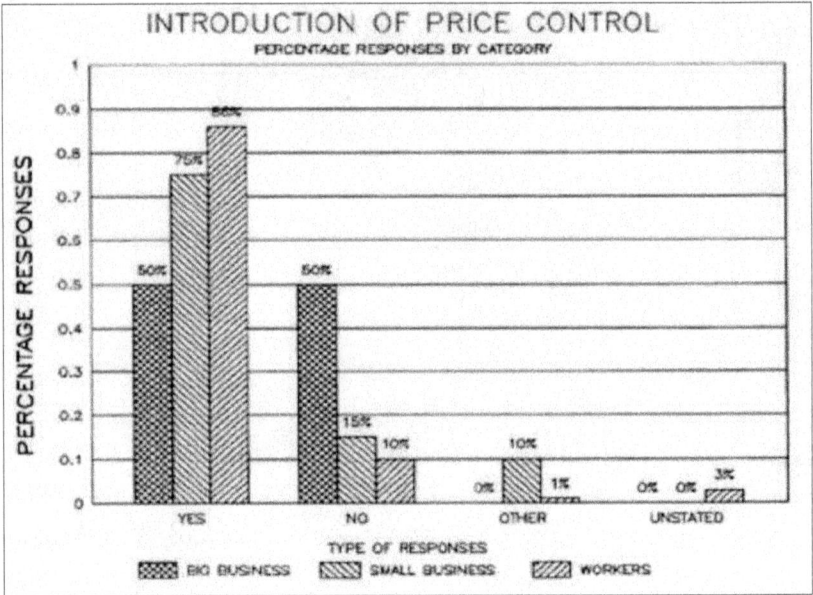

INTRODUCTION OF PRICE CONTROL
PERCENTAGE RESPONSES BY CATEGORY

Figure: 37

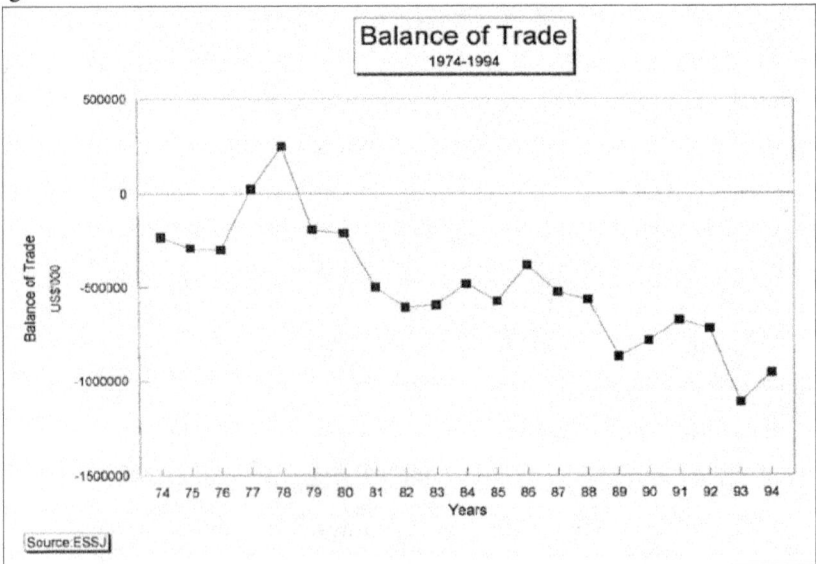

Balance of Trade
1974-1994

Source ESSJ

Q.11

Table: 28   Control of Rent, Interest Rates, Dividends and Profits
                        Responses by Category and Type.

Attitudes to Control

Category of respondents	Yes	No	Other Response	Unstated
Big Business	25	17	-	-
Small Business	74	17	-	-
Workers	416	11	-	2
TOTAL	515	45	-	2
%	91.6	8	-	.4

The breakdown of responses for the items Rent, Interest Rates, Dividends and Profits, separately, would present a clearer idea of the vested interest positions on these issues. One would expect, for example, that the replies with respect to Dividends and Profits would differ significantly between big business and workers, but not with respect to Interest rates. (It would be interesting to know how many would now agree with Trinidad's Ag. Colonial Secretary, Nankivell's view in 1937, that an industry has no right to pay dividends at all until it pays a fair wage to labour and gives the labourer decent conditions" – Singh (1994) p. 173.

Q20:

Table: 29   Introduction of a Fixed Exchange Rate
                            Responses, by Category and Type

Attitude to Fixed Exchange Rate

Category of respondents	Yes	No	Other Response	Unstated
Big Business	38	4	-	-
Small Business	83	4	-	4
Workers	353	60	8	8
TOTAL	474	68	8	12
%	84.34	12.09	1.42	2.13

Responses which were favourable were so vague as to suggest that respondents really knew little of the specifics of the Social Partnership as announced and publicized. Examples of such replies are: "I must say this is a good set-up"; "All parties can sit down and come to a better understanding"; and "A chance for better negotiations in the future".

Very significantly, 83% of the sample replied to the effect "don't know anything". This is concerning a proposal that has been under discussion, with IMF blessing, for some eighteen years in all. It should not therefore be surprising that items viewed by the Government as benefits, that should tend to elicit working-class acceptance, cooperation, and concessions are not so perceived at all. Replies to Questions 17 and 18, as to receipt of benefits from the National Housing Trust and the increase in the income tax threshold, indicate that those benefits are not sufficiently widespread nor substantial enough to have the desired effect, with only 26% of the workers acknowledging the receipt of benefits; equally importantly, beneficiaries do not regard housing benefits as a proper subject matter for bargaining under a Social Contract; rather, they see themselves as simply getting what they are entitled to on the basis of their contributions, with no assistance from government. The relatively low interest rate on loans is taken for granted, it seems, as is the low deposit requirement. Most respondents, 88%, noticed no improvement in their situation as a result of personal income tax changes; many made the point that this was a direct consequence of high inflation.

Question 21, "What means more to you? Healthy profits/decent wages / neither", was intended, without it being too obvious, to test the prevailing mood for meaningful concessions and compromises in Social Contract negotiations and, also, if any agreement arrived at by representative organizations is likely to have any chance of acceptance and of "holding" for any worthwhile period. The findings appear encouraging for Social Contract "give and take", at least at the stage of the discussion of fundamentals. In the business segment, combined, 23% saw profits as more important, 56% indicated wages while 20% said "both", As might be expected the vast majority of workers, 87%, view "decent wages" as being more important.

The notion of "the national interest" is of course central to the idea of a Social Contract. This concept was covered by Items 6,7 and 8 in the survey instrument. There were strong positive replies to Question 6 and 8, across all three sample segments, with "Yes" responses being 81% and 97% respectively (see TABLE 30 for responses to Question 8). There was also found to be a high level of agreement that "the people", "the nation" or "the public" should determine what is in the national interest. Responses referring to "the government", "the state", "the elected representatives" totalled only 29%, which immediately raises the question of the importance of the public's perception of the quality of leadership for IMF style economic adjustment policy success. Could this be because there is merit in the point that the national interest is "invoked by governments when the subordinate classes are about to be squeezed", as Miliband maintains[63] – particularly under IMF structural policy continuity since 1989, when the debate has largely become how to run the same economic and social system, rather than about the merits of different systems. Clearly, it is evident that the exalted Hegelian view of the state as the embodiment and protector of the whole of society, and of its higher reason, hardly prevails in the thinking of the majority of the Jamaican people.

Q. 8:

Table: 30	Poverty as a Threat to the National Interest Responses, by Category and Type			
Category of respondents	Yes	No	Other Response	Unstated
Big Business	38	4	-	-
Small Business	70	21	-	-
Workers	390	37	I	I
TOTAL	498	62	I	I
%	88.6	11.04	0.18	0.18

Note: The high percentage of affirmative responses, notably in the big business sector, 90.5%, may be explained on the basis of their concern for the 'losers', who were seen in the increased numbers of homeless and mentally ill searching routinely through garbage containers, they were absorbed among the numbers of youth recruited into criminal gangs, they were included among the fixed income pensioners whose private poverty could not be relieved by food stamps, they were numbered among those who stood grimly in visa lines, and they were to be found among those whose incomes were increasingly inadequate for the purchase of basis food requirements" (Anderson and Witter, in LeFranc, p.52). An alternative explanation is that, "... like the slave master of by gone days, they fear the resistance that comes sooner or later from those in bondage ... "(Ross-Frankson (ed) P-14)

Given the unimpressive national labour productivity performance over nearly two decades, as revealed by TABLE 14 & FIGURE 10, the attempt to arrive at agreement on a commitment to-and strategies and mechanisms for, productivity enhancement are crucial for economic recovery and transformation, with import liberalization and the trend towards globalization of production. It must therefore be seen as a conspicuous instance of policy failure that although allowance was made in the 1987 IMF Agreement for the wage guideline limit to be exceeded, where justified by productivity improvements, a decade later, whereas 45% of the business sector, noticeably more so in the KMR, could name a company with a productivity incentive scheme, only 18% of the workers could do so. Of that 18%, the figure was much higher among those workers in the enclave export free zone operations where straight piece-rate payment systems invariably exist. What becomes apparent from the responses is that companies are identified as having productivity incentive schemes, not because of interviewees' knowledge of their particular arrangements, but instead, on the basis of the presumption that such companies should have them, because of their size, or their assumed relative technological sophistication.

Generally, the overwhelming majority of respondents, 83%, felt that incentive schemes could be to the worker's advantage. Likewise, they felt that employers could benefit from increased *production*, thus displaying the common failure to distinguish between production and productivity. There was some feeling expressed that employers would benefit to a greater extent than workers but, again, the general nature of responses suggest a lack of familiarity with such schemes. This was emphasized by the striking qualitative difference in the responses of those who had actually worked under a performance-based incentive scheme. It is obvious that "success stories" in this area have not been adequately used to effectively market the idea – one that is alleged, exhortatively, to be "the key to national survival".

The consequence of this failure to properly educate the public, and, more specifically, workers and members of the business community, about productivity-based payment systems is that respondents do not distinguish between traditional piece-rate methods of payment, commission arrangements such as with insurance salesmen, and more specifically designed all-embracing efficiency enhancing approaches.

Item 22[64] seeks to tie the factor of productivity to Item 10 on Prices and Incomes Policy, so as to provide information allowing a better assessment of replies to Questions 4 and 5 on the effect of wage movements on prices and unemployment.

As is evident from FIGURE 38, the majority of all three segments of the sample strongly believe that wages should be directly linked to the cost of living. Needless to say, this has serious implications for the possibility of successful implementation of a Prices and Incomes Policy, whether as an element of a Social Contract or otherwise, given the rate of inflation in recent years. This level of positive response, with the big business sector being the lowest at 70%, in favour of wage indexation, not only confirms the findings on Question 21, but is of explanatory value with respect to the answers previously recorded to Items 4 and 5.

Figure: 38

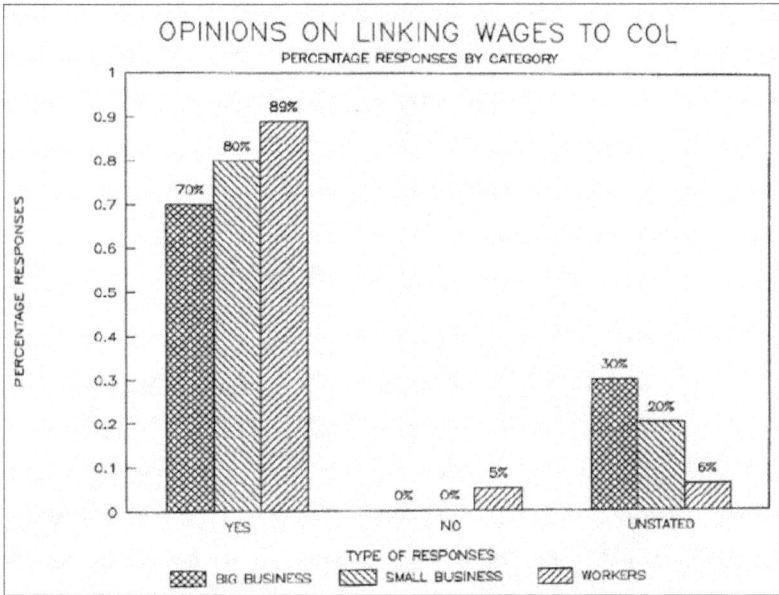

The level of affirmative responses, revealed in FIG, 39, to the idea of linking wages to productivity seems to be based more on the notion of the fairness or justice of the worker being rewarded for any extra effort than on an appreciation of the several possible reasons for productivity improvement, some of which might in fact involve less physical effort from labour. The low worker affirmative response of 50% may come as a surprise to those who are not aware of the fact that, to many, increasing productivity means working harder, not necessarily "smarter". There is the sentiment that with the cost of living moving rapidly upwards, as inexorably as it has been, no further justification is required for wage increases. Some 83% of the business segments, combined, appear to favour wage increases that are tied to productivity, although the indication that the small business sector is more supportive is somewhat unexpected. It also seems to be clearly established that the major argument for the emphasis on productivity, in the fight against inflation, is little understood. There is nothing to suggest that respondents were aware that the productivity factor, in Item 22 (I), could mitigate the effect of wage increases on price movements and thus have such crucial implications for their replies to Items 4 and 5, that their responses might even be reversed. This would represent, in fact, the essence of a Prices and Incomes Policy /Social Contract in Jamaica's economic circumstances of high inflation, high unemployment and virtually no growth in GDP.

Stone's view as to the public's low Level of understanding of the various aspects of policy issues[65] does seem to be confirmed by our findings. This makes determination of the "national interest" even more intractable, without any consideration of the contentious procedural questions involved as to the appropriate mechanism for its expression.

Question 23, as to whether IMF policies created only hardships, proved to be one on which, surprisingly as can be seen in FIG. 40, & TABLE 31, there was a high variance in reply between the big business and the other two sectors. From the nature and extent of media coverage of the views of the big business sector on IMF policies, one would not unreasonably have expected a much greater convergence of perceptions across the segments. In seeking an explanation for this divergence, some assistance may be had from Questionnaire No.2.

Bearing in mind that the responses were aggregated, 82% were absolutely negative and 5% positive in the assessment of the effect of the IMF relationship for Jamaica (Question 2).[66] This must be seen, however, in the light of the fact that in Question 4 of that Questionnaire, (No.2), which asked "Who benefitted/suffered most from the IMF policies?",[67] the "winners" were identified as Big Business/the Private Sector, Banks, Insurance Companies, Hotels and Exporters'" Those who suffered most were seen as "Farmers, Unemployed and Pensioners". But, additionally, with respect to Question 5, requiring that the respondent indicate the IMF policies which were harmful, as against those which were beneficial, it was exactly those policies which most favoured big business which were selected in the beneficial category, namely: "Privatization, Devaluation, Removal of Subsidies, Removal of Price Controls, and Import Liberalization". This is not to deny that particular enterprises in the big business group may have been "losers". However, in this kind of economy and society, it is businesses of large size with, perhaps, the political clout, resources, and leverage that can best cope with significant environmental disturbances and take advantage of new opportunities. While some big companies have been forced to "restructure", "re-engineer", "downsize" or "rightsize", it has tended to the smaller-sized firms that have been forced out of business.

Figure: 39

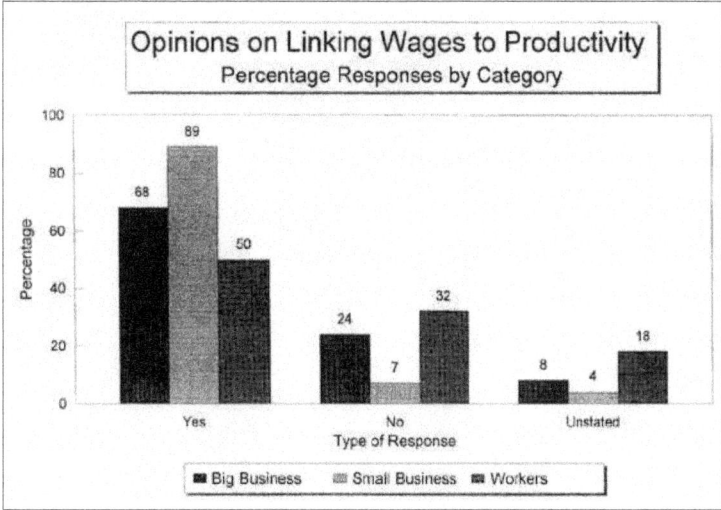

Opinions on Linking Wages to Productivity
Percentage Responses by Category

Figure: 40

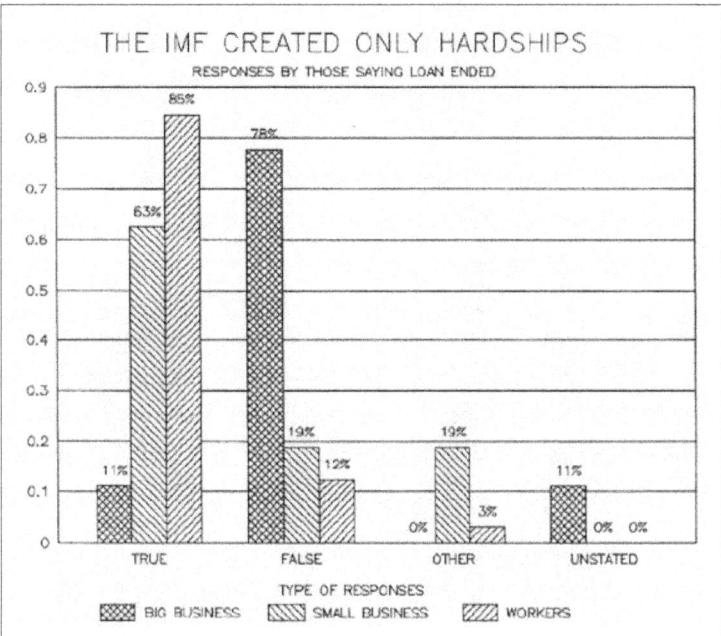

THE IMF CREATED ONLY HARDSHIPS
RESPONSES BY THOSE SAYING LOAN ENDED

Q23:

Table: 31	The IMF Created Only Hardships % of All Respondents			
Category *vis-a-vis* Borrowing	True	False	Other Response	Unstated
Yes, Ended	22.3	16.1	.8	-
No, Not Ended	30.7	18.5	3.1	-
Other Response	.8	3.1	3.8	I
Unstated	-	-	-	.8
TOTAL	70	49	I0	I
%	53.8	37.7	7.7	.8

Note: The high level of "False" responses is due to the linking of Questions 14 and 23 in this Table. The big business sector scored very highly on Question 14, 90% "YES", and at the same time, scored the highest "False", 78% on Question 23.

Of some significance, blame for the state of the economy, since the beginning of the IMF relationship, was almost evenly divided between Governments and the IMF,[68] Hardly any blame was attached to the private sector or trade unions, contrary to occasional trade union and private sector propaganda thrusts against each other.

Given the findings just noted, and the response to Item 15 on Questionnaire No.2, suggesting that 78% would "fight against" the reintroduction of wage guidelines, which were continuously in force for nearly 15 years, why has there been no serious social upheaval?[69] In keeping with the approach of respondents to most of the open-ended questions, Item 24, on the reason for lack of strong sustained policy resistance on the part of the specified groups, Teachers and Nurses, Unionized Workers and the Unemployed produced some variation in the responses. The unemployed were sometimes lumped together with the listed organized groups and in such cases a single response was given. However, there were several differentiated responses, the most noteworthy being:

TEACHERS AND NURSES.

"They believe in law and order",

"They have the nation's interest at heart",

"They are controlled by the leadership",

UNIONIZED WORKERS,

"They are too passive (a silent kind of protest, I suppose)",

"Lack of .leadership",

"No guts",

"Despair",

"All gone to sleep",

"Full of mouth, but no action",

"They are stupid, I would have already",

"Resistance is futile",

"They would only lose more",

"Because of political polarization and disunity", "Political trade union leaders",

"People are coming to realize the realities of the world" "People are too fed up",

"They have thrown in the towel",

"Fear",

"I am puzzled about it myself"

UNEMPLOYED.

"They don't have anyone to lead them"

"They are not organized"

"It wouldn't make any difference"

"That wouldn't create any jobs"

"The security force would just mash it down"

The nature of these responses – alongside little national experience of sustained, stout anti-IMF/Government resistance or any significant – change in the nature of the constitutional order facilitating the suppression of popular protest, stand in firm contradiction of Stone's prediction that,

"The effect therefore (of structural adjustment policies) is likely to be a weakening of support for democracy as efforts are made to impose the hegemony of capital over labour and capitalist interests seek ultra-conservative policy options that are likely to be optimally achieved by authoritarian military regimes rather than by democratic governments accountable to working class and peasant voters".[70]

It is now appropriate to consider, more particularly, the situation of that sector of the labour force most directly and deliberately adversely affected by the retrenchment consequences of wages policy under IMF Structural Adjustment, the public sector. Towards the end of the chapter we will present case studies on instances of redundancy[71] arising from IMF encouraged privatization policy by this third world state that, once upon a time, delighted radical elements with declarations of defiance against "interference in the country's internal affairs", in the name of "national sovereignty" and "independence".

It is a matter of notoriety that reduction of the numbers of public service workers is one of the elements in the IMF formula for the reduction of the budget deficit in client countries. This fits well into the mould designed to minimize the role of the state in economic affairs – put at its crudest and its most graphic "to get the people off the back of the state". As it happens, such sentiments emanate usually from those accustomed to receiving disproportionate rewards for effort. Job evaluation has historically been reserved for those at the 'subordinate' levels of the organizational and social hierarchy.

Putting questions of the socialization into the rationalization of self-perpetuating privilege aside, the Nettleford Committee, as well as the Ministry of the Public Service, were both, according to Stone,

"… misled by data provided by the British High Commission" as to the size of the British public service which … did not take into account some 60% of government workers who are not classified as a part of the civil service".[72]

World Bank figures quoted showed the public-sector staff complement per 1000 of population for industrialized countries at 77%, whereas for developing countries it was less than 50% at 29 per 1000. Regionally, Jamaica was found to be in the order of 5% above the average – no doubt to be explained by the dominance of the middle class in political leadership. But, also, by the traditionally clientelistic nature of multi-class coalition party politics and social mobility into perceived higher-status jobs by children of the more ambitious who have taken advantage of expanding educational opportunities.[73]

The less than satisfactory quality of service provided by the Jamaican Civil Service, generally speaking, is a matter of record.[74]

This places into the realm of deceit, mischief and fantasy the officially published propaganda, accompanying further public-sector retrenchment to meet IMF loan conditionalities, that the Government was committed to,

> "A tighter, leaner, *more responsive* [italics added] public service, under which, layoffs is a must".[75]

The socialist, Rev. Ernie Gordon, placed the blame for the proposed 8000 civil service redundancies in 1992 on both the Government and the staff, and predicted that, "... the country could be seeing the beginning of a return of 1938 [the peak year of the mass labour uprising in the Caribbean colonies] with civil *service* [italics added] agitation".[76] The reading of the situation was, however, totally different by the then President of the JCSA, Eddie Bailey, for whom strike protest would have amounted to nothing more than a "flexing of muscles".

Gordon, observing that, "the attempts in the 1970's to get civil servants to improve their educational levels to make them better equipped for the new technological era was disregarded", failed to attempt a connection between technological sophistication, the number of the public service work force and the size of the government wage bill, as an item of the Budget. At this level of analysis, it is perhaps understandable that his prescription was for the trade union movement to, "... seek to educate and empower its members in order to assert God's option for the poor",[77] [whatever that may be, was not specified].

The Government adopted a more secular approach: The Ministry of the Public Service's advertisement announced that "Layoffs are a must but help is available".[78] The full-page advertisement which, in itself, made the provision of proper notice, human resource planning, and the rationality of the selection process for retrenchment, seem doubtful. It was promised that, "no two bread winners in any one family will be laid off; neither will any handicapped person". A clear case, it would seem, of sentiment and public relations considerations getting the better of concerns about functional efficiency, presumably the appropriate operative guiding principle in the determination of "who goes".

Attempts by Government and the JCSA to help with alternative job placement might well have accelerated the exodus of the better trained, more ambitious, enterprising members of staff from the service: for despite the declared policy of bringing the salaries of qualified upper-level management public employees more in line with levels prevailing in the private sector, the general job insecurity, generated by several massive staff reductions under IMF inspired budget deficit cuts, was probably enough to neutralize any positive appeal in such a policy. In any event, governments have developed a serious credibility problem in relation to promises, projections and "key" policy proposals.

The loss of staff of quality, for the efficient functioning of government services, does not bear contemplation – whether the loss is to the formal private sector, informal sector, self-employed or through migration. Stone expressed his concern as follows,

> "I doubt if any middle-income developing country can function adequately at that low level of public sector manning [at that time there was a planned 40-50% staff cut] unless of course we find a way to get twice the current level of productivity from our government workers"[79]

This hope is quite definitely precluded by the very low level of morale exhibited during the wage dispute, but even more so after the "settlement", judging by the various media reports of public service workers' reaction and general mood.

There is no Jamaican equivalent of the *United States Manpower and Training Act* (1962), providing for the rehabilitation of disadvantaged groups.[80] The extent to which the economics of structural adjustment has ravaged the public sector labour force ought, on any remedial unemployment policy basis, to place those workers in the category of the 'disadvantaged', meriting special consideration. This is particularly so, bearing in mind the absence of unemployment benefits under the National Insurance Scheme,[81] the disqualification of the "normal unemployed" from receiving food stamps, not to mention the stigma attached to applying for benefit from the programme for those who were not so long ago, in the post-colonial and pre-IMF stabilization era, considered to be relatively privileged high- status persons.

ILO Convention No.102 does offer two possibilities for structural adjustment-induced redundancy, which are;[82]

(1) to review the process of adjustment itself with a view to modification of its policies to soften their social impact, particularly on the less well -placed groups, *without undermining the process itself* [italics added] and

(2) the more promising proposal, to provide a degree of incomes support for those who become unemployed (that is), some of the "losers") with measures aimed at employment creation, the promotion of new enterprises, and the training and *timely* vocational education and re-education of potential workers in keeping with industrial/ sectoral changes in the economy, whether internally or externally generated.

The problem with the "more promising proposal", is simply that it conflicts, fundamentally, with IMF anti-welfare state activity and demand management, aimed at curbing consumption of the poorer classes, who are more likely to spend additional income on more labour-intensive, locally-produced "public" goods and services. The IMF most certainly does not encourage the direction of the pattern of investment by the state.

PRIVATIZATION AND REDUNDANCY

Methodology

m method and interviewed, using Interview Schedule at APPENDIX vii. The subjects were identified and selected by references from contact persons still working in the organizations and by seeking referrals from the first person interviewed from the organization. The organizations selected were:

1) Data Bank and Evaluation Division of The Ministry of Agriculture, which was radically downsized in 1992

2) Air Jamaica, which was privatized in 1994

3) The Government Printing Office, which was privatized by way of an employee buy-out in 1992/93.

In selecting the subjects, an attempt was made to compare the experience of those in clerical groups and those in the technical or professional groups (i.e. those higher, as against those lower, in the organizational hierarchy).

In conducting the interviews, it was found that there was some reluctance among the subjects to disclose detailed information about their current and past income, as well as the coping techniques used during the period of their unemployment.

CASE STUDIES ON THE IMPACT
OF PRIVATIZATION AND REDUNDANCY
ON JAMAICAN WORKERS.

Case 1

Case 1 is a female who is 27 years old and was currently employed as a Research Officer in a private sector association. She was employed as a statistician at the Data Bank and Evaluation Division of the Ministry of Agriculture when the major redundancy took place in the public sector in 1992. She had graduated with a B.Sc. degree in Economics from the University of the West Indies in 1991. She heard about the job at the Ministry from someone who worked in the Division, before she graduated, and applied for it. She began working in August 1991. By August 1992 she was informed that her post was being made redundant. She registered with the redundancy assistance service being offered by the Ministry of the Public Service and attended a seminar conducted by them on self-employment. She also registered with a number of private employment and placement agencies and the placement office at the University of the West Indies (UWI). She was referred to a few openings through these sources, but was unsuccessful in getting the jobs, or the jobs did not meet her expectations, in terms of salary and working conditions. It was from the placement office at the UWI that she heard about a post for an Investment Officer at a Merchant Bank in Kingston. She was employed in this position in March 1993, after one month of searching for a job and attending interviews. During the month she was supported by her mother and step-father who live in the United States.[83] She also relied on her savings and the notice pay she received from the Ministry. Her salary in the new post was considerably more than what she was receiving at the Ministry.

Case 2

Case 2 is a female who is 24 years old and is currently employed as a secretary in a statutory construction company. She was employed as a Clerical Officer at the Data Bank and Evaluation Division of the Ministry of Agriculture when the major redundancy took place in the public sector in 1992. She had attended St. Mary's College and later went to the North Street Excelsior College, where she did Business Administration, getting three CXC subjects and elementary typing. She further went on to Fitz-Henley's Business College where she did advanced typewriting. She applied to the Ministry of the Public service in 1991 to work in the government service and was placed at the Ministry of Agriculture by them. She heard about the impending redundancy and began looking for a job, before becoming redundant. In July, she heard about a job-opening for a Receptionist Typist, from a friend at work, and applied for the job and was successful in getting it. She started at the new job the working day immediately following the date the redundancy took effect. Her salary in the new job was marginally more than she was being paid at the Ministry.

Case 3

Case 3 is a male who is 52 years old and currently owns and operates a clothing retail store in an uptown plaza on Constant Spring Road in Kingston. He was employed as a pilot with Air Jamaica before it was privatized by the Government in 1994. He was not retained by the new operators of Air Jamaica, He had received his flight training in Florida and worked with a commercial airline in the United States before joining the staff of Air Jamaica in the early 1980's. Following his redundancy, he became self-employed, engaging in the sale of encyclopaedias. He had started this business some years earlier, while still employed at Air Jamaica, with his wife being the main sales person and manager, while he maintained contacts with the overseas supplier and arranged the shipping of the encyclopaedias. On becoming redundant he devoted all of his time to building and expanding his encyclopaedia business while looking out for more lucrative business opportunities. In 1995 a store in an uptown plaza became available and using his redundancy pay and his pension refund, plus credit from the bank, he was able to capitalize the business, which he said is not doing badly but could be doing better. Case 3 has three teenage sons who are dependent on him for financial support. Immediately following the redundancy, there was a significant drop in his household's income. However, his eldest son was fortunate enough to get a scholarship to a prestigious college in the United States and this took some of the burden off his income. He owns his own home, so he did not have to worry about rent or mortgage payments. The income from the encyclopedia sales, plus minor drawdowns, from his savings, were able to meet the household expenses. The income from the retail business is now adequate to meet his household needs and pay his creditors.

Case 4

Case 4 is a female who is 34 years old and is currently studying for her MBA in the local Nova University programme. She was employed as a flight attendant with Air Jamaica prior to its privatization in 1994. She had graduated from CAST, now the University of Technology (UTECH) in 1984 with a diploma in Commerce. A few years later she joined the staff at Air Jamaica, as a flight attendant. In 1991 she enrolled as a part-time student in Management Studies while maintaining her job with Air Jamaica. She also supplemented her income through informal commercial importing[84] and the selling of the goods bought (toiletries, clothes, shoes, and electronic gadgets) to friends and classmates. On becoming redundant, she continued to trade informally while studying full-time. She graduated in 1995 and enrolled in the Nova MBA programme in 1996. She has one dependent, an eight-year old son and lives with her common-law husband, who is the child's father. She experienced minor difficulties in meeting household expenses and her common-law husband had to contribute a larger proportion of his income to meet household expenses, in particular, the rent for their uptown apartment. He has since gotten a promotion and they are able to live more comfortably, and more easily meet the household and her educational expenses.

Case 5

Case 5 is a male who is 48 years old and is currently self employed as a small trader (higgler).[85] He was employed as a skilled printer in the former Government Printing Office (now Jamaica Printing Service) before it was privatized, through a wholly-owned Employee Share Ownership Programme (ESOP) in 1992. He was not retained by the new management of the printery and was made redundant. He had joined the staff of the Printing Office over twenty years earlier, when he started as a semi-skilled printer and worked his way up to the post of a Grade 3 skilled printer. He has three Jamaica School Certificates subjects. On being made redundant, he used his redundancy money to buy some goods and set up a stall on the side-walk near to a relative of his in downtown Kingston. At first, the transition was somewhat difficult, but within two months he was earning more than he used to earn at the printery. He expanded his operations and engaged his second son in selling mends clothing and accessories (ties and pants material) to office workers. In one of the Municipal operations to clear the street of vendors, he was relocated to the new Oxford Mall where he now has his stall. This relocation has adversely affected sales somewhat, so he uses one of his nieces to man the stall, while he trades in ladies' toiletries and garments among office workers by visiting from office to office. He is married with six children. None of them are dependent on him. His wife migrated to the United States with the two youngest children. The other children are adults. He supplements his income from his stall and other activities, with remittances from his wife, when necessary. He is waiting for her to settle properly, before he attempts to migrate to join her.

Case 6

Case 6 is a female who is 28 years of age and is currently employed as a secretary in a Kingston accounting firm. She was employed as a clerical officer m the Government Printing Service (now the Jamaica Printing Service) before it was privatized through a wholly owned ESOP. She passed four CXC subjects while at Merle Grove High School and went on to Duff's Business College and Excelsior Community College, where she did the diploma course in secretarial studies, before joining the staff at the Government Printing Service in 1990. She was not retained by the new management of the Printery. At first, she had difficulties finding another job and registered with a number of private placement firms and asked her friends at her church if they knew about any openings. After two months of applying for jobs and attending interviews she was accepted for the position of secretary in the accounting firm. She found the job from an advertisement in the press. She is attempting to further her education and is perusing a Diploma in Business Administration at UTECH. She lives at home with her mother and a younger brother and sister. During the two months she was out of work she was supported by her mother. During that period there was some strain on the family income,[86] since she had made monetary contributions to the upkeep of the household when she was employed. Her mother, who is a nurse, was, however, able to support the family for the short period. She used some of her redundancy money to assist her mother each month.

The essential points emerging from this small number of case studies have implications not only for the efficacy of past policy but provide some guidance for policy prioritization in the future, in an environment in which employment dislocation is likely to persist.

Briefly stated, the insights would appear to be appropriately listed as follows:

- the importance of education and training for individual survival in the existing labour market-conditions

- the extent of reliance on personal savings and family support, both local and by way of remittances from abroad, given the absence of any form of unemployment insurance.

- the absence of any significant assistance from the state, in the form of the use of employment services through the Ministry of Labour, for example. Such assistance came from personal contacts and private employment agencies, the latter being confined almost totally to the KMR.

- the absence of any reference to any role played by trade unions in any of these redundancy situations, despite the significant increase in white collar unionization in recent times and the high level of union representation in the public sector.

- the total lack of any sense of shock, anger, outrage, and of wanting to resist redundancy, much less revolting against the traumatic condition of involuntary joblessness.

The points listed prompt the question: does this signify a knowledge and acceptance of "the rules of the game?" As Kornhauser reminds us,

"... those members of society who identify themselves with the central values of a constitutional order are not likely to exploit opportunities to subvert elites ... (especially bearing in mind that) countries undergoing economic growth, rather than economically stagnant ones, manifest the greater discontent when discontinuities in economic conditions occur"[87]

It is thought fitting to conclude the Chapter by reporting the responses to Item 27 on Questionnaire No. 3 and Item I on Questionnaire No. 2. of the IMF survey:

Q27: Questionaire No. 3:

What are your overall comments on the. IMF, social contact, national interest, prices and incomes policy, and productivity incentive schemes?

RESPONSES:

"No policy since 1980 has in any serious way addressed the needs of the Jamaican populace,"

"This country has been abused and mis-managed by morally dishonest politicians who lack the political will to do the right thing."

"They just make the rich get richer and the poor get more pauperized."

"The government is apparently using an economic text book to run the country which clearly is not working."

"My overall comment is that I have said too much already!"

"Live and let live. That's the only way we will survive."

"Why all these questions? I sure know all this research is a waste of people's time. It's not helping our economic situation. So why do it."

"No opinion. I disenchanted with this whole system."

"Tricks to keep black people down."

Ql: Questionaire No. 2:
What is the first word that comes to your mind when you hear 'IMF'?

RESPONSES:

Lending Agency	Debt	Stupidity
Fuekery	Politics	Higher Taxes
Is Manley Fault	Trick	I man '[a]Fraid
Mafia	Headache	Politricks
Devastation	Robbery	Money
Problems	Oppression	Crooks
Help	Slavery	Wickedness

1. Laws of Jamaica Act 1 of 1962, Nov, 29, 1962; Ismail-Sabri Abidulla, "The Inadequacy and Loss of Legitimacy of the IMF" in Development Dialogue 1980: 2 Dag Hammerskjold Foundation, Sweden, pp. 25-53; Herman Daly, a Senior World Bank economist, when leaving office noted the lack of a World Government, "capable of regulating global capital in the global interest"; but he further called for "a few antacids and laxatives to cure the combination of managerial flatulence and organizational constipation and other middle aged infirmities", which afflicted the World Bank, which could hardly foster sustainable development since it had leverage only over the countries of the South – The Daily Gleaner, Jan. 1994, pp.!E,5E.
2. Raymond Forrest, in The Financial Gleaner, May II, 1990, expressed the view that "there is probably no institution throughout the world that invoked as much resentment as the IMF", citing riots and demonstrates in the "the list of countries that have vomited on tasting the bitter IMF medicine"; David Coore, then Opposition spokesman on Foreign Affairs at a Top Management, Seminar sponsored by the Jamaican Institute of Management as reported in The Daily Gleaner, Mar. 15, 1987, asserted that the IMF tended to "take a Poutin's Pilate approach" as to the options appropriate for selection. Ray Hadeed claimed "... Nor can we expect any sympathy from the IMF ... Benevolence is not likely to come from the IMF in the absence of special affinity, such as kith and kin" [experience proven wrong by the British experience after the war again under Harold Wilson in the 1960's and 70's; but also by the influence of U.S. geopolitical and economic interests in the special treatment of E. Europe, especially Russia (after the disintegration of the Soviet Union) and Mexico (as a part of NAFTA) in the present decade] Hadeed a local manufacturer now being to face increased competition from imports, would "tell the IMF to take over the country and run it, but when the money has to be found to close the gap between imports and exports you (the IMF) will have to find it" The Daily Gleaner, Jan. 11, 1990; See also Ted Dwyer "Dangerous politics visionless elite leadership" in The Jamaica Herald Dec. 6, 1995 p.7, who comments "... we had long lost the national honour by handing over our national affairs to the IMF and World Bank ... and reduced our leaders to the status of accountants and underlings taking tests set by those bodies".

3. Some may say that third world countries in their relationships with the Fund and Bank may be compared to the foreigner "who lives in England, and is rightfully subject to a law to which he did not give his consent; if he is unsatisfied to be subject to it, he may go into another kingdom" – C.B. Macpherson, *The Political Theory of Possessive Individualism: Hobbes to Locke*, Oxford University Press, 1962 p.151. Lakshmanna in fact advises that The Report of the South Commission "pleads for the establishment of a South Bank ... liberating these countries from the hold of the World Bank and IMF – Chintamani Lakshmanna "The Challenge to the South (The Report of the South Commission" in the Ramesh Ramsaran (ed) Caribbean Economic Policy and South -South Cooperation, Warwick University Caribbean Studies, Macmillan Caribbean, 1993, p.19; Scott Macdonald, the International Advisor in the office of the Comptroller of Currency, put the matter very bluntly: "if you don't want to play the game, you don't have to ... Countries do not have to implement structural adjustment programmes. They do it because they want to... if you find the terms of the loans too onerous you can always break it off ..." The Daily Gleaner Mar, 17, 1992; Joseph B. Cox a Director of the PSQJ found it necessary to remind the public "that the IMF is not a welfare institution that gives other people's money to incompetent governments, (which) allowed an excessive part of the burden to fall on those with the least political clout" – The Daily Gleaner Jan, 28, 1990, p,19A.

4. Rich Miller, Cana/Reuter, Washington, Sept. 24,1992 referred to "the weak underpinnings of a global economy struggling to work off mountains of debt ... left policy makers (of the Fund and Bank) pointing the finger of blame at each other", as their meeting ended on a divided note.

5. Danny Roberts, of the N.W.U., An Alternative to Structural Adjustment, in the Jamaica Herald Dec. 20, 1994 p, 7 argued for "Social Keynesianism" defined as "a Programme of entitlement for the needy not for the greedy", increased productivity with equitable sharing of the benefit", and a Swedish-type "solidaristic wage policy".

6. Scott. McDonald, gave as the reason for the lack of economic progress under the IMF, the fact that "plans are as good as the people who implement them ..." pointing to the problem of accountability in Jamaica – The Daily Gleaner, Mar. 17, 1992; But see P. Streeter "Structural Adjustment: a survey of issues and options" World Development 1987, 15, 12: 1478 for a more balanced treatment of the reasons for policy failure.

7. See World Development Report, 1990 (New York) Oxford University Press, 1990, p.95, where the removal of subsidies benefitting the poor and the introduction of food stamps was seen as "a success story". Not only has the IMF period been characterized by "missed targets" but, overall, according to Girvan "the Jamaican economy is now (1992) much worse off than before the IMF programme was implemented" – The Jamaica Herald June 28, 1994, p.5; See the Editorial in The Financial Gleaner, Aug. 12, 1994, p.6, titled "Farewell IMF" for a confirmation of Girvans assessment.

8. Camdessus, in a speech to the International Breakfast Forum, U.S. Chamber of Commerce, Washington, is reported to have asserted that whereas Mexico was the first country to have succumbed to debt difficulties "... both countries (Chile included) are now striking examples of success – The Daily Gleaner, May 1, 1992, p.9; But see Wes Van Riel, "IMF and the Third World: Why IMF programmes don't work", in The Jamaican Record, Feb, 4, 1990, p.3B. What has not been admitted is that even when policies have been scrupulously followed the results have failed to meet expectations: the liberalization of the foreign exchange regime which included provision for a market-determined exchange rate for the local currency as against the U.S. dollar "was the very opposite to what, was intended" – within six months the rate jumped from J$12 to US$1 to J$29 to US$1 (an example provided by Best, Girvan and Thomas). And on a more general level, as recent developments in Turkey – previously held up as an example of successful adjustment – as recently as Aug. 1995 the Confederation of Turkish Trade Unions organized marches to protest low wages (the minimum wage being about $100 per month) in the context of inflation then at 86% – The Daily Gleaner Aug. 6, 1995, p.j QC; It has even been claimed that the IMF "appeared to follow the. therapeutic maxim that if the patient is not responding to the treatment then you should change the patient" – David Coore in The Daily Gleaner, Mar. 15, 1987; Stone, however, counters that "... to some extent the IMF has been given unfair blame ... painful and ineffective through the medicine is, some of us pretend that the illness would not exist, but. for the doctor" Carl Stone, "Attacking the IMF", in The Daily Gleaner, Feb. 11, 1987.

9. Belinda Coote, The Trade Trap, Poverty and the Global Commodity Markets, Oxfam, 1993, p. 104. In spite of its mandate to promote the balanced growth of international trade the IMF and other member organizations of the UN system presided in the 1980's Coote notes, over a decade of collapse in which the average real prices of third world export commodities "fell to their lowest level recorded in the twentieth century, with the possible exception of the Great Depression of 1932" – p.4; Immanuel Wallerstein in The Capitalist World Economy, Cambridge. University Press, 1993, p. 66, argues that trade is only relatively free when it "serves effectively to reinforce the existing system of stratification".

10. Carl Stone, in The Daily Gleaner Oct. 18, 1990.

11. The Arusha Initiative, in Development Dialogue, 1980:2 Dag Hammerskjold Foundation, Sweden, which contained a "Resolution of Solidarity with Jamaica" passed at the South/North Conference on the International Monetary System and the New International Economic Order at Arusha, Tanzania, June - July, 1980. Events would prove, however, that if there was "political motivation and calculation within the power structure" of the IMF in its treatment of Jamaica, other countries were not spared essentially similar policies – the lack of country/policy discrimination, indeed, being one of the principal criticisms of the Fund.

12. Despite Jamaica being described as some sort of a "success story" by the World Bank itself in 1992, the noted Caribbean economist, Williams Demas still found it appropriate to prescribe "shock" treatment for the Jamaican economy, which treatment should include a return to wage guidelines or a social contract, restricted imports, and a fixed exchange rate – The Sunday

Gleaner, Nov. 12, 1995, p.1C. It is hardly conceivable that an economy that is in any way associated with successful performance should still need "shock" treatment.

13. Scott McDonald, in The Jamaican Record Oct. 7, 1990 p.8B. See also Andrew Downes, "Structural Adjustment in the Private Sector in the Caribbean" in *Caribbean Affairs*, Vol.5 No,3, 1992, p.178.

14. British T.U.C. Annual Conference Report, 1964, p.383. The period after the 1989 general election provides an interesting throw-back to the British Conservative Chancellor, Reginald Maudling's observation that after the 1964 general election the Labour Party had not only "inherited our problems. They seem also to have inherited our solutions" – Ralph Miliband, Parliamentary Socialism, Merlin Press, London, 1987, pp.363, 162; As Miliband sees it, "lifting the problem above the struggle of party politics" is the perfect formula for the paralysis of policy innovativeness.

15. Clive Y. Thomas, *The Poor and the Powerless*, Monthly Review Press, 1988, p.331.

16. Karl Theodore, Structural Adjustment in the Caribbean", in T*he Role of Trade Unions in Periods of Structural Adjustment Programmes*, ILO Regional Seminar, Barbados Workers Union Labour College, Dec. 1992, pp.2-3. Earle Taylor in The Financial Gleaner, Feb. 16, 1990, p. 12, who notes, with disfavour, that "several presentations have all tended to give the perception to the large masses of our people that Jamaica's problem is basically one with the IMF. Therefore, the average man sees the IMF as Jamaica's traitor, butcher, killer, prosecutor and judge … impression that the sacrifices (are) simply to please the IMF … Looking everywhere else to place blame, and for the solution, except at ourselves … The Government should be bold enough to say … that it is the country's programme – the Governments programme …"; But see Hugh Small, Minister of Finance, Keynote Address, in Patsy Lewis (ed) Jamaica Preparing for the Twenty-first. Century, Ian Randle Publishers, Kingston, for PIOJ, 1994, p.257; Neil Kinnock however then leader of the British Labour Party, on a visit to Jamaica in 1986 as the special guest at the PNP's Annual Conference on Sept. 18, referred to the IMF as the "international pawnbroker imposing conditions that make it impossible for poor countries to pay off their debts [the opposite of the received local wisdom J. an institution whose purpose had been diverted … a puppet, through which the breath of life does not pass" – The Daily Gleaner, Sept. 20, 1986, p.1.

17. Adam Przeworski, *Capitalism and Social Democracy*, Cambridge University Press, 1989, pp.42-43,215-216; He argues that "Any class compromise must therefore have at least two aspects: one concerning the distribution of income and the second concerning investment" (p. 219), neither of which are equitably nor adequately addressed by stabilization programmes, which in effect "… constitute a project for a new society, a bourgeois revolution".

18. Ibid.

19. Derek Gordon, Class, Status and Social Mobility in Jamaica, ISER, U.W.I., 1989 p.35.

20. Ibid p.51.

21. Gordon, 1989, pp.35,48; Earle Taylor, in "Post-IMF Reflections" expressed the view that the mysticism and secrecy surrounding IMF agreements and the pre-occupation with the exchange rate was "clouding the vision of our people … and marginalized skilled and able bodied into unconventional methodologies to survive, imposing a new culture and lifestyle on the nation and making our people self-centred, shortsighted and selfish." (as borne out by the Kirton interviews and our own surveys) – The Financial Gleaner Feb. 16, 1990 p.12; See also Headley Brown, "the IMF Programme and stability" The Financial Gleaner Mar. 20, 1992.

22. Gordon Lewis asserts that "much of what passes for political stability in the self-congratulatory literature is in reality only a reflection of the traditional apathy of the West Indian masses" Gordon Lewis, "The Challenge of Independence in the British Caribbean" in Hilary Beckles and Verene Shepherd (eds) Caribbean Freedom, Ian Randle Publishers, Kingston, 1993, p.512.

23. John Cavanagh, and Walden Bello, "Development: The Market is not Enough", in Foreign Policy No.81, Winter 1990-91 Carnegie Endowment for International Peace, p.152; See also Ramesh Ramsaran "Fact and Fallacy in Economic Liberalization", in Lloyd Best, Norman Girvan and C.Y. Thomas, Economic Liberalization and Caribbean Development, ISER, 1993, p.45 where the additional factors of access to appropriate modern technology and inappropriate pricing of third world commodity exports are considered; See also Teresa Haytei, op cit, 1992, p.68, on the combined effect of adverse terms of trade and import liberalization: increased sale of developed country goods, indirectly paid for by IMF/World Bank loans … repayable at whatever social cost, ("under a system of international trade and division of labour, where the lowly paid workers in developing countries are producing goods sold at inflated prices to developed country consumers … The poor subsidizing the rich!"); George Beckford, in Persistent Poverty, Maroon Publishing House, Jamaica 1988, like Girvan before him in 1971, emphasized the extent to which the island's high propensity to import all categories of goods, "considerably dampens the development, impact deriving from the multiplier effect" (p.187); See also William G, Demas, Essays on Caribbean Integration and Development, ISER, U.W.I., 1976, p.44.

24. Part II, Text of Articles of Agreement of the International Bank for Reconstruction and Development, Article I (Purposes) (III), in Laws of Jamaica Act. I of 1962, Nov. 29, 1962, Those who are attracted by World Bank and/or USAID strategies for development should recall that under their plan conceived for Haiti in 1981/82 involving the "magic of the market" (as Reagan was to describe it in relation to the largely failed Caribbean Basin Initiative) in deeper interdependence with the U.S. economy, Haiti was scheduled to become "the Taiwan of the Caribbean". Instead, the experience was that of increased food imports, inadequate new job creation to keep pace with labour force increase, and rural – urban migration and eventually the "Boat People" phenomenon – Josh De Wind and David H. Kinley III, *Aiding Migration: The Impact of International Development Assistance on Haiti*, Bolder: Westview Press, 1988, pp. 174-175.

25. Jamaica received a total of 12 programme loans from the Fund and Bank during the entire period of the borrowing relationship with the IMF.

26. Richard Downer, Hon, Treasurer of the PSOJ, "Jamaica's current IMF programme," The Daily Gleaner, April 2, 1990 (report of his speech at the AGM of the Trelawny Chamber of Commerce, in which he also claimed that "the private sector had never been given the freedom to achieve its potential", because of bureaucratic, interference and intervention); By 1990 Michael Manley, again Prime Minister, had been converted to the view of the state as the "facilitator" of private enterprise which was now accepted as "the engine of growth" – The Daily Gleaner, April 10, p.8.

27. The Daily Gleaner, Jan. 29, 1990, p.1. The "bang-belly economy" which would be well represented pictorially by the starving African child on the Oxfam poster, was defined to be "an economy that appeared prosperous because there are a lot of [imported and luxury] goods in the shops. But prosperity is not. real as it is not based on production and earnings but borrowed money. Sooner or later, it is a bubble that must burst". The "shock", despite lagging production, was to take the form of high interest rates and tight credit because the alternative to the IMF [for the second time in Manley's political career] would be disastrous, in his view, as "without an IMF agreement, the Jamaican economy would be in serious trouble in four weeks or less"; See also Max E. Lambie, "Now the showdown – IMF Theory vs. reality", The Financial Gleaner, Feb. 16, p.11.

28. Janine Iqbal, "Adjustment Policies in Practice: Case Study of Jamaica 1973-91" in Stanley Lalta and Marie Freckleton (eds) Caribbean Economic Development, Ian Randle Publishers, 1993, p.48; For the worst case prediction of the Haitianization of Jamaica (echoing V.S. Naipaul, on The Caribbean regional level) see Trevor M.A. Farrell "The Caribbean state and its Role in Economic Management" in Lalta and Freckleton (eds) p.200; Both Alan Walker and Elliott Currie in Ian Taylor (ed) The Social Effects of Free Market Policies, Harvester Wheatsheaf, 1990, at pp.38, 302, respectively, address the social consequences of increasing poverty; .and the superficial prosperity (in the United States) that "is also heavy with human tears". See, in contrast, Richard Titmuss, Essays on the Welfare state, Boston: Beacon Press. 1969, p.42

29. PREALC, Meeting the Social Debt, ILO, Geneva, 1988, pp.17-22. The largely failed incentive of low wages induced by devaluation to attract increased foreign investment has been described as "a strategy based on the competitive advantage of misery" – the Nassau Understanding in Carmen Diana Deere (Coordinator) In the Shadows of the Sun, Caribbean Development Alternatives and United States Policy, Westview Press, 1990, pp 46-790. What this effectively means, of course, is that, the poor are being asked to agree to, or at least accept, being deprived of the benefits of better education, health, housing and other welfare amenities and provisions, in the somewhat forlorn hope – given the prolonged austerity experience – that the private sector, "showered with incentives" will export more thus facilitating external debt servicing. See Deere op cit, p. 190; Teresa Hayter, The Creation of World Poverty, London, Pluto Press 1992; Given the consistent failure of the desired response of exports, then costs in government expenditure on essential social and economic infrastructure and including public sector retrenchment and wage restraint are then prescribed as "necessary sacrifice" to the degree required for debt repayment in a situation of a negative net transfer of resources since the mid - 1980's.

30. Those who like to offer the East. Asian NIC's as suitable models of development might ponder the view of the man largely credited with S. Korea's transformation, Sung Sang Park, that "Developing Countries do not have enough foreign exchange to import both consumer goods and machinery" – "The Korean Economic Development Experience: its Relevance to Jamaica", in Patsy Lewis (ed) Jamaica – Preparing for the Twenty- first Century, Ian Randle Publishers, for the PIOJ, 1994, p.118.

31. PREALC, op cit, 1988, p.50, et seq lists the reforms that need to be undertaken by the state so as to create the "social space" necessary for successful negotiation towards meeting the targets of an acceptable social consensus.

32. See Gordon K. Lewis, op cit 1963, p.96; This is not to deny that whereas Carter, Trudeau, and Callaghan were somewhat sympathetic to the Manley cause and used their influence in the IMF accordingly, so did Reagan on Seaga's behalf, when the changed ideological affinity so dictated – Stephens and Stephens 1986, p.175.

33. Gordon K. Lewis, Ibid p.173.

34. George Beckford et al., Pathways to Progress, 1985, ("The People's Emergency Plan, Jamaica, 1977, Maroon Publishing House, Jamaica.

35. George Beckford, Persistent Poverty, Maroon Publishing House, Morant Bay, Jamaica, 1983.

36. Arnold Bertram, "IMF'ed", The Jamaica Record, Jan. 21, 1990, p. 7A; To Van Reil, less radical than Bertram, the situation is one of IMF - phobia, characterized by "frenetic speculation as to what the IMF agreement [for 1990, and in each recurring instance] will contain ... further depressing an already bewildered public" – Wes Van Reil, "Behind the IMF agreement: some simple facts", The Jamaica Record, Jan. 14, 1990, p. 3B; See Claude Clarke, "IMF agreement – A Ticking Economic Time Bomb", The Financial Gleaner, April 16, 1987, p. 2; Basil Buck, in "IMF Announcement – a classic PR job" The Daily Gleaner, Feb. 20, 1987.

37. Evelyne Huber Stephens and John D. Stephens, Democratic Socialism in Jamaica, Princeton University Press, 1986, p. 146; What is certain is that the apathetic poor and demobilized working class are threatened by the crisis of capitalism – it is inevitably on their shoulders that the cost will fall – Adam Przevorski, Capitalism and Social Democracy, Cambridge University Press, 1989, p.43.

38. Carl Stone, Class, Race and Political Behaviour in Urban Jamaica, ISER, U.W.I., 1973, p.31; See also Stone's "The Politics of Expectations" in The Daily Gleaner, May 3, 1988 and his Class, State and Democracy, 1937, pp.108-9,153-4; For when, as between 1986-89, there was "major positive improvements in critical variables", such as growth of 11% cumulatively; 96,000 new jobs created; the balance of payments improved by over US$300M and the net international reserves by more than US$200M; and the level of inflation was restricted to under 9%, the JLP government was nevertheless voted out by a landslide in general elections in 1989. See also Headley Brown "Discussions in a vacuum: the new IMF programme", The Daily Gleaner, Feb. 18, 1990 p.28A»

39. Stephens & Stephens, 1986, p.147.

40. Carl Stone, "The Politics of Expectations", in The Daily Gleaner, May 8, 1988.

41. Prime Minister P.J. Patterson in a speech at the 18th Third World Annual Conference, Kingston, reported in The Financial Gleaner, May 15, 1992, p.9.

42. Keynote Speech as Minister of Finance at the Symposium on "Preparing for the Twenty-first. Century", sponsored by the Ministry of Finance, the PIQJ, in cooperation with UNDP to mark the 30th Anniversary of Jamaica's Independence, 6-7th Oct. 1992, Kingston, reported in Patsy Lewis (ed) *Jamaica Preparing for the Twenty first Century*, Ian Randle Publishers, 1994, pp.252-258, See also Dennis A, Rondinelli, Development Projects as Policy Experiments, Rout ledge, 1 993, p.84. For a comparison with the situation under Democratic Socialism see Vaughan A. Lewis "Political Change and Crisis in the English-Speaking Caribbean" in Alan Adelman and Reid Reading (eds) *Confrontation in the Caribbean Basin*, University Center for International Studies, University of Pittsburg, 1984, p.108; For an excellent short work treating the politics of IMF programme design and implementation see Richard N. Cooper, Economic Stabilization in Developing Countries, International Center for Economic Growth, Occasional Papers No,14, ICS Press, San Francisco, 1991, pp.62-65; Ironically, Gorbachev, the former President of the Soviet Union, who presided over its demise, has been reported as being critical of "rapacious privatization", while the Communist Party leader Gennady Zyuganov declared that "The current government expresses the interests of the bourgeoisie and their patrons abroad, and carries out an antipeople and anti-democracy policy" – The Daily Gleaner, Oct. 27, 1994, p .5 E.

43. Stephens and Stephens in fact while recognizing, with Girvan, Bernal and Hughes, the effect of the world economic conditions of the early 1970's in explaining Jamaica's predicament, rightly, do not accept the deterministic view that there were no options: the contention is in fact, that had there been adequate societal preparation (p.64) for radical change embodied in coherent medium and long term plans (p.102), and the introduction of the Emergency Production Plan in 1974 instead of 1977, the results could hardly have been worse than the results of the IMF engagement. Indeed, they conclude that different and better policy choices (and those always do exist – despite difficulties of recognition) may well have "alleviated the economic deterioration" (p.319); Stephens and Stephens regard the absence of a comprehensive development plan the PNP having ignored the JLP/UN prepared National Physical Plan of 1971) as the "single biggest mistake" of the Manley regime (p.146) – Evelyne Huber Stephens and John D. Stephens, *Democratic Socialism in Jamaica- the Political Movement and Social Transformation in Dependent Capitalism*, Princeton University Press, 1986; On the Emergency Production Plan, itself, see Stephens and Stephens pp.151-2, 161-9, 197, 200-202; There are those, of course, who would have likened a non-IMF path to "changing a one eye horse for one that is blind" – La Guerre op cit., 1982, p. 193.

44. The Daily Gleaner, Aug. 9, 1992, p»6C.

45. Ibid. (Guy Arnold)

46. Ibid. This has been the. case in Jamaica since the end of a progressive redistributive oriented politics under Democratic Socialism in 1980, arid subsequent Fund Bank policies decidedly not social inclusionary . In the absence of a sense of national identity strong enough to facilitate mass mobilization around popular development goals, the increase of the numbers below the poverty line should not come as a surprise against the background of other countries free market experience – Stephens and Stephens, op cit, pp. 83,147.

47. Clive Y. Thomas, *The Poor and the Powerless*, London, Latin America Bureau Monthly Review Foundation, 1988, p.352.

48. John Gaffar La Guerre, *Enemies of Empire*, Extra Mural Studies, U.W.I., Trinidad, 1982, p.xxvi.

49. Claremont Kirton, *Jamaica, Debt and Poverty*, Oxfam, 1992.

50. Carl Stone, 1987, p.93.

51. Kirton, 1992, p. 52 reports the response of one interviewee: "Really the Jamaica Government is riot running the economy any longer. It's the IMF and the World Bank. So it becomes a dreadful escape from responsibility on the part of our governments". Manley saw this as causing a total loss of faith in the country's political leadership and, as a politician, then, was moved to declare that "There must be a better way" in *The Politics of Change*, p.190. From as long ago as 1988 Stone reported that 2 of every 3 wage earners felt that "government has been an obstacle rather than a help in securing fulfilment of labour's aspirations for a better life" – The Daily Gleaner, Jan. 6, 1988.

52. Richard N. Cooper, 1991, p.65. The Skepticism mentioned by Cooper thrives on rumour in the scandal-prone Jamaica society. A recurring question is "What have they done with all the borrowed money?" – See Kirton, 1992, p.59.

53. The Daily Gleaner, June 21, 1992, p.1C.

54. The Daily Gleaner, Sept. 29, 1995, p.1. See also Hugh Small then Minister of Finance, in Patsy Lewis (ed) *Jamaica- Preparing for the Twenty-first Century*, PIOJ Ian Randle Publishers, Jamaica, 1994, p. 257. For the completely opposite view that "Jamaica has been structurally adjusted beyond the limit, of what, any human being can actually endure …". See Beverly Anderson-Manley, Jamaica's representative to the UN's Commission on the Status of Women, at a Conference of the International Coalition of Women Physicians, Wyndham Rose Hall, Jamaica, May 15, 1992 reported in The Daily Gleaner, May 18, 1992. The consequences flowing from the impact on women were listed as: increased tension between mother, mate and children, violence against women, prostitution, drugs, neglect of children, child abuse, delinquency, crime, begging, hunger, malnutrition and teenage pregnancy. Presumably Anderson-Manley's point was that these social problems had been aggravated by structural adjustment. Hyman, more generally, concludes that "… the level of frustration and oppression that the mas of people have endured over the period of continual adjustment have left them suffering from 'adjustment fatigue', The administration must, realize that while its spokesperson use. clichés like 'level playing field' and 'market forces', the man in the street uses ones like

'no better no dey' [things will not get better], 'wey fi do' [what can one do? (nothing)] and 'wi no response' [we are not the ones responsible for the state of affairs] -The Jamaica Herald Oct. 8, 1995, p.6A.

55. The Daily Gleaner, Sept. 29, 1995, p.I; In similar vein, Prime Minister Patterson is reported as stating at his party's Youth Conference that the break from the IMF was necessary to underline the country's economic independence and so that it could "stand on a sound foundation" – The Daily Gleaner, Aug. 3, 1994, p.I, As against this, Headley Brown argued that the critical factors determining whether the time was right to end the borrowing relationship all suggested a negative decision: There had been a decline in net exports; a reduction in local investment in real terms; and a widening of the external current account deficit. This situation was reflected in poor output performance and employment generation and a failure to stabilize prices which suggested that the seemingly impressive build-up in the net international reserves did not represent earned funds which would be available for use as long term development capital – The Financial Gleaner, Jan. 7, 1994, p.8. See also Dennis Morrison's warning that, "If we do not save enough in order to increase investment, exports and growth, then we all end up right back with the IMF" – The Financial Gleaner, Sept. 29, 1995, p.I. Despite the lack of any worthy challenge of Headley Brown's views, the General Secretary of the. ruling PNP having stated that, *Jamaica has had no choice but to borrow from the Fund* [italics added] under the terms and conditions which they have specified concluded "This situation will end in September (1995) and the People's National Party which forms the present Government is justifiably proud of this achievement" – The Jamaica Herald, Aug. 5, 1995, p.6.

56. Butler and Stokes, 1974, p.278.

57. Question 5 has been treated in Joan Ross-Frankson (ed), 1990, p. 7 and Anderson and Witter, in Elsie Le Franc (ed) 1994, p. 52. On Question 12 see Ross-Frankson, 1990, p.14 and Kirton 1992, pp.5-6.

58. Gordon, 1989, p.57.

59. See Rev. Ralston B. Nembhard, "The IMF and the PNP's political agenda" in The Jamaica Herald, Aug. 1, 1995, p.7; Rovan G. Locke, in The Jamaica Herald, Aug. 26, 1994, p. 7A, and the PNP denial, previously referred to, in The Jamaica Herald, Aug. 5, 1995, p.6.

60. Butler and Stokes provide ample evidence … that the influence of the economy on the electorate's mood can depend as much upon impressions of the state of the economy derived from the media as upon direct changes of individual well-being that result from changes of employment, or income or prices" Butler and Stokes, 1974, p.378.

61. Kirton, 1992, p.61; See also C. Roy Reynolds, in The Daily Gleaner, Aug. 7, 1995, p.4A who argues that "… the philosophy of the free market is the state religion from which no deviation is to be tolerated … we have bought, into the consumption element, but the concomitant production aspect, has been ignored".

62. See Mark Wignall, "The needs of the working class" in The Jamaica Herald, April 9, 1995, p.6A, where it. is asked, "Could it. be that … this gulf is now being mirrored in the political parties by failure of middle class political leaders to 'understand' those of the working class that they would dare to govern"; Also see Stephen Fidler, on the Venezuelan government's reluctance to impose economic, austerity, in The Financial Times, Oct. 10, 1994, p.6, Luis Raul Matos Azacer, adviser to the President, is quoted as saying: "We have learned that we have to have an equilibrium between the economic and political aspects of our programme to preserve a climate of social peace".

63. Ralph Miliband, *The State in Capitalist Society*, Basic Books, 1969, pp. 58-9, 73, 81.

64. In the responses to this Question, there is a significant number listed as "Unstated" as some of the respondents answered only one part of the Question (i.e. either 22 (I) or 22 (2).) While it. is possible that the failure to respond to either part could be taken to be tantamount to a negative reply to that part, this could be explained by the belief that the question required a choice to be. made between the two parts, in those cases where Questionnaires were completed in the absence of an interviewer. Further clarification is therefore appropriate, although given the percentage scores the modification of the findings is unlikely to affect the direction of the responses.

65. Stone, 1987, p.148.

66. When asked to give a rating to the IMF policies over the. years (Question 16, Questionnaire No.2) on a scale ranging from 1-10, with 10 being the highest, the average for the total sample was 3.15 (ranging between 0 and 6). In answer to Question 7 (Questionnaire No.2) some 87.5% strongly agreed that the country should break off the IMF borrowing relationship.

67. See Ross-Frankson (ed) 1990, p.7 and Anderson and Witter, in Le Franc (ed) 1994, p. 5 2.

68. This was confirmation of a finding using Questionnaire No.1 which showed twice as many respondents blaming the Government of 1972-80, which entered into the initial agreement with the IMF, as against the political regimes of 1980-89 and 1989 to the present. In any event, as Toye has put it, "New interpretations and new programmes of action cannot support themselves entirely on their own hyperbole" – Toye, 1993, p. 70 .

69. In anticipation of responses emphasizing indifference, disillusionment and frustration etc, it is worth noting Kornhauser's reminder that people are 'available' for mobilization by virtue of being alienated – William Kornhauser, *The Politics of Mass Society*, The Free Press of Glencoe, 1963, pp.177-8. In any event, the lack of revolt obviously does not deny the "yearning for fundamental change which simmers beneath a seemingly placid political surface … in the absence of appropriate political organization, what is possible is turmoil and pressure but. not. revolution" – Miliband, 1969, p. 275. For a particularly insightful treatment of the question of mobilization and resistance from the 1970'sup to the mid 1930's in Jamaica, See Stephens and Stephens, 1986, pp.52, 54, 56, 216, 318. For the positive function of civil unrest, from a historical perspective, See Kelvin Singh, *Race and Class Struggles in a Colonial State – Trinidad 1917-45*, ISER, 1994, pp.172-3, where Governor Fletcher of Trinidad is quoted as remarking about the 1937 strikes, "I think the recent troubles have supplied the colony with a purge it sorely needed …"

70. Stone, 1987, p.4; Singh, 1994, p.3; See also Dennis C. Pirages and Christine Sylvester, *Conflict, Peace and Development in the Caribbean*, St. Martin's Press, 1991, p.228, and Stephens and Stephens, 1986, pp.6, 323 Murick has observed however that, burdensome policies do not necessarily threaten the bourgeois democratic process: it is a dubious third world notion, he argues, "that the most, oppressed strata, be they poor peasants or the 'marginals' would be in the forefront of revolutionary struggle ... the dynamics of revolution are more complex than this ..." – Murick, 1988, p.93; See also Honderich, 1939, p.13, Carl Stone, in The Daily Gleaner, Feb. 17, 1938. As has been contended, as capitalism adapts to its environment, labour's response is not limited simply to, mutually exclusive categories; nor can it be accepted as de Tocqueville would have it, that only those who have *nothing* to lose even revolt – Alexis de Tocqueville, *Democracy in America*, Vol.I, New York: Alfred A. Knopf, Vintage ed., 1945, p.258. See the UNDP Human Development Report., 1994, Oxford University Press, for a quite different perspective, as well as the report of the views of five former Latin American Presidents during panel discussions at the Inter-American Development Bank, reported in The Jamaica Herald, Sept. 29, 1994. But perhaps "... it is not revolution that we should fear, but a kind of spontaneous combustion caused by the despair of people unable to stem the constant erosion of their standard of living" – Morris Cargill, in The Daily Gleaner, Oct. 20, 1994, p.6.

71. The assistance of David Gordon-Rowe of the JTURDC is here specifically acknowledged.

72. The Daily Gleaner, May 20, 1992.

73. See Stone, 1939, p.48.

74. See Girvan, SES, Vol.37 No.4, ISER, U.W.I., Dec. 1988, pp.269-70; *Edwin Jones, Development. Administration – Jamaican Adaptations*, CARICOM Publishers Ltd. 1992, p.5; Beckford et al., Pathways to Progress, 1985, P.116.

75. The Daily Gleaner, May 31, 1994, Jamaica Information Service full page advertisement.

76. The Daily Gleaner, May 25, 1992.

77. Ibid.

78. The Daily Gleaner, May 31, 1992.

79. Stone in The Daily Gleaner, Feb, 17, 1988.

80. Joseph Zeisel, "A Profile of Unemployment", in Stanley Lebergott (ed) Men Without Work- The Economics of Unemployment, Prentice Hall, 1964, p.122.

81. It is generally accepted by the ILO that developing countries with limited sectors of formal employment do not usually have the capacity [given the low level of employment in the formal (especially manufacturing sector in Jamaica) and the low level of productivity and wages and high incidence of Underdevelopment] to engage in unemployment compensation or unemployment insurance on any significant scale.

82. Plant, 1994, p.51.

83. The family frictions and emotional trauma that can accompany redundancy was a matter of concern for Okun in *Prices and Quantities, A Macroeconomic Analysis*, The Brookings Institution, Washington, 1981, p.109.

84. See Norman Girvan "Rethinking Development Out Loud" in Wedderburn (ed) 1991, p.3. Girvan argues that "the real-life experiences of Caribbean people ever since Emancipation seem rather to validate, individual private, informal activity as a survival mechanism and as a means of small scale accumulation" which seems to be borne out by the coping strategies reported here.

85. Ibid.

86. See Alan Walker, "The Strategy of inequality: Poverty and income distribution in Britain 1979-89" in Ian Taylor (ed) 1990, p.38; on the need to study the strategies of survival in relation to the disposable income of the redundant worker over different time periods.

87. William Kornhauser, *The Politics of Mass Society*, The Free Press of Glencoe, 1996, p. 30.

Chapter 7
Policy Resistance?

Transfer of power to new post-independence successor states, Gordon Lewis maintains, is usually merely a consolidation of existing power relations, whereby the ruling class enjoys the major share of the "spoils of office", and the emerging entrepreneurial class expands into the international arena. These developments might well represent a change for the worse, "... for the bourgeois groups understand them (the masses) better, (and so) psychologically their exploitation ... may be made that much easier".[1]

After the regional working-class revolts of 1938, Lewis continues, the "... revolutionary *elan vital* was anaesthetized by being canalized into institutions – trade unions, political parties, cooperative societies – controlled by the bourgeois groups."[2]

For Lewis, like Fanon, it is only the most deprived, the submerged classes, peasants and workers who were capable of meeting the demands of revolutionary action.[3]

The incapacity of the ruling class to initiate fundamental societal change is to be explained not only by structural factors such as the small size of the society and the consequential feature of personalization of relationships, but also the effect of overlapping roles in a cultural context with a strong tendency to the traditionalistic. Indeed, it is suggested by Lewis that by the time of Independence (1960's; Jamaica - 1962) the ordinary people of the West Indies had become "seriously tainted with colonial bourgeois impurities", thus facilitating "the bloodless victory of the bourgeois spirit whether in conservative or reformist garb".[4]

One consequence of this non-revolutionary orientation has been the prominence of propaganda on "self-reliance", while almost every aspect of official government policy has been decidedly dependent in character, in stark contradiction of that rhetoric.

Universal adult suffrage in 1944 has therefore to be viewed as a continuation of that process of conservative politicization in which the psychology of dependency was nurtured in the national personality. The expectation that politics and political leaders was to be the source of the solution of personal and social problems had the effect of distracting the revolutionary potential of the masses into commitment to a political system, the essential feature of which was preservation of *status quo* power relationships.[5]

One direct result of the continued hegemony of the capitalist class, old and new, in the post-independence period has been the reliance of the political parties on capitalists for major financial support, particularly at election time. This mercenary relationship has important policy implications: reforms to benefit the poorer sections of the populace are either not pursued at all or are not taken far enough to make a real difference to the beneficiaries, or are overtaken by compromises and concessions to party financiers, which neutralize their effects. When the parties contending for political power are fairly evenly matched, as in Jamaica, the risk of loss of financial support arising from the determined pursuit of anti-poverty and seemingly anti-capitalist strategies is very real.[6]

With political parties operating under this kind of restraint, the difficulty of organising, coordinating and focusing popular protest cannot be overestimated, as,

> "... its very diversity and spontaneity work against a long term political programme".[7]

But also, Ferguson argues, its very 'success' attracts take-over bids by opportunist rival groups, with varying consequences. Cooptation tends towards energy and image dilution and goal compromise, whereas resistance and independence lead to isolation. Both developments usually give rise to splits, leadership crises, and the establishment of parallel organisations.[8]

In making reference to the deep-seated 'culture of silence', as a factor militating against the effective organization of popular revolt, for the purpose of defending the poor against exploitation, Harrison makes the important point that in a polarized society, "... a representative will usually, only fairly represent people whose interest he shares."[9]

In this respect, Democratic Socialism, under Manley, it has been argued, instead of achieving its ostensible egalitarian goals by its state-centred policies, led instead to, "... further middle-class dominance of the lower classes and reinforcing class inequalities within the society".[10]

If the poor are themselves afflicted by this 'culture of silence', what of the working-class trade union leaders? Edie, in providing a response, seems unaware of the significantly changed nature of party- union relations consequent on the demands of stabilization and structural adjustment. Not only has it become every family and every individual for itself/ himself, as the values of traditional society give way to commercialization, preoccupation with materialistic pressures, urbanization and migration, but economic restructuring has also resulted in a much looser bond between trade union and political party as the interests they see themselves as representing, under prolonged austerity, pushed them further apart in terms of policy preference.[11]

Trade union and worker distrust that was formerly directed mainly at management has increasingly been a feature of the working-class response to government policies, proposals and promises.[12]

Failure to channel and express the resistance of workers to threats to their jobs and standard of living is explained, but not justified, by the risk of loss of membership experienced by the unions during the decade of relative union docility in the 1980's. This was under a JLP government that, seemed not only insensitive to the gravity of the hardship and suffering of the poor but that appeared immune to any form of local leverage or lobby.[13]

Discernment of a reciprocal bond by Edie, as late as 1991, by virtue of which the interests of party and union are served in a manner which ensures the control of the working class[14] thus ignores the emergence of more independent unions and the gradual loosening of the two major union's affiliation to the two major political parties, in the sense of the unions being able to deliver party votes as their membership has become more diversified occupationally, with increased white collar and supervisor level unionization. This is not to deny the legitimacy of Edie's contention that the combination of the forces of both institutions has not undermined support, at least electorally, for the middle-class political order.[15] But then while the PNP displayed mild leftist, Fabian Socialist type, leanings in its earlier years, neither union was afflicted by such strivings.

As the union leader has ceased to depend on the party leader, under the rigidity of the IMF austerity regime, since the area of possible concessionary policy discretion has been very severely curtailed, so has the party leader increasingly ceased to expect the union leader to bring in party votes from an increasingly politically differentiated and disenchanted membership.[16]

Continued electoral support for middle-class political leadership under Fund stabilization and Bank adjustment policies is not to be explained on the basis of patronage, certainly not since the early 1980's, but simple as it may appear, rather on the basis of the absence of a perceived viable alternative. There has in fact been little patronage to dispense with steep cuts in government expenditure. The resources to support clientelism have just not been available under IMF programmes. So that while the lower classes and the poor may rightly be said to have been demobilized[17], the explanation must be sought elsewhere.

The deep apathy, disenchantment and indifference displayed towards the major political parties effectively disputes the thesis that patron- client analysis makes possible the identification of the mechanisms of conflict limitation which regulate and stabilize Jamaican society.[18]

Systemic weaknesses and contradictions of a kind giving rise to unfulfilled predictions of social collapse are incapable of lending support to the proposition that,

> "Focusing on clientilism provides an explanation of the way in which latent tensions are controlled in the society."[19]

It is false logic on Edie's part to further suggest that such a focus reinforces the power of the ruling class and contributes to the equilibrium of the system.

To argue, after fifteen years, during which one of the main planks of neo-liberal IMF policy was the rolling back of the role of the state in the economy to a minimal level, that, "… state expansion has become the thrust of middle-class politics"[20] is to deny the massive cuts in government expenditure, privatization of state owned enterprises, deregulation and trade liberalization – in the attempt to establish that which is insupportable,[21] but self-serving, as viable theoretical analysis.

It is conceded that electable political parties and their leaders have, reluctantly or not, whether by convenient opportunistic conversion or otherwise, embraced with varying degrees of abandon the ideology that best smoothes the path to international financial resources.[22] But to then argue that such resource inflows, "… have been primarily determined not by an economic imperative of industrialization but rather by the politics of clientelism", is little different from the extreme cynicism of the New Right.[23]

The most deprived classes no longer seek benefits through clientelist structures since the economic and financial level on which the scope for patron-client relations still exists allows advantages and benefits to the 'haves' rather than the 'have-nots'. It is in that sense that clientelism may be said to reinforce the racial and class polarizations and to heighten distrust and jealousy and increase the status and class inequalities which characterize the society.[24]

As for the evolving role of the unionized labour movement, it is a matter of history that Caribbean trade unions, which grew out of the social upheavals of the late 1930's, were guided in their early years by officers of the British TUC who passed on the "wisdom of forsaking extreme ideological positions". The models of British unions and political parties presented were anything but revolutionary, with the result that the trade unions from their inception concentrated on bread and butter issues and displayed little ambition to overthrow the political order; not even the colonial, much less one that could, in the approach to independence, be considered their own.

It is well to remember that included among the membership of the West Indies Royal Commission under the chairmanship of Lord Moyne (The Moyne Commission) which carried out investigations into the social and economic conditions which provoked the labour unrest and upheavals in mid-1938 was Sir Walter Citrine, who had been General Secretary of the British TUC since 1928.[25]

British trade union leaders, on the whole, from the late 19th century onwards, "... prided themselves on their practical rather than theoretical approach to industrial problems". Pelling noted that, indeed, "... the TUC would have nothing to do with the Second International founded in 1989."[26] This, despite impatience with the old political parties and the traditional unsympathetic approach of the administrators of the law to labour and trade union interests, which, "might well have impelled the unions to form a political party of their own", but for the emergence of the fledgling Labour Party, "... representing a powerful combination of social forces".[27]

Quite correctly, it is concluded that the fact that militant industrial action appeared deferred until the passage of the *Trade Disputes Act of 1906*, which restored the legal immunity to trade unions from actions in tort, as well as the legality of peaceful picketing, is good enough evidence as to the unions non-revolutionary nature.[28]

In terms of ideology, "it is also not irrelevant", as Shanks puts it somewhat later in time, that a thorough-going (meaning no doubt radical) socialist economic policy would cut across many of the unions' own interests, because of the likely interference with collective bargaining. It is only if the role and goals of trade unions are viewed as fixed and immutable, and in addition the institution of collective bargaining is elevated to an end, in itself, that this observation has merit.

Apart from the influence of advisers, such as Citrine, the umbilical links between the two major political parties and the two main trade unions proved an effective safeguard against union ideological extremism. The party regarded as more radical, traditionally, of the two, and certainly the one with a greater ideological tendency, the PNP, in proclaiming itself socialist in 1939 used the Manifesto of the British Labour Party as a model, rather than that of any of the more doctrinaire continental socialist parties.[29]

Increasing worker dissatisfaction with union-party ties,[30] reflected therefore, not so much a wish to be freed from party conservatism or reformism, but rather, the feeling that some politicians had used the unions to advance their political careers. An important consequence of this was that particularly during the 1980's, the trade unions suffered from a serious loss of leadership as many officers in top positions were coopted into the party-political directorate. It should not be surprising that the working class saw the unions and the labour movement as losing strength and national influence, as their interests had been displaced as a priority for political administrations by concerns about such matters as promoting investment, providing acceptable returns on capital, ensuring a climate of economic stability conducive to "business confidence", and inflation control.[31]

If the union-party alliance has not been perceived as furthering the worker's cause, one might ask, as Thomas does, why is it that, "... (the poor) have failed to seize control of state power", which he regards as, "... a necessary step towards re-ordering social priorities with a view to securing an eventual and permanent end to their poverty and subjugation.[32]

Girvan appears chastened, (as one of the leading radical intellectuals of the 1960's and 70's who was closest to the centre of the democratic socialist project) by the 'betrayal', as the abandonment of the Peoples Plan[33] in favour of the IMF agreement of 1978 is described by Beckford.[34] But, also, the almost universal embrace of the free market ideology, amidst the collapse of communism and the retreat of socialism, appears to have caused him to hold out little chance for radical social change by the revolutionary method.[35] "If radicalism is not to degenerate into a fatalistic pessimism", Girvan argues," it must address the issue of what scope there exists (sic) for the economic and political progress of the majority within the context of *existing* [italics added] political forms ...". As a highly respected student of regional development, one would have expected that, having conceded that substantive change within the context of the present political system was possible, Girvan would have sought to identify some of those prospective changes. Instead, he goes no further than to allow that *such* changes, "... therefore may have occurred...."[36]

Stone, who was probably less afflicted than most in the regional academic community by the pessimism and determinism of the plantation and the dependency school, saw the matter of choice of political form in pragmatic terms. For him the question of whether non-capitalist systems yielded better results was not to be determined, "... by political faith, authoritative text or theoretical insights".[37]

Elsewhere, Stone has argued that, "the majority of the Jamaican people have come to value the democratic system of managing power...." The seizure of power by people who have lost faith in their leaders, contemplated by Thomas, is most unlikely, in Stone's view, as he does not foresee the collapse of existing political institutions as a result of, "... diminishing mass support."[38]

It is significant that the brief period of populist statism, 1972-78, coincided with the political hegemony of the middle-class intelligentsia. With the virtual disappearance of communism and the conversion of most local socialists, somewhat in the mysterious manner of the conversion on the road to Damascus, policy continuity from one party administration to the next has seen the retrenchment of the radical element of the historically socialist PNP. To answer Laguerre's question, therefore, as to whether ideological parties will always be dominated by the intelligentsia, is to make the simple observation that as any manager's pattern of behaviour has some philosophical basis, so it is that political parties are guided by an ideological commitment of one kind or the other whether in pure, diluted or adulterated form, and however articulated.[39]

In fact, it is among the middle and upper classes which can afford to be less dependent on party patronage for survival, that one finds the greatest degree of cynicism and a high enough level of disenchantment with the political process that is most likely to remain substantially unmoved by the mobilizational devices of an election campaign.[40]

Whereas, for Fanon, it was the rural peasantry and lumpenproletariat, "who had nothing to lose," who would be in the forefront of the revolution, in the Jamaican situation it is those and the upper classes, which for different reasons have, by default,[41] ensured the survival of the institutions of liberal democracy.

Significant social mobility and embourgeoisement of substantial numbers of the peasantry and working class during the decades of the 1950's and 60's neutralized whatever revolutionary potential there might have been among the more ambitious members of those classes who remained in the island. It is also likely to have been the more ambitious, dissatisfied, and potentially disruptive elements of the population which accounted for the massive migration of the 1950's and 60's to Britain and later to North America.[42]

The latest Five-Year Development Plan recognised that,

> "... the level of poverty contributes to a high degree of social alienation and dependency ... together with skewed income distribution, creates divisions which weaken the values and social fabric of the nation."[43]

While, however, the Plan seeks to address the poverty issue, by setting, as a matter of "greater equity", one of its targets as improving basic social services "as a social development goal", the actual Jamaican experience has not been very unlike that of Yugoslavia. There, the country was "caught in the dilemma between the plan and the market", reflecting the lack of a clear definition and specification of the principles and aims of economic policy that should be indicative of the resolution of the conflict of counterveiling social and economic forces in society.[44]

Middle and upper class relative immunity to rhetoric, which no doubt stems from their cynicism with regard to party politics and the motives of political leaders, and politicians in general, was confirmed as early as 1982 by content analysis of a sample of Parliamentary speeches of the two-party leaders and Prime Ministers Michael Manley and Edward Seaga. The study by Devon Brown measuring the use of colloquial English, statistical data, personalized speech, and political catchwords, concluded that,

> "... neither leader, by direct references, pays attention or uses emotive techniques to appeal to the upper and middle classes."[45]

This was taken as evidence that they both recognized that their priority area in the electorate, was that of the lower classes, for purposes of mobilizing organizational effort and electoral support.

Using scales to assess ideological tendencies, it was found that neither leader fell in either extreme radical or conservative, but rather in the progressive/moderate categories.[46]

This is perhaps just as well, bearing in mind the Grenadian debacle and the effect of the embargo put on Cuba, particularly since glasnost, perestroika, and the disintegration of the Soviet Union. It is quite possible, of course, that the political leaders had taken their cue from the diplomatic intrigues of the 1970's which caused Fred Mills to state that,

"... Guyana, Jamaica and Barbados have been subjected to the full fury of insidious techniques ... deliberate and well-orchestrated attacks in the media, ... the fomenting of internal unrest, the manipulation of pliant surrogates threatened the uneasy peace in our hemisphere."[47]

Earlier in Guyana, it had been the racial factor which was exploited by the British Colonial Office and the United States Government, through the instrumentality of the International Confederation of Free Trade Unions, the American Institute of Free Labour Development, the local Chamber of Commerce and the transnational sugar and bauxite companies to thwart Jagan's Communist designs; in the Jamaican situation, under Michael Manley and Democratic Socialism, it was the existence of strong ideologically polarized political opposition of a tribal nature which presented the major hurdle in the attempt at mobilization of the masses in support of socialist principles and projects.[48]

Additionally, the insights of the socialist experiment of the German Social Democratic Party in the decade of 1910 had not been heeded: another instance of the repeated failure to benefit from the lessons of history. As Otto Neurath is reported to have noted:

"... the party had not worked out an economic programme and was unable to put forward clear cut demands for socialization. The techniques of socialist economy had been badly neglected. Instead, only criticism of the capitalist society was offered. ... That was why, when revolution broke out a commission for socialization had to be called to discuss the basic principles. Long-winded, sterile debates took place, showing disagreement of all sorts, without producing a uniform programme."[49]

This experience was replicated in almost every respect with the democratic socialist project of the PNP in the 1970's. Stephens and Stephens felt obliged, in assessing the viability of the alternative to the IMF, to conclude that the projects' failure might well have been situation-specific as determined by factors such as the nature of the political system, the implications of which might have been insufficiently considered, and the manner of the attempted implementation of the third path, rather than the substance of the path itself.[50]

It is contended by Vaughan Lewis, in similar vein, that the nationalization of several major foreign owned enterprises in Guyana and the imposition of the fiscally significant bauxite levy by the PNP government in Jamaica in the 1970's triggered an American perception of a "general trajectory of radicalization of domestic and foreign economic and political policy" by these governments. The direct consequence of United States regional and international institutional hegemony was, Lewis notes, a significant fall-off in foreign direct investments, a substantial reduction in visitor arrivals from that country, the major market for the local tourist industry and a notable increase in the difficulty of accessing IMF and World Bank funds, as well as in the harshness of loan terms.[51]

A disproportionate focus on historical and "current 'objective' structural pressures, in explaining and seeking solutions to the problems of the Caribbean region, is a point made by Purcell[52] and Farrell.[53] Indeed, the former goes further by suggesting that social scientists become, in the process, the "enabler" for the politician, who wants to be absolved of responsibility, for electoral reasons, and even for the local bourgeoisie.[54]

Lipset would argue that the British legacy which constrains Jamaican working class industrial and political militancy is an inappropriate inheritance. "A belief in secular reformist gradualism", he maintains, "can be the ideology of only a relatively well-to-do lower class", a category into which the average Jamaican is yet to fall.[55]

In Jamaica, under Manley's Democratic Socialism in the 1970's, the "objective realties seemed to get worse with intensified socialist rhetoric", thus causing an erosion of socialism's credibility.[56] As a result, substantial and profound shifts took place in the balance of forces in the multi-class alliance which had given the PNP its overwhelming election victories of 1972 and 1976. By 1980, it was evident that the electorate had decided that Democratic Socialism was incapable of delivering on its promise of 'social justice'. Hope was thus transferred to the JLP, with its promise of "Deliverance", under the reputed economic managerial competence of party leader, Edward Seaga, in contrast to the populist style and charismatic personality of Michael Manley.

Disillusionment with the ideological politics of socialism, versus the JLP's anti-socialist expedient, called "Nationalism", caused a breakdown of voting trends based on social class, which became noticeable from 1972, and meant that party loyalty became more tenuous as electoral support became increasingly hinged on a perception of tangible benefits received on a personal and/or class level.[57]

Apart from the loss of inter-party ideological differentiation, the acceptance of the deterministic position that there has been no viable alternative to the Fund/Bank stabilization and adjustment paths has had the consequence that development programming has continued to be,

> "... dominated by methodologies which take economic output and the allocation of financial resources – rather than people – as their central focus, despite current development rhetoric".[58]

But as Mishan has been at pains to remind us, "There are no 'musts' in international trade", as, in fact, there are none in the field of economic theory. 'Export or perish' slogans are, it may be retorted, a misleading form of rhetoric, "... due either to ignorance of opportunities or the rejection of alternatives".[59]

The issue raised in the present context, by Girvan, occupied the retrospective attention of Manley himself, who sees the "imposition" of the discipline required by the revolutionary model of development as having possible repercussions at four levels: the party, the labour movement, the nation's political system, and "regional security."[60] At the first level, he testifies to the emergence of "fundamental differences between those in the revolutionary camp." But, as Stephens and Stephens[61] have implied, "... the re-declaration of socialism and the beginning of ideological debate in the society" were hopelessly ill-timed. Internal and societal debate and political education might have been better attempted during the PNP's opposition years between 1962 and 1972, rather than in 1974 in the *middle* of a new term in office, which gave its opponents additional ammunition: the 'right' to question the legitimacy of any socialist mandate, since there had been no mention of this reversion to an ideological posture in the general election of 1972. The fact that "the redefinition of socialism in the 70's caused serious divisions within the Party", might have been taken as indicative of its likely reception in the wider community, stratified by class and tribalized by the patronage relationships between politicians, parties, and electors.

On the level of the labour movement, a distinguished trade unionist himself, Manley put it very well when he advised that, "... if a country has a dynamic trade union movement [as Jamaica did] it cannot be wished away in order that a South Korea can be created".[62]

Whereas, Girvan suggests a consideration of the accommodation of popular political and economic reforms within the existing political system, Manley appears to argue that really fundamental change in the interest of the majority may only be possible by imposition, which is likely to lead to "distortions that hamper or even destroy liberal democratic forms", presumably because of the, "... fatal disjuncture within the system between the nature of the economic process which is demanded and the manner in which the political system works."[63]

Strategies for implementing revolutionary developmental change, within the Caribbean basin, especially after Castro and Grenada, needed to take account of, "the overarching power of U.S. hegemony" in the cold war years before "glasnost", "perestroika" and the ultimate collapse of power block ideological rivalry. However, to an even greater extent, at the present time, any national development- effort needs to he projected within the context of a global economy dominated by trading blocks within and between which the factors of production flow along changed and changing routes, "... supported (to varying degrees) by critical institutions like the IMF, World Bank and GATT."[64]

At the organizational level, Nunes and Draper claimed, in the early 1980's, that the climate "festers with the opportunity for change ... but very few are prepared to initiate the process." The reason given for this lack of catalytic resolve, seems almost too simple: "They seem to be scared: the weight of convention has intimidated them".[65]

The multi-class alliance which provided financial and field support for both major parties has accounted for the peculiar policy configuration which has emerged, as alternatively, and even at one and the same time, governments have attempted to promote the interests of certain strategic groups while appeasing others. The limited nature of project Land Lease, as an attempt at agrarian reform, is one example of the urge to provide benefits to a large electorally important sector, the rural small farmer and peasant, without sacrificing the support of the large land-owning and capitalist-class, in general. The large acreages of privately owned idle lands were, therefore, not compulsorily acquired or nationalized and given or sold to farmers, but were distributed by way of leases, which rarely survived the change of political administration.[66]

This strategy of balancing concerns for conflicting vested interests in policy formation was an effective bar against policy extremes in one direction or the other, and at the same time promoted stability by making one element of the potentially disruptive rural poor[67] even more dependent on favours from the political directorate and its local representatives.

The scandals and charges of corruption and nepotism which accompany the distribution of scarce benefits in a resource-scarce economy – functioning within the framework of a patronage-based liberal multi-party-political system – meant that, so long as this system persisted, governments catered to half the population only. The other half would be in opposition, awaiting its turn to gain access to the personal benefits, which represented the reward for political support and activism. This guaranteed the failure of national mass mobilization, despite grand rhetoric and exhortation directed to the "patriotic" as "nation builders"; it also explains why no programme of non-partisan political education has ever been attempted.[68]

When conflicts between management and labour led in the 1980's to work stoppages, even with a declining incidence of disruptive industrial action, the Seaga Government's response was to amend the Labour Relations and Industrial Disputes Act, introduced by the Manley Government in 1975, and which conferred the right for workers to join the trade union of their choice, as against their employer.[69] The effect of the amendments was to vest wide discretionary powers in the Minister of Labour to intervene in any dispute where he/she is satisfied that the dispute should be settled expeditiously, by referring the dispute to the Industrial Disputes Tribunal for resolution. Further, written instructions can also be given to the parties, "... to pursue such means as he shall specify "... to settle the dispute within such period as he may specify... ."[70] A 1986 amendment further gave the Tribunal the power to Order that actual or threatened industrial action should cease, or not take place, the breach of which Order would make any strike action engaged in unlawful and subject to criminal law sanctions.[71]

It is interesting to note that despite strident criticism of the *Act* by trade unionists,[72] the present PNP Government, even under Manley from 1989-90, has not seen it fit to repeal the offending sections, even when one doubts that any obstacle would have been presented by the principle of 'continuity' with the IMF policy framework of its predecessors, the allegedly more 'pro-capitalist' JLP.

The politics of stabilization and structural adjustment again effectively deprived the working of the intended benefit of originally pro-working-class legislation.

Legislative amendments of the kind outlined were not of course, introduced in a vacuum. Indeed, the policies of the free market,

"... required not only a new ideological orientation ... but a political strategy for handling the transition and the capacity to dismantle the clientelist political conditions that characterized the party system."[73]

Contrary to Edie's view, the contention here is that it is the latter that has been achieved, albeit as an unwelcome if inevitable side-effect of stabilization and structural adjustment austerity measures, while the requisite new political strategy is yet to be revealed. Ample evidence of this is provided by the high-level disenchantment with and antipathy for traditional party politics as indicated by the Carl Stone polls.[74]

Quite apart from the use of legislative enactments and quasi-judicial institutional machinery as instruments of labour control, it has also been contended that the state has "used coercion to protect itself against lower class mobilization." The difficulty in assessing this view inheres in the problem of distinguishing between criminal behaviour partly spawned by the economic crisis, and lower class political dissent made out to be deserving of the use of extraordinary and often extra-legal powers under legislation such as the *Suppression of Crimes Act*,[75] in force for most of the years under the IMF.

There can be little doubt that allegations of the indiscriminate use of unnecessary violence in ghettos or against ghetto-type persons are often well founded. At the same time, there is a conspicuous absence of any evidence indicative of even the genesis of a serious movement of political dissent, lawful or unlawful, organized, coordinated and focused, or otherwise, with the potential to become a threat to the established actors and vested interest groups occupying direct and indirect power positions of prominence in the political system.

This failure to mobilize dissent, or revolt around a 'programme', as against the spontaneous eruption of protest, centered on specific localized issues, is partly to be explained by the exploitation of the advantage, represented by the middle-class and intellectual's, "... command over the symbols and substance of British culture". This has been used, it has been alleged, "... to mystify and mesmerize ordinary Jamaican citizens...."[76]

This pre-Independence belief that middle-class leadership is an essential requirement in giving status and legitimacy to any radical movement, so as to insulate it against the raw excesses of state coercion and repression and to provide "a shield against reactionary challenges[77] has persisted. This was despite Rastafarianism, the black power movement, and the so-called "cultural consciousness" of the 1970's. The lesson is still to be learned, that until some elite is excluded from power, it will not aid, much less lead, the revolution: to do so, while its traditional position in the hierarchical social structure is conceded, would be to revolt against its own kind – the probability of which is remote in a small island state.

The correctness of Lindsay's identification of the problem, as the depth of the left wing's belief in the "supposedly reactionary character of the Jamaican peasantry and working class", which belief was taken to the point where the left-wing itself "became virtually paralysed to face, on their own, the problems and challenges which revolutionary change necessarily involves"... is, at the very least: questionable. The left-wing being itself a part of the nationalist-bourgeoisie is caught in its own class web: it suffers from the consequences of the 'cult of the leader/personality', no less than the established parties; among its members may be found those same know-all, smart, wily intellectuals,

> "... spoilt children of yesterday's colonialism and of today's national governments, they organize the loot of whatever national resources exists".[78]

On the specific question of violence,

> "... the elite (including the leftwing intellectual), are ambiguous. They are violent in their words and reformist in their attitudes."[79]

The reluctance to face this issue squarely and be prepared, *ab initio*, to take whatever action becomes necessary in the furtherance of the radical imperative is a mistake which Lindsay, more defensively, finds common-place among, "... rhetorical advocates of revolutionary change ... who are unwilling to face the cost which revolution demands."[80]

It has been asserted by Munck, that the type of bread and butter unionism which was encouraged and promoted, and that has prevailed in Jamaica, and other islands of the Caribbean, has "aided imperialist penetration", by, "dampening class-consciousness". This has been achieved by an exclusive worker focus on economic issues, in a union organizational culture ideally apolitical.[81]

The defence of living standards on a "reformist cul-de-sac that revolutionary workers can avoid",[82] tends to place limits on supportive working-class action, reflected, for example, in the virtual absence of the use of 'sympathetic' or 'secondary' strike action, as a part of the armoury of industrial strife. This strategy is yet to be placed on the agenda for inter-union debate,[83] there having been no recorded sympathy strikes or secondary boycotts in the official statistics on industrial disputes. Particularly since the establishment of the JTURDC there have been increasing instances of the public expression of support for actual or threatened strike actions by unions not directly involved in the dispute, or by the JTURDC or the JCTU, as representative bodies. But that is as far as sympathy has been taken to date.

Those enclave sections of the labour force such as the 'labour aristocrats', in the bauxite industry, that might be expected to be best able to afford the sacrifice of sympathetic industrial action, have become casualties to the "gross over-development of the acquisitive instinct".[84] An instinct heightened through the influence of the 'demonstration effect', which inhibits the development of any spirit of common interest and struggle, essential for the evolution of consciousness of the working class, as a "class in itself."

The lack of unity and mutual support which exists at the national level is, not surprisingly, even more pronounced at the international level. The growing international division of labour in keeping with increasing mobility of capital and production is unlikely to lead to a uniform pattern of labour control.[85] Even within broadly similar regional economic, political and social environments, labour is formed, exploited, and struggles in a given national context.

Rather than mobilization by the watchwords, "Workers of the World Unite", what one finds, instead, in the Jamaican situation, is that opposition between rich and poor has been mediated by relationships of patronage that transcend ethnic and class boundaries.[86] Analyses which seek to avoid confusing rhetoric with reality, need to critically assess the 'myth' of class harmony, which found expression in the formation of multi-class parties in the prelude to constitutional decolonization.[87]

It is also necessary to evaluate the role of the state and the effect of state corporatism in demobilizing the workers, with the offer of legislative concessions and patronage, such as public works programmes, while at the same time, it engages in anti-labour coercive behaviour through repressive state-designed institutional regulatory mechanisms, such as the Industrial Disputes Tribunal established under the LRIDA.[88]

It has been projected that once the masses begin to,

> "… see through the extent of their exploitation and begin to unite as a single coherent class, Jamaican democracy will collapse under the weight of revolutionary pressure".[89]

It is noteworthy that no assistance is provided as to the specific societal and international conditions that are needed to trigger the beginnings of these developments.

Holstrom visualizes 'salvation' as not coming through the working class, *per se*, but rather through the instrumentality of trade unions, membership of which, it is claimed, often has a strong ideological content:

> "a naive but real longing for a new moral community with universalistic norms and a demand for changes to make them effective".[90]

However, in Post's respected assessment, the labour revolts of 1938 which gave birth to the unions could not be classified as a revolutionary project, neither successful nor failed, which is not to deny that they did call into question "the basic economic structure of Jamaica's social formation". and did bring about profound changes in its political articulation, more so, indeed, than the Democratic Socialist experiment of 1974-80, which had more explicit partisan political goals.[91] Thus, on the basis of Meeks' conclusions as to the necessary convergence of conditions that are conducive to revolution, there has yet to be a modern class rehearsal in Jamaica.[92]

As Lipset observes, trade unions help to "integrate their members into the larger body politic", and, further, where strong unions exist and obtain political representation, "… the disintegrative forms of political cleavages are least likely to be found".[93]

At the same time, while patterns of working-class political action may well be inversely related to the level of national income, it is everywhere observable that economic hardship and poverty are obviously not the main cause of radicalism.[94] If this were otherwise, we would probably in the 1980's, have had the 'world socialist revolution', so optimistically predicted, as a possible path for world history, by Wallerstein.[95]

As it is, the historically evident truth was emphasized by Durkheim that, in a situation where change is not perceived as an option, poverty may very well generate a conservative orientation.[96] Economic deprivation can easily lead to psychological habits of submission and lack of self-confidence, resulting in withdrawal from individual and group interaction with higher-class/status participants.

The working classes of the Dominican Republic, unconstrained by democratic traditions, unlike the case in Jamaica, exhibited a much greater level of resistance to the consequences of IMF austerity measures. In April 1984, widespread revolt and protest, following the announcement of a series of price increases, resulted in the killing of over one hundred people including women and children, the wounding of many more, and the arrest of several hundred.

Most significant among the list of popular demands, was the withdrawal of price increases, the introduction of minimum wage rates, and the cancellation of the recent agreement with the IMF.

As with the Manley Government of 1976-80, the events of April 1984 not only heightened the unpopularity of the Dominican Republic Government, (the PRD), but, because of the scale of the protests and the numbers killed, "... brought to the world's attention the. social costs of the so-called *stabilization* [italics added] programmes which the IMF imposes upon indebted third world countries."[97]

Instead of the stability promised to the people of the Dominican Republic by the IMF technicians, the experience was a 20% fall in real minimum wages from the 1980 level; inflation of 37.5%, up from 4.8% in 1983; unemployment of 27%, an increase of 6% from 1981; negative GDP growth; and debt servicing commitments amounting to 76% of export earnings in 1985."[98]

Again, there were popular protests and a general strike during which four persons were shot and a large number of trade unionists arrested, culminating in the following year, 1986, in the government's electoral defeat, "... in which the IMF played a large part."[99]

Application of the usual IMF policy prescriptions, in the case of the Dominican Republic, has yielded the not unfamiliar results: increase in poverty to 57% in 1991, as against 47% in 1984, and in absolute poverty 30% as against 16% over the same period; decreased spending on and deterioration of the social services; the fall in real wages by 32.5% in the 1980's; increase in prices, especially of food; neighbourhood strikes (led by the Popular Movement consisting of women, youth, the unemployed, marginalized workers of the informal sector); a forty-eight hour general strike in 1988 and again in 1989, with trade union support; widening of the gap between the rich and the poor, with 20% of households in 1991 earning 61% while the poorest 20% earned less than 3% of the national income;[100] increase in the number of street children; more migration of key social service workers like teachers and nurses; and disenchantment with traditional party politics. Although the Popular Movement proved itself quite capable of agitation and mobilization of resistance and revolt, it was found that,

"its very diversity and spontaneity worked against a long term political programme, while efforts to forge such a programme led to divisions and leadership crisis".[101]

Attempts by opportunistic political groups to capture the Popular Movement have not had much better results.

Neither the Independent Peasant Movement founded in 1979, to campaign for agrarian reform, a better standard of living and focusing concern on the debt crisis and the IMF relationship, nor the later Popular Movement, while possessing a great deal of political power, have shown the willingness or ability to seize, or indeed demonstrated any interest in seizing, political power.

Having limited its functions to the arena of strikes, protest and propaganda, on behalf of those "most clearly failed by the political system", and against the payment of IMF debt, it should not be surprising that the sum total of the Movements' efforts has been limited to seeking isolated concessions. Uncertainty as to its proper role – pressure group or change agent – very largely explains its lack of effectiveness, despite geo-political considerations, including the United States of America's regional hegemony.

Despite its lack of a democratic tradition, the lesson of the Dominican Republic's experience seems applicable to other regional reform-minded governments. According to Harrison's advice, somewhat late in the day, perhaps, the thing to do is to keep out of international debt, since failure to do so will cause the government and country to,

> "… fall into the arms of the IMF which will, if it continues according to previous form enforce an austerity programme that will cause riots, jeopardize public support and possibly lead to a coup."[102]

But this is to ignore the blunting of the radical edge of class-consciousness, by mechanisms designed for the institutionalization of political, economic and social conflict, which will ensure that the society remains complacent and apathetic,

> "… lacking the intangible feeling of expectancy, the eagerness to see what the future will bring and the readiness to act to bring the future rapidly to fruition."[103]

One of the weaknesses of 'general unions', which naturally tend, also, to be the major unions in small countries, is the absence of much fraternizing off the job, due to the heterogeneity of membership. What this means, is that, given the nature of 'business unionism', it is only normally, once every two years, during re-negotiation of the labour contract that any part of the membership participates actively in union affairs. Clearly, this will have the effect of encouraging and legitimizing oligarchic leadership .[104]

There would be little dispute aroused by the expression of the view that, contrary to Perlman's suggestion, it is more than likely the "adaptive mechanisms of a security-seeking leadership", conditioned in the Jamaican context, into fearing the worst from industrial militancy, rather than "the social situation of workers" that explains the limited visions, goals, and struggles of the labour movement.[105] This situation is simultaneously reinforced by the pluralism of, and opportunities for social mobility in a middle-class-led society, "... which treats a degree of conflict as no more than an extension of the market".[106] Worker protest as a revolutionary force, it is argued, is likely to emerge only in "certain situations and at certain times" and requires – to be effective by the failed local radical recipe for structural change in Jamaica – mounting a wider class alliance which, for Munck, "... embraces the totality of the labouring poor and even *dissident bourgeois sectors*"[107] [italics added].

Two examples of the "right" situation and time, are given by Lipset, who notes that in Sweden, it was when, and because, the workers were denied both political and economic rights that their struggle for a more equitable distribution of income was, "... superimposed on a revolutionary ideology."[108] On the other hand, he notes that it was the instability of the French unions, and their constant need to maintain militancy, in order just to survive, which, "... made the workers susceptible to the appeals of political groups."[109]

While the conditions for class warfare may still exist[110], even today, the enemy earlier identified as number one, the IMF, benefited from the advantages of 'remoteness and facelessness', and so the cause of revolutionary change suffered to the extent of this wasteful diversion of energy. Governments too, have, to some extent, in exaggerating their helplessness, "in the jaws/embrace of the IMF", succeeded in distracting attention from local sources of hardship and exploitation.

It is not however disputed here that. "... the notion of redeeming violence is inexcusably romantic ... [or that...]the politics of a national peasant revolution are wildly utopian."[111] In similar vein, it can be argued that the assumption by the left that a bourgeoisie which has captured state power in the developing world, cannot he "ridden over rough shod", and its vested interests abolished by anything other than a social revolution, suffers from that analytical determinism which results from being afflicted by dogma.

Failure of radical intellectual leadership, in a cultural environment characterized by low-level literacy, even of the barely functional type [112], may be explained by the inherent lack of confidence in the 'common people', from which the middle class intellectual elite suffers. In doctrinal terms, it can be put down to the absence of a "pure revolutionary class."

As Girvan claims, the transformation of society along radical lines, is more prone to errors and "oversight" and suffers to a greater extent from unpredictability than the gradualist method of change.[113] The fault, however, is usually to be attributed to a failure to engage in detailed contingency planning – an exercise at which radicals are notoriously weak.

If effective revolt against the IMF policies, and the governments implementing them, required political leadership, it was not, according to Farrell, to be expected from the traditional sources. Not when he asserts that,

> "... it is often the greedy, the intellectually limited, the parasitic and generally the flotsam and jetsam of the society that are attracted by the spoils of political office ..."[114]

Effective political leadership of resistance is even less likely, if it is acknowledged that total rejection of the Fund and Bank's stabilization/adjustment policies does not appear to be a feasible alternative for small, open, underdeveloped countries like Jamaica. This is especially so, when the country is already heavily in debt and desperately short of foreign exchange, with an excessive dependence on external sources for financial support, markets, technology, investments, raw material inputs, capital goods, and a wide range of consumer manufactures.[115]

Rejection would most definitely not occur if, as Baker claims, the present groupings which could be expected to be in the vanguard – trade unions and political parties, especially when in opposition – are those which represent the mass movements of the 1930's, and which have, " ... ossified into essentially authoritarian, unresponsive and frequently corrupt institutions.[116]

If the oft-repeated diagnosis of the Jamaican people, as suffering from an overdose of the "dependency syndrome" is correct, then the psychological feelings of inadequacy, hopelessness and helplessness can be imagined when – with raging inflation, massive devaluations, substantial redundancies and devastating erosion of real wages – it was realized that there was now no one on whom to depend for patronage, succour or protection. There are those who indeed claim that the country would be better off if its British colonial status had been maintained.

The consequential feeling of abandonment to little understood and seemingly uncontrollable economic forces let loose by governments which claim, in a display of dependent helplessness, to be under 'IMF duress', did not find expression not in widespread revolt or serious social upheaval. Rather, one witnessed issue-specific, short-lived demonstrations and a one day, largely urban, "national strike", causing the kind of dislocation which did not prevent the resumption of "business as usual" at almost all levels, and in all areas, immediately after each "disturbance".

The political elite has managed to perpetuate itself in office without- achieving any notable degree of success in the economic integration of the rural areas. The rural township development programme announced – not without the sponsorship of the inevitable international agency, this time the World Bank – has managed to achieve the creation of some health centres and concrete slab name-plates of the particular village, overgrow with bush in most cases. And yet there has been nothing remotely resembling the beginning or sounding like the early rumblings of a "peasant" revolt.

The phenomena of social inequality and disguised unemployment, the lot of the economically disadvantaged, have thus been largely untouched by this grand sounding programme.

Clearly, in the context of Jamaica's rural culture it is only the uncritical disciple of Fanon who would argue that, the conditions of unrelieved rural poverty, deprivation, lack of community services, malnutrition and disease constitute, "… the ideal breeding ground for political unrest, disorder or even rebellion".[117]

In the early 1970's, 71% of the total number of farms occupied only 12% of all farm lands while, 97% of the farms accounted for only 34% of the area farmed; the other 3% occupied a massive 60% of lands in farming.[118]

With this pattern of farm land distribution, agrarian reform on the scale and comprehensiveness carried out in Taiwan, for example, was imperative if the radically oriented Emergency Production Plan was to have had any chance of success.

As it was, the combined effects of Project Land Lease, Operation Grow and Pioneer Farms, the latter patterned on the Tanzanian experience, did not do much to alter the disenchantment of the potentially revolutionary rural youth with agricultural work and the stigma attached to the occupation of 'farm labourer'.

Preference for idleness in the larger towns has continued to be manifested by their numbers on the sidewalks, at the street corners, and on the shop piazzas.

The somewhat revised mandate of the World Bank, with respect to rural development, has not managed to make a difference in relation to the problems of lack of capital at affordable cost, marketing, reliable transportation, bad roads and lack of irrigation, not to mention the astronomical increases in the prices of all inputs such as fertilizer, resulting directly from years of devaluations.[119]

The use of modern efficient farm machinery, on the other hand, by taking the drudgery out of agricultural labour, can be of such psychological advantage, as to, "... reduce the general conservatism and inertia of rural areas".[120] But this is a development which has not materialized on a wide scale.

And the emergence of pockets of political radicalism and social protest in the urban ghetto failed to be galvanized into anything more threatening than partisan political violence, later to be generalized into crime against the person and property, showing no discrimination across class boundaries.

If there is one revolution that has been effectively crushed it is that of 'rising expectations' which has been transformed into the cynicism, hopelessness, despair, apathy, alienation and disenchantment with the entire political process which has characterized the mood of the masses for nearly the past three decades. This is to the extent where the Stone surveys showed an astonishing 80% of the population actively interested in migration,[121] in a nation whose national anthem contains the refrain: "Jamaica, Jamaica, Jamaica, land we love!"

The drastic changes in former patterns of social interaction between the lower orders and their betters, characterized traditionally by deference, respect, subordination and the unquestioning obedience of those who knew and kept their places in the social order, did not lead in the direction of organized revolt or resistance against inequality and lack of opportunity. What replaced them was the disregard on a significant scale for virtually all forms of discipline and authority, the essential prerequisites for successful revolutionary social transformation. The photograph displayed on the following page is of great significance in this respect.

The bizarre nature of the ideological elements in Jamaican politics is well illustrated by the massive financial support given by the business community prior to the 1972 election to the then opposition party, the traditionally socialist, PNP, which was to declare itself Democratic Socialist in 1974. The reason for this switching of support being, ironically, the then Government's attempts at Jamaicanization of areas of the financial sector and greater state intervention in the economy, and in particular the public utility companies.

Except for the 1976 election, there can hardly be said to have been "the convergence and crystallization of ideological and sectional issues" between rival social classes championed by political party adversaries. And even then, the country's political history was against undiluted class polarization, along party lines.

Political and social conflict has thus been kept, below boiling point, but for election campaign periods. But political and social revolutions tend not to occur in contexts, it is alleged, where public opinion,

> "… is unstructured, atomized and incoherent and lacks the opinion leadership, organization, and media access through which to articulate responses to the limited public discussion that takes place between coordinate political and economic elites".[122]

The discontent and aggression which have their source in class and racial exploitation and deprivation, is thus diverted, by the promise of patronage through party politics – in the absence of the elements constituting "mass society" or working-class political organization – into politically partisan struggle and the killing of the poor and black by one another, in the majority of incidents.

Radical policies are not likely to be pursued by alliances across class lines which are not cemented together by strong ideological commitment to a cause or movement reflecting and arousing mobili- zational effort of a sustained nature. Controversy therefore tends to surround means, rather than visions, and the essential focus becomes one of the relative efficiency in managing affairs so as to maintain the *status quo*.

SIGN OF THE TIMES

This vendor paid the closest attention possible to this No Vending *sign in the May Pen square by using it as a prop for his stall. Many roadside shacks went up on the busy roadway in defiance of the sign.*

©Greggory Watt Photo

The virtue of maintaining stability and a climate conducive to investor confidence, at all costs, has assumed the importance of a central goal, whatever the quality of life of the population. The result is that middle class party leaders, fearing radical or extremist class mobilization, adopt the strategy of trying to satisfy all social sectors to some degree at all times.

The central preoccupation of the ruling class in its relations with the lower classes is therefore the containment of anger and antagonism resulting in an industrial relations system where the 'mission' of militant trade unionism is limited to the failed attempt at maintaining the workers' share of the national product.

A failure to target fundamental changes in the economic and social structure is understandable given the dissipation of militancy on the relatively limited, but never the less important, day-to-day 'bread and butter' concerns, characteristic of business unionism.

Worker and trade union response to the practice of management, in keeping with this approach to trade unionism, is situation-specific, and therefore, devoid of the guidance of an ideological or philosophical framework, which would guarantee consistency of behaviour by labour. Being thus freed from a concern with the propriety of the production relations of capital and labour, and the equity of the asset ownership structure in the economy and society, the result is that much-admired 'pragmatism' which does not treat the labour process as a problematic within capitalism.[123]

The attempt by Nurse to elevate industrial conflict and, more specifically, the analysis of the structure of strikes according to cause, duration, frequency and worker coverage into an assessment and explanation of the issues around which class struggle is generated, really appears to be a confusion of shadow with substance.[124]

Workers who are not conscious of themselves, as a class "in themselves", much less a class "for themselves", can hardly be conceived of as being engaged in 'class struggle' at any level. "Class struggle", if it is to have any meaning, presupposes the objective of class displacement/substitution, in terms of control, power, and ownership of society's resources.

What is misleadingly referred to as, 'class struggle', by Nurse, and others, in the context of industrial relations conflict, differs little, if at all, conceptually, from keen bargaining between capitalists in commercial contract negotiations.

A recognition of the true nature of the ideological state of the classes in society and of the parties in the industrial relations system, under entrenched capitalism, is one of the major contributions of the Italian Marxist Antonio Gramsci.[125]

Gramsci's concept of hegemony, 'the social glue' that provides the integrating practices, mechanisms and cultural institutions which hold capitalist, societies together on a non-coercive level can with benefit be applied to the Jamaican situation during the IMF years. It is with little difficulty that one is able to identify the agents of domination and subordination from the most cursory glance at, firstly, the class distribution of income and, secondly, at the occupational status of leading members of Cabinets and Governments formed by both political parties in the last three decades.

The right to dissent and engage, however shallowly, in the machinations of adversial politics has left unbroached questions as to the legitimacy, morality, and the social acceptability of the structure of ownership in the society and therefore, by extension, the essential social role and purpose of the political system and its class-affiliated practitioners, if not its visionaries.

The point has been reached with retrogressive income redistribution where some who were once "privileged members of the middle class" must now be categorized among the "new poor".

What the Jamaican state has ensured, therefore, is not so much the expression of class struggle within the industrial relations system but, rather, the hegemonic mediation and definition of political and economic relations in a manner where the socially disadvantaged – casualties of the IMF and World Bank model of capitalism, prescribed for indebted third world countries – are left with the vote as the only concession,[126] a concession that has brought no amelioration of their deprived condition for nearly twenty years.

The evasion of the reality of class stratification in the determination of life chances, due to isolated cases of spectacular social mobility from the lower classes into positions conferring leading capitalist status, demands conscious defence against the tendency of the ruling class to succeed in "turning its enemies into its allies". As Green notes, "… the analysis of hegemony as ideological and cultural domination is more chillingly relevant than ever today".[127]

This tendency of the ruling class is of particular importance, given the fact that concentration of the unions on the 'middle forty percent' of manual and white-collar workers has meant the effective abandonment of the unemployed, the subproletariat, the lumpen-proletariat and the poor to survive by seeking patronage and handouts from the practitioners of a highly polarized partisan political system. It is these members of the labour force, un-touched by the concerns of trade unionism, who fill the role in a labour-surplus economy of eager strike breakers; but, more importantly, the movement thus loses the benefit of the support of those persons most likely to engage in radical transformation activities – those who have the least to lose.

There are not many union officials who, like Frank Cousins, then General Secretary of the British Transport and General Workers Union, have the courage, or commitment to labour's interests, to resign high political office to which they have been co-opted, rather than be parties to policies causing social and economic ruin among their membership. As a strategy to pre-empt vigorous prospective opposition from the most experienced top-level union leaders, both major parties have offered attractive Cabinet and Senate appointments to key union officers. The extent of this practice in the 1970's and 1980's and after, was such that the remaining union leadership could, with a large measure of truth, be described as "debilitated, weakened and lacking in the calibre appropriate at the national level".[128]

Labour's failure to raise real wages and improve other conditions of employment in the 1980's can reasonably be explained by reference to declining export earnings, massive devaluations resulting in substantially reduced purchasing power, and drastic austerity measures that flowed from IMF conditionalities. It is however, precisely the hardships, suffering and dislocations brought about by these policies which might have been expected to lead to major social and political upheaval. The response instead ranged from resignation through alienation to despair.

To say that labour's capacity to engage in militant action was constrained because of the capitalist need for an industrial relations climate conducive to investment, the fear of large scale redundancies, and the general feeling of uncertainty engendered by unrelieved economic crisis, is to indict the leaders of the working class and their intellectual sympathizers for a failure of leadership. After all, the test of the mettle of leadership of any kind is its effectiveness in achieving desired outcomes in moments of severe adversity.[129]

Strike incidence as a measure of economic discontent, or as evidence of labour's confidence in its ability to win concessions through militancy, is in no sense necessarily mutually exclusive. The latter view as the explanation for the level of industrial unrest appears to be not only one of convenience but, is equally cynical, in that it leaves no scope for bold, inspirational system-threatening leadership.

How then does one explain the marked difference in strike statistics between the 1970's and 1980's?

One view is that with the massive public-sector redundancies resulting from substantial cuts in government expenditure so as to reduce the budget deficit, as dictated by the IMF, it became clear to labour and its leaders that the unions could provide no protection in this environment of actual, even if unintended, Government hostility to working-class interests, after the first IMF Agreement of 1977.

A focus on the backgrounds of different political leaders, the populist Michael Manley, a leading trade unionist and President of the NWU up to the time of his becoming Prime Minister in 1972, and Edward Seaga, "the tough managerialist no-nonsense leader, without a background in trade unionism, "… fails to account for the large lag of wages behind the rate of inflation from 1975 onwards.[130] It is equally doubtful that the high interest rate regime, imposed in the attempt to restrain the demand for foreign currency, which resulted in bankruptcies, foreclosures, and consequential unemployment, was a significant factor determining the lack of labour militancy.

'Ability to pay', as an explicit basis for wage claims, tends to be relied on more so in relation to those larger enterprises which are obliged to publish their balance sheets, being public rather than private companies. While such firms are in the minority in the Jamaican corporate world, they are natural targets for union representational claims, particularly in the industrial as against the commercial sector. And while in the earlier part of the period they would have suffered from the severe foreign exchange shortage, their profit levels certainly did not suffer as did wages, having benefited from retrogressive income distribution, despite price controls.

It is agreed that the Westminster-Whitehall model of the Jamaican public administrative sector, in the context of dependent capitalism, spawned an operational style that was "essentially cautious, risk-shy, and precedent-ridden". That, together with other negative factors, would make it appear that the initiation of radical social change is well-nigh impossible in the absence of the occurrence of some cataclysmic event, given the nature of the entrenched competitive political system and the country's geo-political location.[131]

The inheritance of the strong British commitment to the principles of constitutionalism and the rule of law, in a society yet to achieve any acceptable form of "Post-Independence Consensus", has meant that any anxiety to introduce rapid social change has been neutralized by that inherent gradualism that is a feature of more mature bourgeois, democratic political systems.

How else can one explain the Opposition Jamaica Labour Party's response to the State of Emergency declared, a matter of months prior to the 1976 election, clearly for the political purpose of hamstringing that party as the PNP Government's only effective electoral rival?

Challenging the State of Emergency regulations "in the streets", which was advocated by a small minority, as the only appropriate *political*, rather than legal response, was rejected outright under a new leader associated, as rumour would have it, with organized political violence in his own inner-city, economically deprived, so-called "garrison" constituency. The party referred to its own internal legal bureau, the task of getting 'fuller information' on the details of the Regulations. They arrived at an interpretation of the measures contrary to that which the security forces, members of the judiciary, as well as political appointees such as the Attorney General and the Minister of National Security, might eventually put on them. Rather than contestation on the streets, what took place was the search for historical and legal precedents relating to a State of Emergency. Provisions formulated without consultation, and announced to have immediate effect, clearly intended to significantly affect the political balance of power, provoked a response entirely legalistic.

With such a response, the moment for opposition political mobilization was lost. The real objective of the regulations, the demoralization of the Opposition was fully achieved as both leadership and membership at all levels fell into near-total disarray,[132] particularly after the arrest and detention without charge or trial of strategically selected members of its leadership core.

Conflict between any desire for fundamental change in social and economic relations and traditional cultural patterns manifested itself in the ambiguity of the position and role of the church in its concern with the propriety of "political methods, which were expected to conform with political ideals", in the search for "social justice".

The attempt to achieve different objectives, by different means, without prioritization or an agreement on a time schedule – indeed, without even a rudimentary specification of the operational meaning of concepts such as "social justice" – made for misunderstanding, confusion and a fractured focus on the revolutionary project.[133] But this problem of focus has not afflicted the IMF nor the World Bank.

As "the theology of private enterprise" has become the received dogma within the context of state policy-continuity, it has been found necessary for both international lending institutions to provide support to poor countries in the throes of adjustment. This they have done in part by urging the need for "political courage", required for governments to withstand social and political pressures from a plurality of client groups all contending for their maximum share of dwindling resources. At one and the same time, governments are being purportedly rewarded with financial support for engaging in "democratic reforms", while being challenged to adopt an authoritarian posture in confronting popular political pressure deriving from policy resistance.

External institutional encouragement has taken essentially two forms: either emphasis on the prospective benefits of "staying the course", or on the possible disadvantages of distorting market interventions.

It appears as if the self-proclaimed apolitical *modus operandi* of the Fund/Bank is expected to be extended to the practice of national governments, even in competitive multi-party-political systems.

But political parties put themselves in serious electoral danger, under IMF policies, when even the divisions within each class, as Beckford, et al., argue, and, "… the disjuncture between the classes as a whole serve to immobilize the broad mass of the people".[134] The suggested remedies of political education and measures to "eliminate dispossession and alienation", seen as necessary for "a class alliance … capable of turning the pyramid upside down … ", were ill-conceived when attempted under Democratic Socialism. Political education, on a broad mass scale, was never attempted and redistribution in favour of the less privileged has tended to be practised at the level of partisan patronage politics only.[135]

Accepting that the imposed policies of stabilization and structural adjustment were largely anti-labour, certainly in their experienced effects on production relations in the society, it might have been expected that a programme of worker participation would have been welcomed by labour as providing institutional mechanisms of mediation, if not resistance. Commitment and enthusiasm however proved to have existed almost entirely on the part of Government and the 1977 Emergency Production Plain task force.[136]

But perhaps this should not have come as the surprise it proved to be to members of the ruling elite. The history and development of trade unionism, industrial relations, and the political system in Jamaica is far different from that of Tanzania, which, at that time, seemed to be the source of the models of many of our policy and project experiments. Worker participation was established in Tanzania by Presidential Circular[137] and encompassed the establishment of Worker's Councils, Executive Committees and Boards of Directors with the intention of giving full effect to the principle of worker involvement – in aspects of enterprise management such as planning, productivity, quality improvement, marketing, wages and incomes policy arrangements, and, indeed, even the consideration of the balance sheets of their enterprises.

To Jamaican trade unions, worker participation represented the strong possibility, if not the real threat, of diminished representational status and influence at the workplace, and ultimately at the national level. Supposed state benevolence, in this instance, was viewed as suspiciously as the promised 'future benefits', to come from 'present-sacrifices'.

Given the non-ideological orientation of the majority of the island's trade unions, the definition of their role in the Emergency Production Plan as requiring that they forego rivalry, "... which debilitates the working-class movement [which should] be replaced with coordinated efforts to address the wider political needs of the working class, to consolidate and win further rights and to raise their level of consciousness"[138], was certainly forward looking.

In that political context, however, it was probably premature and smacked of what one may term "mission exuberance". The specification of the "wider political needs", and the substance of the "further rights" to be won, is avoided, in a context giving rise to some concern, since the economic reconstruction project, "... implies that workers and their organisations have a responsibility for avoiding unnecessary disruption of the production process".[139]

It goes without saying, that what is perceived to constitute "unnecessary disruptions" , is precisely what distinguishes the vested interest positions of organised labour, as against that of the capitalist classes.

The rejection of the IMF strategy in favour of the "People's Plan", in 1977, would no doubt have involved more, rather than less austerity, certainly in the short term. Contradictions in Plan objectives and between objectives and the structure of the economy were such that it was recognized that any hope for realization of the Plan's technical possibilities rested on the, "... most courageous and tenacious effort at political education, political organization and political mobilization."[140]

Any such popular political mobilization might have had to face the opposition of the World Bank, said to be, "... in the forefront of the West's attempt to crush it".[141] The Bank's criticisms against governments that fail to establish mechanisms for public participation and consultation, in policy formulation, is consequently seen by Hayter, as a "most flagrant bit of hypocrisy".[142]

Unfortunately for the Plan's task force, if for no one else, the changes in attitudes, values and patterns of behaviour necessary for implementation would undoubtedly have proved overwhelming for both a government lacking the requisite confidence and political will and the governed, yet to develop a sense of long-term commitment to a 'mission' and which functioned notoriously on the basis of a short-time perspective.

It is appropriate to note, in this connection, Aldith Brown's observation that the continuing central problem of planning, "presuming that a competitive model of the political process is maintained", is failure to mobilize less than half of the electorate in a commitment to the search for long term solutions.[143]

Following the No-IMF decision by the PNP's National Executive in 1978, a government in power for six years, in having the state of the economy assessed in detail, only then discovered that after more than three hundred years of slavery, colonialism, and imperialism, the economy was deeply "locked" into the world capitalist system.[144]

The people having been exhorted to "Stand Firm" for a PNP non-IMF Third Term[145], the Government's team of planners were now being forced to admit that a dramatic turnaround was unlikely during the Plan period and further that there could well be aggravated economic deterioration.[146] It is evident that planners, particularly those from academia, are not as afflicted with "election-myopia", as their colleagues in the political directorate.

But not surprisingly, the more limited the interest groups from which legitimacy is normally sought, by their participation in the planning process, the greater the likely need for external support. And where the groups excluded include the marginalized, "... the external support will have to be financial if patronage and welfare are to continue".[147]

In the absence of the anticipated external support, and in the midst of austerity and deepening and creeping poverty, the 'calls for sacrifice' and 'worker restraint' is fundamentally contradicted by the "proliferation of stereotypical imagery" [especially through highly popular televised soap operas] which sets up unrealistic pictures of life and life opportunities.[148]

Jamaica's, and the economies of other (British) Caribbean states, are institutionally constrained by the dual legacies of the British colonial experience: a strong and relatively independent economistically-oriented trade union movement and multi-party-political rivalry,[149] which generate tendencies towards stability. The influences of cultural penetration through developments in mass communications may not mediate, by suppressing conflict, as suggested by Aggrey Brown, but might well provoke the outrage and non-conformity so feared by the ruling class.[150]

"It is not", Girvan observes, "that violence is alien to the Jamaican way of life", since – he continues in similar vein as those of the Caribbean intelligentsia, then in the radical New World Group – the society was "conceived in bloodshed and held together by official violence and the threat of it". Violence thus, Girvan concludes, "... comes naturally to a people whose historic womb is the organised brutality of the slave plantation".[151]

Escalating violence in the late 1960's, it was felt, was to be explained by the fact that comparatively spectacular national income growth was accompanied by a less than optimal use of the available labour force. Unemployment was apparently acceptable as a fact of life, in Girvan's view.[152] Had not the safety value of migration to Britain been then available, one is left to speculate as to what the social and political consequences might have been.

The economics of the New Right may be said to complete the vicious circle, relating high and persisting unemployment levels to inner city, and, indeed, society-wide crime and other social problems.

Although the PNP steadily retreated to the ideological centre ground, it never officially abandoned socialism. "It therefore never vacated the left-wing position in the political spectrum for an active socialist (sic) to move into"[153] – hence the peculiar sensation felt by the doctrinally aware that, especially after the "IMF election" of 1980, there existed a vacuum in the political system,[154] occupied by an ideologically embarrassed party that was however, no less electorally ambitious. This vacuum was not effectively filled for long by the "rhetorical investments" by Manley in the 1970's,[155] despite the fact that a "large section of the masses are susceptible to being easily verbally mesmerized",[156] – the less understood the content of the message. It is this fact which explains the major liberal concern that popular mobilization, in the absence of formal or informal institutional provisions for political education and the inculcation of discipline, may simply result in, "… replacing authoritarian regimes of the right with totalitarian ones from the left".[157]

From an historical perspective, by the late nineteen-fifties, any meaningful ideological differentiation between the two major political parties had largely disappeared. There was hardly an identifiable, action-oriented group existing whose transformative potential was worth assessing as a catalyst for structural change.[158] This is discounting the armchair radicals and academic revolutionaries who were comfortable in their reliance on the revolutionary class consciousness of "anonymous discontented masses".[159] What groups there were, tended to be led by members of the middle-class intelligentsia who are inclined to "talk about the people but. (they) do not trust them".[160] This observation is not without significance in the context of Stone's assessment that there has been no really serious social unrest or political upheaval, unlike the case in so many other countries in the wider Caribbean basin and Latin America, despite the comparable prolonged economic hardships experienced by virtually all groups[161] in Jamaica, save and except the really well-off.

One suspects that the zeal to revolt has been tempered by the misadventure of Democratic Socialism of the 1970's, when those who were,

> "… conscious of social evils and [were no doubt] sincerely anxious to remove them merely managed to … set up a new department … invent a new name to express their resolution to effect something more drastic than reform and less disturbing than revolution".[162]

Apart from that, Stone sees the capacity for "crisis management" by both the PNP and JLP governments,[163] as being a large part of the reason for the absence of political turmoil. Further research needs to focus on such factors as: the degree of the secularization of protest experience, in keeping with levels of modernization and differentiation which have occurred in the society; the access of groups, most disturbed by social and economic changes, to the corridors of power responsible for influencing the determination of social policy;[164] the overlap of sectional interests and lines of cleavage, especially given the tradition of multi-class party political alliances and the accompanying feature of clientelism; the degree of cultural invasion,[165] and the kind and extent of foreign infiltration and intervention likely in support of, or opposition to, protest groups. For it is factors such as these that would be decisive in determining the outcome of large scale revolt.[166] What Smelser regards as "one key to political stability", which is "the practice of flexible policies behind the facade of an inflexible commitment to a national mission", is what the IMF's/World Bank's programmes ought, optimally perhaps, to have been – but very conspicuously were not.

"Successful" crisis management has not substantially reduced inequality nor ameliorated misery. Indeed, that the opposite is the case is the fact urged by Honderich as the explanation, and possible justification, for engagement in political violence.[167]

Apart from ideological considerations, the failure of both major political parties to mount a fundamental challenge to the inherited socio-economic system is due not to strategy constraints only, but also to the "pragmatics of electoralism" – the fear of having to face one's own tactics in the hands of "the enemy", when government/opposition roles are reversed.[168] And, additionally, to that failure, conspicuous after 1972, to prepare themselves while in opposition, for the demands of government by adequate alternative policy consideration and formulation. The words of Miliband, in relation to the British Labour Party, that, "... what they were usually trying to discover in their discussions was not a policy for the future but a form of words for the present",[169] can quite fittingly be applied to both the PNP and JLP, as opposition parties, under the IMF.

And this scenario is not improved by the nature of internal party politics under a *de facto* Prime Ministerial dictatorship. In the absence of a considered and shared vision of society grounded in well thought out policies and programmes, career political! progress is likely to depend to a great extent on loyalty to the leader; not "rocking the boat"; not "giving aid and comfort to the other side"; but instead, indulging in "a show of unity", rather than independence – all of which effectively neutralizes any serious radical challenge to the established party leadership. This is especially so, given the patronage capability of the party leader, in the position of Prime Minister, under the Westminster model, and the attraction of the prospective power and glory of high political office to potential dissenters within the party's ranks.

Honderich, contrary to much popular sentiment, not only sees the rules of democracy as "means for securing ends", but, further, as a consequence, argues that political violence – a general justification of which is not here suggested – may certainly "serve the larger ends of freedom and equality", by being instrumental, "… only in the coercion of persuasion".[170]

Some violence, Honderich concludes, being an attempt to more closely approach the democratic ideal of an equality of social influence, thus makes it true to say – "not without dismay"—that, "… some bombs are like votes",[171] It can hardly be disputed that countries now considered models of democratic practice had their fair share of "democratic violence". Almost all the countries of Western Europe had their revolutions of one kind or another, not to mention the American War of Independence and Civil War. Indeed, for Locke, the right of revolution was the only recourse considered available to turn out an unsatisfactory government to those who qualified as members of civil society,[172] which privileged persons did not include the labouring classes since,

> "… the labourer's share (of the national income) being seldom more than a bare subsistence never allows that body of men, time or opportunity to raise their thoughts above that, or struggle with the richer for theirs (as one common interest) unless when some common and great distress, uniting them in one universal ferment, makes them forget respect, and emboldens them to their wants with armed force: and then sometimes they break in upon the rich, and sweep all like a deluge".[173]

Not since the labour upheavals of the 1938 era has anything remotely approaching Locke's scenario of a "common and great distress" and its consequences, materialized in Jamaica. In Stone's view, this is undoubtedly because,

> "… the social history of the lower strata is one of cultural subordination – the result of several factors, socio-economic and political; low education; rigid stratification patterns leading to low levels of self-confidence; dependence on patron-client relationships[174] for a livelihood; employment conditions that are not only physically unsatisfactory but that are psychologically demoralising; and human relations based largely on authoritarianism and paternalism".[175]

The traditional party-supporter clientelistic relationship has had the effect of channelling working- class loyalty to the party rather than to the class, thus diffusing the revolutionary expression of political alienation, as the enemy becomes identified not as the capitalist- employer and his state representative, but accessible supporters of the rival party.[176] Comparatively speaking, there has been a shortage of spoils for distribution under prolonged IMF austerity programmes, with their major emphasis on reducing the degree of state intervention in the economy and, concomitantly, the level of public expenditure. Thus, one of the unrecognized benefits of the association with the Fund and Bank – unacknowledged, because of the highly sensitive nature of the issue, socially and politically – has been the significant reduction in the level of the politics of patronage.

Contrary to Marx's dictum that the party of the workers should be independent from, and opposed to all other classes, the Jamaican party-political system has been characterized – for the reasons already referred to in the works of Stone, Norris, and Stephens and Stephens, in particular – by the very opposite feature: namely, multiple class alliances. And, as parties of workers become diluted by membership spanning all classes, the principle of class conflict between different "internally cohesive collectivities" – each comprising persons with a natural affinity of interests, social, economic, political and cultural – becomes compromised.[177]

Significantly for the Jamaican left, represented by academic intellectuals, such as the late Professor George Beckford,

> "The articulation of socio-economic order which depends on cementing a worker-peasant[178] alliance to administer and direct the society's resources demands critical inputs from the professional and technical strata of the middle class, the state bureaucracy, and the *patriotic capitalist* [italics added] class. It can be safely assumed that once foreign capital is driven out, a large part of the comprador capitalists (i.e. big national capitalists) will depart".[179]

Marxian analysis suggests that the political *status quo* is only maintainable, against the threat, or even the actual use, of force and the ideological commitment of the administrators of the existing system, by the division of the majority into a larger, lower and smaller middle-class element. However, one finds that instead of "the revolutionary call for polarization as a strategy of change", one witnesses instead an emphasis on, "… liberal encomiums to consensus",[180] as a panacea for all the society's ills.

Przeworski concluded, in fact, that in a multi-class party situation, "substantive as against rhetorical opposition to the bourgeoisie could be little more than symbolism".[181] It might be argued, indeed, that Jamaica witnessed little more in the way of attempted radical social transformation than Manley's "rhetorical investments"[182] and, such as they were, those were confined to the 1970's, before his "great (ideological) transformation ."[183]

The lack of confidence in the masses, which explains the persistent self-contradictory proposal for a transformative inter-class collaboration, which is to include patriotic capitalists, is rationalized in Freire's view by cultural invasion – under which the values and attitudes of inferiority are transmitted and also, the manipulation by symbols. The perceived necessity for inter-class unity in action arises because of that failure of sincere and frank party dialogue with the people, while in opposition,[184] the absence of which is the main reason for the continuing policy-paralysis feature of the island's politics.

De-radicalization of the workers and the lower classes, generally, through class coalitions, has meant the deflection of concern towards strategies for personal survival of one sort or the other rather than to the search for collective solutions to social problems on a national level – a development aided and abetted by the role played by the trade union movement, to be discussed later. It is something of a paradox that the existence of multi-class alliances would seem to coincide with, and facilitate the emergence and application of the free market theory whose major achievements, in Britain at least, in cultural and ideological terms, are said to be the,

> "... giving (of) sustenance to a political language articulated around the celebration at the level of ideas, of the pleasures of the individual and private life, on the one hand, and the economic and social beneficence of the culture of enterprise on the other."[185]

As is not at all unusual, Jamaica appears to have reaped the disadvantages of free market doctrines without benefiting noticeably from its reputed advantages. This is even as there has been, at the end of the 1980's, a,

> "... significant rupturing of the progress and popularity of free market theory – especially in those societies, such as Britain, which have been host to its most thorough-going political application".[186]

Despite this evidence, with the encouragement and 'moral support' of the IMF/World Bank, the Government is determined "to stay the (IMF) course", as the current Minister of Finance, the seventh since the engagement with the Fund in 1977, chooses to put it.

But rather than any celebration of the pleasures of the individual, at the level of ideas or otherwise, the responses to Fund/Bank sponsored, and Government implemented, deregulation and Liberalization within the context of neo-liberal demand management economics, have been various and markedly different: substantial migration,[187] (Levitt's "misery index") involving the Loss of the more ambitious with their skills and capital, and often leaving behind the grave social consequences of children bought up in the absence of one and sometimes both parents; the use of informal networks of collective self-help through mutual exchange and aid which, at that time, according to Smith represents, "... more assistance ... to more people in need than the total structure of official and voluntary social services together";[188] the receipt of remittances from friends, but more so relatives, abroad – one of the most profitable, rapidly expanding, and competitive services offered by the financial sector in recent years; official programmes of poverty amelioration – belatedly recognized as an important antidote to the dislocations of the structural adjustment process – ironically, "serving the ends of conquest" as, in Freire's view,[189] they act as an anesthetic, distracting from the causes of, and solutions to the problems of the oppressed", and therefore essentially represent another of the many "instruments of manipulation" (although, as Stone notes, the degree of poverty and inequality [and weaknesses of the tax system] are such as to provide an insufficient income base to sustain a worthwhile social security system); increasing participation in the insecure low-wage, non-unionized, small business and informal petty commodity sector, which represents "ingrained capitalism among the poor and reflects their aggressive survival strategies of creating self-employment in petty-trading, farming, artisan production and services in the face of an economy that, since the 1960's, has displayed a very low propensity to create enough jobs to meet the social needs of a growing population";[190] the increasing incidence of public begging by the young and able-bodied, not to mention the physically and mentally impaired, of all age groups of both sexes, in direct contradiction to the principle that, "self-esteem is essential for national development"; and a marked increase in the female labour force participation rate in relatively low paying, non-unionized work.[191]

By virtue of the above partial catalogue of responses to the prolonged economic crisis, it is clear that discontent by no means necessarily leads to revolt. Aya usefully focuses, therefore, not on collective militant resistance in reaction to

tensions between classes, or between classes and the state, but rather on the, "...
rational satisfying choices human agents make in given conjunctural situations",[192]
in assessing the potential for revolutionary change in specific contexts.

It may be agreed with Salamon that, within the limited context of the industrial
relations system,

> "... the open expression of conflict is an important element in the
> maintenance of stability [in that] it provides the means for identifying
> and balancing different interests...."[193]

With the various forms that the expression of conflict may take, it is
essential that for the purposes of remedial policy-formulation, the full range of
likely responses to the unrelieved economic crisis be individually considered. This
is of some importance since, "... not all conflicts are capable of containment
and absorption by the social structures which give rise to them".[194] As a result,
the effective communication of specific discontent, when suppressed as a less than
legitimate class message, is likely to find expression in, "... a more dispersed an/or
individual manner,[195] with a much-reduced level of predictability and therefore less
susceptibility to institutionalized control".

Some dissatisfied groups, for example, seek to "alleviate their hardships and
express their discontent through flight, or sectarian withdrawal", referred to, by
Munroe, as the option of some oppressed who either, ",,emigrated or sublimated."[196]
Other behaviour may take the form of activities that minimize challenges to, or
clashes with, those whom they view as their oppressors, since rebellion is one of
the "least likely consequences of exploitation". And when rebellion does occur, the
subject matter in the Jamaican context – in which there is not yet even a consciousness
of "a class in itself" – tends to be personal, even if supported by the immediate
community. Further, its scope is often localized, amounting to what Munroe refers
to as, "... individual aggressiveness and ... crowd disorderless so typical of Jamaican
peasant behaviour ...".[197]

Any such manifestation of aggressiveness, however, from the first half of the
1980's would probably not have been directed by an explicit-political intention. In
the absence of overt social protest such behaviour was contained by a pervasive mood
of cynicism, and hopelessness. This development in the country's politics should
not, in retrospect, have been unexpected. Under the IMF/World Bank tutelage, the
state became increasingly perceived as an agent of local and foreign capital vested-

interests and dominance, generating different-forms of resistance, rather than willing compliance, but failing, contrary to Parenti's prediction, to, "... activate a revolutionary class consciousness."[198] Under "... the impact of harsh economic austerity the idea of a just, egalitarian society within the framework of parliamentary democracy and a new international economic order," was, according to Carrington,

> " ... eventually to become a four-letter word, not fit for discussion at respectable gatherings as a consequence of which the guiding ethical notion of social justice has been increasingly discredited ...".[199]

Consent to the nature of existing social relations is thus tentative, and since the "end of ideology" is certainly a misconception, there will always exist "material limits beyond which consent will be withdrawn." This will leave open the door to social crises, despite the extremes which deprivation and suffering may have to attain – given the society's plantation/colonial authoritarian social and cultural traditions – before the boundaries of alienation are crossed and the arena of action is entered.

Distress, being a matter allied to expectations, is less of a motivator to those who have not anticipated anything else. It is, thus, not "some congenital inability" to take responsibility for the determination of the basic direction of the nation's social and economic affairs which explains the docility of the mass public, "... in a situation crying out for militancy",[200] but, instead the fact that, contrary to the faulty analysis of the Peoples Plan, the people, being deprived of power, may well take psychological refuge from feelings of helplessness by simply losing interest in gaining activist political power that is necessary for effective social control.

The docility of the working class and the marginalized can be better understood by recognizing the uncertainty of outcome which always accompanies the revolutionary project, particularly in a context where socialization into the dictates of British constitutionalism has been such that politicization of the security forces is limited to the extent of the bandwagon-effect of the swings in party political popularity. Further, there is unlikely to be any lapse, even temporary, in the monitoring diplomatic vigilance of the geographically omnipresent hegemonic power to the north and the creditor institutions under its influence, if not control.

The loss of any sense of "collective conscience" – never highly developed at the best of times, given the island's social and cultural history – due to a deepening individualistic orientation with increasing urbanization, has been even more pronounced under the materialistic ethic of the free market doctrine. This is made worse by the acute shortage of productive wealth-creating means for achieving socially valued goals. The result has been that with the awesome gap existing at times between wage levels and the trend in inflation, significant numbers of the unemployed, ultimately to become unemployable, refuse employment altogether in favour of "a way of life separated as far as possible from the discipline of industrialism", if not from its useful products. Not surprisingly, the condition of anomie experienced by a substantial section of the poorer classes manifests itself in various patterns of anti-social conflict behaviour: violence of a political, criminal, and domestic nature; crimes against property – including a growing white-collar element; a generally crude and aggressive behaviourial disposition; and an accompanying insensitivity to other people's problems, which precludes the "concern for remote objects" that is necessary for mass action in furtherance of a common cause.

The IMF has led, it has been contended, to, "... the consolidation and enlargement of the militant lumpen stratum which articulates [by word and conduct] many of the social antagonisms which exist in Jamaican society...".[201] But as Kirton reports on the responses to his interviews,

> "... the frightening thing that we are seeing here, in Jamaica, and in the rest of the Third World, is that you cannot put a face onto the oppression. Now it's just the rule of the market Its not ideological anymore you have no way of identifying anybody as culpable. It's all been very much depoliticized".[202]

Politics being increasingly removed, in the tradition of Hayek, from macroeconomic management, by the transfer of decision-making to the market place, and the IMF being a faceless abstraction in Washington,[203] has had the effect of making the "closest enemy" another member of the disadvantaged classes.[204] For that segment of the population for whom misplaced aggression on an interpersonal level was a manifestation of an insufficient outlet for their deep and often subconscious feelings of anger and distress at the country's, and their own, social and economic circumstances, the Kirton interviews would have represented a rare opportunity to be heard, other than by their peers. The Interviews were intended to indicate,

> "... how Jamaicans in almost every sector of society have been affected by rising prices and collapsing living standards. ... They tell of a grim daily struggle to pay for food, clothing and transportation [not to mention housing, health care and education] – even on the part of

people who ten years ago would have been considered middle class and comfortably off".[205]

If the mass public has been incapable of identifying the proper target (s) for resistance and has instead been overwhelmed by the demands of the struggle to survive, what then of the role played by the institution one would expect to be most sensitive to the concerns and interests of the working class and their families, namely, the trade unions?

To begin with, the assessment was made over a decade ago, that,

> "... the IMF programme clearly contributed to dissolving the class alliance which formed the basis of the PNP's political support, discrediting the governments's record of performance and undermining its authority - key elements in this alliance adopted a disillusioned and eventually hostile position".[206]

It should be noted, that the observations apply with equal validity to the successive political administrations, as indicated by opinion polls and election results in 1980, 1983 and 1989.[207] It will be readily recognized that such a disintegrative development in the nature of the politics of the island fitted conveniently the anti-statist/pro-private sector, free market paradigm that, was to become doctrinally dominant as the preferred plith to economic recovery and development, with the Friedman- inspired abandonment and disparagement of the Keynesian "consensus", under "Thatcherism" and "Reaganomics".

The hegemonic status and profitability of the private sector became increasingly enshrined as fundamentals of free market economic ideology with the simultaneous decline in the countervailing role and power of trade unions. This decline has occurred on two levels: individually, with respect to the two major unions in the determination of social and economic policy over their own political party affiliate, when in government, and also as representatives of the labour movement and prospective participants in the tripartite determination of national economic and social policy, regardless of the party which happened to constitute the nation's political directorate. Thus, from the late 1970's onwards,

> "... the (IMF stabilization) measures had the effect of strengthening those very social forces which opposed the attempts of the (sic) changing the traditional power relations in the society."[208]

The understatement of the potency of such forces had been one of the central, but self-servingly espoused, myths[209] in the so-called "march" to independence.[210]

As it became increasingly impossible for the society to "disguise its internal contradictions",[211] to, "... that extent·was strain applied to the umbilical cord attaching and separating the major unions and political parties.

The "business unionism" orientation of the trade unions was to assume the posture, under IMF wage guidelines, demand compression austerity and public and private sector retrenchment, not of struggle for structural economic and social transformation in favour of labour, but rather, competition among themselves over labour's declining share of the national product. One can be certain that in most instances where the owners and managers of enterprises appeared generous in their concessions to labour the true reason, as Currie has pointed out, was probably, "... because the dangers to social stability ... have not been [completely] lost on the corporate community...".[212] Hence, one witnesses substantially greater expenditure on company sponsorship of popular mass activities in the sports and cultural areas, and the attempt to make its place morally secure, or at least acceptable, in the new politico-economic dispensation, through such public relations strategies as the "Adopt a School Scheme" and other such highly publicised, gestures. This at the same time as these seemingly "patriotic nationalist capitalists" further protect themselves with "... 'true insurance' for the creditor banks against (third world debt) repudiation, in the form of their foreign deposits",[213] A debtor-country cartel to make repudiation feasible is therefore, unlikely,[214] for the additional reason that the 'divide and rule' hegemonic regime entrenchment policy still persists at the head tables of the institutions of international finance. Further, the deceptively appealing competition which prevails for scarce foreign capital and aid, guarantees a lack of third world unity but also the entry of transnational investments on highly subsidized terms.

The elevation of the private sector by the state as 'the engine of growth', under Fund/Bank deregulation and liberalization – like everything else that confers benefits – has a price. While certain conflicts have to be tolerated to ensure a minimum level of social cohesion essential for system maintenance, "at the same time the effect of hegemony is that only certain conflicts become organized," in which case, in Gramsci's phrase, "... democracy provides the trenches".[215]

The attitudes and tactics of trade unions have become less differentiated with increasing state/private sector economic policy collaboration. This precludes a radical structural assault[216] on the faults of the existing system of social and economic relations. And the nature and scope of dissent has been determined by, and accommodated within, the macro-economic policy continuity consequent on the loss of substantive sovereignty by the local political directorate. Policy-makers, in the guise of advisers, experts and consultants in Washington, who, understandably, do not see their role as that of, "... starting social revolutions,"[217] have been the seemingly reluctant "beneficiaries" of this abdication.

With the absence of a radical paradigm that seeks to provide other than traditional answers as to how the lower classes should cope with state/capitalistic power, in times which provide less than ideal revolutionary conditions,[218] the search for solutions ought, it would seem, to begin with an ideological situational analysis, not unduly biased by a commitment to any of the "several versions of utopia".[219]

But the Jamaican citizen, Manley has said, "... is not naturally at home to ideas." One would scarcely expect the chief protagonist of Democratic Socialism to be the source of the further statement that,

> "... one of the tragedies of the post-colonial period is that third world countries have permitted themselves the luxury of ideological distraction."[220]

That those claiming to be radicals from the middle class intellectual elite have not served the lower classes well, in contrast to Lenin, in *What is to be Done,* for example, is further illustrated by Meeks' conclusions as to the Caribbean region's revolutionary potential, to the effect that,

> "... even if there is no map for the road ahead ... process of groping ... possibility of a better polity, of humble people playing a greater role in social life ... the open-ended agenda of human history".[221]

Middle class adventurist leadership, in the guise of radicalism, was exposed for what it was and is by Beckford and Witter, who observed that, "the party (PNP) had galvanized an alliance of the dispossessed but did not provide a positive plan for change" – its "Power for the People" slogan "reflects that, party's elitist conception of its fitness to rule deriving from colonial days"; and so, according to the authors, Manley, who, in December of 1976 had declared to the world that "We are the masters in our house, in our house there shall be no masters but ourselves" had, by March 1977, "... turned in the opposite direction and sold Jamaica to imperialism and its central bank, the IMF".[222] As Henry remarked, contemporaneously,

"... they (Caribbean ideological patterns) attract favourable mass response if only for the reason that they denounce the *status quo* and advocate its destruction. Revolutionary, concepts, protest and dissent are indeed therapeutic to poverty and frustration".[223]

In stark contrast to Manley's position, and Henry's assessment, Lenin, in, *What is to be done?* sees the necessity for petit bourgeois intellectuals to provide the ideological foundation for disciplined, focused action, as without a revolutionary theory there can be no revolutionary movement. There should be no doubt, that a non-ideologically polarizing, monolithic, IMF-imposed consensus will be such as to, "... exclude the articulation of any radical options."[224] And since the ideology of the ruling class is adopted, in large measure, by the subordinate classes, including most importantly, the 'conception of the enemy' and the nature of the role assigned to themselves,[225] *traditional* working class parties tend simply to become agents of the prevailing hegemonic order. As Anderson suggests, "... their degeneration is the obverse of their potential for social transformation".[226]

But the Marxist-Leninist parties of the region self-destructed in Grenada and lost all credibility in Guyana and Jamaica as a result of the indulgence in what some saw as a, "... loose combination of (borrowed) emotive and impressionistic cliches",[227] by Caribbean ideologues, of whom Best was to remark, "They too, one fears, are merely idling their resources away in impractical rhetoric".[228]

It is perhaps this lack of the development of an indigenous ideological tradition that has hindered the emergence of a collective consciousness among the working and marginalized classes and, "... prevented, outside isolated incidents, the politicization of industrial militancy".[229] As Tawney might have put it, the IMF/ World Bank's autocracy is yet to be, "... checked by insurgence".[230]

With the ideological teeth of the purportedly radical regional parties being pulled by *glasnost* and *perestroika*, and given the pain involved in 'keeping the faith', as is very apparent in Cuba, a plausible self-extrication from the disintegration of the Soviet system has proved difficult to the point of having terminal consequences in several cases, including the communist Workers' Party of Jamaica. Against the background of the nature of the island's trade union development, there has thus been little ideological offensive against IMF free market doctrines, except in the most apologetic fashion. The strident-voices that have been raised have been few, have not charted a course of action based on a strategy of confrontation and assault, and have thus amounted to little more than voices in the wilderness. Indeed, from as far back as 1980, activist academic intellectual supporters of the

Democratic Socialist path had confessed, despite having contributed to, and even participated in, the formulation of the Emergency Production Plan, that Manley's continuous engagement in discussions and consultations with the trade union leaders had the effect of communicating to them, "... that the alternative to the IMF programme would be widespread unemployment, acute shortages, and virtual economic collapse".[231]

This assessment of the undefined "third path" by the leader of the Democratic Socialist project, who, nevertheless insisted that, "... there must be a better way"[232] (than the IMF strategy for recovery) was hardly facilitative of political ideological commitment, since as Cohen suggests,

> "Political ideologies if they are to work, in the sense of carrying the persuasive force of common sense, must also construct narratives which convince us that the promises they make not only articulate our real wishes, but also possess the means to ensure that they will come true, so that we too will live happily ever after – at least until the next election".[233]

Conspicuous failure, under IMF policy guidance, to deliver on their rhetoric, of whatever variety, by both political parties when given the reins of government has, of course, in a traditionally patronage- based polity, "generated its own crisis of credibility", even among the parties' "most natural supporters". This largely explains, in the Jamaican situation, the prospective social transformer's instinctive fear of staking his fortune on a worsening of the crisis. As Przeworski predicts,[234]

> "... they offer the compromise; they maintain and defend it. [To the would-be reformer] It is better for the working class to be exploited than to create a situation which contains the risk of turning against them".[235]

Nevertheless, the substantive merits of a highly competitive, finely balanced, multi-party-political system, in terms of its social outcomes, has only seriously been questioned by the doctrinally innocent mass public since the paradigmatic entrenchment of structural adjustment.

The economics of liberalization and deregulation imposed and/or embraced in the apparently agreed absence of an "alternative", as the PNP "made peace with capitalism", after years of "ideological posturing", has meant the conquest of the terrain of ideological conflict by the self-proclaimed politically neutral IMF/World Bank version of economic theory. This has found expression in the narrowing of differences between the main parties on ideology and policy – a development which the public has not failed to observe.[236] Effectively, this eliminates the element of real choice from the system of electoral representation and, at the same time, even further consolidates the hegemony of capital by aiding the establishment and maintenance of political stability essential for the maintenance of a climate conducive to the existence of 'business confidence'.

Increasingly, capitalists seek to be guaranteed, and are being allowed to extract, profits free from exposure to risks of any kind whatsoever in developing countries, at least, especially those desperate for foreign investment, given the low national savings rates. Risk here includes even the adverse consequences of serious social protest and unrest in those territories which depend on the fragile tourist industry as a major source of badly needed foreign exchange earnings. It matters little to policy makers, so-called experts and advisors from the international financial institutions that low levels of internal savings and the unfavourable trade balance, owe their deterioration to precisely those policies of demand management and import liberalization prescribed by them as essential for economic recovery.

One can still expect praise for having the courage to 'stay the course' of unpopular policy decisions; IMF and World Bank praise which has not failed to make market converts of former reputedly radically inclined Ministers of Finance. One gets the impression that with the high casualty rate among Ministers holding this pivotal portfolio under the IMF/World Bank stabilization and economic adjustment, it may well be thought that survival is not unrelated to paying homage to these multi-lateral institutions.

Again, one is compelled to inquire, what of the role and influence of worker organizations in mediating between the working class on the one hand and capital and the state[237] on the other? If Galenson was correct, then the island's social and political history would no doubt have been markedly different. He saw the range of leadership forms that were likely to emerge in developing countries as, rather strangely, limited to a variant of Marxism, being either "indigenous radicalism" or "the local branch of World Communism".[238] That this has not been the Jamaican experience is partly due to the colonial heritage. As Cross and Heuman see it,

> "The Labour Department (in the Caribbean) was the institutionalization of the colonial approach to trade unionism, namely to paternalistically

organize labour and encourage 'responsible' labour leaders in order to control the labour movement. The British TUC worked closely with labour advisors of the Colonial Office and various Labour Departments in the colonies to propagate 'responsible' trade unionism by stressing the separation between industrial disputes and militant industrial action",[239] [which ignores the fact, out of ideological convenience that, as Anderson recognizes, the nature of the economy as a system is a highly political issue".]

So that despite having a reputation for militancy bestowed upon them, quite undeservedly,[240] by the rival forces with which they contend Caribbean trade unions have been largely apolitical in outlook. They have fought over 'bread and butter' issues at the micro-level, almost exclusively, tinkering with the "observational details" of capitalism, rather than engaging in its systemic confrontation. It may indeed be true, in this context, that, "... where there is no vision, the people perish".[241] For trade unions being an incomplete and deformed embodiment of a variant of class-consciousness – a proposition to be further considered – they,

"... resist unequal distribution (of the surplus) by wage demands but (they) ratify it by their existence ... a passive reflection of the organization of the workforce ... they merely express the existence of society based on a division of classes (which) has the crucial consequence that their maximum weapon is absence (i.e. strike), (but) the efficiency of this form of action is by nature very limited".[242]

There in fact has been no case of widespread protest demonstrations or even a general strike – from that in Britain in 1926 through those in Jamaica (1978/85) Haiti, Dominican Republic, Chile, Argentina, Brazil, Bolivia (1980's) and Barbados, Nigeria, Panama and Turkey, more recently, in revolt against IMF stabilization policy issues or other circumstances – ever succeeding in overthrowing a socially and politically repressive regime. One important reason is that trade unions on their own produce only a sectoral 'corporate' consciousness and power-potential, as against a universal one. The labour movement thus permits and facilitates a distortion of working-class consciousness by its limited focus on immediate, parochial problems,[243] which is explained but not justified by the class differentiation and fragmentation[244] that has been a feature of the changes accompanying the elaboration of the process of industrialization.

This has been a defining characteristic of the change process in capitalist society, which has enhanced the power of the dominant social and economic classes.

A diffusion of consciousness and a lack of class cohesion makes the assimilation and internalization of 'necessary' constraints, and controls[245] and notions of 'proper' managerial perogatives easier to accept, to an extent that lessens the need to resort, more than infrequently and subtly, to potentially more disruptive coercive means of achieving compliance.

The worker, after all, is always 'free; to leave the job and to 'choose' to be unemployed; courses of action not infrequently resorted to in an environment where the range and degree of trade union action is constrained by institutional inadequacies. Action is also precluded by the absence of a guiding vision of 'the good society', essential in a country where the problems faced are certainly not, as Bierce in the Devils Dictionary would phrase it, "... a file provided for the teeth of the rats of reform".[246]

But trade union leadership cannot be expected to set the pace and tone and determine the structure of action, without some measure of deference to their members general level of consciousness and the "potential for reform inherent in the objective situation". The development of the collective sense of consciousness of being a "class for itself " is dependent on the shared experience of struggles that are at the same time economic, political and ideological.[247]

But legislative restrictions, the competition for jobs in a labour-surplus economy with increasing market differentiation in a class/status-conscious society, and a cultural legacy of slavery and colonialism which promoted self-serving individualistic as against a collectivist action-orientation, together ensure that the leadership of the labour movement can look forward to little widespread sustained commitment towards revolutionary industrial action.

Factors that cannot escape consideration in any attempt to assess the island's potential for social transformation include: the current demobilizational role of partisan political representation under IMF-type adjustment policies; the mass publics' socialized predisposition to pragmatism; the strength of tendencies towards self-reliance; how amenable the majority of the population is to the discipline of political education; the residual consequences of clientelistic patronage-based politics, after the scourge of planned and sustained austerity; the extent to which the purported infallibility of free market doctrines, in ensuring the achievement of desirable social outcomes, has been internalized by the potentially progressive social classes; and the extent to which working and lower class leadership is situationally determined, as against being based on the romanticism of those convinced that they are born with the right to rule. This last factor of the nature of institutional leadership is the more important, if one accepts Anderson's view that,

> "… outside historic trade union institutions the working class has a purely inert identity, impenetrable even to itself".[248]

Of relevance in this connection, is Hyman and Fryer's observation, somewhat in the tradition of Michels, that as trade union leaders become more like managers in terms of their class origins, education and social mobility aspirations the, "… more invincible becomes its (the trade union's) aversion to all aggressive action",[249]

Quite apart from the very questionable alleged inevitability of oligarchically-induced union conservatism, over time, Przeworski notes that,

> "The alleged deradicalization of working class movements constitutes in the eyes of the non-radical proponents of economic determinism a sufficient proof that in the course of economic development workers have themselves discovered the advantages of compromise and abandoned all thought of transformation,"[250] [a position seemingly confirmed indirectly by the Gordon study to which reference has previously been made.]

Southall places the blame for de-radicalization on features of interinstitutional development and leadership. He concludes on the performance of union leaders,

> "Ineffective to the extent that they have been unable to resist state repression, and where they have not been split along party lines, trade union leadership have cooperated with populist and/or more reactionary forms of the state to demobilize the working class and to manipulate and contain its militancy".[251]

Where they did not, or did not appear to the ruling elite to do so, as was the case in Trinidad and Tobago, they could find themselves the subject of a Commission of Inquiry established to investigate, among other matters, the existence and extent of subversive activity within the country with special emphasis on the trade union movement".[252]

Unions do, of course, act in seeking to remedy members' grievances, "… thus making their behaviour more predictable and manageable,"[253] which serves to preserve the *status quo* in that, "Resentment is not permitted to accumulate explosively".[254] As Kerr, et al., wrote some decades ago,

"... systems of industrial relations, almost universally tripartite, develop with a substantial degree of compatibility among the component parts. These systems originate and administer the 'web of rules' that comes to govern daily operations within the system. [Hence the function of the industrial relations system in "institutionalizing industrial conflict" much as parliamentary democracy institutionalizes political conflict]. The organization of the workers becomes more a part of the system than an opponent. The system is subject more to evolutionary change than to revolutionary revision".[255]

This reflects the well-known capacity for self-preservation which characterizes capitalism, manifested – contrary to Marx's deterministic expectations – by its adaptability in the accommodation of seriously threatening challenges to its hegemonic status and indeed systemic survival. As Parenti notes,

"The plutocracy rules but not always in the way it would like. From time to time, those of wealth and power must make concessions to popular resistance, giving a little in order to keep a lot, taking care that the worst abuses of capitalism do not cause people to question and then agitate against the system itself".[256]

There are those employers and managers, in both the private and public sectors who have yet to perceive the vital system-preservation function served by irritating, frustrating, challenging and often dreaded periodic labour contract negotiations. Once routinized, however, it has been argued that collective bargaining.

"... becomes an institutional habit and diverts working class energies into a never ending and never changing routine which makes no inroads into capitalist control."[257]

This, by virtue of its operation on the basis of sectionalism, as in the Jamaican context, blurs, "... any awareness of the common problems of workers inherent in capitalist work relations, which necessitate a class response".[258]

But any pessimism on the part of those concerned about the welfare of the working class and disadvantaged, should perhaps be lessened by the reminder that,

"There is a short-run logic in the formation of a class. It is that the gradual perception of common interests (that is similar relationships to the ownership and control of the means of production and similar sources of revenue) and the construction of some organizational structure(s) to advance these interests is an indispensable aspect of bargaining (which is the form that all short run struggle takes)".[259]

The struggle of the Jamaican state to overcome the inadequacies of the development strategies of import substitution industrialisation by invitation and what Farrell (and to a lesser extent Danns[260] and by implication Iqbal[261] and Harker[262]) has described as, "… a decade of profligacy, riotous living and economic mismanagement",[263] has not had felicitous results[264] for labour.

Abandonment of Keynesianism has meant that policy prescriptions to cope with inflation, balance of payments crises, and unemployment have not proceeded from a commitment to social consensus as an indispensable element in achieving a minimum level of social cohesiveness. The stabilization and structural adjustment programmes which have followed the descent into "the valley of the shadow of debt" have been implemented by imposition, despite the consultative rhetoric of, and the placatory gestures by, IMF and World Bank staff to particularly concerned interest groups, on rare and specially requested occasions.

The architects of these programmes have therefore not seen it fit to, "… incorporate consensus generating measures other than as a response to the hue and cry of resistance.[265]

It may well be the thinking, that the greater the amount of consultation, and the more gradual the process of implementation, the greater the scope and time allowed for lobbying for policy dilution, by negotiation that may be so substantial as to "compromise away" the tough/bitter/harsh medicine that is usually "necessarily" prescribe for recovery and growth; medicine that might be more easily swallowed if the adverse, if not near-fatal, side effects were not so overwhelmingly confined to the poorer classes.

But given the principles of unfettered competition which yield, allegedly, the benefits of market-determined allocation of, and returns to, the resources utilized in the production process, what might be the arguments in explanation of the IMF urging an agreement on the formulation of a social contract as far back as 1978? Harrod's response would be that,

"Third World creditors argue for the incorporatization of trade unions via the 'social democratic' slogan which, in effect, means wage restraint and incomes policies. Both are incompatible with the 'free trade unionism' [in Jamaican terminology, 'free collective bargaining'] slogan of global management in the neo-colonial period. Clearly this tactic assists in the destruction of a broader based labour movement266 by making enclaves of the very workers whose high wages, productivity and strategic position surrounding either high capital [intensive] industries or primary foreign exchange earners, make them a financial and tactical power within any labour movement".[267]

As the so-called 'labour aristocracy' is unlikely to yield to the appeal to submit to the socially levelling restraints of a social contract – whatever the merit of the arguments inherent in such a strategy of development, on the basis of egalitarianism – so too will it be greeted with indifference and cynicism by the non-unionized, the unemployed, the marginalized, the petty self-employed, and the poor and destitute. These are those who face, most devastatingly, the vagaries of individualistic materialism without a social safety net and any effective institutional representation.

Table: 32   Percentage Adopting Radical Positions and Loadings on First Unrotated Factor for Eight Attitudinal

Items in Political Radicalism Index

Items	Per Cent	Loading
1. Support the rise of new, independent union	43	.61
2. Favour more say for workers and delegates in union affairs	51	.49
3. Critical of our present unions and union officials	41	.44
4. Believe big businessmen have too much influence in government	55	.47
5. Feel that P.N.P. and J.L.P. do not sufficiently represents working class interest	56	.40
6. Oppose British and American control of our land and industries	35	.37
7. Regard the social and economic positions of local whites as a result of racial privilege	53	.36
8. Support common ownership of industry	26	.36

Source: Derek Gordon in SES Vol . 27, No. 3, ISER, UWI, Sept, 1978, p.317.

It is difficult to believe that the refuge of the ideologically neutralized – a social contract/partnership – however contrived, will be adequate to the task of defying the logic of the IMF/World Bank's own macro-economic policies, as generated by their chosen brand of economic technicism.

The absence of serious policy resistance is not. to be understood on the basis of the mediating effect of elements of the policies themselves. A more acceptable explanation is provided by Gordon's findings on the percentage of the Jamaican working class with radical inclinations.

Clearly, there has been no sufficient,

> "... breakdown of normal restraints, including the internalized standards of right conduct and established channels of action (which) frees the mass to engage in direct unmediated efforts to achieve its goals and to lay hands upon the most readily accessible instruments of action." [268]

1. Gordon Lewis, "The Challenges of Independence in the British Caribbean", in Hilary Beckles and Verene Shepherd (eds) *Caribbean Freedom,* Ian Randle Publishers, Kingston, 1993, p.515.
2. Ibid, p.515.
3. Frantz Fanon, *The Wretched of the Earth,* Penguin, 1990, p.47.
4. Lewis, 1993, pp.515-516.
5. Ibid, p.516.
6. Paul Harrison, *The Third World Tomorrow,* Penguin, 1991, p.292.
7. James Ferguson, "Pain and Protest: The 1984 Anti-IMF Revolt in the Dominican Republic", in Hilary Beckles and Verene Shepherd(eds)
8. Ibid, p.572.
9. Harrison, 1991, p.297.
10. Carlene J. Edie, *Democracy by Default: Dependency and Clientilism,* Ian Randle Publishers, Kingston, 1991, p.14.
11. Harrison, 1991, p.350. Carl Stone.
12. Clive Dobson, President of the National Workers Union, in The Money Index, No.416, May, 3, 1994, pp.10-11.
13. Carl Stone, in The Daily Gleaner, Feb. 3, 1988.
14. Edie, 1991, p.18.
15. Ibid.
16. The Don Anderson Opinion Poll reported that approximately 50% of the sample surveyed expressed no preference for either major political party – The Daily Gleaner, Mar. 12, 1995; Disillusionment with continued policy failure under the IMF led to a serious loss of credibility by both parties; Carl Stone, The Daily Gleaner, Feb. 3, 1988.
17. Edie, 1991, p. 19.
18. Ibid.
19. Ibid.
20. Ibid. p.26.
21. Ibid.
22. Ibid.
23. Ibid.
24. Ibid, p. 20.
25. Terry Smith, "Sir Walter Citrine and our history", in The Daily Gleaner, p. 8A.
26. Henry Pelling, *A History of British Trade Unionism,* Pelican, 1965, p.7.
27. Ibid, p.91.
28. Ibid, p.133.
29. Trevor Munroe, The Politics of Constitutional Decolonization, Jamaica, 1944-62 ISER, U.W.I., 1983, pp.22,39.
30. In a Carl Stone Survey in 1987, 85% of unionized workers in the survey and 92% of the non-unionized expressed disillusionment with the party union affiliation which they assessed as "not serving their class interests at all". Carl Stone "Trade Unions and Politics", The Daily Gleaner, Feb. 3, 1988.

31. Carl Stone, Class Race and Political Behaviour, in Urban Jamaica, p.** Danny Roberts, Vice President of the NWU, while accepting the correctness of the Stone survey, writing from the perspective of workers, is of the view that that perception does not accord with reality. In providing support for his position he states that while his union was not able to prevent the imposition of the wage guidelines whilst "its" party was in power, despite its most consistent opposition to the measure, the NWU was instrumented in having a number of benefits introduced "to assist workers". He further argues that the union's influence is most effectively exercised in the determination of broad policy goals and objectives, in which respect "the independent unions have a poor record ..." Danny Roberts, *Defending the link between politics, trade unions*, in The Jamaica Herald, July 11, 1994, p.6.

32. C. Y Thomas, *The Poor and the Powerless*, Monthly Review Press, 1988, P-3.

33. See George Beckford, Norman Girvan, Louis Lindsay, and Michael Witter, *Pathways to Progress, The Peoples Socialist Plan*, Jamaica, 1977, Maroon Publishing House, Jamaica, 1985.

34. George Beckford arid Michael Witter, *Small Garden ... Bitter Weed, Struggle and Change, in Jamaica*, ISER, U.W.I., Jamaica, 1980, p.150.

35. Norman Girvan, Review of The Poor and the Powerless, by C. Y Thomas, in *Social and Economic Studies*, Vol.37 No.4, 1988, University of the West Indies, p.257.

36. Ibid.

37. Carl Stone, *Power in the Caribbean Basin: A Comparative Study of Political Economy*, Philadelphia Institute for the Study of Human Issues, 1986, p.viii.

38. Carl Stone, Class State and Democracy in Jamaica, N.Y., Praegar, 1986, p.187.

39. John Laguerre, review of Carl Stone's Power in the Caribbean Basin: A Comparative Study of Political Economy, in SES Vol.39 No.2, U.W.I., 1990, p.230. In Jamaica, as elsewhere, the tendency has been to situate only parties of the left within established politico-economic frameworks. The political economy of the "New Right" is, of course, as much ideological as any version of socialism, or communism for that matter. The extent to which the philosophical foundations of a party are emphasized in propaganda and political rhetoric has, in the Jamaican case, led to questionable ideological categorization of the major parties, as betrayed by not very dissimilar fundamental policy orientations viewed comparatively over the life of the parties.

40. Stone, 1986, p.187.

41. Edie, 1991, pp.9-10.

42. Beckford and Witter 1980, Chapter 6.; Owen Jefferson, *The Post-war Economic Development of Jamaica*, ISER, U.W.I., 1972, Chapter 2.

43. Jamaica, Five Year Development Plan 1990 - 1995, PIOJ, July 30, 1995, p.7

44. Zagorka Coluboric, *The Crisis of the Yugoslav System*, Study No,14, in Research project: Crises in Soviet - type systems, Cologne: Index, p. 25.

45. Devon Brown, A Comparison of the Political Style and Ideological Tendencies of Two Leaders. Michael Manley and Edward Seaga – using Parliamentary Speeches, SES, Vol.31 No.3, U.W.I., 1982, p.202.

46. Ibid, p.209.

47. Fred Wills, Foreign Minister o, Aryana, in a speech to the Non-aligned Nations Conference at Algiers, June 1976, reported in Ralph R. Premdas, "Guyana: Socialism and Destabilization in the Western Hemisphere", CQ, Vol.25 No.3, Sept. 1979, p.25.

48. Ibid, p.35.

49. Otto Neurath, in a lecture to the Sociological Society of Vienna, 1920, in Tom Bottomore, *The Socialist Economy: Theory and Practice*, Harvester Wheatsheaf, 1990, p.24.

50. Evelyne Huber Stephens and John D.Stephens, *Democratic Socialism in Jamaica*, Princeton University Press, 1986, pp.318-45.

51. Vaughan A. Lewis, "The Caribbean in World Political/Economic Trends", in CQ, Vol.25 No.3, Sept. 1979, p.44.

52. Trevor Purcell, "Dependency and Responsibility: A View from West Indians in Costa Rica", CQ, Vol.31 Nos.3&4 Sept, to Dec. 1985.

53. Trevor Farrell, "The Caribbean State and its Role in Economic Management" in Stanley Lalta and Marie Freckleton (eds) *Caribbean Economic Development*, Ian Randle Publishers, Kingston, Jamaica, 1993, p. 207

54. Trevor Purcell, "Dependency and Responsibility: A view from West Indians in Costa Rica", CQ, Vol.31 Nos.3&4, Sept. – Dec. 1985, p.I.

55. Seymour Martin Lipset, *Political Man*, Heinemann, London, 1983, p.45.

56. Carl Stone, *Politics vs Economics: The 1939 Elections in Jamaica*, Heinimann Publishers (Caribbean) Ltd., 1989, p.5.

57. Ibid, p.11.

58. David C. Korten, in David C. Korten and Felipe B. Alfonso, *Bureaucracy and the Poor: Closing the Gap*, Kumarian Press, 1985, p.201.

59. E.J. Mishan, *The Costs of Economic Growth*, Pelican, 1969, p.36.

60. Michael Manley, *The Politics of Change*, Heinemann Publishers (Caribbean) Ltd, 1990, Chapters 2 & 5.

61. Stephens & Stephens, 1986, p.319.

62. Michael Manley, *The Poverty of Nations*, Pluto Press, 1991, p.104.

63. Ibid, Manley pp.70, 105.

64. Ibid, p.74.

65. F.E. Nunes, and Gordon Draper, *Notes on Organization and Change in the Caribbean*, Working Paper No.5, ISER, U.W.I, 1983, p.73.

66. Edie, 1991, p.97.

67. Fanon, 1990, p.47.
68. The denigration of the opposition political party its supporters, then still numbering over 40% of the electorate after the landslide PNP election victories of 1972 and 1976 as well as all other sources of opposition, individual, or institutional, as imperialist agents, traitors and unpatriotic effectively precluded such an effort. Indeed, there was the establishment of the so-called Accreditation Committee whose function was reputedly to ensure that only the doctrinally committed would be selected for employment in certain public positions.
69. Labour Relations and Industrial Disputes Act, (LRIDA), 1975, S.4 (1)(a).
70. Ibid, S. 11A (1)(a) and (b).
71. Ibid, S. 12 (5).
72. Ruddy Spencer, Opposition Senator and Officer of the BITU, in The State of the Nation Debate, in the Jamaican Senate, reported in The Jamaican Herald, Dec. 25, 1994, p.4A.
73. Edie, 1991, p. 123.
74. The Stone Polls reported in The Jamaica Herald, Dec. 5, 1994.
75. This statute which gave wide powers of search, arrest and detention to the security forces, causing frequent allegations of abuse, especially against the poor in urban ghettos was passed in 1974 and remained in force, despite strong protest at the excesses indulged in, for some twenty years.
76. Louis Lindsay, The Myth of Independence: Middle Class Politics and Nonmobilization in Jamaica, WORKING PAPER NO.6, ISER, U.W.I., 1991, P.16.
77. Ibid, p.23.
78. Fanon, 1990, p.37.
79. Ibid.
80. Lindsay, 1991, p.34.
81. Ronaldo Munck, The New International Labour Studies, Zed Books 1988, p. 11.
82. Ibid.
83. This is now a distinctly possible development, given the formation of the trade union umbrella organizations, The JTURDC and the JCTU.
84. Mishan, 1969, p.203.
85. Immanuel Wallerstein, The Modern World System, Academic Press, 1974, p. 87.
86. A worthwhile treatment of the "tempting but ultimately fallacious idea of transnational classes" is to be found in, P. Lloyd, A Third World Proletariat? London: Allen & Urwiri, 1982.
87. Murick, 1988, p.22.
88. The recognized (Munroe, Girvan) predisposition to aggressive and violent behaviour in Jamaican society operates largely at the individual level, even if inspired by class antagonisms. At a collective level, the restraining effect of the legacy of the rule of law as a fundamental tenet of the English legal and Governmental system is very much in evidence and is, of course, not conducive to sustained mass revolt of an extra-legal nature. Institutional arrangements such as the IDT are grounded in these societal characteristics. Thus, the effect of the provision in the LPvIDA S.10 (3) giving the Tribunal the power to declare certain actual or threatened industrial action "unlawful industrial action" is to take the institutionalization of industrial conflict to the point where legalism supplants the free play of bargaining forces, in a manner decidedly anti-labour.
89. Carl Stone, 1986, p.184.
90. M. Holstrom, Industry and Inequality: The Social Anthropology of Indian Labour, Cambridge University Press, 1984, p.287; Marx's view that trade unions provided elementary class training and that they were in fact schools for socialism clearly does not apply to the Jamaican or Caribbean situation – A Lozovsky, Marx and the Trade Unions, London: Martin Lawrence Ltd, 1935.
91. Ken Post, "The Politics of Protest in Jamaica 1938", SES, Vol.18 No.4, 1969, p.394.
92. Brian Meeks, Caribbean Revolutions, Warwick University Caribbean Studies, 1993, p.139.
93. Lipset, 1983, pp.1-2.
94. Ibid, p.47; Herbert Marcuse, the Marxist, concluded that affluence under capitalism had severely limited the scope for working class radical protest as the former antagonists were united by an "overriding interest in the preservation and improvement of the industrial status quo", Herbert Marcuse, One Dimensional Man, Boston: Beacon Press, 1964, PP.xii-xiii.
95. Wallerstein, 1974, pp.118, 279-80.
96. Emile Durkheim, Suicide: A Study in Sociology, Glencoe The Free Press, 1951, pp.253-54.
97. Ferguson, 1993, p.566.
98. Ibid, p.568.
99. Ibid.
100. Comparative figures for Consumption for Jamaica are contained in FIG?
101. Ferguson, 1993, p.572.
102. Harrison, 1991, p.3Q2.
103. Lewis, 1993, p . 517.
104. Robert Michels, Political Parties, Glencoe The Free Press, 1949.
105. Selig Perlman, quoted in Lipset, 1983, pp.427-8.

106. Clark Kerr, John T. Dunlop, Frederick Harbison, and Charles A. Myers, *Industrialism and Industrial Man*, Oxford University Press, 1964, p.184.
107. 1Murick, 1988, p.176.
108. Lipset, 1983, p.73.
109. Ibid.
110. Kerr et al., 1964, p.235.
111. John Toye, *Dilemmas of Development*, Blackwell, 1993, p.29.
112. Elsie Leo Rhynie, The Jamaican Family – Continuity and Change, Grace Kennedy Foundation Institute of Jamaica Publications Ltd. 1993, pp.26 et seq.
113. N. GIRVAN, Review of The Poor and Powerless, 1988, P.262.
114. Trevor M.A. Farrell, "Some notes Towards a Strategy for Economic Transformation", In Lalta arid Freckelton (eds), 1993, p.334.
115. Janine Iqbal, "Adjustment Policies in Practice: Case Study of Jamaica, 1977-91", in Lalta and Freckleton (eds) Ibid p.62. It is highly significant that even leading radical intellectuals who drafted the Emergency Production Plan 1977, as an alternative to the IMF, were forced to make this concession.
116. Peta-Anne Baker, "Search for Transformation Strategies – A Perspective from the NCO Sector", in Lalta and Freekleton (eds) 1993, p.349.
117. Barry Floyd, "Planning for Rural Development in Jamaica: Spartial Systems Analysis", in CQ, Vol.18 No.1, March 1972, p.7.
118. See George Beckford, *Persistent Poverty*, Maroon Publishing House, Morant Bay, Jamaica, 1988, pp.23 et. seq.
119. Horace Payne, "The Role of mini-Research Stations in Increasing Farm Productivity", CQ, Vol.18 No.1, March 1972, p.25.
120. I. Inukai, "Farm Mechanization, Output and Labour Input: A Case Study of Thailand", ILR, Vol.101 No.5, p.467.
121. Stone, 1974, p.16.
122. Ibid, p.62.
123. Lawrence Nurse, "Work and Work place Relations in the Commonwealth Caribbean", in, SES, U.W.I., Vol.42 No.26,3, June & Sept. 1993, p.6.
124. Ibid, p. 17 .
125. Cecelia Green, Advanced Capitalist Hegemony and the Significance of Gramsci's Insights: A Re-statement in, SES, U.W.I., Vol.42 No.2&3, June & Sept.. 1993, p. 179.
126. See Stuart Hall, "The Rise of the Representative/Internationalist State", in Gregor McLennon et al (eds) *State and Society in Contemporary Britain*, Cambridge, Polity Press, 1984, for an interesting treatment of the question of representative democracy.
127. Green, 1993, p.194.
128. Carl Stone, *Power and Policy Making in Jamaica*, undated mimeo p.26.
129. Ibid.
130. Ibid.
131. Edwin Jones, *Development Administration: Jamaican Adaptations*, CARICOM Publishers Ltd., 1992, p.6.
132. The State of Emergency was strategically announced while the JLP was in a pre-election week-end retreat at the Holiday Inn Hotel, Montego Bay in 1976, at which the author was present.
133. Stephens & Stephens 1986, pp.124-25.
134. Beckford et al., 1985, p.21.
135. The cultural dependency trait together with the feature of multi-class political party alliances makes this virtually inevitable.
136. Ibid, p.73.
137. Presidential Circular, No.1, dated Feb. 10, 1970, reported in ILR, Vol.102 No.2, Aug. 1970, p.193.
138. Beckford et al., 1985, p.74.
139. Ibid.
140. Ibid, p.116.
141. Teresa Hayter, *The Creation of World Poverty*, Pluto Press, 1992, p.8.
142. Ibid.
143. Aldith Brown, *Planning as a Political Activity: Some Aspects of the Jamaican Experience*, in SES, U.W.I., Vol.24 No.1, Mar. 1975, p.7.
144. Wallerstein, 1974, pp.7-74.
145. The PNP was in power from 1972-76, and 1976-80.
146. Beckford et al., 1985, pp.123-24.
147. Brown, 1975, p.7.
148. Nancy A. George, in CQ, Vol.27 Nos. 2&3, June-Sept. 1981, p.50.
149. Williams Demas, *Economics of Development, in Small Countries with Special Reference of the Caribbean*, McGill University Press, 1965, P.98.
150. Aggrey Brown, The Dialectics of Mass Communication in CQ, Vol.27 Nos. 2&3, June-Sept. 1981, p.46.
151. Norman Girvan, "Unemployment in Jamaica", in N. Girvan, and Owen Jefferson, (eds) *Readings in the Political Economy of the Caribbean*, New World Publishers, undated p.267.
152. Ibid.
153. Katrin Norris in *Jamaica- Search for an Identity*, Institute of Race Relations, London, Oxford University Press, 1966, p. 70, makes the telling point that "the mass of Jamaican voters have little education and they do not respond strongly to theories", which might explain the absence of any ideologically-based mass party despite the later suggestion at p.96, that the island's class

structure and social conditions present an open invitation to socialist and communist movements, "checked so far by peculiar political circumstances; See also Richard Bernal, "The SELA Debt Proposal: An Evaluation", in SES, Vol.40 No.1, U.W.I., 1991, pp.171-6, where it is argued that, unless there is a substantial reduction in the stock and servicing of external debt – which did not in fact materialize – "the present. (1991) conjuncture ... will inexorably instigate confrontations, inflicting significant costs on all parties".

154. Miliband contends that the capitalist system needs a radical political party, since such a party plays a major role in the management of discontent and helps to keep it within safe bounds – Ralph Milibans, Parliamentary Socialism, Merlin Press, 1987, p.376. Discontent with the potential for social upheaval has been successfully contained in the absence of any such party, at least since the 1980 IMF election. When the then "democratic socialist" PNP was decimated at the polls.

155. Norman Girvan, "Swallowing the IMF Medicine in the 1970's", in Development Dialogue, 1980:2, Dag Hammmerskjold Foundation, Sweden, pp.67-8.

156. Munroe, 1983, p.7. In confirmation of Norris' observation Munroe further notes that "increasingly after 1953 [coincidental with the expulsion of the more radical left wing of the PNP] sycophancy was the only political contribution expected or received from the lower-class party crowd ... (p.82) which was partly responsible for the paradox that the fiercest- political partisanship came precisely from those who suffered most from the joint failure of both parties to cope with massive unemployment (p.93) ... (as) Both parties then became firmly fixed as vote catching mechanisms (p.114). The challenge to this format of political rule was "minoritarian" ... , disorganized, unprofessional, unsustained, fragmented and unfocused electorally – an assortment of what Gray describes as "ideologically potent social movements" – Qbika Gray, Radicalism and Social Change in Jamaica:1960-72, University of Tennessee Press, 1991, p.1.

157. Gray, Ibid, p.4.

158. Stone also notes the absence of a "militant left wing movement able to radically politicize the working class towards the pursuit of long term strategic ends: the problem being that the poor, without the benefit of effective ideological counter socialization to neutralize the effect of the hegemonic indoctrination of the ruling class, are least able to wait benefits", in the long run – See Stone, 1973, p. 53; Colman and Nixson, ask "Can the government inflict a sacrifice on the population for the sake of benefits in the future when there is such an immediate need for output, and employment now?" – David Colman and Frederick Nixson, Economics of Change in LDC's, Harvester Wheatsheaf, 1994, p.401. This is a question that would have been relevant, for the entire IMF experience since 1977. Miliband sees socialist/reformist parties that over time fail to provide any real alternative based on the. longer view, as tending in a direction of "the kind of slow, but sure, decline which, deservedly affects parties that have ceased to serve any distinctive political purpose – Miliband, 1987, p.349.

159. ROD AYA, Rethinking Revolutions and Collective Violence: Studies in Concept Theory and Method, HEB SPINHUIS PUBLISHERS, 1990, P.216.

160. Paulo Freire, Pedagogy of the Oppressed, Penguin, 1990, p.36; This lack of confidence also applies to trade union leaders who are reluctant to propose or instigate action to challenge the status quo because of their own omission in establishing appropriate methods for accurately assessing their members willingness to revolt – Zin Henry, Labour Relations and Industrial Conflict in Commonwealth Caribbean Countries, Columbus Publishers, 1972, p.76; In addition see Karl Kautsky, The Class Struggle, Charles H. Kerr and Co., Chicago 1910 pp.163-4.

161. Stone, 1989, p.176. The Stone Opinion Poll of Oct. 1983 reported that 52% of the. sample had lost hope that life would get better over the next 5-10 years; The potentially destabilizing force represented by the unemployed youth "was either absorbed by populist oriented politics or suppressed depending on its location within the extant political system" – Vaughan A. Lewis "Political Change and Crisis in the English – Speaking Caribbean" in Alan Adelman and Reid Reading (eds) Confrontation in the Caribbean Basin, University of Pittsburg, Centre for Latin America Studies, 1984, pp.93,99-101.

162. R.H. Tawney, The Acquisitive Society, Fontana, 1964, p.11; Robin Blackburn notes that "the morale of the working class is weakened by the labyrinthine manoeuvres of a reformist party" – Robin Blackburn "The Unequal Society", in Robin Blackburn and Alexander Cockburn (eds) The Incompatibles: Trade Union Militancy and the Consensus, Penguin and New Left Review, 1967, p.37.

163. Carl Stone, argues, not altogether convincingly for instance, that the accessibility of the Prime Minister to the trade unions significantly explains (together with whether or not a particular Prime Minister happened to have a trade union background) the relative well-being of the working class – Stone, Ibid, p.109.

164. Carl Stone, argues, not altogether convincingly for instance, that the accessibility of the Prime Minister to the trade unions significantly explains (together with whether or not a particular Prime Minister happened to have a trade union background) the relative well-being of the working class – Stone, Ibid, p.109.

165. Frank, as with Walter Rodney with respect to Africa, saw underdevelopment. in Latin America as the necessary product of four centuries of capitalism itself – Andre Guilder Frank, "The Myth of Feudalism" in, Capitalism and underdevelopment in Latin America, Monthly Review Press, 1967, pp.221-42; According to Frank, it is this historical exposure which explains "the pervasiveness of an ideological commitment to the (capitalist) system as a whole, as a result of the myths propagated and believed by the staff or cadres of the system which places reform movements in the dilemma of being an essential part, (the periphery) of the very system they are seeking to change". See also Immanuel Wallerstein, The Capitalist World Economy, Cambridge University Press, 1993, pp. 22,63 ; See George L. Beckford, Persistent Poverty, Maroon Publishing House, Jamaica, 1988, pp.152-3, where it is argued that the trend seemed to be towards increasing third world dependency by policies directed to "making the environment as hospitable as possible" for further metropolitan enterprise penetration, which was not. likely to be reversed "short of

revolutionary change". The competition for, and fear of losing, investments by transnational corporations may well have the effect of reducing the working class to a state of passivity in the face of deepening global, proletarianization.

166. N.J. Smelser "Mechanisms of Change and Adjustment to Change", in Tom Burns (ed) Industrial Man, Penguin, 1969 pp.59-61. The additional factor decisive of the genesis and the moulding of social disturbances mentioned by Smelser, the scope and intensity of social dislocation created by structural changes, has been more than adequately treated by academics, journalists and the public, through the various sections of the media; Thomas suggests that the path of development chosen must confront the tension between the internal class struggle and the dictates of the capitalist world economy, particularly in the case of small trade and aid dependent and "debt driven" economies such as that of Jamaica, made even more vulnerable to external diplomatic constraints by being located in "imperialism's backyard" – Thomas, 1988, p.361.

167. Ted Honderich, Violence for Equality: Inquires in Political Philosophy, Routledge, 1989; Jean Paul Sartres' Introduction to Fanon, 1990, p.202.

168. This consideration in a two-party system of relatively equal party electoral strength where the "baton" passes at regular intervals (every two terms so far in Jamaica) in itself constitutes a serious restraint on fundamental change in the political system.

169. Ralph Miliband, 1987, pp.359-60,375; Manley, 1990, pp.223 et seq.

170. Ted Hondrich, 1989, p.161; Parenti, 1988, at pp.308-9, expresses the view that since the substance of democracy is about the betterment of the majority, those who fight for substantial benefits are engaged not just in economic issues but in advancing democracy.

171. Ibid, p.166.

172. C.B Macpherson, The Political Theory of Possessive Individualism: Hobbes to Locke, Oxford University Press, 1962, P.224.

173. John Locke, 1759, Works ii, 36, quoted in Macpherson, Ibid, p.224; According to Locke, engagement in manual work is not conducive to the head being "elevated to sublime notions, or exercised in mysterious reasoning".

174. Carl Stone, 1973, pp.46-7. Attachment to and defense of a political party's electoral interests by violent methods, which becomes a substitute for revolutionary militancy among the urban ghetto dwellers and the rural poor becomes not so much a matter of supporting party principles, as an exchange: a vote for the promise of a share of the spoils of victory. As Stone notes, "the desperate are usually susceptible to the bribery of promises"; See also J. Schumpeter, Capitalism, Socialism and Democracy, New York Harper, 1942, pp.316-17.

175. Stone, Ibid p.30.

176. Ibid, p.172.

177. Adam Przeworski, Capitalism and Social Democracy, Cambridge University Press, 1989, p.28.

178. See Fanon to the contrary, 1990, p.98.

179. Beckford and Witter, 1991, p.123.

180. Immanuel Wallerstein, 1993, p.22; Marxism calls for class polarization as an essential requirement for structural transformation of economic relations. The members of the middle class academic intellectual elite who designed the Emergency Production Plan of 1977, as an alternative path to development from that of the IMF programme, claimed that it (The Plan) – was really the work of "the Jamaica people" with the "assistance" of the authors. It was therefore not surprising that given that kind of fantasy, the Plan envisaged delinking from the World Capitalist system. According to the Plan, "Economic reconstruction requires national unity of a type that is based on solidarity among the working class and cooperation with and by patriotic national capitalists" – Beckford et al., 1985, pp.73-74.

181. Adam Przeworski, 1989, p. 51; Louis Lindsay, 1991, p.52.

182. Trevor Munroe's review of David Panton's, Jamaica's Michael Manley in SES, Vol.42 No.1 Mar. 1993, p.193.

183. See David Panton, Jamaica is Michael Manley: The Great Transformation (1972-92) Kingston Publishers, 1993. Beckford and Witter, academics who were actively involved in support of the Democratic Socialism project of 1974-1978, were of the view that "the one individual (Michael Manley) who took the critical decision to keep Jamaica handcuffed to imperialism. One thing is certain: history will never absolve him" – Beckford and Witter, 1991, p.151.

184. Paulo Freire, 1990, pp.36,131 et seq. Democratic Socialism was "declared" in 1974 after the general election of 1972, in which that political philosophy formed no part of the PNP's campaign, or manifesto.

185. Ian Taylor, (ed) The Social Effects of Free Market Policies, Harvester Wheatsheaf 1990, p.4; Macpherson, 1962, p.245 makes the observation that it was necessary for any bourgeois theory claiming to be descended from traditional natural law, to "conceive man in general in the image of rational bourgeois man, able to look after himself and morally entitled to do so".

186. Taylor, Ibid p.3.

187. See Beckford and Witter, 1991, p.53 where, with the growth of the world capitalist economy, migration is seen as one of the important responses to oppression and poverty, See also Karl Levitt, The Origins and Consequences of Jamaica's Debt Crisis, 1970-1990, Consortium Graduate School of Social Sciences, Mona, Jamaica, 1991; The Jamaica Herald, Feb. 2, 1995, and M.G.Smith, Poverty in Jamaica, ISER, 1989, pp.101,159-62; Paulo Freire, 1990, p. 121; Stone, 1987, pp. 36,45 ; Andrew S. Downes, "The Search for a Sustainable Labour Market Response to Structural Adjustment Programmes in the Caribbean", in ILG, The Role of Trade Unions in Periods of Structural Adjustment Programmes, ILO Regional Seminar, Barbados Workers Union Labour College, Dec. 1992; Derek Gordon, Class Status and Social Mobility in Jamaica, ISER, U.W.I., 1989, p.18, reports that of the 4 out of every 5 workers who are employed in the private sector, slightly more than 50% work in enterprises with 10 workers or less, implying personalization of relations and the difficulty of unionization inherent on that scale of operation; Thomas, 1938, p. 189, refers to the effect of small scale enterprise on inhibiting the development of a sense of class identity and solidarity, both of which

are necessary for united class action; Stone, 1973, p.50; Carmen Diana Deere (ed) *In the Shadows of the Sun: Caribbean Development Alternatives and U.S. Policy*, Westview Press, 1990, pp.11-12,97. On the other hand, Korten and Alfonso offer the conclusion that the very ability of the poor to survive under the most unfavourable conditions is testament to their highly developed skills in meeting their basics needs, "even if only at standards intolerable to a socially conscious society" – Korten and Alfonso, 1985, p.183.

188. Smith, Ibid, p.162.

189. Freire, 1990, p.121.

190. Stone, 1986, p.36.

191. This non-traditional export sector has shown what is, for Jamaica, impressive growth, both in terms of foreign exchange earnings and the number of jobs created in assembly-type operations. Apart from the usual foreign investment inducement incentives, foreign based companies are attracted by low wage levels and the "understanding" that they will be free from the fear of unionization. Being "foot, loose" type operations, the ever-present threat of their relocation to a more favourable investment environment exercises a serious restraining influence on governments, unions, and workers.

192. Rod Aya, 1990, pp . 217, 219.

193. Michael Salamon, *Industrial Relations - theory and practice*, Prentice Hall, 1992, p.375.

194. R. Hyman, *Strikes*, Fontana, 1984, pp.108-109.

195. H.A. Turner, G. Clark and G. Roberts, *Labour Relations in the Motor Industry*, Allen and Unwin, 1967, p.190; Malcolm Cross and Gad Henman (eds) *Labour in the Caribbean*, Warwick University Caribbean Studies, Macmillan Press, 1992, p.121; Munroe, 1983, p.17; Parenti, 1988, p.315 ; Norman Girvan, Richard Bernal and Wesley Hughes, The IMF and Third World – The Case of Jamaica 1974-80", in Development Dialogue 1980:2, Dag Hammerskjold Foundation, Sweden, p.13; Przeworski, 1989, pp.139,146; Thomas, 1988, p.361; Gunner Myrdal, *The Challenge of World Poverty*, Penguin, 1971; Honderich, 1989, p. 131; Albert Memmi, *The Colonizer and the Colonized*, Earthscan Publications, London, 1990, p. 161; Rod Aya, 1990, pp.216 et seq; Ian Taylor (ed), 1990, p.15; Claremont Kirton, Jamaica: Debt and Poverty, Oxfam, 1992, p.5; and Stone, 1973, p.149.

196. Illegal migration across the Mexican border into the United States, considered a "safety valve" by the Mexican Government (Levitt's "misery index") is no convincing advertisement for the Mexican development "miracle" – ILO, Report to a Symposium on Employment, Trade, Adjustment and North – South Cooperation, Oct. 1-4, 19S5, ILO, p.74.

197. Munroe, 1984, p.17.

198. Parenti, 1983, p.315.

199. Dr. Edwin Carrington (NIEQ) 4 letter word), A Perspective on North South Relations in Ramesh Ramsaran (ed) *Caribbean Economic Policy and South Cooperation*, Warwick University Caribbean Studies, Macmillan, Caribbean Publishers, 1993, p.28.

200. Memmi 1990, pp. 159,161.

201. Stone, 1973, p.151.

202. Claremont Kirton, 1992, p.51.

203. Ian Shirley, "New Zealand: The Advance of the New Right", in Ian Taylor (ed) 1990, p.363.

204. Stone, 1973, p. 112.

205. Kirton, 1992, p.5.

206. Girvan, et. al, 1980. p.152.

207. The Stone Poll predictions and analyses of these election results may be seen in Stone, 1959, pp.v,1,35,150.

208. Girvan et al., 1930, p.154; That the situation portrayed by the authors was not unique to the Democratic Socialist government of the day is a point made, across the board by Przeworski with respect to social democrats' reform policies in a capitalist economy, especially when faced with a crisis in the world economic and financial system – Przeworski, 1939, p.41.

209. Lindsay, 1991, Ch.iv.

210. Manley, 1990, p.21.

211. Shirley, in Ian Taylor (ed), 1990, p.360.

212. Elliott Currie, "Free Market Policy Inequality and Social Provision in the United States", in Ian Taylor (ed), p.314.

213. Dennis A. Pantin, "Resolving the Foreign Debt Crisis of the Caribbean in the 1990's: A menu Options in ILO, *The Role of Trade Unions in Periods of Structural Adjustment Programmes*, ILO Seminar Barbados Workers Union Labour College, Barbados Dec. 1992, p.20.

214. Pantin advances market/capitalistic solutions such as 'bad debt write off' to the third world debt crisis which, precisely because they are novel, and biased in favour of debtors rather than the lending institutions, are unlikely to find a place in reform proposals acceptable to the ruling international financial powers.

215. Antonio Gramsci, *The Prison Notebooks*, 1971, p.243; Przeworski, 1989, p.201.

216. Stone, 1973, p.69, Stone, 1987, pp.102-3,105, notes that as the unions became less of a political movement with broadly defined national goals, to that extent they abandoned party politics as the primary means of securing institutional power status and benefits for labour in favour of the practice of "business unionism".

217. Peter Phillips, in "Capitalist Elites in Jamaica", in Stone and Brown(eds) Feb. 1976, pp.111-2, considers the policy consequences of private donor support of the major political parties; See also Rupert Lewis, "Black Nationalism in Jamaica in Recent Years", also in Stone and Brown (eds), p . 175.

218. Meeks stresses the importance of timing for maximizing the chances of success for major doctrinal initiatives, such as Democratic Socialism, for which there was virtually no preparation, neither of the would-be leaders of the movement nor the potential supporters on neither the attitudinal level nor that of consciousness, Brian Meeks, *Caribbean Revolutions and Revolutionary*

Theory, Macmillan, 1993 p.207. As a result, Meeks observe that "the structural support for the systemic transformation envisioned was not present" (p.xxxi); See also Manley, 1990, p.222, where it is recognized that the attempted implementation of the Worker Participation Programme "failed due largely to the fall in real wages under IMF austerity after 1977. ... the ideas of worker participation must have seemed remote and fanciful. This was clearly an agenda for another time". With respect to the IMF promoted idea of a Social Contract in 1978, Manley concludes ... "The approach was sound but relations between the government and the private sector were so strained as to make the (National Advisory) Council virtually unworkable".

219. Clark Kerr, et al., "Postscript to Industrialism and Industrial Man", ILR, Vol.103 No.6, June 1971, ILO, p.521.

220. Manley, 1990, p.127. See the Daily Gleaner, Sept. 18, 1992, p.21, for the transformed Manley's statement that "One just can't improve upon Adam Smith". To Luxemburg Manley's claim of a theory-averse citizenry would represent "a paternalistically coarse insult and base aspersion", since for her "the entire strength of the modern labour movement rests on theoretic knowledge" Rosa Luxemburg, Reform or Revolution, Pathfinder, 1988, p.9. The differences in time and place are of course to be taken into account.

221. Brian Meeks, 1973, p. 20 3 ; Peter Phillips, in "Jamaican Elites: 1938 to Present" in Carl Stone and Aggrey Brown (eds), Feb, 1976 p.36, raises the possibility of ... counter elites ... a new series of cataclysms ... the possibility of the better ... which ... must come".

222. Beckford and Witter, 1991, pp.87,92. The authors nevertheless saw the period 1974—76 as a "watershed in the history of Jamaica politics. For Socialism "became legitimized in the political process for the first time, and this put the class question on the agenda of what up to then was nothing more than the politics of tweedle-dum and tweedle-dee".

223. Henry, 1972, pp.168-9; For a more extensive treatment of the frustration/aggression approach to the explanation of social upheaval, see Ted Gurr Why Men Rebel, Princeton University Press 1971. There has yet to be, in the Jamaican experience, that conjuncture conducive to Skocpol's social revolution: the dual coincidence of societal structural change involving class disturbances and, the occurrence of political and social transformation – Theda Skocpol, States and Social Revolution, Cambridge University Press, 1979, p.4.

224. Perry Anderson, "The Limits and Possibilities of Trade Union Action", in Blackburn and Cockburn (eds), 1967, p.271.

225. Memmi, 1990, p.154. The radical, Memmi suggests, "uncertain of being able to convince others, he provokes them" (p.205), a self-defeating tactic evident in the behaviour of the more doctrinaire under Democratic Socialism in Jamaica in the 1970's.

226. Perry Anderson, supra, pp.264,268-9.

227. Zin Henry, 1972, p.168; Catherine A. Sunshine, *The Caribbean: Survival Struggle and Sovereignty*, Epica. Publication, 1994, p .220, Trevor Munroe, then President of the Workers' Party of Jamaica, is quoted as saying "... we have not sufficiently understood and applied a basic principle of Marxism – that principle is that Marxism is not a dogma ... our Party needs to ensure that it is linked more into the concrete conditions of Jamaica and the Jamaican people". Despite this awareness, the Party was a casualty of the changed ideological and geo-political architecture of the world after the collapse of the Soviet Union; Rhetoric, which served to "over-ideologize" the domestic struggle, according to Thomas and expose it to features of the military/diplomatic international environment with which it could not hope to realistically contend – Clive Y. Thomas, 1938, p.224.

228. Lloyd Best, "Independent Thought and Caribbean Freedom" in Girvan and Jefferson (eds) undated, pp.7-28; See also Walter Goldfrank "Theories of Revolution and Revolution without Theory" in Theory and Society, Vol.7 Nos. 1&2, 1979, p.138.

229. Laurie Clements, "Reference Groups and Trade Union Consciousness" in Tom Clark and Laurie Clements (ed), *Trade Unions under Capitalism*, Fontana, 1977, p. 326.

230. Tawney, *The Acquisitive Society*, Fontana, 1964, Tawney's critical examination of the principles upon which capitalist society rests, and more specifically the capitalist production relations is as relevant today as at the time of the first edition in 1921 and makes highly stimulating reading in the context of free market ideological dominance.

231. Girvan, Bernal, and Hughes, 1980, p.143; Social Democracy, not unlike Democratic Socialism, Jamaican style, has according to Wallerstein "turned out to be a monumental failure whose short-term glories have failed to bear the test of time" – Wallerstein, 1993, p.238.

232. Michael Manley's view failed to find substantive expression in the form of any feasible alternative. On the contrary, leading official party spokesman in the 1990's were unanimous in their conclusion that there had been "no choice". Manley's concern was of course, the effect of IMF policies on his leadership popularity both on the personal, and international party levels – See Manley's, 1990, pp.236 et seq.

233. Philip Cohen, "Teaching Enterprise Culture", in Ian Taylor (ed), 1990, p. 49.

234. See also Miliband, 1987, p. 13 7 quoting Harold Laski, who asked "whether evolutionary socialism (had) deceived itself into believing that it can establish itself by peaceful means within the ambit of the political system"; Rosa Luxemburg, 1988, p.28; Ralph Miliband, *The State in Capitalist Society*, Basic Books, 1969, p . 53.

235. These general insights of Przeworski 1983, provide an explanation of the paradox of the alleged "betrayal" of the Jamaican people by Manley by entering into the IMF Agreement in 1978 which was, on the contrary, perceived by Manley as the only recourse, if almost certain and total economic collapse, with all that portended for the poorer classes, was to be avoided. This was a situation which Freire would interpret as a failure of courage to enter into the situation of those with whom the revolutionary intellectuals of the middle class were identifying – Paulo Freire, 1990, p.26; See Beckford and Witter, 1991, p.93.

236. Stone, 1387, p.179. The expanded area of policy continuity between changing political administrations has not however, as against, the performance under the East Asian models of economic growth, produced much by way of a difference in the basic

condition of the working class, the poor, and destitute, to compensate for the loss of real choice between policy alternatives through the ballot box – Jacqueline A. Braveboy – Wagner, *The Caribbean in the Pacific Century*, Lynne Reinner Publishers, 1993, p.79.

237. Allen proposes that unions should free themselves from dependence on the state for labour – protective legislation, for "so long as governments look on much of their statutory labour provisions as concessions to the labour movement", especially given the historical party-union affiliation in Jamaica, they will expect if not demand "equivalent concessions in terms of collaboration or a restriction on union activities in return"Victor Allen, "The Paradox of Militancy", in Blackburn and Cockburn (eds), 1967, p.260; See also Clements, in Clarke and Clements (eds), 1977, p.325. Clements suggests that trade union aggressiveness can expect to be met with "ideological bombardment" by the state, management and financial journalists, a prediction proved to be substantially correct, in the Jamaican context especially since the removal of official wage guidelines in 1991.

238. Walter Galenson, (ed) Labour in Developing Countries, University of California Press, Berkeley and Los Angeles, 1962; Contrary to this prediction, as Lenin and Marx had correctly described their social role, trade unions' transformative capacity is limited precisely by the fact that they are an integral part of the capitalist system since they "incarnate the difference between capital and labour which defines society" – Perry Anderson, in Blackburn and Cockburn (eds), 1967, p.264.

239. Cross, and Heumann, (eds) 1992, p.280; The well-known British Labour Party labour leader, Ernest Bevin is quoted as having said, "… as a trade unionist … our work is eminently practical, and it is to deliver the goods to our members, and we know, as leaders, the absolute folly of putting up programmes that are not. likely to be realized" – Miliband, 19S7, pp.205-6.

240. Describing strikes as the continuation of bargaining by other means [like diplomacy in the case of war] Zin Henry, 1972, p.120; suggests that, given the historical and social background of slavery and colonial/imperialistic exploitation under primitive authoritarian capitalism, "what is surprising is that there are not more and more violent strikes".

241. Proverbs 29 : 18.

242. Perry Anderson, in Blackburn and Cockburn (eds), 1967, p.265.

243. "By not having developed a capacity to mobilize members around wider political non-wage national policy issues and having retreated into … collective bargaining (rather than becoming strong national policy lobby) the trade unions (in the period covered, 1979-34) had no means of defending themselves against anti-labour policies arising from IMF conditionalities" – Stone, 1987, p.108; Lewis and Nurse, in Hilbourne A. Watson (ed), 1994, pp.192 et seq, express sentiments emphasizing the need for unions to eschew their traditional reactive role for a broader class inclusive and pro-active one.

244. Working class differentiation and fragmentation has taken several forms: as represented for example in the "labour aristocracy/ privileged worker "thesis – Lipset, 1983, Ch.4, contra Derek Gordon, "Working class Radicalism in Jamaica: An Exploration of the Privileged Worker Thesis", in SES, Vol.27 No.3, Sept. 1978, U.W.I., pp.332-3; Southall blames fragmentation on workers' historical experiences of struggle: level of proletarianization; uneven development of different segments of the labour force; cultural variations; the strategic location of unions by industrial sectors – (more so in Jamaica on an enterprise, and even departmental, white collar, job classification, occupational, functional, basis); the gender predominance among membership of different occupations and sectors; and the level of unionization within enterprises, sectors, and overall – Southall (ed), 1938, p.27; A further factor militating against working class solidarity in Jamaica is, interunion rivalry, now on the decline – and importantly, given the small size of the country, the feature of general as against craft or specialized unionism, certainly among the larger unions. See William H. Friedland, "Unions and Industrial Relations in Underdeveloped Countries", New York State School of Industrial and Labour Relations Cornell University Bulletin No.47, Jan 1963, p. 3 3; Thomas, 1938, p.192; Laurie Clements, in Clarke and Clements (eds), 1977, p.318.

245. Tom Clarke, Introduction: The Raison D'Etre of Trade Unionism in Clarke and Clements, (eds), 1977, p.15; ILO, Labour Relations and Development in the America's Report 111, 12th Conference of American States, Montreal Mar. 1936, ILO p.17.

246. Paul A. Samuelson, "Functional Fiscal Policy for the 1960's", in Arthur M. Okun, *The Battle Against Unemployment*, New York, W.W. Norton & Co. Inc., 1965, p.110; Quote taken from John Kenneth Galbraith, "The New Position of Poverty, Prentice Hall, New Jersey, 1965, p.53.

247. J. Hinton, and R. Hyman, Trade Unions and Revolution, Pluto Press, 1975, p.59; Wallerstein makes the further point, which should prove sobering to the "adventurer" clique, that "an 'objective' class status is only a reality if it becomes a subjective reality for some group or groups" – Wallerstein, 1993, p.63; Everett M. Kassalow and Ukandi G. Daraachi (eds) The Role of Trade Unions in Developing Societies, ILO, Geneva, 1978, p. 94, where it is stated that "Basically, it is not under anyone's purposive control, either to start up or to slow down "the consciousness raising process …. even astute observers often do not recognize when it is occurring"; Rousseau, reminds us that "The Greeks imprisoned in the cave of the Cyclops lived there very tranquilly, while they were awaiting their turn to be devoured" – Jean-Jacques Rousseau, The Social Contract and Discourses, Everyman, 1993, p. 186. It may therefore be worth considering the merit of Hayter's view, similar to that of Beckford and Witter, that it is exceedingly unlikely that any government in an underdeveloped country will act to eradicate poverty, except under the pressure, and with the assistance of a major popular mobilization"Hayter, 1992, p.95.

248. Perry Anderson, in Blackburn and Cockburn, (eds), 1967, p.274.

249. R. Hyman and R.H. Fryer, "Trade Unions: Sociology and Political Economy", in Clarke and Clements (eds), 1977, p. 161. The simplistic concept of the iron law of oligarchy, which clearly conflicts with the phenomenon of union maturation, connotes a gradual process in which both oligarchic and conservative tendencies should, without more, differ for different unions in different situations over time. Oligarchic tendencies and consequences are further complicated by the phenomenon in Jamaica, and elsewhere in ex-colonial territories, of the not infrequent combination – reflecting the strategy of cooptation to neutralize industrial

opposition to political policy – of the dual roles of career politician and union official. According to Gordon Lewis "… as union and political leadership become at once fused and confused, the objectives of the union side tend to lose out to the political side when a conflict arises between them", due to the greater lobbying from interest groups with which the political structure has to contend. Gordon K. Lewis, *Puerto Rico: Freedom and Power in the Caribbean*, Monthly Review Press, 1963, p.228.

250. Adam Przeworslti, 1989, p. 172; Stone, 1987, p.119, argues that given the depoliticization of the labour movement, "activism and dissent provides a channel by which workers' alienation is articulated", (thus constituting "a safety valve"). See Leon HoSang, "Strikes arid the Public Interest", in The Sunday Gleaner, Nov. 26, 1978, pp.14,21, where the view is expressed that without recourse to the safety valve of Strike action, protest "might otherwise have fed into national anti-systemic political action".

251. Southall, (ed), 1988, Introduction, p.29.

252. Hansard, Trinidad and Tobago, Vol.II, 1962-3, p.293.

253. Counterbalancing this effect of unionism are the exclusion from coverage of the unemployed, self-employed, informal sector workers employees in free zone enclaves, the peasant class, and most female dominated occupations.

254. Parenti, against the background of the almost universal decline in real working-class wages for several years now, is of the view – like Zin Henry – that "what is remarkable is the enormous degree of restraint displayed by workers and their members"; this has not insulated them against attacks for being the cause of both inflation and recession – Parenti, 1988, p.253. The record shows, in fact, that when the unions were overwhelmed by the disparate power of capital in the 1980's the Jamaican economy did not flourish. In keeping with Dubin's "power theory of conflict", Parenti notes that "Unions correlate with prosperity rather than poverty".

255. Clark Kerr, 1971, p.521; Mick Marchington and Philip Parker, *Changing Patterns of Employee Relations*, Harvester Wheatsheaf, 1990, p.25 ; See ILO, "Wage Determination in English-speaking Caribbean Countries", Record of Proceedings ILO/DANIDA Regional Seminar, Kingston, Jamaica Mar. 1978, p.13, on the stabilizing function of collective bargaining as a "mechanism facilitating orderly necessary adaptations … to meet the changing environment in which enterprises operate"; See also ILO, "Labour Relations and development in the Americas", Report 111, 12th Conference of American States, Montreal, Mar. 1936, pp. 1,5,39 and ILO, "Collective bargaining as a means of improving the working and living conditions of the workers in the metal trades", Report 11, Metal Trades Committee, 11th Session, Geneva, 1933, p.30.

256. Michael Parenti, 1938, p.105; See the perspective on trade unions and management "as joint managers of discontent", thus diminishing any fundamental challenge to the *status quo* by persuading the working class and its leadership "to accept ultimately the need for compromise, and by leading them to believe that gains can be made, within the confines of the present system" in Salomon, 1992, p. 377. The "patriotic capitalists" of The Peoples Plan should be expected to be concerned with, among other matters, the creation of a level of employment such that "the operation of the market remained simultaneously conducive to economic efficiency, social harmony and political stability" – Manfred Bienefeld, "In Defence of Nationalism as a Trade Union Perspective", in Southall (ed), 1988, p.332. That this expectation has not been fulfilled testifies to the fact that for trade unions of the developing world "life is a choice of evils" Linden Lewis notes that with increasing job insecurity arising from operations restructuring on the enterprise, national and indeed, international level and accompanying production dispersal, "this has led to the fragmentation of working class solidarity [contrary to Wallerstein] making the task of organizing workers considerably more difficult – Linden Lewis, "Restructuring and Privatization in the Caribbean" in Hilbourne A, Watson (ed), 1994, p. 175; As Marcuse recognized, "… most people have had that sense of their power and their ability systematically stripped from them, not only through their socialization [so that the ideologies they believe tend to disempower them] Could it really be that they have not resisted simply because "they could not"? but also that the realities in which they find themselves gives them relatively little freedom of movement" – Erman M. David, Mary B. Williams, and Claudio Gutierrey (eds) *Computers, Ethics and Society*, Oxford University Press, 1990, p.283. See also Ajeet. N. Mathur, *Industrial Restructuring and Union Power – Macro Economic Dimensions of Economic Restructuring and Industrial Relations in India*, ILO ~ ARTEP, 1991, p.19.

257. Tony Topham, "New Types of Bargaining", in Blackburn and Cockburn (eds), 1967, pp.135, et seq.

258. Tom Clarke in Clarke and Clements, (eds), 1977, p.16; More detailed attention, it has been argued, therefore needs to be paid to broader mechanisms for the distribution of power and rewards in society – Salomon, 1992, p.45. This is necessary so as to mitigate the suboptimal results of the "structural antagonism" of the process of collective bargaining. For the more radical, "the very success of the bargaining process vitiates its polarizing impact on the political system" (Lenin's "economism" and the New Left's "cooptation"); Immanuel Wallerstein, 1993, p.234.

259. Wallerstein, IBID, 1993, p.225.

260. See Karl Theodore, "Structural Adjustment in the Caribbean", in ILO, Dec, 1992, p.3.

261. Jariine Iqbal, in Stanley Lalta and Marie Freckleton (eds) 1993, p.47.

262. Trevor Harker, "Development Planning – Reflections and Reconsiderations", in Lalta and Freckleton (eds) Ibid, pp.356 et seq.

263. Trevor M.A. Farrell "The Caribbean State and its Role in Economic Management", in Omar Davies (ed) *The State in Caribbean Society*, Dept, of Economics, U.W.I., Jamaica, 1986, p.6.

264. But Streeten and Mussa, as reported by Rondinelli have given different and varying reasons for the failures of adjustment policy implementation – some to do with the target areas for, and the efficiency of, government intervention; others representing instances of inadequate institutional analysis by international lending institutions; and, further, the institutions' omission, given their claim of political neutrality, to consider the political conditions necessary for the success of purportedly growth enhancing fiscal and monetary policies. Dennis A. Rondinelli, *Development Projects as Policy Experiments*, Routledge, 1993, pp.87-8; See also

Richard N. Cooper, *Economic Stabilisation in Developing Countries*, Occasional Papers No.14, International Center for Economic Growth, ICS Press, San Francisco, 1991, p.64.

265. See the St. Augustine Alternative (to IMF/Bank designed Adjustment Programmes) in ILO, Dec. 1992, pp.9 et seq; As for the merits of involvement in a Social Contract, Przeworski foresees the prospect of little progressive benefit, from "workers' participation in bourgeois governmental policies" which "cannot have other results than the consolidation of the existing state of affairs and thus would paralyze socialist revolutionary action of the proletariat" – Przeworski, 1989, p.8. One is left to wonder if views such as Przeworskis have undergone any revision since the splintering of the Soviet empire.

266. Gray,1991,p.75.

267. J. Harrod, "Social Relations of Production, Systems of Labour Control and Third World Trade Unions", in Southall (ed), 1988, p.55; The objectives of the failed Worker Participation Project of the late 1970's, according to Stone, included: reducing friction, tension and alienation on the part of rank and file workers and increase their identity with the workplace ...» with top management as well as with the owners of the enterprise; to reduce industrial and class conflict" – Carl Stone "Worker Participation in Industry – A Survey of Workers' Opinions, in Stone and Brown (eds), Jan. 1976, p.437.

268. Philip Selzniek, The organizational Weapon N.Y., McGran Hill, 1952, pp.293-4.

Conclusion

Comments, assessments and an indication as to preferred views have been interspersed throughout the text, as it has been sought to add a dimension of political philosophy, within the limitations of the subject matter and the immediate ideational environment. This, in a universalistic economic context said to be, "tarnished by policy familiarity".

Rather than a continuation of the traditional approach of studies on structural adjustment, involving focus on programme performance criteria, macro-economic indices and their social consequences, the effort here is to examine officially applied and contemplated responses to persistent economic crises. These may be viewed as labour control strategies with the potential of containing organized and/or popular spontaneous revolt, possibly of a system-threatening order.

The views of the working class/man in the street have, for the first time,[1] been canvassed on these specific policy options. Also surveyed has been their perception of the role of the leading international financial institutional force, the IMF, which has, under United States control, it is alleged, been made into a branch of that country's foreign policy and has thus,

> "… taken an equally narrow and ridiculous view of their prescriptions
> which result only in local economies becoming handsome corpses".[2]

Government policy formulation suffered from one of the negative features of the island's political culture – the lack of in-depth study of alternatives, better undertaken while parties are in the political wilderness. As a result, what were intended to be solutions, compounded the traditional internal maladjustments, or were perceived to have that potential inherent in them.

Policy proposals have been formulated in a stressful, practical problem-solving, crisis environment, and have thus been deprived of the advantage of being honed by rigorous theoretical examination. They have suffered from the absence of value challenges, which,

> "… dig to bedrock … (and) require that we cut to the stratum of the
> social unconscious".[3]

Also, they have suffered unjustifiably, from the absence of that guidance from comparative country experience that ought to have been forthcoming from the institutions of the United Nations system, and, in particular, the ILO.

And without deliberately equitable official policy, efficaciously pursued in a free market regime, "social conscience withers" in a conjuncture where trade unions are no more than the "paid agents in the capitalist jungle", lacking a membership representative of a new working-class re-testing its strength, experimenting with new forms of action, and bringing into play a discovery of its power, "… for too long suppressed".[4]

In the Jamaican context, moreover, radical intellectual leadership, which might have been expected to fashion the moulds for more egalitarian policy has taken, "… the safer course of learning from the people",[5] reflecting the national syndrome of avoidance of responsibility for results. This is not to deny that there was a time when an enlightened social vision was confused with 'the politics of the impossible'. But now it appears, that what is un-ambitiously defined to be possible is being pursued without the benefit of any contemplated vision of society. For the history of stabilization and structural adjustment in Jamaica, "documents the process by which events work to alter ideology".

There is no longer a gap of certitude[6] between the now disappearing, if not extinct, native ideologists and "the others". But, that is essential for the possible evolution of the 'politics of bargaining and compromise' that could lead to the formation of a meaningful social consensus.

At the same time, without ideology, society in terms of its potential for transformation must be seen as non-pluralist/homogeneous: violence for equality is the last resort of those without power in such a situation. And this is likely to remain so as long as the power elite remains unchallenged by a social group with the potential and the will to overwhelm them.[7]

Neither Productivity Incentive Schemes nor the Prices and Incomes Policy experiments were attempted with any degree of policy commitment or confidence. Perhaps for this reason, interlocking goals were never really agreed nor adequately specified quantitatively. The result, for example, was that the investment effort, stated to be essential under all proposals for, and versions of a Social Contract, were never reconciled with meeting the legitimate demands that would elicit acceptance from the relatively deprived majority – after eighteen years of consideration.

While governments have had a serious credibility problem, the private sector, has not been able to resolve the dilemma occasioned by a belief that, "… the cleansing disciplines of the marketplace are fundamentally infallible,"[8] while at the same time, harbouring the instinct to place controls on labour.

For the majority, there seems no room any longer for populist rhetoric, given "the politics of despair and disillusionment",[9] which increasingly echoes "...the anxieties and fears of lower-class violence, that have dominated the thoughts of the privileged since slavery".[10] The rhetoric that administers doses of even "temporary hope" for the future does not come easily in the midst of continuous policies urging present sacrifice when that 'present' appears to be everlasting.[11] This leaves the mass of the population, "... without roots to the extent that we have not yet thought out our position in the world ....[12] As a result, as Worrell suggests,

> "Our leaders find themselves pushed to implement policies of which they are skeptical, but we cannot confront the technicians of the multinational institutions with models as convincing as their own ... our ideas must infiltrate the metropole to cast doubt on the pernicious strategies which are often thrust upon us".[13]

For example, the continued presumption, evident in the IMF 1995 Report, of a wage-driven inflationary spiral as the foundation of remedial policy,[14] in spite of the absence of supporting empirical evidence is, to say the least, mesmerizing. Nothing is heard of the problematic consequences of the debt-servicing burden.

Not only has hyper-inflation over a substantial number of these years been accompanied by a significant fall in real wages, but it would be highly unlikely for increases in labour productivity, however caused, to assist, appreciably, in restraining inflation, running at 26.9/25.1% in 1994/95.[15] Anything near that level of productivity increase is simply not achievable in the medium term, even with improbably dramatic technological innovation, which, in the short term at least, has its own troubling unemployment related costs, especially significant in a context of vigorous multi-party contestation, where debt-servicing makes necessary a high level of tax revenue from the employed.

As FIG. 9 makes plain, national debt per capita has increased enormously, achieved amidst much self-congratulatory talk about debt relief/forgiveness and rescheduling. Since 1989/90 external debt has been declining, (FIG. 4I), yet actual debt service payments in 1995 amounted to US$592.56M, being 19.53% of the country's total exports of goods and services. Further, as the external debt has declined, so has there been an astronomical growth of the internal debt, now amounting to some J$56B.[16] Persistent devaluation of the local currency and an absurdly high interest rate regime have aggravated the problem to the extent that

52% of the last Budget was allocated to debt-service as indicated in FIG.42. Indeed, since 1989 there has been a 546% increase in the national debt.

The consequence of the above is simply that there can be no meaningful attempt to improve the social wage and provide publicly-funded special employment projects to the extent necessary to prevent frustration of Social Contract and Prices and Incomes Policy proposals. And even if no more IMF funding is sought, this will not prevent the continuation of debt-service payments for several years.[17]

But the adverse conditions faced by developing countries might, instead of dictating capitulation to multi-lateral agencies proposing policies of "development by exploitation", be treated as "a "challenge to greater boldness ... an opportunity to greater radicalism" in policy design[18] – the stimulus to engage in timely, innovative structural reform, autonomously prescribed and self-imposed. There is a certain usefulness in confrontation[19] with a problem, as against virulent, caustic attacks against, or the opposed attitude of resignation to, the idiosyncrasies of an external source of assistance. This is especially so when what is offered is a less than optimal solution for the client, if the accompanying conditions are reasonably perceived to be deliberately and essentially self-serving.

The explanation for the failure of successful policy identification often is to be found, as Miliband has argued, not in the realm of the intentions of the ruling political elite in peripheral societies, but rather in the fact that they have allowed themselves, as Levitt laments,[20] to become,

> "... the willing prisoners of an economic and social framework which necessarily turns their reforming proclamations, however sincerely meant, into verbiage".[21]

When repeated often enough, this amounts, in the eyes of a populace predisposed to 'await salvation', to the promises of 'false prophets'.

This has led Stone to the conclusion – positively disputed by our surveys – that,

> "Sustaining political order and stability under these conditions will demand a more enlightened and informed electorate that is more able to understand the link between economic and social policies and macro-economic trends ... the limits of the political system to deliver"[22]

The political institutions will not "crumble for lack of people support", because expectations go unfulfilled, the reason being that ignorance, in the ideologically innocent Jamaican context, clearly promotes "the tyranny of the *status quo*". This does not portend the outcome of a "blood bath the likes of which we would not have seen in this country before".[23] There is nothing in the Chapter on Policy Resistance to support this bleak prediction, nor indeed in the survey responses. Nor, most importantly, has there been any such development, in fact.

Figure: 41

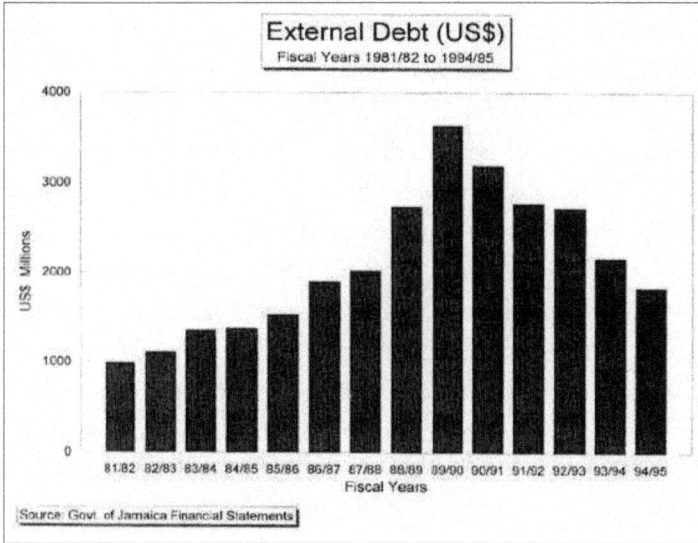

External Debt (US$)
Fiscal Years 1981/82 to 1994/85

Source: Govt. of Jamaica Financial Statements

Figure: 42

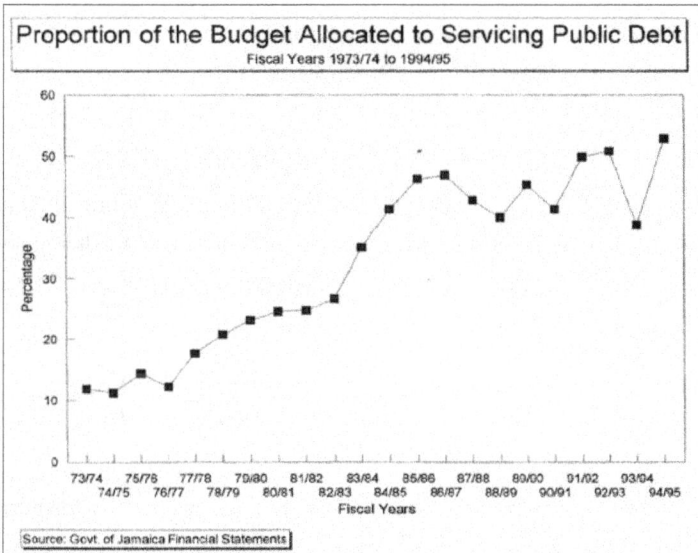

Proportion of the Budget Allocated to Servicing Public Debt
Fiscal Years 1973/74 to 1994/95

Source: Govt. of Jamaica Financial Statements

Those like the leaders of the trade unions, in general, but, more particularly, the teachers and public servants – as the surveys suggest – who might have been expected to resist more firmly, perhaps like Theodore,[24] were probably,

> "... oppressed by the fear that to insist on even half a loaf might spell disaster, and were therefore eager to settle for crumbs".[25]

The expanded and sustainable capacity to earn required amounts of foreign currency has been recognized as the test of stabilization and structural adjustment programme success. It is this, which should lead to an improved quality of life through wages levels in excess of CPI movements, adequate social services and a safety net acceptable to those with the social conscience appropriate for civilized society. But the repeatedly recorded public attitude of apathy towards, and withdrawal of interest in, what ought to be raging public policy issues and concerns, suggests that the moment is now less than propitious for a campaign of political education. All the indications are, that what some regard as the political culture's most precious resource – faith in the legitimacy of the political system[26] – has been all but overwhelmed by the adjustment experience. If this is not in fact so, then importantly, in the popular perception, the formula for freedom, requiring among other things the space to individually pursue one's "schedule of utilities",[27] without the disadvantage of "unnecessary" state interference, appeals only to those to whom deprivation and disadvantage are like strangers at the gate of the manor.

The irony is that, "The new dependency which was engendered by the mounting debt did not sit easily on elements of the leadership of this generation", having strong feelings on the issue of national sovereignty. Those leaders felt obliged, nevertheless, to apply neo-classical principles, under what was seen as economic duress,[28] although, in the end-result, to the material advantage of many of the ruling elite.

This further collision between social and political sentiments and the economic realities of stabilization and adjustment added a further problem to programme implementation. This was not mediated by the fact that the nature of these nationalistic "Independence" concepts and,

> "... the empirical realities they are supposed to reflect, seem to be drawn from different universes, only occasionally intertwined – what the French call a dialogue of the deaf".[29]

Inequality, unemployment, and poverty have clearly not yielded to IMF/government policy prescriptions, exhortations, warnings, threats, and even private sector incentives for development. Economic dynamism is still elusive after eighteen years of an IMF piloted search. Perhaps research on some of the following issues would provide the empirical basis for less impressionistic and sounder, tentative judgements in the process of strategic policy formulation:

:   the determinants of enterprise vulnerability to conditions in the external environment.

:   the effects of economic restructuring on employment in different types of enterprises, according to factors such as the product market situation, whether the operation is in the public or private sector, enterprise size, the nature of the industry, technology, etc.

:   the factors contributing to a high level of industrial disputes and the propensity to strike at the enterprise and national levels.

:   designing wage/inflation/employment policies especially for those priority categories of the labour force, critical to national growth and development, such as teachers and science and technology workers, and others, in growth industries like tourism and potentially significant import-substitution ones, such as agriculture.

:   the relationship between wages and productivity at the micro level with emphasis on all the variables promoting efficiency, based on regular whole-system audits.

:   the factors explaining differences in labour market flexibility.

:   the role of the state in the determination of the investment profile of countries, during periods of rapid industrialization and economic growth.

If government is not to be the servant of private enterprise, and the 'common good' become private property[30], and if one is to avoid the generalized cynicism of "the pathology of politics"[31] of the New Right, then the attempt must be made to resolve the marginalization thesis. This, as Dunn observes, involves an encounter with,

> "... the problem of determining whether working class elements are excluded (from the economic and cultural benefits of economic change) by the existence of traditional values and institutions, or by inequalities and social divisions inherent in the process of development itself".[32]

The latter explanation would be precluded by a rejection of the African structuralist determinism style of "development dictatorship". And the former, seems to be nothing more than the apologist's response of ignoring that "deep malaise" and,

> "... pervasive sense of unfulfilled individual and collective possibilities (which) penetrates and corrodes the climate [not just] of every advanced capitalist society",[33] but now of an increasing number of countries.

At this level, there seems little distinction between the "happy problems of affluence" and the not-so-happy problems of poverty.

It could not, however, be said, with justification, that at the beginning of the 1970's, Jamaica's problems stemmed from premature "senility and decadence", associated, by Baran with "a peculiarly twisted career" of capitalism in developing countries.[34]

As has been recognized – but has not often enough been publicly conceded – the IMF and World Bank, the former in particular, became directly involved with a Jamaican economy, already in crisis. And since their involvement was at the invitation of the Government of Jamaica, they could not reasonably be accused of having caused the crisis. What is arguable is that their programmes have exacerbated the previously existing social and economic inequalities, and further disadvantaged the poorest sections of the community who, on any definition of social justice, ought, one would reasonably expect, to have been the beneficiaries of any measure of growth achieved, or indeed any change introduced.

Oxfam, making reference to Chile – allegedly one of the structural adjustment success cases – reveals data showing that 45% of the employed labour force,

> "... earned less than a subsistence wage under conditions of decreased job security and the erosion of worker benefits and employment rights, euphemistically called 'flexible labour markets.'"[35]

The report, in defending the call for IMF stabilization policy re-orientation, ended on the highly eloquent note that, "Oxfam works with some of the victims of this Latin America miracle".

It was in the midst of a public-sector wage crisis, increasing malnutrition, deepening and widening poverty, and a pervasive mood of public despair that the IMF's President Camdessus expressed the view that he was impressed with Jamaica, which, he expected, would soon be a model of successful economic adjustment, sufficient to provide inspiration for other developing countries.

Contemporaneously, the situation of the victims of IMF policies in Jamaica has been portrayed in the report of Monseigneur Richard Albert, on the inner-city conditions of the Kingston ghettos, in these terms:

> "Unfortunately, there is too much self-interest and not enough national interest .... Mothers are being forced to make decisions that they have never made before – which child will go to school today, who is going to sleep on the bed tonight [all prefaced by Fr. Albert's disclaimer] ... "before you judge me too quickly what I have said is not a political statement".[36]

To the extent that the above portrayal of the widening and deepening of the culture of poverty contradicts the official version of reality,[37] to that extent has it become necessary to re-examine the logic of the situation, so as to derive a different perception of the problems and arrive at an appreciation of alternative economic policy options/solutions.[38] This re-examination is mandated by the need to prevent the deeply embedded feelings of frustration and sense of hopelessness from becoming further psychologically disabling[39] on a mass scale.

The politics of 'continuity' – reflecting agreement as to the lack of an alternative to the "template laid out" by the IMF' World Bank – is indicative of a disturbing lack of awareness of the presence of a spectrum of possibilities in arriving at preferred states of social relations.[40] The result has been to narrow the boundaries of political debate on fundamental macro-economic policy to such an extent that the annual Budget Debate in Parliament is an event no longer thought worthy of attention by the general population.[41] As Bertram said in 1990 – which still holds true – "This time even fewer of them will listen [to the recurring calls for sacrifice on the part of the working class] for by now they know ... ."[42]

What debate there now is – rhetoric having subsided – without a redefinition and pursuit of the national interest in more transcendental terms, and less from a privileged minority perspective, is centered not on the system which generates inequality, poverty, and individual and collective distress. Rather, discussion surrounds the sizes of the slices of the surplus and poverty alleviation,[43] in an economy that continues to fail to grow, significantly, year after year in defiance of official projections.

We thus find, somewhat paradoxically, that ideological convergence resulting in a narrowing of fundamental differences between the ruling political elites as to the appropriate macro-economic policies to be pursued, is inversely related to capital/labour turbulence at the workplace. Profit and wage levels are now ostensibly under the influence of the principle of individualism, as against collectivism, within the context of an increasingly materialistic culture. But also, being the main items readily offered by labour and management in a *quid pro quo* of interest modification and adjustment,[44] which is the essence of any form of social contract, militant industrial action, in defence of demands threatening the fragile stability of the system, tends to be increasingly classified by those at whom it is aimed as a form of "social treason".

How are long-term commitments and the creation of a widely shared set of basic social premises, essential for planning and major problem solving, to be achieved in a society with predominant tendencies to conflict generation?

A patriotic/nationalistic, as against the vested interest hegemonic class definition of the 'National Interest', and the formulation of strategies based on consensus, such as a Social Contract and Prices and Incomes policy and the notion of Productivity Bargaining, becomes even more problematic when, as Reynolds phrases it,

"We have lived with failure for so long that we feel more comfortable with the condition".[45]

The promises of job creation and poverty alleviation[46] are, in the first case, backed by no guarantee, especially since the first promise is from government, but performance is left to the private sector – the capacity of which to spearhead the growth and modernization of industry, and, in the process, create a sufficient number of well-paid jobs, has not ceased to be questioned by commentators, unconnected to that sector. And the second cannot be fulfilled by token financial allocations, to relieve new or deepened poverty: a policy of "taking from the poor to give to the poor", what with retrogressive income distribution and a flat-rate consumption and insufficiently discriminating tax regime income.

Herson notes that in the absence of,

"... long-term planning, narrowly focused interest groups force us into piece-meal legislation, concerned with compromise among the spokesmen [italics added] for the most powerful interest groups".[47]

Mill also reminds us that the ultimate end of democracy is not the laws it produces but the enhancement of the intelligence of its people.[48] But this goal will be highly elusive under an economic model which, in a developing society, encourages the 'tinkering mentality', with 'budgetary constraints' which, among other consequences, fosters functional illiteracy in the educational system.

As Honderich submits,

> "The principle of equality does not derive from a view of life as simply a curious race where all attention is given to an equal start and no attention to some being lame".[49]

So, the "culture of enterprise", appealing as it sounds, is pitched at the, "... very small percentage of the community (that) will exhibit innovative or entrepreneurial qualities ... (in a market economy) ... where uncertainty must be borne individually".[50] People who are unemployed, or otherwise deprived in a semi-literate society, possessing little loan collateral, are not likely to assume the role of investors in enterprises, privatized or otherwise, or speculators on the stock market.[51]

Despite the failure to find solutions acceptable to the majority, and granted that the course of history is never entirely predictable, the radical intellectual option does not, as we have stated, appear viable: that option being that,

> "... only a massive programme of political mobilization and education along with a revolutionary end to the political tribalism engendered by a two-party Westminster political process can correct this situation. Whether such a transition can be effected without a violent upheaval remains quite doubtful".[52]

Parenti's observation is here appropriate, that there has,

> "In the face of class oppression (been) no class struggle; plutocratic dominance but no popular opposition to the policies and social conditions created by state supported capitalism".[53]

His conclusion is confirmed, by any liberal/radical review of the worsened Jamaican social situation, under extended IMF programmes. The response to the survey question specifically directed to the issue of resistance/revolt provides no challenge to this hegemonic class paradigm.

The systemic damage-limitation strategies, which have been the focus of major policy concern, have made little difference to the result.[54] The *status quo* has been preserved by the lack of a sufficiently severe social disruption and the emergence of new class re-alignments, in a society with strong politically conservative tendencies. This is both at the political party and trade union levels.

With the end of the Cold War, the island is now, of course, of less interest to those states that effectively control the International Financial Institutions. There is now, according to Green, "... nothing to protect us from but ourselves"[55] – a background statement, against which some of our survey responses can, with benefit, be assessed. Jamaica, in other words, is no longer geo-politically important, if indeed, it ever truly was.

The ambivalence which allegedly results in the indecisiveness, policy confusion, lack of strong political will in policy implementation and, most importantly, perhaps, the absence of a coherent vision of society, which would enable public policy, "... to climb above the mere give and take of interest group bargainers ... (and instead) solve fundamental and difficult problems",[56] with the majority as the beneficiaries, will, one expects, survive the ending of the borrowing relationship with the IMF.

The indicators thus suggest, that if populist, messianic politics were to re-emerge, then one should at least be entitled to expect that there might be a shortage of people to be "delivered".

1.   The Kirton interviews on behalf of Oxfam have been noted and referred to in the report of our own survey findings in Ch. 6
2.   Dawn Ritch, in The Daily Gleaner, Sept. 11, 1994, p.9A.
3.   Lawrence J.R. Herson, *The Politics of Ideas*, The Dorsey Press, I   984, p. 70.
4.   Abeng, editorial, Mar. 1, 1969.
5.   Obika Gray, *Radicalism and Social Change in Jamaica 1960-72*, University of Tennessee Press, 1991, p.179. Equally relevant to the Jamaican situation are British Labour Party leader, Tony Blair's words: "The core of government is flaccid, its decision-making consistent only for its indecisiveness" and he tenders a diagnosis appropriate to all local political administrations under Fund/Bank tutelage, "It is a government in which tactics have been elevated to the place normally reserved for vision" The Daily Gleaner, Nov. 22, 1995, p.14.
6.   Herson, Ibid, 1984, p. 296; For a similar approach see Paulo Freire, *Pedagogy of the Oppressed*, Penguin, 1990, p.18. Freire uses the term "circle of certainty".
7.   Herson, 1984, pp. 245,296.
8.   Larry Allan and Rita Maldon Ado-Bear, Free Market, *Finance, Ethics and Law*, Prentice Hall, 1994, p.58.
9.   Carl Stone, Race Class and Political Behaviour in Urban Jamaica, ISER, 1973, P.173; Gordon K. Lewis, Puerto Rico – Freedom and Power in the Caribbean, Monthly Review Press, 1963, P.96.
10. Carl Stone, *Class State and Democracy in Jamaica*, Praegar, 1987, p.188.
11. Delisle Worrell, "Economic Thought and Caribbean Economy", SES, U.W.I., Vol.2 Nos. 2&3, ISER, U.W.I., June & Sept. 1980, p.173.
12. Alione Diop, quoted in John Gaffar La Guerres, *Enemies of Empire*, Extra Mural Studies, U.W.I, Trinidad, 1982, p.136.
13. Worrell, 1980, p.174; Those in the private sector, and the multilateral institutions also, who hold out the E. Asian model as worthy of emulation need to ponder Hutton's reminder that "President Park Chung-Hee's first action when he became president of S. Korea in 1961 was to arrest some of the country's leading businessman under the Illicit Wealth Accumulation Act ... Only when they agreed to increase investment *in those industries* [italics added] which the government prioritized were they released creative government intervention (including nationalization of the banking system) unlocked the market failure, and so triggered the investment boom ... that delivered the export growth" – Will Hutton, "Why the Asian tigers burn so bright", in The Guardian Weekly, Aug.6, 1995, p.12; See in contrast, Delroy Lindsay, "Jamaica's industrial climate: a disincentive to investment

and growth", in The Sunday Gleaner, Dec. 24, 1990, p.8C, against the background of the statement to Parliament by the then Minister of Development. Planning and Production on Jan. 31, 1990, reported in The Daily Gleaner Supplement Feb. 7, 1990.

14. The Daily Gleaner, Oct. 18, 1995, p.1; In August of 1994 it was reported that only then had the Government seen it fit to establish a unit, comprising representatives of the BOJ, Ministry of Finance, PIOJ, and the Statistical Institute of Jamaica to monitor and "keep under constant review" *all* [italics added] factors which adversely affect "the monster" of inflation. One can only wait to see the extent to which the results of such monitoring will introduce an element of rationality into IMF wage policy advice. One year later the Prime Minister was warning the population to "Brace yourselves" for tighter monetary and fiscal measures as part of a package to "tame inflation". Among these measures would be the postponement of several items of expenditure, already approved in the current budget – The Jamaica Herald, Nov. 8, 1995, p.1. Relative stability of the exchange rate for 1994 did not prevent actual inflation being some 80% more than the projected rate, nor did it foster economic growth or employment expansion. Government's policy focus therefore, on the value of the local currency, has yielded little benefit in real terms. As the late Headley Brown contends, it is clearly the purchasing power of the local dollar in relation to local goods and services that needs to be the core concern of macro-economic policy. In this respect the rate of inflation of 25.1% for 1995 indicates little Government success in "taming the beast ..."

15. Headley Brown, in The Financial Gleaner, April 8, 1994, p.8 predicted that the chances of achieving the targeted inflation rate of 6.5% for 1994 is zero. This was subsequently adjusted to 12.5% and again to 15% clearly suggesting target setting by guesswork. The rate was actually 26.9%. Brown comments that "If in the fight against inflation in 199495, there is no victory for the monetary authorities, the near-term sacrifices of real output and employment contraction – which the use of high interest rates and crippling tight monetary policy entail – would be in vain".

16. The Jamaica Herald Financial Weekly Magazine "Dollars and Sense", May 6, 1966.

17. The Daily Gleaner, Sept. 24, 1995, p.3A.

18. Ralph Miliband, *The State in Capitalist Society*, Basic Books, 1969, p.101.

19. Lawrence J.R. Herson, *The Politics of Ideas*, The Dorsey Press, 1984, P.267.

20. Kari Levitt, "Stabilization and Structural Adjustment: Rhetoric and Reality", in *Caribbean Affairs*, Jan. 1991, p.11, where the further claim is made that "The IMF has in effect been transformed into the principal agent of an unofficial creditor cartel of the international banks ...". See also pp.17, 22.

21. Miliband, 1967, p.270.

22. Stone, 1987, p.179.

23. Rev. Ralston Nembhard in The Jamaica Herald, Sept. 5, 1995, p.7.

24. Karl Theodore, "Structural Adjustment in the Caribbean" in ILO, *The Role of Trade Unions in Periods of Structural Adjustment Programmes*, Barbados Workers Union Labour College, Dec. 1992, p.3.

25. Ralph Miliband, *Parliamentary Socialism*, Merlin Press, 1987, p.89.

26. Herson, 1984, p.284.

27. Irving Kristol, *Two Cheers for Capitalism*, Mentor Books, New York, 1978, p . 15 .

28. Elsie Le Franc, The Consequences of Structural Adjustment – A Review of the Jamaica Experience, Canoe Press, U.W.I. 1994, p13.

29. Immanuel Wallerstein, *The Capitalist World Economy*, Cambridge University Press, 1993, p.251; see also Michael Manley, *The Politics of Change*, Heinemann (Caribbean) Ltd. 1990, p.223.

30. Michael Harrington, *Twilight of Capitalism*, Touchstone, New York, 1976, p.264.

31. Miliband, 1967, p.270.

32. Leith L. Dunn Review of Manan's: *Social Life and Work in Brazils Free Trade Zone* Les A Despres, State University of N.Y. Press, Albany, 1991, in SES, Vol.41 No.1 ISER, U.W.I., Mar. 1992, p.249.

33. Miliband, 1967, p. 269.

34. P.A. Baran, *The Political Economy of Growth*, Monthly Review Press, 1957, Chap.6.

35. David Bryer, in The Guardian Weekly, Oct. 16, 1994.

36. Address at the Central St. Catherine Management Committee dinner, Kingston, reported in The Jamaica Herald, Dec. 3, 1994, p.6, titled "Economic Liberalization at what Cost?"; Claremont Kirton, *Debt and Poverty*, Oxfam, 1992, pp. 47 et seq, reports the responses in interviews as to experiences of living conditions under structural adjustment; On the practice of "blaming the victim", see William Ryan, *Blaming the Victim*, Vintage Books, New York, 1976.

37. C. Wright Mills, *The Power Elite*, Oxford University Press, New York, 1957, p. 4. "Reality" is viewed by Mills as a social construct and similarly by Gramsci as being defined by the hegemonic social class. On the "culture of poverty" see Oscar Lewis, *La Vida*, Random House, New York, 1966, and Karl Mannheim, *Ideology and Utopia*, Harcourt Brace Jovanovich, 1955.

38. Karl Popper, *The Open Society and its Enemies*, Princeton University Press, 1950.

39. Anderson and Witter assert that "the *new* [italics added] dependency which was engendered by the mounting debt did not sit easily" with those, including politicians, technocrats, academics and entrepreneurs, who had emerged from the peasantry and for whom the belief in national sovereignty had deep roots and "who had grown up to understand the nuances of colonial rule" – Patricia Anderson and Michael Witter, "Crisis Adjustment and Social Change – A Case Study of Jamaica" in Le Franc, 1994, p.13.

40. Such preferred states are here taken to be those of peace, order, harmony and stability.

41. Public Opinion polls have shown a persistently declining percentage of the population which listens to or watches the annual budget debate on radio or television, The Don Anderson Poll of 1994, published in The Daily Gleaner, June 29, 1994, p.3.

42. Arnold Bertram in The Jamaica Record, Jan. 21, 1990. p.7A.

43. Michael Parenti, *Democracy for the Few*, St. Martin's Press, 1988, p.312.

44. This is a problem similar to that of obtaining concessions from unfocused conservatives of the New Right – see Person, 1984, pp. 294,296.

45. C. Roy Reynolds, in The Jamaica Herald, Sept, 7, 1994, p. 7A.

46. Alan Walker refers to this strategy in the U.K. as "Governments pursuit of inequality as a conscious act of social policy" in "The Strategy of Inequality" in Ian Taylor (ed) *The Social Effects of Free Market Policies*, Harvester Wheatsheaf, 1990, p.30.

47. Herson, 1984, p.237; One may here express the view that, in relation to differences over fundamentals, major battles are usually lost by the "decision" to negotiate within the framework provided by the *status quo*; the working class and the poor should from this "angle of vision" be on its guard whenever the representatives of private capital "sing the praises" of governments; Mathur reminds us that "the long-run is unreal to the extent that the future has become less predictable, since global developments now have an increasing impact on internal decision-making at all levels – Ajeet Mathur, *Industrial Restructuring and Union Power*, ILO -ARTEP, 1991, p.57.

48. J.S Mill, 1882, "Representative Government.", in C. B. Macpherson, *Life and Times of Liberal Democracy*, Oxford University Press, New York, 1977.

49. Ted Honderich, Violence for Equality: Inquiries in Political Philosophy, Routledge, 1987, p.61.

50. Immanuel Wallerstein, 1993, p.114.

51. Ibid.

52. George Beekford and Michael Witter, *Small Garden, Bitter Weed: Struggle and Change in Jamaica*, ISER, U.W.I., 1991, p.121.

53. Parenti, 1988, p.308; The unity achieved in the trade union movement indicated by the formation of the JTURDC arid more recently the JCTU has been at a price: sensitivity to continuing union/party affiliation has meant, on the basis of impressionistic evidence, that the militancy of joint action and stridency of criticism of the party in power has been somewhat moderated. This is not to question the integrity of joint bargaining behaviour of officials on the union side – which is a recent development, and one which is to be watched with interest as central trade union organizational leadership, and party-political fortunes, change over times.

54. But see Clive Y. Thomas, *The Poor and the Powerless*, Monthly Review Foundation, 1988, p.231.

55. "Farewell IMF", in The Jamaica Herald Magazine, Dollars and Sense, Oct. 2, 1995, p.5; See also Arnold Bertram, "IMF ed in The Jamaica Record, Jan. 21, 1990, p.7A where it is claimed that the IMF achieved everything it set out to do in Jamaica as "capital reigns supreme and in many instances enjoys a return on investment unheard of since slavery".

56. Herson, 1984, p.237.

Appendices

Appendix i

PRODUCTIVITY INCENTIVE SCHEMES
INTERVIEW SCHEDULE

Name of Organization: _____

When was the productivity scheme introduced?_____

Is the scheme still in operation?

      Yes   [ ]

      No   [ ]

If no please explain why?_____

_____

Why was the productivity scheme introduced?

_____

_____

_____

Whose idea was it initially?

_____

How was the productivity scheme introduced?

      Unilaterally by management   [ ]

      Through a process of consultation [ ]

If there was consultation which of the following groups were involved:

Top Management	[ ]
Middle Management	[ ]
Supervisors	[ ]
Workers	[ ]
Union Leaders	[ ]
Union Officers and Delegates	[ ]
Consultants	[ ]

Did any significant conflict arise during the consultation?

Yes   [ ]

No   [ ]

If yes, what was the conflict over?_____

_____

_____

What proportion of the work force is included in the productivity scheme?_____

Are benefits from the scheme limited to certain groups (if so which groups)?

_____

_____

How were the performance standards set and what are they?

_____

_____

How is increased productivity rewarded under the scheme?

_____

_____

Since the introduction of the scheme has productivity/efficiency increased or decreased?

      Increase   [ ]

      Decrease   [ ]

      Fluctuate   [ ]

What has been the cost or benefit of the productivity scheme in dollar terms to:

      the company   [ ]

      the worker   [ ]

What impact has the productivity scheme have on the morale of the workers involved?_____

_____

What mechanisms are in place to monitor the scheme?

_____

_____

_____

Have any significant changes been made to the scheme since it was first introduced?

    Yes   [ ]

    No   [ ]

If yes what are these changes?

_____

_____

_____

Why were these changes made? _____

_____

_____

Have any lessons been learnt from the company's experience with productivity schemes? _____

_____

_____

_____

Appendix ii

SUMMARY OF JAMAICA'S PERFORMANCE

Date	Nature of Programme	Quota	Agreed Amount	Date of Expiration/ Cancellation
13.06.63	1yr. Stand-by	SDR 20.0 mn.	SDR 10.0 mn.	12.6.64
01.06.73	1yr. Stand-by	SDR 53.0 mn.	SDR 26.5 mn.	31.5.74
11.08.77	2yr. Stand-by	SDR 53.0 mn.	SDR 64.0 mn.	9.6.78
09.06.78	3yr. EFF	SDR 74.0 mn.	SDR 200.0 mn.	10.6.79
11.06.79	2yr. EFF	SDR 74.0 mn.	SDR 260.0 mn.	12.4.81
13.04.81	3yr. EFF	SDR 111.0 mn.	SDR 477.7 mn.	12.4.84
22.06.84	1yr. Stand-by	SDR 145.5 mn.	SDR 64.0 mn.	21.6.85
17.07.85	22mth. Stand-by	SDR 145.5 mn.	SDR 115.0 mn.	16.7.86
02.03.87	15mth. Stand-by	SDR 145.5 mn.	SDR 85.0 mn.	31.5.88
19.09.88	20mth. Stand-by	SDR 145.5 mn.	SDR 82.0 mn.	30.9.89
01.01.90	15mnth. Stand-by	SDR 145.5 mn.	SDR 82.0 mn.	31.3.91
01.04.91	12mnth. Stand-by	SDR 145.5 mn.	SDR 43.7 mn.	31.3.92

UNDER IMF PROGRAMMES

Undrawn Bal. at Expiration/ Cancellation	Comments
SDR 10.0 mn.	Expiration - financing was not necessary.
SDR 13.25 mn.	Expiration - remaining 50% was not needed.
SDR 44.8 mn.	Cancellation - deviation of fiscal performance and breach of bank credit ceiling.
SDR 130.0 mn.	Cancellation - deviation from NIF target of BOJ and breach of criterion to eliminate external arrears by end of 1979.
SDR 175.0 mn.	
SDR 74.9 mn.	Waiver granted (after end March 1983) following breach of NIR Cancellation (after end Sept. 1983) disagreement between IMF and the government concerning technical aspects of performance criteria.
———	Waiver granted (after Sept, and Dec. 1984) following breaches of programme targets on payment arrears.
SDR 73.4 mn.	Cancellation- delays on disbursements of loans - breach
SDR ———	Expiration - 1987/88 programme successfully completed.
SDR 40.9 mn.	Waiver granted (after end March 1989) following breach of targets relating to NIR, external payment arrears, ceiling on short term external public debt, limit on NDA, and financing requirements of public sector. Criteria postponed to June 1989.
	Cancellation (after end Sept. 1989), accumulation of payment arrears and breach of NIR.
———	Waiver granted (after end March and June 1991 following breached of NIR targets.)
	Expiration – 1990/91 programme successfully completed.
———	Out turn not as impressive as that of 1990/91. NIR deteriorated to – US$250. 49m due to liberalization of the foreign exchange market in Sept. 1991. Stand-by programme extended to June 1992, involving removal of Government subsidies etc. Modified performance criteria satisfied.

Appendix iii

QUESTIONAIRE NO. I (Test Instrument)
IMF: SURVEY

1. Was it necessary for Jamaica to go to the IMF in the first place.
    If yes, why_____; If no, why not?_____

2. Was going to the IMF: good/bad/neither good nor bad for Jamaica
    or don't know

3. As long as we are under the IMF does it matter which Party is in power?____

4. What in your opinion have been the main problems created by the
    IMF policies: few new jobs
    high cost of credit/interest rates
    cost of living/inflation
    cut in government spending - government work
                     - health
                     - education
    loss of value of the dollar
    low wages (wage guidelines)
    redundancies/unemployment
    OTHER

5. Who benefited most from the IMF policies? Who suffered most

big business/private sector	banks insurance companies
hotels	exporters
small business	wealthy
workers	farmers
middle class	upper class
unemployed	pensioners
youth	women

6. Which IMF policies brought most benefit/did most harm

        wage guidelines   devaluation

        credit restrictions   high interest rates

        cut in government spending   privatization/divestment

        removal of subsidies   removal of price controls

        import liberalization   removal of exchange controls

7. How has your own position been affected by INF policies?

        not affected: why

        don't know

        better off: why/how?

        worse off: why/how?

        If worse off: how have you coped?

8. How have the IMF policies affected trade unions/trade union representation of workers?

9. Who do you blame for the state of the economy since we went to the IMF:

        Government: which?   72/80   80/89   89/ ?

        Private sector

        Unions

        IMF

10. Do you agree that we should break from the IMF?

        yes: why?   no: why not?

11. How do you expect conditions after the break with the IMF to be for yourself and the country?

        COUNTRY   PERSONALLY

        better: why/how   better: why/how

        worse: why/how   worse: why/how

        no different: why   no different: why

        don't know   don't know

12. Should we repay the IMF debts?

        If yes: why?   If no: why not?

13. In your opinion why has there been no serious IMF

        protest
        revolt
        revolution

14. What are your expectations for the future?

        personally

        for the country

15. Which of the following IMF objectives would you say have been achieved:

        reduce state involvement in the economy
        increase role of private sector in the economy
        increase exports
        reduce balance of payments deficit
        increase investment/stimulate economy growth
        stabilization of exchange rate at market determined rate
        slow down wages increases
        cut fiscal deficit
        cut down excess money supply
        liberalize imports
        removal of price controls

16. What areas of the economy, if any, are showing signs of growth?

17. Do you think the IMF policies have anything to do with the level of crime?

        If yes, why   If no, why not?

18. Can you state the ways in which the country has benefited from the IMF?

19. Can you state the ways in which the country has suffered under the IMF?

20. Have management/labour relations been affected by the IMF policies?

        If yes, how

        If not., why not?

21. What would you say are the most serious problem facing Jamaica?

        now

        over the past 15 years

22. Do you think more people have become self-employed as a result of IMF policies?

23. Has there been business expansion or declinefgeneraIlyf under the IMF?

        Expansion: why?   Decline: why?

24. What have most companies done with most of their profits under the IMF?

        Given more dividends to shareholders

        Put back more into business

        Used it to support high life style

        Paid more wages to workers

        Paid more taxes to Government

        OTHER:

25. How has your ability to save changed over the years?

        1970's

        1980's

        1990's

26. How would you react to the reintroduction of wage guidelines?

        accept

        fight against

        don't know

Appendix iv

INTERVIEWER GUIDE

QI.   Borrowing relationship refers to the loan arrangement which Jamaica started with the IMF in the 1970s.

Q2 & Q3. Q2 refers to the individual and Q3, the country. The respondent is only to answer Q2 and Q3 if the answer to QI is yes. If a respondent does not know "why" or "how" in response to these and other questions, simply write "Don't know" in the lined spaces provided.

Q6.   Protecting workers' rights and benefits means, e.g., ensuring that workers are not paid less than the minimum wage, or that they get agreed time off, housing, lunch and other types of benefits which have been agreed on.

The national interest is generally what is good for the nation or the people in the Country as a whole.

Q7.   If the respondent does not give an immediate answer, the person interviewing may mention, for example: the people, the people through a referendum, the government, the business people, the workers, the trade unions, the church, leaders, etc. The respondent can select one of these or several, or none, or a combination of these and others – depending on what answer he or she wants to give.

Q9.   Q9 is for workers only. Wage guidelines are the increases in wage levels (e.g., 15%) which the government (or the IMF through the government), etc., sometimes establishes and requests that workers and employers follow or adhere to.

If workers, for example, wish to have a 50% increase but they accept only 15%, they would probably wish to have some sort of compensation for the missing 35% (e.g., stable prices, housing and welfare benefits and allowances of various sorts, government bonds, etc.).

QI0.   Prices and incomes policies refer to attempts to regulate prices of goods and services and wages, and possibly other forms of income, such as rent and dividends, so as to keep the rate of inflation at a lower level. Of course, one policy may also be to leave prices and incomes unregulated.

Q11. This asks whether the amounts paid and received should be controlled rather than be left to move freely. The respondent may say Yes (Y) but agree with controls for only two three things. Circle "Y" and underline the two or three things. If the answer is "No" ("N"). do not underline anything.

Q12. A productivity incentive scheme is one which promises or offers benefits to members of an organization if they produce at a higher rate. This may be in the form of weekly pay and end-of-year bonus, a paid holiday, etc.

Q16. This refers to whether the respondent works in a private sector organization (e.g., Desnoes & Geddes or a shoe shop).

Q18. The Income Tax threshold is that level of income up to which people do not begin to pay tax. This involves a basic allowance. Some low-income earners may even pay no tax at all as a result of the level at which the threshold now stands. Q18 asks whether the respondent has benefited from the increase (e.g., has there been a drop in the amount of income tax which he or she pays.).

Q20. A fixed exchange rate is one in which the Jamaican dollar is fixed, for example, in terms of how much (or how many units) have to be paid or a US$. a fixed rate would state, for example that it is J$38 to the US$. It will not normally be J$36 to US$ next week or J$71 to the US$ next month. Next week and next month it would remain at a rate of exchange of $38 to the US$ normally such a fixed rate would be determined by the Government through the BOJ and not market forces.

Q21. Circle or tick one answer of the three possible ones suggested here. Some people might nevertheless find it difficult to decide between, say, "Healthy profits" and "Decent wages" because they feel that they are closely related. Circle or tick the one which is more strongly believed. You could circle and also underline that main answer but put a circle only, or a tick around the other, e.g., Decent wages.

Q22. This is really two questions, although it seems to be an "either/or" question. Please see that both sections are answered.

Productivity is generally the rate at which goods ate produced or at which people or machines work – generally the combination of speed, accuracy, and efficiency. When wages are linked to the cost of living, this should be taken to mean that, for example, if the cost of living goes up, then wages should be increased at least as much so that living standards are maintain? or improved.

Q23 The Y (Yes) or N (No) answer may not suit the respondent. Write the answer which he or she provides. He may feel, for example, that the IMF created some hardships, but also help or has helped in some ways.

Q24 Sustained revolt refers mainly to serious protest here. Rather than making a comment for such of the groups, the respondent could offer one comment for all of them.

Q25. If the respondent does not know of the social contract, write the answer Don't know. Skip Q26, if he or she does not know of the social contract.

Q26. The respondent does not have to give an answer for each of these – economy, trade unions, employers, government. A general answer can be given, if preferred

Q27. This is asking: Do you have a short comment or summary on all that you have been saying?

Appendix v

QUESTIONAIRE No. 2

Good Day Sir/Madam. I am representing an individual who is doing research towards a post-graduate degree on the Jamaican experience under the IMF. I would appreciate if you would answer some questions for this purpose.

1. What' is the first word that comes to your mind when you hear 'I.M.F.'?

   _____

2. Was the decision to go the IMF: Good   Bad   Neither

3. What have been the main problems created by the IMF?
   - fewer new jobs
   - high cost of credit/interest rates
   - high cost of living/inflation
   - cut in government spending (health/education sector)
   - devaluation
   - other:_____
   _____

4. Who benefitted/suffered most from the IMF policies?
   Benefitted _____ Suffered

       Big business/private sector as a whole
       Banks/Insurance companies
       Hotels
       Manufacturers/Trade
       Small business
       Exporters
       Workers
       Consumers
       Farmers
       Unemployed
       Pensioners
       Other: _____

5. Which of the following IMF policies would you rate as having been beneficial/harmful?

    Beneficial _____ Harmful

    Wage guidelines
    Devaluation
    Credit Restrictions
    Privatization/Divestment
    Removal of Subsidies
    Removal of Price Controls
    Import Liberalization
    Removal of Exchange Controls

6. Who do you blame for the state of the economy since we went to the IMF?
    Government; Private Sector; Trade Unions; Neither
    Why?_____
    _____

7. It is best that we break from the IMF?

Strongly Agree	Agree	Don't Know	Disagree	Strongly Disagree	Neither

8. How do you expect conditions in the country after IMF to be?

Definitely Worse	Worse	Better	Definitely Better	Neither

    Why?_____
    _____

9. What are your personal expectations for the future?_____
    _____
    _____
    _____

10. What areas of the economy are showing signs of growth?_____
    _____
    _____
    _____

11. Do you think more people have become self-employed as a result of IMF policies?   Yes [ ]   No [ ]

   (Yes, go to question #12 - No, go to question # 13)

12. What kinds of jobs are created as a result of the self-employment?

   Small Scale Vending   Craft Work
   Taxi Operators   Restaurant Operations
   Jewellers   Other_____

13. What have most companies done with most of their profits under the IMF

   - Contributed to Food for the Poor, etc.
   - Paid Better Wages
   - Expanded their operations/Put back into businesses
   - Donations to Churches
   - Profit-sharing schemes for employees
   - Dividends to Shareholders
   - Paid to Government as taxes
   - Other_____

14. Under the IMF, has your ability to save improved over the years?

   Yes [ ]   No [ ]

15. How would you react to the re-introduction of wage guidelines?

   Accept   Fight Against   Don't Know

   Why?_____

16. On a scale of 1-10, with 10 being for the best results, how would you rate the IMF Policies over the years?   _____

   Why?_____

17. What particular grouse, if any, do you have regarding the IMF Policies

   _____

   Name_____
   Address_____
   Phone_____

Appendix vi

QUESTIONAIRE No. 3

This questionnairs is designed to obtain the views of members of the public in Jamaica on issues such as the International Monetary Fund's (IMF'S) policies and how they affect the Jamaican people and the economy. Your answers to the questions are important to the study of which they will be a part. Thank you for your cooperation.

LEGEND: Y = Yes   N = No   T = True   F = False

Category (respondent) (BB, SB, WC)_____

Title/Occupation _____Organization_____

Location KMR_____ Parish_____

Date of interview _____

1. Has our (Jamaica's) borrowing relationship with the IMF ended?   Y   N

2. If yes, will you be better off as a result?   Y   N
   Why?_____

3. Will the country be better off?   Y   N
   Why?_____

4. Increased wages lead to increased prices.   T   F
   Why?_____

5. Increased wages lead to unemployment.   T   F
   Why?_____

6. Is the protection of workers' rights and benefits in the
   national interest?   Y   N

7. Who should determine what is in the national interest?_____
   _____
   _____

8. Is poverty a threat to the national interest?   Y   N

9. What would you want in exchange for accepting wage guidelines?_____
_____

10. If prices and incomes policies are introduced, what would be their effect on
the economy?_____
_____
_____

11. Should rent, interest rates, dividends and profit levels also be
controlled?   Y   N

12. Can you identify a company with a productivity incentive scheme?
                                      Y   N

If Yes, Please name the company_____

13. Does a productivity incentive scheme benefit the employee?
                                      Y   N
How?_____

14. How does such a scheme benefit the employer?_____
_____

15. Are you a member of a trade union?   Y   N

16. Are you a member of the private sector?   Y   N

17. In what way have you benefited from the National Housing Trust?
_____
_____

18. In what way have you benefited from the increase in the Income Tax threshold?
_____
_____

19. Should price controls be introduced in our liberalized economy?

        Y   N

20. Would a fixed exchange rate benefit our economy? Y   N

21. What means more to you?   Healthy profits   Decent wages   Neither

22. Do you feel wages should be directly linked with increased:

    (i) Worker productivity   Y   N

    (ii) Cost of living?   Y   N

23. IMF policies created only hardships for the Jamaican people.

        T   F

24. Why has there not been more sustained revolt by dissatisfied groups? e.g.

      Teachers and nurses_____

      Unionized workers_____

      The unemployed_____

25. What does the idea of a social contract mean to you?_____

_____

26. Will a Social Contract make any difference to the economy/trade unions/ workers/employers/government? Please comment_____

_____

27. What are your overall comments on the whole issue of the IMF, the social contract, national interest, prices & incomes policies, and productivity incentive schemes?_____

_____

_____

Thank you again for answering the questions.

Appendix viii

INTERVIEW SCHEDULE
FOR CASE STUDIES ON THE IMPACT OF
PRIVATIZATION AND REDUNDANCY
ON JAMAICAN WORKERS

Personal Data

1. Name_____

2. Address_____

3. Age (Last Birthday; DD/MM/YR) [   ]

4. Marital Status_____

5. Number of dependents: Spouse: [   ] Children: [   ] Other [   ]

Educational Data

6. Level of academic attainment:

Primary:

Secondary: No. of 'O' levels [   ]

　　　　　　　No. of 'A' l evels [   ]

　　　　　　　Other_____

Vocational_____

Tertiary_____Certificate [   ]_____

　　　　　　　Diploma　[   ]_____

　　　　　　　Degree　　[   ]_____

7. Age at which education stopped [   ]

Employment Data

8. Employment history prior to redundancy

Occupation	Employer	Duration	How Found

8a. How long did it take you to find a new job? [   ]

9. Employment since redundancy

Occupation	Employer	Duration	How Found

10. How were you made redundant?

    a)   Voluntary Retrenchment   [ ]

    b)   Early Retirement   [ ]

    c)   Declared Redundant   [ ]

    d)   Quit Voluntarily – not influenced by developments   [ ]

    e)   Anticipated redundancy and quit to look for a job   [ ]

    f)   Other (Specify)_____

11. Did the job that you found after redundancy pay you more or less than the job from which you were made redundant?

    a)   More   [ ]

    b)   Less   [ ]

11a. Did the job that you found after redundancy have more or less fringe
benefits than the job from which you were made redundant?

a) More [ ]

b) Less [ ]

11b. If the pay was less how did you deal with the shortage?

a) Reduced household expenditure [ ]

b) Used savings [ ]

c) Used severance pay [ ]

d) Used pension refund [ ]

e) Borrowed money [ ]

f) Informal employment [ ]

g) Remittances [ ]

h) Previously unemployed members have sought work[ ]

i) Other_____

12 Did you receive a pension refund and redundancy payment?

a) Pension Refund [ ]

b) Redundancy Payment [ ]

c) Notice Pay [ ]

12a If yes, what was the money used to do? [ ]

a) Supplement household expenditure [ ]

b) Consumed (Durable items) [ ]

c) Invested/Saved [ ]

d) Capitalize Business [ ]

e) Other_____

13. Through which media did you seek work?

a) Leads from friends or relatives [ ]

b) Newspaper listings [ ]

c) Placement service [ ]

d) Direct applications [ ]

e) Other_____

14. How does you household deal with the absence of your income?

a) Reduced household expenditure [ ]

b) Used savings [ ]

c) Used severance pay [ ]

d) Used pension refund [ ]

e) Borrowed money [ ]

f) Informal employment [ ]

g) Remittances [ ]

h) Previously unemployed members have sought work [ ]

i) Other_____

15. Have you been offered any jobs which you have not accepted?

a) Yes [ ]

b) No [ ]

15a. If yes, why were they not accepted?

a) Regarded the pay as too low [ ]

b) Regarded working conditions as sub-standard [ ]

c) Location [ ]

d) Other_____

16. Were you unable to qualify for any jobs that you found open?

a) Yes [ ]

b) No [ ]

16a. If YES, why were you unable to qualify

    a)   Age   [   ]

    b)   Did not have the skills   [   ]

    c)   Other reason_____

17 What is the lowest wage you would be willing to work for [$]

18 Would you want more training in your same field or would want to be trained in a new area

    a)   More training in same field   [   ]

    b)   Training in new field   [   ]

19 Are you interested in self-employment

    a)   Yes   [   ]

    b)   No   [   ]

19a. If YES, why haven't you started

    a)   Afraid of risk   [   ]

    b)   Lack the startup capital   [   ]

    c)   Other_____

19b. If no, why?_____

BIBLIOGRAPHY

BOOKS

ADDISON, Tony and Lionel DEMERY, *The Alleviation of Poverty Under Structural Adjustment.* Washington DC: World Bank, 1988.

ADELMAN, I. and C.T. MORRIS, *Economic Growth and Social Equity in Developing Countries,* Stanford University Press, 1973.

AKERLOF, G.A. and Y. YELLEN, eds. *Efficiency Wage Models of the Labour Market.* Cambridge University Press, 1987.

ALLEN, V.L. *The Sociology of Industrial Relations.* LONGMAN, 1971.

AMIN, S. *Unequal Development.* New York: Monthly Review Press, 1976.

ARENDT, Hanna. *On Revolution.* New York: Viking Press, 1963.

ARON, Raymond. *Democracy and Totalitarianism.* London: Weidenfeld & Nicholson, 1968.

ASHBY, Timothy. *Missed Opportunities: The Rise and Fall of Jamaica's Edward Seaga.* Indianapolis, Indiana: Hudson Institute, 1989.

AYA, Rod. *Rethinking Revolutions and Collective Violence: Studies on Concept, Theory and Method.* Heb Spinhuis Publishers, 1990.

BALASSA, Bela, and Associates. *Development Strategies in Semi-Industrial Countries.* Baltimore: Johns Hopkins University Press, 1982.

BARAN, P.A. *The Political Economy of Growth.* Harmondsworth: Penguin, 1957.

BAUER, P.T. *Reality and Rhetoric: Studies in the Economics of Development.* London: Weidenfeld & Nicholson, 1984.

BECKFORD, George, ed. *Caribbean Economy Dependence and Backwardness.* Kingston: Mona, ISER, 1975.

—. Michael WITTER, eds. *Small Garden Bitter Weed: Struggle and Change in Jamaica.* Kingston, Mona: ISER, 1986.

BECKLES, Hilary, and Verene SHEPHERD, eds. *Caribbean Freedom: Economy and Society from Emancipation to the Present.* Kingston, Jamaica: Ian Randle, 1993.

BERNSTEIN, Eduard. *Evolutionary Socialism.* New York: Schocken, 1961.

BLACKBURN, Robin, and Alexander COCKBURN, eds. *The Incompatibles: Trade Union Militancy and the Consensus.* Middlesex, Penguin, 1967.

BLACKMAN, C. "Wage Price Policies for Increasing International Competitiveness in the Caribbean," in Yin-Kann Wen and Jayshree Sengupta, eds., *Increasing the International Competitiveness of Exports from Caribbean Countries.* Washington, D. C.: World Bank, 1991.

BOTTOMORE, Tom. *The Socialist Economy Theory and Practice.* New York: Harvester Wheatsheaf, 1990.

BOURNE, Compton, ed. *Inflation in the Caribbean.* Kingston, Mona: ISER, 1977.

—. "Wage Determination in the Caribbean Countries: Trends & Issues," in ILO *Labor-Management Relations Series,* ILO. 57: 1979, 34-50.

BOYD, D. Macro-Economic Stabilization in Jamaica: the lessons of recent experience, Overseas Development Institute, w/p. 1986.

BRAVERMAN, H. *Labour and Monopoly Capital.* Monthly Review Press, 1974.

BRUNO, Michael, "Stabilisation and Stagflation in a Semi-industrialised Economy," In: Rudiger Dornbusch and Jacob A. Frenkel, eds., *International Economic Policy, Theory and Evidence.* Baltimore, Md: Johns Hopkins University Press, 1979.

BUCHANON, Paul. *Community Development in the Ranking Economy: A Socio-Economic Study of the Jamaican Ghetto.* KINGSTON: CAST, 1992.

BURNS, Tom. *Industrial Man.* Middlesex: Penguin, 1969.

BUTLER, David., and Donald Stokes. *Political Change in Britain: The Evaluation of Electoral Choice.* 2nd ed. New York: St. Martin's Press, 1974.

CAMMACK, A.K. 'Dependency and the politics of development' in P.F. Leeson, and M.M. Minogue eds. *Perspectives in Development: Cross-disciplinary themes in development.* Manchester University Press, 1988.

CHENERY, Hollis., et al. eds. *Redistribution with Growth.* London: Oxford University Press, 1974.

CHOWDHURY, A. AND I. ISLAM. *The Newly Industrialising Economies of East Asia.* Routledge, 1993.

CLAPHAM, Christopher, ed. *Private Patronage and Public Power: Political Clientelism in the Modern State.* New York: St. Martins Press, 1982.

CLARKE, Tom. and Laurie CLEMENTS. *Trade Unions Under Capitalism.* – Fontana, 1977.

CLEGG, H.A. *How to Run an Incomes Policy and why we made such a mess of the last one.* Heineman, 1971.

COLE, G.D.H. and Raymond POSTGATE. *The Common People 1746-1946.* London: Methuen, 1961.

COLCLOUGH, C. and J. MANOR, eds. *States or Markets: Neo-liberalism and the Development Debate.* Oxford: Oxford University Press, 1990.

COLMAN, David, and Fred NIXSON. *Economics for Change in Less Developed Countries.* 3rd ed. New York: Harvester Wheatsheaf, 1994.

COOTE, Belinda. *The Trade Trap: Poverty and the Global Community.* Oxford:L Oxfam, 1992.

CORBO, Vittorio, GOLDSTEIN, Morris and Moshin KHAN. *Growth-Oriented Adjustment Programmes,* Washington DC: IMF/World Bank, 1987.

CORNFORTH, Maurice. *Materialism and the Dialectical Method.* N.Y: International Publishers, 1972.

CORNIA, Giovanni, et al. *Adjustment With a Human Face: Protecting the Vulnerable and Promoting Growth.* Oxford, Clarendon Press, 1987.

COSER, Lewis. *The Functions of Social Conflict.* Glencoe: Free Press, 1959.

COWELL, Noel. *A Summary of Test Cases in Jamaican Labour Law,* Kingston, JTURDC.

CROSS, Malcolm, and Gad. HUEMANN. eds. *Labour in the Caribbean: From Emancipation to Independence.* London: Macmillan, 1988.

CROUCH, C. *Class Conflict and the Industrial Relations Crisis,* Heinemann, 1977.

DAHRENDORF, Ralf. *Class and Class Conflict in Industrial Society.* London, 1959.

DEERE, Carmen, et al co-ordinator. *In the Shadows of the Sun: Caribbean Development Alternatives and US Policy.* San Francisco: West View Press, 1990.

DELL, S. 'Stabilization: The Political Economy of Overkill', in Williamson, J., ed. IMF *Conditionality.* Washington, DC: Institute of International Economics, 1983.

DOMHOFF, William G. *Who Rules America?* Englewood Cliffs, N.J.: Prentice Hall, 1967.

DUNCAN, Graeme, ed. *Democracy and the Capitalist State.* Cambridge: Cambridge University Press, 1989.

DUNLOP, J.T. *Industrial Relations Systems.* Mott, 1958.

—. *Wage Determination under Trade Unions.* Macmillan 1944. 45-73.

EDELMAN, Murray. *The Symbolic Uses of Power.* Urbana: University of Illinois Press, 1964.

EDIE, Carlene. *Democracy by Default: Dependency and Clientism in Jamaica.* Kingston, Ian Randle 1991.

EISENSTADT, S.N. *Revolution and the Transformation of Societies.* New York: Free Press, 1978.

EMMANUEL, A. *Unequal Exchange.* New Left Books, 1972.

ESPING-ANDERSEN, G, *Politics Against Markets: The Social Democratic Road to Power.* Princeton: Princeton University Press, 1985.

FANON, Frantz. *The Wretched of the Earth.* London: Penguin, 1963.

FARLEY, RAWLE. *Trade Unions and Politics in the British Caribbean,* Georgetown, 1957.

FEI, J., G. RANIS, and S. KUO. *Growth and Equity: The Taiwan Case.* Oxford: Oxford University Press, 1979.

FEMIA, J. Gramscis. *Political Thought.* Oxford: Clarendon Press, 1981.

FLANDERS, Allan. *The Fawley Productivity Agreements: A Case Study of Management and Collective Bargaining,* London: Faber, 1964.

FOX, A. 'Industrial Relations: A Social Critique of Pluralist Ideology', in J. Child ed. *Man and Organization.* George Allen and Unwin, 1973, 216.

FREIRE, Paulo. *Pedagogy of the Oppressed.* London: Penguin, 1972.

FROEBEL, Folker. "Perspectives on the New International Division of Labour" Conference on The Future of the Caribbean in the World System, Mimeo, Jamaica, May 1988.

FUKUYAMA, F. *The End of History and the Last Man.* London: Hamish Hamilton, 1992.

FURTADO, Celse. *Development and Underdevelopment: A Structural View of the Problems of Development and Underdeveloped Countries.* Berkeley: University Press of California, 1967.

GALENSON, W. and S.M. LIPSET, (eds.) *Labour and Trade Unionism.* New York, Wiley, 1960.

GARCIA, Alvaro, et al. *Meeting the Social Debt.* Geneva: ILO - PREALC, 1988.

GILL, Richard. *Economic Development: Past and Present.* 2nd. ed Englewood Cliffs NJ: Prentice - Hall 1967.

GODFREY, Martin. *Labour Market Monitoring and Employment Policy in a Developing Economy: A Study of Indonesia,* New Delhi ILO - ARTEP, 1993.

GORDON, Derek. Class, *Status and Social Mobility in Jamaica.* Mona, Jamaica: ISER, 1987.

GOROSTIAGA, X. "Towards Alternative Policies for the Region," in G. Irvin and X. Gorostiaga, eds., *Towards an Alternative for Central America and the Caribbean.* London: George Allen and Unwin Ltd., 1985.

GRAMSCI, A. *Selections from Prison Notebooks.* Lawrence and Wishart, 1971.

GREENAWAY, David, and Chris MILNER., *Trade and Industrial Policy in Developing Countries.* London: MacMillan, 1993.

GURR, Ted. *Why Men Rebel.* Princeton: Princeton University Press, 1971.

GWIN, Catherine, and Richard E. FEINBERG, eds *The IMF in a Multipolar World: Pulling Together,* Overseas Development Council, Washington, 1989.

HARRIGAN, Jane. "The Case of Jamaica" in Paul Mosley, Jane Harrigan, and John Toye, *Aid and Power.* (2), Routledge, 1991.

HARRISON, Paul. *The Third World Tomorrow: A Report from the Battlefront in the War against Poverty.* 2nd ed. London: Penquin, 1983.

HAYEK, F.A. *The Road to Serfdom.* London, Rout-ledge & Kegan Paul, 1962.

HAYTER, Teresa, *The Creation of World Poverty,* 2nd ed. London: Pluto Press, 1990.

HEADY, P. and M. SMYTH, *Living Standards During Unemployment.* London: HMSO, 1989.

HENRY, Zin. *Labour Relations and Industrial Conflict in Commonwealth Caribbean Countries.* Port of Spain, Trinidad: Columbus 1972.

HERMAN, Bohuslav. *The Optimal International Division of Labour.* Geneva: ILO, 1975 .

HERSON, Lawrence. *The Politics of Ideas: Political Theory and American Public Policy.* Homewood Ill: Dorsey, 1984.

HICKS, John. *Capital and Growth,* Oxford University Press, 1965.

HINTON, J. and R. HYMAN, *Trade Unions and Revolution,* Pluto Press, 1975.

HOBHOUSE, L.T. *The Elements of Social Justice.* London: Allen and Unwin, 1922.

HONDERICH, Ted. *Violence for Equality: Inquiries in Political Philosophy.* New York: Routledge, 1989.

HYMAN, Ralston. *Industrial Relations: A Marxist Introduction.* Macmillan 1975.

ILO. *Payments by Results. International Labour Office,* Geneva, ILO, 1984.

JEFFERSON, Owen. *The Post-War Economic Development of Jamaica.* Mona: ISER, 1972.

JONES, Edwin. *Development Administration: Jamaican Adaptations.* Kingston: Caricom, 1992.

JONES-HENDRICKSON, Simon. *Public Finance and Monetary Policy in Open Societies.* ISER, 1985.

KALDOR, N. 'Economic Problems of Chile' in: *Essays on Economic Policy,* II, London: Duckworth, 1964.

KASSALOW , Everett, and Damachi UKANDI, eds. *The Role of Trade Unions in Developing Societies.* Geneva: ILO.

KAUTSKY, Karl. *The Class Struggle.* (Erfurt Program) trails. William Bohn. Chicago: Charles H. Kerr, 1910.

KERR, Clark, et al. *Industrialism and Industrial Man: The Problems of Labour and Management in Economic Growth.* New York: Galaxy Books, 1964.

KERR, Madeline. *Personality and Conflict in Jamaica.* Liverpool, University Press, 1952.

KEYNES, J.M. *General Theory of Employment, Interest and Money.* London: Macmillan, 1936.

KIRTON, Claremont. *Jamaica Debt and Poverty.* Oxford: Oxfam, 1992.

KORNHAUSER, A., R. DUBIN, and A.M. ROSS, eds. *Industrial Conflict.* McGraw-Hill, 1954.

KORNHAUSER, William. *The Politics of Mass Society.* — Free Press, 1959.

KORPI, Walter. *The Working Class in Welfare Capitalism: Work, Unions, and Politics in Sweden.* London: Routledge & Kegan Paul, 1978.

KORTEN, David, and Philipe ALFONSO, *Bureaucracy and the Poor: Closing the Gap*. Hardford, Ct: Kumarian Press, 1983.

KRISTOL, Irving. *Two Cheers for Capitalism*, New York: Mentor Books, 1978.

KIIZNETS, S. *Modern Economic Growth*. New Haven, Ct.: Yale University Press, 1966.

LACEY, Terry. *Violence and Politics in Jamaica: 1960-1970*. London: Manchester University Press, 1972.

LaGUERRE, John. *Enemies of Empire*. St. Augustine, Trinidad: U.W.I.

LAL, D. *The Poverty of 'Development Economics'*, Hobart Paperback 16 London: Institute of Economic Affairs, 1983.

LALTA, Stanley, and Marie FRECKLETON, eds. *Caribbean Economic Development: The First Generation*. Kingston: Ian Randle, 1993.

LASSWELL, Harold. Politics: *Who Gets What, When, and How*. New York: McGraw-Hill, 1936.

LEBERGOTT, Stanley, ed. *Men Without Work: The Economics of Unemployment*. Englewood Cliffs, NJ: Prentice Hall 1964.

LE FRANC, Elsie. *Consequences of Structural Adjustment: A Review of the Jamaican Experience*. Mona; Jamaica: Canoe Press, 1994.

LEE, Eddy. ed. *Export Led Industrialization and Development*. Geneva: ILO, 1981.

LENIN, V.I., *What Is to Be Done*. Moscow: Progress Publishers, 1964.

LEVINSON, Harold. *Determining Forces in Collective Wage Bargaining*, New York: John Wiley & Sons, 1966.

LEVITAS, R. ed. *The Ideology of the New Right*. Cambridge: Polity Press, 1986.

LEWIS, Gordon. *Puerto Rico: Freedom and Power in the Caribbean*. New York: Monthly Review, 1963.

LEWIS, W.A. *Development Planning: The Essentials of Economic Policy*. Allen and Unwin, 1966.

—, *The Principles of economic Planning*. 3rd ed. London: Urwin, 1969.

LIPPMANN, Walter. *The Public Philosophy*. Mentor Books, 1955.

LIPSET, Seymour, ed. *Political Man: The Social Bases of Politics*. London: Heinemann, 1983.

LLOYD, Peter, *A Third World Proletariat?* George Allen & Unwin, London, 1982.

MACPHERSON, C. *The Political Theory of Possessive Individualism: Hobbes to Locke*. New York: OUP, 1962.

—. *The Rise and Fall of Economic Justice and Other Papers*. New York: Oxford University Press, 1985.

MANNHEIM, Karl. *Ideology and Utopia*. New York: Harcourt Brace Jovanovich, 1955.

MANLEY, Michael. *The Politics of Change: A Jamaican Testament*, rev. ed. Kingston: Heinemann, Caribbean, 1990.

—. *The Poverty of Nations: Reflections on Underdevelopment and the World Economy*. Concord, Mass: Pluto, 1991.

MARCHINGTON, Mick, and Phillip PARKER, *Changing Patterns of Employee Relations*. Hentfordshire: Harvester, 1990.

MARCUSE, Herbert. *One-Dimensional Man*, Boston: Beacon Press, 1964.

MARX, Karl, *Wage Labour and Capital*. Moscow: Progress Publishers, 1952.

—. *Capital*, 3 volumes, New York: International Publishers, 1967.

MATHUR, Ajeet. *Industrial Restructuring and Union Power*. Micro-Economic Dimensions of Economic Restructuring and Industrial Relations in India. New Dehli ILO, 1991.

McDERMOTT, John. *Class, Property and Contemporary Capitalism*, Boulder: Westview Press, 1991.

MCKERSIE, R.B. AND L.C. HUNTER, *Pay, Productivity and Collective Bargaining*, Macmillan, 1973.

MEEKS, Brian. *Caribbean Revolutions and Revolutionary Theory: An Assessment of Cuba, Nicaragua and Grenada.* London: Macmillan, 1993.

MEMMI, Albert. *The Colonizers and the Colonized.* trans Howard Greenfeld, London: Earthscan, 1990.

MICHELS, Robert. *Political Parties.* New York: Dover Publications, 1959.

MILIBAND, Ralph. *Parliamentary Socialism: A Study in the Politics of Labour.* 2nd ed. London: Merlin, 1972.

—. *The State in Capitalist Society: An Analysis of the Western System of Power.* New York: Basic, 1969.

MISHAN, E. *The Cost of Economic Growth.* Harmondsworth Middlesex, Pelican 1969.

MOSLEY, Paul, et al. *Aid and Power: The World Bank and Policy Based Lending.* 2 Vols. New York Routledge, 1991.

Moyne Commission. 'West. Indian Royal Commission Report, HMSO, CMD, 6607, 1945.

MUNCK, Ronaldo, *The New International Labour Studies: An Introduction*, New Jersey: Zed Books, 1988.

MUNROE, Trevor. *The Politics of Constitutional Decolonization:* Jamaica 1944-62. Mona: ISER, 1972.

—. *Jamaican Politics: a Marxist Perspective in Transition*, Kingston: Heinemann, 1990.

NELSON, Joan. ed. *Economic Crisis and Policy Choice: the Politics of Adjustment in the Third World*, Pronceton, NJ: Princeton University Press, 1990.

NORRIS, Katrin. *Jamaica: The Search for an Identity.* London: Oxford, 1962.

NOVE, Alec. *The Economics of Feasible Socialism.* London: Allen and Unwin, 1983.

OKUN, Arthur., ed. *Prices and Quantities: A Macro-economic Analysis.* Washington DC: Brookings Institution, 1981.

OLSON, M. *The Logic of Collective Action. Public Goods and the Theory of Groups.* rev. ed, New York: Schocken Books 1971.

PAINE, Thomas. *Rights of Man.* ed. Henry Collins., Harmondsworth Middlesex, Pelican 1969.

PANTIN, Drnnis. *Into the Valley of Debt. An Alternative Road to the IMF/World Rank Path in Trinidad and Tobago.* St. Augustine Trinidad: Dennis Pantin, 1989.

PANTON, David. *Jamaica's Michael Manley: The Great Transformation.* 1972-92 Kingston: Kingston Publishers, 1993.

PARENTI, Michael. *Democracy for the Few.* 5th ed. New York: St. Martin's, 1988.

PASTOR, M. 'The Effects of IMF Programmes in the Third World: Debate and Evidence from Latin America', *World Development*, forthcoming, 1986.

PAYER, Cheryl. *The Debt Trap: The International Monetary Fund and the Third World.* New York: Monthly Review Press, 1974.

PEARSON, Lester B. et al. *Partners in Development: Report of the Commission on International Development*, London and New York: Praeger, 1969.

PEDEN, G. *British Economic and Social Policy: Lloyd George to Margaret Thatcher*, 2nd. ed. London: Phillip Allen, 1991.

PELLING, Henry. *A History of British Trade Unionism.* Harmondsworth: 1963.

PIRAGES, Dennis C. and SYLVESTER, Christine., *Conflict Peace and Development in the Caribbean.* St. Martin's Press, 1991.

PLANT, Roger. *Labour Standards and Structural Adjustment.* Geneva: ILO, 1994.

POST, K. *Arise Ye Starvelings: The Jamaican Labour Rebellion of 1938 and its Aftermath.* Martinus Nijhoff The Boston 1978.

POULANTZAS, Nicos. *Social Classes and Political Power.* London: Verso, 1978.

PEOPLES NATIONAL PARTY, *PNP Manifesto: Democratic Socialism, the Jamaican model,* Kingston: PNP, 1974.

—. *Principles and Objectives of the Peoples National Party.* Kingston: PNP, 1979.

PREALC. Meeting the Social Debt, ILO, 1988.

PRZEWORSKI, Adam. *Capitalism arid Social Democracy.* New York: Cambridge, 1985.

RAMANANADHAM, V. ed. *Privatization in the UK.* London: Routledge, 1988.

RAMSARAN, Ramesh. ed. *Caribbean Economic Policy and South - South Co-operation.* London: Macmillan Caribbean, 1993.

REID, Stanley. "An Introductory Approach to the Concentration of Power in the Jamaican Corporate Economy and Notes on its Origin." In Carl Stone and A. Brown, eds., *Essays on Power and Change in Jamaica.* Kingston, Jamaica: Kingston Publishing, 1977, 15-44.

ROASSEAU, Jean Jacques. *The Social Contract and Discourses.* Trans. G Coke. London: JM Bent, 1993.

ROEMER, John. *A General Theory of Exploitation and Class.* Cambridge, MA.: Harvard University Press, 1982.

RONDINELLI, Dennis A. *Development Projects as Policy Experiments.* Routledge 1993, Ch.3.

ROSS, A.M. *Trade Union Wage Policy,* Berkeley: University of California Press,1948.

ROSTOW , W.W. *The Stages of Growth: A Non-Communist Manifesto.* Cambridge University Press, 1960.

ROTHSCHILD, K. ed. *Power in Economics.* Harmondsworth: Penguin, 1971.

Royal Commission. Report on Trade unions and Employers' Association, HMSO, Cmnd 3623, 1968.

—. *Productivity Bargaining/Restrictive Labour Practices.* HMSO, 1967, 50.

RUNGIMAN, W., *Relative Deprivation and Social Justice,* Routledge and Kegan Paul, 1966.

RYAN, William. *Blaming the Victim,* New York: Random House, 1972.

SANDBROOK, Richard. *The Politics of Basic Needs.* University of Toronto Press, 1982.

SCHUMPETER, J.A. *Capitalism, Socialism and Democracy.* Allen and Unwin, 1943. J.K. Galbraith, American Capitalism, Penguin, 1967.

SEERS, D. *The Political Economy of Nationalism.* Oxford: Oxford University Press, 1983.

SHARPLEY, J., "Jamaica: 1972-1980" in T. Killick ed. *The IMF and Stabilization: Developing Country Experiences,* London: Heinemann, 1984.

SINGER, Peter. *Democracy and Disobedience,* Oxford: Oxford University Press, 1973.

SINGHAM, A. W. *The Hero and the Crowd in a Colonial Polity,* New Haven, CT.: Yale University Press, 1968.

SKOCPOL, T., *States and Social Revolution.* Cambridge: Cambridge University Press, 1979.

SOLOW, Robert M. *Growth Theory: An Exposition.* Oxford: Clarendon Press, 1970.

STEPHENS, E.H. and J.D. STEPHENS. *Democratic Socialism in Jamaica.* London: Macmillan, 1985.

STETTNER, N. *Productivity Bargaining and Industrial Change,* Pergamon, 1969.

STONE, Carl. *Work Attitudes Survey: A Report to the Jamaican Government,* Jamaica: Earle Publishers, 1982.

—. *Democracy and Clientelism in Jamaica.* New Brunswick, N.J.: Transaction Books, 1980.

—. "Jamaica: From Manley to Seaga." In Donald E. Schulz and Douglas A. Graham, eds., *Revolution and Counter-Revolution in Central America and the Caribbean.* Boulder: Westview Press 1984, 385-419.

—, and BROWN, A. eds. *Essays on Power and Change in Jamaica,* Kingston: Jamaica Publishing House, 1977.

—. *Class State and Democracy in Jamaica,* Kingston: Blackett Publishers 1986.

STRINATI, D. *Capitalism, the State and Industrial Relations,* Croom Helm, 1982.

SUSSES, Edward. 'Workers and Trade Unions in a Period of Structural Change', WEP Working Paper No. 25, ILO, Geneva, 1987.

TAWNEY, R.H. *The Acquisitive Society.* London: Collins, 1961.

TAYLOR, Ian. ed. *The Social Effects of Free Market Policies.* New York: Harvester Wheatsheaf, 1990.

THE SHEFFIELD GROUP. *The Social Economy and the Democratic State.* London: Lawrence & Wishart, 1989.

THERBORN, Goran. *What Does the Ruling Class Do When It Rules?* London: New Left Books, 1978.

TOYE, John. *Dilemmas of Development. Reflections on the Counter-Revolution in Development Economics.* Oxford: Blackwell, 1989.

ULMAN, Lloyd and J. FLANAGAN, *Wage Restraint: A Study of Incomes Policy in Western Europe.* University of California Press, 1971.

WADE, R. *Governing the Market. Economic Theory and the Role of Government in East Asian Industrialisation.* Princeton NJ: Princeton University Press, 1990.

WALLERSTEIN, Immanuel, *The Capitalist World Economy,* Cambridge University Press, 1993.

WALTON, John. *Reluctant Rebels: Comparative Studies of Revolution and Underdevelopment.* New York: Columbia, 1984.

WATSON, Hilbourne A. ed. *The Caribbean in the Global Political Economy,* Kingston: Ian Randle, 1994.

WEDDERBURN, Judith, ed. *Rethinking Development.* Mona, Kingston: Consortium Graduate School of Social Sciences 1991.

WELDON, Thomas. *States and Morals: A Study in Political Conflicts.* London: John Murray, 1946.

WESTERBURY, J. "The Political management of economic adjustment and Reform" in J. Nelson ed *Fragile Coalitions: The Politics of Economic Adjustment,* New Brunswick, N.J., Transaction Books, 1989.

WESTERGAARD, J, 'Sociology: The Myth of Classlessness' in R. Blackburn ed., *Ideology and Social Science.* Fontana, 1972.

—. I. NOBLE, and A. WALKER, *After Redundancy.* Oxford: Polity Press, 1989.

WOLF, Eric. *Peasant Wars and Revolution in the Twentieth Century.* Harper and Row, 1969.

ZUCKERMAN, Elaine. *Adjustment Programs and Social Welfare.* Washington, DC.: The World Bank, 1989.

JOURNALS

ADDISON, John J. and Barry T. HIRSCH, 'Union Effects on Productivity Profits and Growth: Has the Long run Arrived? ', *Journal of Labour Economics.*(1989) : Vo 1.7, 1.

ADELMAN, I. "Growth, income distribution and equity-oriented development strategies", *World Development.* 2-3, 3 (1975): 67-76.

AHLUWALIA, M. "Inequality, Poverty and Development", *Journal of Development Economics.* 3. 4 (1976).

AMBURSLEY. F, "Populism in Jamaica." *New Left Review.* 128 (July/August) (1981): 76-87.

ARNDT,H.W. "The 'Trickle-Down' Myth", *Economic Development and Cultural Change,* Vol. 32, 1, (1983).

BACHA, E.L. "IMF conditionality: conceptual problems arid policy alternatives", *World Development.* 15, 12: 1987, 1469-82.

BERNAL, Richard. 'The IMF and Class Struggle in Jamaica 1977-1980', *Latin American Perspectives,* issue 42, vol.11, 3, (Summer, 1984).

BEST, Lloyd. 'Size and Survival', *New World Quarterly,* 2. 3, (1966).

BHAGWATI, J.N. "Development Economics: What Have We Learned", *Asian Development Review,* Vol.2, 1, (1986).

BOURGUIGNON, Francois, William BRANSON, and Jaime De MELO, "Poverty and Income Distribution During Adjustment: Issues and Evidence from the OECD Project", *World Development.* 19. 11: 1991, 1485-508.

BROAD, R., J. CAVANAGH, and W. BELLO, "Development: The Market is not Enough." *Foreign Policy.* No.81 (Winter 1990-91): 144-162.

BROWN, Aldith. "Issues of Adjustment and Liberalization in Jamaica: Some Comments." *SES* Vol. 31, 4 ISER, UWI (December 1982): 192-200.

BROWN, William, and Peter NOLAN, 'Wages, and Labour Productivity: The contribution of Industrial Relations Research to the Understanding of Pay Determination', BJTR: (November 1988).

DAVIES, R.J. 'Economic activity, incomes policy and strikes: a quantitative- analysis', BJIR, vol. XVII, (1979): 205-23.

DOWNES, Andrew S. "Structural Adjustment and the Private Sector in the Caribbean" in *Caribbean Affairs.* Vol.5. 3, (1992).

—. C.A. HOLDER and H.L. LEON, "A Model of Output, Wages, Prices and Productivity in Barbados", *Money Affairs.* Vol.1 .1, (January-June, 1988): 55-69.

Economist Intelligence Unit. *Jamaica: Country Profile,*1986 – 1990. London: Economist Publications (1990).

EDWARDS, P.K. 'Strikes and unorganized conflict; some further considerations', BJIR, vol.XVII. 1, (1979).

FIGUEROA, Mark. "The Formation and Framework of Middle Strata National Leadership in Jamaica: The Crisis of the Seventies and Beyond." *Caribbean Studies.* Vol. 21. 1-2 (June 1988): 44-66.

FLANDERS, Allan 'Productivity Bargaining as a Rule-Changing Exercise', in the BJIR, vol. xiii. 2, (1975).

FRIEDMAN, Milton. "The Role of Monetary Policy," *American Economic Review.* vol. 58 (March 1968), 7-11.

FROBEL, F., J. HEINRICHS and O. KREYE, 'The World Market for Labor and the World Market for Industrial Sites', *Journal of Economic Issues.* vol.XII. 4, (1978): 843-58.

GANGA, Gobind. "Structural Adjustment in Guyana: The Human Impact" *Caribbean Labour Journal.* Vol.I. 1, (Sept. 1991): 61-67.

GENNARD, J. 'The financial costs and returns of strikes', BJIR. vol.XX (1982): 247-56.

GIRVAN, Norman., Richard BERNAL, and Wesley HUGHES, "The IMF and the Third World: The Case of Jamaica, 1974-80." *Development Dialogue.* No. 2: (1980). 113-144.

GIRVAN, N. 'Liberalization increases Jamaica's hardships' in *Caribbean Contact.* (March, 1992).

GQLDFRANK, Walter. 'Theories of Revolution and Revolution Without Theory', *Theory and Society.* Vol. 7. 1&2, (1979).

GOLDSTEIN, M. and P. MONTIEL, 'Evaluating Fund stabilisation programmes with multi-country data', IMF Staff Papers. Vol. 33. 2., (1986)

GREEN, J. and C.N. KAHN, 'Wage employment contracts', *Quarterly Journal of Economics.* 98 (Supplement), (1983).

GREGORY, Robert. 'Wages Policy and Unemployment in Australia', *Economica,* (1986).

HAWKINS, K. 'Productivity bargaining: a reassessment'. *Industrial Relations Journal,* (Spring 1971): 20.

HOBSBAWN, Eric. The Forward March of Labour Halted? *Marxism Today.* (September 1978): 279-86.

HOLDER, C. and D. WORRELL, "A Model of Price Formation for Small Economies: Three Caribbean Examples", *Journal of Development Economics.* Vol. 18. 2-3, (August, 1985).

HORTON, Susan., Ravi KANBUR, and Dipak MAZUMDAR, "Labour markets in an era of adjustment: Evidence from 12 developing countries", in ILR. Vol.130. 5-6, Geneva: ILO, (1991).

HYMAN, Ralston. 'Ideology, Inequality, and Industrial Relations', BJIR, (1974): 179.

IBRD 'Economic Memorandum on Jamaica', report no. 2076-JM, (26 May 1978).

IBRD 'Jamaica: Structural Adjustment, Export Development and Private Investment', report no. 3955-JM, (3 June 1982).

ICFTU/CCL International Confederation of Free Trade Unions/Caribbean Congress of Labour, *A Trade Union Program for the Structural Transformation of the Caribbean.*

ICFTU/CCL conference and special session of the general council, Barbados, (April 9-11, 1986).

Jamaica Labour Party. Manifesto, "Change Without Chaos: A National Development Programme for Reconstruction". Kingston: JLP, (1980).

JOHNSON, Harry. 'The Keynesian Revolution and the Monetarist Counter Revolution'. *American Economic Review.* 61, Papers and Proceedings, (May,1971).

KAPLINSKY, R. 'Myths about the 'Revolutionary Proletariat' in Developing Countries", *Institute of Development Studies Bulletin,* Vol.3. 4, (1971).

KORPI, W. and M. SHALEV, 'Industrial Relations and Class Conflict in Capitalist Societies', *British Journal of Sociology,* 30 (1979): 164-87.

LEVITT, K. "Stabilisation and structural adjustment: rhetoric and reality", *Caribbean Affairs* Vol. 3. 1.

LUCAS, Robert E. Jr. and L, RAPPING, 'Real wages, employment and inflation', *Journal of Political Economy,* (1969).

MAGRI, Lucio, Problems of the Marxist Theory of the Revolutionary Party. *New Left Review.* 60: (1970): 97-128.

MARCUSE, Herbert. 'Industrialization and Capitalism. in *New Left Review,* 30, (March-April 1965).

MCDONALD, I.M. and R.M. SOLOW, 'Wage bargaining and employment', American *Economic Review.* (1981).

MISHEL, L. 'The Structural Determinants of Union Bargaining Power', *Industrial and Labour Relations Review,* (Oct. 1986).

MUSCATELLI, V.A. and D. VINES, "Third World Debt and Macro-economic Interactions between North and South", *Journal of Development Studies.* 27. 3, (1991).

NELSON, Joan, "Organized labor, politics and labor market flexibility in developing countries", in *World Bank Research Observer.* Vol.6. 1, (January 1991).

—. 'The Political economy of stabilisation: commitment, capacity and public response', *World Development* 12 (Development): 983-1006.

OLSEN, M.E. "Alienation and Political Opinion," *Public Opinion Quarterly.* Vo 1. 29, (1965).

PAGE, Benjamin and Robert SHAPIRO, "Effects of Public Opinion on Policy,". *American Political Science Review.* 77, (1983).

PAYNE, Anthony. "From Michael with Love: The Nature of Socialism in Jamaica." *Journal of Commonwealth and Comparative Politics,* Vol. 14. 1 (1976): 82-100.

—. "Seaga's Jamaica after One Year," *World Today,* Vol. 37. 11 (1981): 434-440.

PHELPS, Edmund S. "Phillips Curves, Expectations of Inflation and Optimal Unemployment Over Time," *Economica.* n.s., vol. 34. (August 1967): 254-81.

PRZEWORSKI, Adam, arid Michael WALLERSTEIN, The Structure of Class Conflict in Democratic Capitalist Societies. *American Political Science Review.* 76. 215-38.

RAO MATURE, M. 'Nutrition and Labour Productivity', ILR, 118:1/1-12.

ROBINSON, R.V, and W. BELL, 'Attitudes Towards Political Independence in Jamaica After Twelve Years of Nationhood', *British Journal of Sociology,* 29.2. (1978): 208-33.

ROSENBERG, M. "Some Determinants of Political Apathy," *Public Opinion Quarterly,* Vol.18. (1954).

SACHS, Jeffrey D. "Theoretical Issues in International Borrowing", *Princeton Studies in International Finance,* 54, 1984, Princeton University.

SEN, A.K. "Development: Which Way Now", *Economic Journal*. Vol.93. (December 1983).

SKOCPOL, T. 'A Critical Review of Barrington Moore's Social Origins of Dictatorship and Democracy', *Politics and Society*. 2. 1. (1980): 1-34.

SOLOW, Robert M. 'Insiders and, Outsiders in Wage Determination', *Scandinavian Journal of Economics*. 87. 2. (1985).

STEWART, F. ed. 'The Fragile Foundations of the Neoclassical Approach to Development'. *Journal of Development Studies*. 21. 2. (January, 1985).

SUTHERLAND, R.J. 'Redundancy: perspectives and policies', *Industrial Relations Journal*, vol.11, no.4, 1980.

TURNBULL, Peter J. 'The Economic Theory of Trade Union Behaviour: A Critique', BJIR, (March 1988).

WHITE, P.J. 'The management of redundancy', *Industrial Relations Journal*, vol. 14. 1. (1983).

WITTER, M. and P. ANDERSON, "The Distribution of the Social Cost of Jamaica's Structural Adjustment", (prepared for ILO), (May, 1991).

WORLD BANK. *Report on Adjustment Lending 11: Policies for the recovery of Growth*. March, 1990; Cocument R, 90-99.

OTHER SOURCES

BRANDT REPORT, North-South: A Programme for Survival, *The Report of the Independent Commission on International Development Issues under the Chairmanship of Willy Brandt*. London: Pan Books, 1980.

LIPTON, M. *Labour and Productivity*. World Bank Staff Working Paper 616. Washington, DC: World Bank, 1983.

CAMPBELL, T. "The Restructuring Process in the World Capitalist Economy and its Implications for the Social Classes in the Caribbean." Paper presented at the National Conference of Black Political Scientists Annual Conference, Washington D.C., March 1988.

Commonwealth Secretariat, *The Debt Crisis and the World Economy*. Report by a Commonwealth Group of Experts, London, 1984.

GANNON, John C. "The Origins and Development of Jamaica's Two-Party System, 1930-1975." Ph.D. dissertation, Washington University, 1976.

MAMDANI, Mahmood. "Uganda: Contradictions of the IMF Programme and Perspective". Papers presented at a conference on "Economic Crisis and Third World Countries: Impact and Response", Kingston, 3-6 April 1989.

NBPI, Report No. 23: *Productivity and Pay during the Period of Severe Restraint*. HMSO, 1966, P. 13.

UNDP. *Human Development Annual Reports*. New York: Oxford University Press, 1992.

World Bank. *Report on Adjustment Lending*. Document R88-199, Country Economics Department, August, 1988.

—. *Report on Adjustment Lending 11: Policies for the recovery of Growth.* Document R 90-99, March, 1990.

—. *World Development Reports Several Issues.* New York, Oxford University Press, 1930.

—. *The Challenge of Development. World Development Report 1991.* Washington D.C., 1991.

—. *Poverty in Latin America: The Impact of Depression.* Report 6369, Latin America and the Caribbean Regional Office. Washington, DC: World Bank, 1986.

WORRELL, DeLisle. 'The relation between the exchange rate and the rate of economic growth', Central Bank of Barbados/Ford Foundation seminar paper, January 1978.

Acknowledgements

Sincere gratitude is owed and expressed to several individuals who made the task more manageable. Chief among them are David Gordon-Rowe then of the Joint Trade Union Research and Development Centre, Autherine Spence, Dr. Paul Martin and Lynval Hall for their help with statistical data, case studies and conducting surveys; Errol Richards, Gilbert Young and Yvonne Nelson for putting the material on the computer and their persistence in the face of several technical problems; the late Professor Norman Girvan, then Director of the Consortium Graduate School of Social Sciences of the University of the West Indies for the benefit of his library, and not least my brother, George, for his constant encouragement and support.

Finding an editor who could bridge the economic/political arenas, particularly given the contentious nature of the former was solved when my editor/publisher, Lena Joy Rose, and her team, assumed the task.

AUTHOR BIOGRAPHY

Leon HoSang, a Jamaican Attorney at Law, is a graduate of London and City Universities where he studied Law and Management, respectively. He was called to the English bar at Lincoln's Inn.

In returning to Jamaica he taught full-time in the Department of Management Studies, University of the West Indies, Mona Campus, and subsequently completed a doctoral thesis: "Wage Policy, Life and Labour Under the IMF; Jamaica 1977-1994", which has become his latest book *The Working Class Under the IMF*. In addition, he is the author of *Money & Politics – Towards a Legal Framework* (2015).

A member of the Senate in the 1970's, the author contested the general parliamentary election in 1976. Having lost, he decided that once was enough. Since then he has practiced law full-time, taught law courses and Industrial Relations, occasionally, and provided consultancy services in the latter.

He has also contributed articles to newspapers, regional labour and law magazines and journals (including a critique of the 'Jamaican Bail Act of 2000', and 'The Right to Strike: A Reformulation', published in the *West Indian Law Journal*.

The author has made presentations at several seminars, sponsored by his law firm, and in the past for the trade union movement and business organisations.

HoSang has also made submissions containing suggested changes of a radical nature to Parliamentary Committees established to consider the amendment of labour legislation. His major writings to date have involved engagement in empirical research.

Other Works by the Author
Money & Politics: Towards a Legal Framework
Available in select bookstores, on Amazon and wherever books are sold online.

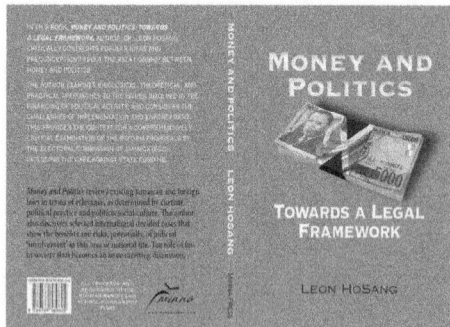

www.ingramcontent.com/pod-product-compliance
Lightning Source LLC
Chambersburg PA
CBHW031427180326
41458CB00002B/472